Crime and Criminals

Crime and Criminals

Contemporary and Classic Readings in Criminology

Frank R. Scarpitti
University of Delaware

■

Amie L. Nielsen
University of Miami

■

J. Mitchell Miller
University of Texas at San Antonio

SECOND EDITION

New York   Oxford
OXFORD UNIVERSITY PRESS
2009

Oxford University Press, Inc., publishes works that further Oxford University's
objective of excellence in research, scholarship, and education.

Oxford   New York
Auckland   Cape Town   Dar es Salaam   Hong Kong   Karachi
Kuala Lumpur   Madrid   Melbourne   Mexico City   Nairobi
New Delhi   Shanghai   Taipei   Toronto

With offices in
Argentina   Austria   Brazil   Chile   Czech Republic   France   Greece
Guatemala   Hungary   Italy   Japan   Poland   Portugal   Singapore
South Korea   Switzerland   Thailand   Turkey   Ukraine   Vietnam

Published by Oxford University Press, Inc.
198 Madison Avenue, New York, New York 10016
http://www.oup.com

Library of Congress Cataloging-in-Publication Data

Scarpitti, Frank R.
  Crime and criminals : contemporary and classic readings in
  criminology / Frank R. Scarpitti, Amie L. Nielsen, J. Mitchell Miller.—2nd ed.
    p. cm.
  ISBN 978-0-19-537090-4 (alk. paper)
  1. Criminology.   I. Nielsen, Amie L., 1970–   II. Miller, J. Mitchell.   III. Title.
  HV6025.S339 2008
  364—dc22   2008022560

Printed in the United States of America
on acid-free paper

Contents

SECTION I: Defining Criminology and Crime

J. Mitchell Miller

Criminology is often misunderstood relative to criminal justice and its practitioner orientation; this reading defines the academic discipline of criminology in terms of social scientific theory–methods symmetry.

C. Ronald Huff

This reading summarizes the history of explanations of criminal behavior in chronological order, tracing early views rooted in superstition and religion through the scientific revolution and contemporary empirically based integrated theories.

Edwin H. Sutherland and Donald R. Cressey

In this reading, criminal behavior is shown to be dependent on criminal law, a body of rules distinguished from other rules by specific characteristics.

William J. Chambliss

Chambliss demonstrates that law does not emerge from value consensus alone but depends largely on differences in power in various groups and conflicts created by social class divisions.

SECTION II: Extent and Nature of Crime

SECTION III: Correlates of Crime

SECTION IV: Theories of Crime

SECTION V: Types of Crime

SECTION VI: **Responses to Crime**

Preface

Crime and Criminals: Contemporary and Classic Readings, Second Edition, is designed for courses that seek to provide students with a comprehensive introduction to the discipline of criminology. The selections deal with the full range of subjects typically covered in a criminology class, including how our society attempts to control crime and criminal behavior. The readings are written by sociologists, criminologists, and scholars from related disciplines concerned about crime.

This new edition reflects changes that maintain the text's original purposes of compiling a set of readings that represent the breadth and diversity of research on the causes of crime, its control, and related social policy issues, and the nature of contemporary criminology. Crime is a dynamic, challenging, and ever-changing reality that is reflected in many of the new entries to this edition. Sociologist J. Mitchell Miller joins the editorial team in assembling an easy-to-read and engaging set of selections that will enable students to understand the core concepts and fundamental theories in the field. This new edition is appropriate as either a primary text or as a supplement for criminology, criminal justice, and sociology of deviance courses.

Crime and Criminals: Contemporary and Classic Readings, Second Edition, features forty-three selections (twenty-four new) that represent the major areas and issues in the discipline of criminology. The selections include both "classics" and contemporary pieces by leading scholars shaping the discipline today. The readings have been edited to promote an increased understanding, readability, and interest by undergraduate students. There are six sections in

the book; at the beginning of each is an introduction that provides an overview of the major issues in the area. The introductions are intended to help facilitate the student's understanding of the area, to acquaint him or her with the major issues, and to provide a broader context for the readings that follow. In addition, preceding each selection is an introduction that provides a succinct overview of the reading and discusses the importance of the selection for the student. Each reading is followed by discussion questions that are intended to help students to understand the main contributions of each article, to think critically about the issues each raises, and to integrate the ideas from the specific reading with those of the larger field.

In Section I, the readings deal with issues related to what behaviors are defined as crime and possible explanations concerning why some behaviors are criminalized and others are not. A new reading also provides an overview of criminology as a social science and how it differs from criminal justice. Section II addresses the extent and nature of crime in the United States, including the types of data used to assess these issues. Section III includes readings on the major correlates of crime, such as age and gender. The selections in Section IV represent the major theoretical approaches in criminology, with biological, psychological, and sociological approaches included. In Section V, which deals with types of criminal behavior, we include several pieces that discuss various types of criminal behavior from organized crime to drug dealing to school violence. In the last section, Section VI, the readings deal with how our society reacts to crime and criminal behavior, focusing on various components of the criminal justice system.

Acknowledgments

Several people facilitated the work represented in this second edition of *Crime and Criminals: Contemporary and Classic Readings.* We are especially appreciative of the editorial assistance provided by Holly Ventura Miller and the graduate research assistance of Natalie Dominguez, both at the University of Texas at San Antonio. We also thank Roxbury Editor Claude Teweles who was instrumental in bringing J. Mitchell Miller onto the book for this edition and Sherith Pankratz for patience and guidance during conversion to Oxford University Press.

About the Contributors

Patricia A. Adler is Professor in the Department of Sociology at the University of Colorado.

Robert Agnew is Professor and Chair of the Department of Sociology at Emory University.

Ronald L. Akers is Professor in the Department of Sociology at the University of Florida.

Elijah Anderson is Professor in the Department of Sociology at the University of Pennsylvania.

Linda S. Anderson is a Visiting Assistant Professor of Legal Skills at Stetson University College of Law.

Michael L. Benson is Professor in the Department of Criminal Justice at the University of Cincinnati.

Alan A. Block is Professor in the Department of Crime, Law, and Justice at Penn State University.

Avshalom Caspi is Professor of Personality Development at the Institute of Psychiatry, King's College London and Professor of Psychology at the University of Wisconsin.

William J. Chambliss is Professor in the Department of Sociology at George Washington University.

Theodore G. Chiricos is Professor in the Department of Criminology and Criminal Justice at Florida State University.

Lawrence E. Cohen is Professor in the Department of Sociology at the University of California, Davis.

George F. Cole is Professor Emeritus in the Department of Political Science at the University of Connecticut.

The late **Donald R. Cressey** was Professor and Chair in the Department of Sociology at the University of California, Los Angeles.

Scott H. Decker is Professor in the Department of Criminology and Criminal Justice at the University of Missouri–St. Louis.

Delbert S. Elliott is Professor in the Department of Sociology and Director of the Institute of Behavioral Research at the University of Colorado.

Marcus Felson is Professor in the School of Criminal Justice at Rutgers University.

Michael Geerken is the chief administration officer in the Orleans Parish Criminal Sheriff's Department, New Orleans.

Chris L. Gibson is an Assistant Professor in the Department of Criminology at the University of Florida.

Michael Gottfredson is the Executive Vice Chancellor and Professor in the Department of Criminology, Law, and Society at the University of California, Irvine.

Walter R. Gove is Professor in the Department of Sociology at Vanderbilt University.

W. Byron Groves is Professor in the Department of Sociology at the University of Green Bay, Wisconsin.

David A. Harris is Balk Professor of Law and Values at the University of Toledo College of Law.

Travis Hirschi is a Regents Professor in the Department of Sociology at the University of Arizona.

C. Ronald Huff is Professor and Dean of Social Ecology at the University of California, Irvine.

Michael Hughes is an Associate Professor in the Department of Sociology at Virginia Polytechnic Institute and State University.

David Huizinga is a senior research associate at the Institute of Behavioral Research, located at the University of Colorado.

Gary F. Jensen is Professor and the Chair in the Department of Sociology at Vanderbilt University.

Maryaltani Karpos is an instructor in the Department of Sociology at the University of Miami in Florida.

Carl B. Klockars is Professor in the Department of Sociology and Criminal Justice at the University of Delaware.

Robert F. Krueger is Professor in the Department of Psychology at the University of Minnesota.

Matthew T. Lee is Professor in the Department of Sociology at the University of Akron.

The late **Cesare Lombroso** was an Italian criminologist and the founder of the Italian School of Positivist Criminology.

Michael J. Lynch is Professor in the Department of Criminology at the University of South Florida.

Ramiro Martinez, Jr. is Professor in the School of Policy and Management at Florida International University.

The late **Joan McCord** was Professor in the Department of Criminal Justice at Temple University.

The late **Henry McKay** was affiliated with the Department of Sociology at the University of Chicago.

Daniel P. Mears is Professor in the Department of Criminology and Criminal Justice at Florida State University.

Robert F. Meier is Professor in the Department of Sociology at Iowa State University.

Scott Menard is Professor in the College of Criminal Justice at Sam Houston State University.

Steven F. Messner is Professor in the Department of Sociology at the State University of New York-Albany.

J. Mitchell Miller is a Professor in the Department of Criminal Justice at The University of Texas-San Antonio.

The late **Walter B. Miller** served as an Adjunct Research Consultant for the Institute for Intergovernmental Research (IIR) in Tallahassee, Florida.

Terrie E. Moffitt is Professor in the Department of Psychology at the University of Wisconsin at Madison.

Matthew Ploeger is an attorney with the law firm of Vinson & Elkins in Houston, TX.

Allison K. Redfern was a graduate student at the University of Missouri-St. Louis.

Albert J. Reiss, Jr., is Professor Emeritus in the Department of Sociology at Yale University.

Richard Rosenfeld is Professor in the Department of Criminology and Criminal Justice at the University of Missouri-St. Louis.

Jeffrey A. Roth is a criminologist and associate director for research at the University of Pennsylvania's Jerry Lee Center of Criminology.

The late **David C. Rowe** was Professor in Family Studies at the University of Arizona.

Frank R. Scarpitti is Professor in the Department of Sociology and Criminal Justice at the University of Delaware.

Pamela S. Schmutte is a graduate student in developmental psychology at the University of Wisconsin, Madison.

Christopher J. Schreck is an Associate Professor in the Department of Criminal Justice at the Rochester Institute of Technology.

The late **Clifford R. Shaw** was affiliated with the Department of Sociology at the University of Chicago.

Phil A. Silva is Director of the Dunedin Multidisciplinary Health and Development Research Unit at the University of Otago Medical School, Dunedin, New Zealand.

Dietrich L. Smith was a graduate student at the University of Missouri-St. Louis.

Darrell J. Steffensmeier is Professor in the Department of Sociology at Penn State University.

Magda Stouthamer-Loeber is Professor at the Western Psychiatric Institute at the University of Pittsburgh.

The late **Edwin H. Sutherland** was head of the Department of Sociology at Indiana University.

Charles R. Tittle is Professor in the Department of Sociology at Washington State University.

Kenneth D. Tunnell is Professor in the Department of Police Studies at Eastern Kentucky University.

Jeffrey T. Ulmer is Professor in the Department of Sociology and Crime, Law, and Justice at The Pennsylvania State University

Gordon P. Waldo is Professor in the College of Criminology and Criminal Justice at Florida State University.

Samuel Walker is Professor in the Department of Criminal Justice at the University of Nebraska at Omaha.

Mark Warr is Professor in the Department of Sociology at the University of Texas at Austin.

Ronald Weitzer is Professor in the Department of Sociology at The George Washington University.

Richard Wright is Professor in the Department of Criminology and Criminal Justice at the University of Missouri-St. Louis.

The late **Richard A. Wright** was Professor and Chair in the Department of Criminal Justice at Chicago State University.

Crime and Criminals

Defining Criminology and Crime

Most U.S. citizens believe there is far too much crime in our society, even if they do not know that about one major crime is committed every two seconds and one violent crime every eighteen seconds. Knowing such facts would probably elevate one's already heightened fear of crime, a fear that has been growing in recent years. Fear of crime undermines the very quality of our lives, making us suspicious of one another, restricting our willingness to walk city streets, and increasing our demand for harsh penalties. But what is it that we fear? What is crime?

Ask the woman passing on the street, who may feel certain she knows what it is. An ordinary citizen would probably define crime as any one of a number of actions, such as rape, murder, robbery, assault, burglary, and a host of others. All of these might be included in the broad category of conventional, or street crime. They might also include vandalism, disturbing the peace, driving while intoxicated, and traffic offenses such as speeding, running a red light, or reckless driving. An informed citizen might even include the relatively newly defined crimes of marital and date rape, stalking, and computer fraud, as well as currently well-publicized crimes such as child abuse, spousal battering, elder abuse, nonpayment of child support, and credit card fraud. This list, in all probability, would include primarily crime featured in the popular media, which mention few, if any, white-collar, corporate, or political "crimes."

Not all crime seems to arouse the fear associated with conventional personal and property violations. Although average citizens know far less about white-collar and corporate crimes than about street crimes, they view them as less threatening and frightening even when they are aware of them. Corporate executives who rig bids on government contracts or who knowingly manufacture defective cars that may cause thousands of accidents and deaths are not defined as criminals in the same way that burglars or purse snatchers are. Similarly, public officials who accept bribes to overlook some wrongdoing or to help a friend obtain a lucrative government contract tend not to be seen as criminals, although such crimes may involve greater financial loss and greater potential personal harm than do street crimes.

The Legal Definition of Crime

This first section of the book will begin the study of crime and criminals by considering what is legally defined as crime and why. Most studies of law-violating behavior are based on a legal definition of the phenomenon; nevertheless, it is important to consider nonlegal definitions as well. Although nonlegal definitions do not determine the actions of the criminal justice system, they allow the student of crime to explore the ramifications of potentially harmful, even deadly, behavior that the criminal law ignores. The same law, however, does not apply to all violators, because juveniles are governed by different statutes and treated differently by the state in view of their age. This distinction says a great deal about American society's definition of justice. Lastly, where do victims fit into the definition of crime and the application of law and order? Understanding these issues and the questions they raise provides the foundation needed for a knowledge of crime and criminals.

The legal definition of crime is relatively straightforward. Simply stated, a crime is any action that is in violation of law, or criminal statutes. Edwin H. Sutherland refers to crime as "behavior which is prohibited by the State and against which the State may react" (1949: 31). Paul W. Tappan says, "Crime is an intentional act or omission in violation of criminal law (statutory and case law), committed without defense or justification, and sanctioned by the state as a felony or misdemeanor" (1960: 10). Acts of omission, such as not reporting a felony of which one has been made aware, even if not personally involved, add a dimension to the definition of crime that the average citizen seldom thinks of.

Crime is a social construction; that is, what is defined as criminal behavior depends on the subjective meaning we attach to the behavior. No behavior is criminal until it is defined as such. Therefore, the definition of acts as criminal or noncriminal is not consistent across jurisdictions or time. That is why paparazzi in France could be charged with a crime for failing to assist persons in need (the 1997 car crash involving Princess Diana and Dodi Fayed), whereas in the United States such failure would not be a crime at all. It is also why actions not previously defined as criminal become crimes with the passage of new legislation (e.g., the Harrison Act, which outlawed most narcotics and cocaine), and why some actions previously considered to be crimes no longer are (e.g., distilling alcohol was no longer illegal following the repeal of Prohibition). Additionally, there is political and social ambivalence toward many crimes, which is why many crimes that have been on the books for years are no longer enforced (certain adult sexual activities) or are enforced sporadically (prostitution, small-time gambling).

Social context is an important factor that must also be considered. Some actions, such as killing, are not considered a crime in all situations—killing is not murder when carried out by police officers in the line of duty, when the state carries out the death penalty, or when carried out by soldiers in times of war. The social context and circumstances involved in a situation are thus important for whether an act is defined as a crime. As we see, even the simple legal definition of crime is fraught with inconsistencies and ambiguities. The preceding examples are only a small sample of the problems inherent in defining crime and reaching any agreement about these definitions.

The reason some acts are defined as crime in the first place is that they are believed to be deviant, outside society's boundaries of acceptable behavior. Although all crime is considered deviant, not all deviance is criminal. What differentiates behavior defined as crime from deviant behavior generally? Deviance is determined by a group or a society through a social and political process. Rules and laws are a response to individual behaviors and actions that the group disapproves of or perceives as harmful to its well-being. According to Kai Erickson, society imposes sanctions for actions it considers dangerous, embarrassing, or irritating to the group; society labels deviance and deviants. Deviant behavior deemed very offensive or antisocial is usually codified by law. Criminal law, therefore, addresses behavior that is considered detrimental to society in general, behavior that may compromise the "safety and order of the state" (Inciardi 1987: 50). Codified laws represent society's strongest negative feelings about individual behavior. Although it might appear from this perspective that the most harmful actions are prohibited by law, many experts think some of the worst offenses, often falling into the categories of corporate or political wrongdoing, are not defined as crime at all.

Once an action is defined as a crime, it is thought of as more precise and more specific than natural law or moral concepts. Criminal statutes share four characteristics that distinguish them from civil statutes or other rules of conduct: politicality (created by a constitutionally authorized body), penalty (a state-imposed punishment for a crime), specificity (strict definition of a crime and its penalty), and uniformity (applied equally to everyone in the jurisdiction) (see Reading 3).

Making Law

Three different perspectives suggest differing reasons that some behaviors are declared criminal and others not: conflict, pluralistic, and value consensus. Many theorists share the conflict perspective, which argues that laws in general reflect the values and protect the interests of the politicians, the wealthy, the powerful, the corporate leaders, and other elites, who have historically and overwhelmingly been white, male, older, middle or upper class, and often Protestant. According to conflict theorists, "law originated with the emergence of social inequality" (Bierne and Messerschmidt 1991: 23), and its purpose is to permit the socially powerful to control those who might challenge their privileged position. This perspective can be seen in the prevalence of civil penalties instead of criminal penalties in instances of corporate wrongdoing. It can be seen in the populations of our prisons, where most inmates have been convicted of conventional street crimes rather than white-collar or corporate crimes, and those few who are convicted of white-collar crimes tend to go to "country club" prisons, rather than maximum-security prisons, where violence, racial tensions, overcrowding, and other unsavory conditions are common. It can also be seen in the great multitude of laws created to protect private property, the cornerstone of capitalist economies, or to maintain the status quo (see Reading 4). Indeed, many theorists view early rape laws as being aimed at protecting the property of the male (i.e., his wife) rather than protecting the female from harm. Whether or not one wholly subscribes to this theory, at the very least it can be observed that "those social classes who control the resources of society are more likely to have their interests represented by the state through the criminal law than are any and all other social groups" (Chambliss 1974: 8-9). At the same time, it must be acknowledged that many laws, such as those outlawing assault or murder, are good for the entire society.

According to the pluralistic perspective, law results from struggle by competing groups for the legal protection of their economic, social, and moral interests (Voigt et al. 1994). This view may be observed in the creation of Prohibition, which, according to Joseph R. Gusfield, reflected not only Protestant beliefs but also the efforts of the declining Federalist "aristocracy," as well as "native" (as opposed to immigrant or ethnic) Americans, to maintain their status by enacting laws outlawing the consumption of alcoholic beverages. Alcohol was customarily used and abused by the outgroups, such as the Irish, whose status they were attempting to diminish.

The third view of law creation, the value-consensus perspective, postulates law is based on the social contract, by which everyone concedes some freedoms in exchange for the good of the entire society. In this view, law supports the values and norms of society. Changes in the laws that uphold these norms can occur as a result of the efforts of special-interest groups, the efforts of an individual, or a triggering event and a resulting public grassroots outcry. Herbert Blumer suggests that there are five stages to this process, starting with the emergence of a problem, continuing with an awareness campaign through mass media, and ending with the implementation of a solution or response. Marital rape, a once inconceivable offense, began to be perceived as a crime after a woman in the state of Oregon brought divorce proceedings against her husband, accusing him of raping her during the course of their marriage (*State v. Rideout* 1978, Oregon). "Megan's law," requiring released sexual molesters of children to register with local law enforcement officials, came about as the result of a massive campaign spearheaded by outraged citizens when seven-year-old Megan Kanka of New Jersey was raped and murdered by a convicted sex offender living in her neighborhood.

In an ever changing society, laws are made, changed, or repealed in response to perceived needs, changing attitudes, public opinion, political rhetoric, special-interest groups, investigative reporting, and other catalysts. As technology changes and society evolves, conditions may be perceived to be a social problem, and new laws are created. According to Roscoe Pound (1994), laws grow out of "social, economic, and psychological conditions." Laws can be created as a result of political pressures, maneuvers, and campaign issues. Crime first became a major political issue in 1964, when Barry Goldwater made it a key platform plank in his presidential campaign against Lyndon Johnson. This political ploy, aimed at making Johnson appear responsible for a perceived increase in the rate of crime, caused

Johnson to create his President's Commission on Law Enforcement and Administration of Justice (President's Crime Commission) in 1965 and led to the passage of the Omnibus Crime Control and Safe Streets Act of 1968. This act appeared to have the political goal of soothing the public's fear of crime and their attitudes toward recent Supreme Court decisions that were perceived as giving offenders too many rights at the expense of the police.

Laws are often a belated response to advances in technology. This delay may be seen as legislatures' and courts' struggle to deal with sophisticated computer crimes, assisted suicide, advanced fertilization techniques, surrogate parents, frozen sperm, cloning, medical procedures such as organ transplants, and the medical use of marijuana.

Some laws are created as a response to the nonuniform enforcement of other laws. Perhaps the best example is the creation of federal "violation of civil rights" laws, which compensate for the lack of convictions by state courts for racially motivated violent crimes. Because criminal laws permit a penalty only after a crime has actually been committed, stalking laws were created in an effort to charge offenders with a crime before they are able to do something much worse to their victims.

Laws are created by legislatures, both state and federal, and all laws are subject to the conditions spelled out in the federal Constitution, despite the fact that only one specific crime—treason—is mentioned in it. State laws are also subject to the constitutions of the individual state. Laws may vary from one jurisdiction to another; a crime in one state may not be a crime in another.

Laws are also clarified and refined by the courts, especially the U.S. Supreme Court. The Supreme Court interprets the Constitution, decisions from the lower courts, and previous Supreme Court cases. Although the Supreme Court, or any court, does not have the power to create the laws, the Court's interpretation of the Constitution and of legislative intent often has the same effect. Because Supreme Court justices are presidential appointees, presidents who have the opportunity to fill a number of Supreme Court vacancies have the potential to have the tenets of their particular party reflected in Supreme Court decisions for years to come.

Most of the processes already mentioned apply to laws governing an individual's behavior. Administrative law, the rules and guidelines of administrative agencies, generally governs corporate behavior. Persons staffing these agencies are often from the ranks of those who identify with big business; sometimes they are retirees from the very corporations they regulate. It is not unusual for corporate officers to be drawn from the ranks of the governing agencies. This practice gives some insight into why cases of corporate deviance are seldom treated as crime.

Nonlegal Definitions of Crime

The social philosopher Jeffrey Reiman contends that "Many of the ways in which the well-off harm their fellows (deadly pollution, unsafe working conditions, and the like) are not even defined as crimes though they do more damage to life and limb than the acts that are treated as crimes" (1998: viii) Those agreeing with him generally hold that the definition of "crime" should be much broader than the legal definition (see Reading 4).

There are good reasons for this view, ranging from the altruistic to the practical. For one thing, social scientists would not then be limited to definitions provided by other fields, such as law or politics. They would be free to speculate and conduct research in areas far beyond those covered in the statutes. They could illuminate areas of deviance and harm that could be covered by criminal laws but that are not, due to the interests of those who control the law-making process. By extending the definition of crime, social scientists would be able to "uncover injustices for purposes of reform" (Voigt et al. 1994: 36) and to discover "wrongs which are absolute and eternal rather than mere violations of a statutory and case law system which vary in time and place" (Tappan 1947: 96).

Broadening the definition of crime also frees social scientists from the biases against race and class that are inherent in the criminal law, which deals primarily with conventional, or street crimes. It allows them to look at crime not only as a working-class phenomenon, but also as misdeeds by those of upper socioeconomic status (Greenberg 1993). In other words, a broad definition puts the relative danger or harm of conventional crimes in perspective. Above all, it keeps the field of criminology from being "a status quo handmaiden of political systems" (Hagan 1994: 17) by allowing criminologists to examine the ways in which laws are created and the forces behind the laws, instead of just accepting them at face value. In this way, social scientists are forced to look beyond the punishment of the offender to the structural elements that contribute to the definitions of what constitutes crime in the first place.

Piers Bierne and James Messerschmidt identify four specific sociological definitions of crime: "(1) crime as a violation of conduct norms, (2) crime as a social harm, (3) crime as a violation of human rights, and (4) crime as a form of deviance" (1991: 16). Conduct norms, a concept described by Thorsten Sellin, include normal and abnormal forms of conduct, varying, of course, from group to group. Although it would not be possible to study all abnormal forms, Sellin proposes that at the very least we should question why some of these are considered to be crime and some are not.

Crime as social harm incorporates Sutherland's ideas about white-collar crime, namely that because white-collar offenses cause harm and are punishable by fines, they meet the criteria for being defined as a crime. Crime as a violation of human rights would include any action violating one's "natural and inalienable rights," or injuries resulting from "imperialism, sexism, racism and poverty" (Bierne and Messerschmidt 1991: 18-19). Finally, crime as a form of deviance would include any acts violating social norms for which an individual is penalized. As pointed out, not all deviant acts are labeled as crime. But the concept brings up important questions regarding why some acts are regarded as deviant, who defines the behavior, what the consequences of an act for the individual are, and why certain deviant acts are criminal and certain other deviant acts are not.

Juvenile Justice

In the U.S. criminal justice system, juveniles constitute a special class and usually receive special treatment. This custom has not always been so. Before the sixteenth century, children were regarded as little adults (Hart 1991); as such, they were tried in adult courts and thrown into jails with adults. "Children were ignored, abandoned, abused, sold into slavery, and mutilated" (Hart 1991: 53). During the sixteenth, seventeenth, and eighteenth centuries, children were considered chattel; their value was in what they could contribute economically to the family. They were replaceable and interchangeable. During the eighteenth century, children began to be regarded as a special class, and parents were expected to assume responsibility for their maintenance, education, and protection. Schools were also given some responsibility for the welfare of children. Laws were created to handle difficult children. Children, though still regarded as property, were now regarded as valuable and vulnerable property.

In the nineteenth century, children were regarded as innately good (as Jean Jacques Rousseau taught), innately sinful (the Calvinist theory), or neither good nor evil but malleable (according to John Locke) (Hart 1991). People began to believe that the protection and care that a child received could influence him or her one way or the other, and so the child began to assume more importance, to be regarded as not just a throwaway, interchangeable commodity, but as a person to be cared for. In the United States, a variety of public and private agencies began to work for the improvement of family life.

By the start of the twentieth century, the child-as-redeemer theory had come into play. From this perspective, the child was regarded as a valuable human resource who would "determine the future of society" (Hart 1991: 53). This belief fostered a number of reform movements in the United States, including the advocating of a juvenile court system. The Juvenile Court Act created the first court for children and adolescents in Illinois in 1899.

The juvenile court was ushered in hand in hand with the idea of *parens patriae*. This concept determined that the child was entitled to certain rights of care and nurturing, and if the parent was not providing these things, or if there was no parent, the state would, in effect, become the parent for the purpose of protecting and providing for the child and guiding him or her in the right direction. It was this principle that caused the juvenile courts to be set up quite differently from adult courts. Where it was the purpose of adult courts to determine guilt and punish the guilty, it was the purpose of juvenile courts to protect and treat the child, without attaching the stigma of a criminal label (Drowns and Hess 1990). Originally, a child was defined as an individual under the age of eighteen, or under the age of twenty-one who had committed a delinquent act before age eighteen.

Children may be heard in a juvenile court for both offenses that would be crimes if committed by adults and in a number of states for "status offenses," or actions that would not be considered criminal if committed by an adult. Status offenses include running away from home, incorrigibility, and truancy. Under the philosophy of the juvenile justice system, proceedings are informal and private: the court does not release information to the press, and at the age of majority a child's court records are supposed to be sealed. Children cannot be sent to adult jails and prisons except under special circumstances and unique legal provisions, and in most states they cannot be given the death penalty. Correctional alternatives often include releasing them into the custody of their parents, or sending them to a facility for juveniles.

Even the language of a juvenile court differs from that of an adult court to avoid giving the impression of a criminal proceeding. A child is taken into custody, not arrested; has an adjudicatory hearing, not a trial; is held in detention, not jail; is petitioned, not accused or indicted; has a preliminary inquiry, not an arraignment; is found delinquent, not guilty; receives an adjudication, not a conviction; receives a disposition, not a sentence; receives aftercare, not parole, and so on (Drowns and Hess 1990).

Because the proceedings are not considered criminal and the court is cast in the role of parent, it is felt that the court is watching out for the best interests of the child; therefore, for many years, children had no constitutional procedural rights such as those guaranteed to adults. Because the court was nonadversarial, there appeared to be no need for the right to counsel, the right to remain silent, the right to confront witnesses, and other constitutional guarantees. Thus, children often received

"treatment" out of proportion to their acts; they were confined to juvenile facilities for long periods for being status offenders, even for being abused or neglected (throwaways). Not only was their freedom taken away, but they were confined with more violent juvenile offenders, at risk of being bullied, abused, or injured in this setting as well.

Eventually, it came to people's attention that these children were receiving neither fair treatment nor the paternal protection of the state as had been assumed. They had the worst of both worlds: no treatment and no procedural rights. Supreme Court decisions, such as In Re *Gault*, *Kent v. The United States*, and In Re *Winship* began to change this situation. Children received some rights, including the right to counsel, the privilege to defend themselves from self-incrimination, and the due-process right of proof beyond a reasonable doubt before being deprived of liberty. The only right they were denied (*McKeiver v. Pennsylvania*) was the right to a jury trial.

Although juveniles in the last ten years have been receiving more of the legal rights enjoyed by adults, there has also been a shift toward the criminalization of many of the behaviors for which they are brought to court. This shift is changing the very face and function of the juvenile court. Instead of protecting the child, the court has pretty much washed its hands of the status offender, who may still need help, and has endorsed a get tough policy toward the delinquents who are left. During the 1990s many states changed their laws to allow delinquents to be transferred to adult courts at younger and younger ages (Bartol and Bartol 1998), and some states are now allowing children to receive the death penalty. Although a growing number of states are demanding that violent offenders over fourteen years old be tried in criminal courts, there are instances of even younger children being tried as adults, usually for committing particularly heinous crimes.

According to some critics (Bartol and Bartol 1998), there are two current trends in attitudes toward justice for juveniles: (1) a law and order mentality, which includes tough new state and federal laws and a reluctance of courts to interfere with them, and (2) a retributive response toward seriously violent adolescents. From 1989 to 1993, the number of juvenile cases waived to adult court increased 41 percent. Thus the full circle can be seen, whereby children are once more regarded as little adults in the criminal justice system.

Victims of Crime

Ironically, the formal definition of crime does not mention victims, who are often considered the forgotten element in the criminal justice process. Who are the victims of crime? Statistically speaking some people have a greater likelihood than others of becoming the victims of conventional crime. (The odds even up a bit when considering white-collar crime; more people run the chance of being victimized by it.) In general, and for violent crimes in particular, victims are likely to be young (teenagers and young adults); male; African American or Latino; poor; single, divorced, or separated; unemployed; renters; and city dwellers (Voigt et al. 1994; see also National Commission 1969). Place of residence and socioeconomic status play a part, as does lifestyle. Lifestyles of the young make them especially vulnerable to street crime because they go out partying; use or are exposed to drugs, alcohol, and gangs; and, in general, place themselves at greater risk.

Although most people are blameless in contributing to their becoming victims, others precipitate the crime in some way, either by carelessness or some deliberate act. Putting up with spousal abuse, starting a fight in a bar, or leaving one's keys in the ignition are examples of victims precipitating crimes. Such precipitation brings up some interesting possibilities. Marvin E. Wolfgang found that women are twice as likely to be the killer in victim-precipitated homicides as in homicides not precipitated by the victim. He thought that fact justified the "police thoroughly investigat[ing] every possibility of strong provocation by the male victim when he is slain by a female—and particularly…if the female is his wife" (1957). Studying the relationship between the victim and the offender helps society to understand, and perhaps even prevent, crimes.

Other people are victimized because they are more vulnerable, on account of their gender (female) or age (very young or old). Women are the usual victims of rapes and domestic violence. Although the elderly are not so frequently victimized compared to other age groups, they are greatly affected by the fear of crime, and when they are actually victims, the injury or loss may be more devastating because of their delicate physical condition or the marginal economic status of many elderly persons. Each year one million children are abused or neglected, one million are runaways (from dangerous situations), and one in five young females and one in ten young males are affected by sexual abuse (Voigt et al. 1994). Children who are not abused themselves are often the psychological victims of their parents' spousal abuse.

Who cares about the victim? In preindustrial societies, victims and their families played a direct role in meting out retribution or in receiving compensation for a wrong committed against them. But as society grew more complex and diverse, it was no longer in the best interests of the state to allow people to carry out personal vendettas or take the law into their own hands. Over time, the government replaced the victim as the wronged or injured party in crime. The victim's role was reduced to making the crime known and testifying in court. Punishment became the purview of the state. Victims were overlooked, and little thought was given to their pain and loss, inconvenience (missing work to appear in court), trauma, fear, stigma, medical expenses, health, and other detrimental effects of the crime. Some victims were treated so poorly by the system that it was akin to being victimized twice, first by the offender, and then by the system.

One frequent response is that of blaming the victim, a practice engaged in by almost everyone, from the offender to the victim. Domestic violence offers a particularly poignant example of this tendency. The offender invariably blames the victim ("Now see what you made me do"), the authorities often think the offender was provoked, and the victim herself (victims are usually women) begins to see herself as the problem ("If I'd just kept the kids quiet," or "If I hadn't burned the dinner," "Now look what I've made him do"). Blaming themselves is one reason why some women do not leave abusive relationships. Outsiders, too, often blame the victim, deciding it is her fault, there is something wrong with her if she does not leave, and even, perhaps subconsciously, she wishes to be beaten (Goode 1990). If the police blame the victim, they are strongly tempted not to intervene or make an arrest.

In rape cases, blaming and attempting to discredit the victim are common. Rapists justify their actions by asserting, "All women want to be raped," "No woman can be raped against her will," or "She was asking for it," (Brownmiller 1975: 311). According to Diana Scully and Joseph Marolla (1993: 103), several common themes appear in rape justification: "(1) women as seductresses; (2) women mean 'yes' when they say 'no'; (3) most women eventually relax and enjoy it; (4) nice girls don't get raped." Unfortunately, it is not only rapists who blame the victims. Unsympathetic spouses, the general public, and law enforcement officials often wonder, to one degree or another, if or how the victim contributed to her victimization: Was she dressed provocatively? Did she lead him on? Did she willingly participate then cry "rape" when she was caught or regretted her decision? Often the victim wonders what she has done to provoke the rape. In court, she feels as if she is on trial, as the defense brings up things from her past and lifestyle that cast aspersion on her character. Similar facts about the victim are often reported in the media.

Police sometimes refuse to make arrests in domestic disputes (instead telling the husband to cool off) and in situations that seem to involve a homosexual relationship. A young boy would be alive today if police officers had not taken him back to a violent, homosexual (and deadly!) situation with Jeffrey Dahmer.

With the advent of the victims' rights movement, a number of advances have been made in the general attitude toward victims and the general willingness to assist them where possible. Stalking laws have been created to keep potential victims from greater harm. Victim-impact statements are often allowed in the sentencing phase of criminal trials. Victim advocacy groups, such as Mothers Against Drunk Driving (MADD), influence legislation that affects victims, and draw media attention to problems (such as drunk driving) that affect victims. Some cities have encouraged citizen groups

to patrol neighborhoods at night to decrease crime. In some instances, victims may receive restitution (payment to the victim by the criminal) or compensation (assistance from government agencies for expenses incurred as a result of being a victim). Battered women's shelters have been opened to give women and their children a chance to escape from abusive mates. Most states have passed rape-shield laws to protect the private lives of rape victims who testify against their attackers in court.

In some cases, police departments have created victim-assistance units. For example, the Rochester (New York) Police Department has two: Victim Assistance Unit and Family Crisis Intervention Team (FACIT) (Roberts 1990). The Victim Assistance Unit, started in 1975, provides various services for victims, such as notification of legal court proceedings, transportation, filing for compensation for personal property damaged during a crime, and accompaniment to court (especially when the victim is afraid of or intimidated by the offender). FACIT is a crisis intervention unit, which follows up, often by going to victims' homes to prevent bad situations from deteriorating. FACIT counselors provide liaisons between clients and agencies that offer services and counseling pertinent to their problems, and it intervenes on the spot when necessary.

Though some people still claim that criminals enjoy more rights than victims do, victims have made headway in being acknowledged and in many instances helped. A number of recent changes in legal statutes and judicial procedures indicate that the law does care about victims. No changes, however, will prevent victims of crime from wondering why they were chosen to be victimized and why society did not protect them from harm.

Crime, the violation of legal statutes, exists because those with constitutional authority enact certain values into law. Understanding the lawmaking process becomes essential, then, to knowing why some behaviors are criminalized and others are not. Nonlegal definitions of crime, used mainly by researchers and those advocating social change, expand the range of behavior considered criminal and raise questions about the extent to which law serves all segments of society. Although the uniform application of criminal law is one of its tenets, it is applied differentially to juveniles because of their age. Although the definition of crime implies that an act is considered a crime because of the harm it does, victims of crime are often overlooked by the justice system. In the readings that follow, each of these issues pertaining to the question, "What is crime?" is examined in greater detail.

References

Bartol, Curt R. and Anne M. Bartol. 1998. *Delinquency and Justice: A Psychological Approach* (2nd ed.). Upper Saddle River, NJ: Prentice-Hall.

Bierne, Piers and James Messerschmidt. 1991. *Criminology*. San Diego: Harcourt Brace Jovanovich.

Blumer, Herbert. 1971. "Social Problems as Collective Behavior," *Social Problems* 18: 298-306.

Brownmiller, Susan. 1975. *Against Our Will: Men, Women and Rape*. New York: Simon and Schuster.

Chambliss, William J. 1974. "The State, the Law, and the Definition of Behavior as Criminal or Delinquent." In D. Blaser (ed.), *Handbook of Criminology*. New York: Rand-McNally.

Drowns, Robert W. and Karen M. Hess. 1990. *Juvenile Justice*. Saint Paul, MN: West.

Erickson, Kai T. 1966. *Wayward Puritans: A Study in the Sociology of Deviance*. New York: Wiley.

Goode, Erich. 1990. *Deviant Behavior* (3rd ed.). Englewood Cliffs, NJ: Prentice Hall.

Greenberg, David F., ed. 1993. *Crime and Capitalism: Readings in Marxist Criminology*. Philadelphia: Temple University Press.

Gusfield, Joseph R. 1986. *Symbolic Crusade: Status Politics and the American Temperance Movement* (2nd ed.). Urbana, IL: University of Illinois Press.

Hagan, Frank E. 1994. *Introduction to Criminology* (3rd ed.). Chicago: Nelson-Hall.

Hart, Stuart N. 1991. "From Property to Person Status: Historical Perspective on Children's Rights," *American Psychologist* 46: 53-59.

Inciardi, James A. 1987. *Criminal Justice* (2nd ed.). San Diego: Harcourt Brace Jovanovich.

National Commission on the Causes and Prevention of Violence. 1969. "Violent Crime: Homicide, Assault, Rape, Robbery," *To Establish Justice and Ensure Domestic Tranquility, Final Report of the National Commission*. Washington, DC: Government Printing Office.

Pound, Roscoe. 1994. "The Scope and Purpose of Sociological Jurisprudence." In John Monahan, and Laurens Walker (eds.), *Social Science in Law: Cases and Materials* (3rd ed.). Westbury, CT: The Foundation Press.

Reiman, Jeffrey. 1998. *The Rich Get Richer and the Poor Get Prison: Ideology, Class, and Criminal Justice* (5th ed.). Boston: Allyn and Bacon.

Roberts, Albert R. 1990. *Helping Crime Victims: Research, Policy, and Practice*. Newbury Park, CA: Sage.

Scully, Diana and Joseph Marolla. 1993. "Convicted Rapists' Vocabulary of Motive: Excuses and Justifications." In H. Delos Kelley (ed.), *Deviant Behavior: A Text-Reader in the Sociology of Deviance* (4th ed.). New York: St. Martin's.

Sutherland, Edwin H. 1949. *White Collar Crime*. New York: Dryden.

Tappan, Paul W. 1947. "Who Is the Criminal?" *American Sociological Review* 12: 92-102.

——. 1960. *Crime, Justice and Correction*. New York: McGraw-Hill.

Voigt, Lydia, William E. Thornton, Jr., Leo Barrile, and Jerrol M. Seaman. 1994. *Criminology and Justice*. New York: McGraw-Hill.

Wolfgang, Marvin E. 1957. "Victim-Precipitated Criminal Homicide," *Journal of Criminal Law, Criminology, and Police Science* 48: 1-11.

CHAPTER 1

Criminology as Social Science

J. Mitchell Miller

In recent years, criminology has embraced an increasingly interdisciplinary orientation that, although broadening the scope of criminology, has generated debate over definition and purpose. The following introductory reading, "Criminology as Social Science," provides a brief and straightforward distinction between traditional academic criminology and criminal justice, as well as outlining the defining characteristics of criminology. Criminology is portrayed as a standard social science rooted in a theory–methods symmetrical approach to inquiry and discipline commitment to both pure and applied research.

Comparison and contrast with the academic discipline of criminal justice revolves around the role of commitment, moreso than subject matter. Indeed, theories, specific types of crimes, and control of crime are addressed from a criminological orientation according to social science precepts toward the goals of: (1) establishing and maintaining an empirically sound knowledge base on the nature of crime and its control, and (2) refining criminal justice practices and policies. These two general objectives are directly related in that changes toward improved performance are informed and guided by criminological research. Through the identification of scientifically based best practices, criminology seeks to realize betterment in the criminal justice system, then, through a social scientific approach.

From *Encyclopedia of Criminology* (pp. 337-339) by R.A. Wright and J.M. Miller, 2005. New York, New York: Routledge Publisher.

Criminology consists of the study of the social problem of crime, including the processes of making and breaking laws as well as society's reaction to the phenomenon (Sutherland, 1939). As an academic field of study, criminology meets the standards of a social science, defined as:

> The entirety of those disciplines, or any particular discipline, concerned with the systematic study of social phenomena. No single conception of science is implied by this usage, although there are sociologists who reject the notion that social studies should be seen as scientific is in any sense based on the physical sciences (Jary and Jary, 2001).

The social sciences (e.g., sociology, political science, anthropology, economics) differ from the natural or hard sciences (e.g., chemistry, physics, biology) in more ways than just addressing dissimilar subject matter. The natural sciences enjoy a much longer history, dating back to the European Enlightenment era, whereas most of the social sciences did not appear on the university setting prior to the 20th century. The utilization of society as laboratory yields implications for inquiry surrounding the inability of social scientists to adequately eliminate mitigating factors in hypothetic, deductive, and experimental research designs. As an alternative methodological approach, social science largely relies on quasi-experimental research design, which emulates hard science, generally.

The social sciences are heavily rooted in and subscribe to the major philosophies of science, most notably positivism and subjectivism. Positivism has been the dominant paradigm influencing research theory symmetry throughout the social sciences for several decades. According to the *Dictionary of the Social Sciences* (Gould and Kolb, 1964, 530), positivism is "a philosophical approach, theory or system based on the view that in the social as well as in the natural sciences sense experiences and their logical and mathematical treatment are the exclusive source of all worthwhile information." Derived from the social thought of Comte, Newton, and the Vienna Circle, the logic of positivism sets the standard for contemporary social science theory testing and both pure and applied research, primarily through the logic and use of variable analysis. Variable analysis emphasizes reductionism, categorization, and measurement toward the goals of establishing correlation and causality. This style of inquiry, called positivistic criminology, is rooted in empiricism, which is often erroneously thought to characterize quantitative research featuring statistical analyses.

Subjectivism, or interpretivism, differs from positivism in its fundamental assumptions concerning the nature of inquiry. A dynamic and developmental perspective that fosters a qualitative naturalistic research style, subjectivism, also known as interpretivism, has become established as the foremost inquiry alternative to positivism in the social sciences, generally, and in criminology, specifically. Subjectivism is a methodological approach to inquiry positing that social phenomena cannot be objectively observed per se, rather each concept is constructed and understood by shared meanings. Whereas positivism seeks to eliminate any subjectivity or bias from both the researcher and the subject, interpretivism encourages consideration of participant perception of human actions. Qualitative research methods, both observational and interactional, facilitate this approach, which, despite the widespread equaling of empiricism and statistical analysis, is inherently sense oriented and thus empirical.

Another standard by which to define a field of study as a science is theory, that is, a set of explanations specific to the field in question. The various social sciences are shaped by specific theories, typically derived from larger social perspectives,

namely functionalism, power conflict, and symbolic interactionism. Criminology certainly draws on each of these larger perspectives in its leading theories. Functionalism and its emphasis on normative consensus clearly influences classical criminology and its more modern extensions of deterrence and rational choice theories. Virtually all of critical criminology is either directly or indirectly derived from social conflict perspectives on society and symbolic interactionism affects a variety of crime causation and response theories, such as routine activities theory, reintegrative shaming theory, and labeling theory.

Whether attempting to validate a theory, exploring new phenomena, or evaluating the operational effectiveness of a juvenile or criminal program, criminologists employ a broad range of research methods, both quantitative and qualitative, but strive to do so from a theoretical orientation. Accordingly, a strong case can be made for criminology as a social science.

The issue of criminology as a social science stems from both its embeddedness in sociology and the erroneous assumption that criminology and the complimentary field of criminal justice are synonymous. Although it is clear that criminology is a social science, the boundaries between and hierarchal order of the other crime-focused academic fields relative to criminology are muddled. Criminology, historically, has been considered a major area of specialization within its mother discipline, sociology, the refinement and evolutionary outcome of the sociology of deviance. Criminology today remains both a primary research focus and formal track of undergraduate and graduate studies within sociology departments, but has also splintered from sociology at many colleges and universities to become an independent discipline (a trend in the social sciences since the 1970s responsible for several relatively "young" fields such as child and family studies, women's studies, and African American studies).

Criminology is often confused and contrasted with criminal justice, which emerged on the college setting during the 1970s—about the time criminology was becoming somewhat independent from sociology. Criminal justice was largely shaped by and reflected the spirit of the times, which included the civil rights movement, the Vietnam War, and a general liberalization of the popular culture.

These social movements, along with unprecedented levels of juvenile delinquency, presented widespread challenges for law enforcement management and social order maintenance. The nation's response was the Law Enforcement Administrative Act (LEAA) that sought to resource criminal justice and enhance the professionalism of police administrators. Accordingly, criminal justice (originally known as "police studies" or "police science") programs of study were established in institutions of higher education throughout the country. The LEAA served to define criminal justice as an applied and practitioner-oriented field of study, contrasting it with the more theoretical orientation of criminology.

Today, the paradigmatic conflict between criminal justice as applied science and criminology as social science lingers, but has been largely resolved. The two are naturally complementary and have become so intertwined in coverage and research focus that differences are often a matter of semantics.

References

Gould, J. and Kolb, W.L., Eds. (1964). *A Dictionary of the Social Sciences*. New York, NY: The Free Press of Glencoe.

Jary, D. and Jary, J. (2000). *Sociology: The HarperCollins Dictionary*. New York, NY: HarperCollins.

Schuetz, A. (1943). The problem of rationality in the social world, *Economica*, 10, 130–149.

Schuetz, A. (1953). Common-sense and the scientific interpretation of human action, *Philosophy and Phenomenological Research*, 14, 1–38.

Schuetz. A. (1973). *Collected Papers*. Natanson. M. The Hague: Martinus Nijhoff.

Sutherland. E.H. (1939). *Principles of Criminology*. 3rd ed. Philadelphia, PA: J.B. Lippincott.

CHAPTER 2

Historical Explanations of Crime: From Demons to Politics

C. Ronald Huff

The following article by C. Ronald Huff reviews the development and evolution of philosophical, ideological, and scientific thought on crime. From supernatural explanations of demonic possession to the emergence of free will and rationalism that has significantly shaped formal social control for over two centuries, a chronologically ordered development of philosophies of crime is presented. Accordingly, this reading provides quick yet thorough coverage of precriminological views of crime, the emergence of positivism, and the scientific perspective to contemporary sociological theories. These diverse perspectives situate the fundamental causes of crime in a variety of sometimes conflicting sources ranging from external factors argued to be largely beyond the individual's control such as economics and environment to free will values and belief systems that are considered internal to individuals.

Man's historical concern with the existence of crime has been reflected in his diverse attempts to explain how and why crime occurs. Long before there was a scientific approach to the crime problem, there were speculative "explanations" of criminal behavior. Some of these earlier views concerning the nature of crime may seem absurd according to contemporary standards, but they must be viewed as symbolic expressions of the prevailing ideas and concerns of their own era. Similarly, it would be surprising if our currently fashionable theories of crime are not viewed as naive and unsophisticated in the next century.

Before discussing the major historical explanations of crime, it seems appropriate to ask what, if any, relevance such a discussion can have for students of criminology and criminal justice. While intellectual inquiry is justifiable for its own sake, the current discussion has contemporary relevance in at least two ways: (1) it presents an overview of the development of criminological theory, which should permit a greater understanding of contemporary explanations and their place in the continuity of thought on the subject of crime; and (2) since society's responses to crime depend, to a large extent, on its theories and its assumptions about the nature of crime, an understanding of those views is useful in attempting to analyze the numerous attempts to "prevent...control," "deter," "cure," or otherwise contain criminal behavior. The operations of the various components of the criminal justice system (such as the police, the courts, and the prisons) can perhaps best be viewed by understanding the various assumptions which underlie their policies and procedures. Every major theory, explanation, or assumption about the nature and causes of crime may be viewed as having important implications for the strategies of social control which society elects to implement. The following discussion examines the existence of such connections between theory and practice.

From *Crime and the Criminal Justice Process* (pp. 208-220) by C. R. Huff, 1978, Dubuque, Iowa: Kendall Hunt Publishing Company. Edited by J. Inciardi and K. Haas. Copyright © 1978 by Kendall Hunt Publishing Company. Reprinted by permission of James A. Inciardi.

Supernatural Explanations

Primitive man's basic explanation of "criminal" behavior was that of diabolical possession. Criminal behavior was viewed as evidence that the culprit was under the control of evil spirits, or demons. This view of deviant behavior was simply an extension of the prevailing view of nature—that is, that every object or being was controlled by spiritual forces. Obviously, such an explanation requires *belief or faith*, since it does not lend itself to scientific verification. Nevertheless, demonology had important implications for man's responses to crime.

Given such an explanation of crime, the only sensible solution was to try to exorcise the demons which were responsible for the behavior or, failing that, to do away with the criminal, either by exile or by execution. In a society where the gods were perceived as omnipotent and omnipresent, it was clearly a matter of the highest priority to appease them, no matter what the costs. Thus, the fate of the criminal was less related to the protection of society than to compliance with the will of the gods. The failure of the group to punish the wrongdoer was believed to leave the tribe open to the wrath and vengeance of the gods. As the noted historian and criminologist Harry Elmer Barnes noted:

Not only does this transgression of the customary code expose the offending individual to untold woes, but it also renders his whole social group liable to the vengeance of the gods, for in early days, responsibility is collective from the standpoint of both the natural and supernatural world. In primitive society a crime and a sin are practically identical. Hence, to supplement the individual fear of violating the prescribed modes of conduct on account of danger from unseen powers, there is the certain knowledge on the part of the offender that his group will summarily avenge themselves upon him for rendering it open to destruction from the intervention of both human and spiritual forces.... [T]he most generally accepted way of wiping out a crime and sin in primitive society is "to wipe out the sinner."

One who violated the norms dealing with endogamy, witchcraft, or treason was likely to receive the harshest punishment in primitive society. The offender might be hacked to pieces, exiled, or even eaten. All three of these sanctions accomplished the same goal—the removal of the offender from the group. Offenses of a private, rather than public, nature were generally dealt with by the victim's clan through the process known as "blood feud." Essentially, it was the duty of each member of a clan to avenge a fellow clan member. The principle which guided this pursuit of retaliation was the well-known *lex talionis* ("an eye for an eye and a tooth for a tooth"). The idea of *lex talionis*, roughly, was that the punishment should fit the crime. Primitive obsession with making the retaliation exact was in some cases so fanatical that inanimate objects which had been instrumental in accidental deaths were actually "punished."

There was very little use of any form of incarceration in primitive society, except for periods of detention while awaiting disposition and the incarceration related to cannibalistic practices. The only other major type of punishment did not appear until the late stages of primitive society. It was a form of compensation or restitution. This practice developed in response to the failure of blood feud as a method of criminal justice. Blood feuds all too often resulted in prolonged vendettas which exacted heavy tolls on both sides. The practice of paying a fixed monetary penalty therefore evolved as an alternative to the potentially genocidal blood feuds. Later, in the feudal period, the extended families or clans established a system of *wergeld* (man-money) by which the victim's status determined the amount assessed against the offender. This concept was gradually broadened to include differences in degree of responsibility, the individualization of responsibility, and even a distinction between "intent" and "accident." Eventually, a specified value was set for each type of offense, and the system of restitutive fines paid by the offender to the victim came to be preferred over the blood feud. With the subsequent development of an appeal procedure whereby either party could protest an injustice, the roots of the modern-day court system emerged in embryonic form. Finally, through the absolute authority which accompanied kingships, especially in early historic society and during feudalism, all crimes became "crimes against the king's peace"; in other words, crimes came to be regarded as offenses against the public welfare. At that point, man had, in a sense, come "full circle" in his efforts to rationalize law and punishment:

> The heavy fines imposed on places and people became an important source of revenue to the crown and to the barons and the lords of manors.
>
> The State was growing strong enough to take vengeance; the common man was no longer feared as had been the well-armed Saxon citizen of old, and to the "common" criminal was extended the ruthless severity once reserved for the slaves…and the idea of compensation began to wane before the revenge instinct now backed by power.

Rationalism and Free Will

Just as demonological explanations dominated the thinking of early man, the so-called classical period of criminology (roughly, 1700–1800) was characterized by its own conceptions of the nature of man. Man was seen as being rational, having free will, and seeking that which would be most productive of pleasure or happiness. Such views, of course, represented a significant departure from the idea that man was under the control of supernatural forces and that criminal behavior was a function of demons. For an understanding of the magnitude of this shift in thinking during the eighteenth century, it is best to examine the ideas of the two most influential contributors to classical criminology—Cesare Beccaria and Jeremy Bentham.

Beccaria, who was influenced by French rationalism and humanitarianism, strongly attacked the arbitrary and inconsistent "criminal justice" practices of the mid-eighteenth century. In his major work, Beccaria reacted against the secret accusations, inhumane punishments, and lack of concern for the defendant's rights that characterized criminal justice. He articulated the framework of what came to be known as the classical school of criminology, that is, (1) that the motivation underlying all social action must be the utilitarian value of that action (the greatest happiness for the greatest number); (2) that crime is an injury to society and can only be measured by assessing the extent of that injury (focus on the act and the extent of damage, not intent); (3) that the prevention of crime is more important than its punishment; (4) that secret accusations and torture should be eliminated and the trial process ought to be speedy and the accused treated fairly and humanely throughout the process; (5) that the only valid purpose of punishment is deterrence, not social revenge; and (6) that incarceration should be used more widely, but at the same time, conditions for those confined must be vastly upgraded and systems of classification developed to prevent haphazardly mixing all types of inmates.

Beccaria had enormous influence on the reformation of criminal justice. For example, he proposed that the courts should mete out punishments to the offender in direct proportion to the harm caused by the crime. To accomplish this, it was necessary that all crimes be classified according to some assessment of their social harm and, further, that the penal codes must prescribe for each crime exact penalties that would be useful deterrents to crime:

> A scale of crimes may be formed of which the first degree should consist of those which immediately tend to the dissolution of society; and the last, of the smallest possible injustice done to a private member of society. Between those extremes will be comprehended all actions contrary to the public good, which are called criminal.…Any action which is not comprehended in the above mentioned scale, will not be called a crime, or punished as such.

One need only observe the deliberations of state legislatures today during the process of revising a state's criminal code to understand and appreciate the lasting effect which Beccaria has had on our criminal laws. The arguménts and considerations of lawmakers today are, for the most part, still influenced by this concept of the criminal as a rational person who acts as a result of free will on a pleasure-seeking basis. Contemporary punishments prescribed by the law are generally well defined, even though they are administered in a very inexact manner. And the widespread belief that the enactment of laws is the best method of social control clearly has at least some of its intellectual roots in the work of Beccaria.

Several of Beccaria's other ideas have contemporary significance. Perhaps the most notable of these is his assertion that the speed and certainty of punishment, rather than its severity, are the most critical factors in deterrence. The modern criminal justice system, characterized by broad discretion on the part of the police, prosecutors, judges, guards, and parole boards; discrimination against the poor and minorities; court delays and months of pretrial detainment; and the use of plea bargaining, offers neither swiftness nor certainty. Furthermore, Beccaria's advocacy of the humane treatment of incarcerated offenders has certainly never been fully realized. Indeed, many contemporary reformers claim that we have largely replaced corporal punishment with psychological and social persecution.

Jeremy Bentham, a contemporary of Beccaria, was also a major figure in utilitarian social philosophy, and he proposed that all acts must be evaluated so that "the greatest happiness for the greatest number" results. To make such assessments, one would obviously need some method of calculation; Bentham happened to have just such a method. His "felicity calculus" was a superficial, quasi-mathematical attempt to quantify the utility of all conceivable acts. Humorous in retrospect, his attempt to catalogue the almost infinite varieties of behavior was nevertheless understandable, given the uncertainties of the criminal justice system he was attempting to reform.

Bentham's theory of human motivation—that man pursues pleasure and tries to avoid pain—led him to argue that criminal penalties should prescribe a degree of punishment (pain) just sufficient to offset the potential gains (pleasure) of criminal behavior, so that the net result (negative utility) would be deterrence. Bentham further believed that the punishment should "fit the crime," and he generally seemed to favor restitution over physical punishment. Given Bentham's concept of deterrence, punishment in general was regarded as a necessary evil intended to prevent greater harm or evil.

The social control philosophy that characterized classical criminology, then, was based on the assumption that the would-be criminal could be deterred by the threat of punishment if that punishment was swift, certain, appropriate for the offense, and sufficiently unpleasant to offset any potential gains to be realized by committing the act. These principles were advocated by classicists across the entire range of available punishments, whether they involved the loss of money, the loss of freedom, or the loss of life. The impact of classical criminology on the penal codes remains clear, even though in actual practice much of the vagueness and arbitrary abuse of discretion remains problematic.

Despite the anticipated ability to administer the principles of the classical school, the fact was that enforcement and implementation were quite problematic. Especially controversial was the classical position that individual differences and particular situations were irrelevant in assigning responsibility. The focus on the act committed, rather than on any characteristics or qualities of the person, came to be regarded as imprudent as did the practice of treating persons who clearly were incompetent, for various reasons, as competent solely because of commission of a given act. These principles were criticized strongly because they did not promote justice anywhere except on paper, in an abstract sort of way.

The idealized concept of justice held by the classicists, perhaps best symbolized by the familiar image of a blindfolded Lady Justice holding scales in her hand, was regarded by neoclassical revisionists (1800–1876) as too impersonal and rigid. The classical theorists, in their indignation over the inconsistencies and other inadequacies of the criminal justice system, had overreacted. They had designed a system which was so dispassionate and "objective" that it could not deliver justice to a society of human beings not identical to one another.

The neoclassicists were successful in introducing some modifications of the free-will doctrine. Criminological thought was revised to readmit some determinism—not the magical, supernatural determinism of demonology, but rather an awareness that certain factors could operate to impair one's reason and thereby mitigate personal responsibility to an extent. While retaining the essential positions articulated by the classicists, considerations involving individual differences began to appear during the neoclassical period. Age, mental status, physical condition, and other factors which could alter one's ability to discern right from wrong were acknowledged grounds for a decision of partial responsibility.

Far from regarding their views as a general theory of human behavior, the neoclassicists were actually focusing on what they viewed as a small minority of the population. There was no attempt to assert that all persons (not even all criminals) are partially shaped and controlled by deterministic forces. On the contrary, neoclassicists continued to view man as a rational, pleasure-seeking being who was personally responsible for his behavior except in abnormal circumstances or in the case of children who were not old enough to know right from wrong.

The neoclassical revisions outlined above meant that criminology had developed a dominant theoretical perspective that viewed man as essentially rational and behavior as volitional, but allowed for some mitigation of responsibility under certain circumstances. This theoretical framework provided the foundation for many legal systems, including that of the United States. The implications for sentencing and for the criminal justice system included the recognition that a particular sentence could have different effects on different offenders and an awareness that the prison environment could affect the future criminality of the offender. This allowed for much more flexibility than did the classical school in determining the appropriate punishment. Many recent "reforms" in penology, such as probation, parole, suspended sentences, and many programs designed for certain "types of offenders, would be inconsistent with the classical emphases on uniformity and certainty of punishment.

Determinism

A book written in 1876 by an Italian psychiatrist was to provide the impetus necessary to shift the focus of criminology from the crime to the criminal. The book was called *The Criminal Man*, and its author was Cesare Lombroso; the result was the development of the "positive school" in criminology. Lacking the moralistic tones of the earliest positivist Auguste Comte, Lombroso's approach was clearly Darwinian, focusing on biological determinism.

As the title of his classic book implies, Lombroso believed that there was indeed a criminal type, or "born criminal," who was discernibly different from noncriminals in physical ways. In short, he was convinced that criminals bore bodily stigmata which marked them as a separate class of people. Following Darwin's monumental work by less than two decades, Lombrosian theory postulated that criminals had not fully evolved but were, instead, inferior organisms reminiscent of apelike, preprimitive man, incapable of adapting to modern civilization. Specifically, Lombroso described the criminal as "atavistic" (a concept used earlier by Darwin) in that the criminal was physically characteristic of a lower phylogenetic level. From his extensive physical measurements, autopsy findings, and other observations, Lombroso concluded that criminals disproportionately possessed an asymmetrical cranium, prognathism (excessive jaw), eye defects, oversized ears, prominent cheekbones, abnormal palate, receding forehead, sparse beard, woolly hair, long arms, abnormal dentition, twisted nose, fleshy and swollen lips, and inverted sex organs. He also noted such non physical anomalies as a lack of morality, excessive vanity, cruelty, and tattooing.

It would be misleading to imply that Lombroso held firmly to the idea that his was the sole explanation for crime. While continuing to believe that his theory explained part of the difference between criminals and noncriminals, Lombroso ultimately accepted environmental and other factors as equally valid contributing causes of crime.

While positivism, since Lombroso's day, has taken in a lot of intellectual territory, there remains a unifying framework that is visible in the work of his successors. That general framework consists of the following:

1. A general rejection of metaphysical and speculative approaches.
2. Denial of the "free-will" conception of man and substitution of a "deterministic" model.
3. A clear distinction between science and law, on one hand, and morals, on the other.

4. The application, as far as practicable, of the scientific method.

These principles of positivism have been applied to the study of the criminal from various and diverse theoretical perspectives. Although these perspectives differ in significant ways, they retain the essence of positivism as described above. The theories to be discussed range from purely individualistic approaches to more macrolevel, sociological theories.

The "Italian School"

The origins of positivism in criminology have a decidedly Italian character. Besides Lombroso, the other Italian pioneers in this school of thought were Enrico Ferri and Raffaele Garofalo. Although emphasizing different points as critical in the study of the criminal, both Ferri and Garofalo were adamant in their espousal of, and adherence to, the positivist approach.

Enrico Ferri, a pupil of Lombroso, is perhaps best known for his classification of criminals as insane, born, occasional, habitual, and drawn to criminality as a result of passion. This topology of offenders represented an attempt by Ferri to conceptualize in anthropological categories the continuum of criminality. He believed that the differences between categories were differences of degree and of the danger represented for society.

The third member of the "Italian school," Raffaele Garofalo, attempted to construct a universal definition of crime—one that would be based on the concept of "natural crime," or acts that offend the basic moral sentiments of pity (a revulsion against the voluntary infliction of suffering on others) and probity (respect for the property rights of others). Garofalo's approach to the crime problem was primarily psychological and legal. He perceived some criminals as psychological degenerates who were morally unfit. His background as a jurist led him to advocate reforms in the criminal justice system so that the criminal could be dealt with in a manner more in line with his theory. Garofalo believed that the criminal must be eliminated, citing Darwin's observations on the functions of biological adaptation as a rationale for this "remedy." Since, according to this bio-organismic analogy,

the criminal was one who had not adapted to civilized life, Garofalo saw only three alternatives—all of which involved some type of elimination: (1) death, where there is a permanent psychological defect; (2) partial elimination for those suitable to live only in a more primitive environment, including long-term or life imprisonment, transportation, and relatively mild isolation; and (3) enforced reparation, for those whose crimes were committed as a result of the press of circumstances.

Physical-Biological Theories

The prototype for all physical-biological theories of crime were the early (and nonpositivist) craniologists-phrenologists, who believed that the "faculties of the mind" were revealed by the external shape of the skull. This vastly oversimplified and pseudoscientific approach nevertheless predates all other theories of a physical-biological nature.

Such theories have grown increasingly sophisticated and scientific since those earliest attempts to explain man's function by analyzing his cranial structure. In addition to the Italian school, there have been a number of other intellectual contributions to this physical-biological tradition.

Charles Goring has been widely credited with refuting Lombroso's contention that there is a criminal "physical type." However, Goring's critique was aimed at Lombroso's methodology, not necessarily his theory or his conclusions, for which Goring had a certain affinity. In Goring's famous book, *The English Convict*, he presented an analysis of 3,000 English convicts, and as a matter of fact, he did find what he regarded as a positive association between certain physical differences and the offender's crime and social class. As Mannheim noted:

> In the controversy "heredity or environment"…he was on Lombroso's side, and perhaps even more than the latter he was inclined to underrate environmental influences: "Crime is only to a trifling extent (if to any) the product of social inequalities, of adverse environment or of other manifestations of…the force of circumstances."

Goring's general interpretation of the height and weight deficiencies of the criminal population he studied was that the criminal suffered from hereditary inferiority. He also believed that criminals were most different from noncriminals with respect to their intelligence, which he found to be defective. Finally, Goring added a third category—that of moral defectiveness—to account for those whose criminality could not be explained by either of the first two factors. But the main thrust of Goring's theoretical position was a physiological one, thus placing him within this tradition of thought.

Not everyone agreed that Goring's criticisms of Lombroso's methodology were valid. The leading skeptic was Earnest Hooton, an anthropologist at Harvard University. In *The American Criminal*, Hooton presented data and interpretations based on a twelve-year study of 13,873 criminals and 3,203 noncriminals. After analyzing 107 physical characteristics, Hooton concluded that criminals, when compared with the control group, were "organically inferior." Describing their distinctive characteristics, he included low foreheads, high pinched nasal roots, compressed faces, and narrow jaws. These he cited as evidence for his assertion of organic inferiority, and he attributed crime to "the impact of environment upon low grade human organisms."

Hooton also constructed a topology of criminals based on physical constitution. He argued that murderers and robbers tended to be tall and thin; tall, heavy men were most likely to be killers and to commit forgery and fraud as well; undersized men were disposed to commit assault, rape, and other sex crimes; and men lacking any notable physical characteristics had no criminal specialty. The primary problem with all of this is that Hooton had considered only the offender's *current* crime, whereas in fact half or more of Hooton's prisoners had previously been imprisoned for an offense other than that noted by Hooton.

Studies by Ernst Kretschmer and William Sheldon are typical of the work of more recent proponents of the constitutional inferiority-body type theorists. Although differing in the details of their approaches, both men advocated the idea that body type and temperament are closely related. Both developed topologies relating body types to certain forms of behavior, including crime.

Some investigators have focused specifically on the effects of heredity, especially genetic deficiencies, in producing criminality. In this regard, the studies of "criminal families" were quite interesting. Perhaps the most well-known efforts along these genealogical lines were those of Richard Dugdale and Henry Goddard, both of whom attempted to analyze the apparently excessive criminality of entire families by relating it to feeblemindedness. The term *mental testers* has often been applied to this method of inquiry.

More recently, another line of inquiry has focused on the criminality of twins. Lange, Rosanoff, Christiansen, and others have studied twins in an attempt to determine the effect of heredity in producing criminality. The basic idea has been that if a greater percentage of monozygotic ("identical") twins than of dizygotic ("fraternal") twins are concordant in being criminal, that is, if they are both criminal, then the effect of heredity would, theoretically at least, have to be given greater weight than other factors. Although the methodological criticisms aimed at Rosanoff have been less damaging than those directed at Lange, the fact remains that neither study can be regarded as conclusive in finding that identical twins are far more likely to be concordant in terms of criminality.

Finally, some of the most sophisticated research employing a physical-biological model has been focused on the neuroendocrine system. The essential proposition of these theories has been that criminal behavior is often due to emotional disturbances produced by glandular imbalance. Often using the electroencephalogram (EEG) as a diagnostic aid, this biochemical approach to crime thus far offers more promise than clear-cut and unequivocal findings.

Psychopathology

A number of positivist theories of crime have used the paradigm based on individual psychopathology. The father of this approach was, of course, Sigmund Freud. His work, along with that of his intellectual successors, has focused on man's unconscious. The explanation for criminal behavior which grew out of this approach was that such behavior is largely the result of drives which are uncontrolled because of a defective personality structure. There are a seemingly endless number of applications of psychoanalytic theory to crime. Conditions such as psychosis and neurosis have been related to criminal behavior by psychoanalysts, as have most forms of deviant behavior. The essential contention of the psychoanalytic approach is that all behavior is purposive and meaningful. Such behavior is viewed as the symbolic release of repressed mental conflict. From this perspective, the criminal is one who acts not out of free will, as the classicists believed, but as an expression of deterministic forces of a subconscious nature. Such a view, of course, leads to a theory of social control based on a clinical model of therapeutic rehabilitation.

A derivation of the psychoanalytic approach and the "mental testers" has been the emphasis on personality deviation as an explanation for crime. Relying on theoretical constructs of the "healthy" personality and the "abnormal" personality, the personality deviation approach has become increasingly popular, though not well validated. Using psychological tests such as the Rorschach, the Wechsler Adult Intelligence Scale, the Minnesota Multiphasic Personality Inventory, the Thematic Apperception Test, and many others, psychologists have led in this attempt to construct causal theory. Advocates of this approach generally attempt to diagnose the psychopathological features of one's personality and then focus on these "target areas" using a variety of interventions.

Economic Factors

The effects of economic inequality are undeniably instrumental in producing great variability in one's "life chances." The pervasive day-to-day realities of poverty limit the chances of millions of people in securing adequate health care, housing, education, jobs, and opportunities. The crippling effects of poverty can hardly be comprehended by those not confronted with them on a daily basis. For these and related reasons, some theorists have attempted to relate at least some crimes to economic inequality. Such a theoretical position has had a special attraction for Marxists.

Historically, the most extensive application of Marxist theory to criminology was provided by Willem Bonger. The central argument Bonger

made is that capitalism, more than any other system of economic exchange, is characterized by the control of the means of production by relatively few people, with the vast majority of the population totally deprived of these means. The economic subjugation of the masses, he argues, stifles men's "social instincts" and leads to unlimited egoism, insensitivity, and a spirit of domination on the part of the powerful, and the poor are subjected to all sorts of pathogenic conditions: bad housing, constant association with "undesirables," uncertain physical security, terrible poverty, frequent sickness, and unemployment. Bonger maintained that the historical condition of this class of people was severely damaged by these conditions of economic subjugation. He attempted to demonstrate connections between certain types of crime (e.g., prostitution, alcoholism, and theft) and economic inequality. This explanation of crime suggests that the socioeconomic system is causally related to crime and would have to be restructured to reduce crime.

Although Bonger did not deny the influence of hereditary traits, he attributed no causal power to them in the absence of criminogenic environmental conditions. Throughout most of his writings, he stressed a socioeconomic view of crime and attacked the views of Lombroso and others of a physical-biological persuasion. His deterministic approach, along with his application of quantitative methods and his rejection of metaphysical, speculative "explanations" for crime, places Bonger in the positivist school, even though his primary focus was on the social structure, rather than the individual. Bonger's theory, which illustrates the economic approach to criminal etiology, is quite near the sociological approach in many ways, especially in its macrolevel focus on the structure of society.

Sociological Explanations

The economic depression of the 1930s and the social problems which accompanied it helped further an interest in socioeconomic factors related to crime. Not only the economic condition of the nation but also the seemingly disorganized condition of many areas of major American cities were causes for great concern on the part of those seeking explanations for crime. The so-called Chicago school dominated criminological thought for a number of years, focusing on a social disorganization model. Specifically, this school of thought held that the interstitial areas of our major cities (heavily populated at the time by immigrants) reflected a high degree of sociocultural heterogeneity. This, they believed, resulted in a breakdown in social organization and norms, which made deviant behavior much more commonplace. Using analogies based on plant ecology, the Chicago school believed that rapid social change in "natural areas" of the city was undermining the basic social controls of a stable cultural heritage.

The theoretical successor to the Chicago school and its social disorganization approach was the culture conflict perspective, best articulated by Thorsten Sellin. The essential contention of culture conflict theory is that crime results from the absence of one clear-cut, consensual model of normative behavior. The increasing conflict in norms that came with immigration and the rapid pluralization of our society provided the most fertile ground for culture conflict theory. Although still applicable in nations with significant levels of immigration (such as Israel), it has largely been replaced in the United States by other perspectives.

There have been several sociological theories of cultural transmission, each of which has stressed different dynamics. One, known generally as "subcultural theory," had its general intellectual origins in the work of Emile Durkheim, but was initially applied in the United States by Robert Merton. For Merton, the explanation for crime rested in the disjunction existing for many between culturally defined success goals and the institutionalized means available to meet those goals. For some, this discrepancy results in criminal behavior, according to Merton.

Elaborations of this same general statement were made later by Albert Cohen, who saw the subculture which developed from this disjunction as a negative one that attempted to invert society's success goals and create its own, more realistic goals; and by Richard Cloward and Lloyd Ohlin, who added the idea that illegitimate, as well as legitimate, opportunity structures were differentially accessible to individuals and that one could become either a criminal or a respected citizen, depending on which means were available.

Walter Miller offered an alternative view of the lower-class subculture. He saw it as essentially characterized by its own value system and goals, not perpetually seeking to emulate the higher strata to gain status. Crime, for Miller, was a function of the normal socialization occurring in the subculture.

Another type of cultural transmission theory is that of Edwin Sutherland. Known as differential association theory, it is essentially a learning theory suggestive of the earlier work of Gabriel Tarde, a French social psychologist.

Sutherland's theory was later modified by Daniel Glaser to take into account the perceived effect of the mass media and other methods of transmitting culture. Glaser's differential identification theory substituted for Sutherland's required personal interaction the following definition of the dynamics:

> A person pursues criminal behavior to the extent that he identifies himself with real or imaginary persons from whose perspective his criminal behavior seems acceptable.

The foregoing presentation of positivism has been intended to provide an overview of the various types of theories comprising this school. No attempt has been made to be exhaustive, but merely illustrative. Numerous other theoretical and empirical contributions could have been discussed; however, the above provide a representative sampling of positivist thought. Unlike either the demonologists of the preclassical period or the classical advocates of a free-will, rational view of man, the positivists' concepts of causation were deterministic and antimetaphysical. Therefore, their theories of social control have also been vastly different. They have advocated change—change of the personality, of the economic system, of the social system. Each of the positivist perspectives on crime developed its own ideas of how to deal with the crime problem, and these "solutions" were, of course, of a physical-biological, psychiatric-psychological, or social-economic nature. Their effect on penal policy is perhaps best symbolized in the name changes of our prisons—from "penitentiaries" to "correctional institutions."

But positivism is not the final chapter of this story. More recent theoretical developments have tended to concentrate on crime as a phenomenon which is determined by factors such as societal reaction (labeling), a system of laws which disproportionately reflects the interests of the wealthy and the powerful, and/or a corrupt and corrupting political system which is itself viewed as producing crime and criminals.

The New Emphasis: "The System"

If positivism shifted society's focus from the crime to the criminal, then clearly that focus has shifted again with the development of the labeling and conflict perspectives, and especially with the emergence of a "radical" criminology perspective in the United States. While these theories differ substantially in their interpretations of crime, one central feature which they have in common is their emphasis on the social and political systems as factors which help to generate the crime problem. Frequently, "the system" is identified as the "cause" of crime because of its unequal distribution of social and political power. Increasingly, the criminal is viewed as a victim—a victim of class struggle, racial discrimination, and other manifestations of inequality.

While there is, to be certain, some continuity between these relatively recent theories and some earlier sociological and economic perspectives, the general thrust of these new explanations is quite different. Most important, there is a much more pervasive political emphasis in current theoretical perspectives.

Labeling, Conflict, and Radical Perspectives

The labeling or "social reaction" approach to crime is reflected in the works of Becker, Lemert, Erikson, Kitsuse, and Schur. This approach represents a significant departure from the absolute determinism of the positivists. The essence of labeling theory is its assertion that crime is relative and is defined

(and thus *created*) socially. The often-quoted statement of Howard Becker perhaps best sums up the approach:

> *Social groups create deviance by making the rules whose infraction constitutes deviance,* and by applying those rules to particular people and labeling them as outsiders. From this point of view, deviance is *not* a quality of the act the person commits, but rather a consequence of the application by others of rules and sanctions to an "offender." The deviant is one to whom that label has successfully been applied; deviant behavior is behavior that people so label.

The labeling approach clearly shifts the focus of inquiry from the individual being labeled and processed to the group and the system doing the labeling and processing.

Finally, recent contributions to what has been called "radical" or "critical" or "Marxist" criminology include Richard Quinney, Ian Taylor, Paul Walton, Jock Young, Anthony Platt, Barry Krisberg, and Herman and Jules Schwendinger. While there are some theoretical differences among these writers, they occupy common intellectual ground within the overview of the development of criminological theory. Their analysis of crime and social control, essentially Marxist in nature, is to be distinguished from the applications of conflict theory to criminology made by Austin Turk and other non-Marxian conflict theorists, as well as the positivist approach taken by the formal Marxist Willem Bonger.

The "radical Marxist" criminologists focus their analysis on the state as a political system controlled by the interests of the "ruling capitalist class," especially through the use of law as a tool to preserve existing inequalities. Much of the work of these theorists deals with the historical conditions of classes which they link, theoretically, with the development and differential enforcement of criminal law. They reject the traditional (functionalist) view that law reflects society's consensus on the norms and values which should control behavior; instead, they argue that law emerges from a conflict of competing interests and serves the interests of the elite "ruling class."

Turk, on the other hand, essentially continues the intellectual tradition of Ralf Dahrendorf and other non-Marxist conflict theorists who have analyzed crime as a result of conflict concerning the distribution of power and authority within society. Rather than isolating the economic system and the class structure related to it, this perspective takes a broader view of the structural factors which produce conflict.

The implications of these perspectives for a philosophy of social control and for the criminal justice system are dramatically different from those suggested by earlier theorists. Again, the centrality of the political dimension is inescapable, whether one is discussing labeling theory, conflict theory, or "radical Marxist" theory. The labeling perspective, which emphasizes the discrepancy between actual criminal behavior and officially detected crime, is a societal reaction theory. It is not the deviance itself that is so important, but the way in which society reacts. This perspective generally is interpreted as advocating less intervention and less labeling of people as "criminal." The criminal justice system is viewed as one which exacerbates the problem of crime; therefore, that system should be reduced and made less powerful.

Conflict and radical Marxist theory also would suggest that there is a need for societal restructuring. However, from these perspectives the criminal justice system merely reflects broader structural arrangements (i.e., the economy, the class system, and/or the distribution of power and authority). Radical Marxists advocate the abolition of capitalism and the development of a socialist society. They tend to view anything less than that as piecemeal "liberal tinkering" with a fatally flawed system. The alternative conflict view would argue that the particular economic system (e.g., capitalism) is not the basic problem and that crime exists in noncapitalist states as well. Crime is viewed as a structural problem resulting from the distribution of power and authority and as a reflection of unstable relationships between legal authorities and subjects.

In conclusion, it should be apparent that while man's attempts to explain crime have covered a tremendous range of ideas, there are parallels among these ideas. The idea that crime is a result of demonic possession is perhaps not a great deal different than the "mental illness" explanation advanced at a much later point in history. Both are largely deterministic, even though one is "magical" and the other "scientific."

Similarly, the rationales cited by the state for the use of imprisonment have varied from "moral reform" to "deterrence" to "rehabilitation," "public protection," and "punishment." Meanwhile, the perceptions of those imprisoned by the state have also changed, from passive acceptance of society's reaction to the increasing tendency to view themselves as "political prisoners" of an unjust legal and political system. It is apparent, therefore, that the linkage between theories of crime and social control philosophies must be evaluated on two levels: (1) the connections between theoretical explanations and formal policies, and (2) the changing rationales for employing essentially similar social control practices (e.g., "punitive" imprisonment vs. "therapeutic" correctional rehabilitation).

Discussion Questions

1. Why were offenders often executed in "primitive" societies?

2. What are six tenets advocated by Beccaria?

3. What assumption underlies classical criminology?

CHAPTER 3

Characteristics of the Criminal Law

Edwin H. Sutherland ■ Donald R. Cressey

It is fitting that the classic definition of crime, offered in the following excerpt, be presented by two legendary criminologists, Edwin H. Sutherland and Donald R. Cressey. As they explain, crime emanates from the criminal law, a body of rules containing unique characteristics that differentiate it from other rules and regulations found in a society. Although crime is the codification of social values shared by those possessing political authority, it is variable in nature, changing from time to time and place to place. Nevertheless, unlike personal grievances or individual wrongs, crime is believed to do social harm, harm that threatens the entire group or the social order. For that reason the state becomes the injured party in a crime, and it is the state that uses its power to control crime and punish criminal offenders.

At the same time that Sutherland and Cressey present the legal definition of crime, discuss those characteristics that differentiate it from civil, or tort, law, and establish its legal parameters, they also point out that this definition represents an ideal type that may be difficult to find in reality. This definition of crime may satisfy certain legal requirements, but it is difficult to make behavioral sense of it. The term crime represents broad categories of behavior that are vastly different in nature and motive, often sharing little more than violation of the criminal code. When grouping crimes

into broad, general categories, such as felony and misdemeanor, important behavioral differences are lost and offenders may be judged on inaccurate and misleading criteria. The legal definition of crime prevails, however, in structuring the discipline of criminology.

Criminal behavior is behavior in violation of the criminal law. No matter what the degree of immorality, reprehensibility, or indecency of an act, it is not a crime unless it is prohibited by the criminal law. The criminal law, in turn, is defined conventionally as a body of specific rules regarding human conduct which have been promulgated by political authority, which apply uniformly to all members of the classes to which the rules refer, and which are enforced by punishment administered by the state. The characteristics which distinguish the body of rules regarding human conduct from other rules are, therefore, *politicality, specificity, uniformity,* and *penal sanction.* However, these are characteristics of an ideal, completely rational system of criminal law; in practice the differences between the criminal law and other bodies of rules for human conduct are not clear-cut. Also, the ideal characteristics of the criminal law are only rarely features of the criminal law in action.

The vast majority of the rules which define certain behavior as crime are found in constitutions, treaties, common law, enactments by the legislatures of the state and its subdivisions, and in judicial and administrative regulations. However, the criminal law is not merely a collection of

Reprinted from: Edwin H. Sutherland and Donald R. Cressey, "Characteristics of the Criminal Law." In *Criminology,* 9th Edition, pp. 4-8, 12-17. Copyright © 1974 by J.B. Lippincott: New York. Reprinted by permission from Elaine Cressey.

written proscriptions. The agencies of enforcement are the police and the courts, and these agencies, rather than the legislature, determine what the law is. According to one school of thought, police and courts merely "apply" the law in an evenhanded manner to all persons who come before them. However, both the techniques used by justice administrators in interpreting and applying the statutes and the body of ideals held by them are a part of the law in action, as truly as are the written statutes.

The court decision in one controversy becomes a part of the body of rules used in making decisions in other controversies. Consequently, law students must read court decisions in order to learn law. Further evidence supporting this view that the courts as well as the legislatures make law is found whenever the nation is confronted with the problem of selecting a justice of the Supreme Court. At such times it is explicitly recognized that the nature of the law itself, not merely its administration, is determined to a considerable extent by the proportion of liberals and conservatives on the supreme bench. Thus, behind the behavior of courts is public opinion. Also, between the courts and the legislature are intermediate agencies such as the police. Many statutes are never enforced; some are enforced only on rare occasions; others are enforced with a striking disregard for uniformity. Enforcement and administrative agencies are affected by shifts in public opinion, budget allocations, and in power. As a consequence, the law often changes while the statutes remain constant.

Politicality is regarded almost universally as a necessary element in criminal law. The rules of the trade union, the church, or the family are not regarded as criminal law, nor are violations of these rules regarded as crimes. Only violations of rules made by the state are crimes. This distinction between the state and other groups is not only arbitrary but also is difficult to maintain when attention is turned to societies where patriarchal power, private self-help, popular justice, and other forerunners of legislative justice are found. This may be illustrated by the gypsies, who have no territorial organization and no written law, but who do have customs, taboos, a semijudicial council which makes definite decisions regarding the propriety

of behavior of members of the group and often imposes penalties. These councils have no political authority in the territory in which they happen to be operating, but they perform the same function within the gypsy group that courts perform in the political order. Similarly, early Chinese immigrants in Chicago established an unofficial court which had no political authority, but which, in practice, exercised the functions of an authorized court in controversies among the Chinese people. The American "Cosa Nostra" has a legislative and judicial system for administering the functional equivalent of the criminal law among its members.[1] Thus, the element of politicality is arbitrary and is not sharply defined. The earlier systems of law, together with the present relation between public opinion and legal precepts, raise the question, When should the rules of a group be regarded as the law and violations of these rules as crimes?[2]

Specificity is included as an element in the definition of criminal law because of the contrast in this respect between criminal law and civil law. The civil law may be general. An old German civil code, for instance, provided that whoever intentionally injured another in a manner contrary to the common standards of right conduct was bound to indemnify him. The criminal law, on the other hand, generally gives a strict definition of a specific act, and when there is doubt as to whether a definition describes the behavior of a defendant, the judge is obligated to decide in favor of the defendant. In one famous case, for example, the behavior of a person who had taken an airplane was held to be exempt from the consequences of violating a statute regarding the taking of "self-propelled vehicles," on the ground that at the time the law was enacted "vehicles" did not include airplanes.[3] Some laws, to be sure, are quite general, as the laws in regard to nuisances, conspiracy, vagrancy, disorderly conduct, use of the mails to defraud, and official misfeasance. The criminal law, however, contains no general provision that any act which, when done with culpable intent, injures the public can be prosecuted as a punishable offense.[4] Consequently it frequently happens that one act is prohibited by law while another act, which is very similar in nature and effects, is not prohibited and is not illegal.[5]

Uniformity or regularity is included in the conventional definition of criminal law because law attempts to provide evenhanded justice without respect to persons. This means that no exceptions are made to criminal liability because of a person's social status; an act described as a crime is crime, no matter who perpetrates it. Also, uniformity means that the law-enforcement process shall be administered without regard for the status of the persons who have committed crimes or are accused of committing crimes. This ideal is rarely followed in practice, principally because it results in injustices. Rigid rule is softened by police discretion and judicial discretion. Rigid rule treats all persons in the class to which the law refers exactly alike, while police and judicial discretion take cognizance of the circumstances of the offense and the characteristics of the offender, a process which has come to be called "individualization."[6] Much of what happens to persons accused of delinquency or crime is determined in a process of negotiation. Equity, also, developed as a method of doing justice in particular situations where iron regularity would not do justice. As precedents in equity have accumulated, the decisions tend to become uniform, and thus similar to law. In line with the present tendency toward judicial discretion, authority has been conferred by legislative assemblies upon many administrative bodies to make regulations applicable to particular situations such as length of prison term and parole.

Penal sanction, as one of the elements in the orthodox definition of law, refers to the notion that violators will be punished or, at least, threatened with punishment by the state. Punishment under the law differs from that imposed by a mob in that it is to be applied dispassionately by representatives of the state in such a manner that it may win the approval of the cool judgment of impartial observers. A law which does not provide a penalty that will cause suffering is regarded as quite impotent and, in fact, no criminal law at all. However, the punishment provided may be very slight; in the courts of honor a verdict was reached, a party was declared guilty, and the disgrace of the declaration of guilt was the only punishment. In view of the difficulty of identifying the criminal law of nonliterate societies, where the institution of "the state"

is not obvious, the suggestion has been made that the penal sanction is the only essential element in the definition of criminal law, and that wherever proscriptions are enforced by a penal sanction, there criminal law exists. This is in contrast to the tort law, where the court orders the defendant to reimburse the plaintiff, but does not punish him for damaging the plaintiff.

The punitive aspect of criminal law clearly is on the wane. In the juvenile court and to a smaller extent in the criminal courts, the tendency is to discover and use methods which are effective in forestalling crime, whether they are punitive or not. By using juvenile court procedures, we have attempted to avoid applying the "stigma of crime" to the acts of children. In theory, the juvenile court does not determine the guilt or innocence of a criminal; it merely acts in behalf of a child who is in need of help. The court's objective is treatment, not the meting out of penalties. However, except for children who are called delinquent because they have been neglected, or are "predelinquent," juvenile delinquencies are acts which would be crimes if committed by an adult. Consequently, juvenile delinquencies continue to be acts which are punishable by law, even if the punishment is kept in the background.[7] Similarly, the states and the federal government for a generation or two have been enacting laws for the regulation of manufacturing, commerce, agriculture, and other occupations. The persons affected by such laws are ordinarily respectable and powerful, and the legislatures have adapted the procedures to the status of these persons. Violations of these laws are crimes, but they are not always tried in the criminal courts. Instead, they are handled in civil and equity courts or in administrative commissions; the conventional penalties of fine and imprisonment are kept in the background to be used only as a last resort, and coercion in the first instance consists of injunctions and cease-and-desist orders. Thus these persons of social importance avoid the "stigma of crime," just as, to a lesser degree, juvenile delinquents do. The acts remain as crimes, however, for they are punishable by law.[8]

The conventional view is that a crime is an offense against the state, while, in contrast, a tort in violation of civil law is an offense against an individual. A particular act may be considered as an offense against an individual and also against the state, and is either a tort or a crime or both according to the way it is handled. A person who has committed an act of assault, for example, may be ordered by the civil court to pay the victim a sum of $500 for the damages to his interests, and he may also be ordered by the criminal court to pay a fine of $500 to the state. The payment of the first $500 is not punishment, but payment of the second $500 is punishment.

This distinction between individual damage and social harm is extremely difficult to make in the legal systems of nonliterate societies, where court procedures are relatively informal. Even in modern society, the distinction is dubious, for it rests upon the assumption that "individual" and "group" or "state" are mutually exclusive. For practical purposes, the individual is treated as if he were autonomous, but in fact an act which harms an individual also harms the group in which he has membership. Also, in modern society the indefiniteness of the distinction between torts and crimes is apparent when the victim of an act which is both a tort and a crime uses the criminal law as a method of forcing restitution which could not be secured with equal facility in the civil courts. Prosecutors frequently complain about the use of the criminal law as a collecting agency, especially because the victim who is reimbursed by the offender prior to trial then refuses to act as a witness....

The rules of criminal law contain only definitions of specific crimes, such as burglary, robbery, and rape, but legal scholars have been able to abstract certain general principles from such definitions. These general principles are said to apply to all crimes and are the criteria ideally used in determination of whether any particular behavior is or is not criminal. They are consistent with the ideal characteristics of the whole body of the criminal law—politicality, specificity, uniformity, and penal sanction—and, in fact, they may be viewed as translations of the ideal characteristics of the criminal law into statements of the ideal characteristics of all crimes. The concern is shifted from determination of the characteristics of a body of rules to determination of the general characteristics of the many specific acts described

in those rules. Thus, for example, penal sanction is a general characteristic of the criminal law, and liability to legally prescribed punishment is a characteristic of all acts or omissions properly called crime. Obviously, a set of criteria used for deciding whether or not any specific act is a crime must be more precise than statements of the general characteristics of a body of rules.

One extensive and thorough analysis of crimes has resulted in a description of seven interrelated and overlapping differentiae of crime.[9] Ideally, behavior would not be called crime unless all seven differentiae were present. The following brief description of the differentiae is greatly simplified.

First, before behavior can be called crime there must be certain external consequences or "harm." A crime has a harmful impact on social interests; a "mental" or emotional state is not enough. Even if one decides to commit a crime but changes his mind before he does anything about it, he has committed no crime. The intention is not taken for the deed.

Second, the harm must be legally forbidden, must have been proscribed in penal law. Antisocial behavior is not crime unless it is prohibited by law. As indicated previously, the law must have specifically prohibited the harm which occurs. Penal law does not have a retroactive effect; there is a long-standing tradition against the enactment of ex post facto legislation.

Third, there must be "conduct"; that is, there must be an intentional or reckless action or inaction which brings the harmful consequences about. One who is physically forced to pull the trigger of a gun does not commit murder, even if someone dies from the bullet.

Fourth, "criminal intent," or *mens rea*, must be present. Hall suggests that legal scholars have often confused intentionality (deliberate functioning to reach a goal) and motivation (the reasons or grounds for the end-seeking).[10] *Mens rea* is identified with the former, not with the latter. The "motives" for a crime might be "good," but the intention itself might be an intention to effect a harm forbidden by the criminal law, a criminal intent. Thus if a man decides to kill his starving children because he feels that they will pass on to a better world, his motive is good, but his intention is wrong. Persons who are "insane" at the time they perpetrate legally forbidden harms do not commit crimes, for the necessary *mens rea* is not present.[11]

Fifth, there must be a fusion or concurrence of *mens rea* and conduct. This means, for example, that a policeman who goes into a house to make an arrest and who then commits a crime while still in the house after making the arrest cannot be considered a trespasser from the beginning. The criminal intent and the conduct do not fuse or concur.

Sixth, there must be a "causal" relation between the legally forbidden harm and the voluntary misconduct. The "conduct" of one who fails to file an income tax return is his failure to take pen and ink, fill out the form, etc.; the "harm" is the absence of a return in the collector's office. In this case, the "causal" relation between the two obviously is present. But if, for example, one man shot another (conduct) and the victim suffocated while in a hospital recovering from the wound, the relationship between conduct and harm (death) is not so clear-cut.

Seventh, there must be legally prescribed punishment. Not only must the harm be proscribed by law but, as indicated above, the proscription must carry a threat of punishment to violators. The voluntary conduct must be punishable by law.

These differentiae of crime are all concerned with the nature of the behavior which can properly be called crime, but in making decisions about most cases each criterion need not be considered separately but individually. If the *mens rea* conduct, the legally proscribed harm are obviously present for example, the "causal" relation between harm and misconduct almost certainly will be present. In sum, the differentiae represent the kinds of subject matter with which both criminal lawyers and criminal-law theorists must deal.

There are, of course, many exceptions to the generalization that these are the elements of all crimes. Criminal-law theory is not a body of precise principles, and consequently there are deviations from that which is logical and ideal. For purposes of illustration, we may cite two major exceptions to the above differentiae.

First, criminal intent, in the ordinary meaning of the concept, need not be present for some crimes. In some cases—the so-called strict-liability

cases—the offender's intent is not considered. Instead, the person is held responsible for the results of his conduct, regardless of his intention. The handling of "statutory rape" is a case in point—no matter how elaborate the calculations, inquiries, or research which a male utilizes in reaching the conclusion that his female companion is above the age of consent, if he has sexual relations with her and it is subsequently shown than she was below the age of consent, he has committed statutory rape. Certain "public welfare" offenses, such as traffic offenses and the selling of adulterated food, are handled under the same rule. Similarly, under the "felony-murder–misdemeanor-manslaughter doctrine" defendants are held criminally liable for much more serious offenses that they intended to commit. If one sets fire to a building and a fireman dies trying to extinguish the flames, the offender is liable for murder; if the offense had been a misdemeanor rather than arson, he would have been liable for manslaughter.

Hall has severely criticized this doctrine and the general conception of strict liability in the criminal law. He contends that it is "bad law," stating that "there is no avoiding the conclusion that strict liability cannot be brought within the scope of penal law."[12] A behavioristic school in jurisprudence, however, insists that the intent can be determined only by the circumstances of the act, and that a translation of these circumstances into mental terms confuses rather than clarifies the procedure. It contends that the doctrine of *mens rea* should be greatly modified or even abandoned. In criminology, the inclusion in the concept "crime" of behavior which was not intended by the actor makes general theoretical explanation of all crime extremely difficult. No current theoretical explanation of criminal behavior can account for the strict-liability offenses.

Second, "motive" and "intention" are confused in many court decisions. In the crime of libel, for instance, motive is explicitly considered. In many states, one cannot publish truthful, albeit damaging, statements about another unless his motive is good. Criminal conspiracy also frequently involves consideration and evaluation of a defendant's motives as well as his intention. In most instances, however, motivation ideally is taken into account only in the *administration* of the criminal law, i.e., in making a decision as to the severity of the punishment which should be accorded a criminal.

Crime is relative from the legal point of view and also from the social point of view. The criminal law has had a constantly changing content. Many early crimes were primarily religious offenses, and these remained important until recent times; now few religious offenses are included in penal codes.[13] It was a crime in Iceland in the Viking age for a person to write verses about another, even if the sentiment was complimentary, if the verses exceeded four stanzas in length. A Prussian law of 1784 prohibited mothers and nurses from taking children under two years of age into their beds. The English villein in the fourteenth century was not allowed to send his son to school, and no one lower than a freeholder was permitted by law to keep a dog. The following have at different times been crimes: printing a book, professing the medical doctrine of circulation of the blood, driving with reins, sale of coin to foreigners, having gold in the house, buying goods on the way to market or in the market for the purpose of selling them at a higher price, writing a check for less than one dollar. On the other hand, many of our present laws were not known to earlier generations—quarantine laws, traffic laws, sanitation laws, factory laws.

Laws differ, also, from one jurisdiction to another at a particular time. The laws of some states require automobile owners to paste certificates of ownership or inspection certificates on the windshield, while adjoining states prohibit the pasting of anything on the windshield. Georgia has a $1,000 fine or six months' incarceration as the maximum penalty for adultery, while in Louisiana adultery is not a crime at all.[14]

In a particular jurisdiction at a particular time there are wide variations in the interpretation and implementation of the law. These variations are related to the specific characteristics of the crimes, to the status of the offenders, and to the status of the enforcers. Sudnow has shown that what is "burglary" or "robbery" or almost any other crime is highly negotiable.[15] Further, gross forms of fraud, such as those committed by confidence men, are easily detected by the regular police, but expert investigators must deal with the subtler forms of fraud which flourish in many areas of business and of the professions. When such experts are provided by politicians interested in making subtle fraud "real crime," what has been mere chicanery is interpreted and dealt with as crime. In this sense, also, crime is relative to the status of the criminals and the situations in which they violate law.

Since crime is not a homogenous type of behavior, efforts have been made to classify crimes. They are frequently classified in respect to atrocity as felonies and misdemeanors. The more serious are called felonies and are usually punishable by death or by confinement in a state prison; the less serious are called misdemeanors and are usually punishable by confinement in a local prison or by fines. As a classification of crimes this is not very useful, as was pointed out long ago by Sir James Stephen, and it is difficult to make a clear-cut distinction between the classes. Though one may agree that assaults, as a class, are more serious offenses than permitting weeds to grow on a vacant lot in violation of a municipal ordinance, the effects of permitting the weeds to grow, in a particular case, may be more serious because of the hay fever produced by the pollen and the resulting incapacitation of many people. The fact that many things which are classed as felonies in one state are classed as misdemeanors in nearby states shows how difficult it is to make a real distinction between them. Even within a single state the distinction is often vague.

The greatest objection to the classification of crimes as felonies and misdemeanors is that it is used also as a classification of criminals. The individual who commits a felony is a felon; the individual who commits a misdemeanor is a misdemeanant. It is assumed that misdemeanants are less dangerous and more susceptible to rehabilitative measures than felons. But it is quite fallacious to judge either dangerousness or the probability of reformation from one act, for an individual may commit a misdemeanor one week, a felony the second week, and a misdemeanor the third. The acts do not represent changes in his character or changes in his dangerousness.

Moreover, the definition of a crime as misdemeanor or felony is influenced by various considerations other than atrocity or dangerousness. Since 1852, when a felony was first defined in

Massachusetts as a crime punishable by confinement in the state prison, at least four changes have been made in the laws of that state determining the conditions under which a sentence is served in state prison rather than in a jail or house of correction. These changes, which also changed crimes from felonies to misdemeanors or the reverse, were not made because of alterations in views regarding the atrocity of crimes but for purely administrative reasons, generally to relieve the congestion of the state prison. In the administration of justice, thousands of persons charged with committing felonies successfully arrange to have the charge reduced to a misdemeanor, and the distinction between the two classes of offense is lost. Consequently there seems to be good reason to abandon this classification....

Discussion Questions

1. Which group (legislature, police, courts) exerts the most influence over the definition/interpretation of what law is? Do you agree/disagree with the authors' contention that it is not the legislature that really defines the law?

2. These authors discuss a number of ways in which police and courts affect the nature and intent of criminal law. Is it desirable for this to take place, or does this undermine the purpose and effects of criminal law?

3. What are some of the problems associated with the classification of crimes by type of crime and by seriousness of crime? How might differences in classification affect the offender, the court, and the prison?

Notes

1. See Jean-Paul Clebert, *The Gypsies*, trans. Charles Duff (London: Vista Books, 1963), pp. 123-33; and Donald R. Cressey, *Theft of the Nation: The Structure and Operations of Organized Crime in America* (New York: Harper and Row, 1969), pp. 162-220.
2. See E. Adamson Hoebel, *The Law of Primitive Man: A Study in Comparative Legal Dynamics* (Cambridge: Harvard University Press, 1954).
3. *McBoyle v. United States*, 283 U.S. 25 (1931).
4. A German law of June 28, 1935, seems to be an exception to this generalization. It provided: "Whoever commits an action which the law declares to be punishable or which is deserving of punishment according to the fundamental idea of a penal law and the sound perception of the people, shall be punished. If no determinate penal law is directly applicable to the action, it shall be punished according to the law, the basic idea of which fits it best." Lawrence Preuss, "Punishment by Analogy in Nationalist Socialist Penal Law," *Journal of Criminal Law and Criminology*, 26: 847, March-April, 1936. See also Frederick Hoefer, "The Nazi Penal System," *Journal of Criminal Law and Criminology*, 35:385-393, March-April, 1945, and 36: 30-38, May-June, 1945.
5. See Jack P. Gibbs, "Crime and the Sociology of Law." *Sociology and Social Research*, 51:23-38, October, 1966.
6. See Donald R. Cressey, "Control of Crime and Consent of the Governed, An Introduction," chap. in Gresham M. Sykes and Thomas E. Drabeck, eds., *Law and the Lawless* (New York: Random House, 1969), pp. 271-287.
7. Edwin H. Sutherland and Donald R. Cressey, *Criminology*, 9th Edition, chap. 20, pp. 440-461. Copyright © 1974 by J.B. Lippincott: New York.
8. Edwin H. Sutherland, "Is 'White Collar Crime' Crime?" *American Sociological Review*, 10:132-139, April, 1945; idem, *White Collar Crime* (New York: Dryden Press, 1949), pp. 29-55.
9. Jerome Hall, *General Principles of Criminal Law*, 2d ed. (Indianapolis: Bobbs-Merrill, 1960). See especially pp. 14-26.
10. Ibid., pp. 84-93.
11. See Edwin Sutherland and Donald R. Cressey, *Criminology*, 9th Edition, pp. 156-157. J.B. Lippincott: New York.
12. Hall, *General Principles of Criminal Law*, p. 336. See also Jerome Hall, "Analytic Philosophy and Jurisprudence," *Ethics*, 77: 14-28, October, 1966; and Colin Howard, *Strict Responsibility* (London: Sweet and Maxwell, 1963).
13. Kai T. Erikson, *Wayward Puritans: A Study in the Sociology of Deviance* (New York: John Wiley, 1966).
14. Robert C. Bensing, "A Comparative Study of American Sex Statutes," *Journal of Criminal Law, Criminology, and Police Science*, 42:57-72, May-June, 1951.
15. David Sudnow, "Normal Crimes: Sociological Features of the Penal Code in a Public Defender Office," *Social Problems*, 12:255-276, Winter, 1965.

CHAPTER 4

The State, the Law, and the Definition of Behavior as Criminal or Delinquent

William J. Chambliss

Why are some acts considered criminal and others are not? A number of sociologists have answered this question by asserting that the violation of values that are in the public interest are the ones that are codified into the criminal code. In other words, some values are so important to the public good that they must be protected by the state from transgression. Hence, a "collective conscience" determines which acts are legislated as criminal and which are not. But maybe it is not quite that simple. The noted conflict theorist William Chambliss takes issue with that belief and concludes that a collective conscience is not important in determining law. Instead, crime is a political phenomenon and can be understood as the product of special interests seeking to gain advantage over political and economic competitors. He tells us that "The state, rather than being value-neutral, is, in fact, an agent of the side which controls the production and distribution of the society's available resources."

Answering the question posed earlier, then, depends on our understanding of the relationship between the political process and social stratification. Conflicts emerging out of class divisions cause some acts to be seen as crime or delinquency by state representatives who favor the economic and political status quo. Those acts that might disrupt or threaten the position of the privileged are the ones

likely to be labeled criminal. Thus, by understanding the process of creating law one is better able to understand crime. This is true whether one believes in the collective conscience or the conflict theory of why some acts are criminal and others are not.

It was fashionable, a few years back, to speak of crime and delinquency as though these were characteristics possessed by some people but not by others. In the heyday of such thinking, the search was on for physical, biological, or psychological traits and social experiences which led people to become "criminal" or "delinquent."[1] There is still a recognized need to look for characteristics and experiences of people which lead them to live lives different from those of their neighbors—whether the difference is in commitment to criminality, Catholicism, or cooking.

It is now generally recognized, however, that the starting point for the systematic study of crime is *not* to ask why some people become criminal while others do not, but to ask first why is it that some acts get defined as criminal while others do not. Criminology begins, then, with the sociology of law: the study of the institutions which create, interpret, and enforce the rules that tolerate and encourage one set of behaviors while prohibiting and discouraging another....

Models of Law Creation

Until recently the prevailing view in modern social thought—both legal and social science—has centered on one or more of the following propositions:

1. The law represents the value-consensus of the society.
2. The law represents those values and perspectives which are fundamental to social order.
3. The law represents those values and perspectives which it is in the public interest to protect.
4. The state as represented in the legal system is value-neutral.
5. In pluralistic societies the law represents the interests of the society at large by mediating between competing interest groups.

Among sociologists the work of Emile Durkheim is the outstanding example of the systematic analysis of law from this perspective. It is, therefore, worth spending some time appraising Durkheim's thesis as put forth in *The Division of Labor in Society* (1893). My concern here will not be to point out contradictions, inconsistencies, or tautologies in Durkheim's work but only to explore how closely Durkheim's thesis fits with extant empirical data.

Durkheim stated his central thesis quite clearly: for an act to be a crime that is punishable by law, it must be (1) universally offensive to the collective conscience of the people, (2) strongly opposed, and (3) a clear and precise form of behavior. In his words:

the only common characteristic of crimes is that they consist…in acts universally disapproved of by members of each society…crime shocks sentiments which, for a given social system, are found in all healthy consciences (1893:73).

The collective sentiments to which crime corresponds must, therefore, singularize themselves from others by some distinctive property; they must have a certain average intensity. Not only are they engraven in all consciences, but they are strongly engraven (p. 77).

The wayward son, however, and even the most hardened egoist are not treated as criminals. It is not sufficient, then, that the sentiments be strong; they must be precise (p. 79).

An act is criminal when it offends strong and defined states of the collective conscience (p. 80).

Those acts, to offend the common conscience, need not relate "…to vital interests of society nor to a minimum of justice" (1893:81). Durkheim argues that a single murder may have less dire social consequences than the failure of the stock market, yet the former is a crime for the reasons stated and the latter is not.

Durkheim distinguishes two types of law: Restitutive and Repressive. Restitutive law "is not expiatory, but consists of a simple *return to state*" (1893:111). Repressive law is one which "in any degree whatever, invokes against its author the characteristic reaction which we term punishment" (p. 70). Restitutive laws, or as he sometimes says, "co-operative laws with restitutive sanctions" (p. 129), are laws that invoke rule enforcement but which (a) do not reflect the collective conscience (they reflect only the opinions of *some* of the members of society), and (b) do not reflect sentiments that are strongly felt. Therefore, these laws do *not* invoke penal sanctions but only rule enforcement. The more specialized the functions of law, the less the laws represent the common conscience. As a result, they cannot then offend the common conscience since they are in fact marginal and not common to all. Thus expiatory responses are likely. "The rules which determine them cannot have the superior force, the transcendent authority which, when offended, demands expiation" (1893:127).

There is very little evidence in the studies of the process by which laws are created that would support Durkheim's thesis. It is obvious that, contrary to Durkheim's expectations, industrial societies have tended to pass more and more repressive laws (Kadish, 1967) and that these laws have reflected special interests to a greater extent than they reflect the feelings of "all healthy consciences." Indeed, the reverse is closer to the mark: the collective conscience is largely irrelevant to the creation of laws. What relationship there is tends to be a consequence rather than a cause of new laws.

A view closely related to Durkheim's has also held considerable influence. This is the often-expressed belief that criminal law represents an attempt to control acts which it is in the "public interest" to control. Auerbach et al. attempted a listing of minimal elements of "the public interest":

a) It is in the "public interest" that our nation be free from outside dictation in determining its destiny; that it have the power of self-determination.…

b) It is in the public interest to preserve the legitimated institutions through which conflicts in our society are adjusted and peaceful change effected, no matter how distasteful particular decisions reached by these institutions may be to particular groups in our society. In other words, the preservation of democracy—government with the freely given consent of the governed—is in the public interest.

c) It is in the public interest that no group in our society should become so powerful that it can submerge the claims of all other groups.

d) It is in the public interest that all claims made by individuals and groups in our society should at least be heard and considered by the law-making authorities. This proposition, which calls for recognition of the freedom to speak and to associate with others in pursuit of group interests, is a fundamental assumption of the democratic order.

e) It is in the public interest that every individual enjoy a minimum decent life and that the degree of inequality in the opportunities open to individuals be lessened (1961:661).

A variety of arguments suggest that this statement of a national public interest is invalid. Even assuming that there were a value-consensus on these propositions, the range of questions that come before lawmaking agencies and the state is largely outside their scope. Such a view is not a very useful or interesting guide to the study of lawmaking, for very few questions coming before lawmakers actually touch on any of these generalized objectives. Rather, they tend to be much narrower: What should the penalty be for prostitution? Should the patron be punished? Does the law of theft include "breaking bale and carrying away"? Are amphetamines to be included as dangerous drugs? Should students engaged in disruption in state universities automatically be expelled upon conviction? The usual questions coming before lawmaking authorities only rarely touch on the large questions suggested by any list of supposed "public interests."

Second, even if one were to accept these statements of "the public interest," the actual questions coming before lawmakers that even touch on these objectives are never very simple. Whether or not the United States ought to simply turn itself over to a foreign power, for example, is a question that has never come and doubtless never will come before any legislature. Rather, the question is always partial and problematic: Is joining the United Nations, and the surrender of sovereignty *pro tanto*, for example, too serious an invasion of the "public interest" in independence? If "freedom to speak" is "a fundamental assumption of the democratic order," then it can be argued that no private individual or corporation ought to control newspapers, television, or other institutions of the mass media, which instead should be equally available to all without regard to their financial resources. That would require government control of the mass media, which might well be regarded as the negation of free speech. While, no doubt, it is in the public interest that every individual should enjoy the minimum essentials of a decent life, exactly how much is a "minimum"? Is it in the public interest to reduce the size of "big business" in order to keep that group from attaining too much power, even if it can be shown that large economic units are more efficient than smaller ones? And if one decides to reduce the size of "big business," what is to be the standard of acceptable maximum size?

Third, is it true that even this list of "the minimal elements of the public interest" would be unanimously accepted? It is notable for omitting any reference to minimum protection for property. Many members of the propertied classes, at least in the American society, would insist that such a guarantee is an essential component of the "public interest." The list omits any statement that equality of treatment before the law regardless of race or color is a necessary ingredient of "the public interest"; white racists would hardly complain of this omission but others surely would.

Fourth, what a majority conceives of as "the public interest" at any period in history is not a constant. Not so long ago a majority of the lawmakers believed that it was in the public interest to prevent any citizen from buying alcoholic beverages. Not very long before that, in the long view of history, no doubt a majority believed that it was in the public interest to burn wretched old women at the stake as witches. How can one be sure that today's perception of "the public interest" is not merely an evanescent reflection of the value-sets of the majority?

Finally, consider the second of the propositions put forward, the broadest and most overarching of all: "It is in the public interest to preserve the legitimated institutions through which conflicts in society are adjusted and peaceful change effected." So long as real poverty exists, it seems clear that the fifth assertion of "the public interest," i.e., "that every individual enjoy a minimum decent life," is sharply in conflict with the second. Which of these interests is to be overriding? The repeated phenomenon of urban rioting in the ghettos of America suggests that there is no value-consensus on the relative weight to be given to any of these propositions which purport to define "the public interest."

The reason why this or any other set of claimed "public interest" elements, a commonly held *summum bonum*, can never adequately describe the actual state of affairs can be explained philosophically as well as empirically. John Dewey (1938) has argued that a distinction must be made between *that which is prized* and the *process of valuation*. No doubt we all have general, culturally acquired objectives, i.e., things which are prized. In any specific instance, however, how we define these generalized goals depends on a complex process of considering objective constraints, relative costs and benefits, and the valuation of alternative means. In this process of valuation, our generalized objectives are necessarily modified and changed as they become concrete and definite—i.e., in Dewey's language, as they become ends-in-view. Whatever the relative cultural agreement on general, broad prizings, there is never any complete agreement on any specific end in view.

The particular norms prescribed by law always are specific. They always command the role-occupant to act in specific ways. It is always a statement, not of generalized prizings, but of a specific end in view. It is the result of a process of valuation. On that valuation there is never complete agreement, for there is no complete agreement on the relative weightings to be given the various prizings held in different strata of the society, nor on the relative valuation to be given to different means.

In short, every assertion that a specific law should have a certain content must necessarily reflect the process of valuation of its proponents, and by the same token, it will be opposed to the processes of valuation of its opponents. The nature of law as a normative system, commanding what ought to be done, necessitates that it will favor one group as against another. The proof, whatever academic model-builders may say, lies in the fact that there is some opposition to *every* proposed new rule, whether or not the lawmakers themselves are unanimous. Even a declaration of war in the face of armed attack is never supported by the *entire* population.

That the law necessarily advances the values of some groups in society and opposes others reflects the fact that in any complex, modern society there is no value-consensus that is relevant to the law. That is so because of the very nature of the different "webs of life" that exist. It is a function of society itself.

For many of the same reasons, the view that the state is a value-neutral agent which weighs competing interests and distributes the available resources equitably is equally untenable. There are, indeed, competing interests but the competitors enter the arena with vastly different resources and, therefore, much different chances of success (Reich, 1964; Domhoff, 1970). The state, rather than being value-neutral, is, in fact, an agent of the side which controls the production and distribution of the society's available resources. The criminal law is then first and foremost a reflection of the interests and ideologies of the governing class—whether that class is private industry or state bureaucracy. Only secondarily, and even then only in minor ways, does the criminal law reflect the value-consensus, the public interest, or the sifting and weighing of competing interests.

A model more consistent with the realities of legal change must take into account differences in power which stem largely from differences in control over the economic resources of the society. More importantly, an adequate model to account for the definition of behavior as criminal or delinquent must recognize that in societies with social class divisions there is inevitably conflict between social classes and it is this class conflict which is the moving force for legal changes. Actions of the ruling class or representatives thereof as well as the machinations of moral entrepreneurs and the mobilization of bias all reflect attempts by various social classes to have their own interests and ideologies implemented by the state through the legal system.[2] It is, of course, true that the conflicts that are the basis of legal changes are not fought by equals. Thus those who control the economic and political resources of the society will inevitably see their interests and ideologies more often represented in the law than will others.

There are, of course, issues that are of only minor consequence to the established economic and political relations in the society. Such issues may be described by the pluralist perspective that sees different interest groups of more or less equal power arguing in the value-neutral arena of state bureaucracies. It seems clear that such instances are rare, and, in fact, even when the issue is the wording of prostitution laws or the changes in juvenile court laws there are differences in power between groups and these differences will usually determine the outcome of the struggle.

Summary and Conclusion

From the Black Death in feudal England where the vagrancy laws emerged and were shaped, through the Star Chamber in the fifteenth century where judges defined the law of theft in order to protect the interests of the ruling classes, to the legislatures of New York and California and the appellate courts of the United States lies a vast array of criminal laws that have been created, contradicted, reformulated, and allowed to die. Constructing a general theory that can account for such a wide range of events is no simple task. It is not surprising that such efforts often fall short of their goal.

Looking only at the two most general models of rule creation: the "value-consensus" and the "ruling class" models and pitting them against the extant empirical data leaves little doubt but that both fall short of the mark. The value-consensus model which suggests that community consensus

is the moving force behind the definition of behavior as criminal and delinquent finds little support in the systematic study of the development of criminal law. The ruling class model falls short as an adequate explanation to the extent that it posits a monolithic ruling class which sits in jurisdiction over a passive mass of people and passes laws reflecting only the interests of those who rule.

On the other hand, the importance of the ruling class in determining the shape of the criminal law cannot be gainsaid—whether that influence is through direct involvement in the law-creating process or merely through the mobilization of bias. Nor, for that matter, can the influence of "public opinion" (especially as this is organized around moral entrepreneurs) be ignored as a source of criminal law. Thus both general models contain some valuable truths to which must be added the important role played by bureaucracies, vested interest groups, and even individuals acting virtually alone (Lewis, 1966).

An alternative model compatible with the data is best described as a conflict theory of legal change. The starting point for this theory is the recognition that modern, industrialized society is composed of numerous social classes and interest groups who compete for the favors of the state. The stratification of society into social classes where there are substantial (and at times vast) differences in wealth, power, and prestige inevitably leads to conflict between the extant classes. It is in the course of working through and living with these inherent conflicts that the law takes its particular content and form. It is out of the conflicts generated by social class divisions that the definition of some acts as criminal or delinquent emerges.

So long as class conflicts are latent, those who sit at the top of the political and economic structure of the society can manipulate the criminal laws to suit their own purposes. But when class conflict breaks into open rebellion, as it often does in such societies (Rubenstein, 1970), then the state must enact legislation and the courts reinterpret laws in ways that are perceived as solutions to the conflict. During times of manifest class conflict, legislatures and courts will simultaneously create criminal laws that provide greater control over those groups who are engaged in acts disruptive to the status quo and laws which appear to alleviate the conditions which are seen as giving rise to the social conflicts.

In between crises or perhaps as an adjunct to the legislative-judicial innovations taking place because of them, bureaucracies can mobilize and moral entrepreneurs organize to plead their case before the lawmaking bodies. Without the changes in economic structure that accompanied England's transition from feudalism to capitalism the laws of theft and vagrancy (to mention only two) would not have taken the form they did, just as the Supreme Court decisions and legislative enactments of the 1960s that effectively refocused substantial areas of the criminal law would not have taken place without the riots, rebellions, and overt social conflicts which characterized that historical period in America.

Crime is a political phenomenon. What gets defined as criminal or delinquent behavior is the result of a political process within which rules are formed which prohibit or require people to behave in certain ways. It is this process which must be understood as it bears on the definition of behavior as criminal if we are to proceed to the study of criminal *behavior*. Thus to ask "why is it that some acts get defined as criminal while others do not" is the starting point for all systematic study of crime and criminal behavior. Nothing is inherently criminal, it is only the response that makes it so. If we are to explain crime, we must first explain the social forces that cause some acts to be defined as criminal while other acts are not.

Discussion Questions

1. What is meant by the term "public interest"? How is it different from the "collective conscience"? In order to protect the "public interest," what sacrifices might individuals have to make? In your view, is that a good trade-off? Does the law really protect a "public interest"? In what areas is the concept of "public interest" impractical to achieve?

2. How do differences in power or resources affect the formation of law? How do they

affect the outcome of the application of law to individuals?

3. Compare the value-consensus model of law creation with the ruling class model. Describe the theory behind each one. What are the weaknesses of each? How might the ruling class model affect law creation in subtle ways (other than direct involvement in the law-creation process)? Suggest some laws for which each model might be explanatory (what laws might reflect the value consensus model? The ruling class model?).

Notes

1. See, for example, Cohen (1955), Merton (1957), Miller (1958), and Cloward and Ohlin (1960). Donald Cressey has pointed out that an earlier generation of criminologists, particularly Sutherland (1924), Sellin (1938), and Tannenbaum (1938), were less likely to ignore the importance of the criminal lawmaking process; see Cressey (1968) and Sutherland and Cressey (1970).

2. Most broadly conceived, each of these sources of law may be summarized under the concept of "interest groups" (Quinney, 1970). But such a general concept does little more than provide an umbrella under which to put these various social processes. Further, the notion of "interest groups" often leads to the erroneous implication that competition for control of or influence over the state is a battle between equals where social class differences are largely irrelevant. It seems analytically wiser to deal with all the sources of criminal law creation and to see them as stemming from basic conflicts within the society.

References

Auerbach, D., K. Garrison, W. Hurst, and S. Mermin. 1961. *The Legal Process: An Introduction to Decision-Making by Judicial, Legislative, Executive, and Administrative Agencies.* San Francisco: Chandler.

Cloward, Richard A., and Lloyd E. Ohlin. 1960. *Delinquency and Opportunity: A Theory of Delinquent Gangs.* New York: Free Press of Glencoe.

Cohen, Albert K. 1955. *Delinquent Boys.* Glencoe, Ill.: Free Press.

Cressey, Donald R. 1968. "Culture conflict, differential association, and normative conflict." Pp. 43-54 in Marvin Wolfgang (ed.), *Crime and Culture: Essays in Honor of Thorsten Sellin.* New York: Wiley.

Dewey, John. 1938. *Logic: The Theory of Inquiry.* New York: Holt.

Domhoff, G. William. 1970. *The Higher Circles.* New York: Random House.

Durkheim, Emile. 1893. *The Division of Labor in Society.* Translation by George Simpson. Glencoe, Ill.: Free Press (1947 edition).

Kadish, Sanford H. 1967. "The crisis of overcriminalization." *Annals of the American Academy of Political and Social Science 374* (November):157-170.

Lewis, Anthony. 1966. *Gideon's Trumpet.* New York: Vintage Books.

Merton, Robert K. 1957. "Social structure and anomie." Chap. 4 in Robert K. Merton, *Social Theory and Social Structure.* Glencoe, Ill.: Free Press.

Miller, Walter B. 1958. "Lower class culture as a generating milieu of gang delinquency." *Journal of Social Issues* 14 (3): 5-19.

Quinney, Richard. 1970. *The Social Reality of Crime.* New York: Little, Brown.

Reich, Charles A. 1964. "The new property." *Yale Law Journal 73* (April): 733-787.

Rubenstein, Richard E. 1970. *Rebels in Eden.* Boston: Little, Brown.

Sellin, Thorsten. 1938. *Culture Conflict and Crime.* New York: Social Science Research Council. Bulletin 41.

Sutherland, Edwin H. 1924. *Criminology.* Philadelphia: Lippincott.

Sutherland, Edwin H., and Donald R. Cressey. 1970. *Criminology.* Eighth Edition. Philadelphia: Lippincott.

Tannenbaum, Frank. 1938. *Crime and the Community.* New York: Columbia University Press.

Extent and Nature of Crime

Newspapers and television portray crime in a particular way. Local and even national evening news programs provide coverage of the most sensationalistic kinds of offenses. The media frenzy surrounding the O. J. Simpson cases is perhaps the best example of overzealous reporting and the highly sensationalized picture of crime with which most Americans are familiar. Popular television shows also present a good deal of violence; such shows as *CSI* and numerous others depict homicide and other forms of violence as extremely prevalent crimes in the United States.

Criminologists are interested in learning more about the actual extent and nature of crime than the distorted picture portrayed in print and on radio and television. Some of the questions they study include the following: How many crimes are committed in the United States? What are the characteristics of people who commit offenses? How widespread is criminal offending? How widespread is criminal victimization? Who are the criminals? Who are the victims?

The answer to these questions, in part, is that it depends. That is, it depends on how we measure crime as well as the kinds of crimes in which we are most interested. As Section V of this book describes, there are many different types of crime. What we measure, and how we measure it, have important implications for what we know about the nature and extent of crime. Unfortunately, reliable and valid data are not available for many crimes, including public-order crimes, professional crimes, organized crimes, and white-collar

crimes. There are a variety of reasons for this lack of data, including the nature of the offenses themselves. These matters will be dealt with in more detail in Section V.

Unlike data for the previously mentioned offenses, better data are available for crimes of violence and property offenses. Even for these offenses, however, the type of data that we use is important for determining the picture of crime that we have. Criminologists typically rely on three types of data to determine the nature and extent of crime: "official" data, victimization surveys, and self-report surveys. Each type provides a different picture of crime, and much effort has been expended to identify the strengths and weaknesses of each type.

This section will consider the three different types of data and their strengths and weaknesses. It will then discuss the nature and extent of crime in the United States as revealed by these data sources. Finally, it will consider issues related to "overcriminalization," that is, whether U.S. society labels too many offenses as criminal. The five readings that follow this introduction examine the strengths and weaknesses of the three types of data.

Official Data

When criminologists discuss "official data," they are usually referring to information available in the Uniform Crime Reports (UCR), which are compiled and published by the Federal Bureau of Investigation (FBI). The UCR is an annual report published since 1930 that incorporates data from 95 percent of the police precincts in all fifty states. It includes crimes known to the police (either through citizen reports or through police discovery), information about the number of arrests, and some characteristics of the people arrested. Each reporting unit collects this information for its jurisdiction; this information is forwarded to the FBI, which publishes the Uniform Crime Reports (Federal Bureau of Investigation 1997).

The crimes recorded in the UCR are of two types: Part I offenses, usually called index crimes, and Part II offenses. There are eight index crimes, which are offenses that we usually think of as "serious" crimes. The four violent index crimes are murder and nonnegligent homicide, forcible rape, aggravated assault, and robbery. All these crimes include an element of force or threat of force, and include attempts to commit these crimes. The element of force differentiates them from the four property index crimes, which are larceny-theft, burglary, motor vehicle theft, and arson.

Although states have somewhat different definitions for each of the eight index crimes, the UCR data incorporate crimes that are consistent with a standard set of definitions. The definitions for the violent index crimes provided by the FBI are as follows: murder and nonnegligent homicide is "the willful (nonnegligent) killing of one human being by another"; rape is "the carnal knowledge of a female forcibly and against her will"; aggravated assault is "an unlawful attack by one person upon another for the purpose of inflicting severe or aggravated personal injury"; robbery is "the taking or attempting to take anything of value from the care, custody, or control of a person or persons by force or threat of force or violence and/ or by putting the victim in fear" (Federal Bureau of Investigation 1997: 13, 23, 31, and 26, respectively). The definitions of the index property crimes are: larceny-theft is "the unlawful taking, carrying, leading or riding away of property from the possession or constructive possession of another" and includes such crimes as shoplifting; burglary is "the unlawful entry of a structure to commit a felony or theft"; motor vehicle theft is "the [unlawful] theft or attempted theft of a motor vehicle" (p. 49); arson is "any willful or malicious burning or attempt to

burn, with or without intent to defraud" the property of another (Federal Bureau of Investigation 1997: 43, 38, 49, and 53, respectively).

In addition to the number of crimes known to the police, the UCR also reports information about arrests for the index crimes. Several different types of information are reported. Clearance rates are reported for each type of index crime; these are the percentage of crimes known to the police that are "cleared" or "when at least one person is arrested, charged with the commission of the crime, and turned over to the court for prosecution" (Federal Bureau of Investigation 1997: 203). (Note that just because a crime is "cleared" does not mean that the person(s) arrested will necessarily plead guilty or be found guilty.) Also included in the UCR is the number of people arrested and the characteristics of those arrested, such as age, gender, and race.

The UCR also provides information about Part II offenses. As a whole, they are generally considered less serious than Part I index crimes. Part II offenses include a variety of crimes, such as drug abuse violations, prostitution, simple assaults, drunkenness, disorderly conduct, vagrancy, weapons offenses, and two status offenses (runaways and curfew violations). For these offenses, arrest information, rather than the number of offenses known to the police, are usually reported. This is because of the nature of the Part II offenses: Many of them are not necessarily reported to the police but rather are detected through the proactive efforts of the police themselves.

The UCR is an important source of data about the nature and extent of crime in the United States. Nevertheless, the UCR data have both strengths and weaknesses that can make their use somewhat problematic. Walter R. Gove, Michael Hughes, and Michael Geerken discuss some of the problems with the UCR, as well as other sources of crime data, in Reading 5, although they conclude that the UCR provides valid information about most index crimes.

The UCR provides the longest-running source of crime data in the United States. As such, we are able to measure long-term trends in crimes known to the police. With the increased professionalization of police forces over time, we can have increased confidence that many crimes reported to the police are recorded and counted as crimes. The arrest data provide some insight into the characteristics of offenders who are committing the crimes that result in arrest.

The UCR data have a number of limitations, however. A substantial number of crimes are *not* reported to the police (see the discussion later). Thus, using the UCR to determine the number of crimes that are committed seriously underestimates the true number of crimes. The crimes that are reported to the police are more serious (in terms of injury or loss) than those that are not reported (Bureau of Justice Statistics 1997b). Further, although arrest data provide some insight into demographic characteristics of criminals, using this information is problematic. The clearance rates for violent, and particularly property, index crimes indicate that only about half of violent crimes are cleared by arrest; for property crimes, only about 20 percent. Thus, even if we assume that the persons arrested for crimes that are cleared are the actual perpetrators (a somewhat questionable assumption), in one of two cases the perpetrator of violent crimes is not apprehended; for property crimes, this number is four in five! It cannot be assumed, therefore, that the people who are arrested are representative of all offenders.

There are other problems with UCR data. The police have discretion in whom they arrest; although the seriousness of the offense is an important factor, extralegal factors also seem to play a role in the decision to arrest (Smith and Visher 1981; Lundman 1996; Worden and Shepard 1996; but see also Klinger 1994, 1996). Limited information other than demographic information is available about arrestees; for example, no information is available about their socioeconomic status (an important factor in criminological theories as discussed in Section III) or motivations for committing the offense.

Despite its weaknesses, the UCR is an important data source available to criminologists, and as discussed in Reading 5, its data are generally considered valid for the index crimes.

Victimization Surveys

Partly in response to some of the problems with the UCR, however, alternative sources of crime data

were developed. One of these is victimization surveys. The primary victimization survey, which is discussed here, is the National Crime Victimization Survey (NCVS). The National Crime Survey (NCS), as it was originally called, was initiated in 1973 by the Bureau of Justice Statistics (BJS). The NCVS consists of interviews with a nationally representative sample of approximately 100,000 people age twelve and over living in 50,000 households in the United States. Everyone in this sample is interviewed every six months about his or her personal experiences as a victim in the previous six months (that is, whether he or she has been the victim of a crime in the six months prior to the interview). In addition, one adult member of the household provides information about whether the household itself has been victimized by a property crime. Households remain in the study for three years and then are replaced (Bureau of Justice Statistics 1997b).

In the interview, respondents are asked whether they were the victims of specific crimes, such as robbery. They are asked about each crime separately, to obtain information about different offenses. The crimes asked about are similar to the Part I index crimes (except homicide), but identical definitions are *not* used. As indicated in Readings 5 and 7, respondents were not explicitly asked about rape until 1993, when the survey was changed to address this limitation. Also obtained is information related to characteristics of respondents and households, such as socioeconomic status and number of household residents, and about the crime, such as where it occurred and whether the victim resisted (Bureau of Justice Statistics 1997b).

Although originally envisioned as a measure of the true crime rate, the NCVS is not without strengths and weaknesses. Some of these are discussed in Readings 5 and 7, but they will be briefly considered here.

The NCVS has several strengths. It provides an alternative estimate of the number of crimes that occur in the United States each year. In addition, it provides information on crime and victims that is unavailable in official data. For example, when possible, NCVS respondents provide information about the perpetrator(s) (e.g., the age and the relationship to the victim), the situation (e.g., when and where the crime occurred), and the amount of damage (e.g., physical injury or financial loss). The NCVS also obtains important information about whether a crime was reported to the police and the reasons behind the decision to report it or not. Thus, the NCVS makes it possible to estimate the number of crimes that have occurred, characteristics of the victims, characteristics of the offenders, factors associated with the crime, and the percentage of crimes reported to the police and reasons why many crimes go unreported.

The NCVS also has a number of weaknesses. The interviewer can have important effects on the situation and on the respondent, thus potentially influencing whether victimizations are reported, which in turn affects the total number of victimizations. Further, respondents may be unwilling to report their experiences as victims, particularly those offenses also not reported to the police (and most likely not reported to the interviewer for the same reasons they were not reported to the police). Other problems arise because respondents may "telescope" (say an event occurred during a given time period when it actually occurred outside of it), forget that a crime occurred, or report a nonserious event as a serious one.

As a whole, the NCVS provides some important information about the nature and extent of crime that the UCR does not and therefore, is an important data source. Like the UCR, however, the NCVS is not without weaknesses, some of which are shared by self-report surveys, which are considered in the next section.

Self-Report Surveys

The third major data source widely used by criminologists is self-report surveys. Where victimization surveys ask respondents about whether they have been the victim of a crime, self-report surveys are primarily interested in obtaining information about respondents' own delinquent and criminal behavior. Use of the self-report method in criminology became popular after the publication of an article in 1958 by James F. Short and F. Ivan Nye that used this methodology; since that time, numerous self-report surveys have been developed. The National Youth Survey (see Reading 6) and the Rochester Developmental Youth Survey are but two examples. The surveys include questions not only about criminal and delinquent behavior but also about a variety of other topics, such as demographic characteristics, familial relationships, attitudes, and a host of related issues.

As with the other data sources, self-report data have strengths and weaknesses. With regard to strengths, self-report surveys give researchers access to information that official data and victimization surveys do not. Their delinquency and crime measures are generally considered reliable and valid (see Reading 6; Hindelang, Hirschi, and Weis 1981) and allow estimation of the prevalence and incidence of offending, regardless of whether offenders are caught for the crimes. Further, these surveys allow researchers to obtain information about why an individual commits crimes, and factors associated with an individual's behavior, such as whether he or she has delinquent friends, socioeconomic status, attitudes, and a number of other topics.

Self-report studies also have important weaknesses. Responses to such surveys may have different degrees of validity, with the validity of responses from African American males about delinquent and criminal activity coming particularly under scrutiny (see Reading 6; Hindelang, Hirschi, and Weis 1981). Self-reports rely on the willingness and ability of an individual to report his or her behavior; several factors limit this ability, such as telescoping, forgetting, and social acceptability. Further, questions related to the frequency of a behavior are particularly susceptible to problems of underreporting and overreporting; that is, a person may underestimate or overestimate the number of times he or she committed an offense. Although a number of techniques in the interview situation can be utilized to reduce these problems, they cannot completely eliminate them.

Self-reports are subject to other problems. Many items included in the surveys are trivial (nonserious) and overlap (they do not measure distinct behaviors). More important, serious persistent offenders are underrepresented for a variety of reasons, thus disallowing examination of factors associated with their offending patterns and factors that differentiate this group from other offenders (Elliott and Ageton 1980; Cernkovich, Giordano, and Pugh 1985).

Crime in the United States

An understanding of the strengths and weaknesses of the three major sources of criminological data is necessary if one is to be able to think critically about what each shows about the nature and extent of crime in the United States. As discussed in Section III, the discrepant results obtained from different data sources create controversy over the nature of the relationship between several of the correlates and crime, as well as have implications for theories of crime.

Crimes Known to the Police

The United States, in comparison to other countries, and particularly Westernized countries, has extremely high crime and violence rates (Archer and Gartner 1984; United Nations 1997). In 1996 there were 13,473,614 index crimes known to the police, or 5,079 per 100,000 people (Federal Bureau of Investigation 1997). Despite these high numbers, they reflect the fifth straight year of decline in crime in the United States. This decline is a relatively recent pattern, however, as crime rates increased in almost every year between 1960 and 1991, the peak year of offenses known to the police. More specifically, in 1960, there were 3,384,200 offenses (1,887 per 100,000) known to the police; by 1991, there were 14,872,900 offenses known to the police (5,898 per 100,000), reflecting almost a threefold increase in the thirty-year period (Maguire and Pastore 1997).

Of the index crimes, the vast majority are property crimes rather than violent crimes. In any given year, property crimes comprise approximately 88 percent and violent offenses 12 percent of index crimes known to the police. Of the index crimes, the one most often reported to the police is larceny-theft (7,894,620 known to the police in 1996); homicide, the crime that receives the most attention in the media, is the smallest category among serious offenses (with 19,645 offenses in 1996) (Federal Bureau of Investigation 1997).

Within the United States, crime is not evenly distributed; that is, crime rates vary by geographic region and by size of locale. In particular, both property and violent index crime rates are highest in the South, followed by the West (Nelsen, Corzine, and Huff-Corzine 1994; Federal Bureau of Investigation 1997). This finding is consistent with a "subculture of violence" (Wolfgang and Ferracuti 1967) often attributed to the South. In addition, index crime rates are highest in large cities and their surrounding areas (i.e., Metropolitan Statistical Areas), followed by cities outside of metropolitan areas, and then rural counties, which have the lowest crime rates (Federal Bureau of Investigation 1997).

Arrests and Characteristics of Arrestees

Despite the large number of index crimes known to the police, arrests for these crimes are fairly infrequent, as indicated by the clearance rates. In 1996, for violent crimes overall, about 47 percent were cleared, with variations ranging from 67 percent for homicide to 27 percent for robbery. Clearance rates were lower for property crimes, with 18 percent of the four crimes cleared (Federal Bureau of Investigation 1997). Despite the low clearance rates, close to 3 million people were arrested for an index crime in 1996. Not surprisingly, the majority were arrested for property crimes, with larceny-theft leading the way.

What are the characteristics of the people arrested? Although we cannot be certain that those arrested are representative of all offenders, the UCR arrest data suggest their characteristics (Federal Bureau of Investigation 1997). As a whole, arrestees are young; in 1996, 56 percent of those arrested for all index crimes were under the age of twenty-five (46 percent of violent arrestees and 59 percent of property crime arrestees). Further, juveniles (under age eighteen) accounted for almost 31 percent of all people arrested for index crimes. Over the past decade, the number of juvenile arrests has increased at a greater pace than adult arrests. This increase is particularly true of violent index crimes, with arrests for homicide for juveniles up 51 percent, arrests for robbery up 57 percent, and arrests for aggravated assault up 70 percent between 1987 and 1996; the comparable arrests for adults declined 10 percent and 3 percent and rose 39 percent, respectively (Federal Bureau of Investigation 1997).

Gender and race patterns are also evident in arrest data. Arrestees are disproportionately male: males represented 79 percent of those arrested for index crimes in 1996. The situation is even more disproportionate for violent crimes, with males making up 85 percent of such arrestees in 1996; 72 percent of those arrested for property crime were male. With regard to race, African Americans are disproportionately represented relative to their size in the population. Although they comprised approximately 12.6 percent of the U.S. population in 1996 (U.S. Bureau of Census 1997), they accounted for about 35 percent of index arrestees overall. In 1996 they represented approximately 43 percent of those arrested for violent crimes and about 32 percent of those arrested for property crime. Overall, whites accounted for the majority of all arrestees for index crimes (62 percent), violent crime arrestees (55 percent), and property crime arrestees (65 percent) (Federal Bureau of Investigation 1997). Whites, however, are almost 83 percent of the population in the United States (because Hispanics may be of any race and are not differentiated in the UCR statistics, they are not treated separately here) (U.S. Bureau of Census 1997). The reasons for these differences across demographic groups are discussed in more detail in Section III.

Comparison of the UCR and NCVS

Despite the seemingly large number of offenses revealed by the UCR, the NCVS reveals what is often called "the dark figure of crime." That is, the NCVS indicates that substantially more crimes are committed than are reported to the police. For example, in 1996 the NCVS estimates that there were approximately 36,800,000 crimes against persons and households. Of these, 27.3 million were property offenses and 9.1 million were personal offenses. Although there are differences in definitions and measurement, the figure of almost 37 million (Bureau of Justice Statistics 1997a) dwarfs the number of similar crimes known to the police in 1996 (about 13 million) (Federal Bureau of Investigation 1997).

A potential problem arises with regard to comparisons of the NCVS and UCR. Although the two are not directly comparable in terms of definitions

used and crimes included, crime rates derived from the two sources have been compared by a number of criminologists (e.g., Blumstein, Cohen, and Rosenfeld 1991; McDowall and Loftin 1992). In many cases, the NCVS and UCR patterns are parallel, but the NCVS reveals higher rates than the UCR. When the NCVS and UCR show widely discrepant crime rates, which should criminologists use to base their estimates of the true number of crimes? This issue is discussed in Reading 7, by Gary Jensen and Maryaltani Karpos, who attempt to reconcile discrepant patterns of rape rates.

That the number estimated by the NCVS is much higher than reported in the UCR is not altogether surprising given the low percentages of people who report the offense to the police. The NCVS reveals that in 1996 for all violent crimes, only 43 percent were reported to the police; this figure varied substantially by the type of crime, with 54 percent of robberies and only 31 percent of rapes reported. For property crimes against the household, only 35 percent overall were reported, again with variations by crimes (76 percent of motor vehicle thefts, compared to only 28 percent of thefts, were reported to the police) (Bureau of Justice Statistics 1997a). The rationale for not reporting a crime to the police varies across and within the categories of violent and property crimes. For violent crimes, respondents were most likely to cite the reason for not reporting was that it was a "private or personal matter." "Object recovered; offender unsuccessful" was the most frequently cited reason for not reporting property crimes to the police (Bureau of Justice Statistics 1997b).

Victims of Crime

Who are the victims of all these crimes? The answer is related to the extent and nature of crime in society. The NCVS suggests that the characteristics of victims closely resemble those of offenders. The results of the 1996 NCVS indicate that for violent crimes (excluding homicide), victims tend to have the following characteristics: they are male (except for rape); young (between the ages of twelve and twenty-four); more likely to be African American than white; more likely to be Hispanic than non-Hispanic; poor (household incomes under $7,500); single, separated, or divorced; live in the West; and live in urban areas (Bureau of Justice Statistics 1997a).

For property crimes in 1996, the characteristics of the heads of households that were victimized resemble those of victims of violence with one notable exception. Specifically, property victimization rates are highest for households headed by African Americans rather than whites and Hispanics rather than non-Hispanics, located in the West or in an urban area, and rented rather than owned the home. Overall, however, property victimization rates are highest for households with incomes of $75,000 and over, although this figure varies by specific offense: burglaries are highest for households under $7,500, thefts for those over $75,000, and motor vehicle thefts for those in the category of $35,000 to $49,999 (Bureau of Justice Statistics 1997a). It should be noted that the characteristics of victims are considered here separately (e.g., considering race without also considering household income), an approach that Section III reveals is problematic, but the results do suggest who tends to be victimized by conventional street crimes in U.S. society.

The relationship between offender and victim often differs from stereotypes. For example, most violent crimes are intraracial rather than interracial. This fact is particularly illustrated by homicide: In cases in which there is a single victim and a single offender who has been identified, 84 percent of whites are killed by other whites and 92 percent of African Americans are killed by other African Americans (Federal Bureau of Investigation 1997). Further, many crimes of violence are not committed by strangers but rather by people the victims know. For violent crimes (completed and attempted) overall, the NCVS indicates that the offender was a stranger in just over half the cases in 1994. For robbery, the offender was a stranger in 78 percent of cases, and for aggravated assault the offender was a stranger in 61 percent of cases. For rape, however, the victim and offender were strangers in only 36 percent of cases and were at least acquainted with each other in the remaining 64 percent (Bureau of Justice Statistics 1997b).

Self-Report Information

Self-report studies provide a picture that is fairly different from that of the UCR or NCVS. Specifically, self-report studies reveal that crime is much more prevalent, or widespread, among the general population than was generally assumed prior to extensive use of the surveys. In addition, these studies reveal that a large number of crimes are committed by people who are never caught or punished. For example, results from Monitoring the Future, an annual nationally representative self-report survey of high school students and young adults, indicate that for twelfth graders in 1996, 14 percent had "hurt someone bad enough to need bandages or a doctor," 32 percent had "taken something not belonging to you worth under $50," and 24 percent had "gone into some house or building when you weren't supposed to be there" at least once in the previous year. Overall, however, only 10 percent had "been arrested and taken to a police station" during that year, suggesting that relatively few people are caught or punished for their crimes (Maguire and Pastore 1997).

Further, self-report studies indicate that gender, race, and class differences revealed by official data on crime, and the basis of many theories, are not found in self-report studies or, if found, the relationships are smaller than indicated in official data (e.g., Huizinga and Elliott 1987; Tittle and Meier 1990). Although these findings are not always consistent and may be due to measurement issues (e.g., Elliott and Ageton 1980; Farnworth et al. 1994), they have important implications for criminology. These issues, and their implications, are discussed in more detail in Section III.

Part II Offenses and Overcriminalization

The attention in this section thus far has been primarily on the eight index crimes, which are considered the most serious and have been used to gauge crime in the United States. Recall, however, that the UCR provides information about both the index crimes and Part II offenses. The data for Part II offenses are presented in terms of arrests, rather than offenses known to the police. Indeed, arrests for Part II offenses largely reflect the proactive enforcement efforts of the police and other law enforcement agencies.

The Part II offenses are important to consider for several reasons. First, arrests for them are the majority of arrests made in any given year and thereby have a huge impact on the criminal justice system in terms of police, court, and prison resources. Second, many of these offenses are "victimless crimes," those that may involve harm to the person engaged in the behavior itself but not directly to others (Federal Bureau of Investigation 1997). Whether some of these offenses should be considered criminal, or whether our society is "overcriminalized," are important issues that may be studied by examining these offenses.

Part II Offenses

In 1996 an estimated 15,168,100 people were arrested. Of these, only 18 percent were arrested for index crimes. The remaining 82 percent can be accounted for by Part II offenses. Not including the residual category of "all other offenses," drug abuse violations represent the single offense, of either Part I or Part II offenses, for which the most people were arrested in 1996. Indeed, 10 percent of all people arrested were arrested for drug abuse violations. Further, the minority of arrests for drug abuse were for sale or manufacture (25 percent) and the majority (75 percent) for possession; of the possession arrests, half were for marijuana. These figures are in stark contrast to the picture of crime portrayed on television or suggested by examination of Part I crime data. The combined categories of prostitution and commercialized vice, drug abuse, gambling, liquor law violations, drunkenness, disorderly conduct, and vagrancy, all offenses that may be considered victimless, account for more than 25 percent of all arrests (Federal Bureau of Investigation 1997).

One of these Part II offenses—drug abuse—has had serious implications for the criminal justice system. The number of people arrested for drug abuse violations has increased dramatically since 1980, from 600,000 in 1980 to about 1.5 million in 1996 (Federal Bureau of Investigation 1997) and to nearly 2 million in 2005 and the percentage of

inmates incarcerated for drug-related offenses has also increased greatly (Bureau of Justice Statistics 1992). Surveys of high school students reveal that despite the war on drugs, use of marijuana and other illicit drugs is currently on the rise, following a period of decline in the 1980s (Johnston, O'Malley, and Bachman 1996).

Overcriminalization

The point is not to argue that the use of drugs specifically should be decriminalized, although there are scholars who do argue for their legalization (see Inciardi 1991, and Trebach and Inciardi 1993, for the pros and cons of this issue). Instead, drug abuse provides a striking example that allows us to pose the question of whether the United States as a society is "overcriminalized," that is, does our society define as criminal many behaviors that are of little, if any, threat to society? Should our laws focus only on behaviors that are truly harmful to society and its citizens? Some scholars answer these questions in the affirmative. Sanford H. Kadish, for example, argues that laws have been misused to criminalize offenses such as drug use, prostitution, drunkenness, vagrancy, and others, and the "existence of these crimes and attempts at their eradication raise problems of inestimable importance for the criminal law" (1971: 57).

Overcriminalization has several important effects, according to Kadish. First, when laws are used to legislate morality, the nonenforcement of these laws undermines their intent, produces indifference and cynicism in the public, and may lead to discriminatory law enforcement. Second, such laws may result in the "diversion of police resources; encouragement of use of illegal means of police control [and] degradation of the image of law enforcement; discriminatory enforcement against the poor; and official corruption" (Kadish, 1971: 60). Additional problems may also result from such laws. Prohibiting behavior has little effect on how often people engage in it, and enforcement efforts might actually lead to more criminal behavior, as they produce greater organization and profit for those involved, thereby attracting more people and making enforcement even more difficult. With drug trafficking, increased enforcement efforts led to greater organization of the trade and the use of more sophisticated techniques and technology, resulting in traffickers being harder to detect (e.g., Johnson et al. 1990; Adler 1993). Kadish also states that there is "a cost of inestimable importance, one which tends to be a product of virtually all the misuses of criminal law…. That is the substantial diversion of police, prosecutorial and judicial time, personnel, and resources" from protecting society from truly harmful behaviors (1971: 63).

The implications for the extent and nature of crime are important. As outlined in Section I, the laws that are created reflect changing social attitudes and political processes. Law enforcement efforts and resources are expended to enforce laws related to victimless offenses that seem to reflect efforts to regulate morality. Further, people arrested for these offenses are taking up valuable resources, including jail and prison space, and are clogging the court system. People convicted of such offenses are labeled with a criminal record that will plague them for the rest of their lives. Despite the fact that many of these behaviors are ones that society disapproves of, defining them as crimes reflects the notion that our society may be overcriminalized.

The readings that follow deal with issues particularly related to the strengths and weaknesses of data sources available to criminologists for studying the extent and nature of crime. One article focuses on UCR data, another on the NCS, and a third on the reliability and validity of self-report data. Readings 8 and 9 describe novel ways in which criminologists can better ascertain the nature and extent of crime in the United States.

References

Adler, Patricia A. 1993. *Wheeling and Dealing: An Ethnography of an Upper-Level Drug Dealing and Smuggling Community* (2nd ed.). New York: Columbia University Press.

Archer, Dane and Rosemary Gartner. 1984. *Violence and Crime in Cross-National Perspective*. New Haven, CT: Yale University Press.

Blumstein, Alfred J., Jacqueline Cohen, and Richard Rosenfeld. 1991. "Trend and Deviation in Crime Rate: A Comparison of UCR and NCS Data for Burglary and Robbery," *Criminology* 29:237-264.

Bureau of Justice Statistics. 1992. *Prisoners in 1991*. Washington, DC: U.S. Department of Justice.

——. 1997a. *Criminal Victimization 1996: Changes 1995-96 with Trends 1993-96*. Bulletin NCJ-165812. Washington, DC: U.S. Department of Justice.

——. 1997b. *Criminal Victimization in the United States, 1994*. NCJ-162126. Washington, DC: U.S. Department of Justice.

Cernkovich, Stephen A., Peggy C. Giordano, and Meredith D. Pugh. 1985. "Chronic Offenders: The Missing Cases in Self-Report Delinquency Research," *Journal of Criminal Law and Criminology* 76:705-732.

Elliott, Delbert S. and Suzanne S. Ageton. 1980. "Reconciling Race and Class Differences in Self-Reported and Official Estimates of Delinquency," *American Sociological Review* 45:95-110.

Farnworth, Margaret, Terence P. Thornberry, Marvin D. Krohn, and Alan J. Lizotte. 1994. "Measurement in the Study of Class and Delinquency: Integrating Theory and Research," *Journal of Research in Crime and Delinquency* 31:32-61.

Federal Bureau of Investigation. 1997. *Crime in the United States, 1996*. Washington, DC: U.S. Government Printing Office.

Hindelang, Michael J., Travis Hirschi, and Joseph G. Weis. 1981. *Measuring Delinquency*. Beverly Hills, CA: Sage.

Huizinga, David and Delbert S. Elliott. 1987. "Juvenile Offender Prevalence, Incidence, and Arrest Rates by Race," *Crime & Delinquency* 33:206-233.

Inciardi, James A. (Ed.). 1991. *The Drug Legalization Debate*. Newbury Park, CA: Sage Publications.

Johnson, Bruce D., Terry Williams, Kojo A. Die, and Harry Sanabria. 1990. "Drug Abuse in the Inner City: Impact on Hard-Drug Users and the Community." In Michael Tonry and James Q. Wilson, (eds.). *Drugs and Crime*. Chicago: University of Chicago Press.

Johnston, Lloyd D., Patrick O'Malley, and Jerald G. Bachman. 1996. *National Survey Results on Drug Use from The Monitoring the Future Study 1975-1995*. Volume I, Secondary School Students. NIH Publication No. 96-4139. Washington, DC: U.S. Government Printing Office.

Kadish, Sanford H. 1971. "Overcriminalization." In L. Radzinowitz and M. Wolfgang (eds.), *The Criminal in Society*. New York: Basic Books.

Klinger, David A. 1994. "Demeanor or Crime? Why 'Hostile' Citizens Are More Likely to Be Arrested," *Criminology* 32:475-493.

——. 1996. "More on Demeanor and Arrest in Dade County," *Criminology* 34: 61-79.

Lundman, Richard J. 1996. "Demeanor and Arrest: Additional Evidence from Previously Unpublished Data," *Journal of Research in Crime and Delinquency* 33:306-323.

Maguire, Kathleen and Ann L. Pastore (Eds.). 1997. *Sourcebook of Criminal Justice Statistics 1996*. U.S. Department of Justice, Bureau of Justice Statistics. Washington, DC: U.S. Government Printing Office.

McDowall, David and Colin Loftin. 1992. "Comparing the UCR and NCS Over Time," *Criminology* 30: 125-132.

Nelsen, Candice, Jay Corzine, and Lin Huff-Corzine. 1994. "The Violent West Reexamined: A Research Note on Regional Homicide Rates," *Criminology* 32:149-161.

Short, James F., Jr. and F. Ivan Nye. 1958. "Extent of Unrecorded Juvenile Delinquency: Tentative Conclusions," *Journal of Criminal Law and Criminology* 49:296-302.

Smith, Douglas A. and Christy Visher. 1981. "Street-Level Justice: Situational Determinants of Police Arrest Decisions," *Social Problems* 29:167-177.

Tittle, Charles R. and Robert F. Meier. 1990. "Specifying the SES/Delinquency Relationship," *Criminology* 28:271-299.

Trebach, Arnold S. and James A. Inciardi. 1993. *Legalize It?: Debating American Drug Policy*. Washington, DC: American University Press.

United Nations. 1997. *Demographic Yearbook 1995*. New York: United Nations.

U.S. Bureau of Census. 1997. *Statistical Abstract of the United States: 1997*. Washington, DC: U.S. Government Printing Office.

Wolfgang, Marvin E. and Franco Ferracuti. 1967. *The Subculture of Violence*. New York: Tavistock.

Worden, Robert E. and Robin L. Shepard. 1996. "Demeanor, Crime, and Police Behavior: A Reexamination of the Police Services Study Data," *Criminology* 34:83-105.

CHAPTER 5

Are Uniform Crime Reports a Valid Indicator of the Index Crimes? An Affirmative Answer with Minor Qualifications

Walter R. Gove ▪ Michael Hughes ▪ Michael Geerken

The type of data used to measure crime has important implications for the picture of crime that society sees. Within criminology, there has been a great deal of debate about the merits of the three major types of data available: official data, victimization surveys, and self-report surveys. In this selection, Walter R. Gove, Michael Hughes, and Michael Geerken illuminate some of the issues raised in this debate.

The primary emphasis in the selection is on the validity of official data and the Uniform Crime Reports (UCR) specifically. The authors examine the validity of the UCR data for Part I index crimes, excluding arson. Their results suggest that as a whole, the UCR data provide valid measures of the index crimes, and in some cases, measures more valid than those provided by victimization surveys. Overall, the authors conclude that the UCR data are generally valid measures of the crimes that are perceived by both the police and citizens as the most serious.

A number of other issues important for criminology are also discussed. As the authors note, official data, victimization data, and self-report data all provide somewhat different pictures and, in some instances, discrepant pictures of crime, and all have important limitations that render none ideal for all types of studies in criminology. In official data, not all crimes that are known about are reported to the police, nor are all crimes reported to the police eventually recorded in the UCR. Official data are constructed, in the sense that two types of "filter" processes are involved: the victim must be aware of the crime and decide to report it to the police, and the police must determine if a crime actually occurred and record it as such, with the offense eventually counted by the FBI. A number of factors can impinge upon this process, although the authors indicate that the seriousness of the crime and the victim's wishes are two of the most important considerations.

Two recent assessments (Gibbs, 1983; Gove, 1983) of the field of criminology during the past 20 years conclude that the key methodological issue (and, in many respects, the key theoretical issue) confronting the field is a clear determination of how official crime rates are constructed and what they reflect. Both assessments hold that the field of criminology cannot substantially advance without using official crime rates for scientific purposes.

The present paper attempts to assess the validity and scientific utility of the Uniform Crime Reports (UCR). It is argued that the UCR have a clear interpretation and for most purposes are a valid measure of the FBI index crimes. In reaching this conclusion we draw on a variety of evidence including studies of citizen and police behavior, victimization studies, and, to a lesser extent, self-report studies of deviant behavior. The conclusion that the UCR are reasonable measures of the various index crimes is in part based on the proposition that official statistics provide good measures of certain types of criminal behavior, and we recognize that they are less adequate as measures of other types of criminal behavior. Thus, part of the conclusion is based on developing a fairly clear understanding of what the UCR actually measures. The conclusion also requires an understanding of what is measured by self-reports and, particularly, victimization surveys.

This position is controversial and runs counter to what has been a very common view of the UCR....

Much of the justification for questioning the validity and/or utility of the Uniform Crime Reports is based on empirical evidence. Introduced by Porterfield (1946), self-report studies have shown *drastically higher rates* of unofficial delinquency and *much weaker* correlations by class and race than are disclosed by official statistics. Furthermore, victimization surveys indicate that the majority of crimes are not reported to the police (Decker, 1980: 50; Cohen and Lichbach, 1982: 261). These data are commonly interpreted as indicating that the vast majority of crime goes unrecorded, and the large number of unreported crimes, commonly called the "dark figure of crime," is used to call into question the validity of official statistics. It is also argued that the victimization surveys and the UCR appear to be measuring different things....

Official Crime Statistics and Self-Reports: The Illusion of a Difference

The apparent sharp disparity between self-reports and official statistics which has plagued criminologists for a number of years has, to our satisfaction, been resolved. This resolution effectively answers one of the issues used to question the validity of official statistics and provides a step towards understanding what official statistics in general and the UCR in particular measure. Recently there have

been at least four major attempts to interpret the apparent disparity between official delinquency rates and self-reported delinquency rates....

These studies indicate that at least most of the apparent disparity in the rates in the self-report studies and official statistics is due to the very high rates of nonserious crime found in the self-report studies. This suggests that a substantial part of the "dark figure of crime" involves relatively trivial criminal acts. The studies indicate that class, race, sex, and age are related to crime in the direction reported by official statistics of arrest rates, and the study by Thornberry and Farnworth (1982) suggests the strength of the relationship is roughly consistent with that found in official statistics. However, these analyses focus on offender characteristics and provide no direct evidence of the factors determining what the police record as a crime; they only tangentially touch on the central issue raised by Kitsuse and Cicourel (1963)—namely, the factors that determine how the official statistics are constructed. These studies do not tell us what the UCR means and how we should interpret them. How do the unreported crimes differ from the reported crimes? Are there systematic differences? Unless we have a fair understanding of the characteristics of crimes that become official and those that do not, we are on very tenuous ground when we use official statistics to try to determine if crime is related to such things as income, racial inequality, urban density, city size, governmental structure, or a variety of other variables, for we do not know what the crime rates measure (Booth et al., 1977; Decker, 1980; Decker et al., 1982; O'Brien, 1983).

A Critical Issue: Understanding What the Victimization Surveys Measure

In attempting to determine the validity of the UCR and to interpret what they mean, we will draw heavily on the victimization survey, analyses of the surveys, and studies of police behavior. In many respects victimization surveys can be seen as an attempt to estimate the amount of criminal behavior using techniques that are entirely independent of the process that leads to officially recorded crime. The first victimization survey of a normal population was conducted in the U.S. in 1966 (Biderman and Reiss, 1967; Biderman, 1967).

Since 1973, the U.S. Census Bureau has fielded a large national victimization survey of households (Penick and Owens, 1976; Garofalo and Skogan, 1977). There have been attempts to relate changes over time in the rates found in the national victimization survey with changes in the national rates in the UCR. Although an early study by Eck and Riccio (1978) interpreted the data as indicating that the variations over time in the UCR did not reflect real difference in the crime rate, the more recent study by Biderman, Lynch, and Peterson (1982) suggests that the variations over time in the UCR correspond to variations in the national victimization survey and thus reflect real differences.

From 1971 to 1975, the Bureau of the Census performed victimization surveys in the 26 largest United States cities, each survey consisting of a sample of 10,000 households (approximately 22,000 individuals). Residents were asked if they had been victims of certain types of crime during the preceding year. Persons over 12 years of age were questioned about crimes against the person (rape, robbery, aggravated and simple assault, and personal larceny) and one adult in each household was questioned about crimes against household (burglary, auto theft, and household theft). Information about the circumstances surrounding each incident and about characteristics of the respondent and the household were collected. Similar data were obtained from businesses, except that no questions were asked about larceny. The number of businesses sampled ranged from 1,000 to 5,000 depending on the city sampled. It should be noted that 13 of the 26 cities were sampled twice.

Because data were obtained from both individuals and businesses in the 26 cities surveyed, it is relatively easy to compare victimization crime rates with the UCR (except for larceny). Furthermore, it is possible to compare characteristics of the cities with the two crime indexes, something that is not possible with the national victimization surveys. We know of eight comparisons of the UCR and the

city victimization surveys (Skogan, 1974; Clarren and Schwartz, 1976; Decker, 1980; Booth et al., 1977; Nelson, 1979; Decker et al., 1982; Cohen and Lichbach, 1982; Cohen and Land, 1984). Although Skogan (1974) in his preliminary analysis is relatively optimistic about the implications of the victimization survey for the UCR, most of the other investigators have concluded that the city victimization surveys raise serious questions about the UCR....

Before turning to how the Uniform Crime Reports are constructed, and particularly the light that the victimization surveys shed on the UCR, it is necessary to discuss what the victimization surveys measure. It is particularly important to focus on the methodological problems characteristic of the victimization surveys, because they are generally viewed as a more valid indicator of the crime rate than the UCR (Decker et al., 1982; Cohen and Land, 1984).

Conceptual Issues

In the victimization surveys, "victimizations" are conceptualized as discrete incidents with a beginning and an end, which are sharply bounded in time and space. As a result the surveys do not measure well continuous processes that are not clearly delineated discrete events but that instead resemble enduring conditions. Furthermore, they only measure events that can be uniquely described and ignore classes of crimes for which victimization is quite prevalent but the frequency of individual incidents is unknown. This procedure of operationalizing victimizations implies that crimes can be understood apart from their social context, that they are discrete events which are bounded in time and space, and that crimes are knowable as discrete individual incidents (Skogan, 1981a: 7, 1981b; Biderman, 1981).

Context
The victimization survey presupposes that through description behavior can be identified as criminal or noncriminal. However, criminality is a concept which in law is not strictly defined in terms of behavior. An example will help to illustrate the problem. The UCR definition of "aggravated

assault" is an unlawful attack by one person against another for the purpose of inflicting severe bodily injury, usually accompanied by the use of a weapon or other means likely to produce death or severe bodily harm (United States Department of Justice, F.B.I., 1973: 11). A number of sources of potential confusion lie in this definition. The "attack" does not have to produce any injury or even harm, since the definition includes attempts (as we will see, the inclusion of "attempts" is especially problematic in the victimization surveys). Furthermore, the issue of intent is crucial. Yet the establishment of intent is often difficult for the average citizen and the uniformed patrolman (who usually acts on secondhand information). Whether an attack is "unlawful" is likewise a difficult decision for the average citizen to make, particularly in the case of heated disputes where both parties (and their respective friends) feel aggrieved or threatened by the other. In fact, the victimization surveys do not determine who is the "aggressor" and who is the "victim," because the issue is never even broached in the interview. It would appear that most "aggressors" would be categorized as "victims" in the surveys. Furthermore, what is a "severe injury"? Injuries obviously fall along a continuum of seriousness and gray areas will always exist. The issue is complicated by the fact that the categories such as aggravated assault, simple assault, assault and battery, and fighting specifically exclude consideration of injury (United States Department of Justice, F.B.I., 1973: 55)....

Such serious definitional problems exist for almost all crimes. Among the index crimes, rape and minor burglary are almost as difficult (in some cases more difficult) to define and apply to concrete situations than are definitions of aggravated assaults (Clarren and Schwartz, 1976). In fact, it is not clear that a definition of a crime can refer only to objectively measurable behavior without some reference to intent of the offender, the unique circumstances, and the general attitude or condition of the victim.

The problem of social meaning is not as important a methodological issue with street robbery or anonymous assaults, but physical aggression among family and friends, and theft and robberies in which the offender is known to the victim are

much more difficult to interpret. The "crimininality" of such incidents depends heavily on the attitudes of those involved. Victimization surveys find such incidents tend not to be reported to the police and the most common reason given for not reporting is that "it was not a police matter," which suggests the victim did not wish to treat it as a crime. Nevertheless, such incidents are reported as crimes in the surveys (Hindelang, 1976; Gottfredson and Gottfredson, 1980.)

Discrete Events Versus Continuous Processes

Several crimes such as child abuse, spouse abuse, and robberies of children at school are perhaps better viewed as ongoing processes than as discrete events. Consider the family in which the father regularly comes home drunk, beats his wife, and threatens to beat his children. Occasionally, the conflict may escalate so that a family member or neighbor calls the police, so the police are apt to have an episodic record of such events. In the crime surveys these processes are treated as "series offenses." Series offenses are those incidents that are so frequent, similar in character, or otherwise difficult to separate that the victim cannot disentangle them during the interview into concrete events occurring at specific times. About 100 series incidents are recorded every month in the National Crime Surveys and they make up about 3% of all incident reports (Dodge, 1975). Overall, series incidents are disproportionately violent crimes. In the National Crime Survey and in the City Victimization Surveys, series incidents are completely excluded when the data are processed to produce crime rate estimates (Skogan, 1981a: 9)....

Reliance on the Victims' Definition of Criminal Acts

Because victimization surveys rely only on the report of the victims, the data may be distorted by variation in how respondents define crime. This appears to be a key issue with assaultive behavior. As Skogan (1981a: 10) notes, victimologists have always assumed the bulk of victims of assault come from the lower reaches of the social ladder because lower status persons are heavily overrepresented among victims of such crime on police files. However, in survey data, education is typically positively associated with victimization by assault. In 1976, for example, persons with college degrees recalled three times as many assaults as those with only an elementary education (U.S. Department of Justice, 1979: Table 15). This finding is extremely stable, being found in the United States (Dodge et al., 1976), Germany (Stephan, 1976), the Netherlands (Steinmetz, 1979), Norway, Finland, and Denmark (Wolf, 1976).

Skogan (1981a: 10) notes there are two competing explanations for this relationship, both of which assume that assaults tend to be more common in the lower class. The first is that educated persons are better respondents and give more complete information, and there is evidence to support this position (Skogan, 1981a: 22; Sudman and Bradburn, 1974; Sparks, Genn, and Dodd, 1977). However, it seems unlikely that this characteristic of respondents is sufficient to account for the relationship observed with education. The second is that persons in a lower-class environment may see a certain act as a normal aspect of daily life, while persons who have had very little contact with physically assaultive behavior may see the same act as a brush with criminal violence....

Subcultural differences in the salience of aggressive behavior may also explain some of the perplexing racial differences in reported assault victimization. For example, white residents of Washington, D.C., reported a rate of assault victimization that was two and one half times what blacks reported, a racial difference that is entirely due to nonserious assaults (U.S. Department of Justice, 1975: Table 3, 247)....

Sampling and Interviewer Effects

Interviewer Effects

... The categorization of many crimes is quite sensitive to individual discretion at the lower end of the seriousness scale, whether the discretion is of police officers (in the UCR crime estimates) or of respondents and their interviewers (in the victimization surveys). In an excellent discussion of the problem, Clarren and Schwartz (1976: 129) conclude that "the upper bound for the number of 'crimes' that could be elicited is limited only by the persistence of the interviewer and the patience of the respondent." Bailey, Moore, and Bailer (1978) show that a considerable amount of the variation in reported crime in the victimization surveys is due to interviewer effects—that is, variation due to the fact that some interviewers elicit more and/or different kinds of information from respondents than others. The extent of these effects varies both across cities and across crimes....

The Issue of the Distribution of Crime

While crime is relatively infrequent in the general population, this is not the case among certain subgroups. For example, in 1970 two thirds of the reported robberies in the United States were concentrated in 32 cities which contained 16% of the national population. Within those cities crime was very heavily concentrated within a few places (Skogan, 1979). As a result, a very small proportion of the population is exposed to extremely high levels of risk and contains a disproportionate number of victims. The relatively extreme spatial concentration of victims, especially victims of violent crime, poses a serious problem in drawing probability samples that will accurately reflect the proportion of criminal victimizations. As Skogan (1981a: 5) indicates, this problem has not been solved. A further difficulty is that factors associated with the victimization rates are also associated with the nonresponse rate, which tends to be particularly high among crime victims (Martin, 1981)....

Response Bias

Nonrecall

One way of checking the accuracy of victimization surveys is to take incidents from police files and to interview the victims. The San Jose reverse record check found that violent crimes of assault and rape were much less likely to be reported in the survey than property crimes (Turner, 1972); the prime determinant in whether the violent crimes were reported to the police was the relationship of the offender to the victim....

Classification

Another key finding of the record checks is that the police frequently classify a crime differently than the victims do in the survey. In general, the police tend to classify the crimes as less serious than do the victims.... A major reason why the police classification may differ from the victim's is that the data from police records and police decisions reflect information gathered from a variety of sources other than the victim, including their own observations and reports of witnesses (Skogan, 1978, 1981a: 13).

Other Sources of Error

It has consistently been found that interviewing a single informant in a household produces considerably fewer victimization reports than if all residents were interviewed (Biderman and Reiss, 1967; Sudman and Bradburn, 1974; Ennis, 1967; Stephan, 1976; Dodge, 1977). This is a source of some error in the city interview, because not all household respondents were interviewed, and even when all household respondents were interviewed, not all were asked about certain crimes (Dodge, 1977; Skogan, 1981a). Furthermore, a substantial number of crimes are not recalled unless they occurred in the very recent past, and the rate at which incidents are forgotten increases with time (Skogan, 1981a; Woltman, Bushery, and Carstensen, 1975; Penick and Owens, 1976). In addition to respondents forgetting or not telling about some crimes, other crimes that occurred prior to the time frame covered in the interview (one year in the city surveys) tend to be telescoped in the interview....

Assessment of the Victimization Data

Property Crimes

As it is presently constructed, the National Crime Survey appears to measure serious property crimes adequately—that is, successful robberies, burglaries, and auto theft. The measure of larceny appears to be much less satisfactory because (1) most

larceny involves offenses of small value, and (2) data on larceny are not obtained from businesses (Skogan, 1981a; Gottfredson and Gottfredson, 1980). For these crimes the city victimization surveys are much more problematic, in part because they occurred before many of the refinements in the current victimization surveys were made. Nevertheless, for serious robberies, burglaries, and auto thefts the estimated crime rates should have a rough correspondence with reality. By using the term seriousness we are concerned with such issues as the success of the crime, who committed it, the loss incurred, where the crime was committed, and, with robbery, such issues as the weapon used and the extent of bodily harm. Most cases of larceny where substantial loss is incurred are probably reported. However, because larceny primarily involves items of little value (Gottfredson and Gottfredson, 1980), it is not clear that the relatively few cases of "serious larceny" that occur in a city will be closely related to the rates estimated in the victimization survey.

Assault and Rape

There is substantial evidence that the data from the victimization surveys substantially underreport assaults and rapes among acquaintances, friends, and relatives. In the national survey 60% of the assaults were attributed to strangers and in the city survey 70% of interpersonal violence was attributed to strangers. As Skogan (1981a: 29) notes, these data do not correspond to what is known about the dynamics of interpersonal violence, namely that a much higher proportion of assaults and even rapes take place among family, friends, and acquaintances. Numerous studies of police homicide files suggest that strangers account for only 25% of all urban murders; homicide and assault typically are very similar in origin although the processes differ in outcome. (For review of the evidence, see Zimring, 1972; Curtis, 1974; Ennis, 1967; Skogan, 1978, 1981a; U.S. Department of Justice, F.B.I., 1971). Skogan (1981a:30) indicates that the victimization surveys are particularly suspect because police files contain three and one half times more violence between acquaintances than is reported in interviews. A study conducted in Washington, D.C., by the Law Enforcement

Assistance Administration (LEAA, 1977) found that in 1973, according to the victimization survey, 30% of the victims were assaulted by nonstrangers, whereas 75% of the persons arrested for assault were nonstrangers. The LEAA data on rapes are even more striking. They found that only 9% of the rapes reported in the victimization survey included nonstrangers whereas the official statistics indicated that 57% of the rapes included nonstrangers....

The LEAA (1977: 19) study concludes that the data are "substantial enough to cast serious doubt on the victimization surveys' ability to measure the incidence of assault and rape between nonstrangers." The report goes on to assert that "either the survey should be restructured to obtain better information on nonstranger violence or estimates from the survey should be limited to data about assault and rape between strangers" (1977: 19)....

It should be quite clear that for rape and assault, the measures of "crime" in the victimization surveys and in the UCR are completely different. We have focused on the issue of stranger/nonstranger violence, and to a lesser extent on the differences between blacks and whites, but probably a substantial part of the difference is due to the nature of the instruments used. In the UCR, the police must determine to their satisfaction that an assault or rape occurred. To do so they must conduct an investigation to determine if the incident fits the criteria for that particular crime. For aggravated assault, these criteria are (1) an unlawful attack of one person upon another, (2) for the purpose of inflicting severe or aggravated bodily injury, which (3) usually involves the use of a weapon or by means likely to produce death or severe bodily injury. In the victimization surveys, an aggravated assault is defined as having occurred if the respondent answers survey questions which indicate that he or she was (1) attacked with a weapon resulting in any injury, or (2) attacked without a weapon resulting either in serious injury (e.g., broken bones, loss of teeth, internal injuries, loss of consciousness) or an undetermined injury requiring two or more days of hospitalization, or (3) attacked in an attempted assault with a weapon. Note that in the victimization definition there is no determination of lawfulness or of intent.

For rape, the factors the police must determine to their satisfaction before a rape incident appears in the UCR are that a man must have had (1) carnal knowledge of a woman, (2) forcibly, and (3) against her will. In the victimization surveys a woman is never asked if she has been raped. To be recorded as rape the woman had to answer that she was raped to one of the following questions: (1) "Did anyone threaten to beat you up or threaten you in some other way?" or (2) "Did anyone *try* to attack you in some other way?" In the interview rape is never mentioned, no definitions are given, and no follow-up or probing questions are asked to find out the nature of the rape....

In summary, there is little if any reason to believe that across cities the victimization rates for aggravated assault and rape will correlate with the UCR rates. (For a more detailed discussion of this issue, see Skogan, 1978, 1981a; LEAA, 1977).

The Construction of UCR Offense Rate Statistics

UCR Index offense rates can be conceptualized as the final product of a filtering process which selects from a wide range of illicit behavior those specific acts reported to the FBI as serious crime. The most crucial step in the creation of an official crime statistic is the police becoming aware that a crime has been committed. The evidence consistently indicates that in this process the police are primarily reactive rather than proactive; that is, the crime is detected by a citizen who then notifies the police.... Thus, the process can most conveniently be considered as occurring in two stages: (1) a citizen detecting the offense, deciding to report it to police, and actually doing so, and (2) a police officer interpreting the reported offense, deciding to record it as an official crime, and later reporting it to the FBI under some UCR category....

Citizen Reporting and Nonreporting

Detection of a criminal offense involves both observing an event and defining that event as a criminal act. An attempted burglary where the burglar leaves no sign of an attempted entry or where the potential victim misinterprets the sign will not be labeled as a crime. Further, an event might be observed, yet not reported as a crime either (1) because the illegal nature of the act is not known, (2) because the citizen disagrees with the legal definition of an act as criminal, or (3) the cost of reporting the crime is not worth the benefit. It should be noted that citizens quite often cannot make the proper legal classification of an incident.... Among other things, this suggests that citizens in an interview may describe an incident as in a different category than police would have. This finding is supported in the reverse record checks; it is also found in studies which attempt to match victims' reports with police records (e.g., Schneider, 1977).

Reporting. Two issues crucial to deciding if there is a systematic bias in citizen reports of crimes to the police are whether among the different segments in our society (1) there are differences in the perceived severity of various crimes, or (2) there are differences in how serious a person must perceive a crime to be before reporting it to the police.... In short, with regard to the first issue it appears that the different segments of society agree on the severity of the various crimes covered by the FBI index crimes and that differences in perceived severity would not be a source of systematic bias affecting citizen reports of crime to the police.[1]...

Thus, the evidence from the victimization surveys provides very strong support for the view that perceived seriousness of the crime is the key determinant of reporting a crime to the police and the attributes of the individual and where the person lives play only a very minor role.

Another way to assess the reasons for citizens not reporting crimes is simply to ask the respondent why the crime was not reported. The two most frequently given reasons are that the offense "was not serious enough" to report and that "the police could not be effective." For the crimes of rape, assault, and motor theft a large percent of the victims reported that the victimization was "a private matter." Fear of reprisal is infrequently given as a reason for not reporting a crime

(Biderman, Johnson, McIntyre, and Weir, 1967: 154; Ennis, 1967: 44; Hawkins, 1973; Hindelang, 1976: 5; Gottfredson and Gottfredson, 1980; U.S. Department of Justice, F.B.I., 1974)....

In summary, the perceived seriousness of a crime appears to be the prime determinant of whether it is reported to the police. Furthermore, there is no evidence in the studies reviewed to suggest that different segments of society differ in the level of perceived seriousness (of the FBI index crimes) required before a crime is reported to the police.[2]

Police Recording and Nonrecording

The second major filter through which crime counts pass is the police organization itself, from the first patrolman's contact with the complaining citizen through the final classification of a crime into UCR categories for official recording and publication. It is the alleged bias in this screening process which has traditionally caused the most concern about the usefulness of official police statistics. As was noted, the initiation of the recording process is almost always in response to a citizen's complaint.

There are a number of ways of measuring law enforcement bias in the recording of crime. One is to look at characteristics of individuals and see if they are treated differently by legal officials. Another is to look at police departments and their reporting behavior. A third is to look at independent indicators of the crime rate.

Characteristics of individuals and police behavior. Perhaps the best direct-observation study is that of Black and Reiss (1970). The study consists of systematic observation of police-citizen transactions occurring in lower-class areas of Boston, Chicago, and Washington, D.C., during the summer of 1966. Black and Reiss (1970: 76) found that

1. Most police encounters with juveniles arise in direct response to citizens who take the initiative to mobilize the police to action.
2. The probability of arrest increases with the legal seriousness of alleged juvenile offenses,

in particular as that legal seriousness is defined in the criminal law for adults.

3. Police sanctioning of juveniles strongly reflects the manifest preferences of citizen complainants in field encounters.

4. The presence of situational evidence linking a juvenile to a deviant act is an important factor in the probability of arrest.

Note that the key determinants of official action were perceived seriousness of the offense and the desires of the complainant. In no instance did the police initiate official action when the complainant manifested a preference for informal action. When no complainant was present, the police very rarely initiated official action even though the suspect was found with incriminating evidence of some sort (Black and Reiss, 1970: 76). Second, there was no evidence of racial discrimination on the part of the police. Third, the deference of the offender had little effect on police action, with 22% of the antagonistic suspects and 22% of the very deferential suspects being arrested.[3] These findings have recently been replicated by Lundman, Sykes, and Clark (1978).[4]...

Block and Block (1980), using secondary data from a victimization survey and police records in Chicago, look at the process by which robbery is transformed into statistics. Rates of victimization are based on a survey conducted in 1974 and the rates of official records are based on a sample of police records for different months in 1975, with the rates projected for the entire year.... Block and Block found that (1) age, sex, and race of the victim had no effect on the decision probabilities at any stage in the decision process; (2) victim and police decisions are primarily affected by the seriousness of the incident as indicated by whether a gun was used or robbery completed; (3) most of the serious cases that are eliminated are eliminated by the victim and not by the police, and in fact no crimes were eliminated by the police when a robbery was completed and a gun was used; and (4) upon responding to a robbery reported by a victim, the police "found" 79% (officially reported a robbery had occurred), while 21% received a different categorization (this most frequently occurred when the victim reported a completed robbery with no

gun, and it is likely that many of these were categorized as burglaries).

By far the best studies of the validity of UCR figures regarding race, sex, and age characteristics of offenders are those by Hindelang (1978; 1981). Hindelang (1978) compared UCR estimates of the racial distribution of offenders for four common-law personal crimes—robbery, rape, aggravated assault, and simple assault—to those obtained from the national victimization survey.... Hindelang (1978: 101) concludes that "these data suggest there is virtually no criminal justice system selection bias for either rape or robbery."

The pattern is quite different with assault, particularly aggravated assault. The UCR arrest rate for aggravated assault is 41% black, and the victimization survey rate is 30% black (Hindelang, 1978: 100). When we look at the respondents in the victimization surveys who said they had reported the crime to the police, the percent black drops to 26 (Hindelang, 1978: 102), and so the disparity between the UCR and the NCS increases....

More recently, Hindelang (1981) compared offender characteristics using the victimization surveys and the UCR. He looked at crime rates by sex, race, and age for personal crimes (rape, robbery, assault, and personal larceny) and for household crimes (burglary, household larceny, and vehicle theft).... Hindelang demonstrates a remarkable correspondence between the survey data and official statistics. Hindelang (1981: 473) concludes, "the general agreement between UCR and NCS (National Crime Survey) on the offenders' sex, race, and age characteristics increases the probability that both are acceptably valid."...

Other evidence also suggests that professionalism is related both to more complete and more accurate crime reporting.... With the increase in both federal money and federal guidelines for police departments across the country during the 1970s, it is likely there was an increase in the level and uniformity of the professionalism of police departments, and that this variable is less important as a determinant of variation in the official crime rate across cities than it was in the past. Note also that in the past three decades there has been a very sharp increase in the number of agencies reporting to the FBI and at the present time virtually all relevant agencies report....

In summary, there are four factors which appear to play a significant role in whether the police, upon responding to a complaint, report a crime. The first is whether upon investigation the police conclude that the evidence fairly clearly indicates a crime has occurred (remember that the police and the citizens often differ regarding the appropriate categorization of a crime). Second, the police very rarely report a crime if the victim would prefer to treat the matter informally. Third, the more serious the crime, the more likely the police are to report it; with regard to this point it is worth emphasizing that police and citizens use very similar criteria for the "seriousness." Fourth, the more professional the police department, the more likely its officers are to report a crime. There has been a substantial increase in the professionalism of the police departments over the past four decades. In evaluating police behavior in the reporting of a crime, it is very important for the reader to keep in mind that the key determinant of whether a crime is officially recorded is the decision of the victim to notify the police, while police behavior plays a much more modest role.

A Comparison of UCR and Victimization Estimates

The best way to answer questions about the validity of the UCR is to relate them to the "true" crime rate. Since one can only estimate this rate (it can never be measured directly) and since all estimates of the true rates contain error, the next best test is to compare the UCR rates to another, maximally different indicator of the same variable, that is, to compare it to another flawed measure of the true rate. If the two measures share no method variance, if there is no common source of error which will bias both measures (in the same or in opposite directions), then the relationship between the two can be treated as a validity coefficient because the only source of common variance is taken to be the true rate (Skogan 1974)....

The correlations are higher for crimes involving theft (including robbery) than for purely personal crimes (aggravated assault and rape), and there tends to be less agreement among the investigators regarding the correlations for purely personal crimes. One can interpret this lack of agreement for the personal crimes among investigators as due to different decisions about the proper categorizations in the victimization surveys. Motor theft is consistently found to have the highest correlation and all the studies find burglary and robbery to have relatively high correlations. As expected, Nelson (1979) finds higher correlations with motor theft and robbery than most of the other investigators, while Clarren and Schwartz (1976) and Decker (1980) find a higher correlation with burglary. Nelson *also* found the correlation with robberies committed with a weapon to be substantially stronger than robberies without weapons, which is consistent with the fact that when weapons are used the crimes are much more likely to be reported to the police and the police are much more likely to record that a robbery occurred. Except for the study by Decker (1980), all of the studies found essentially no correlation between the measures of rape, and all studies found a negative correlation between the two measures of aggravated assault.

Motor Theft, Robbery, and Burglary

The victimization surveys and the UCR have similar rates for motor theft, and in the victimization surveys the respondents almost always indicated that they reported the crime to the police; however, with burglary and robbery the victimization rate is approximately three times as large as the UCR and the majority of the crimes are not reported to the police (Decker, 1980: 50). We would thus expect the correlations between the victimization survey and the UCR to be higher with motor theft than with burglary and robbery.... In short, for these crimes our analysis indicates the UCR rates are very highly correlated with the true crime rates and are a valid measure of serious motor theft, robberies, and burglaries....

Larceny

Among the FBI index crimes considered here, the larceny crime rate has received the least attention.

However, it is clear that larceny is (1) the most frequent index crime, (2) the most difficult to detect, (3) the crime least likely to be reported to the police (Schneider, 1981) and (4) the crime most amenable to reporting manipulation in response to political pressures (Clarren and Schwartz, 1976). The victimization surveys clearly indicated that for larceny the greater the value of the object stolen, the greater the likelihood that the crime will be reported and recorded.... However, because the vast majority of larcenies involve property of modest value, the official larceny rate will not primarily reflect stolen objects of considerable value (even though these crimes are the most likely to be reported and recorded). On reverse record recall checks, larceny is considerably less likely to be recalled than robbery or burglary but much more likely to be recalled than assault or rape (Penick and Owens, 1976: 39).

...The results of Decker and of Cohen and Lichbach indicate that the UCR larceny rate is fairly highly correlated with the true larceny rate. In contrast, the results of Decker et al. and Cohen and Land suggest that while the UCR larceny rate is clearly correlated with the true larceny rate, the relationship is not particularly robust. Thus, all four studies provide support for the position that the UCR larceny rate is correlated with the true larceny rate, but the results are equivocal with regard to the strength of that relationship, ranging from modest to strong....

Overall, unlike the other property index crimes, larceny needs more research before one can conclude that the official rate is a valid indicator. In our view the evidence is sufficient to support the position that the official larceny rate is adequate as a rough indicator of the actual larceny rate, meaning that *marked* variation in the official larceny rate will reflect real variation. However, the evidence is insufficient to conclude that modest changes in the actual larceny rate will be reflected in the official larceny rate.

Homicide

Hindelang (1974b) examined sources of homicide using data from the NORC, the Center for Health Statistics, and the UCR, and the comparisons indicated a high level of accuracy in the official homicide rates. More recently, Cantor and Cohen (1980) compared the UCR with the homicide rate measured by the vital statistic reports, and their analysis also shows that (at least since 1949) the UCRs provide an accurate measure of the homicide rate.

Aggravated Assault

There is a relatively large negative correlation between aggravated assault reported in victimization surveys and in the UCR, and in most analyses this relationship is statistically significant. Given the small sample size (n = 26), this is a remarkable finding. In the victimization surveys most of the aggravated assaults involve strangers, injury is rare, and serious injury is very rare. Furthermore, reverse record checks show that assaults by acquaintances, particularly by relatives, are rarely recalled in survey interviews. Also, official records have much higher rates of violence between acquaintances than are shown in the surveys, and many investigators have concluded that victimization surveys are unable to measure violence.

According to the U.S. Department of Justice, F.B.I. (1971: 11-12), "most aggravated assaults occur within the family unit or among neighbors or acquaintances. The victim and the offender relationship as well as the nature of the attack makes this crime similar to murder." And there is an extensive literature indicating homicides and aggravated assaults typically occur among a certain segment of the population which has a very high rate of violence (Mulville, Tumin, and Curtis, 1967; Wolfgang, 1958; Curtis, 1974; Luckenbill, 1984; Skogan, 1981a: 29-31).... Thus, the evidence involving police behavior indicates that stranger assaults are more likely to be reported than non-stranger assaults; if this is correct, then the high rate of stranger assaults reported in the victimization surveys is even more misrepresentative than a simple comparison with official statistics indicates.

What may be occurring with aggravated assault is the following. Serious assaults typically involve significant bodily injury, or at least a serious attempt to inflict such injury. Such assaults are likely to lead to police involvement due to someone else's effort to stop a serious altercation by calling the police, or when serious injury does occur (such as a knife or gunshot wound), the police become involved when medical attention is sought. The evidence suggests that the UCR rate of aggravated assaults largely reflects such cases....

It is also likely that in victimization surveys the nonreporting of aggravated assaults, particularly those committed by family members and acquaintances, occurs for the following reasons. First, such assaults typically arise over very trivial matters (Mulville et al., 1967; Curtis, 1974) and when one has a close relationship with an individual one tends, over time, to put the assault into the context of one's overall relationship with the person and as a consequence the incident tends to become normalized.[5] Second, because the assaults tend to occur in an environment where there is a high level of verbal and physical conflict, they would be fairly common experience to those involved and thus more easily forgotten and less likely to be reported to strangers.[6]

It is clear that many "aggravated assaults" are not recorded in the UCR. However, given the inability of the victimization surveys to measure non-stranger assaults and the very high proportion of "nonserious aggravated assaults" in the victimization surveys, it appears that the UCR provide a better measure....

Rape

Victimization surveys appear to be unable to measure rape adequately and, according to official statistics, they vastly undercount nonstranger rape. As with other assaults, the majority of rapes reported in the victimization surveys were attempted and not completed, and in a substantial majority of the rapes reported the victims received no physical injury. Unfortunately, because the victimization surveys contain no probes for either attempted or completed rapes, it is very difficult to grasp what the victimization surveys are measuring.

According to the UCR, rape is carnal knowledge of a female against her will through the use of force or the threat of force. In 1970, 71% of the official rape offenses involved a complete rape while the remaining 29% were attempted (U.S. Department of Justice, F.B.I., 1971: 14). According to official records rape is more likely than most of the index crimes (all except homicide and aggravated assault) to involve someone known to the victim.... Thus, official statistics on rape are much more likely to deal with completed rapes than are victimization surveys and report a vastly higher rate of nonstranger rapes than are reported in victimization surveys.

Of all the index crimes, rape appears to be the most problematic in terms of both the willingness of victims to contact the police and the ability to establish that the incident meets the legal criteria. That rape is difficult to prove is indicated by the fact that in 1970, for the nation as a whole, 18% of the reported rapes were determined to be unfounded (U.S. Department of Justice, F.B.I., 1971: 14), and the rate appears to be relatively constant over the years. As the UCR makes clear, the fact that upon investigation the police decided a citizen-reported rape was unfounded does not mean a rape did not occur, but that in most cases it was difficult to establish that force or threat of force was used because a prior relationship existed between the victim and the offender (U.S. Department of Justice, F.B.I., 1971: 14)....

It is argued that when a rape occurs it is primarily the severity of the turmoil, anguish, and bodily harm that determines whether the rape is reported to the police. Nonstranger rapes are probably less likely to be reported to the police than stranger rapes. However, it is likely that the victim's relationship with the offender tends to play a relatively modest role at the time a rape occurs but the nature of the relationship becomes increasingly important with the passage of time. Rapes reported in the UCR are probably a relatively poor indicator of rape as a social phenomenon but are probably a relatively accurate indicator of rapes which meet the established legal criteria (Lizotte, 1985).

It is not argued that only true rapes are reported in the UCR and that the victimization surveys are measuring trivial events. What is proposed is that the UCR tend to measure violent rapes where the legal evidence is clear.[7] In contrast, many of the rapes measured in the victimization surveys may be highly traumatic to the victim, but they are probably less serious in terms of violence, and in terms of legal criteria the evidence is more ambiguous. Such rapes appear to be fairly common and to be particularly difficult to contain by formal means of social control.

Conclusion

For a number of decades social scientists have recognized that the UCR are the result of a set of social processes which result in some crimes becoming "official" while other crimes do not become public "social facts." Since the recognition that the UCR were the product of a social process which selected out a large number of crimes, it has not been clear what the UCR represent. This paper, drawing on recent research, has attempted to interpret the meaning of the UCR and thus to assess their validity.

Running throughout this discussion of the factors involved in the development of crime rates are a few important themes. Both citizens and the police are involved in a decision-making process concerning the classification of an incident as an official crime. In the United States and most other democracies, the primary responsibility for serious crime detection is lodged in the citizenry rather than the police. The uniformed patrol division is geared for the reaction to citizen calls for help through a centralized radio communications system. In the majority of crime situations, the police act in response to citizens' telephone calls and give great weight to the preference of the complainant for action. The key factor in the decision of the citizen to notify the police, as well as in the police response to the complaint, is the perceived *seriousness* of the incident, especially if seriousness is defined very generally.

It appears that both the citizen and the police are in general agreement as to what is a serious crime, particularly if it involves bodily injury (or serious threat of bodily injury), if the property stolen is of high value, if the act is committed by a stranger, or it involves breaking and entering. The perceived seriousness of the crime, first and primarily as defined by the victim, and secondarily as defined by the police, appears to account for most

of the variance in whether a crime is officially reported....

Legal seriousness, victim-offender relationship, desires of the complainant, and the extent to which citizen and police see an incident as a public or private matter are all criteria related to reporting. They all concern the extent to which the victim of a crime sees himself or herself as substantially injured by another citizen in a way he or she cannot control.... Thus, official crime rates are in part a measure of the extent to which the citizens feel injured, frightened, and financially hurt by a criminal act. In this sense they may be a better measure of social disruption than are "true rates," where more objectively definable behavior is measured. In short, the rates of the index crimes presented in the UCR appear to be reasonably good approximations of true crime rates when the latter are defined as what both citizens and the police view as serious violations of the laws which codify the fundamental personal and property norms of society.[8]

Thus, the "dark figure" of crime uncovered in victimization surveys primarily involves rather trivial events; as Skogan (1978: 14) states, "Most victimizations are not notable events. The majority are property crimes in which the perpetrator is never detected. The financial stakes are small, and the costs of calling the police greatly outweigh the benefits." (See also Gottfredson and Gottfredson, 1980: 28-36). For those crimes when the victim knows the offender and does not notify the police the major reason that the police are not notified is that the victim views the "crime" as a "private matter." The aggravated assaults committed by strangers that are uncovered by victimization surveys and are not officially reported almost invariably involve no injury, and it is likely that most would not meet the legal criteria in aggravated assault. Similarly, most of the rapes committed by strangers and which are not reported by the police involve rapes that were not completed and that did not cause injury. Apparently, like self-reported delinquency, the criminal behavior picked up by victimization surveys but not reported to the police involves a different domain of behavior than that which is officially recorded (Hindelang et al., 1979).

The analysis suggests that the UCR appear to reflect fairly accurately what the citizens and the police perceive as violations of the law which pose a significant threat to the social order. For motor vehicle theft, robbery, burglary, and homicide, the evidence supporting this interpretation is also quite strong. For aggravated assault and rape the evidence is quite strong, but in reaching this conclusion one must recognize that one is making choices about the validity of various pieces of conflicting evidence. In particular, we are largely ignoring the data from the victimization surveys on assaults and rape on the grounds that they vastly underreport nonstranger assaults and rape and record a large number of aggravated assaults and rapes by strangers that do not meet the legal criteria.

Although there is general support for the utility of official larceny rates, in many respects the evidence on larceny is the most equivocal. As the rate of larceny is very high, even though most larcenies are not reported to the police, the official larceny rate is substantially higher than the other index crime rates. This means that the overall index crime rate disproportionately reflects the official rate of larceny, and given our questions about the validity of the larceny rate it is probably better not to look at the overall rate but to look at the crimes separately. In summary, it is concluded that the index crimes, with the possible exception of larceny, are valid indicators of crimes which members of society perceive as serious.

Most criminologists agree that the actual or "true" crime rate should correlate with urban structural characteristics and that if we had a valid indicator of the crime rate we could determine the relationship between crime and those structural characteristics (Shaw and McKay, 1931, 1969; Lander, 1954; Chilton, 1964; Bordua, 1958-1959; Schuessler, 1962; Land and Felson, 1976; Cohen and Felson, 1979; Hughes and Carter, 1983; Crutchfield, Geerken, and Gove, 1982; Cohen and Lichbach, 1982; Blau and Blau, 1982). Furthermore, a valid indicator of the crime rate is essential to study an etiological theory of criminality (see especially Gibbs, 1981, 1983). It is clear that the UCR provide a valid indicator of the index crimes and can be used in studies of the relationship between crime and social structural characteristics and in etiological studies.

When the UCR are used it should be made clear that one is dealing with the relatively serious crimes which tend to pass through the citizen and the police filters and are officially reported. Finally, it is important to note that if one defines crime as criminal acts serious enough to be reacted to by both citizens and the police, then from the evidence reviewed above, the UCR are at least as valid and probably more valid than the data from victimization surveys. In fact, with regard to rape and aggravated assault the rates obtained from the UCR have much more validity than the victimization rates.[9]

Discussion Questions

1. What are the Uniform Crime Reports? What are the strengths of these data? What are some of their limitations?

2. In what senses are official data (Uniform Crime Reports) socially constructed? What factors are important for determining whether an offense is actually reported to the police? What factors are important for determining whether the police record an "offense" as a crime?

3. Overall, for what offenses are the UCR data valid? For what offenses are the UCR less valid? What are the implications of this for criminologists' use of official data to study crime?

Notes

1. Miethe (1982) argues that perhaps some of the apparent consensus on the perceived seriousness of crimes may be a methodological artifact. However, because his argument only applies to minor crimes, which are not part of the FBI index crimes, this possibility has no relevance to the present discussion.

2. A reviewer of this paper has suggested that different segments of society (blacks and possibly persons from the lower class in general) are less likely to report comparable crimes to the police, with those segments requiring a higher "threshold level" (that is, a more serious crime) before reporting a crime to the police. This argument suggests that, because blacks (and

possibly members of the lower class in general) are less likely to report comparable crimes to the police than other members of the population, and because there are class and ethnic variations across cities, there could be a systematic bias in the UCR statistics across cities. The studies just reviewed appear to contradict such an argument. However, many assaults and some rapes that are reported to the police are not reported in victimization surveys, and many of those reported to the police are not reported in victimization surveys, and many of those reported come from educated whites, so these data do not conclusively address the issue for auto theft, burglary, robbery, or homicide. We argue later in the paper that with regard to reporting assaults and rapes to the police, at the time the crime is committed the threshold level is relatively comparable across the different components of society. However, the evidence for this proposition is largely inferential.

3. In an earlier study, Piliavin and Briar (1964) reported that the demeanor of the juvenile had a very strong effect on the field disposition of the suspect, even stronger than the type of offense. However, as Hirschi (1980: 282) notes, because offenses did not vary in this study, "anything and everything will be more important than offense in determining the severity of disposition."

4. The reader may want to look at Hirschi's (1980: 295-297) discussion of the interpretation of Lundman et al.'s (1978) findings in evaluating this summary of their findings.

5. We would argue that with aggravated assault, because there is a serious threat to one's life, the issue of stranger versus acquaintance tends to be ignored at the time the crime is committed. Furthermore, when someone other than the victim reports the assault to the police, the person reporting the crime is likely to be relatively unconcerned with the issue of the relationship between the offender and the victim. Thus, if correct, the victim's relationship to the assailant often only becomes an issue after the crime has occurred.

6. This analysis is consistent with the hypothesis that a subculture of violence is causally linked to a high level of violence; however, these assumptions do not require that the "subculture of violence" hypothesis be correct. All we are assuming is that when violence is common (1) it tends to be normalized, and (2) people will tend to be more distrustful of strangers.

7. First, at the time they occur nonstranger rapes are likely to be perceived as less serious. Second, victims are aware that the issue of force is more difficult to establish when the victim has an established relationship with the offender.

8. It should be clear from the discussion that what most citizens and police perceive as serious crimes tend not to include most white-collar crime, which many sociologists see as particularly serious crimes (Chambliss and Seidman, 1971; Quinney, 1975, 1978; Johnson and Wasicklewski, 1982).

9. In recent years the second most common source of data in the study of crime has been the victimization survey. If the analysis presented here is correct, then some of those studies are of questionable value. At the minimum investigators should be as cautious in drawing conclusions from victimization studies as they are in drawing conclusions from studies based on the UCR.

References

Akman, Dogan, Andre Normandeau, and Steven Turner. 1967. "The Measurement of Delinquency in Canada" in *Journal of Criminal Law, Criminology, and Police Science* 58: 330-337.

Bailer, Barbara, Leroy Bailey, and Joyce Stevens. 1977. "Measures of Interviewer Bias and Variance" in *Journal of Marketing Research* 14: 337-343.

Bailey, Leroy, Thomas F. Moore, and Barbara A. Bailer. 1978. "An Interviewer's Variance Study of the National Crime Survey City Sample" in *Journal of the American Statistical Association* 73: 16-23.

Beattie, Ronald H. and John P. Kenney. 1966. "Aggravated Crimes" in *Annals of the American Academy of Political and Social Sciences* 364: 73-85.

Berk, Richard, Donileen Loseke, Sarah Fenstermaker Berk, and David Rauma. 1980. "Bringing the Cops Back In: In Study of Efforts to Make the Criminal Justice System More Responsive to Incidents of Family Violence" in *Social Science Research* 9: 193-215.

——. 1982. "Throwing the Cops Back Out: The Decline of a Local Program to Make the Criminal Justice System More Responsive to Incidents of Domestic Violence" in *Social Science Research*.

Berk, Sarah and Donileen Loseke. 1981. "Handling Family Violence: The Situational Determinants of Police Arrests in Domestic Disturbances" in *Law and Society Review* 15: 317-346.

Biderman, Albert D. 1966. "Social Indicators and Goals" in Raymond A. Bauer (ed.), *Social Indicators*. Cambridge, MA: MIT Press.

Biderman, Albert D. 1967. "Surveys of Population Samples for Estimating Crime Incidence" in *The Annals* 374: 16-33.

——. 1975. *A Social Indicator of Interpersonal Harm.* Washington, D.C.: Bureau of Social Science Research.

——. 1981. "Sources of Data for Victimology" in *Journal of Criminal Law and Criminology* 72: 789-817.

Biderman, Albert D. and Albert Reiss. 1967. "On Exploring the 'Dark Figure' of Crime" in *The Annals* 374: 1-15.

Biderman, Albert D., James P. Lynch, and Joseph L. Peterson. 1982. "Why NCS Diverges From UCR Index Trends." Unpublished manuscript. Washington, D.C.: Bureau of Social Science Research.

Biderman, Albert D., Louise A. Johnson, Jennie McIntyre, and Adrianne W. Weir. 1967. "Report on a Pilot Study in the District of Columbia on Victimization and Attitudes Toward Law Enforcement." Field Surveys I. President's Commission on Law Enforcement and Administration of Justice. Washington, D.C.: U.S. Government Printing Office.

Black, Donald. 1970. "Production of Crime Rates" in *American Sociological Review* 35: 733-748.

Black, Donald and Albert Reiss, Jr. 1970. "Police Control of Juveniles" in *American Sociological Review* 35: 63-77.

Blau, Judith R. and Peter M. Blau. 1982. "Metropolitan Structure and Violent Crime" in *American Sociological Review* 47: 114-128.

Block, Richard. 1974. "Why Notify the Police? The Victim's Decision to Notify the Police of an Assault" in *Criminology* 11: 555-566.

——. 1981. "Victim-Offender Dynamics in Violent Crime" in *Journal of Criminal Law and Criminology* 74: 743-761.

Block, Richard and Carolyn Block. 1980. "Decision and Data: The Official Transformation of Robbery Incidents into Official Robbery Statistics" in *Journal of Criminal Law and Criminology* 171: 622-636.

Booth, Alan, David Johnson, and Harvey Choldin. 1977. "Correlates of the City Crime Rate: Victimization Surveys Versus Official Statistics" in *Social Problems* 25: 187-197.

Bordua, David J. 1958-1959. "Juvenile Delinquency and Anomie: An Attempt at Replication" in *Social Problems* 6: 230-238.

Bordua, David J. and Albert Reiss, Jr. 1967. "Organization and Environment: A Perspective on the Police" in David J. Bordua (ed.), *The Police: Six Sociological Essays*. New York: Wiley.

Braithwaite, John. 1981. "The Myth of Social Class and Crime Reconsidered" in *American Sociological Review* 46: 36-57.

Cantor, David and Lawrence Cohen. 1980. "Comparing Measures of Homicide Trends: Methodological and Substantive Differences in the Vital Statistics and the Uniform Crime Report Time Series (1933-1975)" in *Social Science Research* 9: 121-145.

Catlin, Gary and Susan Murry. 1979. "Report on Canadian Victimization Survey Methodological Pretests. Ottawa, Canada": Government Statistics.

Chambliss, William J. and Robert B. Seidman. 1971. *Law, Order, and Power.* Reading, MA: Addison Wesley.

Chilton, Roland J. 1964. "Continuity in Delinquency Area Research: A Comparison of Studies for Baltimore, Detroit, and Indianopolis" in *American Sociological Review* 29: 71-83.

Clarren, Summer N. and Alfred I. Schwartz. 1976. "Measuring a Program's Impact: A Cautionary Note" in Wesley Skogan (ed.), *Sample Surveys of the Victims of Crime*. Cambridge, MA: Ballinger.

Clelland, Donald and Timothy Carter. 1980. "The New Myth of Class and Crime" in *Criminology* 18: 391-396.

Cohen, Larry J. and March I. Lichbach. 1982. "Alternative Measures of Crime: A Statistical Evaluation" in *The Sociological Quarterly* 23: 253-266.

Cohen, Lawrence E. and Marcus Felson. 1979. "Urban Social Structural Determinants of Discrepancies Between Crime Reports and Crime Surveys." Presented at the annual meeting of the American Sociological Association.

Cohen, Lawrence E. and Kenneth Land. 1984. "Discrepancies Between Crime Reports and Crime Surveys: Urban Social Structural Determinants." *Criminology* 22: 499-530.

Cohen, Lawrence E. and Rodney Stark. 1974. "Discriminatory Labelling and the Five-Finger Discount: An Empirical Analysis of Differential Shoplifting Dispositions" in *Journal of Research in Crime and Delinquency* 11: 25-39.

Crutchfield, Robert, Michael Geerken, and Walter Grove. 1982. "Crime Rate and Social Integration: The Impact of Metropolitan Mobility" in *Criminology* 20: 467-478.

Cullen, Frances T., Bruce G. Link, and Craig W. Pozanzi. 1982. "The Seriousness of Crime Revisited: Have Attitudes Toward White-Collar Crime Changed?" in *Criminology* 20: 83-102.

Curtis, Lynn A. 1974. *Criminal Violence.* Lexington, MA: D.C. Heath.

Decker, David, David Shichor, and Robert O'Brien. 1982. *Urban Structure and Victimization.* Lexington, MA: Lexington.

Decker, Scott. 1980. *Criminalization, Victimization and Structural Correlates of Twenty-Six American Cities.* Saratoga, CA: Century Twenty-one Publishing.

Dodge, Richard. 1970. *Victims Recall Pretest— Washington, D.C.* Unpublished paper. Washington, D.C.: U.S. Census Bureau.

——. 1975. *Series Victimization: What is to be Done?* Washington, D.C.: U.S. Census Bureau, Crime Statistics Analysis Staff.

——. 1977. *Analysis of Screen Questions on the National Crime Survey.* Unpublished paper. Washington, D.C.: U.S. Census Bureau, Crime Statistics Analysis Staff.

Dodge, Richard and Harold Lentzner. 1978. "Patterns of Personal Series Incidents in the National Crime Survey." Presented at the annual meeting of the American Statistical Association.

Dodge, Richard, Harold Lentzner, and Frederick Shenk. 1976. "Crime in the United States: A Report on the National Crime Survey" in Wesley Skogan (ed.), *Sample Surveys of the Victims of Crime.* Cambridge, MA: Ballinger.

Dunbow, Frederic L. and David E. Reed. 1976. "The Limits of Victims Surveys: A Community Case Study" in Wesley Skogan (ed.), *Sample Surveys of the Victims of Crime.* Cambridge, MA: Ballinger.

Eck, J. Ernst and Lucius Riccio. 1978. "Relationship Between Reported Crime Rates and Victimization Survey Results: An Empirical and Analytic Study" in *Journal of Criminal Justice* 7: 293-308.

Elliot, Delbert S. and Suzanne S. Ageton. 1980. "Reconciling Race and Class Differences in Self-Reported and Official Estimates of Delinquency" in *American Sociological Review* 45: 95-110.

Ennis, Philip H. 1967. "Criminal Victimization in the United States: A Report of a National Survey" in *Field Surveys II.* Washington, D.C.: U.S. Government Printing Office.

Figlio, Robert M. 1975. "The Seriousness of Offenses: An Evaluation by Offenders and Non-offenders" in *Journal of Criminal Law and Criminology* 66: 189-200.

Garofalo, James and Michael J. Hindelang. 1977. *An Introduction to the National Crime Survey.* Washington, D.C.: U.S. Department of Justice.

Geerken, Michael and Walter R. Gove. 1977. "Deterrence, Overload and Incapacitation: An Evaluation of Three Explanations of the Negative Correlation Between Crime and Punishment" in *Social Forces* 56: 424-27.

Gibbs, Jack. 1981. *Norms, Deviance and Social Control: Conceptual Matters.* New York: Elsevier.

——. 1983. "The State of Criminology Theory." Presented at the annual meeting of the American Society of Criminology.

Gibbs, Jack and Maynard Erickson. 1976. "Crime Rates of American Cities in an Ecological Context" in *American Journal of Sociology* 82: 605-20.

——. 1979. "Conceptions of Criminal and Delinquent Acts" in *Delinquent Behavior* 1: 71-100.

Gottfredson, Michael and Don Gottfredson. 1980. *Decisionmaking in Criminal Justice.* Cambridge: Ballinger.

Gottfredson, Michael and Michael J. Hindelang. 1979. "A Study of the Behavior of Law" in *American Sociological Review* 44: 3-18.

Gove, Walter R. 1983. "Criminology: The Current State of the Field." Presented at the annual meeting of the Southern Sociology Society.

Hagan, John. 1972. "The Labelling Perspective, the Delinquent and the Police: A Review of the Literature." *Canadian Journal of Criminology and Corrections* 14: 150-165.

Hawkins, Danell. 1980. "Perceptions of Punishment for Crime" in *Deviant Behavior* 1: 193-216.

Hawkins, Richard O. 1973. "Who Called the Cops? Decisions to Report Criminal Victimization" in *Law and Society Review* 7: 427-444.

Hindelang, Michael J. 1974a. "Decisions of Shoplifting Victims to Involve the Criminal Justice Process" in *Social Problems* 21: 580-593.

——. 1974b. "The Uniform Crime Reports Revisited" in *Journal of Criminal Justice* 2: 1-17.

——. 1976. *Criminal Victimization in Eight American Cities.* Cambridge, MA: Ballinger.

——. 1978. "Race and Involvement in Common Law Personal Crimes" in *American Sociological Review* 43: 93-109.

——. 1981. "Variation in Rates of Offending" in *American Sociological Review* 46: 461-74.

Hindelang, Michael J., Michael Gottfredson, and James Garofalo. 1978. *Victims of Personal Crime: An Empirical Foundation for a Theory of Personal Victimization*. Cambridge, MA: Ballinger.

Hindelang, Michael J., Travis Hirschi, and Joseph G. Weis. 1979. "Correlates of Delinquency: The Illusion of Discrepancy Between Self-Report and Official Measures" in *American Sociological Review* 44: 995-1,014.

——. 1982. "Reply to 'On the Use of Self-Report Data to Determine the Class Distribution of Criminal and Delinquent Behavior" in *American Sociological Review* 47: 433-435.

Hirschi, Travis. 1980. "Labelling Theory and Juvenile Delinquency: An Assessment of the Evidence and Postscript" in Walter R. Gove (ed.), *The Labelling of Deviance* (2nd ed.). Beverly Hills: Sage.

Hsu, Marlene. 1973. "Cultural and Sexual Differences in the Judgment of Criminal Offenses: A Replication of the Measurement of Delinquency" in *Journal of Criminal Law and Criminology* 64: 348-353.

Hughes, Michael and Timothy J. Carter. 1983. "A Declining Economy and Sociological Explanation of Crime" in Kevin N. Wright (ed.), *Crime and Criminal Justice in a Declining Economy*. Cambridge, MA: Oelgeschlager, Gunn, and Hain.

Jacob, Herbert. 1975. "Crimes, Victims and Statistics: Some Words of Caution." Unpublished paper. Evanston, IL: Northwestern University.

Johnson, Kirk and Patricia Wasicklewski. 1982. "A Commentary on Victimization Research and the Importance of Meaning Structures" in *Criminology* 20: 205-222.

Kitsuse, John and Aaron Cicourel. 1963. "A Note on the Use of Official Statistics" in *Social Problems* 10: 131-139.

Kleck, Gary. 1982. "On the Use of Self-Report Data to Determine the Class Distribution of Criminal and Delinquent Behavior" in *American Sociological Review* 47: 427-433.

Land, Kenneth C. and Marcus Felson. 1976. "A General Framework for Building Dynamic Macro Social Indicator Models: Including an Analysis of Changes in Crime Rates and Police Expenditures" in *American Journal of Sociology* 82: 565-604.

Lander, Bernard. 1954. *Understanding Juvenile Delinquency*. New York: Columbia University Press.

Law Enforcement Assistance Administration. 1977. *Expanding the Perspective of Crime Data: Performance Implication for Policy Makers*. Washington, D.C.: U.S. Government Printing Office.

Lizotte, Alan. 1985. "The Uniqueness of Rape: Reporting Assaultive Behavior to the Police" in *Crime and Delinquency* 31: 169-190.

Luckenbill, David. 1984. "Murder and Assault" in Robert Meier (ed.), *Major Forms of Crime*. Beverly Hills: Sage.

Lundman, Richard. 1978. "Shoplifting and Police Referral: A Re-examination" in *Journal of Criminal Law and Criminology* 69: 395-408.

Lundman, Richard, Richard Sykes, and John Clark. 1978. "Police Control of Juveniles: A Replication" in *Journal of Research on Crime and Delinquency* 15: 74-91.

Martin, Elizabeth. 1981. "A Twist on the Heisenberg Principle—Or How Crime Affects Measurement" in *Social Indicators Research* 9: 191-223.

McCleary, Richard, Barbara Nienstedt, and James Erven. 1982. "Uniform Crime Reports on Organizational Outcomes: Three Time Series Experiments" in *Social Problems* 29: 361-372.

Miethe, Terance. 1982. "Public Consensus on Crime Seriousness" in *Criminology*: 515-526.

Miller, Frank, Robert Dawson, George E. Day, and Raymond Parnas. 1971. *Cases and Materials on Criminal Justice Administration and Related Process*. Mineola, NY: Foundation.

Miller, Walter B. 1967. "Theft Behavior in City Gangs" in Malcolm W. Klein (ed.), *Juvenile Gangs in Context: Theory, Research and Action*. Englewood Cliffs, NJ: Prentice-Hall.

Mulville, Donald, Melvin Tumin, and Lynn Curtis. 1967. *Crimes of Violence*. National Commission on the Causes and Prevention of Violence. Washington, D.C.: U.S. Government Printing Office.

Nelson, James. 1979. "Implications for the Ecological Study of Crime: A Research Note" in William Parsonage (ed.), *Perspectives of Victimology*. Beverly Hills: Sage.

Neter, John and Joseph Woksberg. 1964. "A Study of Response Errors in Expenditures Data From Household Interviews" in *Journal of American Statistical Association* 59: 17-53.

Newman, Graeme R. 1976. *Comparative Deviance: Perception and Law in Six Cultures*. New York: Elsevier.

O'Brien, Robert. 1983. "Metropolitan Structure and Violent Crime: Which Measure of Crime?" in *American Sociological Review* 48: 434-437.

Penick, Bettye, K. Eidson, and Maurice Owens. 1976. *Surveying Crime.* Washington, D.C.: National Academy of Sciences.

Piliavin, Irving and Scott Briar. 1964. "Police Encounters with Juveniles" in *American Journal of Sociology* 70: 206-214.

Pontell, Henry, Daniel Granito, Constance Keenan, and Gilbert Geis. 1984. "Seriousness of Crime: A Survey of the Nation's Chiefs of Police" in *Journal of Criminal Justice* 13: 1-13.

Porterfield, Austin. 1946. *Youth in Trouble.* Fort Worth: Leo Potishman Foundation.

Price, James. 1966. "A Test of the Accuracy of Crime Statistics" in *Social Problems* 14: 214-221.

Quinney, Richard. 1970. *The Social Reality of Crime.* Boston: Little, Brown.

——. 1975. *Criminology: Analysis and Critique of Crime in America.* Boston: Little Brown.

——. 1978. *Class, State and Crime.* New York: Longman.

Reiss, Albert J., Jr. 1967. "Studies in Crime and Law Enforcement in Major Metropolitan Areas" in *Field Surveys III*, Vol. 1. Washington, D.C.: U.S. Government Printing Office.

——. 1978. *Final Report for Analytical Studies of Victimization in Crime Using National Crime Survey Data.* New Haven, CT: Yale University, Institute for Policy Studies.

Rossi, Peter, Emily Waite, Christine Bose, and Richard Berk. 1974. "The Seriousness of Crimes: Normative Structure and Individual Differences." *American Sociological Review* 39: 224-237.

Schneider, Anne. 1977. *The Portland Forward Check of Crime Victims: Final Report.* Eugene Oregon: Institute for Policy Analysis.

——. 1981. "Methodological Problems in Victimization Surveys and Their Implications for Research in Victimology" in *Journal of Criminal Law and Criminology* 72: 818-838.

Schneider, Anne, Jaine Burcert, and L.A. Wilson. 1976. "The Role Attitudes in the Decision to Report Crimes to the Police" in William McDonald (ed.), *Criminal Justice and the Victims.* Beverly Hills: Sage.

Schrager, Laura and James F. Short, Jr. 1980. "How Serious a Crime? Perceptions of Organizational and Common Crimes" in Gilbert Geis and Ezra Stotland (eds.), *White-Collar Crime: Theory and Research.* Beverly Hills: Sage.

Schuessler, Karl. 1962. "Components of Variation in City Crime Rate" in *Social Problems* 9: 314-323.

Seidman, David and Michael Couzens. 1974. "Getting the Crime Rate Down: Political Pressure and Crime Reporting" in *Law and Society Review* 8: 457-493.

Sellin, Thorsten and Marvin Wolfgang. 1964. *The Measurement of Delinquency.* New York: Wiley.

Shaw, Clifford R. and Henry D. McKay. 1931. "Social Factors in Juvenile Delinquency" in *Report on the Causes of Crime*, Vol. 2. National Commission on Law Observance and Enforcement. Washington, D.C.: U.S. Government Printing Office.

——. 1969. *Juvenile Delinquency and Urban Areas* (revised ed.). Chicago: The University of Chicago Press.

Shenk, Frederick and William McInerney. 1978. "Issues Arising From Application of the National Crime Survey." Presented at the annual meeting of the Southwestern Political Science Association.

Skogan, Wesley. 1974. "The Validity of Official Crime Statistics: An Empirical Investigation" in *Social Science Quarterly* 55: 25-38.

——. 1976. "Crime and Crime Rates" in Wesley Skogan (ed.), *Sample Surveys of Victims of Crime.* Cambridge, MA: Ballinger.

——. 1978. *Victimization Surveys and Criminal Justice Planning.* National Institute of Law Enforcement and Criminal Justice, Washington, D.C.: U.S. Government Printing Office.

——. 1979. "Crime in Contemporary America" in Hugh Graham and Ted Gurr (eds.), *Violence in America.* Beverly Hills: Sage.

——. 1981a. *Issues in the Measurement of Victimization.* Washington, D.C.: U.S. Government Printing Office.

——. 1981b. "Assessing the Behavioral Context of Victimization" in *Journal of Criminal Law and Criminology* 72: 727-742.

Skogan, Wesley and William Klecka. 1977. *The Fear of Crime.* Washington, D.C.: American Political Science Association.

Sparks, Richard, Hazel Genn, and David Dodd. 1977. *Surveying Victims.* New York: Wiley.

Steinmetz, Carl. 1979. "An Empircally Tested Analysis of Victimization Risks." Presented at the Third International Symposium on Victimology.

Stephan, Egon. 1975. "Die ergebnisse der stuttgater opferbefrangung unter beruchksicthtigung vergleichbarer Amerikanischer daten." Kriminolostatistic 5: 210-306.

——. 1976. *Die Stuttgarter Opferbefragung.* Wiesbaden, Germany: Bundeskriminalant.

Sudman, Seymour and Norman Bradburn. 1974. *Response Effects in Surveys: A Review and Synthesis.* Chicago: Aldine.

Sullivan, Peggy and Walter Gove. 1984. "The Perceived Utility of the Uniform Crime Reports: An Analysis of Current Criminology Textbooks." Unpublished paper. Nashville: Vanderbilt University.

Thornberry, Terence and Margaret Farnworth. 1982. "Social Correlates of Criminal Involvement: Further Evidence on the Relationship Between Social Status and Criminal Behavior" in *American Sociological Review* 47: 505-518.

Tittle, Charles R., Wayne J. Villemez, and Douglas A. Smith. 1978. "The Myth of Social Class and Criminality: An Empirical Assessment of the Empirical Evidence" in *American Sociological Review* 43: 643-656.

Turk, Austin T. 1969. *Criminality and Legal Order.* Chicago: Rand-McNally.

Turner, Anthony. 1972. *The San Jose Methods Test of Known Crime Victims.* Washington, D.C.: National Criminal Justice Information and Statistics Service, U.S. Department of Justice.

U.S. Department of Justice. 1975. *Criminal Victimization in 13 American Cities.* Washington, D.C.: National Criminal Justice Information and Statistics Service.

——. 1979. *Criminal Victimization in the United States, 1976.* Washington, D.C.: National Criminal Justice Information and Statistics Service, U.S. Department of Justice.

——. 1982. *Violent Crime by Strangers.* Washington, D.C.: Bureau of Justice Statistics.

U.S. Department of Justice, Federal Bureau of Investigation. 1971. *Uniform Crime Reports, 1970.* Washington, D.C.: U.S. Government Printing Office.

——. 1973. *Uniform Crime Reports, 1971.* Washington, D.C.: U.S. Government Printing Office.

——. 1974. *Uniform Crime Reporting Handbook.* Washington, D.C.: U.S. Government Printing Office.

Velez-Dias, Angel and Edwin I. Megargee. 1970. "An Investigation of Differences in Value Judgments Between Youthful Offenders and Non-Offenders in Puerto Rico" in *Journal of Criminal Law, Criminology, and Police Science* 61: 549-553.

Wilson, James Q. 1976. *Varieties of Police Behavior.* Cambridge, MA: Harvard University Press.

Wolf, Preben. 1976. "On Individual Victims of Certain Crimes in Four Scandinavian Countries 1970-74: A Comparative Study." Presented at the Second International Symposium of Victimology.

Wolfgang, Marvin. 1958. *Patterns in Criminal Homicide.* Philadelphia: University of Pennsylvania Press.

Wolfgang, Marvin and Simon Singer. 1978. "Victim Categories of Crime" in *The Journal of Criminal Law and Criminology* 69: 779-94.

Woltman, Henry, John Bushery, and Larry Carstensen. 1975. "Recall Bias and Telescoping in the National Crime Survey." Unpublished paper. Washington, D.C.: U.S. Census Bureau, Statistical Methods Division.

Yost, Linda and Richard Dodge. 1970. "Household Survey of Victims of Crime: Second Pretest—Baltimore, Maryland." Unpublished paper. Washington, D.C.: U.S. Census Bureau.

Zimring, Franklin. 1972. "The Medium is the Message: Firearms Caliber as a Determinant of Death From Assault" in *Journal of Legal Studies* 1: 97-123.

CHAPTER 6

Reassessing the Reliability and Validity of Self-Report Delinquency Measures

David Huizinga ■ Delbert S. Elliott

Extensive use of self-report data in criminology began in the 1950s and continues to be used. At the same time that this method was gaining in popularity, however, criticisms were being leveled against it. In response, numerous attempts have been made to determine if self-reports are valid and reliable measures of delinquent and criminal behavior. David Huizinga and Delbert S. Elliott have developed and administered the National Youth Survey, one of the best known and most widely analyzed self-report studies in criminology. In this selection they address the issues of reliability and validity.

Reliability, and particularly validity, are important for all forms of measurement. Huizinga and Elliott consider several different types of reliability and validity and provide definitions for them. Reliability can be loosely defined as the ability to replicate results; although reliability varies depending on the method used to assess it, self-reports are generally considered reliable. Validity, which can be defined as whether a measure assesses what it is intended to measure, is more questionable in self-reported delinquency. Huizinga and Elliott examine several types of validity, including content validity and empirical validity. They indicate that overall, self-reports are generally valid. The evidence suggests that there is differential validity in

different groups. In particular, they report that the validity of self-reports for black males is lower than for other groups, with underreporting of behavior the most serious problem. Huizinga and Elliott conclude that overall, self-reported delinquency data are generally reliable and valid, although the empirical results suggest that neither reliability nor validity is overwhelmingly high and this cannot be ignored when using such data.

Introduction

General Objectives

Few issues are as critical to the study of crime and delinquency as the question of the reliability and validity of our measures of this phenomenon. Much of the earlier debate on this issue centered on the relative merits and disadvantages of self-report measures as compared to official record measures, and for a number of years now criminologists have been polarized with respect to these two approaches to measuring crime. This resulted in part because there was limited information available on the reliability and validity of self-report measures and in part because these measures appeared to generate different basic findings regarding the volume and distribution of crime in the population and a different partitioning of subjects into criminal and noncriminal subgroups. These measure-related differences quickly became linked to ideological differences and theoretical preferences.

The concern over the measurement of crime has now taken a slightly different direction. Currently

Reprinted from: David Huizinga, and Delbert S. Elliott, "Reassessing the Reliability and Validity of Self-Report Delinquency Measures." In *Journal of Quantitative Criminology* 2, pp. 293-327. Copyright © 1986 by Plenum Publishing Corporation. Reprinted by permission of David Huizinga, Delbert S. Elliott, and Plenum Publishing Corporation.

many crime and delinquency researchers consider self-report measures to have acceptable levels of reliability and validity, i.e., the reliability and validity of these measures compare favorably to those of other standard measures employed routinely by social scientists (Hindelang et al., 1981). It is also clear that official record measures of crime have *not* been replaced by self-report measures, and there is no sign that they are likely to be replaced in the near future. Further, there is recent evidence that at least some of the earlier observed discrepancies in findings between self-report and official record measures were the result of differences in measure content and form, i.e., comparisons involving different offense sets and/or prevalence with incidence measures (Reiss, 1975; Hindelang et al., 1979, 1981; Elliott and Ageton, 1980; Elliott and Huizinga, 1983). As a result, self-reported offender measures, self-reported victimization measures, and official record measures now tend to be viewed as alternative measures of crime which compliment one another, each having some strengths or advantages which the others lack and some limitations which are better addressed by the others. Each is considered a reasonably reliable and valid measure of crime which is more appropriate for certain research purposes than others (Garofalo and Hindelang, 1977).

The accumulated research on the reliability and validity of self-report delinquency measures has consistently supported the conclusion that these measures have acceptable levels of reliability and validity as judged by conventional social-science standards (e.g., Hindelang et al., 1981; Sampson, 1985; Wyner, 1981; Hardt and Petersen-Hardt, 1977; Huizinga and Elliott, 1983). Still, the question of the reliability and validity of self-report measures continues to be a major issue. There are several reasons for this. First, the approach to validation has relied heavily (but not exclusively) upon official record measures of crime as the validation criterion. While correlation with alternative measures is a standard form of measure validation, since the validity of neither arrest nor self-report measures is beyond question, it leaves the issue of the true validity of these two measures unanswered. Second, there are conceptual, methodological, or interpretation problems with much of the earlier

validation work. Third, a number of important validity issues have simply not been addressed. For example, the major emphasis has been on deliberate falsification and recall problems as sources of underreporting; relatively little attention has been given to sources of error leading to overreporting. Fourth, there is some evidence that while self-report measures are reliable and valid in general, they are differentially valid within certain subpopulations. For example, Hindelang et al. (1981) found that self-report measures have a lower reliability and validity for blacks and delinquents than for whites and nondelinquents. There are grounds for questioning this finding (see Elliott, 1982), but if it were sustained by further research, it would seriously limit the appropriateness of self-report measures for certain research purposes. Finally, while these measures may meet minimum standards, it cannot be said that estimates of reliability and validity are uniformly high; there is an obvious need to work toward the further improvement of self-report measures of crime and delinquency.

In the following sections, several issues related to the reliability and validity of self-report delinquency measures are raised. Discussions of these issues include prior research findings and incorporate new information from the National Youth Survey.[1] In light of the problems described, some cautions about the use of self-report measures are made.

Reliability

Definition of Reliability

The reliability of a measuring instrument is commonly defined as the level of precision of the instrument. In this context, the level of precision refers to the extent to which the measuring instrument would produce identical scores if it were used to make multiple measures of the same object or, equivalently, the amount of measurement error, when each measurement is considered as the sum of true score and error components....

Reported Levels of Reliability in Prior Research

In a brief and nonexhaustive review of the reliabilities reported in earlier delinquency studies, it became apparent that although only a few studies had formally examined the reliability of the SRD indices employed, those that had were reasonably consistent in reporting relatively high reliabilities for the total samples.... In general, it appears that the reliability of SRD indices is quite high and would be considered adequate by the prevailing standards for attitude and other social-psychological measures.

There are, however, some findings which are not as positive. In a more comprehensive study of the reliability of SRD measures, Hindelang et al. (1981) examined reliabilities of different scoring procedures within different sex, race, and police-court record groups. All but one group had test-retest reliabilities in the 0.84-0.97 range. For black males with a police record, however, the reliabilities varied from 0.62 to 0.81, depending on scoring procedure. Patterson and Loeber (1982) report on the reliabilities of various subscales of a larger general measure of SRD and note that a scale consisting of only nonserious items had a reliability of 0.69. Thus there is some indication that the high reliabilities for total samples and total scales may not carry over to certain subgroups or subscales. It should also be noted that there is an indication that when a variety measure (i.e., a count of the number of different offenses committed) is used, the reported reliabilities are slightly higher than when a frequency measure (i.e., the number of all reported offenses) is used (Belson, 1968; Hindelang et al., 1981).

In the National Youth Survey (NYS) test-retest reliabilities were obtained for a sample of respondents. The total set of respondents participating in the fifth-wave survey was stratified by race (white, black) and four levels of delinquent involvement. Within each of the eight strata, approximately 20 individuals were randomly selected to be included in the test-retest study. A total of 177 retest interviews was completed. All retest respondents were reinterviewed approximately four weeks after their initial interview. (The distribution of test-retest intervals is bell shaped, with a range of 21-35 days. The mean, median, and mode, however, all fall on the 28- to 29-day interval.) The retest interview was conducted in the same manner as the initial interview and in most cases involved identical interview

situations, i.e., the same interview setting and interviewer. Complete details of the test-retest study are given by Huizinga and Elliott (1983)....

In general, the reliabilities of the individual items included in the NYS delinquency measure are over 0.5, with the majority of reliabilities ranging from 0.65 to 1.00. Although there are some items with low reliabilities, for the most part the reliabilities at the item level are in the same range as the reliabilities for scales. Thus, the reliabilities of the scales do not result from a fortuitous combination of item scores, but reflect the reliabilities of the underlying items....

Some Empirical Evidence of the Correlation Between Scores and Magnitude of Errors

Some notion of differences in the magnitude of the errors made by less frequent and more frequent offenders is indicated by the proportions of these offender types who change their responses by more than two behaviors.... Defining a low-delinquency group as having five or fewer reported offenses and a high-delinquency group as having six or more reported offenses, approximately 60% of the low-delinquency group had test-retest differences on the general SRD measures that were two or less, and only about 20% of the high-delinquency group were this precise. While the exact magnitude of error is not indicated by these data, they clearly suggest that errors made by high-frequency offenders are likely, on the average, to be larger than those made by less frequent offenders. While the proportion of individuals within these two delinquent groups with difference scores of less than two varies by particular scales, the low-delinquency group always has the largest such proportions....

Percentage of Persons Who Change Their Response From Positive to Never or From Never to Positive

Although not directly involved in the usual examination of reliability for delinquency measures, it is of interest to examine a particular kind of change in SRD scores from test to retest. While small changes in reported delinquency would be expected, it might be anticipated that individuals will accurately remember and report whether they ever engaged in particular behaviors during the last year. Thus, it would be expected that never (or zero) responses on the original test would remain never on the retest and, similarly, that positive responses would remain positive....

The magnitude of the percentages of individuals who change their mind about whether or not they have engaged in various kinds of delinquent behavior clearly suggests a moderate level of error in many of the SRD indices. Although for group analyses the positive-to-never and never-to-positive changes may "cancel" much of the error, for individual data the "error" is rather large. As noted above, this is especially true for the less serious or minor scales, where over a quarter of some subgroups changed their minds about whether they had ever (in the last year) engaged in certain minor delinquent behaviors. Thus, the lack of response consistency to the question of ever committing particular offenses suggests that at least the minor SRD indices may not be very reliable.

Summary

In the preceding it has been noted that because delinquent behavior is most likely not a homogenous domain, the use of test-retest correlations as measures of the reliability of SRD indices is more appropriate. The vast majority of studies examining the reliability of SRD indices has followed this prescription and generally has found the reliabilities to lie in the eighties and nineties. While this level of reliability is often said to be adequate in the light of prevailing standards for attitude measurement, there are some major difficulties inherent in the reliabilities of SRD indices....

Clearly, the reliability of SRD scales is an issue that requires further examination and it would be inappropriate to assume on the basis of current evidence that the reliability of SRD indices is adequate for all subgroups or for all purposes. While the current evidence is promising and the reliabilities reported compare favorably with those of other social-psychological measures, further effort in determining and improving the reliability of SRD measures is necessary and some care should be taken in the use of these scales in future delinquency research....

Validity

Definition

The validity of a psychological or behavioral test is commonly defined as the evidence that the test measures what it was intended to measure or that it represents what it appears to represent. Thus to determine the validity of indices of delinquent or criminal behavior, it becomes important to delineate carefully what is being measured or represented. The term delinquent has been used in various ways, e.g., to describe persons or groups, to describe illegal behaviors, and as a synonym for deviant, with the result that the meaning of the term delinquent is often ambiguous. However, what is being measured by a delinquency index for most current researchers is the commission of behaviors that are violations of criminal statutes or such violations that are actually acted upon by formal law-enforcement agencies. This definition is important not only because it is a necessary prerequisite to determining if a measure is valid but also because it indicates what ostensibly is being measured is a count of specific behaviors. Underlying the delinquency measures are, although perhaps unknowable, absolute true scores of delinquent behavior. Thus delinquency is not an abstract construct and a variety of empirical indicators can play a more prominent role in the determination of the validity of a given measure of delinquent behavior.

Given a relatively precise definition of what is being measured, three major approaches to the demonstration of validity are often described. Content validity refers to the subjective evaluation that the test items seem plausible and relevant and that the universe of behavior being measured is adequately sampled by the test items. Empirical or criterion validity refers to the relationship between test scores and some known external criterion that accurately indicates the quantity being measured. Construct validity involves the use of theoretical hypotheses about the relationship of test scores to other theoretical variables and the empirical justification of those hypotheses.

In general, based on the first or second of these indicators of validity, almost all researchers in crime and delinquency that have investigated the validity of their self-reported measures of delinquent behavior conclude that these measures are reasonably valid or are valid in the sense that they compare favorably with the validity of other measures employed in the social sciences (cf. Hindelang et al., 1981, pp. 114, 213). However, it should be carefully noted that most such researchers, including the authors of this article, have a vested interest in producing a positive evaluation of the validity of either official data or self-reports of delinquency (or both), since a negative evaluation would challenge years of individual research effort. The conclusions concerning validity are not made by disinterested parties. In the validity literature, only two articles provide strong cautionary notes. Gould (1969) suggests that given the problems inherent in both arrest and self-report data, there may be no measure of delinquent behavior in which criminologists can place a high degree of trust, and Bridges (1978) concludes from a more technical examination that biases and correlated errors may seriously distort our measures of crime and delinquency.

Construct validity has seldom, if ever, been used in delinquency research. The problem of simultaneously examining both tests of theory and validity issues within the same study generally precludes examination of construct validity. However, many variables theoretically linked to delinquency have been shown to be correlated with self-reported delinquency measures, and even when the correlations are not those specified by a given theory, the researchers have concluded that the theories are misspecified and not that the self-report measures are invalid. Thus, in a very loose sense, there is some indication of the construct validity of SRD measures.

In the following sections a brief review of findings relative to the content and empirical validity of self-reported measures of delinquency is given. A more detailed review of some of the studies cited is given by Hindelang et al. (1981).

Content Validity

Face Validity. Face validity refers to the evaluation of what the items included in an index appear to measure. Many of the indices of self-reported delinquency that have been used include items that do not involve violations of criminal statutes or involve such trivial infractions that they would rarely result in official action even if observed or discovered. Although many of the items included in some SRD indices are about criminal violations, others are not, and the summative scales or indices constructed from the total set of items thus do not appear to have a uniform or consistent face validity. More recently this problem has been recognized and at least partially corrected by the elimination of items that involve only trivial or noncriminal infractions. However, many of the SRD indices in use include such items and thus may fail the test of validity [a notable exception is the set of items employed by Hindelang et al. (1981)].

A related problem concerns the nature of responses to items which, on the surface, appear to be about serious-offense behavior. Questioning respondents about offenses they have reported reveals that some responses are about trivial events that do not match the severity of the offense described. This source of error results in inflated estimates of involvement in delinquent behavior, i.e., it constitutes a form of overreporting....

The vast majority of overreporting (trivial responses) in the NYS involved items concerning minor assault. However, the remaining items, especially felony assault (including robbery) and property damage items, also had a sizable proportion of responses that were considered trivial. There was no evidence, however, of a differential distribution of trivial responses by sex, race, social class, or place of residence (urban, suburban, rural). Exactly why the interview situation, instruction sets, or wording of items causes some respondents to report trivial events to serious items is not clear, but some combination of those factors illicited reports of trivial events.... Since there were no sex, race, class, or age differentials in the reporting of trivial events, this overreporting problem may not be a serious one for estimating the social correlates of criminal behavior. But it poses a serious problem for comparisons of self-reported offense rates with NCS or UCR rates and potential problems for etiological studies....

Empirical or Criterion Validity

In examining the empirical validity of SRD measures, various means of determining the relationship between SRD and some external criterion have been employed. These include known groups—in which the differences in SRD between groups presumed to have differences in delinquent behavior are demonstrated; correlational—in which the relationship of SRD scales with a criterion variable is examined; and official record checks—in which a check is made to determine if an individual with an officially recorded offense reports a behavior matching the offense behavior.

Known Group Validity. Differences in SRD between various groups expected to have different levels of delinquency have been examined by several studies....

In all cases involving official records or self-report of official contact, the groups that would be anticipated to have higher delinquent involvement (those with greater official involvement) had substantially and usually statistically significant higher mean SRD scores. Although few formally examined the ability of the SRD measures actually to discriminate between groups, most studies would appear to allow some moderately accurate classification into the known groups. In terms of this rather minimal check in validity, self-report measures of delinquency are clearly indicated as being valid.

Differences between the mean SRD scores of groups defined by different levels of variables related to delinquent behavior have also been investigated.... As with official records, again all groups anticipated to have greater delinquent involvement have higher mean SRD scores. Thus, those who teachers nominate, who have a greater number of delinquent friends, who have lower socialization scores, who have a low perceived risk of punishment, who are less obedient, or who are class bullys, as groups, have higher SRD scores. As a result, in terms of the differences between the groups defined by these other variables, the SRD indices would appear to be valid.

Correlational Validity. Stronger evidence for the validity of a measure is provided by its correlation with a criterion related to the behavior being measured. A number of factors important to SRD measures affect the magnitude of the measure-criterion correlation, however.... Because most criterion measures used in the examination of the validity of SRD measures are not particularly accurate indicators of the volume of delinquent behavior, correlations between SRD and criterion variables are not expected to be high....

The correlational validity of SRD measures has been examined using official data, other self-reported indicators of delinquent involvement, reports on respondents' behavior by others, and other variables presumed to be related to SRD as criterion measures. The correlations among SRD and arrests or official contacts are generally low.... The relationship between SRD and self-reported official contacts is much higher, with correlations ranging in the 0.60s for various scales (Hindelang et al., 1981).

The level of these relationships between SRD and official contacts or self-reported official contacts raises a number of issues that are beyond the scope of this paper. Clearly if official data are an accurate reflection of individual involvement in delinquent behavior, then SRD measures do not appear to be very valid. It is more likely, however, that the frequency of delinquent behavior is not tied very tightly to arrests or contacts, and other problems with the accuracy of official data coupled with problems of reliability result in the low reported correlations....

Record Checks. One of the most frequently used methods for investigating the validity of SRD measures has been an examination of whether offenses or official actions reported by others will be admitted on a self-report index. These examinations have included whether individuals will self-report the behaviors evidenced by peer reports of their offense behavior and whether they will self-report acts reported or known to the police. While only indirectly related to SRD indices, examinations have also been made of whether individuals will self-report known arrests, court appearances, and convictions....

Record checks that examine whether offenses known to the police are reported on SRD indices have shown that a high proportion of such offenses is in fact admitted....

Hindelang et al. (1981), employing a community sample of youth found that the self-reporting rate of official offenses varies by race, with whites admitting 90% of their official offenses and blacks

65% of their official offenses. While there is, thus, some evidence of differential validity by offense type and by race, it appears that a high percentage of offenses known to police is reported on SRD indices.

While the above record checks have examined offense *behavior*, it is also useful to determine how many *individuals* are concealing their delinquent behavior. Conceivably, only a few individuals may account for the majority of unreported official offenses. Gibson et al. (1970), in a sample of British schoolboys, found that 83% admitted all official convictions on a SRD inventory, 9% made at least partial admissions, and only 8% made no relevant admissions. Thus only 8% deliberately concealed or failed to recall their convictions....

Record checks of self-reported official contacts also provide some indication of the amount of overreporting on self-report measures. Although there is some question whether self-reported official actions that cannot be verified result from inaccuracies in the official record (see Chaiken and Chaiken, 1982) or from exaggeration on the part of respondents, high levels of overreporting would seem suspicious. Estimates of the number of individuals who report official contact when there is no official record vary from 10 to 30% (Hardt and Petersen-Hardt, 1977; Hathaway et al., 1960; Hirschi, 1969).... There is thus some indication of potential exaggeration on the part of respondents to self-report questionnaires....

Given the findings from the various official record checks, what conclusions seem warranted? First, it appears that the majority of arrested individuals will self-report officially known offenses. The assertion that most such individuals will deliberately hide their delinquent behavior on survey instruments does not appear to be true. Second, whether self-reported measures of delinquency are seen as valid is an issue for debate. Clearly, on the basis of the official record checks, SRD measures are not perfectly valid and the degree to which the measures appear to be valid depends on whether one "sees the cup as being mostly full or partially empty." Using the NYS data, which present perhaps the lowest record-check validity estimates for juvenile studies, and assuming that the official records are accurate and

that the findings from the arrested sample can be generalized to the total sample, it then appears that at least 20% of the respondents may be concealing or forgetting some part of their delinquent behavior and that, overall, approximately 20% of the delinquent behavior among respondents is not being reported on the SRD measure. If the necessary assumptions are correct, clearly this is a substantial error, and even allowing some leeway for inaccurate official records, the findings suggest a sizable level of *underreporting* on the part of youthful respondents. Third, because of potential errors in official records, the magnitude of *overreporting* in self-report instruments is difficult to determine. However, if the errors in official records are not too large, the official record checks also give some indication of *overreporting* on the part of respondents. Further, the earlier discussion of the rate of reporting trivial events suggests substantial levels of overreporting (i.e., 22–32% of all reported offenses). Overall, the magnitude of overreporting appears to be at least as great as that of underreporting. While these two sources of error tend to offset one another on a global measure of delinquency, this may not be the case on more specific scales or for particular subgroups (e.g., blacks).

Differential Validity of SRD

In the preceding review there has been some indication that the level of validity of SRD measures may differ in different subgroups. In this section the question of differential validity is examined more completely. It should be noted that most of the evidence concerning differential validity comes from record checks and is thus limited to samples of arrestees and arrest behaviors. Whether these findings can be generalized to total samples or to all offense behaviors of arrestees requires some questionable assumptions....

Assuming that the findings can be generalized from arrested to general samples, several conclusions appear warranted. While it appears that there are some sex differences on particular items, overall levels of underreporting do not vary by sex. Findings concerning social class are mixed, but generally there are few substantial or consistent class differences. The two largest studies with comprehensive arrest and SRD data clearly provide evidence of differentials by race. Most extreme is the underreporting by black males and, in one study, evidence of underreporting by black females as well. In addition, there is some indication that rates of underreporting are greater for the more serious offenses. While it is possible that the magnitudes of the differentials encountered are in part dependent on police practices and errors and biases in official data, they nevertheless provide a cautionary note about the interpretation of results from SRD studies, especially results concerning race. A description of some of the factors that may influence the size of the race differential and analyses of problems arising from this differential are given by Hindelang et al. (1981).

Assuming that there is a potential for blacks, and black males in particular, to have a larger underreporting rate on record checks of official data, a major issue arises as to why this is the case. There are a number of possibilities including lying or deliberate falsification, forgetting and lower salience of events, difficulty with coding behavioral events, difficulty with "paper-and-pencil" tests, acquiescence and social desirability, and inaccurate or invalid arrest data. There is, however, relatively little evidence concerning this issue....

In light of the above, unequivocal answers about why there is a white-black differential in the underreporting of officially recorded offenses are unknown, as is the exact magnitude of the differential. It is our judgment that the strength of the evidence suggests that while various factors may reduce the level of the differential, some difference in the reporting of known arrest offenses remains, and a research effort directed at understanding the reasons underlying this differential would be profitable.

Summary

As an overview of the validity of self-reported offender measures, the consideration of the content validity of these measures indicated some potential problems. Examination of the face validity of these measures suggested that they often included trivial items that either were not law violations or were such trivial infractions that in

only very specialized circumstances would they result in official action. There is also evidence that items involving seriously delinquent behaviors lead to reports of trivial behaviors and thus to overreporting on some items. The sampling validity of the items contained in self-reported measures is also of concern. The construction of these measures needs to ensure that the full range of delinquent behavior is included. Often, serious offenses have not been adequately represented in prior measures.

In examining the empirical validity of the self-reported offender measures, the examination of known group validity consistently indicated substantial and often large differences on self-report measures between groups presumed to have a low or high involvement in delinquent behavior. The correlational validity of these measures, as indicated by their correlation with other criterion variables presumed to indicate levels of delinquent behavior, was generally quite small. However, none of the criterion variables that have been used are very good indicators of the level of individual delinquent behavior, and as a result, the low correlations would be anticipated. The lack of any good criterion variables provides a major obstacle to the examination of the validity of self-reported offender measures. Without such variables, no truly adequate test of validity can be made. Finally, official record checks indicate that some, and usually the majority of, "officially known" individuals will report the majority of their known offenses, including their serious offenses. However, these record checks also indicate sizable levels of underreporting, especially among blacks, and in general the rate of underreporting was larger for more serious offenses.

Conclusion

It has become customary, as Hindelang et al. (1981) note, for researchers employing self-reported offender data to preface their work with a brief review of research on the reliability and validity of these measures and to reach the general conclusion that these measures are reasonably reliable and valid or that at least the reliability and validity of these measures compare favorably with those of other social-science measures. However, the discussion of the reliability and validity of self-reported offender data presented above suggests that the quality of these measures cannot be taken for granted, nor are the reliabilities and validities sufficiently high that these measures can be used without question. Although at times the psychometric properties of SRD compare favorably with those of other social-science measures, there are instances where they clearly do not meet this criteria. Particularly problematic are the lower validities among black respondents. In addition, because these are measures of countable behaviors, not loosely defined attitudes, matching the levels of reliability and validity of other social-science variables does not mean that the SRD measures are particularly good or that they would meet the standards commonly required in other academic fields.

We believe that self-report measures are among the most promising of our measures of criminal behavior and are, perhaps, the only measures capable of meeting the needs of both descriptive and etiological research efforts. As a result, while research projects employing SRD measures are likely to be continuing, attempts to improve this methodology should be undertaken.... Such research is necessary if the full potential of self-report offender measures is to be realized.

Discussion Questions

1. Based on the Huizinga and Elliott article, what is the definition of reliability? What is the definition of validity? What are the different types of validity these scholars consider? Why are issues related to reliability and validity of data important to consider in criminology?

2. What do Huizinga and Elliott conclude about the reliability of self-reported delinquency? What does the empirical evidence suggest about the validity of self-reported delinquency?

3. What are the implications of Huizinga and Elliott's findings for studying race differences in offending behavior? What are the implications of these findings for studying criminal and delinquent behavior in general through use of self-reports?

Note

1. The National Youth Survey (NYS) is a projected longitudinal study of delinquent behavior, alcohol and drug use, and problem-related substance use in the American youth population. To date, six waves of data have been collected on this national youth panel ($N = 1725$), covering the period from 1976 to 1993. The NYS employed a probability sample of households in the continental United States based upon a self-weighting, multistage, cluster sampling design. Annual involvement in delinquent behavior and substance use was self-reported by members of the youth panel in confidential, personal (face-to-face) interviews. In 1980 a search of police records was completed for each respondent in each location where the respondent lived between 1976 and 1978.

References

Belson, W. A. 1969. "The extent of stealing by London boys and some of its origins." *Adv. Sci.* 25: 171-184.

Bridges, G. 1978. "Errors in the measurement of crime: An application of Joreskogs method of analysis of general covariance structures." In Wellford, C. (ed.), *Quantitative Studies in Criminology*. Sage, Beverly Hills, pp. 9-29.

Chaiken, J. M., and Chaiken, M. R. 1982. *Varieties of Criminal Behavior*. Rand Corp., Santa Monica.

Elliott, D. S. 1982. "A review essay on 'Measuring Delinquency' by M. J. Hindelang, T. Hirschi, and J. G. Weis." *Criminology*, 20: 527-537.

Elliott, D. S., and Ageton, S. S. 1980. "Reconciling race and class differences in self-reported and official estimates of delinquency." *Am. Sociol. Rev.* 45(l): 95-110.

Elliott, D. S., and Huizinga, D. 1983. "Social class and delinquent behavior in a national youth panel: 1976-1980." *Criminology*, 21: 149-177.

Garofalo, J., and Hindelang, M. J. 1977. *An Introduction to the National Crime Survey*. U.S. Government Printing Office, Washington, D.C.

Gibson, H. B., Morrison, S., and West, D. J. 1970. "The confession of known offenses in response to a self-reported delinquency schedule." *Br. J. Criminol.* 10: 277-280.

Gould, L. C. 1969. "Who defines delinquency: A comparison of self-reported and officially reported incidences of delinquency for three racial groups." *Soc. Problems*, 16: 325-336.

Hardt, R. H., and Peterson-Hardt, S. 1977. "On determining the quality of the delinquency self-report method." *J. Res. Crime Delinq.* 14: 247-261.

Hathaway, R. S., Monachesi, E. D., and Young, L. A. 1960. "Delinquency rates and personality." *J. Crim. Law Criminal. Police Sci.* 50: 433-440.

Hindelang, M. J., Hirschi, T., and Weis, J. G. 1979. "Correlates of delinquency: The illusion of discrepancy between self-report and official measures." *Am. Sociol. Rev.* 44: 995-1014.

Hindelang, M. J., Hirschi, T., and Weis, J. G. 1981. *Measuring Delinquency.* Sage, Beverly Hills.

Hirschi, T. 1969. *Causes of Delinquency.* University of California Press, Berkeley.

Huizinga, D., and Elliott, D. S. 1983. "A preliminary examination of the reliability and validity of the national youth survey self-reported delinquency indices." *National Youth Survey Project Report 27.* Behavioral Research Institute, Boulder, Colo.

Patterson, G. R., and Loeber, R. 1982. "The understanding and prediction of delinquent child behavior." *Research proposal to NIMH.* Oregon Social Learning Center, Eugene.

Reiss, A. J., Jr. 1975. "Inappropriate theories and inadequate methods as policy plaques: self-reported delinquency and the law." In Demerath, N. J., III, et al. (eds.), *Social Policy and Sociology.* Academic Press, New York.

Sampson, R. J. 1985. "Sex differences in self-reported delinquency and official records: A multiple group structural modeling approach." *J. Quani. Criminol.* 1: 345-366.

Wyner, G. A. 1981. "Response errors in self-reported number of arrests." In Bohrnstedt and Borgatta (eds.), *Social Measurement.* Sage, Beverly Hills.

CHAPTER 7

Managing Rape: Exploratory Research on the Behavior of Rape Statistics

Gary F. Jensen ■ Maryaltani Karpos

Victimization surveys originated in an attempt to measure the "true" crime rate in society and to offset the problems involved in using the UCR to measure crime rates (see Reading 5). The best known and longest running such survey is the National Crime Victimization Survey (NCVS). This survey reveals that a "dark figure" of crime exists, that is, a large number of crimes occur that are not reported to the police or included in official data. Introduction of the survey did not solve all questions about the true crime rate, however. Instead, comparisons of the crime rates obtained from both the UCR and the survey have been made, with claims of one or the other being a more valid measure of crime. This selection, by Gary F. Jensen and Maryaltani Karpos, is one example of a comparison between the UCR and NCVS. The authors attempt to reconcile differences evidenced in rape rates over time that are found in the two data sources.

Jensen and Karpos demonstrate that while UCR rape rates have increased over time, those obtained in the NCVS have declined. They argue that the differences in rates may be attributable to a number of factors. Under the assumption that the NCVS rates more closely resemble the "true" rape rates, they show that the UCR data may reflect the larger number of civilian (and particularly female) law

enforcement employees and the greater number of rape crisis centers. These factors result in a higher rape rate found in official statistics, although the true rape rate may have declined over time. Although rape is perhaps the most likely of the index crimes to be affected, this selection is illuminating in that it demonstrates how social factors, as well as increased attention to a particular type of crime, can combine to produce an apparent increase in rates although the actual rate may remain stable or decline.

It is commonplace in discussions of official statistics on crime to note that variations over time and space in police-recorded crime can reflect changes in public willingness to report crimes to the police and in the police response to crime, in addition to variation in actual criminal events (see, e.g., Barlow, 1990; Conklin, 1989; Kelly, 1990; Siegel, 1989). As one technique for circumventing such influences and more directly measuring some types of criminal events, the annual National Crime Survey (NCS) of household and personal victimizations was developed and has become a major alternative to the Federal Bureau of Investigation's Uniform Crime Reports (UCR) for determining trends and spatial variations in crime.

With both types of data available since 1973, numerous analyses have assessed the degree to which the UCR and NCS measure similar or disparate phenomena. There appears to be mounting agreement that for some types of crime they yield similar results when comparing cities (see Gove et al., 1985, for a review). However, there is an ongoing debate about the degree to which they measure the same trends and fluctuations in underlying criminal events over time....

The focus of this analysis is an offense for which there is either explicit agreement that NCS and UCR data are *not* measuring the same phenomenon or that methodological problems preclude an adequate comparison—forcible rape. Blumstein et al. (1992: 117-118) state that, in contrast to burglary and robbery, they are prepared to accept that NCS and UCR measures of rape share little common variance due to sampling error (small numbers of cases for NCS rape) and systematic, nonsampling errors (e.g., upward shifts in rape reporting).

In Figure 7.1 we have plotted the NCS and UCR data for rape and the two offenses deemed to "share variance"—burglary and robbery.[1] This comparative context is important for assessing whether NCS rape statistics behave more strangely or erratically over time than statistics for other offenses and for discerning the nature and magnitude of disparities involving the two types of data.... In terms of the significance, direction, and fit of a linear trend, *NCS measures of rape behave the same as the burglary and robbery measures.* The NCS data may be based on a small number of victimizations compared with robbery and burglary, but they behave in an orderly manner. In fact, the upward shift of UCR rape rates, coupled with the downward shift of the NCS rates, generates a high level of "shared variance" between the series. But, in contrast to burglary and robbery, that shared variance stems from a strong inverse relationship: The greater the rate of officially recognized rape (UCR rapes "known to police"), the lower the rape victimization rate (NCS rape rates). This negative relationship could reflect a deterministic causal process at work (see concluding section) or could be totally spurious....

Thus, one of a variety of issues that must be addressed in a theory of crime statistics is the disparity in rape statistics generated by an upward trend in UCR rape rates coupled with an apparent downward trend in NCS rape rates. Prior literature has concentrated on cultural and organizational

Figure 7.1 UCR and NCS Crime Rates, 1973-1990

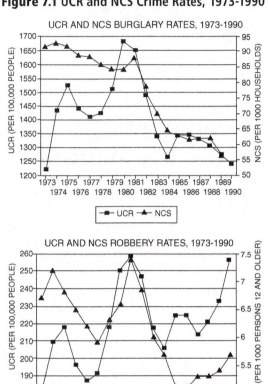

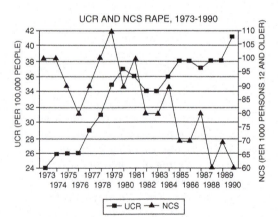

factors that can cause the UCR rape rate to increase, regardless of actual rape, and we deal with that topic first. We then consider the exploratory hypothesis that the downward trend in NCS rape data reflects actual trends in rape.

Victimizations Reported to Police

The most common interpretation of the disparity in trends for rape is that the trends differ because of changes in the willingness of women to report such offenses to the police. The most often cited research on the topic (see, e.g., LaFree, 1989; Seigel, 1989) is a study by Orcutt and Faison (1988) examining trends in reporting of rape victimizations in National Crime Surveys from 1973 through 1985. Orcutt and Faison report increases in the percentage of female victims indicating that they reported the rape to the police. The increases were particularly prominent for nonstranger rape. Moreover, they report that the increase is correlated with increases in the acceptance of liberated sex role attitudes. Increases in acceptance of liberated feminist sex role definitions are thought to lead to increases in reports of rape victimizations to police, which in turn lead to increases in UCR rape rates.

Figure 7.2 summarizes the percentage of stranger, nonstranger, and all rape victimizations involving female victims reported to police from 1973 through 1990.[2]...

Orcutt and Faison argue that this upward movement is a product of changes in sex role attitudes....

We used data from the annual Monitoring the Future surveys (MFS) carried out among a representative sample of high school seniors to measure feminist or liberated gender beliefs in 1975 through 1988 (Johnston et al., 1975-1988). The MFS is more likely to be representative of the population of young adults than college surveys. Moreover, it includes numerous items relevant to acceptance or rejection of traditional gender stereotypes or endorsement of liberated gender beliefs....

For 1975 through 1988, there is no significant correlation between gender beliefs and nonstranger victimizations reported to the police.... Thus, the relationship reported by Orcutt and Faison was due to either their specific measure of gender beliefs or, more likely, the more prominent upward shift in percentage of nonstranger victimizations reported for the 1973-1985 period. Endorsement

Figure 7.2 NCS Rapes Reported to Police, 1973-1990

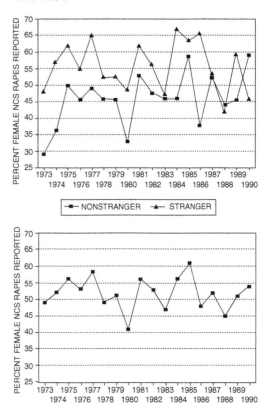

of feminist gender beliefs has increased over time, and such beliefs may be relevant to the behavior of crime statistics. But, the mechanism generating that relevance does not appear to be willingness to report victimizations to the police, at least not as measured in the National Crime Survey.

While the slight upward trend in nonstranger rapes reported cannot be attributed to shifts in gender beliefs, there is a small correlation between percentage of nonstranger rape victimizations reported to police and the UCR rape rate.... Thus, consistent with Orcutt and Faison's argument, one possible source of the upward trend in UCR rape rates is a slight increase in reports of NCS nonstranger rape victimizations to police. However, alternative sources of the UCR trend in rape must be considered, not only because that relationship is quite weak, but because overall reporting of rape victimizations has not increased over the 1973-1990 time span.[3]

Organizational and Employee Change

Literature on the organizational management of crime has suggested a number of variables that can lead to general increases in recorded crime, and some of them are particularly relevant to rape processing. For example, McCleary et al. (1982) report that a shift to civilian dispatchers can lead to increases in "crimes-known-to-police." If that shift coincided with a shift to female civilian dispatchers and female dispatchers were found to filter out fewer potential rapes, the official recognition of rape in crime statistics would increase as a product of changes in the composition of police departments.

Data on law enforcement employees in cities of 2,500 or more population are available in the Uniform Crime Reports over a considerable period and more detailed data are available beginning with the 1971 report (Federal Bureau of Investigation, 1960-1991).... The percentage of police employees who are civilian...has increased considerably over time. In 1960, 10% of urban law enforcement employees were civilian employees as distinct from sworn police officers. By 1975 that percentage had risen to 17%, and by 1990, 22% of employees were civilian. This increase was highly correlated with an increase in female law enforcement employees. The percentage of all law enforcement personnel in the female civilian category...increased from 7% in 1971 to 16% in 1990. The percentage of females among sworn officers increased from 1% to 8%. Thus, when compared with NCS data on victimizations reported to police, changes in the composition of law enforcement personnel are far more promising candidates for explaining artificial increases in rape rates.

Some specific changes in the organizational management of rape victimizations occurred during the 1970s and are potentially relevant to changes in UCR rape statistics as well. While rape crisis centers are a well-publicized component of the contemporary rape enforcement scene, there were no rape crisis centers nor specialized agencies to support rape victims until late 1969. By 1970 there were six or seven such agencies, by 1973 there were 61, and by 1981 there were at least 740 such agencies around the United States. There was relatively little growth of such centers in the 1980s, and some observers consider the period since the early 1980s to be one of retrenchment and withering financial support (Harvey, 1985; Koss and Harvey, 1987). In short, the major period of growth in organizations that could affect the official management of rape was the 1970s.

Police departments also changed the internal management of rape cases by creating specialized units and changing their procedures for managing rape cases. If those changes lessened the tendency to dismiss certain types of reports as unfounded, they would have led to an increase in UCR rape rates. LaFree's analysis (1989) of rape processing in Indianapolis supports this interpretation. LaFree reports that the establishment of a special sex offender unit was followed by a decline in the percentage of cases that the police deemed "unfounded." He did not find significant changes at other stages in the processing of rape cases....

Given the magnitude of bivariate relationships, it should not be surprising that when (a) female reports to police of nonstranger rape victimizations and (b) organizational or employee variables are considered simultaneously, only the latter are significantly associated with UCR rape rates.[4] Female victimizations reported to the police are not significantly related to UCR rape rates when organizational and employee variables are introduced.

Figure 7.3 illustrates the nature of the shared trends between the UCR rape rate and percent civilian from 1960 to 1990. However, the span of time in the UCR series during which the UCR rate accelerates more rapidly than percent civilian would predict is exactly the period in which organizational change also occurred. Indeed, if the sample is limited to the 1968-1990 period, both percent civilian and estimated number of rape crisis centers are significantly related to the UCR rate.... The UCR rape rate can be predicted with considerable accuracy based on percent civilian alone, and anomalies in the prediction can be

Figure 7.3 UCR Rape, Percent Civilian, and Crisis Centers

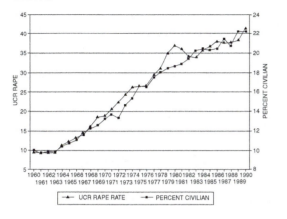

explained by introducing organizational innovations during specific periods of time.

These data do not prove that the UCR rape rate is a product of changes in the management of rape cases. However, they do show that, given available measures, such changes are a far more plausible source of trends than variations in NCS victimizations reported. Moreover, since the relationships are limited to common trends, one has to be very wary of spurious correlations. However, in this instance, the coincidence of trends is consistent with prior theory and research and is presented as a counter to other, much weaker, coincidences proposed in the literature. Moreover, this deterministic interpretation is strengthened when the downward shift in the NCS rape rate is considered.

The Downward Trend in NCS Rape Rates

Despite the annual collection of two types of data on rape by separate government agencies, we cannot answer the simple question "Has the rate of rape increased, decreased, or been stable in the past two decades?" An alarmist could point to the UCR data and claim marked increases in the risk of rape in the United States. In contrast, an optimist could point to NCS data as evidence that there has been progress in reducing the risk of rape for most of the past two decades. While there are other sources of survey data for many types of offenses,[5] there is no third measure of rape that would allow an adjudication between the two measures. Third sources have suggested that both the UCR and NCS underestimate rape (see Eigenberg, 1990), but supporting data are not available over time.

One potential indirect measure is public opinion poll data on women's fear of crime. It is not an ideal candidate for adjudicating between the two measures because it can be a product of the publicity accorded crime statistics themselves. Hence, a correspondence between trends for fear and measures of rape may reveal nothing about actual rape rates. Numerous researchers have noted that public fear of crime does not necessarily coincide with actual risks of crime (see Warr, 1991). However, there is also evidence that rape is "at the heart of fear of crime" for women (Warr, 1991: 7).

The Roper Opinion Research Center has asked a question about such fears periodically since 1973 ("Is there any area right around here—that is, within a mile—where you would be afraid to walk alone at night?"), and those data have been summarized in other sources (Bureau of Justice Statistics, 1974-1991). If fear of rape is central to women's fear of walking alone and if UCR-based "increases" are more likely to be publicized and attended to by the public than news of decreases, one would anticipate an upward trend in women's fear over time. In contrast, if women are responding to publicity regarding NCS data or to a real downward trend in the risk of rape, one would expect a decrease in fear of walking alone at night.

The actual trend in women's fear of walking alone at night has been downward—from a high of 63% in the mid-1970s to about 55 percent in the late 1980s. Women do not appear to have been more fearful in the 1980s than in the 1970s, despite the higher levels of rape indicated by the Uniform Crime Reports. Indeed, the trend in the NCS rape rate and women's fear of walking alone at night are very similar. However, the shared trends are both downward and both are contrary to the trend in the UCR rape rate. While additional data would be necessary to test the implied hypotheses adequately, the data are consistent with a scenario in which women's fear can be interpreted as a response to a decline in the rate of rape—a decline that is captured by the NCS data. Advocacy of the UCR as the best data for discerning the real trend in rape would necessitate a far less parsimonious explanation of the sum total of findings. If we were to argue that the UCR data over time approximate the real trend, we would have to (a) develop an explanation for the contrary trends in fear and the UCR as well as the contrary trends in UCR and NCS rape rates, (b) ignore plausible theories and research findings that would explain why the UCR rate exhibits an upward, nonlinear trend, and (c) propose a better explanation for a downward trend in NCS rape rates....

... In their analysis of research on NCS and UCR crime rates, Gove et al. (1985: 483) cite prior research (Geerken and Gove, 1977) to defend the position that UCR data accurately reflect the true larceny rate on the grounds that "as deterrence theory predicts...there is a strong negative correlation between the larceny crime rate and the larceny clearance rate."...

The two NCS rape rates, the UCR rape rate, and the UCR percent cleared are plotted in Figure 7.4.... There is no significant correlation between the UCR rape rate and the percentage of rapes cleared. In contrast, there are significant negative relationships between the NCS rape rate and percent cleared.... Hence, regardless of measure, fluctuations in rape are negatively related to fluctuations in the percentage of rapes cleared by arrest....

Since deterrence theory would predict inverse trends as well as inverse relationships for annual changes, the NCS data behave in a manner more consistent with deterrence theory than does the UCR rape rate. Following the logic of Gove et al.'s argument, we can propose that the NCS female rape rate is a closer approximation of the real rate than is the UCR rape rate. Both types of data behave as expected when annual fluctuations are considered.

There is another sense in which the NCS data on rape could be interpreted in a manner consistent with deterrence theory. Prior discussions of the disparity between UCR and NCS data have interpreted the upward trend in UCR rates as a reflection of "systematic" errors in the form of changes in victim reporting or law enforcement

Figure 7.4 Trends in Percent Cleared and Measures of Rape

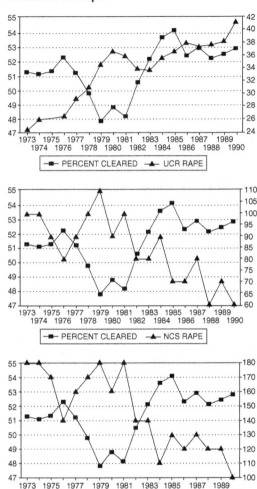

procedure. While such an interpretation has been used to exclude rape from arguments that the UCR and NCS measure the same phenomenon, the full implications of such systematic errors have not been addressed. If systematic error takes the form of an upward trend in official attention to rape, we can propose that increases in UCR rape rates can have deterministic consequences for the level of the NCS rape rate. The transformation of criminal events into "crimes known to the police" is a first step in the official recognition and control of crime. If NCS rape data and women's fear of walking alone are indicators of the actual rate of rape events, the data are consistent with the argument that the rate of rape is inversely related to the level of official recognition and attempts to control the problem. These observations are, admittedly, highly speculative, but they are quite plausible given our overall pattern of findings. Indeed, if the UCR rape rate and rape clearance are treated as measures of attempted official control, they can be used to predict the level of NCS rape with a high degree of accuracy.... Thus, disparate data on rape may reflect a deterministic relation between the two measures whereby an upward trend in attempted control is associated with a downward trend in the rate of rape.[6]

Summary and Conclusions

The pattern of findings reported in this paper makes sense if two assumptions are made: First, the NCS rate is a better approximation of the true rate of rape over time than the UCR rate. Second, trends in UCR data primarily reflect trends in the organization and management of rape victimizations. The first assumption is consistent with findings for trends in fear and with deterrence theory. The second assumption is supported by (a) prior research (i.e., LaFree's observations), (b) the close fit of trends in organizational and employee variables thought to affect rape processing as compared with the slight relation found for nonstranger rapes reported to police, and (c) by the contrary trends in the UCR and fear data.

It is important to emphasize that while the NCS data are proposed as a closer approximation to the true rate of rape in this analysis, the NCS data do not directly measure rape. Eigenberg (1990) has stressed that since the NCS measures rape by follow-up questions on assault, one cannot be certain what the NCS is measuring.[7] However, this has been true throughout the history of the NCS, and it is plausible to assume that this problem should not lead to a systematic downward trend. If there has been a systematic change in the manner of collecting or categorizing the NCS data that would lead to a downward trend, such a change should be identified and measured.

While there is mounting evidence that the UCR rape rate is sensitive to the amount of official attention accorded rape, the NCS data are not impervious to such influences. In January 1991, Steven Dillingham (1991:iii), the director of the Bureau of Justice Statistics announced that the NCS was going to pay special attention to improving the measurement of rape in victimization surveys.... While UCR police statistics on rape may have increased due to increases in the amount of organized and recorded police attention to rape, the increase in interviewer attention to rape in the NCS is likely to lead to an increase in NCS rape rates as well. Indeed, the NCS is going to pay more attention specifically to rape and assault precisely because they are presumed to be underestimated. With increased interviewer attention to the problem of rape, the long, downward shift in NCS rape victimization rates is likely to end regardless of stability or change in actual rape. Thus, while victimization surveys were designed to avoid problems with variation in "official" police statistics, the NCS is itself a body of data garnered through officials who have announced their intention to vary the amount of attention accorded certain types of crimes. If the changes have their intended effect, there will be another source of systematic error to complicate analyses over the next several years. Once the changes announced are fully implemented, analysts will have a better measure of rape but it will be many years before they can hazard any statements about trends in rape events over time. Thus, the behavior of the NCS rate of rape, like the behavior of the UCR rate, is likely to be affected by changes in the collection and management of information on rape.

Discussion Questions

1. According to Jensen and Karpos, what do the UCR data reveal about rape rates over time? What do the NCS data reveal about the rape rates in society? Based on their analysis, do you agree that rape rates have declined over time?

2. What factors influence the rising rape rates seen in the UCR data? The declining rape rates revealed by the NCS?

3. What are the potential implications of having social factors influence the data available for criminologists to use to study crime? Do you think that it will ever be possible to determine the "true" crime rate without error?

Notes

1. Basic data on victimization rates over time were compiled drawing on the 1980 and 1991 issues of the Bureau of Justice Statistics' *Sourcebook of Criminal Justice Statistics*, edited in 1980 by Hindelang, Gottfredson, and Flanagan, and in 1991 by Flanagan and Maguire. The UCR crime rates are summarized in the 1991 *Sourcebook of Criminal Justice Statistics*.

2. These more detailed data on rape were derived from the 1973 through 1990 issues of the Bureau of Justice Statistics' *Criminal Victimization in the United States*.

3. While victimizations reported to police are not correlated with gender beliefs, there is a significant correlation between liberated gender beliefs and the UCR rape rate ($b = .18$, $r^2 = +.64$, $p = .000$). However, the relation between the two disappears when first differences are used ($r^2 = .00$). Note that the absence of a significant relation between gender beliefs and victimizations reported to police does not rule out other mechanisms through which changing beliefs can affect the behavior of crime statistics. For example, if the upward shift of liberated gender beliefs is relevant to the upward shift in UCR rape rates, it may be through correlated changes in the processing of rape cases rather than through victimizations reported to police.

4. When introduced into regression analyses with any of the organizational or employee variables, the relationship of victim reporting to the UCR rape rate disappears. For 1973-1990, the number of rape crisis centers and an employee variable generated R^2s ranging from .89 to .92. Moreover, there are no relationships using differenced series. However, since gender beliefs were available for a shorter period (1975-1988) than the other variables, the results of regression analyses including such beliefs differ from the results of analyses for longer periods. However, they differ in a manner that strengthens the argument that changes in the official management of rape are a source of variation in UCR rape rates. When first differences for female reports of nonstranger rapes, crisis centers, and gender beliefs are used, the annual change in crisis centers comes very close to being a significant correlate of fluctuations in UCR rape rates ($b = .016$, $p = .06$). Hence, whether considering similarities in trends or

fluctuations, organizational and employee changes are more promising candidates for explaining UCR rates than other variables suggested in the literature.

5. National poll data on assault victimizations and annual surveys of victimization and self-reported offenses involving high school seniors are available for a sufficient period of time to consider them as a third source of data (see Bureau of Justice Statistics, *Sourcebook of Criminal Justice Statistics, 1990*). The authors know of no third source of data for rape over time.

6. An alternative interpretation of UCR-NCS rape trends is that our statistics compiling agencies are "converging" on a common rate. The disparity in the two measures has been declining over time. We interpret that decline as reflecting meaningful contrary trends in disparate phenomena rather than some sort of convergence on the "real" rate. If a convergence on the "real" rate is reflected in the variations over time, the organizational and political processes that would lead to such increasing agreement in data compiled by different types of agencies and officials would have to be specified. If the NCS detected fewer rapes over time by refining its measures or training its interviewers differently, such changes should be identified and their impact studied.

7. While we have concentrated on rape, the same changes could account for other UCR-NCS disparities. For example, the only offense showing a greater negative correlation with its UCR counterpart than that found for rape is aggravated assault. Blumstein et al. (1992) did not expect a correspondence between NCS and UCR data for assault because of classification problems. With growing emphasis on domestic violence, shelters for abused women, and how spousal violence is classified, increases in UCR aggravated assault rates could reflect changes in the management of violence against women in general. In contrast, we would not expect such organizational and employee changes to make as much difference for property-oriented crimes. Considering the correlations between the organizational and employee variables and other UCR offenses, the closest relationships are found for rape and aggravated assault.

References

Barlow, Hugh. 1990. *Introduction to Criminology*. Glenview, Ill.: Scott, Foresman.

Blumstein, Alfred, Jacqueline Cohen, and Richard Rosenfeld. 1991. "Trend and deviation in crime rates: A comparison of UCR and NCS data for burglary and larceny." *Criminology*, 29: 237-263.

——. 1992. "The UCR-NCS relationship revisited: A reply to Menard." *Criminology*, 30: 115-124.

Bureau of Justice Statistics. 1973. *Criminal Victimization in the United States.* Washington, D.C.: Bureau of Justice Statistics.

——. 1974. *Sourcebook of Criminal Justice Statistics.* Washington, D.C.: Bureau of Justice Statistics.

Conklin, John E. 1989. *Criminology.* New York: Macmillan.

Dillingham, Steven D. 1991. Foreword. In Caroline Wolf Harlow, *Female Victims of Violent Crime.* Washington, D.C.: Bureau of Justice Statistics.

Eigenberg, Helen M. 1990. "The National Crime Survey and rape: The case of the missing question." *Justice Quarterly*, 7: 655-671.

Federal Bureau of Investigation. 1960-1991. *Crime in the United States. Uniform Crime Reports.* Washington, D.C.: 1991 Federal Bureau of Investigation.

Geerken, Michael and Walter R. Gove. 1977. "Deterrence, overload and incapacitation: An evaluation of three explanations of the negative correlation between crime and punishment." *Social Forces*, 56: 424-427.

Gove, Walter R., Michael Hughes, and Michael Geerken. 1985. "Are Uniform Crime Reports a valid indicator of the index crimes? An affirmative answer with minor qualifications." *Criminology*, 23: 451-501.

Harvey, Mary. 1985. *Exemplary Rape Crisis Programs.* Rockville, Md.: National Institute of Mental Health.

Johnston, Lloyd D., Jerald G. Bachman, and Patrick M. O'Malley. 1975-1988. "Monitoring the Future: Questionnaire Responses from the Nation's High School Seniors." Survey Research Center. Ann Arbor, Mich.: Institute for Social Research.

Kelly, Delos H. 1990. *Criminal Behavior: Text and Readings in Criminology.* New York: St. Martin's Press.

Koss, Mary and Mary Harvey. 1987. *The Rape Victim.* Lexington, Mass.: The Stephen Greene Press.

LaFree, Gary D. 1989. *Rape and Criminal Justice: The Social Construction of Sexual Assault.* Belmont, Calif: Wadsworth.

McCleary, Richard and Richard A. Hay, Jr., with Errol E. Meidinger and David McDowall. 1980. *Applied Time Series Analysis for the Social Sciences.* Beverly Hills, Calif.: Sage.

McCleary, Richard, Barbara C. Nienstedt, and James M. Erven. 1982. "Uniform Crime Reports as organizational outcomes: Three time series experiments." *Social Problems*, 29: 361-372.

McDowall, David and Colin Loftin. 1992. "Comparing the UCR and NCS over time." *Criminology*, 30: 125-132.

McDowall, David, Richard McCleary, Errol E. Meidinger, and Richard A. Hay, Jr. 1980. *Interrupted Time Series Analysis.* Beverly Hills, Calif.: Sage.

Menard, Scott. 1992. "Residual gains, reliability, and the UCR-NCS relationship: A comment on Blumstein, Cohen, and Rosenfeld (1991)." *Criminology*, 30: 105-113.

Orcutt, James D. and R. Faison. 1988. "Sex-role attitude change and reporting of rape victimization, 1973-1985." *The Sociological Quarterly*, 29: 589-604.

Seigel, Larry J. 1989. *Criminology.* St. Paul, Minn.: West.

Warr, Mark. 1991. "America's perception of crime and punishment." In Joseph F. Sheley, *Criminology: A Contemporary Handbook,* Belmont, Calif.: Wadsworth.

CHAPTER 8

A Snowball's Chance in Hell: Doing Fieldwork with Active Residential Burglars

Richard Wright ▪ Scott H. Decker ▪ Allison K. Redfern ▪ Dietrich L. Smith

Criminologists have long recognized the limitations of studying crime through traditional methods such as surveys and interviews. Typically, however, offenders and victims alike are queried for information after the fact. So as to minimize validity issues such as memory loss, selective memory, and other data quality concerns related to time lapse, criminologists have sought to study criminals "in the wild."

The following article by Richard Wright and his colleagues, based on research with more than 100 active residential burglars, demonstrates how criminologists can identify active offender populations and develop relationships toward research objectives. The authors also address the difficulties of doing research with chaotic and volatile groups—a process worthwhile in terms of advancing the existing knowledge base about offender characteristics and criminal processes.

Criminologists long have recognized the importance of field studies of active offenders. More than 2 decades ago, for example, Polsky (1969, p. 116) observed that "we can no longer afford the convenient fiction that in studying criminals in

their natural habitat, we would discover nothing really important that could not be discovered from criminals behind bars." Similarly, Sutherland and Cressey (1970) noted that:

> Those who have had intimate contacts with criminals "in the open" know that criminals are not "natural" in police stations, courts, and prisons, and that they must be studied in their everyday life outside of institutions if they are to be understood. By this is meant that the investigator must associate with them as one of them, seeing their lives and conditions as the criminals themselves see them. In this way, he can make observations which can hardly be made in any other way. Also, his observations are of unapprehended criminals, not the criminals selected by the processes of arrest and imprisonment. (p. 68)

And McCall (1978, p. 27) also cautioned that studies of incarcerated offenders are vulnerable to the charge that they are based on "unsuccessful criminals, on the supposition that successful criminals are not apprehended or at least are able to avoid incarceration." This charge, he asserts, is "the most central bogeyman in the criminologist's demonology" (also see Cromwell, Olson, and Avery 1991; Hagedorn 1990; Watters and Biernacki 1989).

Although generally granting the validity of such critiques, most criminologists have shied away from studying criminals, so to speak, in the wild. Although their reluctance to do so undoubtedly is attributable to a variety of factors (e.g., Wright and Bennett 1990), probably the most important of these is a belief that this type of research

The research on which this article is based was funded by Grant No. 89-IJ-CX-0046 from the National Institute of Justice, Office of Justice Programs, U.S. Department of Justice. Points of view or opinions expressed in this document are those of the authors and do not necessarily represent the official position or policies of the U.S. Department of Justice.

JOURNAL OF RESEARCH IN CRIME AND DELINQUENCY, Vol. 29 No. 2, May 1992 148-161 © 1992 Sage Publications, Inc.

is impractical. In particular, how is one to locate active criminals and obtain their cooperation?

The entrenched notion that field-based studies of active offenders are unworkable has been challenged by Chambliss (1975) who asserts that:

> The data on organized crime and professional theft as well as other presumably difficult-to-study events are much more available than we usually think. All we really have to do is to get out of our offices and onto the street. The data are there; the problem is that too often [researchers] are not. (p. 39)

Those who have carried out field research with active criminals would no doubt regard this assertion as overly simplistic, but they probably would concur with Chambliss that it is easier to find and gain the confidence of such offenders than commonly is imagined. As Hagedorn (1990, p. 251) has stated: "Any good field researcher...willing to spend the long hours necessary to develop good informants can solve the problem of access."

We recently completed the fieldwork for a study of residential burglars, exploring, specifically, the factors they take into account when contemplating the commission of an offense. The study is being done on the streets of St. Louis, Missouri, a declining "rust belt" city. As part of this study, we located and interviewed 105 active offenders. We also took 70 of these offenders to the site of a recent burglary and asked them to reconstruct the crime in considerable detail. In the following pages, we will discuss how we found these offenders and obtained their cooperation. Further, we will consider the difficulties involved in maintaining an on-going field relationship with these offenders, many of whom lead chaotic lives. Lastly, we will outline the characteristics of our sample, suggesting ways in which it differs from one collected through criminal justice channels.

Locating the Subjects

In order to locate the active offenders for our study, we employed a "snowball" or "chain referral" sampling strategy. As described in the literature (e.g., Sudman 1976; Watters and Biernacki 1989), such a strategy begins with the recruitment of an initial subject who then is asked to recommend further participants. This process continues until a suitable sample has been "built."

The most difficult aspect of using a snowball sampling technique is locating an initial contact or two. Various ways of doing so have been suggested. McCall (1978), for instance, recommends using a "chain of referrals":

> If a researcher wants to make contact with, say, a bootlegger, he thinks of the person he knows who is closest in the social structure to bootlegging. Perhaps this person will be a police officer, a judge, a liquor store owner, a crime reporter, or a recently arrived Southern migrant. If he doesn't personally know a judge or a crime reporter, he surely knows someone (his own lawyer or a circulation clerk) who does and who would be willing to introduce him. By means of a very short chain of such referrals, the researcher can obtain an introduction to virtually any type of criminal. (p. 31)

This strategy can be effective and efficient, but can also have pitfalls. In attempting to find active offenders for our study, we avoided seeking referrals from criminal justice officials for both practical and methodological reasons. From a practical standpoint, we elected not to use contacts provided by police or probation officers, fearing that this would arouse the suspicions of offenders that the research was the cover for a "sting" operation. One of the offenders we interviewed, for example, explained that he had not agreed to participate earlier because he was worried about being set up for an arrest: "I thought about it at first because I've seen on T.V. telling how [the police] have sent letters out to people telling 'em they've won new sneakers and then arrested 'em." We also did not use referrals from law enforcement or corrections personnel to locate our subjects owing to a methodological concern that a sample obtained in this way may be highly unrepresentative of the total population of active offenders. It is likely, for instance, that such a sample would include a disproportionate number of unsuccessful criminals, that is, those who have been caught in the past (e.g., Hagedorn 1990). Further, this sample might exclude a number of successful offenders who avoid associating with colleagues known to the police. Rengert and Wasilchick (1989, p. 6) used a probationer to contact active burglars, observing that the offenders so located "were often very much like the individual who led us to them."

A commonly suggested means of making initial contact with active offenders other than through criminal justice sources involves frequenting locales favored by criminals (see Chambliss 1975; Polsky 1969; West 1980). This strategy, however, requires an extraordinary investment of time as the researcher establishes a street reputation as an "all right square" (Irwin 1972, p. 123) who can be trusted. Fortunately, we were able to short-cut that process by hiring an ex-offender (who, despite committing hundreds of serious crimes, had few arrests and no felony convictions) with high status among several groups of Black street criminals in St. Louis. This person retired from crime after being shot and paralyzed in a gangland-style execution attempt. He then attended a university and earned a bachelor's degree, but continued to live in his old neighborhood, remaining friendly, albeit superficially, with local criminals. We initially met him when he attended a colloquium in our department and disputed the speaker's characterization of street criminals.

Working through an ex-offender with continuing ties to the underworld as a means of locating active criminals has been used successfully by other criminologists (see e.g., Taylor 1985). This approach offers the advantage that such a person already has contacts and trust in the criminal subculture and can vouch for the legitimacy of the research. In order to exploit this advantage fully, however, the ex-offender selected must be someone with a solid street reputation for integrity and must have a strong commitment to accomplishing the goals of the study.

The ex-offender hired to locate subjects for our project began by approaching former criminal associates. Some of these contacts were still "hustling," that is, actively involved in various types of crimes, whereas others either had retired or remained involved only peripherally through, for example, occasional buying and selling of stolen goods. Shortly thereafter, the ex-offender contacted several street-wise law-abiding friends, including a youth worker. He explained the research to the contacts, stressing that it was confidential and that the police were not involved. He also informed them that those who took part would be paid a small sum (typically $25.00). He then asked the contacts to put him in touch with active residential burglars.

Figure 8.1 outlines the chain of referrals through which the offenders were located. Perhaps the best way to clarify this process involves selecting a subject, say 064, and identifying the referrals that led us to this person. In this case, the ex-offender working on our project contacted a street-wise, noncriminal acquaintance who put him in touch with the first active burglar in the chain, offender 015. Offender 015 referred 7 colleagues, one of whom—033—put us in touch with 3 more subjects, including 035, who in turn introduced us to 038, who referred 8 more participants. Among these participants was offender 043, a well-connected burglar who provided 12 further contacts, 2 of whom—060 and 061—convinced 064 to participate in the research. This procedure is similar to that described by Watters and Biernacki (1989, p. 426) in that "the majority of respondents were not referred directly by research staff." As a consequence, our sample was strengthened considerably. After all, we almost certainly would not have been able to find many of these individuals on our own, let alone convince them to cooperate.

Throughout the process of locating subjects, we encountered numerous difficulties and challenges. Contacts that initially appeared to be promising, for example, sometimes proved to be unproductive and had to be dropped. And, of course, even productive contact chains had a tendency to "dry up" eventually. One of the most challenging tasks we confronted involved what Biernacki and Waldorf (1981, p. 150) have termed the "verification of eligibility," that is, determining whether potential subjects actually met the criteria for inclusion in our research. In order to take part, offenders had to be both "residential burglars" and "currently active." In practice, this meant that they had to have committed a residential burglary within the past 2 weeks. This seems straightforward, but it often was difficult to apply the criteria in the field because offenders were evasive about their activities. In such cases, we frequently had to rely on other members of the sample to verify the eligibility of potential subjects.

Figure 8.1 "Snowball" Referral Chart

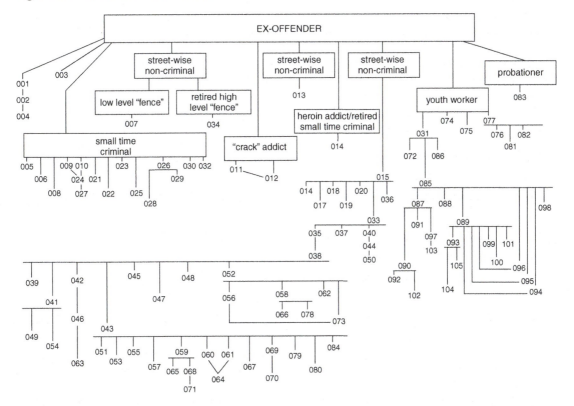

We did not pay the contacts for helping us to find subjects and, initially, motivating them to do so proved difficult. Small favors, things like giving them a ride or buying them a pack of cigarettes, produced some cooperation, but yielded only a few introductions. Moreover, the active burglars that we did manage to find often were lackadaisical about referring associates because no financial incentive was offered. Eventually, one of the informants hit on the idea of "pimping" colleagues, that is, arranging an introduction on their behalf in exchange for a cut of the participation fee (also see Cromwell et al. 1991). This idea was adopted rapidly by other informants and the number of referrals rose accordingly. In effect, these informants became "locators" (Biernacki and Waldorf 1981), helping us to expand referral chains as well

as vouching for the legitimacy of the research, and validating potential participants as active residential burglars.

The practice of pimping is consistent with the low level, underworld economy of street culture, where people are always looking for a way to get in on someone else's deal. One of our contacts put it this way: "If there's money to make out of something, I gotta figure out a way to get me some of it." Over the course of the research, numerous disputes arose between offenders and informants over the payment of referral fees. We resisted becoming involved in these disputes, reckoning that such involvement could only result in the alienation of one or both parties (e.g., Miller 1952). Instead, we made it clear that our funds were intended as interview payments and thus would be given only to interviewees.

Field Relations

The success of our research, of course, hinged on an ability to convince potential subjects to participate. Given that many of the active burglars, especially those located early in the project, were deeply suspicious of our motives, it is reasonable to ask why the offenders were willing to take part in the research. Certainly the fact that we paid them a small sum for their time was an enticement for many, but this is not an adequate explanation. After all, criminal opportunities abound and even the inept "nickel and dime" offenders in the sample could have earned more had they spent the time engaged in illegal activity. Moreover, some of the subjects clearly were not short of cash when they agreed to participate; at the close of one interview, an offender pulled out his wallet to show us that it was stuffed with thousand dollar bills, saying:

> I just wanted to prove that I didn't do this for the money. I don't need the money. I did it to help out [the ex-offender employed on our project]. We know some of the same people and he said you were cool.

Without doubt, many in our sample agreed to participate only because the ex-offender assured them that we were trustworthy. But other factors were at work as well. Letkemann (1973, p. 44), among others, has observed that the secrecy inherent in criminal work means that offenders have few opportunities to discuss their activities with anyone besides associates—which many of them find frustrating. As one of his informants put it: "What's the point of scoring if nobody knows about it." Under the right conditions, therefore, some offenders may enjoy talking about their work with researchers.

We adopted several additional strategies to maximize the cooperation of the offenders. First, following the recommendations of experienced field researchers (e.g., Irwin 1972; McCall 1978; Walker and Lidz 1977; Wright and Bennett 1990), we made an effort to "fit in" by learning the distinctive terminology and phrasing used by the offenders. Here again, the assistance of the ex-offender proved invaluable. Prior to entering the field, he suggested ways in which questions might be asked so that the subjects would better understand them,

and provided us with a working knowledge of popular street terms (e.g., "boy" for heroin, "girl" for cocaine) and pronunciations (e.g., "hair ron" for heroin). What is more, he sat in on the early interviews and critiqued them afterwards, noting areas of difficulty or contention and offering possible solutions.

A second strategy to gain the cooperation of the offenders required us to give as well as take. We expected the subjects to answer our questions frankly and, therefore, often had to reciprocate. Almost all of them had questions about how the information would be used, who would have access to it, and so on. We answered these questions honestly, lest the offenders conclude that we were being evasive. Further, we honored requests from a number of subjects for various forms of assistance. Provided that the help requested was legal and fell within the general set "of norms governing the exchange of money and other kinds of favors" (Berk and Adams 1970, p. 112) on the street, we offered it. For example, we took subjects to job interviews or work, helped some to enroll in school, and gave others advice on legal matters. We even assisted a juvenile offender who was injured while running away from the police, to arrange for emergency surgery when his parents, fearing that they would be charged for the operation, refused to give their consent.

One other way we sought to obtain and keep the offenders' confidence involved demonstrating our trustworthiness by "remaining close-mouthed in regard to potentially harmful information" (Irwin 1972, p. 125). A number of the offenders tested us by asking what a criminal associate said about a particular matter. We declined to discuss such issues, explaining that the promise of confidentiality extended to all those participating in our research.

Much has been written about the necessity for researchers to be able to withstand official coercion (see Irwin 1972; McCall 1978; Polsky 1969) and we recognized from the start the threat that intrusions from criminal justice officials could pose to our research. The threat of being confronted by police patrols seemed especially great given that we planned to visit the sites of recent successful burglaries with offenders. Therefore, prior to beginning our fieldwork, we negotiated an agreement with police authorities not to interfere in the conduct of the research, and we were not subjected to official coercion.

Although the strategies described above helped to mitigate the dangers inherent in working with active criminals (see e.g., Dunlap et al. 1990), we encountered many potentially dangerous situations over the course of the research. For example, offenders turned up for interviews carrying firearms including, on one occasion, a machine gun; we were challenged on the street by subjects who feared that they were being set up for arrest; we were caught in the middle of a fight over the payment of a $1 debt. Probably the most dangerous situation, however, arose while driving with an offender to the site of his most recent burglary. As we passed a pedestrian, the offender became agitated and demanded that we stop the car: "You want to see me kill someone? Stop the car! I'm gonna kill that motherfucker. Stop the fuckin' car!" We refused to stop and actually sped up to prevent him jumping out of the vehicle; this clearly displeased him, although he eventually calmed down. The development of such situations was largely unpredictable and thus avoiding them was difficult. Often we deferred to the ex-offender's judgment about the safety of a given set of circumstances. The most notable precaution that we took involved money; we made sure that the offenders knew that we carried little more than was necessary to pay them.

Characteristics of the Sample

Unless a sample of active offenders differs significantly from one obtained through criminal justice channels, the difficulties and risks associated with the street-based recruitment of research subjects could not easily be justified. Accordingly, it seems important that we establish whether such a difference exists. In doing so, we will begin by outlining the demographic characteristics of our sample. In terms of race, it nearly parallels the distribution of burglary arrests for the City of St. Louis in 1988, the most recent year for which data are available. The St. Louis Metropolitan Police Department's Annual Report (1989) reveals that 64% of burglary arrestees in that year were Black, and 36%

were White. Our sample was 69% Black and 31% White. There is divergence for the gender variable, however; only 7% of all arrestees in the city were female, while 17% of our sample fell into this category. This is not surprising. The characteristics of a sample of active criminals, after all, would not be expected to mirror those of one obtained in a criminal justice setting.

Given that our research involved only currently active offenders, it is interesting to note that 21 of the subjects were on probation, parole, or serving a suspended sentence, and that a substantial number of juveniles—27 or 26% of the total—were located for the study. The inclusion of such offenders strengthens the research considerably because approximately one third of arrested burglars are under 18 years of age (Sessions 1989). Juveniles, therefore, need to be taken into account in any comprehensive study of burglars. These offenders, however, seldom are included in studies of burglars located through criminal justice channels because access to them is legally restricted and they often are processed differently than adult criminals and detained in separate facilities.

Prior contact with the criminal justice system is a crucial variable for this research. Table 8.1 sets out whether, and to what degree, those in our sample have come into official contact with that system. Of primary interest in this table is the extent to which our snowball sampling technique uncovered a sample of residential burglars unlikely to be

TABLE 8.1 Contact with Criminal Justice System

	Frequency	Percent
Subject ever arrested (for any offense)?		
No	28	28
Yes	72	72
	100	
Subject ever arrested, convicted, incarcerated (for burglary)?		
No arrests	44	42
Arrest, no conviction	35	33
Arrest, conviction, no jail/prison	4	4
Arrest, conviction, jail/prison	22	21
	105	

encountered in a criminal justice setting, the site of most research on offenders.

More than one-quarter of the offenders (28%) claimed never to have been arrested. (We excluded arrests for traffic offenses, "failure to appear" and similar minor transgressions, because such offenses do not adequately distinguish serious criminals from others.) Obviously, these offenders would have been excluded had we based our study on a jail or prison population. Perhaps a more relevant measure in the context of our study, however, is the experience of the offenders with the criminal justice system for the offense of burglary, because most previous studies of burglars not only have been based on incarcerated offenders, but also have used the charge of burglary as a screen to select subjects (e.g., Bennett and Wright 1984; Rengert and Wasilchick 1985). Of the 105 individuals in our sample, 44 (42%) had no arrests for burglary, and another 35 (33%) had one or more arrests, but no convictions for the offense. Thus 75% of our sample would not be included in a study of incarcerated burglars.

We turn now to an examination of the patterns of offending among our sample. In order to determine how many lifetime burglaries the offenders had committed, we asked them to estimate the number of completed burglaries in which they had taken part. We "bounded" this response by asking them (a) how old they were when they did their first burglary, (b) about significant gaps in offending (e.g., periods of incarceration), and (c) about fluctuations in offending levels. The subjects typically estimated how many lifetime burglaries they had committed in terms of a range (e.g., 50-60), then were prompted with questions about the variation in their rate of offending over the course of their burglary career. We recorded what offenders agreed was a conservative estimate of the number of lifetime burglaries. More than half of the sample (52%) admitted to 50 or more lifetime burglaries. Included in this group are 41 offenders (40% of the total) who have committed at least 100 such crimes.

The measure of lifetime burglaries, of course, does not provide an estimate of the *rate* of offending. For that, we calculated "lambda" (Blumstein and Cohen 1979)—that is, the annual number of lifetime burglaries—for each subject by using our interview data. We arrived at this figure by subtracting age at first burglary from age at time of initial interview; from this, we subtracted the number of years each offender spent "off the street" in a secure residential facility (prison, jail, secure detention, or treatment center). This gave us the denominator for the lambda measure, the number of years at risk. The number of lifetime burglaries was divided by years at risk to get lambda. Approximately two thirds of the sample (68%) averaged 10 or fewer burglaries a year over the course of their offending careers—a finding not out of line with lambda estimates for burglary derived from arrest data (Blumstein and Cohen 1979). It should be noted, however, that there was great variability in the rate of offending among our sample; 34% committed, on average, less than five burglaries a year while, at the other extreme, 7% committed more than 50 such crimes yearly. This subgroup of exceptionally high rate offenders accounted for 4,204 of the 13,179 residential burglaries (32%) reported by our subjects. This result compliments previous research based on self-reports by prison inmates that has shown great variability in individual crime rates, with a small group of very active criminals being responsible for a disproportionate number of offenses (e.g., Greenwood 1982; Petersilia, Greenwood, and Lavin 1977).

The final portion of the analysis compares offenders who have and have not ever been arrested *for anything* in terms of (a) their total lifetime burglaries, and (b) their lambda (see Table 8.2).

The differences for these measures are pronounced. The mean lifetime burglaries for those who have never been arrested for anything is nearly double that for those who have been arrested. The variability in the group that has not been arrested is evident in the standard deviation (s = 324). A small subsample of this group has committed very few lifetime burglaries. Those in this subsample are mostly juvenile females who have offended infrequently over a very short period of time. But for this, there would be even larger differences between the groups. The mean lambda for those who have not been arrested is twice that for their arrested counterparts. This measure also displays

TABLE 8.2 Comparisons of Sample Members by Any Previous Arrest Status

	Number	Mean	s	t*
Total lifetime burglaries by any previous arrest				
Yes	67	120	166	
No	20	232	324	.04
	N = 87			
Lifetime burglary lambdas				
Yes	67	13	21	
No	20	28	38	.03
	N = 87			

*Because sample selection was not random, the *t*-test results must be interpreted cautiously.

considerable variation, as evidenced by the high standard deviation. Nevertheless, among those who have not been arrested, there are a number of offenders whose existence often has been doubted, namely high-rate criminals who successfully have avoided apprehension altogether.

Conclusion

By its nature, research involving active criminals is always demanding, often difficult, and occasionally dangerous. However, it is possible and, as the quantitative information reported above suggests, some of the offenders included in such research may differ substantially from those found through criminal justice channels. It is interesting, for example, that those in our sample who had never been arrested for anything, on average, offended *more* frequently and had committed *more* lifetime burglaries than their arrested counterparts. These "successful" offenders, obviously, would not have shown up in a study of arrestees, prisoners, or probationers—a fact that calls into question the extent to which a sample obtained through official sources is representative of the total population of criminals.

Beyond this, researching active offenders is important because it provides an opportunity to observe and talk with them outside the institutional context. As Cromwell et al. (1991) have noted, it is difficult to assess the validity of accounts offered

by institutionalized criminals. Simply put, a full understanding of criminal behavior requires that criminologists incorporate field studies of active offenders into their research agendas. Without such studies, both the representativeness and the validity of research based on offenders located through criminal justice channels will remain problematic.

REFERENCES

Bennett, Trevor and Richard Wright. 1984. *Burglars on Burglary: Prevention and the Offender*. Aldershot, England: Gower.

Berk, Richard and Joseph Adams. 1970. "Establishing Rapport with Deviant Groups." *Social Problems* 18: 102-17.

Biemacki, Patrick and Dan Waldorf. 1981. "Snowball Sampling: Problems and Techniques of Chain Referral Sampling." *Sociological Methods & Research* 10:141-63.

Blumstein, Alfred and Jacqueline Cohen. 1979. "Estimation of Individual Crime Rates from Arrest Records." *Journal of Criminal Law and Criminology* 70:561-85.

Chambliss, William. 1975. "On the Paucity of Research on Organized Crime: A Reply to Galliher and Cain." *American Sociologist* 10:36-39.

Cromwell, Paul, James Olson, and D'Aunn Avary. 1991. *Breaking and Entering: An Ethnographic Analysis of Burglary*. Newbury Park, CA: Sage.

Dunlap, Eloise, Bruce Johnson, Harry Sanabria, Elbert Holliday, Vicki Lipsey, Maurice Barnett, William Hopkins, Ira Sobel, Doris Randolph, and Ko-Lin Chin. 1990. "Studying Crack Users and Their Criminal Careers: The Scientific and Artistic Aspects of Locating Hard-to-Reach Subjects and Interviewing Them about Sensitive Topics." *Contemporary Drug Problems* 17:121-44.

Greenwood, Peter. 1982. *Selective Incapacitation*. Santa Monica, CA: RAND.

Hagedorn, John. 1990. "Back in the Field Again: Gang Research in the Nineties." Pp. 240-59 in *Gangs in America*, edited by C. Ronald Huff. Newbury Park, CA: Sage.

Irwin, John. 1972. "Participant Observation of Criminals." Pp. 117-37 in *Research on Deviance*, edited by Jack Douglas. New York: Random House.

Letkemann, Peter. 1973. *Crime as Work*. Englewood Cliffs, NJ: Prentice-Hall.

McCall, George. 1978. *Observing the Law*. New York: Free Press.

Miller, S. M. 1952. "The Participant Observer and Over-Rapport." *American Sociological Review* 17: 97-99.

Petersilia, Joan, Peter Greenwood, and Marvin Lavin. 1977. *Criminal Careers of Habitual Felons*. Santa Monica, CA: RAND.

Polsky, Ned. 1969. *Hustlers, Beats, and Others*. Garden City, NJ: Anchor.

Rengert, George and John Wasilchick. 1985. *Suburban Burglary: A Time and a Place for Everything*. Springfield, IL: Thomas.

———. 1989. *Space, Tune and Crime: Ethnographic Insights into Residential Burglary*. Final report submitted to the National Institute of Justice, Office of Justice Programs, U.S. Department of Justice.

Sessions, William. 1989. *Crime in the United States—1988*. Washington, DC: U.S. Government Printing Office.

St. Louis Metropolitan Police Department. 1989. *Annual Report–1988/89*. St. Louis, MO: St. Louis Metropolitan Police Department.

Sudman, Seymour. 1976. *Applied Sampling*. New York: Academic Press.

Sutherland, Edwin and Donald Cressey. 1970. *Criminology—8th Edition*. Philadelphia, PA: Lippincott.

Taylor, Laurie. 1985. *In the Underworld*. London: Unwin.

Walker, Andrew and Charles Lidz. 1977. "Methodological Notes on the Employment of Indigenous Observers." Pp. 103-23 in *Street Ethnography*, edited by Robert Weppner. Beverly Hills, CA: Sage.

Watters, John and Patrick Biernacki. 1989. "Targeted Sampling: Options for the Study of Hidden Populations." *Social Problems* 36: 416-30.

West, W. Gordon. 1980. "Access to Adolescent Deviants and Deviance." Pp. 31-44 in *Fieldwork Experience. Qualitative Approaches to Social Research*, edited by William Shaffir, Robert Stebbins, and Allan Turowitz. New York: St. Martin's.

Wright, Richard and Trevor Bennett. 1990. "Exploring the Offender's Perspective: Observing and Interviewing Criminals." Pp. 138-51 in *Measurement Issues in Criminology*, edited by Kimberly Kempf. New York: Springer-Verlag.

CHAPTER 9

Covert Participant Observation: Reconsidering the Least Used Method

J. Mitchell Miller

Criminologists and others concerned with the study of crime often refer to the "gray figure," a general reference to the actual empirical uncertainty of crime statistics. A great deal of crime is simply not known for a variety of reasons. Many crimes are either not reported (e.g., rape) or the perpetrators are never identified (e.g., burglary). Much of the nature of crime (and related control efforts) is not known and thus unavailable to the social scientific community for study. Clearly, the study of crime is often controversial, sensitive, and restricted for ethical, practical, legal, personal safety, and security reasons.

The following essay in support of covert participant observation, acknowledging both the unknown level of crime in society and the difficulties involved in studying crime, presents a marked contrast to traditional approaches of collecting and analyzing criminal foci. It is contended that only by being submersed in the immediacy of criminal and deviant contexts can the true nature of crime and its control be fully understood. The practice of criminology in the midst of active criminals presents ethical concerns that covert participant observers must address.

> "The goal of any science is not willful harm to subjects, but the advancement of knowledge and explanation. Any method that moves us toward that goal is justifiable" (Denzin 1968).

Reprinted from J. Mitchell Miller, "Covert Participant Observation: Reconsidering the Least Used Method" in Journal of Contemporary Criminal Justice," 11, pp. 97–105.

Social scientists have virtually ignored the qualitative technique covert participant observation. This variation of participant observation is either not mentioned or described in less than a page's length in social science research methods texts. The majority of qualitative methods books provide a few illustrative examples, but scarcely more in terms of detailed instruction. Manifested in the selection of alternative field strategies, this disregard has made covert observation the truly least used of all the qualitative research methods.

It is unfortunate that covert research is so rarely conducted because a veiled identity can enable the examination of certain remote and closed spheres of social life, particularly criminal and deviant ones, that simply cannot be inspected in an overt fashion. Consequently, covert research is well-suited for much subject material of concern to criminology and the criminal justice sciences. Also applicable in some situations where overt designs appear the appropriate or only option, covert schemes are infrequently considered. Clearly, complicated ethical issues inherent to secret investigations have created a methodological training bias that has suppressed their application. New generations of researchers therefore remain unfamiliar with a potentially valuable research option.

This brief commentary reintroduces covert participant observation and presents the principal advantages of using the technique. Theoretical, methodological, and pragmatic grounds are offered for exercising covert research. Ethical matters long associated with the stifling of its use are also reconsidered in the context of criminal justice research. The ethicality of secret research, relative to other qualitative methods, is upheld for some research problems with certain stipulations.

Defining Covert Participant Observation

Covert participant observation is a term that has been used rather interchangeably with other labels: "secret observation" (Roth 1962), "investigative social research" (Douglas 1976), "sociological snooping" (Von Hoffman 1970), and most frequently "disguised observation" (Erickson 1967: 1968: Denzin 1968). Disguised observation has recently been defined as "research in which the researcher hides his or her presence or purpose for interacting with a group" (Hagan 1993:234). The distinguishing feature is that the research occurrence is not made known to subjects within the field setting.

Disguised observation is too inclusive a term often used in reference to those who simply hide in disguise or secret to observe, such as Stein's (1974) observation via a hidden two-way mirror of prostitutes servicing customers. Covert participant observation likewise involves disguise, however, the researcher is always immersed in the field setting. Additional elements—intentional misrepresentation, interpersonal deception, and maintenance of a false identity over usually prolonged periods of time are entailed. "Covert participant observation" is therefore a more technically correct term than "disguised observation" because it better indicates the active nature of the fieldwork essential to the technique (Jorgensen 1989).

Covert participant observation is essentially "opportunistic research" (Ronai and Ellis 1989) conducted by "complete-member researchers" (Adler and Adler 1987) who study phenomena in settings where they participate as full members. Admission to otherwise inaccessible settings is gained by undertaking a natural position and then secretly conducting observational research. Examples of the method include Steffensmeier and Terry's (1973) study of the relationship between personal appearance and suspicion of shoplifting involving students dressed either conventionally

or as hippies, Stewart and Cannon's (1977) masquerade as thieves, Tewksbury's (1990) description of adult bookstore patrons, and most recently Miller and Selva's (1994) assumption of the police informant role to infiltrate drug enforcement operations.

The most pronounced example of covert research, however, is Laud Humphreys' infamous Tea Room Trade (1970). Shrouding his academic interest in sexual deviance, Humphreys pretended to be a "watchqueen" (i.e., a lookout) for others so that he might observe homosexual acts in public bathrooms. He also used this role to record his subjects' license plate numbers to obtain their names and addresses in order to interview them by means of another disguise—survey researcher interested in sexual behaviors and lifestyles.

There are other versions of disguised or covert participant observation wherein certain confederates are made aware of the researcher's true identity, purpose and objectives (Formby and Smykla 1981: Asch 1951). The reasons for working with cooperatives are plain: to facilitate entry and interaction in the research site, to become familiar with nomenclature and standards of conduct, to expedite the happening of that which the researcher hopes to observe, and to avoid or at least minimize potential danger. Such reliance may be counterproductive, though, in that observations and consequent analysis of the social setting may be tainted by confederates' values, perceptions, and positions within the research environment.

If only a few individuals within a research site are aware of the researcher's true identity, it is possible, indeed likely, that interaction will be affected and spread to others within the setting. Hence, data distortion can become a potential validity and reliability problem with the use of confederates. The researcher must be completely undercover to avoid this problem and utilize the coven role so as to optimally exploit a social setting.

The goals of covert participant observation are no different than the standard objectives of overt participant observation: exploration, description, and, occasionally, evaluation (Berg 1989). Epistemological justification is similarly derived from an interpretive, naturalistic inquiry paradigm (Patton 1990). Most aspects of the methodological process, such as defining a problem, observing and gathering information, analyzing notes and records, and communicating results, are nearly identical to conventional participant observation as well. The covert approach may thus be considered a type of participant observation rather than a distinctive method.

There are aspects of the covert participant observation research cycle, however, that are unconventional. One controversial point is gaining entry to a setting through misrepresentation. It is the closed nature of backstage settings and the politics of deviant groups that negates announcement of the researcher's objectives and requires deception via role assumption if certain topics are to be examined.

The character of the participation is also much different and more demanding on the researcher. Covert role assumption means full participation in various group and individual activities, many of which contain risks. The direct study of crime by means of an undercover role can be doubly enigmatic to both the researcher's well-being and the inquiry. Assuming a role either as a criminal or in close proximity to crime for the purpose of research does not absolve the researcher from real or perceived culpability; thus moral decisions and the possibility of arrest and legal sanction must be considered prior to the onset of fieldwork.

The recording of notes from a clandestine position would divulge the researcher's cover and is obviously inadvisable. Extended periods of time in the field often yield rich and rare insight, but, without a chance to withdraw and log events, recollection of temporal/causal sequence can become muddled due to information overload and understandable fatigue. Resolves to this concern have been the use of mnemonics—a process of memorizing through abbreviation and association (Hagan 1993: 193), taking photographs when possible, and the use of hidden mini-tape recorders and even body wires (Miller and Selva 1994).

The Ethics of Covert Observation

The ethicality of disguised or covert observational techniques has long been controversial,

as evidenced by the "deception debate" (Bulmer 1980: Humphreys 1970: Roth 1962: Gallther 1973). Participants in this debate have tended to assume one of two polarized positions: moralistic condemnation or responsive justification. Deception is explicitly equated with immorality and is so unconscionable for some they would have covert observation banned from social science research altogether (Erikson 1967). The major objection is that deceptive techniques often violate basic ethical principles including informed consent, invasion of privacy, and the obligation to avoid bringing harm to subjects.

Critics further contend that misrepresentation not only causes irreparable damage to subjects, but also to the researcher, and to science by evoking negative public scrutiny and making subject populations wary of future researchers (Polsky 1967). Risk to the researcher, however, is a matter of individual decision. To set restrictions on academic investigations in an a priori fashion on the basis of potential harm is at odds with both the ideals of an open, democratic society (individual freedom and autonomy) and traditional social science precepts (free inquiry and, ironically, informed consent).

The argument of isolating future research populations is seemingly unsound as well. Many settings of interest to criminal justice researchers are essentially restricted and typically occupied with subjects already suspicious of strangers due to the threat of legal penalty associated with disclosure. Because researchers as outsiders will usually be distrusted and excluded from such settings, it is logical to assume that its occupants are already ostracized from researchers. The more substantial points that remain and must be confronted are interrelated: the use of deceit and the harm subjects may encounter as a result of the research process.

The topic of dishonesty in covert research is not as clear as opponents of the method suggest and nebulous in comparison to the frequent disregard for ethical standards demonstrated in other qualitative deviance research. Klockars' award winning The Professional Fence, for example, describes research conduct far more offensive than the duplicity intrinsic to covert participant observation. This case history of a thirty year career of dealing in stolen goods was enabled by an intentionally misrepresentative letter in which the researcher admittedly lied about: 1. his academic credentials. 2. his familiarity and experience with the subject of fencing. 3. the number of other thieves he had interviewed, and most seriously 4. the possible legal risks associated with participating in the project (Klockars 1974:215). Klockars' deception is reasoned in near blind pursuit of his research objective:

> "I thought the claim would strengthen the impression of my seriousness" and "the description of what I wanted to write about as well as the whole tone of the letter is slanted…and did not warn Vincet (the research subject) of his rights" (Ibid).

Surprisingly, Klockars' book and similar projects have not produced controversy on par with covert strategies. The terms "case history" and "personal interview" simply do not provoke the interest and suspicion generated by the labels "covert" and "disguise." Covert methods can be considered, relative to the exercise of some techniques, forthright in that the level of deception is predetermined and calculated into the research design (Stricker 1967). The decision of whether or not to use deception to gain entry and thus enable a study can be made based on the ends versus the means formula described below.

A Basis for Covert Research?

Justifications for the use of covert techniques have been presented on various levels. The most common practical argument is that those engaged in illegal or unconventional behavior, such as drug dealers and users, simply will not submit to or participate in a study by overt methods. Likewise, those in powerful and authoritative positions have been considered secretive and difficult to openly observe (Shils 1975). Police chiefs, white-collar criminals, prison wardens, and drug enforcement agents benefit from the existing power structure which inhibits study of their behavior in these official roles. A covert design is often the only way to conduct qualitative evaluation research of certain enforcement and intervention programs closed to principal participants.

Beyond a "last-resort" rationale, there are other reasons, methodological and theoretical, for employing the covert technique. An evident reason is that of qualitative methodology in general—the desirability of capturing social reality. By concealing identity and objective, researchers can avoid inducing a qualitative Hawthorne effect (i.e., a covert approach can minimize data distortion). Covert participant observation is justified theoretically by dramatulurgical and conflict perspectives. If Goffman (1959) is to be taken seriously, then all researchers should be viewed as wearing masks and the appropriateness of any inquiry viewed in its context. Following Goffman, Denzin has also argued that ethical propriety depends upon the situation:

> "the sociologist has the right to make observations on anyone in any setting to the extent that he does so with scientific intents and purposes in mind" (1968:50).

Dramatulurgy also provides a theoretical framework from which to assess topics of concern to the covert observer. The duplicity of roles already present in criminal settings under analysis (e.g., undercover police, fence, snitch, racketeer) are only multiplied when such a role is assumed with the additional post of social scientist.

Consideration of the well known consensus-conflict dialectic also provides logic supportive of covert research. Conventional field methods, such as in-depth interviewing and overt observation, are based on a consensus view of society where-in most people are considered cooperative and willing to share their points of view and experiences with others (Patton 1990). This assumption is highly suspect, however, in stranded and culturally diverse societies. To the extent that acute conflicts of interests, values, and actions saturate social life to the advantage of some and not others, covert methods should be regarded proper options in the pursuit of truth.

This rationale should resonate with critical criminologists as it is in sync with the accepted view of much crime and delinquency as definitions and labels unjustly assigned to persons and events by operatives of an oppressive criminal justice system. John Galliher, well-known for commentaries on research ethics, supported a critical approach to covert research at a recent meeting of the Society for the Study of Social Problems by qualifying "upward snooping that might expose institutionalized corruption."

Perhaps the most compelling basis for the use of disguise in some research, however, is "the end and the means" position first stated by Roth (1962), then Douglas (1972) and Homan (1980), and most recently Miller and Selva (1994). Employing this reasoning in defense of covert observation, Douglas (1972:8-9) notes:

> "Exceptions to important social rules, such as those concerning privacy and intimacy, must be made only when the research need is clear and the potential contributions of the findings to general human welfare are believed to be great enough to counterbalance the risks."

That the purpose may absolve the process has also been acknowledged by the British Sociological Association, which condones the covert approach "where it is not possible to use other methods to obtain essential data" (1973:3); such is the case in many criminal justice research situations. The benefits of investigating and reporting on expensive, suspicious, and dysfunctional facets of the criminal justice system, then, may outweigh its potential costs. Failure to study how various initiatives and strategies are actually implemented on the street could condemn other citizens to misfortune and abuse should the behavior of the system be inconsistent with stated legitimate objectives.

To rule out study of covert behavior, whether engaged in by the powerful or the powerless, simply because it cannot be studied openly places artificial boundaries on science and prevents study of what potentially may be very important and consequential activities in society. The propriety and importance of research activities must always be judged on a case by case basis. Drug enforcement's use of asset forfeiture, for example, has been questioned by the press and media with such frequency and intensity that scholarly evaluation is warranted. The very nature of the allegations, however, have prompted the police fraternity

to close ranks, thus compelling covert analysis. Abandoning such a study because it can not be carried out overtly would mean that potential misconduct and betrayal of public trust by government officials would remain unexposed.

The means and end rule, of course, requires the subjective interpretation of plausible harm to subjects, what exactly constitutes benefit, and who will be beneficiaries. To assess the balance between these elements it is necessary that they be highly specified, a requirement that is not easily met. The means and end formula is thus ambiguous and the choice to use a covert technique must be carefully deliberated. Certainly, deceptive observation carries ethical baggage less common to other qualitative methods, yet its ethicality is negotiable through detailed purpose and design.

Conclusion

The study of crime invites and sometimes requires the covert method as does examination of the clandestine nature of many facets of the formal social control apparatus. How other than through covert participant observation can topics such as undercover policing and inmate-correctional officer interaction be fully understood and evaluated? Those in the criminal justice system, as well as criminals, have vested interests in maintaining high levels of autonomy which require degrees of secrecy. This is evident in various labels such as "police fraternity," "gang," and "confidential informant."

The very things that make a criminal justice or criminological topic worthy of investigation and suitable for publication in a social science forum can preclude overtly exploring it. Methodologically sustained by the theoretical foundations of qualitative inquiry, covert designs tender opportunities to reach relatively unstudied topics.

The solidification of criminology and criminal justice as independent academic disciplines have resulted in a greater number, breadth, and specification level of refereed journals-all of which may indicate a general research surplus (Vaughn and del Carmen 1992). This is a debatable point for new technologies and the ever evolving nature of the criminal law present still developing and unstudied forms of deviance; but it is also true that the last thirty years have witnessed the near-exhaustion of most obvious crime oriented research foci. It is not uncommon to hear the sagely professor remark how much more difficult it is to now market one's intellectual work in choice outlets (e.g., Justice Quarterly, Criminology) than in years past. Covert research is simply one particularly inviting means by which to meet the expectations and competitive realities of today's social science arena.

This comment has briefly surveyed the methodological, theoretical, and practical reasons to utilize covert participant observation in criminal justice research. The most difficult facet of using this method will undoubtedly remain ethical factors that must be dealt with on a case by case basis. But these too can be overcome with caution, conviction, and adherence to established scientific guidelines for qualitative research (Glaser and Strauss 1967). The spirit of selecting methods on technical merit and relevance to research objectives rather than ethical pretense is an outlook consistent with the goals of social science. To the extent that this perspective thrives, covert participant observation may well become more commonplace: perhaps to the point of no longer being the least used method.

References

Adler, P. A. and P. Adler. (1987) "The Past and Future of Ethnography." *Contemporary Ethnography* 16:4-24.

Asch, Solomon E. (1951) *"Effects of Group Pressure upon the Modification and Distortion of Judgement,"* in H. Guetzkow (Ed.) Groups, Leadership and Men. Pittsburgh: Carnegie Press.

Berg, Bruce L. (1989) *Qualitative Research Methods for the Social Sciences.* Boston: Allyn and Bacon.

British Sociological Association. (1973) Statement of Ethical Principles and their Application to Sociological Practice.

Bulmer, Martin. (1980) "Comment on the Ethics of Covert Methods". *British Journal of Sociology* 31: 59-65.

Denzin, Norman. (1968) "On the Ethics of Disguised Observation". *Social Problems* 115:502-504.

Douglas, Jack D. (1976) *Investigative and Social Research: Individual and Team Field Research.* Beverly Hills. CA: Sage.

Erikson. Kai T. (1967) "Disguised Observation in Sociology". *Social Problems* 14:366-372.

Formby, William A. and John Smykla. (1981) "Citizen Awareness in Crime Prevention: Do They Really Get Involved?" *Journal of Police Science and Administration* 9:398-403.

Galliher, John F. (1973) "The Protection of Human Subjects: A Reexamination of the Professional Code of Ethics". *The American Sociologist* 8:93-100.

Glaser, Barney G. and Anselm Strauss. (1967) *The Discovery of Grounded Theory.* Chicago: Aldine.

Goffman, Erving. (1959) *The Presentation of Self in Everyday Life.* New York: Doubleday.

Hagan, Frank E. (1993) *Research Methods in Criminal Justice and Criminology.* 3rd ed. New York: Macmillian Publishing Co.

Homan, Roger. (1980) "The ethics of covert methods". *British Journal of Sociology* 31:46-59.

Humphreys, Laud. (1970) *Tearoom Trade: Impersonal Sex in Public Places.* New York: Aldine Publishing Co.

Jorgensen, Danny L. (1989) *Participant Observation: A Methodology for Human Studies.* Newbury Park. CA: Sage.

Klockars, Carl B. (1974) *The Professional Fence.* New York: The Free Press.

Miller, J. Mitchell and Lance Selva. (1994) "Drug Enforcement's Double-Edged Sword: An Assessment of Asset Forfeiture Programs." *Justice Quarterly* 11: 313-335.

Patton, M.Q. (1990) *Qualitative Evaluation and Research Methods.* 2nd ed. Newbury Park. CA: Sage.

Polsky, Ned. (1967) *Hustlers. Beats. and Others.* New York: Anchor Books.

Ronal, C.R. and C. Ellis. (1989) "Turn-ons for money: Interactional strategies of the table dancer". *Journal of Contemporary Ethnography* 18:271-298.

Roth, Julius A. (1962) "Comments on Secret Observation". *Social Problems* 9: 283-284.

Shils, Edward A. (1975) *"Privacy and Power"* in Center and Periphery Essays in Macrosociology. Chicago: University of Chicago Press.

Stein, Martha L. (1974) *Lovers. Friends, Slaves...: The Nine Male Sexual Types.* Berkeley: Berkeley Publishing Corp.

Stewart, John E. and Daniel Cannon. (1977) "Effects of Perpetrator Status and Bystander Commitment on

Response to a Simulated Crime. *"Journal of Police Science and Administration* 5:318-323.

Stricker, L.J. (1967) "The True Deceiver." *Psychological Bulletin* 68:13-20.

Tewksbury, Richard. (1990) "Patrons of Porn: Research Notes on the Clientele of Adult Bookstores." *Deviant Behavior* 11:259-271.

Vaughn, Michael and Rolando del Carmen. (1992) "An Annotated List of Journals in Criminal Justice and Criminology: A Guide For Authors." *Journal of Criminal Justice Education* 3:93-142.

Von Hoffman, N. (1970) *"Sociological Snoopers".* Washington Post (Jan. 30).

Correlates of Crime

Crime is unevenly distributed through the social system. Because not all of us are criminals and crime occurs more often in some areas than in others, sociologists and criminologists have devoted much time and attention to understanding how and why crime is concentrated as it is. Even the casual observer is able to see that most conventional criminals seem to represent a constellation of social characteristics that have come to be associated with such crime. They are of lower socioeconomic status, often minority-group members, male, young, and from troubled families. Although those with quite different characteristics do commit crimes and are prosecuted in the courts, they represent a decided minority of such cases. Why? What is the relationship of class, race, gender, age, and family to crime and delinquency? These correlates of crime tell an interesting story about where crime occurs and who its perpetrators are. In many cases, the correlates of those committing the offenses closely resembles those of the victims.

Although the correlates of crime just listed are often thought of independently of one another, they seldom exert influence on behavior in isolation. More realistically, they operate in combination, reinforcing one another while affecting the person's behavior in a variety of ways. In the profile of a typical conventional offender, for example, which is more important, race, gender, age, citizenship, intelligence or family stability? More likely, no single factor is solely responsible for the offender's behavior, but interacting together

they have a powerful influence. These factors are discussed and their contribution to criminality examined.

Social Class and Crime

Many persons who are known to commit the ordinary, or index, crimes come from lower socioeconomic backgrounds, which include unemployment, little money, and poor education. These characteristics are particularly true of young offenders. Various studies of delinquents and young adults who are arrested for street crimes confirm their lower-class status (Byrne and Sampson 1985; Thornberry and Farnsworth 1982). This finding is so prevalent that underprivileged status is an important element in many theories of the causes of crime.

But there is another view, supported by self-report studies involving subjects of all social classes, that lower-class men and women are simply more likely to be arrested and convicted, whereas middle-class and upper-class offenders often manage to avoid arrest and particularly conviction. Although social class plays a major role in most criminological theories, there is still debate over its significance in the causation of crime (see Reading 10). For example, Charles R. Tittle, Wayne J. Villemez, and Douglas A. Smith (1978) believe that there is little or no inverse relationship between class and criminality and that such a relationship cannot be demonstrated in either official statistics or in self-report studies. They believe that crime is just more visible in lower-income neighborhoods. They state quite plainly that "In short, class and criminality are now, and probably never were related, at least not during the recent past." Indeed, they interpret Sutherland's differential association as being an absence of "countervailing interpersonal influences [rather] than of class position or place of residence," and they observe, as Sutherland would agree, that "definitions favorable to deviance are... distributed over the classes" (1978: 653). Others (Voigt et al. 1994: 93-94) point out that some self-report studies even indicate a higher incidence of serious deviant behavior among the upper class than among the lower. This finding, however, is not consistent in all such studies.

Although John Braithwaite (1981) acknowledged that not all self-report studies support a relationship between class and crime, he thought that too many of them do support a connection to be considered mere chance. He disagreed with Tittle and his associates, indicating his belief that self-report studies exaggerated the delinquency of middle-class youth. He cited the National Youth Survey to prove his point. Although there was not much difference in numbers of victimless crimes (public disorder, status offenses, drug use) committed, the lower class committed four times as many "predatory crimes against persons" and about two times as many "predatory crimes against property" as middle-class youth. Furthermore, he said, one is more likely to become the victim of certain types of crimes in lower-class neighborhoods and that social class accounts for more variance than any other urban ecological factor. Finally, he demonstrated that most studies not showing a relationship between class and crime were conducted in rural areas, where class distinctions may not be as strong.

Scholars who agree that there is a relationship between social class and crime offer various explanations. W. Bonger, for example, writing in 1916, found criminal attitudes of both the upper and the lower class to be tied to capitalism. The lower class is affected by the misery imposed upon them by the capitalists, and the upper class is influenced by a greedy desire for more wealth.

According to Thomas J. Bernard (1988), those who are the truly disadvantaged suffer from high

levels of angry aggression, brought about by the urban environment (population density, noise pollution), low social position, racial or ethnic discrimination, and social isolation. As some people in these circumstances experience frequent and intense "situation arousal," they are unable to cope; they become angry and engage in some form of intentional harm.

William Julius Wilson (1996) attributes much crime to joblessness (which is rapidly increasing in urban areas) and high levels of neighborhood deterioration, partly the fault of corporations and businesses moving out. He equates this situation with high levels of social disorganization, which then lead to the problems of gang violence, drug use and drug dealing, and crime in general. Nearly 40 years earlier, Walter Miller (1958) saw the lower-class community as one which has created its own tradition of behavior and values that influences its members (see Reading 22). These "focal concerns," as he refers to them, are trouble, toughness, smartness (ability to outsmart), excitement, fate (luck), and autonomy. These distinct concepts are part of a culture that encourages a young person to become involved in gang delinquency to attain these valued characteristics.

Differences in social class certainly create different opportunities for engaging in crime. One cannot commit embezzlement, for instance, when one is unemployed. As John Braithwaite (1981) points out, the lower class commits more of the conventional crimes likely to be handled by the police, whereas the middle class engages in crimes connected to their occupations. These are the same crimes, of course, that are lightly penalized.

Social class certainly affects how one is processed through the system; it is the lower class who cannot afford bail, who must depend on public defenders, who cannot pay for private investigators. Reiman (1988: 162) sees the bias in the criminal justice system as blurring the distinction between "criminal classes" and "lower classes," creating instead the concept of the "dangerous classes." This situation results in the fact that "Fear and hostility are directed toward the predatory acts of the poor [rather] than toward the acts of the rich" (1988: 162). Although many agree that social class affects crime, almost all agree that it affects the way offenders from different backgrounds are treated by the criminal justice system.

Race, Ethnicity, and Crime

Crime rates vary among African Americans, Whites, Hispanics, Asians, Native Americans, and other racial and ethnic groups. Because of data limitations, this brief discussion will be primarily limited to differences between African Americans and whites, with references made to other groups where possible. Evidence on the relationship between race and ethnicity and crime rates is often conflicting. Although they are only 12 percent of the population, African Americans represent 63 percent of those arrested for robbery, 54 percent of those arrested for homicide, and 31 percent of those arrested for burglary (LaFree, Drass, and O'Day 1992). Thus, relative to their size in the population, African Americans are disproportionately involved in crime, with the glaring exception of white-collar crime. As Marvin E. Wolfgang (1966: 46) points out, "Most corporate crime reflects not only the collar but of the skin as well, and neither becomes part of the arrest statistics available for analysis by race."

A number of critics claim that this picture of African American crime is not accurate, and they offer explanations of the existing rates that place them in a different context. Probably the two most widely held explanations are the confounding effects of social class and prejudice within the justice system. One theory is that conventional crime is highly correlated with social class, and blacks are overrepresented in the lower classes and underclasses. It is theorized that when social class is taken into consideration, the effects of race are greatly diminished (see the previous section of this introduction).

Others point out that self-report studies indicate that crime is more evenly distributed by social class than official reports show. One study of delinquency among college students found that the main difference between their delinquency and that of others who went to court seemed to be the relative immunity given them because of their status, and proportionately fewer African Americans than whites attend college (Wolfgang 1966).

Gary LaFree, Kriss A. Drass, and Patrick O'Day (1992) also challenge some common assumptions about social class pertaining to crime. Looking at economics, they found that economic stress and unemployment had little effect on African American crime, though it did have an effect on white crime rates. The deprivation of African Americans relative to whites (interracial deprivation) also had little effect on African American crime. However, they did find support for an intraracial polarization effect, based on a widening gap between middle-class and underclass African Americans. Interestingly, they found a similar effect for whites.

Bias or prejudice against African Americans in the criminal justice system can be observed at many levels. African Americans have higher rates of arrest, conviction, and imprisonment, combined with longer lengths of incarceration than other groups (Mauer 1990). They are more likely to be subject to illegal arrests and detentions, to be arrested and convicted on skimpy evidence, to go to jail rather than receive bail, and to receive harsher sentences (Kappeler, Blumberg, and Potter 1996). Adult African American males have a one-in-five chance of going to prison at some point in their lifetime, and for the twenty–to–twenty-nine age group there are currently more African American males under criminal justice supervision (incarceration, probation, and parole) than there are in colleges and universities (LaFree 1995). African Americans have a proportionately greater chance of receiving the death penalty than whites. African American juveniles are also more likely than whites to experience higher rates of formal processing, court referral, and adjudication as a delinquent, and are more likely to receive harsher dispositions (Bishop and Frazier 1988). LaFree and his associates (1992) confirm that African Americans usually commit crimes against other African Americans (thus creating a high victimization rate similar to rates of offending) and point out that African American men have a one–in–twenty-one chance of being murdered in their lifetimes.

Although few official statistics have been gathered on groups other than African Americans and whites, there is some evidence "that Latinos ages

15 to 19 may have the highest homicide victimization rates of any minority group" (Bartol and Bartol 1998: 41). Ramiro Martinez, the author of Reading 15, looked at Latino violence as related to poverty and inequality. He noted that the 1980 Latino homicide rate of 20 per 100,000 was not dissimilar to African American rates of 27 per 100,000, and twice the national rate. Like LaFree, Martinez concluded that intraracial inequality (similar to LaFree's polarization) has more impact on crime than poverty does, as a widening gap persists between poor and middle-class Latinos.

Other evidence indicates that Native Americans also have high violent crime rates, although the accuracy of official data is questionable (Bartol and Bartol 1998). Ronet Bachman looked at homicide rates per 100,000 from 1980 to 1984 and found African American rates to be 33.1, American Indian rates to be 9.6, and white rates to be 4.6, making American Indian rates much lower than African American rates, but still twice those of whites. Bachman also indicated that these numbers are somewhat deceiving, because on some reservations rates are as high as 100, even 127, per 100,000 population. A few of the contributing factors include economic deprivation, alcohol and drug use, social disorganization, and a subculture of violence. Bachman's research also discovered that during 1985, more than 15 percent of American Indians engaged in domestic violence (slightly higher than white rates at just under 15 percent); three out of every hundred women were severely assaulted by their husbands.

The relationship between race and crime is exceedingly complex, with the effects of race and ethnicity masked by complex factors that may be operating in subtle and indirect ways. The overlap between race and social class, noted earlier, may mean that race and ethnic differences in crime are the product of socioeconomic status rather than race per se. If so, we may expect the crime rates of today's minorities to decline if and when their economic circumstances improve.

Gender and Crime

It is a well-known fact that men commit a great many more crimes than women. They also commit different types of crimes. Men are more likely to commit violent crimes, such as aggravated assault. Women are seldom violent; they tend to commit such crimes as prostitution, shoplifting, and welfare fraud. They also commit child abuse and elder abuse; middle-age daughters are the most common abusers of aged parents (Alston 1996). There has been a trend in the last twenty years for some women to be involved in white-collar crime, probably corresponding to their entry into business and professional careers (Simpson 1989).

Sally S. Simpson (1991) has made a distinction between African American and white females, indicating that social class greatly affects the different rates of crime found for women of different races. The African American female crime rate is quite similar to that for white males, both of which are greater than the rate for white females but much less than the rate for African American men. This fact illustrates once again that no one variable can be considered in isolation, and many variables affect crime rates among different groups. Simpson points out that both lower-class crimes and female crimes reflect the powerless status of these groups. But powerless men turn to violent street crime; powerless women turn to vice crimes such as drugs and prostitution and to nonviolent property crimes.

Until very recently, status offenses figured heavily in the labeling of young girls as delinquent (Chesney-Lind 1989). In 1983, for instance, 34 percent of girls referred to juvenile or family court were there for such offenses as truancy or running away from home, but only 12 percent of boys in the system were referred for these types of offenses, even though evidence indicates that boys engaged in these acts as frequently as girls did. Because the courts failed to recognize that many of these acts were committed as a result of girls' being physically assaulted or sexually abused in the home, the courts tended to criminalize the very acts (such as running away or stealing to survive once on the street) that facilitated their survival.

Violence among teenage girls appears to be on the rise (Kelley et al. 1997). In Denver, serious violence among thirteen- to fifteen-year-old girls is more than half that of boys, a number substantially higher than found among adults. In Rochester, at age thirteen, boys' prevalence rate for serious violence is 16 percent, and girls' is 18 percent! At age twelve, 15 percent of Rochester girls and 19 percent of boys were involved in serious violence. For every 100 fourteen-year old girls in Rochester, more than eighteen had committed an average of 5.5 offenses each.

For most crimes, overall gender stability exists; men far outnumber women and have done so for a long time. Where evidence points to gender convergence, with women offenders beginning to rival men, it is for less serious property crimes and substance abuse (Belknap 1996). Where gender convergence exists, it can likely be explained by one of the following reasons: (1) changes in law enforcement practices (women are treated more like men), (2) feminization of poverty (an increasing number of poor women are forced into crime), (3) changes in data collection methods (minor offenses get recorded as major crimes), and (4) increases in women's crimes with small original base numbers (it does not take much to show an increase when the base is small).

Just as males commit more violent crimes, they are also more often the victims of those types of crimes, with the exception of rape. Women are more often victims of rape and domestic violence. Of criminal homicides, 36 percent are intergender and 64 percent are intragender. When one gender kills the other, two-thirds are men killing women and one-third are women killing men (Goode 1990: 232), and when women do kill, they usually kill someone they know (lovers, husbands, children). Many woman who kill have been the victims of abuse.

After years of being neglected in the study of crime and deviance, women are finally gaining a new and well-deserved level of importance in such research. Previously, when female offending was studied, female criminals were accused of being biological atavists, rebellious toward feminine roles, inferior to men, deceitful, narcissistic, dull, devoid of sexuality, and a host of other uncomplimentary descriptions (Klein 1973). Recently, feminist scholars have developed a perspective that takes into account "points of reference, underlying assumptions, and understandings about crime, victimization, and the justice process" (Simpson 1989: 606). Instead of looking at women's crime in terms of masculinization or sexuality, for example, contemporary research looks at women's economic plight, abusive backgrounds, and similar areas that give insight into differences in male and female offending. For example, rape has been reinterpreted by feminist scholars as a crime of male power and domination. Pornography, incest, battering, and sexual harassment are now examined as various ways of victimizing women. The introduction of feminist scholarship into the study of crime has changed the way criminologists think about female offenders and female victims. Theories of crime causation offered from a feminist point of view have broadened the perspective on crime and brought us closer to an explanation of female criminals and their offenses.

Age and Crime

Studies of the relationship between age and crime indicate that for most offenders, crime peaks in adolescence or young adulthood and then declines, often sharply (Steffensmeier et al. 1989). Ages of peak involvement and ages and rates of decline differ for different crimes, however. For instance, burglary peaks at age sixteen, then rapidly declines. A study of nonviolent offenses found the peak age for male involvement to be fifteen and through eighteen, with decline beginning at nineteen (Farrington 1986). Researchers have found vandalism, auto theft, arson, burglary, theft, and liquor violations most prevalent among young offenders with median ages of seventeen and eighteen. Handling stolen property, abuse of narcotics, violence, disorderly conduct, prostitution, sex offenses (other than rape or prostitution), forgery and fraud, and family abuse are found most frequently in the next group, with median ages between twenty and twenty-eight. Drunkenness, drunk driving, and gambling are most prevalent among an older group of violators, those with median ages between thirty-five and thirty-seven. Although there are slight differences in peak ages based on gender, the overall pattern is similar, with a peak age of fifteen for arson for both males and females, a peak age for murder of twenty for males and twenty-three for females, and peak ages for auto theft, burglary, and aggravated assault falling in between with a one- or two-year difference in peak age for males and females. In contrast to Darrell J. Steffensmeier and his associates, who placed peaks and declines at earlier ages, David P. Farrington concludes in his study that the average age of offenders is between twenty-five and thirty. (It must be noted that some discrepancies arise from the fact that different studies focus on a different array of crimes).

Some crimes do not decline much with age. Gambling, for instance, rises dramatically in one's twenties and then remains high into one's sixties. There is evidence (Steffensmeier et al. 1989) that older people commit less visible, less likely-to-be-reported, and more lucrative crimes, such as corporate crime, racketeering, and political corruption. Crimes that have lower risks decline with age at a slower rate. One study (Farrington 1986) indicated that the ages of victims of violent crime also peak at sixteen to nineteen.

Age affects the rate of crime in a number of ways. For example, on the one hand, the younger one is at the onset of criminal activity, the more likely one is to pursue crime in later life, and the more likely one is to be involved in serious crime (Farrington 1986). On the other hand, the older a person is when released from prison, the less likely it is that he or she will return to crime. Changes in crime patterns as one ages encompass a number of factors (see Reading 11). They may be due at least partially to crime switching, in which offenders shift from burglary, for instance, to something like drug- and alcohol-related offenses. Specialization increases with age, but seriousness of offense often does not increase.

A large number of offenders outgrow crime. This fact can be explained in a number of ways. For example, some believe that aging criminals apply a cost–benefit analysis and determine that as one gets older, the cost (possibility of longer prison sentences, greater likelihood of losing family or job) outweighs the benefits (Farrington 1986). James Q. Wilson and Richard J. Herrnstein (1985) believe that as offenders age they become better at delaying gratification and considering the future consequences of their criminal actions. Other

criminologists, such as Letitia T. Alston, note a decrease in speed, physical stamina, and other physical characteristics as one ages.

Although burglary, robbery, and shoplifting all decrease with age, there has been an exceptional upswing in shoplifting among the elderly, as well as a general "reported increase in crimes committed by older people" (Alston 1996: 4). The elderly who are involved with crime are likely to be involved in victimless crimes, such as being drunk and disorderly ("geriatric delinquency") or body exposure. Larceny-theft accounts for 79.8 percent of the elderly arrests for index crimes. Some reasons why crime by the elderly might be increasing, besides a general decline in economic status, include their becoming a larger portion of the population (thus, even if the rate remains the same, sheer numbers will increase), their remaining healthier longer (sustained health and vigor facilitate crime commission), and the number of elderly alcohol abusers has been increasing.

Family and Crime

Sheldon Glueck and Eleanor Glueck (1950) determined that broken homes were a major contributor to juvenile delinquency. Although other studies have since confirmed their findings (Sampson and Laub 1993), their studies came under attack for problems with methodology (Drowns and Hess 1990). Since that time, it has been shown that a number of family variables, among them broken homes, have some impact on delinquency. It is believed by some that "…the best predictor of the onset of offending is poor parental control" (Farrington 1986: 231). Farrington is quick to point out, however, that as children near their teenage years, other influences become important in their lives, and they become influenced less by their family and more by their peers.

A number of factors relating to the family are thought to play a part in the decision to engage in delinquency and crime. Travis Hirschi believes that whether or not children commit delinquent acts depends on the strength of their attachment to their parents and whether or not they have internalized parental standards for their behavior.

A study conducted by Walter R. Gove and Robert D. Crutchfield (1982), which examined the variables of family structure, poor parental characteristics, household characteristics, and parent–child relationships, supports Hirschi's contention that attachment is the strongest predictor of delinquency. Important aspects of parental attachment are the time shared between parent and child; parents' "psychological presence," even when they are not there; intimacy of their communication; and the affection, love, and respect they and their children share. Males and females appear to be affected differently by the nature of family relationships. Characteristics of the parents' marriage are more important for males, whereas parent–child interaction and parental control are important for females in predicting delinquency. In reviewing the literature, Gove and Crutchfield found that a number of family variables appear to be related to delinquency, including broken homes, poor marital relationships, lack of parental control, ineffectual parental behavior, and poor parent–child relationships. The authors caution, however, that many of the studies specifying these variables have severe limitations.

Joseph H. Rankin and Roger Kern (1994) took the study of attachment one step further, to determine whether it mattered if the child was attached to both parents or just one. They found that a strong attachment to both parents was a better predictor of nondelinquent behavior than a strong attachment to just one parent. This finding has implications for the single-parent home even when there is a strong attachment to the custodial parent. In addition to attachment, Lawrence Rosen (1985) lists lack of role modeling, parental conflict (with each other), large family size, and erratic discipline or the absence of direct social control as variables that might contribute to delinquency. Farrington suggests there is little informal social control for juveniles when parents are working.

There are other hypotheses related to the absence or presence of parents in the home, as well as to their employment status. Hirschi believes that boys are more likely to engage in delinquency when their fathers are unemployed or their family is on welfare (the family is not self-sufficient). Although the idea that children in households headed by women are more likely to engage in delinquent acts has been discussed, LaFree (1995) found that there was often less crime in such African American households than in two-parent households.

There are situations, of course, when families can have a devastating effect on children. One such case is when a child is being physically or sexually abused in the home. Another is when the child observes spousal abuse in the home. One of the strongest predictors of the child's growing up to be an abuser is having grown up in an abusive home. Although Joan McCord cites neglect and rejection as well as abuse as predictors of delinquency and crime, her research indicates that parental rejection is a more significant factor in determining law-violating behavior (see Reading 16).

Explanations of all of these relationships—class and crime, race and crime, gender and crime, age and crime, and family and crime—have been advanced in various theories of crime. As will soon be described, learning theory, strain theory, control theory, and social disorganization theory, to name the most prominent, have viewed one or more of these correlates of crime as essential parts of their explanations of crime. Indeed, knowledge of these correlates makes it easier to understand why certain groups are more likely than others to commit certain types of crimes. Nevertheless, the exact relationship between these correlates and crime remains unclear, and more research is clearly needed. The following readings illustrate some of the research that explores the relationship between class, race, gender, age, citizenship, intelligence, and family and crime and delinquency.

References

Alston, Letitia T. 1996. *Crime and Older Americans.* Springfield, IL: Charles C. Thomas.

Bachman, Ronet. 1992. *Death and Violence on the Reservation: Homicide, Family Violence, and Suicide in American Indian Populations.* New York: Auburn House.

Bartol, Curt R. and Anne M. Bartol. 1998. *Delinquency and Justice: A Psychological Approach* (2nd ed.). Upper Saddle River, NJ: Prentice Hall.

Belknap, Joanne. 1996. *The Invisible Woman: Gender, Crime, and Justice*. Belmont, CA: Wadsworth.

Bernard, Thomas J. 1988. "Angry Aggression Among the 'Truly Disadvantaged'," *Criminology* 28: 73-96.

Bishop, Donna M. and Charles E. Frazier. 1988. "The Influence of Race in Juvenile Justice Processing," *Journal of Research in Crime and Delinquency* 25: 242-263.

Bonger, W. 1916. *Criminality and Economic Conditions*. Boston: Little, Brown.

Braithwaite, John. 1981. "The Myth of Social Class and Criminality Reconsidered," *American Sociological Review* 46: 36-57.

Byrne, James and Robert Sampson. 1985. *The Social Ecology of Crime*. New York: Springer-Verlag.

Chesney-Lind, Meda. 1989. "Girls' Crime and Woman's Place: Toward a Feminist Model of Female Delinquency," *Crime and Delinquency* 35: 5-29.

Drowns, Robert W. and Karen M. Hess. 1990. *Juvenile Justice*. Saint Paul, MN: West.

Farrington, David P. 1986. "Age and Crime." In Michael Tonry and Norval Morris (eds.), *Crime and Justice*. Chicago: University of Chicago Press.

Glueck, Sheldon and Eleanor T. Glueck. 1950. *Unraveling Juvenile Delinquency*. New York: Commonwealth Fund.

Goode, Erich. 1990. *Deviant Behavior* (3rd ed.). Englewood Cliffs, NJ: Prentice Hall.

Gove, Walter R. and Robert D. Crutchfield. 1982. "The Family and Juvenile Delinquency," *The Sociological Quarterly* 23: 301-319.

Hirschi, Travis. 1969. *Causes of Delinquency*. Berkeley: University of California Press.

Kappeler, Victor E., Mark Blumberg, and Gary W. Potter. 1996. *The Mythology of Crime and Criminal Justice* (2nd ed.). Prospect Heights, IL: Waveland.

Kelley, Barbara Tatem, David Huizinga, Terence P. Thornberry, and Rolf Loeber. 1997. "Epidemiology of Serious Violence," *Juvenile Justice Bulletin*, June 1997. Washington, DC: U.S. Department of Justice, Office of Juvenile Justice and Delinquency Prevention.

Klein, Dorie. 1973. "The Etiology of Female Crime: A Review of the Literature." In Susan Datesman and Frank Scarpitti (eds.), *Women, Crime and Justice*. New York: Oxford.

LaFree, Gary. 1995. "Race and Crime Trends in the United States, 1946-1990." In D.H. Hawkins (ed.), *Ethnicity, Race and Crime*. Albany: State University of New York Press.

LaFree, Gary, Kriss A. Drass, and Patrick O'Day. 1992. "Race and Crime in Postwar America: Determinants of African-American and White Rates, 1957-1988," *Criminology* 30: 157-188.

Loeber, Rolf and Thomas Dishion. 1983. "Early Predictors of Male Delinquency: A Review," *Psychological Bulletin* 94: 68-99.

Martinez, Ramiro, Jr. 1996. "Latinos and Lethal Violence: The Impact of Poverty and Inequality," *Social Problems* 43: 131-146.

Mauer, Marc. 1990. *Young Black Men and the Criminal Justice System: A Growing National Problem*. Washington, DC: The Sentencing Project.

McCord, Joan. 1991. "Family Relationships, Juvenile Delinquency, and Adult Criminality," *Criminology* 29: 397-417.

Miller, Walter B. 1958. "Lower Class Culture as a Generating Milieu of Gang Delinquency," *Journal of Social Issues* 14: 5-19.

Rankin, Joseph H. and Roger Kern. 1994. "Parental Attachments and Delinquency," *Criminology* 32: 495-515.

Reiman, Jeffrey. 1998. *The Rich Get Richer and the Poor Get Prison: Ideology, Class, and Criminal Justice* (5th ed.). Boston: Allyn and Bacon.

Rosen, Lawrence. 1985. "Family and Delinquency: Structure or Function?" *Criminology* 23: 553-573.

Sampson, Robert J. and John H. Laub. 1993. *Crime in the Making*. Cambridge: Harvard University Press.

Simpson, Sally S. 1989. "Feminist Theory, Crime, and Justice," *Criminology* 27: 605-631.

——. 1991. "Caste, Class, and Violent Crime: Explaining Difference in Female Offending," *Criminology* 29: 115-135.

Steffensmeier, Darrell J., Emilie Andersen Allan, Miles D. Harer, and Cathy Streifel. 1989. "Age and the Distribution of Crime," *American Journal of Sociology* 94: 8-3-31.

Thornberry, Terence and Margaret Farnsworth. 1982. "Social Correlates of Criminal Involvement: Further Evidence of the Relationship Between Social Status and Criminal Behavior," *American Sociological Review* 47: 505-518.

Tittle, Charles R., Wayne J. Villemez, and Douglas A. Smith. 1978. "The Myth of Social Class and Criminality: An Empirical Assessment of the

Empirical Evidence," *American Sociological Review* 43: 643-656.

Voigt, Lydia, William E. Thornton, Jr., Leo Barrile, and Jerrol M. Seaman. 1994. *Criminology and Justice*. New York: McGraw-Hill.

West, Donald J. 1982. *Delinquency: Its Roots, Careers, and Prospects*. London: Heinemann.

Wilson, James Q. and Richard J. Herrnstein. 1985. *Crime and Human Nature*. New York: Simon and Schuster.

Wilson, William Julius. 1996. "Work," *The New York Times Magazine*, August 18: 26-30.

Wolfgang, Marvin E. 1966. "Race and Crime." In H. Klare (ed.), *Changing Concepts of Crime and Its Treatment*. New York: Pergamon.

Wolfgang, Marvin E., Thorsten Sellin, and Robert Figlio. 1972. "Delinquency in a Birth Cohort." In Joseph E. Jacoby (ed.), *Classics of Criminology*. Prospect Heights, IL: Waveland.

CHAPTER 10

Specifying the SES/Delinquency Relationship

Charles R. Tittle ■ Robert F. Meier

For a long time, sociologists and criminologists believed that there was a direct relationship between socioeconomic status (SES) and crime and delinquency. Lower-class persons, they believed, were more likely to break the law than middle- and upper-class persons because of the social and economic deprivations and hardships they had to endure. Official data on known crimes supported this contention. Questions began to arise, however, when self-report studies indicating offenses unknown to the police showed offending behavior to be more evenly distributed across the classes than was previously believed. As this selection by Charles R. Tittle and Robert F. Meier explains, scholars lined up on both sides of the debate that followed, often with study results supporting their chosen position. What, then, is the student to believe about the relationship between class and crime?

This selection examines several categories of studies that purport to test the relationship between SES and delinquency. The results are both illuminating and perplexing, demonstrating that under some conditions, SES and delinquency are significantly related, leading some scholars to proclaim a relationship between class and crime. But Tittle and Meier are more skeptical, questioning the lack of "systematic patterns whereby those relationships occur." They conclude that SES may not be

as important as some researchers have believed, although its precise role in delinquency prediction remains to be determined. Actual reviews of many of the studies have been omitted.

It is no overstatement that the relationship between social class and criminal behavior is one of the most important and perennial issues in the sociology of crime. The centrality of the dispute is undeniable and on its resolution presumably hinges the fate of many theories of crime and delinquency (but see Tittle, 1983). An apparently simple question—What is the relationship between social class and criminality?—has generated a large research literature, but the results of empirical investigations are inconsistent. The relationship is said to be positive (direct), negative (inverse), conditional, or some combination of the three. Different studies have used different samples, measures of social class, measures of delinquency or crime, and analytic procedures, and some of the discrepant findings are attributable to those different methodologies. But regardless of the conceptual or methodological reasons, criminologists seem no closer to resolving the issue and identifying the nature of the relationship than 50 years ago.

Most criminological data collected prior to the 1950s seemed to demonstrate strong SES differences between delinquents and nondelinquents. Indeed, the existence of a negative relationship between SES and delinquency was accepted as fact by most social scientists, and it became the basis for several theories of delinquency. But not all scholars accepted this conventional wisdom uncritically. Some observed that the official data on which the SES/delinquency correlation was based could be biased because much delinquency was hidden from official view and those hidden acts might have been more equally distributed among the various social strata than the officially known acts. But real controversy about an SES/delinquency relationship did not emerge until self-report studies became common.

Early self-report research by Nye and Short (1957; Nye et al., 1958) suggested that there was no statistically significant relationship between delinquency and SES. Numerous subsequent studies, using a variety of techniques, measures, and analytic procedures, confirmed that conclusion (e.g., Akers, 1964; Arnold, 1966; Clark and Wenninger, 1962; Dentler and Monroe, 1961; Hirschi, 1969; Vaz, 1966; Winslow, 1967). But still other research contradicted the Nye and Short conclusion and reaffirmed the original finding of a negative relationship between SES and delinquency (e.g., McDonald, 1968; Reiss and Rhodes, 1961; Slocum and Stone, 1963; West and Farrington, 1973). In addition, by the late 1960s critics began to challenge the validity of self-report evidence (see Hindelang et al., 1981).

The controversy became acute with the publication of a paper by Tittle et al. (1978). Their meta-analysis of official data and self-report studies, which provided data reducible to a comparable, contingency-table format, revealed that the association between SES and crime/delinquency was negative and at best small, that this negative association had diminished in magnitude over four decades, and that temporal changes were mainly for results based on official statistics rather than self-reports.

There were strong reactions to the Tittle et al. paper. Some scholars challenged the conclusions and presented alternative analyses or interpretations (Braithwaite, 1981; Clelland and Carter, 1980; Kleck, 1982; Nettler, 1978, 1985; Stark, 1979; see also responses to the critics: Tittle et al., 1979, 1982; Tittle, 1985; Tittle and Villemez, 1978). Others, however, were stimulated to further thought and research, reasoning that although there may be no general correlation between SES and delinquency or criminal behavior, there might well be specific conditions under which SES and deviance are related. The product of those additional efforts is a substantial literature published in the last decade that has focused on three categories of specific conditions under which SES effects on delinquency might emerge.[1] They are (1) specific conditions of measurement, (2) specific demographic conditions, and (3) contextual conditions.

Conditions of Measurement

The Independent Variable

Several efforts to pinpoint an SES/delinquency relationship have focused on the meaning and method of measuring socioeconomic status.

The Underclass Specification. Some (e.g., Clelland and Carter, 1980) have proposed that it is only at the very lowest point on an SES Continuum that differences in delinquency can be found. They argue that research using gradational measures, which array respondents on a continuum, are inappropriate for examining the SES/delinquency relationship, and they propose instead a two-category measurement that delineates an "underclass" from all others....

Notwithstanding interpretations set forth by the authors of the above studies (which are contradictory, in any case), it appears that the evidence concerning the effect of SES, as reflected in measures differentiating an underclass from others, is problematic. One study shows one significant correlation (of –.08) out of two. Another shows a range of correlations from –.11 to –.02 for five measures, none of which would likely be statistically significant in a sample of only 110. A third study shows four significant effects out of eight tests, with no measures of association (a sample of approximately 1,500 would usually show significance with only a very small correlation coefficient). A fourth study shows a higher SES/delinquency relationship using an underclass measure, but both the underclass and the conventional occupational measures revealed significant and fairly large effects of SES. Finally, a fifth study, focusing on adults, found mixed results. Thus, it appears that "underclass/overclass" measures of SES that have been used do not unambiguously specify an SES/delinquency relationship.

The Gradational Specification. It has also been argued that the SES/delinquency relationship will emerge if the correct, specific indicator of social rank, conceived in terms of a gradational continuum, is employed in the test (Thornberry and Farnworth, 1982)....

...Again, the evidence provides little confidence that using particular indicators of social rank will specify the SES/delinquency relationship. Of the four studies reviewed, one finds education the superior predictor, one finds occupation superior, one presents inconsistent evidence, and the fourth shows almost imperceptible differences between the two. And in no instance was the association between any of the indicators and the measures of delinquency consistently negative and strong.

Marxian Class Specification. A third approach contends that the true SES/delinquency relationship will not be found until SES is reconceptualized in terms of the parents' positions in the social structure relative to the means of production (Brownfield, 1986; Colvin and Pauly, 1983). Two studies conducted since 1978 address this potential specification....

...The two studies employing a measure of SES based on a Marxian class conception provide no evidence that such a shift in conceptualization will specify a potential link between SES and delinquency. Indeed, if anything, the results suggest a complete negation of the expected inverse association, because most of the effects in the Hagan et al. data were positive (a result consistent with their theoretical argument) and the Brownfield data show no effects at all (it is not possible to determine directional tendencies from his presentation).

The Youth Status Specification. Fourth, it has been suggested that the SES/delinquency relationship will be discovered if SES is measured in terms of the youth's own position within the social structure of the school rather than in terms of the parents' SES (Stark, 1979). To our knowledge, no studies examining this relationship were reported within the past decade. Indeed, we are not sure any exist prior to 1978. Although Stark emphasizes that this finding is uniform in delinquency

research, he refers specifically only to Hirschi's Richmond Youth Study, which shows that youths who are attached to the school are less likely to be delinquent. It is not at all clear, however, that attachment to the school or academic success is synonymous with status within "teenage society" or standing in "the status system of the school." Clearly, Stark assumes that academic success is equivalent to success in the teenage high school social system: "The better a person is doing in school, the higher a person stands among his or her peers" (p. 669). Braithwaite (1981) makes a similar assumption: "If we assign adolescents a class position of their own derived from their location on the success ladder of the school, then a powerful class-crime relationship can be demonstrated. The weight of empirical evidence that school failure is a strong correlate of delinquency is beyond question" (p. 50). Yet, research by Coleman (1961) suggests that academic success is indicative of social success in a student culture in only some type of schools. We contend, therefore, that the potential specification of the SES/delinquency relationship by measuring the status of the juvenile in the teenage social system rather than in terms of the family's SES has not really been investigated, and until the social status of youths is directly measured and related to delinquency, one cannot know if this condition will unmask the true SES/delinquency relationship.

The Dependent Variable

Various scholars have suggested that the SES/delinquency relationship is contingent on how the dependent variable, delinquency, is measured.

The Data Source Specification. It has often been suggested that a negative relationship between SES and delinquency can be shown if one uses official police or court data rather than self-report data (but see Hindelang et al., 1979, for a contrary argument), presumably because lower status persons are more likely to underreport their offenses, thereby reducing the true relationship between SES and delinquency (Kleck, 1982; Nettler, 1978), or because of other methodological artifacts of self-report data (Elliott and Ageton, 1980). Testing this specification has been difficult, however, because most official published data, particularly the Uniform Crime Reports, do not include information about the SES of the offenders. It was customary for many years to attempt to overcome this limitation by substituting areal/ecological measures of SES for individual measures or by substituting racial categorization for SES categorization. But it is now recognized that using areal measures is likely to inflate artificially the magnitude of the true associations between the individual variables of interest (Hindelang et al., 1981) and that racial proxies suppress any effects potentially attributable to low-status whites and high-status blacks. Thus, it is necessary to use data that include direct measures of the individual's SES, perhaps from survey responses, as well as measures of delinquency from official records....

Overall, then, recent analyses concerning the strength of an SES/delinquency relationship as revealed by officially recorded measures relative to self-report measures show mixed results. In one case no differences are observed, in another a possibly significant difference is reported, and in the third the evidence is diffuse and contradictory. Hence, it has not been demonstrated that an SES/delinquency relationship is contingent on the source of the data.

The Seriousness Specification. Numerous scholars have asserted that an SES/delinquency relationship is contingent on whether the measure of delinquency is focused exclusively on serious, criminal acts rather than on a full range of delinquencies or mainly on less serious delinquencies. According to some observers, a negative association between SES and delinquency applies only to serious criminal acts (Clelland and Carter, 1980; Elliott and Ageton, 1980; Nettler, 1978; see also Hindelang et al., 1981, for an argument that self-report studies cover a less serious domain of behavior). Because of its plausibility, this argument has been one of the most frequently addressed specifications in the post-1978 literature, and nine studies bear on it....

The nine studies relevant to the seriousness specification show no consistent support for the idea that an SES/delinquency relationship will be found when researchers measure serious delinquency. Of the nine, two provide evidence supporting the

argument, four provide mixed findings, and three report evidence contrary to the argument.

The Frequency Specification. Elliott and Ageton (1980) contend that the SES/delinquency relationship will become clear when researchers measure delinquency in such a way that the full frequency of various offenses can be captured. In much research, investigators do not use actual frequencies at all, opting instead for such response categories as never, sometimes, often, very often, and always. And sometimes, when investigators collect information about frequency, they end up analyzing the data in terms of the proportion of the various SES levels that reports some involvement or involvement above a particular magnitude (prevalence). In other instances, researchers use numerical categories but collapse the upper one; for example, a researcher might inquire about how often the respondent committed a certain act during the past year, presenting numbers 1 through 10 and a final number of 10+ (alternatively, the researcher might collect the actual number of offenses, but code all answers above 10 as an inclusive category of 10+). Thus, if lower SES respondents commit offenses far more frequently than those of other statuses, this difference will be concealed by the manner in which the data are collected or managed....

The four data sets compiled since 1978 that used measures of delinquency based on frequency of offense show inconsistent results. The two most extensive data sets—the National Youth Survey and the Philadelphia cohort follow-up—produce weak, contrary or inconsistent findings, one of the more limited studies finds contrary evidence, and the other finds weak but supportive evidence. Thus, it appears that the SES/delinquency relationship cannot be specified by focusing on the full frequency of offenses, even for serious criminal acts.

Demographic Conditions

Specification by Race

Hagan (1985: 121) suggests that an SES/delinquency relationship will be greater among blacks than among whites. Recent studies based on three important data sets bear on this possibility....

These three data sets do not demonstrate that an SES/delinquency relationship is specific to one race or the other. Moreover, those instances revealing some tendency toward one race or the other suggest that if a racial specification were present, an association between SES and delinquency would probably be more likely among whites than blacks—the opposite of the association suggested by Hagan.

Specification by Gender

Although no theorist, to our knowledge, has set forth a specific rationale suggesting that an SES/delinquency relationship will be confined to one gender or the other, or even that such an association will be greater for one gender than the other, three studies have examined the SES/delinquency association within categories of gender.[2] Theories usually invoked as postulating SES/delinquency relationships (see Tittle 1983), however, would logically lead to the expectation that such relationships would be more prevalent among males than among females. For instance, since males are expected to achieve more than females, one might imagine that anomie will induce males to innovate more often than females....

The three studies relevant to gender specification, therefore, do not demonstrate that SES and delinquency are more highly related among one gender than the other. One study reports some evidence of greater effects among males, but the other two both show contradictory internal findings depending on the measures of SES used or the method of analysis.

Context and the SES/ Delinquency Relationship

Specification by Urbanness

At least two publications (Hagan, 1985: 121; Krohn et al. 1980:314) suggest that an SES/delinquency relationship will be more evident in urban than in other places. But we were able to locate only one study reporting comparative evidence on this point.

Using a sample of youths from 15 schools (nine junior high and six senior high) in three types of communities in two states, Krohn et al. (1980) calculated correlations between respondent's individual social status, as reflected by father's occupation, and three factor-score-based scales of self-reported delinquency (social and hard drug use and serious delinquent behavior), as well as an additive index of minor delinquency, separately for each of the schools. Only 10 of the 60 (17%) situations showed statistically significant correlations, but seven of the eight urban junior high schools showed significant relationships between individual SES and at least one of the four delinquency measures. No significant correlations were present for any of the other junior high schools. This seemed to indicate specification by urbanness, but the pattern was not there when the senior high schools were considered. Hence, the results are only suggestive of an urbanness specification. Although the SES/delinquency relationship is more prominent in the urban schools for the younger adolescents, the fact that even among them only seven of 32 correlations proved significant calls into question even the narrower specification by urbanness and age. Moreover, the absence of any trend along those lines among the high school students is contrary to the specification in question.

An alternative method for evaluating a possible urbanness specification is to consider the magnitude and/or consistency of associations between SES and delinquency in studies using only urban samples. Ten such data sets have been used for studies since 1978. Only three of those data sets (Cernkovich, 1978; Ouston, 1984; and Simcha-Fagan and Schwartz, 1986) show significant effects in a majority of the conditions examined. Five yield contradictory results (1—Johnson, 1980; 2—Johnstone, 1978; 3—Thornberry and Christenson, 1984; Thornberry and Farnworth, 1982; Tracy, 1987; 4—Hindelang et al., 1981; Sampson, 1986; 5—Farrington, 1983; West, 1982), and two (Cernkovich and Giordano, 1979; Hagan et al., 1985) produce no significant negative associations between SES and delinquency. Although these studies collectively fail to sustain the idea that SES and delinquency are highly related in larger sized places, one must be cautious in rejecting the urbanness specification on this basis. Not only does the diversity of the studies make interpretation difficult, but there are no reasonable comparisons with smaller sized places.

Specification by Heterogeneity

Ideas about a potential specification by the heterogeneity of the social environment were formulated even before the post-1978 flurry of research into specification. Reiss and Rhodes (1963) hypothesized greater SES/delinquency associations in SES-heterogeneous schools. They reasoned that relative deprivation among lower status youths, which was thought to motivate delinquency, would be greater in heterogeneous contexts. The hypothesis was not supported by the data, however; in fact, it was more consistent with the idea that status frustration is greater in the more homogeneous schools.

Harry (1974) hypothesized the same outcome as Reiss and Rhodes, but his reasoning focused on heterogeneity of cultural influences rather than heterogeneity of social status. He believed that a pro-law culture would permeate all students in culturally homogeneous middle-class schools regardless of any individual variation in status. This would vitiate any SES/delinquency relationship. And in mixed-class schools a homogeneous amalgamated general culture would presumably emerge to contradict any SES/delinquency association. But he contended that the middle-class culture of school officials in predominantly working-class schools would conflict with the youths' working-class culture, causing such youths to form a subculture. This putative subculture would presumably cause delinquency among its members, leaving the non-subculturally involved higher status youths in such schools to be guided into conformity by school officials. The result would be a negative SES/delinquency relationship only in the culturally heterogeneous contexts.

Only the previously described Krohn et al. (1980) research has tried to test the heterogeneity specification hypothesis, however, and its data are of only indirect relevance. By aggregating individual-level information for sampled individuals within each school, Krohn et al. were able to estimate the SES characteristics of their 15 schools. The schools were then grouped into three categories based on the percentage of the sample in each school with fathers in various occupational categories. This permitted study of the associations between individual SES and four measures of self-reported delinquency within each type of school context. In trying to test the Harry hypothesis, they *assumed* more cultural heterogeneity in the working-class schools, expecting an SES/delinquency relationship among only those in the working-class schools.

The results were not favorable. Only three (15%) of the 20 associations based on those in working-class schools (5 schools and 4 measures of delinquency), proved to be statistically significant, and the middle- and upper-middle-class schools produced seven (18 percent) significant correlations out of 40. Thus, it appears that cultural or social heterogeneity is not the key to specifying the SES/delinquency relationship. But again, a firm conclusion would be premature because Krohn et al. had no actual measure of heterogeneity.

Specification by SES of the Context

Johnstone (1978) maintains that lower status youths will experience severe relative deprivation in higher status contexts, leading to high rates of delinquency, and that higher status youths, lacking deprivation, will have relatively low rates of delinquency. Conversely, lower status youths in lower status contexts will experience little deprivation because they will compare themselves with other lower status youths and will therefore commit relatively little delinquency. But higher status youths will also feel little relative deprivation in the lower status context. Although Johnstone was mainly interested in explaining variations in absolute levels of delinquency, his argument implies that the association between SES and delinquency will be confined to higher status contexts because the large discrepancy in status there should motivate lower status youths to delinquency. But in lower status contexts there will be little variation in delinquency among the SES levels because no status group is relatively deprived. By extension, modest associations between SES and delinquency should prevail in middle-status contexts.

Although various authors have measured the SES characteristics of social contexts and of the individuals therein (e.g., Sampson, 1986; Simcha-Fagan and Schwartz, 1986; Thornberry and

Farnworth, 1982), only two recent studies have examined the strength of association between an individual's SES and delinquency within contexts that vary in overall SES. Although Krohn et al. (1980) interpret their data only with respect to a potential heterogeneity specification, the SES specification can also be evaluated from their data. They found slightly more instances of an SES/delinquency relationship in the middle and upper status schools, which provides some small support for the Johnstone hypothesis.

Johnstone (1978) himself reported results from a survey of 1,200 youths in the Chicago SMSA, which he combined with information from the 1970 census. Individual SES was measured with a composite, trichotomized index using weighted educational and occupational components from the survey. The SES of the census tract where the youth lived was measured by the average educational, occupational, and income characteristics as revealed in the census (each component was trichotomized and summed and the resulting sum was trichotomized). Delinquency was measured with eight indices reflecting differing types of self-reported offenses and degrees of seriousness. The relationship between SES and delinquency proved to be lowest in the low-status contexts for all eight measures of delinquency. But the highest associations between SES and delinquency were not in the high-status contexts as he predicted. Rather, they were in the medium-status contexts for seven of the eight measures. Thus, Johnstone's own data only partially confirm his hypothesized SES contextual specification. Moreover, because his method of presentation prohibits measuring associations between SES and delinquency directly (he used rank-order analysis), one cannot tell how strong even the supporting data are. These two studies, therefore, do not confirm or negate the hypothesis of an SES/delinquency specification by the SES of the context. One of them is contradictory and the other is only partially supportive.

The evidence concerning specification of an SES/delinquency relationship by characteristics of the social context is both meager and generally nonsupportive. Thus, although too little research has been done to draw a firm conclusion, it appears from the research that has been conducted that characteristics of the social context will not specify when delinquency and SES will be related.

Summary

Research published since 1978, using both official and self-reported data, suggests again (cf. Tittle et al., 1978) that there is no pervasive relationship between individual SES and delinquency. Although 18 of 21 studies (including three—Cernkovich, 1978; McCord, 1979; Wadsworth, 1979—that report the magnitude of this association only for a whole sample) report finding *at least one condition* under which there is a significant relationship between SES and delinquency,[3] the overall proportion of investigated conditions in which such relationships were found is less than 20%.[4] Nevertheless, since this figure exceeds chance, it confirms the wisdom of searching for specific circumstances under which an SES/delinquency relationship might exist. If SES is related to delinquency only sometimes, then scientific imperatives require one to look for systematic patterns whereby those relationships occur. Only then can we construct theories with statements of scope (Walker and Cohen, 1985) that enable one to account for reality.

The search for specification has so far proven disappointing, however. Our review of the recent evidence concerning 12 hypothesized specifying conditions has failed to find any hypothesized specification that is sustained by the evidence. Perhaps it is premature to conclude from this that none of the hypothesized conditions does in fact specify an SES/delinquency relationship. After all, some of the conditions have hardly been researched at all. Particularly lacking is research on contextual specifications and on the youth's status specification suggested by Stark (1979). In addition, much of the research about some of the hypothesized specifications is not directly addressed to the relevant issue, and some of the measures of the specifying conditions may be questionable. Finally, drawing general conclusions about the hypotheses requires aggregation of diverse studies, many of which may not be comparable. For all these reasons, it would be erroneous to conclude that an SES/delinquency relationship is not specifiable. However, it is correct to say that it has not yet been specified.

Discussion

Where does this leave us, then, in trying to account for delinquency with the help of SES? It appears, on the basis of the recent evidence, that SES may not be nearly so important as many seem to think (Braithwaite, 1981; Kleck, 1982; Nettler, 1978, 1985), but it may well be more important than others have concluded (Tittle et al., 1978). But the circumstances under which individual SES plays a role in delinquency production remain elusive. Sometimes SES does appear to predict delinquency; most of the time it does not.

One response to this reality is to continue to try to find the conditions under which SES predicts delinquency. Much remains to be investigated, and the quality of research can surely be improved. Moreover, scientists are always intrigued by a puzzle, and this is a puzzle of the highest order, particularly since the unruliness of the SES variable seems to challenge a number of theories (but see Tittle, 1983, for a contrary point of view).

A second approach, pioneered by Colvin and Pauly (1983) and by Hagan and his associates (1985), would reconceptualize the problem in terms of interactions among SES and other variables that ultimately have import for delinquency. The focus then is neither on whether SES is generally related to delinquency nor on the conditions wherein it might be so related. Rather, the focus is on the way in which SES sets the parameters within which social structural and other factors impinge on delinquency. Within that framework there would be little reason to expect a direct effect of SES on delinquency, although there would be many reasons to expect indirect effects that would only become apparent after the intricate processes of social life were explicated. Once the scholarly community as a whole moves to that more sophisticated level, dogged attempts to prove that SES, in some form or circumstance, must be related to delinquency will probably seem primitive.

A third strategy would be to rethink the whole idea of SES and its potential effects on delinquency. After all, SES, no matter how conceptualized, is no more than a configurative concept, presumably amalgamating many specific attributes (Loeber and Dishion, 1983). To achieve a general summary measure of a concept like this, one must blur particular details. But in reality it may be the blurred details that are important in understanding delinquency. For instance, if SES supposedly predicts youthful misbehavior because more lower status than higher status youths are deprived, it would make more sense to measure deprivation directly than to measure SES, which is a step removed from the real variable at issue. In addition, since deprivation is usually perceived by the individual in relative terms, it may better be conceived as a subjective variable. Hence, it is quite likely that many higher status youths *feel* relatively deprived even though they may not be objectively deprived. Indeed, many higher status youths may actually be objectively deprived of intelligence, looks, athletic ability, or other attributes. Thus, SES may be a poor proxy for the numerous causal variables that are supposedly embodied within it.

If our reasoning is correct, the knotty problem of individual delinquent behavior would best be approached by attempting to build better theory that owes no allegiance to SES. This need not be an intellectually painful process, but it will require a shift from the use of a configurative concept to a more precise identification of those variables that may really matter with respect to delinquency, possibly including values, bonding, peer structure, relative deprivation, community social climate, attitudes, and others. It will also require an examination of the assumptions and underlying logic that have for generations led scholars to focus on the potential interrelationship of such factors around "social class" (see Meier, 1985). Some might see this agenda as possibly calling for dismantling extant theories, supposedly based on SES as an explanatory variable, in order to identify the crucial underlying factors that presumably affect juvenile misconduct (Cernkovich, 1978). Still others might view this agenda as preliminary to the construction of integrated models in which the variables so identified are combined with others to build new theories. But regardless of how the process is viewed, some disaggregation of the social class concept appears necessary for improvement of existing theories and development of new ones. Although involving hard conceptual and theoretical work, such an approach would appear to be in everyone's best interests.

Discussion Questions

1. Why is the evidence concerning the effect of SES on delinquency seen as "problematic"? What are the findings?

2. Discuss the ways in which the SES/delinquency relationship is contingent on how the dependent variable, delinquency, is measured.

3. What demographic conditions interact with the SES/delinquency relationship? In what ways do they affect it? How does the context affect the SES/delinquency relationship?

Notes

1. In dealing with this issue it is useful to differentiate the literature concerning delinquency from that concerning adult crime. Because overlap between the two is often incomplete, it may be misleading to generalize from one to the other. This is particularly true because studies of SES and delinquency include status offenses and/or other misbehaviors that are not criminal but are relevant to tests of theories of deviance and/or delinquency. Therefore, our concern is specifically the delinquency literature.

2. Other studies (Cernkovich and Giordano, 1979; Figueira-McDonough et al., 1981) examine gender differences in delinquency but do not examine an SES/delinquency relationship within gender categories.

3. Some scholars would regard this as overwhelming evidence of the generality of an SES/delinquency relationship (e.g., Braithwaite, 1981). It appears to us, however, that the real issue is not whether one can usually find some condition that will yield a significant negative SES/delinquency relationship, but rather whether such a relationship is persistent across a variety of conditions, and if not, can the circumstances under which it emerges be specified in a systematic and empirically supportable way.

4. It is practically impossible to establish this figure exactly because some researchers do not report measures of significance; some researchers report their data in such a way that it is difficult to ascertain even the magnitude of association; some of the instances examined involve analyses of the same data by different researchers with contradictory results; and sometimes it appears that the failure to achieve significance is the result of researchers having broken the samples into subgroups with N's too small to demonstrate a significant relationship even when the association is relatively large. We counted all instances in which the SES/delinquency relationship was examined by some scholar for a specific subgroup or for some specific condition of measurement and then divided into the number that were statistically significant (or appeared that they might if it were possible to calculate an appropriate statistic or the N of the subsample was of a reasonable size), using the significant finding in those cases in which different authors found contradictory results from the same data. This produced a percentage of 16%, but in order to allow for possible error we prefer to grant the possibility of as many as 20% of the instances yielding significant associations.

References

Akers, Ronald L. 1964. "Socioeconomic status and delinquent behavior: A retest." *Journal of Research in Crime and Delinquency*, 1:38-46.

Arnold, William R. 1966. "Continuities in research: Scaling delinquent behavior." *Social Problems*, 13: 59-66.

Braithwaite, John. 1981. "The myth of social class and criminality reconsidered." *American Sociological Review*, 46:36-57.

Brown, Stephen E. 1984. "Social class, child maltreatment, and delinquent behavior." *Criminology*, 22: 259-278.

Brownfield, David. 1986. "Social class and violent behavior." *Criminology*, 24:421-438.

Cernkovich, Steven A. 1978. "Value orientations and delinquency involvement." *Criminology*, 15: 443-458.

Cernkovich, Steven and Peggy Giordano. 1979. "A comparative analysis of male and female delinquency." *Sociological Quarterly*, 20:131-14.

Clark, John P. and Eugene P. Wenninger. 1962. "Socioeconomic class and area as correlates of illegal behavior among juveniles." *American Sociological Review*, 27:826-834.

Clelland, Donald and Timothy J. Carter. 1980. "The new myth of class and crime." *Criminology*, 18: 319-336.

Coleman, James S. 1961. *Adolescent Society.* New York: Free Press.

Colvin, Mark and John Pauly. 1983. "A critique of criminology: Toward an integrated structural marxist theory of delinquency production." *American Journal of Sociology,* 89:513-551.

Dentler, Robert A. and Lawrence J. Monroe. 1961. "Social correlates of early adolescent theft." *American Sociological Review,* 26:733-743.

Elliott, Delbert S. and Suzanne S. Ageton. 1980. "Reconciling race and class differences in self-reported and official estimates of delinquency." *American Sociological Review,* 45:95-110.

Elliott, Delbert S. and David Huizinga. 1983. "Social class and delinquent behavior in a national youth panel." *Criminology,* 21:149-177.

Farrington, David P. 1983. "Further Analyses of a Longitudinal Survey of Crime and Delinquency." *Final report to the National Institute of Justice.* Washington, D.C.

Figueira-McDonough, Josefina, William H. Barton, and Rosemary C. Sarri. 1981. "Normal deviance: Gender similarities in adolescent subcultures." In Marguerite Q. Warren (ed.), *Comparing Female and Male Offenders.* Beverly Hills, Calif.: Sage.

Hagan, John. 1985. *Modern Criminology: Crime, Criminal Behavior, and Its Control.* New York: McGraw-Hill.

Hagan, John, A. R. Gillis, and John Simpson. 1985. "The class structure of gender and delinquency: Toward a power-control theory of common delinquent behavior." *American Journal of Sociology,* 90: 1151-1178.

Harry, Joseph. 1974. "Social class and delinquency: One more time." *Sociological Quarterly,* 15:294-301.

Hindelang, Michael, Travis Hirschi, and Joseph G. Weis. 1979. "Correlates of delinquency: The illusion of discrepancy between self-report and official measures." *American Sociological Review,* 44: 995-1014.

——. 1981. *Measuring Delinquency.* Beverly Hills, Calif.: Sage.

Hirschi, Travis. 1969. *Causes of Delinquency.* Berkeley: University of California Press.

Johnson, Richard E. 1980. "Social class and delinquent behavior: A new test." *Criminology,* 18:86-93.

Johnstone, John W. C. 1978. "Social class, social areas and delinquency." *Sociology and Social Research,*63:49-72.

Kleck, Gary. 1982. "On the use of self-report to determine the class distribution of criminal and delinquent behavior." *American Sociological Review,* 47: 427-433.

Krohn, Marvin D., Ronald L. Akers, Marcia J. Radosevich, and Lonn Lanza-Kaduce. 1980. "Social status and deviance." *Criminology,* 18:303-318.

Loeber, Rolf and Thomas Dishion. 1983. "Early predictors of male delinquency: A review." *Psychological Bulletin,* 94:68-99.

McCord, Joan. 1979. "Some child-rearing antecedents of criminal behavior in adult men." *Journal of Personality and Social Psychology,* 37:1477-1486.

McDonald, Lynn. 1968. *Social Class and Delinquency.* New York: Archon.

Meier, Robert F. (ed.) 1985. *Theoretical Methods in Criminology.* Beverly Hills, Calif.: Sage.

Nettler, Gwynn. 1978. "Social status and self-reported criminality." *Social Forces,* 57:304-305.

——. 1985. "Social class and crime, one more time." *Social Forces,* 63:1076-1077.

Nye, F. Ivan and James F. Short. 1957. "Scaling delinquent behavior." *American Sociological Review,* 22: 326-331.

Nye, F. Ivan, James F. Short, and Virgil Olson. 1958. *Socioeconomic Review,* 63:381-389.

Ouston, Janet. 1984. "Delinquency, family background, and educational attainment." *British Journal of Criminology,* 24:2-26.

Polk, Kenneth, Christine Adler, Gordon Bazemore, Gerald Blake, Sheila Cordray, Gary Coventry, James Galvin, and Mark Temple. 1981. "Becoming Adult: An Analysis of Maturational Development from Age 16 to 30 of a Cohort of Young Men." *Final Report, Grant No. MH14806, Center for Studies of Crime and Delinquency, National Institute of Mental Health.* Washington, DC: U.S. Department of Health and Human Services.

Reiss, Albert J. and Albert L. Rhodes. 1961. "The distribution of juvenile delinquency in the social class structure." *American Sociological Review,* 26: 720-732.

——. 1963. "Status deprivation and delinquent behavior." *Sociological Quarterly,* 4:135-149.

Sampson, Robert J. 1986. "Effects of socioeconomic context on official reaction to juvenile delinquency." *American Sociological Review,* 51: 876-885.

Sellin, Thorsten and Marvin Wolfgang. 1978. *The Measurement of Delinquency.* 1964. Montclair, N.J.: Patterson Smith.

Simcha-Fagan, Ora and Joseph F. Schwartz. 1986. "Neighborhood and delinquency: An assessment of contextual effects." *Criminology*, 24:667-703.

Slocum, Walter L. and Carol L. Stone. 1963. "Family culture patterns and delinquent type behavior." *Journal of Marriage and Family Living*, 25:202-208.

Stark, Rodney. 1979. "Whose status counts?" *American Sociological Review*, 44:668-669.

Thornberry, Terence P. and R. L. Christenson. 1984. "Unemployment and criminal involvement: An investigation of reciprocal causal structure." *American Sociological Review*, 49:398-411.

Thornberry, Terence P. and Margaret Farnworth. 1982. "Social correlates of criminal involvement: Further evidence of the relationship between social status and criminal behavior." *American Sociological Review*, 47:505-518.

Tittle, Charles R. 1983. "Social class and criminal behavior: A critique of the theoretical foundation." *Social Forces*, 62:334-358.

——. 1985. "A plea for open minds, one more time: Response to Nettler." *Social Forces*, 63:1078-1080.

Tittle, Charles R. and Wayne J. Villemez. 1978. "Response to Gwynn Nettler." *Social Forces*, 57:306-307.

Tittle, Charles R., Wayne J. Villemez, and Douglas A. Smith. 1978. "The myth of social class and criminality: An empirical assessment of the empirical evidence." *American Sociological Review*, 43:643-656.

——. 1979. "Reply to Stark." *American Sociological Review*, 44:669-670.

——. 1982. "One step forward, two steps back: More on the class/criminality controversy." *American Sociological Review*, 47:435-438.

Tracy, Paul E., Jr. 1987. "Race and class differentials in official and self-reported delinquency." In Martin E. Wolfgang, Terence P. Thornberry, and Robert M. Figlio (eds.), *From Boy to Man, From Delinquency to Crime*. Chicago: University of Chicago Press.

Vaz, Edmund W. 1966. "Self-reported juvenile delinquency and socioeconomic status." *Canadian Journal of Corrections*, 8:20-27.

Wadsworth, Michael. 1979. *Roots of Delinquency: Infancy, Adolescence and Crime*. New York: Barnes and Noble.

Walker, Henry A. and Bernard P. Cohen. 1985. "Scope statements: Imperatives for evaluating theory." *American Sociological Review*, 50:288-301.

West, Donald J. 1982. *Delinquency: Its Roots, Careers, and Prospects*. London: Heinemann.

West, Donald J. and David P. Farrington. 1973. *Who Becomes Delinquent?* London: Heinemann.

Winslow, Robert H. 1967. "Anomie and its alternatives: A self-report study of delinquency." *Sociological Quarterly*, 8:468-480.

Wolfgang, Marvin E., Robert M. Figlio, and Thorsten Sellin. 1972. *Delinquency in a Birth Cohort*. Chicago: University of Chicago Press.

Wright, Eric O. and Luca Perrone. 1977. "Marxist class categories and income inequality." *American Sociological Review*, 42:32-55.

CHAPTER 11

Age and the Patterning of Crime

Darrell J. Steffensmeier ■ Jeffrey T. Ulmer

Age has long been established as one of the strongest correlates of criminal behavior. Empirical evidence has supported the age–crime relationship and its strength has been demonstrated both temporally and spatially. Early statisticians first discovered the link between age and crime and noted that the proportion of the population involved in criminal activity tended to peak in late adolescence or early adulthood and then decline as one ages. Although much has changed in the nearly two centuries since this initial research was conducted, the age–crime curve has remained relatively constant, although variations in peak age, median age, and rates of decline are observable.

In the following selection, "Age and the Patterning of Crime," Darrell J. Steffensmeier and Jeffrey T. Ulmer discuss the curvilinear relationship between crime and one of its strongest correlates, age. After first examining official UCR statistics documenting age-specific rates of index crimes, the authors move beyond the bivariate relationship to review the etiology of the age–crime curve. Variations in the age curve such as cross-cultural, historical, race, and sex differences are explored prior to a concluding discussion of "aging out" of crime.

The relationship between aging and criminal activity has been noted since the beginnings of criminology. For example, Adolphe Quetelet, the 19th century geographer and criminologist who in the mid-1800s pioneered the statistical analysis of crime across space, gender, and age, found that the proportion of the population involved in crime tends to peak in adolescence or early adulthood and then decline with age. This age–crime relationship is remarkably similar across historical periods, geographic locations, and crime types. That the impact of age on criminal involvement is one of the strongest factors associated with crime has prompted the controversial claim that the age–crime relationship is invariant (Hirschi and Gottfredson, 1983). However, considerable variation exists among offenses and across historical periods in specific features of the age–crime relationship (for example, peak age, median age, rate of decline from peak age). A claim of "invariance" in the age–crime relationship, therefore, overstates the case (Steffensmeier et al., 1989).

Age–Crime Patterns for the U.S.

The FBI's Uniform Crime Report (UCR) data, particularly the Crime Index (comprising homicide, robbery, rape, aggravated assault, burglary, larceny-theft, and auto theft), document the robustness of the age effect on crime and also reveal a long-term trend toward *younger* age–crime distributions in more modern times. Today, the peak age (the age group with the highest age-specific arrest rate) is younger than 25 for all crimes reported in the FBI's UCR program except gambling, and rates

From, *Encyclopedia of Criminology* (pp. 22–58) by R.A. Wright and J.M. Miller, 2005. New York, New York: Routledge Publisher begin to decline in the teenage years for more than half of the UCR crimes. In fact, even the median age (50% of all arrests occurring among younger persons) is younger than 30 for most crimes. The National Crime Victimization Survey (NCVS), self-report studies of juvenile and adult criminality, and interview data from convicted felons corroborate the age–crime patterns found in the UCR data (Rowe and Tittle, 1977; Elliott et al., 1983).

Explaining Youthful Offending

In a general sense, physical abilities, such as strength, speed, prowess, stamina, and aggression are useful for successful commission of many crimes, for protection, for enforcing contracts, and for recruiting and managing reliable associates (for a review, see Steffensmeier, 1983). Although some crimes are physically more demanding than others, persistent involvement in crime is likely to entail a lifestyle that is physically demanding and dangerous. Declining physical strength and energy may make crime too dangerous or unsuccessful, especially where there are younger

or stronger criminal competitors who will not be intimidated, and thus might help to explain the very low involvement in crime of small children and the elderly.

However, available evidence on biological aging reveals very little correspondence between physical aging and decline of crime in late adolescence. The research literature on biological aging (see especially, Shock, 1984) suggests that peak functioning is typically reached between the ages of 25 and 30 for physical factors plausibly assumed to affect one's ability to commit crimes (strength, stamina, aerobic capacity, motor control, sensory perception, and speed of movement). Although decline sets in shortly after these peak years, it is very gradual until the early 50s, when the decline becomes more pronounced (Shock, 1984). Other commonly mentioned physical variables like testosterone levels peak in early adulthood but then remain at peak level until at least the age of 50. In contrast, the age curves for crimes like robbery and burglary that presuppose the need for physical abilities peak in mid-adolescence and then decline very rapidly. In short, although biological

Table 11.1 Male and Female Arrest Rates per 100,000 (All Ages), Female Percentage of Arrests, and Male and Female Arrest Profiles (1965-2000 Uniform Crime Reports)

Offense	Male Rates*				Female Rates*				Female Percentage (of Arrests)[†]				Offender-Profile Percentage[‡]			
													Males		Females	
	1965	1980	1990	2000	1965	1980	1990	2000	1965	1980	1990	2000	1965	2000	1965	2000
Violent																
Homicide	9	16	17	12	2	2	2	1	17	12	10	10	0.1	0.1	0.2	0.1
Weapons	78	140	174	141	5	10	13	12	6	7	7	8	1	2	0.6	0.5
Simple assault	279	369	697	817	32	56	127	221	10	13	15	21	4	9	4	9
Property/Drugs																
Larceny	466	755	894	685	125	298	391	351	21	28	30	34	7	8	14	15
Fraud	62	145	169	160	15	96	128	126	20	40	43	44	1	2	2	5
Drug abuse	66	450	800	1010	10	65	150	182	13	13	16	15	1	11	1	8

*Rates are calculated based on 3-year averages and are sex-specific rates (e.g., female rate = no. of female arrests/no, of females in the population × 100.000).
[†]The female percentage of arrests adjusts for the sex composition of the population. It is calculated as follows: [female rate/(female rate + male rate)] × 100.
[‡]The offender profile percentage is the percentage of all arrests within each sex that are arrests for a particular offense; this measure indicates the distribution of arrests by gender.

and physiological factors may contribute toward an understanding of the rapid increase in delinquent behavior during adolescence, they cannot by themselves explain the abrupt decline in the age–crime curve following mid-to-late adolescence.

A variety of social and cognitive factors can help explain the rapid rise in age-specific rates of offending around mid-adolescence. Teenagers generally lack strong bonds to conventional adult institutions, such as work and family (Warr, 1998). At the same time, teens are faced with strong potential rewards for offending: money, status, power, autonomy, identity claims, strong sensate experiences stemming from sex, natural adrenaline highs or highs from illegal substances, and respect from similar peers (Wilson and Herrenstein, 1985; Steffensmeier et al., 1989). Further, their dependent status as juveniles insulates teens from many of the social and legal costs of illegitimate activities, and their stage of cognitive development limits prudence concerning the consequences of their behavior. At the same time, they possess the physical prowess required to commit crimes. Finally, a certain amount of misbehavior is often seen as natural to youth and seen as simply a stage of growing up (John and Gibbons, 1987; Hagan et al., 1998).

For those in late adolescence or early adulthood (roughly age 17–22, the age group showing the sharpest decline in arrest rates for many crimes), important changes occur in at least six spheres of life (Steffensmeier et al., 1989; Sampson and Laub, 1993; Warr, 1998):

1. Greater access to legitimate sources of material goods and excitement: (including jobs, credit, alcohol, and sex).
2. Patterns of illegitimate opportunities: with the assumption of adult roles, opportunities increase for crimes (for example, gambling, fraud, and employee theft) that are less risky, more lucrative, or less likely to be reflected in official statistics.
3. Peer associations and lifestyle: reduced orientation to same-age–same-sex peers and increased orientation toward persons of the opposite sex or persons who are older or more mature.
4. Cognitive and analytical skill development leading to a gradual decline in egocentrism, hedonism, and sense of invincibility; becoming more concerned for others, more accepting of social values, more comfortable in social relations, and more concerned with the meaning of life; and seeing their casual delinquencies of youth as childish or foolish.
5. Increased legal and social costs for deviant behavior.
6. Age-graded norms: externally increased expectation of maturity and responsibility; internal anticipation of assuming adult roles, coupled with reduced subjective acceptance of deviant roles and the threat they pose to entering adult status.

As young people move into adulthood or anticipate entering it, most find their bonds to conventional society strengthening, with expanded access to work or further education and increased interest in "settling down" (Warr, 1998; Hagan et al., 1998). Leaving high school, finding employment, going to college, enlisting in the military, and getting married all tend to increase informal social controls and integration into conventional society. In addition, early adulthood typically involves a change in peer associations and lifestyle routines that diminish the opportunities for committing these offenses (Warr, 1998). Furthermore, at the same time when informal sanctions for law violation are increasing, potential legal sanctions increase substantially.

Variations in the Age Curve

Crime tends to decline with age, although substantial variation can be found in the parameters of the age–crime curve (such as peak age, median age, and rate of decline from peak age). "Flatter" age curves (i.e., those with an older peak age or a slower decline in offending rates among older age groups) are associated with at least three circumstances: (1) cultures and historical periods in which youth have greater access to legitimate opportunities and integration into adult society; (2) population groups for whom legitimate opportunities and integration into adult society do not markedly increase with age (i.e., during young adulthood); and (3) types of crime for which illegitimate opportunities increase rather than diminish with age.

Cross-Cultural and Historical Differences

In simple, nonindustrial societies, the passage to adult status is relatively simple and continuous. Formal "rites of passage" at relatively early ages avoid much of the status ambiguity and role conflict that torment modern adolescents in the developed world. Youths begin to assume responsible and economically productive roles well before they reach full physical maturity. It is not surprising, therefore, to find that such societies and time periods have significantly flatter and less skewed age–crime patterns (for a review, see Steffensmeier et al., 1989). Much the same is true for earlier periods in the history of the U.S. and other industrial nations, when farm youths were crucial for harvesting crops and working-class children were expected to leave school at an early age and do their part in helping to support their families (Horan and Hargis, 1991). By contrast, today teenagers typically work at marginal jobs that provide little self-pride and few opportunities for adult mentorship, and instead segregate them into a separate peer culture. Youth has always been seen as a turbulent time, although social processes associated with the coming of industrialization and the postindustrial age have aggravated the stresses of adolescence, resulting in increased levels of juvenile criminality in recent decades. The structure of modern societies, therefore, encourages crime and delinquency among the young because these societies "lack institutional procedures for moving people smoothly from protected childhood to autonomous adulthood" (Nettler, 1978, 241).

Unfortunately, reliable age statistics on criminal involvement are not available over extended historical periods. Nonetheless, we can compare age–crime distributions over the past 60 years or so in the U.S. and also compare these to early 19th century age–crime distributions reported in

Figure 11.1 Age distribution of homicide offenders across four historical periods.

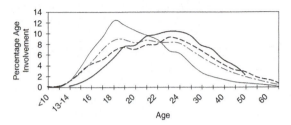

Source: Uniform Crime Reports

Quetelet's pioneering study. The age–crime plots are shown in Figure 11.1 for total offenses and homicide (the most reliable crime statistic). The plots clearly show a trend toward younger age distributions and younger peak ages.

The shift toward a greater concentration of offending among the young may be due partly to changes in law enforcement procedures and data collection. Nevertheless, the likelihood that real changes have in fact occurred is supported by the consistency of the changes from 1830 to 1940–1980, and even from 1980 to roughly 2000. Support for the conclusion that real change has taken place over the past century also is found in the age breakdown of U.S. prisoner statistics covering the years 1890–1980 (Steffensmeier et al., 1989). As with the UCR statistics, the prison statistics show that age curves are more peaked today than a century ago and that changes in the age–crime curve are gradual and can be detected only when a sufficiently large time frame is used. Moreover, research shows that more recent birth cohorts of juveniles are more violent than ones in the past (Tracey et al., 1985; Shannon, 1988).

Together, these findings are consistent with the view that contemporary teenagers in industrialized nations are subject to greater status anxiety than in previous periods of history and that the transition from adolescence to adulthood is more turbulent now than in the past (Friday and Hage, 1976; Greenberg, 1977a; Glaser, 1978). In comparison to earlier eras, youths have had less access to responsible family roles, valued economic activity, and participation in community affairs (Clausen, 1986). This generational isolation has fostered adolescent subcultures oriented toward consumption and hedonistic pursuits (Hagan, 1991; Hagan et al., 1998). The weakened social bonds and reduced access to valued adult roles, along with accentuated subcultural influences, all combine to increase situationally induced pressures to obtain valued goods; display strength, daring, or loyalty to peers; or simply to "get kicks" (Briar and Piliavin, 1965; Gold, 1970; Hagan et al., 1998).

Minority Differences

For black inner-city youths, the problems of youth described above are compounded by persistent racial discrimination and blocked conventional opportunity (Wilson, 1987; 1996). As inner-city blacks move into young adulthood, they continue to experience limited access to high quality adult jobs and are more likely to associate primarily with same-sex peers. As UCR data show, adult offending levels among blacks continue at higher levels than among whites, and the proportion of total black crime that is committed by black adults is greater than the proportion of total white crime that is committed by white adults (Steffensmeier and Allan, 1993). Arrest statistics for homicide or robbery from California further document the flatter age–crime curves among blacks than whites.

Crime Types

The offenses that show the youngest peaks and sharpest declines are crimes that fit the low-yield, criminal mischief, "hell-raising" category: vandalism, petty theft, robbery, arson, auto theft, burglary, and liquor law and drug violations. Personal crimes like aggravated assault and homicide tend to have somewhat "older" age distributions (with median ages in the late twenties), as do some of the public order offenses, public drunkenness, driving under the influence, and certain of the property crimes that juveniles have less opportunity to commit, like embezzlement, fraud, and gambling (with median ages in late twenties or thirties).

The offenses with flatter age curves are often those for which the structure of illegitimate opportunities increases rather than disappears with age. For example, some opportunities for fraud exist for young people (such as falsification of identification to purchase alcohol or gain entry to "adult" establishments), but as they are too young to obtain credit, they lack the opportunities for common frauds such as passing bad checks, defrauding an innkeeper, or credit card forgery. Similarly, young people have more opportunities for some kinds of violence (for example, street fights or gang violence) but less opportunity for other kinds of violence (for example, spousal violence).

Older people may also shift to less visible crimes such as bookmaking or receiving stolen goods. Or as a spinoff of legitimate roles, they may commit surreptitious crimes or crimes that, if discovered, are unlikely to be reported to the authorities, such as embezzlement, stock fraud, bribery, or price-fixing. Unfortunately, we know relatively little about the age distribution of persons who commit these and related lucrative crimes, but the fragmentary evidence that does exist suggests that they are likely to be middle aged or older (Shapiro, 1984; Pennsylvania Crime Commission, 1991). Evidence also suggests that the age curves for lucrative crimes in the underworld like racketeering or loan-sharking not only peak much later but tend to decline more slowly with age (Steffensmeier and Allan, 1993; Steffensmeier, 1986).

Still less is known of the age distribution of "respectable" or upperworld offenders who commit lucrative business crimes like fraud, price-fixing, or bribery, as such data are not plentiful. However, data from *New York Times* articles on profitable business crimes (those involving gains of $25,000 or more) during the 1987–1990 period reveals a preponderance of middle-aged or older offenders, with a modal age between 40 and 50 (Steffensmeier and Allan, 1993).

Sex Differences in the Age–Crime Relationship

There appears to be considerable similarity in the age–crime relationship between males and females (Steffensmeier and Streifel, 1991). The UCR arrest statistics from 1940–2000 show that the age curves of male and female offenders are very similar within any given period and across all offenses, with the exception of prostitution. To the extent that age differences between the sexes exist, the tendency is for somewhat lower peak ages of offending among females—apparently because of their earlier physical maturity and the likelihood that young adolescent females might date and associate with older delinquent male peers. But overall, although male levels of offending are always higher than female levels at every age and for virtually all offenses, the female-to-male ratio remains fairly constant across the life span (Steffensmeier and Streifel, 1991). Also, the trend toward younger and more peaked age–crime distributions holds for both sexes.

Variations in Criminal Careers

The youthful peak and rapid drop-off in offending that constitutes the most common societal pattern for conventional crimes is only one of a number of patterns identified when criminal careers are tracked for individual offenders (see Jolin and Gibbons, 1987; D'Unger et al., 1998). Other interesting trends pertain to older offenders.

"Aging Out" of Crime

Research suggests that exiting from a criminal career requires the acquisition of meaningful bonds to conventional adult individuals and institutions (Sampson and Laub, 1993; Warr, 1998). One important tie to the conventional order is a job that seems to have the potential for advancement and that is seen as meaningful and economically rewarding. A good job shifts a criminal's attention from the present to the future and provides a solid basis for the construction of a noncriminal identity. It also alters an individual's daily routine in ways that make crime less likely (Meisenhelder, 1977; Shover, 1983). Other bonds that may lead people away from crime include involvement in religion, sports, hobbies, or other activities (Irwin, 1970).

The development of conventional social bonds may be coupled with burnout or a belated deterrent effect as offenders grow tired of the hassles of repeated involvement with the criminal justice system and the hardships of a life of crime. They may also have experienced a long prison sentence that jolts them into quitting or that entails the loss of street contacts that make the successful continuation of a criminal career difficult. Or offenders may develop a fear of dying alone in prison, especially as repeated convictions yield longer sentences. Still other offenders may quit or "slow down" as they find their abilities and efficiency declining with increasing age, loss of "nerve," or sustained narcotics or alcohol use (Prus and Sharper, 1977; Adler and Adler, 1983; Shover, 1983; Steffensmeier, 1986).

Older Criminals

Older offenders typically fall into two categories: (1) those whose first criminal involvement occurs relatively late in life (particularly in shoplifting, homicide, and alcohol-related offenses) and (2) those who started crime at an early age and continue their involvement into their forties and fifties and beyond. What evidence is available on first-time older offenders suggests that situational stress and lack of alternative opportunities play a primary role. The unanticipated loss of one's job or other disruptions of social ties can push some individuals into their first law violation at any age (Alston, 1986; Jolin and Gibbons, 1987; Agnew 1992).

Older offenders who persist in crime are more likely to belong to the criminal underworld. These are individuals who are relatively successful in their criminal activities or who are extensively integrated into subcultural or family criminal enterprises. They seem to receive relational and psychic rewards (e.g., pride in their expertise) as well as monetary rewards from lawbreaking and, as a result, see no need to withdraw from lawbreaking (Reynolds, 1953; Klockars, 1974; Steffensmeier, 1986). Alternatively, such offenders may "shift and oscillate" back and forth between conventionality and lawbreaking, depending on shifting life circumstances and situational inducements to offend (Adler and Adler, 1983). These older offenders are also unlikely to see many meaningful opportunities for themselves in the conventional or law-abiding world. Consequently, "the straight life" may have little to offer successful criminals, who will be more likely to persist in their criminality for an extended period. But they, too, may slow down eventually as they grow tired of the cumulative aggravations and risks of criminal involvement, or as they encounter the diminishing capacities associated with the aging process.

Effects of Population Age Structure on Crime Rates

The dramatically higher age-specific offending rates for young people suggest that shifts in the age-composition of the population could produce considerable changes in societal crime rates. The so-called "baby-boom" generation born between the end of World War II and the early 1960s brought a large and steady increase in the proportion of the population aged between 12 and 25—the most crime-prone age group—during the 1960s and 1970s, a period when the nation's crime rate was also increasing steadily. Ferdinand (1970) found that about 50% of the increase in the Index crime rate during the 1960s could be attributed to population shifts such as the baby-boom generation's movement into the crime-prone years. Similarly, Steffensmeier and Harer (1989) found that virtually all the reported decreases in the UCR and NCVS Index crime rates during the early 1980s could be attributed to the declining proportion of teenagers in the population, that is. to a "baby-bust" effect.

More recently, Steffensmeier and Harer (1999) report that the large impact of age composition on crime rates during the 1980s has diminished during the 1990s, and that the broad decline in both the UCR and NCVS crime rates since 1992 (the Clinton presidency years) cannot be solely attributed to changes in population age composition. One explanation of the recent downtrend has attributed the decline to dramatic increases in incarceration rates that presumably incapacitate or prevent crimes by locking up high-frequency offenders who commit a disproportionate amount of all crimes. However, the rise in incarceration rates extends backward to at least the late 1970s, and therefore, considerably predates the 1990s drop in crime. Therefore, it appears unlikely that higher imprisonment rates explain much, if any, of the recent drop in crime—just as they do not account for its rise in the late 1980s.

Alternative explanations for recent downward trends in crime rates include the strong economy and low unemployment of the 1990s, an abatement of the crack epidemic of the late 1980s, and the wide variety of community-level criminal justice initiatives undertaken in the past decade, such as Operation Weed and Seed, Pulling America's Communities Together, Safe Futures, and community policing (Kelling, 1998). Also, Steffensmeier and Harer (1999) speculate that offenders may be shifting from risky, low-return offenses like burglary (also robbery) to others that are more lucrative (drug dealing) or less risky (fraud).

Conclusion

Age is a consistent predictor of crime, both in the aggregate and for individuals. The most common finding across countries, groups, and historical periods shows that crime—especially "ordinary" or "street" crime—tends to be a young person's activity. However, the age–crime relationship is not invariant, and in fact varies in its specific features according to crime types, the structural position of groups, and historical and cultural contexts. On the other hand, relatively little is known about older chronic offenders. Clearly, the structure, dynamics, and contexts of offending among older individuals are rich topics for future research.

References

Adler, P. and Adler, P. 1983. Shifts and oscillations in deviant careers: The case of upper-level drug dealers and smugglers. *Social Problems* 31: 195–207.

Coontz, S. 1997. *The Way We Really Are: Coming to Terms with America's Changing Families.* New York, NY: Basic Books.

Federal Bureau of Investigation. 1935–1997. *Crime in the United States.* Washington, DC: U.S. Government Printing Office.

Ferdinand, T. 1970. Demographic shifts and criminality: An inquiry. *British Journal of Criminology* 10: 169–175.

Glaser, D. 1978. *Crime in Our Changing Society.* New York, NY: Holt, Rinehart, and Winston.

Greenberg, D. 1979. Delinquency and the age structure of society. *Contemporary Crisis* 1: 66–86.

Greenberg, D. 1982. Age and crime. In *Encyclopedia of Crime and Justice,* Vol. 1, Sanford, K. (Ed.). New York, NY: Macmillan, pp. 30–35.

Hagan, J. 1991. Destiny and drift: Subcultural preferences, status attainments, and the risks and rewards of youth. *American Sociological Review* 56: 567–581.

Hagan, J., Heffler, G., Classen, G., Boehnke, K., and Merkens, H. 1998. Subterranean sources of subcultural delinquency beyond the American dream. *Criminology* 36: 309–342.

Hirschi, T. and Gottfredson, M. 1983. Age and the explanation of crime. *American Journal of Sociology* 89: 522–584.

Irwin, J. 1970. *The Felon.* Englewood Cliffs, NJ: Prentice-Hall.

Jolin, A. and Gibbons, D. 1987. Age patterns in criminal involvement. *International Journal of Offender Therapy and Comparative Criminology* 31: 237–260.

Monkkonen, E. 1999. New York City offender ages: How variable over time. *Homicide Studies* 3: 256–270.

Nettler, G. 1978. *Explaining Crime.* New York, NY: McGraw-Hill.

Pennsylvania Crime Commission. 1991. *1990 Report-Organized Crime in America: A Decade of Change.* Commonwealth of Pennsylvania.

Quetelet, A. 1833 (1984). *Research on the Propensity for Crime at Different Ages.* (Translated by Sawyer Sylvester.) Cincinnati, OH: Anderson Publishing Co.

Sampson, R. and Laub, J. 1993. *Crime in the Making: Pathways and Turning Points through Life.* Cambridge, MA: Harvard University Press.

Shannon, L. 1988. *Criminal Career Continuity: Its Social Context.* New York, NY: Human Sciences Press.

Shapiro, S. 1984. Wayward Capitalists: Target of the Securities and Exchange Commission. New Haven, CT: Yale University Press.

Shock, N. 1984. *Normal Human Aging: The Baltimore Longitudinal Study of Aging.* Washington, DC: U.S. Government Printing Office.

Shover, N. 1983. The later stages of ordinary property offender careers. *Social Problems* 30: 208–218.

Steffensmeier, D. 1986. *The Fence: In the Shadow of Two Worlds.* Totowa, NJ: Rowman & Littlefield.

Steffensmeier, D. and Allan, E. 1995. Criminal behavior: Gender and age. In *Criminology: A Contemporary Handbook,* Joseph, S. (Ed.), pp. 83–114.

Steffensmeier, D., Allan, E., Harer, M., and Streifel, C. 1989. Age and the distribution of crime. *American Journal of Sociology* 94: 803–831.

Steffensmeier, D. and Harer, M. 1991. Did crime rise or fall during the Reagan presidency? The effects of an 'aging' U.S. population on the nation's crime rate. *Journal of Research in Crime and Delinquency* 28: 330–359.

Steffensmeier, D. 1999. Making sense of recent U.S. crime trends, 1980–98: Age composition effects and other explanations. *Journal of Research in Crime and Delinquency* 36: 235–274.

Steffensmeier, D., and Cathy, S. 1991. Age, gender, and crime across three historical periods: 1935, 1960, and 1985. *Social Forces* 69: 869–894.

Tracey, P., Marvin, W., and Robert, F. 1990. *Delinquency Careers in Two Birth Cohorts.* New York, NY: Plenum.

Ulmer, J. and William, S.J. The contributions of an interactionist approach to research and theory on criminal careers. *Theoretical Criminology* 3: 95–124.

Warr, M. 1998. Life-course transitions and desistance from crime. *Criminology* 36: 183–216.

Wilson, J.Q. and Richard, H. 1985. *Crime and Human Nature.* New York, NY: Simon and Schuster.

CHAPTER 12

Explaining the Gender Gap in Delinquency: Peer Influence and Moral Evaluations of Behavior

Daniel P. Mears ■ Matthew Ploeger ■ Mark Warr

Gender is one of the most prominent correlates of criminal behavior. For nearly every offense committed, males are more likely to be the perpetrator. Although some research on the correlates of crime may suffer from methodological biases, the link between gender and crime is supported by official, self-report, and victimization data. The consistency of this finding over a number of studies and data sources suggests the saliency of the relationship and necessitates its consideration in criminological theorizing.

Explanations for crime have long noted the importance of sex differences in offending. Cesare Lombroso, sometimes referred to as the father of modern or positivistic criminology, suggested in the late nineteenth century that females were inherently less criminal than males. Other criminological theories such as Sutherland's differential association did not specifically address gender differences in offending but nonetheless provide a usable framework for understanding the phenomenon. In this selection, "Explaining the Gender Gap in Delinquency: Peer Influence and Moral Evaluations of Behavior," Daniel P. Mears, Matthew Ploeger, and Mark Warr employ differential association theory to explain gender disparity in criminal offending. The authors explore three key research questions: (1) Do male and female adolescents differ in their exposure to

delinquent peers? (2) Are males and females who are exposed to delinquent peers differentially affected by them? (3) If males and females are affected differently by exposure to delinquent peers, why is this the case? Their findings offer a greater understanding between gender, crime, and another salient factor, delinquent peers.

Gender is one of the strongest and most frequently documented correlates of delinquent behavior. Males commit more offenses than females at every age, within all racial or ethnic groups examined to date, and for all but a handful of offense types that are peculiarly female. Unlike some putative features of delinquency that are method-dependent (e.g., social class differences), sex differences in delinquency are independently corroborated by self-report, victimization, and police data, and they appear to hold cross-culturally as well as historically. So tenacious are sex differences in delinquency, in fact, that it is difficult to argue with Wilson and Herrnstein's conclusion that "gender demands attention in the search for the origins of crime."

Explanations for gender differences in offending have been promulgated at least since the time of Lombroso, who opined that the female criminal is "of less typical aspect than the male because she is less essentially criminal." Lombroso's observations notwithstanding, efforts to explain the gender/crime relation have not fared well, and some sharp philosophical and methodological differences have arisen as to how investigators ought to

Reprinted from: "Explaining the Gender Gap in Delinquency: Peer Influence and Moral Evaluations of Behavior" by D. Mears, M. Ploeger and M. Warr, 1998, *Journal of Research in Crime and Delinquency* 35 (3):251-66. Reprinted by permission of Sage Publications, Inc.

proceed. Some analysts argue that conventional theories of delinquency were largely designed to explain male delinquency and that separate theories are required to account for male and female delinquency. Smith and Paternoster, however, strongly warn against premature rejection of existing theories: "Since most empirical tests of deviance theories have been conducted with male samples, the applicability of these theories to females is largely unknown. Moreover, the fact that most theories of deviance were constructed to account for male deviance does not mean that they *cannot* account for female deviance."

Rather than postulating separate etiological theories for males and females, Smith and Paternoster join a number of investigators in suggesting that males and females differ in their rates of delinquency because they are *differentially exposed* to the *same* criminogenic conditions. In a close variant of this position, other investigators have suggested that males and females are *differentially affected* by exposure to the same criminogenic conditions. If such arguments are correct, then it is pointless to construct entirely separate theories to explain the delinquent behavior of males and females.

One traditional theory of delinquency that holds promise for a unified explanation of gender differences in offending is Sutherland's theory of differential association. In this classic sociological theory, Sutherland argued that delinquency is learned behavior and that it is learned in intimate social groups through face-to-face interaction. When individuals are selectively or differentially exposed to delinquent companions, Sutherland argued, they are likely to acquire "an excess of definitions favorable to violation of law over definitions unfavorable to violation of law" and consequently engage in delinquent conduct. Sutherland's theory was subsequently recast in modern social learning terms and enjoys considerable empirical support today. Although Sutherland did not limit his theory to peer influence, tests of the theory have generally concentrated on peers, and association with delinquent peers remains the single strongest predictor of delinquent behavior known today.

Several studies suggest that differential association may be a critical factor in explaining gender differences in delinquency. Using self-report data from a sample of Iowa teenagers, Simons et al. found that males and females experienced substantially different levels of exposure to delinquent peer attitudes in their everyday lives. "Males were much more likely than females to have friends who were supportive of delinquent behavior." But although these investigators were able to establish sex-linked differences in exposure to delinquent friends, they did not isolate and quantify the effect of such exposure on sex-specific rates of delinquency.

Other studies illustrate the variant approach described earlier. Johnson tested an integrated model of delinquency containing family, school, socioeconomic, deterrence, and peer variables. Among both sexes, the effect of delinquent associates outweighed all other variables in the model. But the effect of delinquent peers on self-reported delinquency was substantially stronger among males than females. Smith and Paternoster examined the ability of strain theory, differential association, control theory, and deterrence theory to explain sex differences in adolescent marijuana use. They, too, found that association with deviant peers had the largest effect on marijuana use among both males and females, but the effect was once again stronger for males than females. Despite the strikingly similar findings of these two studies, not all investigators have obtained similar results. Most, however, have failed to employ appropriate interaction terms or tests of significance in making gender comparisons, or have used widely divergent measures of peer influence.

This article draws on Sutherland's theory on differential association with a view to explaining gender differences in delinquency. Following the logic of Sutherland's theory, the analysis is organized around three general questions: Do male and female adolescents differ in their exposure to peers, and, more specifically, in their exposure to delinquent peers? Are males and females who are exposed to delinquent peers differentially affected by those peers? And if males and females are affected differently by exposure to delinquent peers, why is this true?

The third question is the most fundamental, and it requires elaboration. Some analysts have speculated that same-sex friendships among male and female adolescents are qualitatively different, with male culture placing greater emphasis on daring or risk-taking. Without denying that possibility, the present analysis stems from a rather different premise. That is, we suspect that females ordinarily possess something that acts as a barrier to inhibit or block the influence of delinquent peers.

What might that barrier be? One possible answer lies with moral evaluations of conduct. The notion that individuals refrain from conduct because they morally disapprove of it has a long history in criminology, but it appears in a wide variety of theoretical guises (e.g., subcultural theory, religiosity and crime, deterrence theory), and research on the issue, although promising, is not systematic, comparable, or cumulative.

Nevertheless, if moral evaluations do affect conduct, how does that bear on gender differences in offending? Gilligan has suggested that females are socialized in such a way that they are more constrained by moral evaluations of behavior than are males. In her influential book, Gilligan argued that moral development in females is guided by the primacy of human relationships and by an overriding obligation to care for and to avoid harming others. This other-oriented quality of female moral development, she added, contrasts sharply with the moral socialization of males. If the moral imperative of women is "an injunction to care," Gilligan argued, men tend to construe morality in more utilitarian terms, that is, as a set of mutually acknowledged rights that protect them from *interference* from others. Thus, the driving principle of male morality is not responsibility to others, but the freedom to pursue self-interest. These gender-linked differences in socialization described by Gilligan imply that females will be more reluctant than males to engage in conduct that harms others, including criminal conduct.

Gilligan did not present direct empirical evidence for her thesis, but research on moral development in children and adolescents provides support for her argument. Although males and females evidently do not differ in the complexity of moral reasoning, there appear to be qualitative differences in such reasoning. In longitudinal and cross-sectional studies of children and adolescents, Eisenberg, Fabes, and Shea have observed

that from the age of about 11 or 12, girls "are more other-oriented in their prosocial moral reasoning than are boys." Similarly, Gibbs, Arnold, and Burkhart report that moral judgments among females rely on a greater degree of "empathic role-taking," and Bebeau and Brabek found that females display a higher degree of "ethical sensitivity" to others than do males.

If moral evaluations of conduct do function as a barrier to peer influence, and if that barrier is higher for females than for males, then we ought to observe a strong difference in the effect of delinquent peers on males and females, a difference that is itself conditioned by sex-linked differences in moral evaluations....

Data and Measures

Data for this study come from the National Youth Survey (NYS), a continuing longitudinal study of delinquent behavior among a national probability sample of 1,725 persons aged 11 to 17 in 1976. The NYS sample was obtained through a multistage probability sampling of households in the continental United States. In each wave of the study, respondents were asked a series of questions about events and behavior that occurred during the preceding year. Although the first wave of interviews was conducted in 1976, data for the present analysis come from Wave III of the NYS ($N = 1,626$), which captured respondents during the period of adolescence (ages 13 to 19).

The NYS collects self-report data on a wide range of delinquent behaviors, using the general question, "How many times in the last year have you [act]?" In addition to their own behavior, respondents are asked questions about the friends who they "ran around with," friends who they are asked to identify by name and who they are requested to think of whenever answering questions about peers. For our purposes, the crucial variable of interest is the number of delinquent friends reported by the respondent, measured by the question, "Think of your friends. During the last year how many of them have [act]?" (1 = *none of them*, 2 = *very few of them*, 3 = *some of them*, 4 = *most of them*, 5 = *all of them*). Respondents' moral evaluations of each act were measured by responses to the following question: "How wrong do you think it is for someone your age to [act]?" (1 = *not wrong at all*, 2 = *a little bit wrong*, 3 = *wrong*, 4 = *very wrong*).

Although the NYS collects data on a large number of offenses, questions concerning peer delinquency, respondents' delinquency, and moral evaluations are asked about different sets of offenses, sets that only partially overlap. Precisely comparable data on all three of these dimensions are available for only a small number of offenses. Three of these—marijuana use, alcohol use, and cheating—exhibit only minimal sex differences (the smallest, in fact, of any offenses measured in the NYS). Another three—burglary, grand theft, and selling hard drugs—are among the most highly sex-differentiated offenses, but they are so rare among females that virtually none of the females in the sample committed the offenses. Fortunately, there is one offense—theft of property worth less than $5—that exhibits a large sex difference (a male/female ratio of 2.0) and is sufficiently common among both sexes to afford statistical analysis. The analysis will therefore concentrate on this offense, but we have taken care to include data on other offenses in the analysis whenever possible.

Findings

The first aim of the analysis is to describe sex differences in delinquent behavior using data from the NYS.... Gender differences in delinquency are quite pervasive, but they vary a good deal from one offense to the next. The largest differences are found among the most serious offenses, where the ratio of male to female offenders exceeds 5:1 (grand theft) and even 8:1 (burglary). By contrast, drug offenses (alcohol and marijuana use), as stated earlier, exhibit little or no sex difference in prevalence, as does cheating on school tests. These patterns are evident regardless of whether one considers the prevalence of offenders...or the mean incidence of offending.

...Are males and females differentially exposed to delinquent peers? The data...show that, compared to females, males spend more time on average with their friends (delinquent or not) on weekday afternoons and evenings, but not on weekends. The differences are not large, however, amounting to less than half an afternoon or evening per week. A much more stark contrast between the sexes, however, is evident...[when looking at] the percentage of male and female respondents who reported that at least some of their friends had committed each offense. The differences are once again minimal for cheating and for drug and alcohol use. Among the remaining offenses, however, the proportion of males who have delinquent friends exceeds that of females by factors of approximately 1.5 to 2.5, or by differences in the range of about 10 to 25 percent. The most general or inclusive item, simply "break the law," has a male/female ratio of roughly 2:1.

Males, it seems, are substantially more likely than females to be exposed to delinquent friends....

Now recall the second major question: Are males and females *affected* differently by delinquent friends?...

The evidence...points to an initial conclusion: males are more strongly affected by delinquent friends than are females. Why is this true? As we postulated earlier, the answer may lie in the constraining effect of moral evaluations. Before turning to a direct test of that hypothesis, let us first consider some preliminary evidence. [Concerning] the percentage of male and female respondents who rated each offense in the NYS as "very wrong," [t]he difference between the sexes in these ratings is statistically significant in every case, with females more apt than males to rate the offenses as very wrong. But consistent though these differences may be,...sex differences in moral evaluations are not in themselves sufficient to explain sex differences in delinquency. The sex effect...remains strong and statistically significant even after controlling for differences in moral evaluations of the offense....

Much more critical is the role of moral evaluations in regulating or conditioning the effect of delinquent peers....A close look at the [data] reveals that the effect of delinquent peers diminishes very rapidly as moral disapproval increases. Moral evaluations, then, do appear to mitigate or counteract the influence of delinquent peers.

Having laid the necessary foundation, we may now turn to the central hypothesis of this study: Do moral evaluations of conduct provide a stronger barrier to peer influence among females than among males?…

…Among both males and females, moral evaluations act to regulate or restrain the effect of delinquent peers.… But the impact of those evaluations is different for the two sexes. Among males and females who show little or no disapproval of the act…, the effect of delinquent peers is very similar; both groups exhibit strong sensitivity to peers. As moral disapproval increases, however, males and females diverge from one another, with females showing less susceptibility than males to peer influence. In fact, among females who strongly disapprove of the offense…, the effect of delinquent friends is effectively *eliminated*…, meaning that females in this category are essentially immune to peer influence. But the same cannot be said of males, for whom peers continue to have a statistically significant effect even when moral disapproval is strong.

Conclusion

The findings of this study point to several tentative conclusions. Males and females differ in exposure to delinquent peers, with males substantially more likely than females to have delinquent friends. This differential exposure contributes to sex differences in delinquency, but it is not the sole source of those differences. Quite aside from differences in exposure to peers, males appear to be more strongly affected by delinquent peers than are females. This fact, in turn, evidently reflects the greater effect of moral evaluations in counteracting peer influence among females. Although the number of delinquent peers an adolescent has is the strongest known predictor of delinquent behavior, the moral judgments of females are apparently sufficient to reduce and even eliminated the impact of delinquent peers.

Why are moral evaluations of behavior so effective in combating peer influence among females? Given the results of our analysis, it would be difficult to reject the argument by Gilligan and others that the primary socialization of women instills moral values that strongly discourage behavior that hurts or harms others. To be sure, our analysis is not a direct test of Gilligan's thesis, if only

because it focused on the intensity rather than the quality of moral evaluations and did not examine the socialization process itself. Nevertheless, the results of this analysis clearly attest to the power of moral evaluations among females, and they demonstrate that the consequence of those evaluations is to reduce the frequency of antisocial behavior among females.

Our analysis also suggests that it is fruitless to construct utterly different theories to explain the delinquency of males and females. As we have seen, both males and females are affected—though to different degrees—by a common factor: association with delinquent friends. What differs between the sexes, it seems, are not the *generative* factors that give rise to delinquency, but rather the *inhibitory* factors that prevent or counteract it. Although we have focused on peer influence in this analysis, it may be the case that, among females, moral evaluations counteract a variety of criminogenic conditions, from economic deprivation to dysfunctional family organization. If the present analysis is any indicator, there may be few, if any, generative factors that can overcome the moral constraints of most females. Viewed that way, the enormous sex ratios in offending observed in these and other data seem less startling or inexplicable.

There is at least one factor, however, that may neutralize the moral evaluations of females, one that bears directly on the phenomenon of peer influence. Several studies conducted during the past two decades suggest that, for some females, delinquency is a consequence of exposure to delinquent males. Giordano, for example, reported that girls who spend time in mixed-sex groups are significantly more likely to engage in delinquency than are girls who participate in same-sex groups. Warr found that females were much more likely than males to report that the instigator in their delinquent group was of the opposite sex. Stattin and Magnusson discovered that elevated levels of delinquency among females who experience early menarche is attributable to their tendency to associate with older males, and Caspi et al. observed that New Zealand girls in all-female schools were significantly less likely to engage in delinquency than were girls in mixed-sex schools.

Despite this evidence, it remains unclear just how often males contribute to the delinquency of females, and it is equally unclear whether the relations that link male and female offenders are ordinarily romantic in nature or similar to those of same-sex offenders. Nevertheless, there remains the intriguing possibility that relations with males are one of the few generative factors capable of overcoming the strong moral objections that females commonly hold toward illegal behavior.

One final theoretical issue deserves attention. Although the conceptualization of delinquency employed here borrows heavily from Sutherland's theory of differential association, it nonetheless differs from that theory in at least one respect. According to Sutherland's theory, delinquency is a consequence of attitudes or "definitions" acquired from others, attitudes that ostensibly include moral evaluations of behavior. Individuals, in short, become delinquent by adopting the attitudes of significant others. Tests of differential association. however, consistently indicate that attitude transference among peers is not the primary mechanism by which delinquency is transmitted, implying that

other, more direct, mechanisms of social learning (e.g., imitation, direct and vicarious reinforcement) may be at work. Our findings, too, cast doubt on the notion of attitude transference that undergirds Sutherland's theory. It appears from our analysis that the moral evaluations of adolescents—especially females—are frequently a barrier that restrains peer influence rather than a conduit that transmits it. If that interpretation is correct, then Sutherland's theory may require modification.

Discussion Questions

1. Which gender commits more offenses at every age, within all racial or ethnic groups examined to date?

2. For which gender do moral evaluations of conduct provide a stronger barrier to peer influence?

3. What is one of the few generative factors capable of overcoming the strong moral objections that females commonly hold toward illegal behavior?

CHAPTER 13

Intelligence (IQ) and Criminal Behavior

Scott Menard

Whereas gender and age are considered very strong correlates of crime, some factors are weakly linked and highly disputed. Intelligence is one of those factors. In one of the earliest positivistic theories of crime, Lombroso argued that criminals were less intelligent, less evolved atavists who differed significantly from the general population. More precise tests of the link between intelligence and crime have produced mixed results. Overall, it appears that there is a weak to moderate correlation between intelligence, as measured by IQ, and criminal offending. What is less known is the precise nature and direction of this relationship.

In the following selection, "Intelligence (IQ) and Criminal Behavior," Scott Menard examines the causal nature of the relationship after first reviewing the historical work on IQ and crime. In the second section, he discusses major limitations to measuring both crime and intelligence. Neither of these concepts is necessarily easy to operationalize and even more difficult to accurately ascertain through available data. The seven major hypotheses related to the IQ–crime link are examined prior to a summary of the major research conducted to date.

Historically, a relationship between intelligence and crime was suggested as early as 1876 by Cesare Lombroso, who suggested that at least some criminals were atavisms, biological throwbacks to

Reprinted from *Encyclopedia of Criminology*, 2005 by R.A. Wright and J.M. Miller (Eds) pp. 750–754 New York, New York: Routledge Publisher.

an earlier stage of human evolution, inferior to normal, law-abiding individuals both physically and mentally. In 1905, Alfred Binet and Theodore Simon developed a test of general intelligence for use in the public schools, then revised the test in 1908 to incorporate the concept of mental age. Subsequent revisions of Binet's intelligence test, with the addition of the concept of mental age and the intelligence quotient (IQ), equal to the mental age divided by the chronological age and multiplied by 100, produced the familiar IQ test. (For a general review of early studies of intelligence and crime, see Vold et al., 1998, Chapt. 5.)

Henry Goddard translated the Binet intelligence test and administered it to all of the inmates of the Training School for the Feeble-Minded at Vineland, New Jersey, where he was the director of the research center. Goddard found that none of the inmates had a mental age over 13. Based on this, he concluded that mental age 12 (IQ 75) marked the upper limit of feeblemindedness. He also examined studies of feeblemindedness in institutionalized criminals, and found that 28–89% were feebleminded by this criterion. In his 1914 book *Feeble-Mindedness: Its Causes and Consequences*, he estimated that 70% of the criminal population was feebleminded. In a related finding, W. Healy and A.F. Bronner in their book *Delinquency and Criminals: Their Making and Unmaking*, published in 1926, showed that 37% of tested delinquents in Chicago and Boston were subnormal in their intelligence, and concluded that delinquents were 5–10 times more likely to be mentally deficient than

139

nondelinquents. Later research using Goddard's criterion for feeblemindedness, however, found that 37% of white and 89% of black draftees during World War I were feebleminded. Subsequently, the definition of feeblemindedness was revised downward to an IQ of 50 (mental age 8) or below, and Goddard abandoned not only his original criterion for feeblemindedness but also some of his more extreme positions, in which he had denied the possibility of ameliorating feeblemindedness through education, and in which he had espoused segregating feebleminded individuals in institutions and preventing them from reproducing.

Measuring Intelligence and Measuring Crime

IQ became the principal criterion used in studies of the relationship between intelligence and crime for the remainder of the 20th century. The early researchers in the field of intelligence and crime generally contended (or assumed) that IQ was an innate, genetic characteristic of individuals. Critics of the IQ–delinquency or IQ–crime hypothesis argue that despite strong test–retest correlations for IQ, there is extensive evidence indicating that IQ scores are responsive to social environmental factors (Simons, 1978; see also Menard and Morse, 1984, 1352, note 7). In evaluating the relationship between intelligence and crime, this is a peripheral issue. The assumption that IQ is "constant" over the life span, or "innate," or predominantly "genetic," is *not* critical to the hypothesis that intelligence affects illegal behavior. Instead, the combination of constancy (at least in *differences* in IQ scores) and innateness of IQ, plus the correlation between IQ and crime, is used to argue that some individuals are innately (and by implication genetically) more predisposed to crime than others.

A second, more critical question that has been raised in studies of the relationship between IQ and crime is, what exactly is the IQ test measuring? Advocates of IQ testing argued that it measured a general ability for abstract reasoning and problem solving. Detractors argued that it measured social learning rather than native intelligence, and also noted that IQ tests were sensitive to conditions of administration of the test and to the motivation

and stress level of the test takers. To the extent that IQ tests systematically measure something other than or in addition to intelligence, differences in IQ between criminals and noncriminals (and also, incidentally, between members of higher and lower socioeconomic groups, or majority and minority ethnic groups) may be attributable to that "something else": testing conditions, motivation, or cultural bias. Although this does not invalidate the existence of a correlation between the *IQ test* and crime, it may not reflect a correlation between *intelligence* and crime. Instead, the relationship between IQ test scores and crime may reflect, for example, differences between criminals and noncriminals in how well they have learned mainstream culture. In the context of comparing incarcerated criminals with nonincarcerated individuals, it may reflect differences in how benign or hostile the test environment is in a criminal justice institution as opposed to an educational institution, rather than differences in intelligence. In the latter case, moreover, because the condition of test administration may occur *after* one has been arrested or otherwise processed by the justice system, it would be more reasonable to interpret any correlation between IQ test scores and crime as indicating that involvement in the justice system is a cause of lower IQ test scores, rather than indicating that lower IQ is a cause of involvement in the justice system.

In addition to issues regarding the measurement of intelligence, studies of the relationship between intelligence and crime have been beset with problems in how to measure illegal behavior. The use of official data on arrests and convictions has been criticized by Scott Menard and Barbara Morse (1984, 1348), among others, who suggest that self-reported illegal behavior is a more valid measure of illegal behavior. Menard and Morse based their criticisms on an extensive literature on the reliability and validity of self-report as opposed to official measures of illegal behavior, which generally indicated a much higher validity for self-report studies than for official data on most offenses (about 80% accuracy for self-reports, about 25–50% for official data on more serious offenses, and less than 5% for official data on illicit drug use and some less serious offenses; but official homicide and motor vehicle theft data are probably over 90% valid). Comparisons between incarcerated offenders and the general population are especially problematic, first because the general population includes criminals who are not presently incarcerated (offenders who are undetected, or on probation or parole), and second because incarcerated offenders may disproportionately consist of offenders unintelligent enough (low IQ) to get caught. This latter possibility is made all the more plausible by the finding that low IQ scores are more highly correlated with official than with self-reported crime and delinquency (Hirschi and Hindelang, 1977).

Richard J. Herrnstein and his associates (Wilson and Herrnstein, 1985; Hermstein and Murray, 1994) and other proponents of the hypothesis that intelligence is a risk factor for crime have acknowledged that incarcerated offenders may have lower intelligence than offenders who are not incarcerated. Possible explanations include: the simple proposition that more intelligent criminals are less likely to get caught; the possibility that more intelligent offenders have the opportunity to commit crimes such as embezzlement and other white-collar crimes that pose less risk of detection and apprehension than "street crimes" like robbery and burglary; the possibility that more intelligent respondents are more likely to conceal their illegal behavior on self-reports; and the assertion that incarcerated offenders account for most of the crime anyway, so there is little left to be accounted for by the nonincarcerated offenders. The first two propositions are plausible. There is no evidence to support the third (and it could be argued with equal force that less intelligent respondents might underreport or over report their illegal behavior because of their inability to fully understand the questions). The last assertion is highly suspect, relying on official statistics' underestimates of the actual amount of illegal behavior that occurs.

Research Evidence on the IQ–Crime Relationship

Evidence contrary to the hypothesis that low intelligence leads to crime began to accumulate not long after the publication of the studies by Healy and Bronner and by Goddard. (Again, see Vold et al., 1998, Ch. 5, for a review of earlier studies of the relationship between intelligence and crime.) In his book *Brothers in Crime,* published in 1938, Clifford R. Shaw reported that delinquents generally were not different, with respect to intelligence, from people in conventional society. Evidence from a longitudinal study of treatment outcomes for boys, the Cambridge–Somerville Youth Study, published in William and Joan McCord's (1959) *Origins of Crime,* indicated that intelligence was not strongly related to crime. Similarly, the research of Sheldon and Eleanor Glueck, later reanalyzed by Robert J. Sampson and John H. Laub in their (1993) *Crime in the Making,* indicated no consistent relationship between intelligence and delinquency.

Other research indicated that there was a weak-to-moderate relationship between intelligence and delinquency. Marvin E. Wolfgang, Robert M. Figlio, and Thorsten Sellin's (1972) *Delinquency in a Birth Cohort* found that in their cohort of Philadelphia boys, the IQ scores for delinquents were 8–11 points lower than for nondelinquents, controlling for black or white ethnicity and higher or lower social class. In England, D.J. West (1982) in *Delinquency: Its Roots, Careers, and Prospects* found a six-point difference in IQ at ages 8–10 between boys who did and did not become delinquent during their teen years. Robert Gordon (1987) reported consistency in several studies of modest negative correlations (in the low-to-high 0.20s) between IQ and delinquency in populations whose average IQ would be close to 100. Reviews by Herbert Quay (1987) and by Travis Hirschi and Michael Hindelang (1977) indicate that IQ differences of 8–12 points, and correlations of 0.17–0.27, are commonly found in studies of IQ and delinquency or crime, with the delinquents consistently having lower IQ scores than the nondelinquents.

More detailed examination of the IQ–crime relationship indicates that there is a difference between verbal intelligence and nonverbal or performance intelligence. Using the Wechsler IQ test, which distinguishes between verbal and performance IQ, delinquents disproportionately had higher performance IQ than verbal IQ scores, a result that is more evident for boys than for girls (Quay, 1987). Although the results reported by

Quay are somewhat mixed, it appears that the discrepancy between verbal and performance IQ is attributable primarily to lower verbal IQ scores for delinquents. This once again raises the issue of social learning as opposed to innate ability, as language learning is dependent on socialization.

In a variant of the intelligence–crime relationship, learning disabilities have also been found to be related to illegal behavior (Keilitz et al., 1979). Although learning disabilities should not be equated with intelligence, the pattern of the relationship is the same, with learning disability being correlated with illegal behavior, more so for official than for self-report data. Keilitz et al. (1979) reported that learning-disabled children were more likely to be official delinquents than children in the general population (and official delinquents were twice as likely to be learning disabled as children in the general population), but there were no differences in self-reported illegal behavior between learning-disabled children and children who were not learning disabled.

Several possible explanations of the relationship between intelligence and crime have been proposed, and are stated here as hypotheses.

Hypothesis 1: Intelligence has a direct influence on crime, with criminal behavior resulting from an inability to understand or conform to norms and laws, or from lower levels of moral reasoning or development that result from lower intelligence (Wilson and Herrnstein, 1985, 169).

Hypothesis 2: Low intelligence has an indirect influence on crime, with criminal behavior resulting from a weakening of social controls or from strain, where the weakened controls or strain are caused by low intelligence. One variation on this theme is suggested by Hirschi and Hindelang (1977), who argue that low IQ leads to school failure and negative attitudes toward the school and teachers, producing a lower level of social control, which in turn results in delinquency. Keilitz et al. (1979, 101) describe a similar "school failure rationale" that has been used to explain the relationship of learning disabilities to delinquency.

Hypothesis 3: Low intelligence is a risk factor, not for crime itself, but for getting caught if you commit a crime, as discussed above (Wilson and Herrnstein, 1985; Herrnstein and Murray, 1994).

Hypothesis 4: Low intelligence is a source of social discrimination, which in turn may produce strain and weaken social controls (Menard and Morse, 1984). In this explanation, it is not low intelligence itself, but the negative social response to low intelligence, that would properly be regarded as the cause of crime, and which would need to be modified in order to reduce illegal behavior. This explanation parallels the differential treatment hypothesis suggested by Keilitz et al. (1979) as an explanation for the relationship between learning disabilities and illegal behavior. It is also consistent with differences between official and self-report data in intelligence-delinquency and learning-disability–delinquency correlations.

Hypothesis 5: The relationship between intelligence and illegal behavior is spurious. In particular, low social class and ethnic minority status produce both lower IQ scores and higher rates of illegal behavior.

Hypothesis 6: Low intelligence may be an indirect effect of, rather than an indirect cause of, illegal behavior. For example, Deborah Denno (1985) suggests that there is no direct link between mental ability and delinquency, and raises the possibility that delinquency leads to low school performance, which in turn is reflected in low IQ scores.

Hypothesis 7: Although low intelligence may not be a risk factor for crime, high intelligence is a protective factor, not in the sense that it reduces crime for everyone, but in the sense that it reduces criminal behavior in individuals *who are otherwise at risk* for committing crimes (Werner and Smith, 1982).

Hypotheses 1, 2, and, more indirectly, 3 and 4, have been tested in empirical research on the "school failure" model. Both Menard and Morse (1984) and David A. Ward and Charles R. Tittle (1994) tested variants of the model suggested by Hirschi and Hindelang, incorporating measures of IQ, school performance, school attitudes, and self-reported delinquency. For all of the models tested (two by Menard and Morse, three—one with two different methods of estimation—by Ward and Tittle), the explained variance was small, with IQ accounting for only 4–5% of the differences in delinquency. Menard and Morse (1984) also tested two pairs of models (one each for minor and serious delinquency), one of which included only variables from an integrated theory of illegal behavior, and the other of which added IQ, scholastic aptitude (the Differential Aptitude Test or DAT), and school performance (grade point average or GPA). The integrated theory used by Menard and Morse suggested that lack of access to desirable social roles could lead to premature and inappropriate negative labeling, which could in turn exacerbate the lack of access to desirable social roles. Taken together, lack of access plus negative labeling could lead to alienation from conventional social contexts (home and school) and association with delinquent peers, which in turn led to delinquency.

The models with only the variables from the integrated theory explained 20% of the variance (differences) between individuals in serious delinquency, and 29% of the variance in minor delinquency. The addition of IQ, scholastic aptitude, and school performance resulted in a negligible increase (less than 1%) in explained variance. None of these models indicated a direct effect from IQ to delinquency, as suggested in Hypothesis 1, and the results from Menard and Morse (1984) suggest that there is no need to include even an indirect effect as suggested by Hypothesis 2. Menard and Morse interpreted their results as being consistent with a differential reaction model, as described by Keilitz et al. (1979).

In general, the suggestion in Hypothesis 5 that the relationship between intelligence and crime is spurious, and in Hypothesis 6 that illegal behavior affects intelligence, is speculative, with little or no basis in empirical research. Studies have examined socioeconomic status or race as explanations for both intelligence and crime with the finding that IQ is more closely related to crime than race or social class, and that IQ is related to crime even controlling for social class or ethnicity (Hirschi and Hindelang, 1977; Gordon, 1987), findings contrary to the suggestion that the relationship is spurious with social class or ethnicity. Neither race nor social class is terribly strongly related to illegal behavior to begin with, however, especially when illegal behavior is measured by self-reports (Menard and Morse, 1984, 1348), so the persistence of a relationship between IQ and illegal behavior

controlling only for these variables is insufficient to establish the importance of intelligence as a cause of crime. There is some limited research evidence in support of Hypothesis 7 that higher intelligence may reduce the probability of involvement in crime for individuals who are otherwise at high risk for illegal behavior (Werner and Smith, 1982; Herrnstein and Murray, 1994).

Conclusion

Most criminologists would probably agree that there is a small, consistently replicated correlation between intelligence and crime. Some would suggest that there is a direct influence of intelligence on illegal behavior, either as a risk factor for crime or as a protective factor, reducing the probability of illegal behavior for individuals otherwise at risk. Still others would argue that the relationship between intelligence and crime, although causal, is indirect. None of these positions, however, receives strong support from research, especially when self-report data and adequate controls for theoretically important variables are included. A serious limitation on this research, however, is the focus on juvenile delinquency. Comparable research has not been done on adults, not surprisingly, given the dearth of self-report data on adult respondents. On balance: (1) a good case can be made that intelligence is weakly correlated with illegal behavior; (2) the evidence is inadequate to support the contention that low intelligence *causes* criminal behavior, and in fact is more consistent with the contention that intelligence is neither a direct nor an indirect cause of crime; but (3) it would be advisable to conduct further research into the relationship between intelligence and crime for adults, and also the possible contribution of intelligence as a protective factor for individuals who are otherwise (based on characteristics other than intelligence) at high risk of involvement in illegal behavior.

References

Denno, D. 1985. Sociological and human developmental explanations of crime: Conflict or consensus, *Criminology* 23.

Gordon, R.A. 1987. SES versus IQ in the Race-IQ-Delinquency Model, *International Journal of Sociology and Social Policy* 7.

Herrnstein, R.J. and Murray, C. 1994. *The Bell Curve: Intelligence and Class Structure in the United States,* New York, NY: Free Press.

Hirschi, T. and Hindelang, M.J. 1997. Intelligence and delinquency: A revisionist review, *American Sociological Review* 42.

Keilitz, I., Zaremba, B.A., and Broder, P.K. 1979. The link between learning disabilities and juvenile delinquency: Some issues and answers, *Learning Disability Quarterly* 2.

Menard, S. and Morse, B.J. 1984. A structuralist critique of the IQ-delinquency hypothesis: Theory and evidence, *American Journal of Sociology* 89.

Quay, H.C. 1984. Intelligence, *Handbook of Juvenile Delinquency,* Quay, H.C. (Ed.), New York, NY: Wiley.

Simons, R.L. 1978. The meaning of the IQ-delinquency relationship, *American Sociological Review* 43.

Vold, G.B., Bernard, T.J., and Snipes, J.B. 1998. *Theoretical Criminology,* 4th ed., New York, NY: Oxford University Press.

Ward, D.A. and Tittle, C.R. 1994. IQ and delinquency: A test of two competing explanations, *Journal of Quantitative Criminology* 10.

Werner, E.E. and Smith, R. 1982. *Vulnerable but Invincible: A Longitudinal Study of Resilient Children and Youth,* New York, NY: McGraw-Hill.

Wilson, J.Q. and Herrnstein, R.J. 1985. *Crime and Human Nature,* New York, NY: Touchstone.

CHAPTER 14

Family Relationships, Juvenile Delinquency, and Adult Criminality

Joan McCord

The role of the family in juvenile delinquency has long been debated by criminologists and family sociologists. Because the family is the child's primary socializing agent, it has been natural to look there for explanations of antisocial behavior. This tendency has been strengthened by the popularity of personality-development theories, which seem to place responsibility for all behavior on early family experiences. Do bad parents create bad children who grow up to become bad adults? Some people seem to think so. Researchers have also looked at birth order to determine its impact on the behavior of children. Although personality differences can apparently be found among siblings by order of birth, this difference has not been related to delinquency and crime. Broken homes have been singled out for blame by many critics who see the family instability caused by divorce and separation as detrimental to the behavioral development of the child. And these are but a few of the family variables that have been hypothesized to be related to juvenile delinquency and even to adult crime.

This selection by Joan McCord uses longitudinal data from a classic study of delinquency to address two important questions: Do family interactions in childhood influence criminality among males, and if so, what is the nature of these interactions? Do maternal or paternal interactions influence

the child's delinquency? McCord found that childhood family relationships and interactive patterns do influence criminal behavior. The mother's competence in carrying out the maternal role and the expectations the family had of the child influenced the likelihood of delinquency. Competent mothers with high expectations of their child seem to insulate him against juvenile delinquency in the adolescent years. This insulation has an impact on adult criminality as well, as boys who do not become delinquent are less likely to engage in adult crime. Although it is the mother who insulates and nurtures the child as a juvenile, it is the father who appears to provide the role model for the son as an adult. The father's interaction with the family is more probable to have a direct influence on the son's adult criminality.

McCord's work establishes the important role family relationships play in determining delinquency and crime. Although mothers appear to play the more important role in determining the juvenile's behavior, paternal influence is also important, as fathers teach sons how to behave as adults.

Theoretical Perspective

Historically, family interactions have been assumed to influence criminal behavior. Plato, for example, prescribed a regimen for rearing good citizens in the nursery. Aristotle asserted that in order to be virtuous, "we ought to have been brought up in a particular way from our very youth" (Bk.II, Ch. 3:11048). And John Locke wrote his letters on the education of children in the belief that errors "carry

Reprinted from: Joan McCord, "Family Relationships, Juvenile Delinquency, and Adult Criminality." In *Criminology* 29, pp. 397-417. Copyright © 1991 by American Society of Criminology. Reprinted by permission of Joan McCord and American Society of Criminology.

their afterwards-incorrigible taint with them, through all the parts and stations of life" (1693:iv).

Twentieth century theorists ranging from the analytic to the behavioral seem to concur with the earlier thinkers in assuming that parental care is critical to socialized behavior. Theorists have suggested that inadequate families fail to provide the attachments that could leverage children into socialized lifestyles (e.g., Hirschi, 1969). They note that poor home environments provide a backdrop for children to associate differentially with those who have antisocial definitions of their environments (e.g., Sutherland and Cressey, 1974). And they point out that one feature of inadequate child rearing is that it fails to reward desired behavior and fails to condemn behavior that is not desired (e.g., Akers, 1973; Bandura and Walters, 1959).

Over the past several decades, social scientists have suggested that crime is a product of broken homes (e.g., Bacon et al., 1963; Burt, 1925; Fenichel, 1945; Freud, 1953; Goode, 1956; Murdock, 1949; Parsons and Bales, 1955; Shaw and McKay, 1932; Wadsworth, 1979), maternal employment (e.g., Glueck and Glueck, 1950; Nye, 1959), and maternal rejection (Bowlby, 1940, 1951; Goldfarb, 1945; Newell, 1934, 1936). Some have linked effects from broken homes with the impact parental absence has on sex-role identity (Bacon et al., 1963; Lamb, 1976; Levy, 1937; Miller, 1958; Whiting et al., 1958), and others have suggested that parental absence and maternal employment affect crime through contributing to inadequate supervision (e.g., Dornbusch et al., 1985; Hirschi, 1969; Hoffman, 1975; Maccoby, 1958; Nye, 1958).

Despite this long tradition, empirical support demonstrating the link between child rearing and criminal behavior has been weak. Accounting for this fact, Hirschi (1983) suggested that attributing behavioral differences to socialization practiced in the family is "directly contrary to the metaphysic of our age" (p. 54). Hirschi criticized the few studies that refer to family influences for using global measures of inadequacy, noting that they cannot yield information about the practices or policies that might reduce criminality.

Most of the evidence made available since Hirschi's appraisal has depended on information from adolescents who have simultaneously reported their parents' behavior and their own delinquencies (e.g., Cernkovich and Giordano, 1987; Hagan et al., 1985; Jensen and Brownfield, 1983; van Voorhis et al., 1988). Because these studies are based on data reporting delinquency and socialization variables at the same time, they are unable to disentangle causes from effects.

Two studies based on adolescents' reports have addressed the sequencing issue. Both used data collected by the Youth in Transition Project from adolescents at ages 15 and 17 years (Bachman and O'Malley, 1984). Liska and Reed (1985) looked at changes in delinquency related to parent-adolescent interaction; their analyses suggest that friendly interaction with parents (attachment) retards delinquency, which in turn, promotes school attachment and stronger family ties. Wells and Rankin (1988) considered the efficacy of various dimensions of direct control on delinquency; their analyses suggest that restrictiveness, but not harshness, inhibits delinquency. Although the same data base was used for the two studies, neither considered variables that appeared in the other, so the issues of relative importance and of collinearity among child-rearing parameters were not examined.

Relying on adolescents to report about their parents' child-rearing behavior assumes that the adolescents have correctly perceived, accurately recalled, and honestly reported the behavior of their parents. There are grounds for questioning those assumptions.

Experimental studies show that conscious attention is unnecessary for experiences to be influential (Kellogg, 1980); thus adolescents' reports reflecting this bias would tend to blur real differences in upbringing.

In addition, studies of perception and recall suggest that reports about child rearing are likely to be influenced by the very features under study as possible consequences of faulty child rearing. For example, abused children tend to perceive their parents as less punitive than revealed by objective evidence (Dean et al., 1986; J. McCord, 1983a); aggressive children tend to perceive behavior justifying aggression (Dodge and Somberg, 1987); and painful experience tends to exaggerate recall of painful events (Eich et al., 1990). Yet, criminologists have paid little attention to measurement issues related to ascertaining the impact of socialization within families.

Studies of the impact of child rearing suffer from special problems. When the source of data is children's reports on their parents' behavior, effects and causes are likely to be confounded. When parents report on their own behavior, they are likely to have a limited and biasing perspective and to misrepresent what they are willing to reveal. These biases have been shown in a study that included home observations as well as mothers' reports. The child's compliance was related to observed, although not to reported, behavior of the mother (Forehand et al., 1978). Eron and his coworkers (1961) discovered that even when fathers and mothers reported similarly about events, "the relation to other variables was not the same for the two groups of parents" (p. 471). Additionally, regardless of the source of information, if data are collected after the onset of misbehavior, distortions of memory give rise to biases.

Attention to problems of measurement characterize two studies of juvenile crime. In one, Larzelere and Patterson (1990) combined interviews with the child and his parents, observations, and the interviewer's impressions to create measures of discipline and monitoring. They found strong collinearity and therefore used a combined measure of "parental management." Data on family management were collected when the children were approximately nine years old. This variable mediated a relationship between socioeconomic status and delinquency as reported by the boys when they were 13. Larzelere and Patterson acknowledge that their measure of delinquency may be premature, but they point out that early starters tend to become the more serious criminals.

In the other study, Laub and Sampson (1988) reanalyzed data from the files compiled by Sheldon Glueck and Eleanor Glueck (1950). They built measures of family discipline, parent-child relations, and maternal supervision from multiple sources of information. The variables indicated that child-rearing processes bore strong relations to juvenile delinquency, as measured through official records. Laub and Sampson concluded that "family process and delinquency are related not just independent

of traditional sociological controls, but of biosocial controls as well" (p. 374).

Other researchers have focused on different parts of the child-rearing process. Selection seems to be more a matter of style than a result of considered evidence. In reviewing studies of family socialization, Loeber and Stouthamer-Loeber (1986) concluded that parental neglect had the largest impact on crime. They also suggested the possibility of a sleeper effect from socialization practices, although they noted that reports by different members of the family have little convergence.

Problems in collecting information make the few extant longitudinal data sets that include family interactions particularly valuable. The Cambridge-Somerville Youth Study data provided evidence about childhood milieu and family interaction collected during childhood. The data were based on observations of family processes by a variety of people over a period of several years.

Prior analyses of the data, based on a follow-up when the men were in their late twenties, have provided evidence of predictive validity for many of the measures. The results of these earlier studies suggested that child-rearing practices mediate the conditions under which sons follow the footsteps of criminal fathers (J. McCord and W. McCord, 1958). They showed that child-rearing practices are correlated with concurrent aggressive behavior among nondelinquents (W. McCord et al., 1961) and contribute to promoting antisocial directions for aggressive behavior (J. McCord et al., 1963a). Analyses also indicated that the stability of family environments mediated results of maternal employment on concurrent characteristics of dependency and sex anxiety; only among unstable families did maternal employment seem to contribute to subsequent delinquency (J. McCord et al., 1963b). Probably the most critical test of the predictive worth of the coded variables appeared in the analyses of their relation to alcoholism (W. McCord and J. McCord, 1960). Spurred on by these results, I collected additional information from and about the men two decades later.

Prior analyses from this extended data base have suggested that parental affection acts as a protective factor against crime (J. McCord, 1983b,

1986) and alcoholism (J. McCord, 1988). Analyses also suggested that how parents responded to their son's aggressive behavior influenced whether early aggression continued through adolescence and emerged as criminal behavior (J. McCord, 1983b).

In tracing the comparative results of child abuse, neglect, and rejection, analyses indicated both that parental rejection was more criminogenic than either abuse or neglect and that vulnerability to alcoholism, mental illness, early death, and serious criminality was increased by having had an alcoholic, criminal, or aggressive parent (J. McCord, 1983a).

Prior analyses from these data have also shown that single-parent families are not more criminogenic than two-parent families—provided the mother is affectionate (J. McCord, 1982). Additional analyses of family structure indicated that although parental absence had a detrimental effect on delinquency, only when compounded by other family-related stresses did it have an apparent effect on serious criminal behavior, alcoholism, or occupational achievement (J. McCord, 1990).

Theories have emphasized one or another description of family life as important to healthy child development. Research concerned with bonding to, or identification with, socialized adults has focused on affection of parents for their children (e.g., Hirschi, 1969; W. McCord and J. McCord, 1959). Research based on either conditioning or dissonance theories has emphasized discipline and controls (e.g., Bandura and Walters, 1959; Baumrind, 1968, 1978, 1983; Lewis, 1981). And differential association and social learning theories give special weight to the nature of available models (e.g., Akers, 1973; Bandura and Walters, 1963; Sutherland and Cressey, 1974).

Because criminologists have rarely gone beyond describing home environments in globally evaluative terms, the same data could be interpreted as confirming the importance of family bonding or of providing firm control. In order to distinguish among effects, equally valid and reliable measurement of the different dimensions is needed, and collinearity among the measures must be taken into account. Although it is known that child rearing influences adult criminality (J. McCord, 1979, 1983b), there is little ground for judging the

extent to which one or another dimension of child rearing is important at different times. Thus, the question remains: In what ways does child rearing affect criminal behavior?

This study addresses two questions: (1) Are there particular features of child rearing that influence criminal outcomes or does only the general home atmosphere of childhood account for the relationship between conditions of socialization and crime? (2) Do similar influences operate to increase criminality at different ages?

Method

This study includes 232 boys who had been randomly selected for a treatment program that, although designed to prevent delinquency, included both well behaved and troubled youngsters. The boys were born between 1926 and 1933. They lived in congested, urban areas near Boston, Massachusetts. Counselors visited their homes about twice a month over a period of more than five years. Typically, the boys were between their tenth and sixteenth birthdays at the time of the visits.

One emphasis of the youth study was on developing sound case reports. Staff meetings included discussion of cases not only from the perspective of treatment but also to provide rounded descriptions of the child's life circumstances. After each visit with a boy or his parents, counselors dictated reports about what they saw and heard (see Powers and Witmer, 1951). The reports from visits to the boys' homes provided the raw material for subsequent analyses.

Child-Rearing Variables

In 1957, records were coded to describe the 232 families of the 253 boys who had remained in the program after an initial cut in 1941 (see W. McCord and J. McCord, 1960). Codes included ratings of family structure, family conflict, esteem of each parent for the other, parental supervision and disciplinary characteristics, parental warmth, self confidence, role, and aggressiveness. Codes also included parental alcoholism and criminality. The coding was designed for global assessments;

this type of rating helps to circumvent problems that would occur when measures depend on specific items of information that might be missing from any particular data collection effort.

Among the 232 families, 130 were intact through the boys' sixteenth year. There were 60 families in which mothers were not living with a man; 23 fathers had died and 37 were living elsewhere. There were 30 families with mother substitutes and 29 with father substitutes, including 17 in which both natural parents were absent. Information about absent parents came from their concurrent interactions with the boys or their mothers. Thirteen substitute fathers and 13 substitute mothers were rated.

Ratings for the mother's self-confidence were based on how she reacted when faced with problems. If she showed signs of believing in her ability to handle problems, she was rated as self-confident (N = 66). Alternative ratings were "no indication," "victim or pawn," and "neutral."

The attitude of a parent toward the boy was classified as "affectionate" if that parent interacted frequently with the child without being generally critical. Among the parents, 110 mothers and 59 fathers were rated as affectionate. Alternative classifications were "passively affectionate" (if the parent was concerned for the boy's welfare, but there was little interaction), "passively rejecting" (if the parent was unconcerned for the boy's welfare and interacted little), "actively rejecting" (if the parent was almost constantly critical of the boy), "ambivalent" (if the parents showed marked alternation between affection and rejection of the child), and "no indication."

Parental conflict reflected reports of disagreements about the child, values, money, alcohol, or religion. Ratings could be "no indication," "apparently none," "some," or "considerable." Parents were classified as evidencing (N = 75) or not evidencing considerable conflict.

A rating of each parent's esteem for the other was based on evidence indicating whether a parent showed respect for the judgment of the other. Ratings could be "no indication," "moderate or high," or "low." In this study, each parent was classified as showing or not showing moderate or high esteem for the other. Almost an equal number of mothers (N = 109) and fathers (N = 106) revealed relatively high esteem for their spouse.

Maternal restrictiveness was rated as "subnormal" if a mother permitted her son to make virtually all his choices without her guidance (N = 83). Alternative ratings were "no indications," "normal," and "overly restrictive."

Parental supervision was measured by the degree to which the boy's activities after school were governed by an adult. Supervision could be rated "present" (N = 132) or, alternatively, "sporadic," "absent," or "no information."

Discipline by each parent was classified into one of six categories. "Consistently punitive, including very harsh verbal abuse," identified a parent who used physical force to control the boy. A parent who used praise, rewards, or reasoning to control the boy was rated as "consistent, nonpunitive." Alternative categories were "erratically punitive," "inconsistent, nonpunitive," "extremely lax, with almost no use of discipline," and "no information." Fathers were difficult to classify for consistency, so for this analysis, their discipline was coded as "punitive" (N = 39) or "other." Mother's discipline was coded as "consistent and nonpunitive" (N = 70), or "other."

A mother's role in the family was classified as "leader," "dictator," "martyr," "passive," "neglecting," or "no indication." The leadership role involved participating in family decisions. Mothers in this analysis were classified either as being (N = 144) or not being leaders.

The aggressiveness of each parent was rated as "unrestrained" if that parent regularly expressed anger by such activities as shouting abuses, yelling, throwing or breaking things, or hitting people. Thirty-seven fathers and 23 mothers were rated as aggressive. Alternative classifications were "no indication," "moderately aggressive," or "greatly inhibited."...

Follow Up Measures

Between 1975 and 1980, when they ranged from 45 to 53 years in age, the former youth study participants were retraced. Twenty-four were found through their death records.[1] Police and court records had been collected in 1948. Those records of juvenile delinquency were combined with records gathered in 1979 from probation departments in Massachusetts and in other states to which the men had migrated.

The measure of criminality depended on official records of convictions. Such records do not reflect all crimes committed (Murphy et al., 1946), but they do appear to identify those who commit serious crimes and those who break the law frequently (Morash, 1984). In addition, several studies show convergence between results from official records and from well-designed self-reporting instruments for measuring serious criminality (Elliott and Ageton, 1980; Farrington, 1979; Hindelang et al., 1979; Reiss and Rhodes, 1961).

A boy was considered a juvenile delinquent if he had been convicted for an index crime prior to reaching the age of 18 years. Fifty boys had been convicted for such serious crimes as auto theft, breaking and entering, and assault. Of the 50 juvenile's convicted for serious crimes, 21 also were convicted for serious crimes as adults; additionally, 29 men not convicted as juveniles were convicted for at least one index crime as an adult....

Results

Comparisons for the impact of child rearing showed that Mother's Competence, Father's Interaction with the family, and Family Expectations were related to juvenile delinquency. Considered separately, poor child rearing in each of these domains reliably increased risk of delinquency....

Joint effects of poor child rearing can be seen by examining their combinations in relation to juvenile delinquency. Only 5% of the boys reared by competent mothers in families with good paternal interaction and high expectations had become delinquents. In contrast, almost half (47%) had become delinquents among those who had been raised by incompetent mothers in homes that had poor paternal interaction and low expectations....

Serious criminality as a juvenile was strongly related to both the mother's competence and to family expectations for the boy. Together, these accounted for 12% of the variance in juvenile delinquency, p = .0001. Father's poor interaction with the family showed a weaker relationship with

juvenile delinquency; it accounted for an additional 1.5% of the variance, p = .0617.

A different picture emerges from analyses of the impact of child-rearing variables on adult criminality.[2]... Father's interaction with the family increased in importance. With the exception of affection, each of the variables contributing to this dimension was related to adult criminality. The impact of the mother's competence had weakened—only the mother's self confidence clearly contributed to adult criminality. The dimension of family expectations was not reliably related to adult convictions, although supervision and maternal control apparently had enduring effects. The categorical analysis of variance, controlling collinearity, indicated that only the father's interactions bore a significant independent relationship to adult criminality....

Conviction as a juvenile was related to being convicted as an adult. As noted above, among the 50 boys who had been juvenile delinquents, 21 (42%) had been convicted for serious crimes as adults. In contrast, among 182 boys who had not been convicted for serious crimes as juveniles, 27 (15%) had been convicted for serious crimes as adults....

Summary and Discussion

This study reexamined the ways in which family interactions during childhood influence criminal behavior. By considering families whose socioeconomic backgrounds were similar, it was possible to look beyond effects of poverty, social disorganization, and blighted urban conditions.

Case records based on repeated visits to the homes of 232 boys allowed analyses that included the dynamics of family interactions. The variables resulting from observations in the homes were reduced to three dimensions in order to minimize problems of collinearity. A reasonable conclusion from the data is that the mother's competence and family expectations influenced the likelihood that a son became a juvenile delinquent.

Competent mothers seem to insulate a child against criminogenic influences even in deteriorated neighborhoods. Competent mothers were self-confident and provided leadership; they were consistently nonpunitive in discipline and affectionate. Coupled with high family expectations, maternal competence seems to reduce the probability that sons become juvenile delinquents. The influence of these child-rearing conditions on adult criminality appears to be largely through their impact on juvenile delinquency.

Compared with the mother's influences, the father's interactions with his family appeared less important during the juvenile years. Father's interactions with the family became more important, however, as the boys matured.

Fathers who interact with their wives in ways exhibiting high mutual esteem, who are not highly aggressive, and who generally get along well with their wives provide models for socialized behavior. Conversely, fathers who undermine their wives, who fight with the family, and who are aggressive provide models of antisocial behavior. Both types of fathers, it seems, teach their sons how to behave when they become adults.

The evidence from this study raises doubts about two currently prevalent views. One view holds that regardless of age of the criminal, crime is merely a particular symptom of a single underlying "disorder." The other view holds that causes of crime are basically the same at all ages. This study indicates that the causes of juvenile crime are different from those of adult criminality. Juvenile delinquency might be explained through elements of control, as represented by maternal competence and high expectations, but adult criminality appears to hold a component based on role expectations. If these interpretations are correct, criminality cannot be attributed to a single type of cause, nor does it represent a single underlying tendency.

Discussion Questions

1. It has often been said that broken homes contribute to crime and delinquency. Does empirical data support this theory? Are broken homes linked with juvenile delinquency? What is problematic about studies on this topic?

2. What are some of the problems associated with adolescents' reporting parents' child-rearing behavior? What are some of the problems

associated with parents reporting their own behavior?

3. What family characteristics do seem to have an effect on crime and delinquency? Exactly how does this work (how do certain characteristics affect crime)? Can measurement of any of these characteristics predict future criminal tendencies? Do any family characteristics seem to deter entry into crime?

Notes

1. None of the subjects died before the age of 20. Of those who died in their twenties, nine had no convictions and one was convicted only as a juvenile. Of those who died in their thirties, three had no convictions, two were convicted only as juveniles, and two were convicted only as adults. Of those who died in their forties, three were not convicted, two were convicted only as adults, and two were convicted both as juveniles and as adults.

2. The range in age among the 20 who had died prior to the follow-up and did not have criminal records as adults was 20 to 50 years. The median age was 39. Only six were under age 25. Because there was no attempt to ascertain rates of criminality, no correction was attempted for time of "exposure."

References

Akers, R.L. 1973. *Deviant Behavior: A Social Learning Approach*. Belmont, CA: Wadsworth.

Aristotle. 1941. *Ethica Nicomachea*, trans. W.D. Ross. In R. McKeon (eds.), *The Basic Works of Aristotle*. New York: Random House.

Bachman, J.G. and P.M. O'Malley. 1984. *The Youth in Transition Project*. In S.A. Mednick, M. Harway, and K.M. Finello (eds.), *Handbook of Longitudinal Research*. New York: Praeger.

Bacon, M.K., I.L. Child, and H. Barry, Jr. 1963. "A Cross-Cultural Study of Correlates of Crime" in *Journal of Abnormal and Social Psychology* 66: 291-300.

Bandura, A. and R.H. Walters. 1959. *Adolescent Aggression*. New York: Ronald.

——. 1963. *Social Learning and Personality Development*. New York: Holt, Rinehart & Winston.

Baumrind, D. 1968. "Authoritarian vs. Authoritative Parental Control." *Adolescence* 3: 255-272.

Baumrind, D. 1978. "Parental Disciplinary Patterns and Social Competence in Children." *Youth and Society* 9(3):239-276.

——. 1983. "Rejoinder to Lewis's Reinterpretation of Parental Firm Control Effects: Are Authoritative Families Really Harmonious?" *Psychological Bulletin* 94(1):132-142.

Bowlby, J. 1940. "The Influence of Early Environment on Neurosis and Neurotic Character." *International Journal of Psychoanalysis* 21:154.

——. 1951. "Maternal Care and Mental Health." *Bulletin of the World Health Organization* 3: 355-534.

Burt, C. 1925. *The Youth Delinquent.* New York: Appleton & Co.

Cernkovich, S.A. and P.C. Giordano. 1987. "Family Relationships and Delinquency." *Criminology* 25(2):295-319.

Cohen, J. 1960. "A Coefficient of Agreement for Nominal Scales." *Educational and Psychological Measurement* 20:37-46.

Dean, A.L., M.M. Malik, W. Richards, and S.A. Stringer. 1986. "Effects of Parental Maltreatment on Children's Conceptions of Interpersonal Relationships." *Developmental Psychology* 22(5): 617-626.

Dodge, K.Q. and D.R. Somberg. 1987. "Hostile Attributional Biases Among Aggressive Boys are Exacerbated Under Conditions of Threats to the Self." *Child Development* 58:213-224.

Dornbusch, S.M., J.M. Carlsmith, S.J. Bushwall, P.L. Ritter, H. Leiderman, A.H. Hastorf, and R.T. Gross. 1985. "Single Parents, Extended Households, and the Control of Adolescents." *Child Development* 56: 326-341.

Eich, E., S. Rachman, and C. Lopatka. 1990. "Affect, Pain, and Autobiographical Memory." *Journal of Abnormal Psychology* 99(2):174-178.

Elliott, D.S. and S.S. Ageton. 1980. "Reconciling Race and Class Differences in Self-Reported and Official Estimates of Delinquency." *American Sociological Review* 45:95-110.

Eron, L.D., T.J. Banta, L.O. Walder, and J.H. Laulicht. 1961. "Comparison of Data Obtained From Mothers and Fathers on Child-Rearing Practices and Their Relation to Child Aggression." *Child Development* 32(3): 455-472.

Farrington, D.P. 1979. "Environmental Stress, Delinquent Behavior, and Convictions." In I.G. Sarason and C.D. Spielberger (eds.), *Stress and Anxiety.* Vol. 6. New York: John Wiley & Sons.

Fenichel, O. 1945. *The Psychoanalytic Theory of Neurosis.* New York: Norton.

Forehand, R., K.C. Wells, and E.T. Sturgis. 1978. "Predictors of Child Noncompliant Behavior in the Home." *Journal of Consulting and Clinical Psychology* 46(1):179.

Freud, S. 1953. "Three Essays on the Theory of Sexuality." In *Standard Edition.* Vol. VII. London: Hogarth.

Glueck, S. and E.T. Glueck. 1950. *Unraveling Juvenile Delinquency.* New York: Commonwealth Fund.

Goldfarb, W. 1945. "Psychological Privation in Infancy and Subsequent Adjustment." *American Journal of Orthopsychiatry* 15:247-255.

Goode, W.J. 1956. *After Divorce.* Glencoe, IL: Free Press.

Hagan, J., A.R. Gillis, and J. Simpson. 1985. "The Class Structure of Gender and Delinquency: Toward a Power-Control Theory of Common Delinquent Behavior." *American Journal of Sociology* 90: 1151-1178.

Hindelang, M.J., T. Hirschi, and J.G. Weis. 1979. "Correlates of Delinquency: The Illusion of Discrepancy Between Self-Report and Official Measures." *American Sociological Review* 44: 995-1014.

Hirschi, T. 1969. *Causes of Delinquency.* Berkeley: University of California Press.

——. 1983. "Crime and the Family." In J.Q. Wilson (ed.), *Crime and Public Policy.* San Francisco: Institute for Contemporary Studies.

Hoffman, L.W. 1975. "Effects on Child." In L.W. Hoffman and F.I. Nye (eds.), *Working Mothers.* San Francisco: Jossey-Bass.

Jensen, G.F. and D. Brownfield. 1983. "Parents and Drugs." *Criminology* 21(4):543-555.

Kellogg, R.T. 1980. "Is Conscious Attention Necessary for Long-Term Storage." *Journal of Experimental Psychology* 6(4):379-390.

Lamb, M.E. 1976. "The Role of the Father: An Overview." In M.E. Lamb (ed.), *The Role of the Father in Child Development.* New York: John Wiley & Sons.

Larzelere, R.E. and G.R. Patterson. 1990. "Parental Management: Mediator of the Effect of Socioeconomic Status on Early Delinquency." *Criminology* 28(2):301-323.

Laub, J.H. and R.J. Sampson. 1988. "Unraveling Families and Delinquency: A Reanalysis of the Gluecks' Data." *Criminology* 26(3):355-380.

Levy, D. 1937. "Primary Affect Hunger." *American Journal of Psychiatry* 94:643-652.

Lewis, C. 1981. "The Effects of Parental Firm Control: A Reinterpretation of Findings." *Psychological Bulletin* 90(3):547-563.

Liska, A.E. and M.D. Reed. 1985. "Ties to Conventional Institutions and Delinquency: Estimating Reciprocal Effects." *American Sociological Review* 50(Aug):547-560.

Locke, J. 1693. "Some Thoughts Concerning Education." Vol. 8, *Collected Works*. 9th ed. London: T. Longman.

Loeber, R. and M. Stouthamer-Loeber. 1986. "Family Factors as Correlates and Predictors of Juvenile Conduct Problems and Delinquency." In M. Tonry and N. Morris (eds.), *Crime and Justice*. Vol. 7. Chicago: University of Chicago Press.

Maccoby, E.E. 1958. "Effects Upon Children of Their Mothers' Outside Employment." In National Manpower Council, Work in the Lives of Married Women. New York: Columbia University Press.

McCord, J. 1979. "Some Child-Rearing Antecedents of Criminal Behavior in Adult Men." *Journal of Personality and Social Psychology* 37:1477-1486.

——. 1982. "A Longitudinal View of the Relationship Between Paternal Absence and Crime." In J. Gunn and D.P. Farrington (eds.), *Abnormal Offenders, Delinquency, and the Criminal Justice System*. Chichester: John Wiley & Sons.

——. 1983a. "A Forty Year Perspective on Effects of Child Abuse and Neglect." *Child Abuse and Neglect* 7:265-270.

——. 1983b. "A Longitudinal Study of Aggression and Antisocial Behavior." In K.T. Van Dusen and S.A. Mednick (eds.), *Prospective Studies of Crime and Delinquency*. Boston: Kluwer-Nijhoff.

——. 1986. "Instigation and Insulation: How Families Affect Antisocial Behavior." In J. Block, D. Olweus, and M.R. Yarrow (eds.), *Development of Antisocial and Prosocial Behavior*. New York: Academic Press.

——. 1988. "Identifying Developmental Paradigms Leading to Alcoholism." *Journal of Studies on Alcohol* 49(4):357-362.

——. 1990. "Longterm Effects of Parental Absence." In L. Robins and M. Rutter (eds.), *Straight and Devious Pathways from Childhood to Adulthood*. New York: Cambridge University Press.

McCord, J. and W. McCord. 1958. "The Effects of Parental Role Model on Criminality." *Journal of Social Issues* 14(3):66-75.

——. 1962. "Cultural Stereotypes and the Validity of Interviews for Research in Child Development." *Child Development* 32(2):171-185.

McCord, J., W. McCord, and A. Howard. 1963a. "Family Interaction as Antecedent to the Direction of Male Aggressiveness." *Journal of Abnormal and Social Psychology* 66:239-242.

McCord, J., W. McCord, and E. Thurber. 1963b. "The Effects of Maternal Employment on Lower Class Boys." *Journal of Abnormal & Social Psychology* 67(1):177-182.

McCord, W. and J. McCord. 1959. *Origins of Crime*. New York: Columbia University Press.

——. 1960. *Origins of Alcoholism*. Stanford, CA: Stanford University Press.

McCord, W., J. McCord, and A. Howard. 1961. "Familial Correlates of Agression in Nondelinquent Male Children." *Journal of Abnormal & Social Psychology* 1:79-93.

Miller, W.B. 1958. "Lower Class Culture as a Generating Milieu of Gang Delinquency." *Journal of Social Issues* 14:5-19.

Morash, M. 1984. "Establishment of a Juvenile Police Record: The Influence of Individual and Peer Group Characteristics." *Criminology* 22:97-111.

Murdock, G.P. 1949. *Social Structure*. New York: Macmillan.

Murphy, F.J., M.M. Shirley, and H.L. Witmer. 1946. "The Incidence of Hidden Delinquency." *American Journal of Orthopsychiatry* 16:686-696.

Newell, H.W. 1934. "The Psycho-Dynamics of Maternal Rejection." *American Journal of Orthopsychiatry* 4: 387-401.

——. 1936. "A Further Study of Maternal Rejection." *American Journal of Orthopsychiatry* 6:576-589.

Nye, F.I. 1958. *Family Relationships and Delinquent Behavior*. New York: John Wiley & Sons.

——. 1959. "Maternal Employment and the Adjustment of Adolescent Children." *Marriage and Family Living* 21(August):240-244.

Parsons, T. and R.F. Bales. 1955. *Family, Socialization and Interaction Process*. Glencoe, IL: Free Press.

Plato Laws, trans. B. Jowett. *In the Dialogues of Plato* (1937). NY: Random House.

Powers, E. and H. Witmer. 1951. *An Experiment in the Prevention of Delinquency: The Cambridge-Somerville Youth Study.* New York: Columbia University Press.

Reiss, A.J., Jr., and A.L. Rhodes. 1961. "Delinquency and Class Structure." *American Sociological Review* 26(5):720-732.

Robins, L.N. 1966. *Deviant Children Grown Up.* Baltimore: Williams & Wilkins.

SAS Institute. 1985. *SAS User's Guide: Statistics.* 1985 ed. Cary, NC: SAS Institute.

Scott, W.A. 1955. "Reliability of Content Analysis: The Case of Nominal Scale Coding." *Public Opinion Quarterly* 19(3):321-325.

Shaw, C. and H.D. McKay. 1932. "Are Broken Homes A Causative Factor in Juvenile Delinquency?" *Social Forces* 10:514-524.

Sutherland, E.H. and D.R. Cressey. 1974. *Criminology.* 1924. 9th ed. Philadelphia: Lippincott.

van Voorhis, P., F.T. Cullen, R.A. Mathers, and C.C. Garner. 1988. "The Impact of Family Structure and Quality on Delinquency: A Comparative Assessment of Structural and Functional Factors." *Criminology* 26(2):235-261.

Wadsworth, M. 1979. *Roots of Delinquency.* New York: Barnes and Noble.

Weller, L. and E. Luchterhand. 1983. "Family Relationships of 'Problem' and 'Promising' youth." *Adolescence* 18(69):43-100.

Wells, L.E. and J.H. Rankin. 1988. "Direct Parental Controls and Delinquency." *Criminology* 26(2): 263-285.

Whiting, J.W.M., R. Kluckhohn, and A. Anthony. 1958. "The Function of Male Initiation Ceremonies at Puberty." In E.E. Maccoby, T.M. Newcomb, and E.L. Hartley (eds.), *Readings in Social Psychology.* New York: Holt, Rinehart & Winston.

Yarrow, M.R., J.D. Campbell, and R.V. Burton. 1970. "Recollections of Childhood: A study of the Retrospective Method." *Monographs of the Society for Research in Child Development* 35(1):1-83.

CHAPTER 15

On Immigration and Crime

Ramiro Martinez, Jr. ■ Matthew T. Lee

Immigration has emerged as one of the foremost social issues in contemporary American society. Within the larger immigration debate on legal status, workforce dependency, and cultural conflict, the immigration and crime relationship is perhaps the most alarming and controversial. Criminology, in an effort to inform this quickly intensifying problem, has generated additional controversy to the discussion. Conventional wisdom suggests that the large number of social variables and risk factors that are predictive of crime (e.g., socioeconomic status, educational attainment, alcohol and illicit substance misuse, social disorganization, and family size) are characteristic and indicative of immigrant communities. Alternatively, immigrant groups also maintain culturally based protective factors such as traditional family structures, community homogeneity, and collective efficacy that seemingly retard criminogenic social learning and crime rates.

The issue of immigration and crime is only further complicated by additional germane realities such as assimilation, acculturation, and minority confidence and trust in the police. The following essay by Martinez and Lee surveys much of the vast body of theoretical and empirical knowledge base concerning the connection between immigration and crime, largely to the conclusion that the relationship is a complex one presenting multiple questions for future research.

From The Nature of Crime: Continuity Change, Criminal Justice Vol. 1 (Gary La Free, Ed) pp 485–524

The linkage between immigrants and crime is one of the most controversial contemporary social issues. Discussions of this relationship are notably contentious; they are also not new, as debates on the matter date back more than 100 years. The one point on which writers both pro- and anti-immigration agree is that as we enter the new millennium the latest wave of immigration is likely to have a more significant impact on society than any other social issue (Suarez-Orozco 1998; Brimelow 1996). If the past is any guide, the immigrant-crime relationship will be at the center of attempts to make sense of this impact.

Historically, public opinion about immigration, and the immigrant-crime link especially, has been formed by stereotypes more often than reliable empirical data (Espenshade and Belanger 1998; Simon 1985). Similarly, early 20th-century immigration policy was guided more by questionable research and prejudicial beliefs than a solid foundation of knowledge based on the existing scientific literature (as cited in Sellin 1938). It is therefore essential to systematically review the scholarly literature on immigration and crime so that current public and policy debates may be better informed....

Theoretical Perspectives

Opportunity Structure

Opportunity structure theories stress the material and social structures that shape the values and activities of groups in American society (Bankston

1998). Because legitimate opportunities for wealth and social status are not equally available to all groups, some will "innovate" by taking advantage of available illegitimate opportunities. This type of explanation was popularized by Merton (1938) and draws attention to the ways in which disadvantaged groups (which often includes immigrants) may be denied the legitimate means (e.g., jobs) to attain culturally prescribed goals (e.g., a middle-class lifestyle). Cloward and Ohlin (1960) added the notion that some groups, particularly those living in "high crime" urban areas, have more illegitimate opportunities than others.

Scholars have long noted the tendency for new immigrants to settle in urban neighborhoods characterized by poverty, substandard housing, poor schools, and high crime rates (Thomas and Znaniecki 1920; Taylor 1931; Shaw and McKay [1942] 1969; Hagan and Palloni 1998). Segregated into such neighborhoods, immigrants may turn to crime as a means to overcome blocked economic opportunities or to organized crime to gain a foothold in politics (Whyte 1943). Other writers have suggested that previously noncriminal immigrant groups may simply be "contaminated" by the criminal opportunities that abound in their neighborhoods (Lambert 1970, 284; compare Sampson and Lauritsen 1997 on the "proximity" hypothesis). According to this view, immigrant criminality is more a function of preexisting structural factors like poverty (Yeager 1997); a preponderance of young, unattached males (Taft 1936; Gurr 1989); or the availability of alcohol (see Alaniz, Cartmill, and Parker 1998) than either the biological makeup or cultural traditions of immigrant groups.

Contemporary immigrant gangs can be viewed as an alternative means of securing wealth and status in urban areas in which immigrants are concentrated and a loss of blue-collar jobs has eroded the principal basis of upward mobility used by earlier generations of immigrants (Gans 1992). Patterns of factory life associated with the industrial revolution socialized earlier waves of immigrants (e.g., Irish, Italians) and facilitated their economic stability and assimilation into American culture, thus suppressing their crime rates (Lane 1997). But the contemporary loss of industrial jobs, traceable to the recent transition of the economy from a manufacturing to a service orientation, has had drastic consequences on the legitimate (and illegitimate) opportunities in American cities (cf. Wilson 1987; Anderson 1990). Although deindustrialization impacts both immigrants and nonimmigrants, newcomers (who are both economically and culturally marginal in American society) may find the potential benefits of the "informal economy" particularly attractive (Bankston 1998; see also Vigil and Long 1990). Since the possibility of gang membership is not open to everyone and is, in fact, usually based on ethnic identity, among other things (see Sanchez-Jankowski 1991), the availability of illegitimate opportunities in gangs is one structural variable that differentially influences immigrant crime across social units such as cities or neighborhoods.

Cultural Approaches

In addition to this list of structural issues, scholars have viewed cultural forces as influencing criminal involvement, and immigrant crime in particular. The "culture of poverty" thesis—where low-income people adapt to their structural conditions in ways that perpetuate their disadvantaged condition—is one example of a cultural explanation (Lewis 1965). Thus, engaging in crime as a means of acquiring social status draws children away from schoolwork, which reduces the probability of future economic advancement. A variant of this explanation for crime, the "subculture of violence" thesis, suggests that violence can become a "normal" and expected means of dispute resolution in economically disadvantaged areas (Wolfgang and Ferracuti 1967).

One prominent strain of cultural theory that is especially well suited to the immigration-crime relationship can be found in Sellin's (1938) writings on "culture conflict." Sellin (p. 21) recognized that the criminal law reflects the values of the "dominant interest groups" in society, and that the values of other social groups, particularly immigrants, were quite different. In cases in which the cultural codes of subordinate and dominant groups conflict, legal agents label as deviant the behavior of members of the subordinate classes. Nevertheless, the criminal may be acting according to subculturally accepted norms and feel no "mental conflict" when violating the law. Sellin (p. 68) provides a classic example:

> A few years ago a Sicilian father in New Jersey killed the sixteen-year-old seducer of his daughter, expressing surprise at his arrest since he had merely defended his family honor in a traditional way. In this case a mental conflict in the sociological sense did not exist.

Thus, Sellin (p. 69) distinguishes "internal" (mental) conflict that may involve guilt or shame from "external" (i.e., at the level of cultural codes) conflict that does not. As society becomes more complex through processes of differentiation (of which immigration is just one), the potential for conflict among operative "cultural codes" also increases.

Four years earlier, Sutherland (1934, 51–52) offered a similar explanation, stating that "the conflict of cultures is therefore the fundamental principle in the explanation of crime [and] . . . the more the cultural patterns conflict, the more unpredictable is the behavior of the individual." This thesis has broad applicability to all social groups, but it clearly provides a key reason why immigrants are likely to engage in crime, perhaps suggesting that immigrants should have higher crime rates than the native population, other factors being equal.

Another body of literature in the cultural tradition has focused on the processes by which immigrants adapt to the traditions of the host country (Padilla 1980). It has long been asserted that acculturation to a new environment involves "adjustment to heterogeneous conduct norms" and this, in turn, can lead to higher crime rates (Sellin 1938, 85). Immigrant gangs, for example, usually owe as much to American cultural traditions as to those of the immigrant culture; adult Vietnamese refer to Vietnamese delinquents as "Americanized" (Bankston 1998). Immigrant gangs also form as a reaction to ethnic tensions in diverse neighborhoods; they provide physical protection from other ethnic-based gangs and maintain ethnic identities in the face of pressures for assimilation (Chin 1990; Du Phuoc Long 1996).

Other theoretical and empirical work on acculturation and crime found that delinquency among Korean-American youths varied by mode of acculturation: separation, assimilation, and marginalization. Interestingly, assimilated youths were more likely to be delinquent than those who were separated or marginalized (Lee 1998). Similarly, Stepick (1998) reports that Haitian children in South Florida adjust to extreme anti-Haitian sentiment by trying to "pass" as being African-American. Increasingly, these children are becoming part of the criminal justice system as a result of alienation from both their Haitian background and American society (p. 120).

Social disorganization

The social disorganization perspective, although not denying the importance of cultural or structural forces, adds to the other perspectives a concern with the breakdown of community social institutions that results from social change. Bursik (1988, 521) concisely describes disorganized areas as possessing an "inability to realize the common values of their residents or solve commonly expressed problems." In organized neighborhoods, local community institutions work together to realize community goals, protect values, and generally control the behavior of community members in ways that conform to these goals and values. Bankston (1998) notes that immigration may undermine established institutions via a process of population turnover, while it also makes agreement about common values more difficult. The implication is that when social control is weakened in this manner crime will flourish.

One early influential statement of this perspective was set forth by Thomas and Znaniecki in their five-volume work published between 1918 and 1920 titled *The Polish Peasant in Europe and America*. Thomas and Znaniecki wrote about the many social changes affecting Polish peasants in this time period, including the disorganizing influences inherent in moving from simple, homogeneous, rural areas of Poland to the complex, heterogeneous, urban areas of the United States. They defined social disorganization as "a decrease of the influence of existing social rules of behavior upon individual members of the group" (Thomas and Znaniecki 1920, 2). The effectiveness of social rules (i.e., laws) derived from the individual's investment in them (i.e., attitudes favorable to laws). In the organized society, there was congruence between group rules and individual attitudes. Disorganization implied a gap between rules and attitudes, such that an individual did not feel bound by the rules and was free to disobey them (i.e., engage in crime). Viewed in this light, disorganization was a neutral term that suggested the possibility of social change, both positive and negative, and individual liberation from oppressive community standards, although it has generally been applied to studies of crime. One contribution to this literature is the recognition that crime not only is a function of economic (e.g., poverty) or cultural (e.g., subculture of violence) forces, but is intimately tied to the fundamental processes of social change.

Thomas and Znaniecki (1920, 82–83) describe two general types of disorganization that affect communities (and other organizations such as the family). The first, especially relevant to immigrant communities, causes a decay in solidarity when the young generation adopts the values of the new community rather than the traditional "old world" values of the parent's generation (see also Schneider 1995 on "cultural anomie"). One example is the influence of American schools on immigrant children—learning a new language and values generates new desires in children for experiences that the older generation cannot provide, simultaneously reducing parental and communal ability to control their behavior (see also Young 1936). The second type of disorganization occurs among members of the old generation as values are subjected to differential interpretations over time or as rules are simply not enforced, leading to "social disharmony." For Thomas and Znaniecki, this second type of disorganization is rooted in the individual's unique temperament and may be expressed through a lack of compliance with social rules, even though there is no explicit rejection of the rules themselves. Control is thus weakened gradually through the cumulative actions of individuals who contribute to social change, even if this is not their intention.

Although not chiefly concerned with crime, Thomas and Znaniecki ([1920] 1984) did apply the idea of disorganization to the crimes of Polish immigrants. Murder among the Polish, for example, had a very different etiology in Poland as compared with the United States. Murder among the Polish in Poland was predominantly confined to one's own small communal group—murders of strangers were rare. The motive (e.g., revenge) in these cases was most often strongly felt and was preceded by long periods of brooding and a sense of violation of deeply held values. In contrast, murder in America by Polish immigrants was more likely to involve a victim who was a stranger or not well known to the offender and less likely to involve a concern with the seriousness of violating standards of the community. In the disorganized areas of America into which Polish immigrants settled, the social ties of the old country were weakened and community controls were loosened. Freed from traditional social controls, and subjected to social forces that influenced their lives in ways they could not control or sometimes understand, some Polish immigrants exhibited a "general nervousness" and "vague expectation of hostility" (Thomas and Znaniecki 1984, 286) that was virtually unknown in the old country. In such circumstances, murder could be provoked by seemingly trivial offenses partly because the immigrant feels the need to take individual action against affronts since:

> the murderer does not feel himself backed in his dealings with the outside world by any strong social group of his own and is not conscious of being the member of a steadily organized society. His family is too weak and scattered to give him a safe social refuge…where he could ignore outside provocations in the feeling of his social importance and security. (Thomas and Znaniecki 1984, 286)

Thus, the weakened Polish community in America was not able to solve disputes and organize behavior as it had in the old country, and this had implications for a host of social problems, including increased crime.

Despite the voluminous work of Thomas and Znaniecki, scholars most often associate the social disorganization perspective with the writings of Shaw and McKay (1931, [1942] 1969; see also Ross 1937; Kobrin 1959) on the ecological distribution of delinquency. Shaw and McKay utilized the concept of social disorganization to great effect by using quantitative data from Chicago neighborhoods to specify the role of community disorganization in producing high crime rates, other conditions (e.g., residential poverty, ethnicity) being equal. Their most important finding was that "within the same type of social area, the foreign born and the natives, recent immigrant nationalities, and older immigrants produce very similar rates of delinquents" (Shaw and McKay 1969, 158). Or, in the words of one of their critics, "nativity and nationality have no vital relationship to juvenile delinquency" (Jonassen 1949, 613). The Chicago data suggested to Shaw and McKay (though not to Jonassen) that certain areas had consistently high rates of delinquency, regardless of which immigrant groups lived there, and that as immigrant groups moved out of these areas and into better neighborhoods, their juvenile delinquency rates fell as well.

Inspired by Thomas and Znaniecki, the theoretical explanation suggested by these patterns was that neighborhoods characterized by "disorganizing" factors such as high population turnover and ethnic heterogeneity will be less likely than other neighborhoods to control the behavior of their inhabitants. According to this view, immigrants will have high crime rates only when they settle in disorganized neighborhoods, not because of biological factors or criminal cultural traditions. Thus, Lind (1930a, 1930b) stresses the value of distinguishing homogeneous but poor "ghettos" from heterogeneous, disorganized, and poor "slums." According to this view, crime might flourish in slums but not in ghettos, even though both are characterized by economic deprivation and other deleterious social conditions, because ghetto residents exert a degree of control over neighbors that is missing in disorganized slums (Lind 1930a). However, recent work on nonimmigrant black ghettos has found that homogeneous areas are not better organized for social control (Anderson 1990) and suffer from the concentration of multiple social problems (Sampson and Wilson 1995). Contemporary studies on immigrants in this tradition are lacking.

Recent theoretical work by Sampson and Lauritsen (1997) has attempted to demonstrate how macrosocial and local community-level structural forces can be combined to improve on the classic disorganization framework. Although this work developed from an attempt to explain black-white crime differences as well as the wide variation in black crime rates across structurally different community areas, the theory can also advance our knowledge of the link between immigration and crime. Sampson and Lauritsen suggest that powerful factors (e.g., segregation, housing discrimination, structural transformation of the economy) coincide with local community-level factors (e.g., residential turnover, concentrated poverty, family disruption) to impede the social organization of inner cities (p. 340; see also Sampson and Wilson 1995). A deeper understanding of the interaction effects of these variables would enhance existing theories by better incorporating the role of the "massive social change" (Sampson and Lauritsen 1997, 340) experienced by the mostly black residents in U.S. inner cities in the 1970s and 1980s. Since the post-1965 immigration wave brought newcomers into these same structural conditions, we might expect high rates of immigrant crime during this time period. This question is the subject of the next section on empirical studies of immigration and crime.

Empirical Studies

Early Studies

The earliest studies on crime among the first wave of immigrants, which ended in 1924, were based on evidence that was uneven at best (Tonry 1997, 21). These studies suggested that newcomers were less likely to be involved in crime than the native born. A special report issued by the Industrial Commission of 1901 found that "foreign-born whites were less criminal than native whites," while the 1911 Immigration Commission concluded that "immigration has not increased the volume of crime" and that the presence of immigrants may have even suppressed criminal activity (Tonry 1997, 21). A review of other early immigrant-crime studies discovered that, contrary to stereotypes, most researchers did not find first-wave immigrants to be crime prone (McCord 1995), although results did vary by city (e.g., immigrants in Boston, but not in Chicago, were disproportionately involved in crime). These studies generally found that children of immigrants had crime rates higher than their immigrant parents but not higher than native-born children. This suggests that the acculturation to American life of the second generation of immigrants, and not the assumed "criminal traditions" of immigrant groups, was related to immigrant crime rates (Hagan and Palloni 1998; Sellin 1938; Sutherland 1934). Acculturation was apparently weakening the impact of traditional social controls in immigrant communities.

Even so, studies of the first wave of immigration support the conclusion that immigrants were not as highly involved in crime as natives (Abbott 1915; Lind 1930b; Taft 1936; Ferracuti 1968). A prominent report published in 1931 by the National Commission on Law Observance and Enforcement, popularly known as the Wickersham Report, noted that immigrants had lower overall crime rates than nonimmigrants, although some groups appeared disproportionately involved in specific types of crime. Mexicans in one study, for example, displayed higher rates of arrest for some violent crimes than native whites (though lower than native blacks; see Bowler 1931, 119). However, as Taylor (1931) and later Sellin (1938, 76) pointed out, these rates are "untrustworthy" because reliable Mexican population estimates were not available because of the migratory nature of that group, a situation made worse by the fact that the 1930 census figures were not yet available (Taylor 1931).

Immigrant rates were untrustworthy for other reasons as well. Another author of the 1931 report discussed ways in which prejudice against Mexicans by criminal justice personnel worked to inflate their arrest rates (Warnshuis 1931). For example, police in a community with a large Mexican presence expressed the belief that most crimes were committed by Mexicans, while an examination of arrests revealed that only 4 Mexicans out of 252 total persons arrested were booked in 1 month; 3 of these were for "disorderly conduct," and none were convicted. In terms of official statistics, police prejudice had practical consequences when serious crimes occurred: Police would sometimes arrest "all the Mexicans they could find" (p. 283), artificially inflating Mexican crime rates.

Despite the limitations of the Mexican crime data, Taylor (1931) was able to draw several conclusions. First, the number of Mexican crimes committed was about what could be expected by the number of Mexicans in the population and the crime rates were similar to those of other groups. Second, patterns of criminal arrest varied considerably across cities and were shaped by a host of social factors, including poverty and the age and sex distributions of the immigrant population. Taylor (p. 235) also discovered that Mexican criminal involvement displayed "interesting diversity within the same locality," suggesting the need to examine structural factors differentially affecting immigrants in socially meaningful areas such as neighborhoods, rather than in larger political divisions such as cities and States. In short, there was no single conclusion that could be drawn about "Mexican crime rates" independent of the local community context.

This last point was investigated by Lind (1930a, 1930b) in work on immigration and crime in the ethnically diverse city of Honolulu, Hawaii. Following proponents of the Chicago school of sociology like Robert Park and Louis Wirth, Lind (1930a, 206-207) stressed the distinction between "slums"—ethnically diverse, unstable, and poor neighborhoods—and "ghettos," which were also economically depressed but characterized by a stable, organized, and racially homogenous group of residents (see also Whyte 1943 on "rooming house" verses "settlement" districts). Lind found that due to neighborhood heterogeneity and instability, groups in slums had multiple moral codes and were less effective in organizing families and community organizations to control the behavior of residents who were members of that group. Thus, delinquency was rare in poor but stable Japanese neighborhoods and high among native Hawaiians residing in economically better off, but disorganized, areas (Lind 1930b). In addition, Lind (1930a, 209) documented that Japanese delinquency rates also varied by the degree of neighborhood segregation and population concentration. Such findings provided empirical support for the argument that immigrant crime is a function of generic processes (i.e., disorganization) associated with urban living rather than the cultural traditions or predispositions of immigrants (see also Shaw and McKay 1969).

Other research found that compared with native groups, some immigrant groups were able to resist the disorganizing effects of slum areas to a higher degree than native groups. One study showed that although Seattle's Japanese immigrants lived in an economically deprived, high-crime, disorganized area, their "strong family and community organization" was able to keep their children's delinquency rates low (Hayner 1933, 319). This is consistent with results reported by Taft (1936, 736) showing that immigrants usually displayed lower crime rates than nonimmigrants and that variations could be explained by some combination of "adverse conditions" found in high-crime areas and the insulating effect of the "cultural values which different national groups bring." Von Hentig (1945, 793; contra Glueck and Glueck 1930) reports similar findings: Descendants of native-born groups were much more involved in serious crime than descendants of immigrants or of mixed parentage, though there were "vast diversities by States." Again, some combination of ecological conditions and cultural factors seemed important for explaining the involvement, or lack thereof, of immigrants in crime.

Contemporary Studies

Some writers have suggested that immigrant criminality was becoming an increasingly serious problem in the 1990s, as evidenced by the increase in prosecutions in U.S. district courts of noncitizens from 1984 to 1994 (3,462 cases to 10,352 cases, respectively; see Marshall 1997). Yet this finding does not take into account the tremendous increase in immigration over this time period and is largely the result of increased prosecution for drug offenses as well as for immigration offenses to which natives are not subject. As we discuss in the following section, public opinion continues to associate immigrants with crime, so it is important to review recent studies that have investigated this relationship.

The 1994 U.S. Commission on Immigration Reform compared crime in cities along the U.S.-Mexico border with nonborder cities in order to assess the impact of Mexican immigrants on crime rates. The Commission concluded that crime rates in border cities such as El Paso, Texas, were generally lower (in some cases much lower) than rates in nonborder cities. In addition to city rate comparisons, regression analysis revealed that "crime is lower on average in border areas than in other U.S. cities when the characteristics of the urban population are held constant" (1994, 20). A followup study conducted a more direct statistical test of the effect of immigration on levels of crime and found "no consistent or compelling evidence at the SMSA [Standard Metropolitan Statistical Area] level that immigration causes crime" (Hagan and Palloni 1998, 380).

Much of the recent work on immigration and crime has focused on gangs (see Bankston 1998; Marshall 1997). This is not surprising, since new immigrants often settle in urban areas characterized by a high level of gang activity, and many immigrant gangs form as a means of protection from these existing threats (Chin 1990). Although there have been numerous studies of specific immigrant gangs (cf. Du Phuoc Long 1996), there has been no research that systematically compares the level of immigrant involvement versus native involvement in gangs or suggests reasons to suspect that immigration increases gang activity (Bankston 1998).

Post-1965 studies of nongang criminal involvement of specific immigrant or ethnic groups have been rare (Martinez and Lee 1999). The studies that have been conducted tend to agree with research on the first wave: Immigrants are not disproportionately involved in crime and often are much less involved than native groups. For example, research on homicide in San Antonio found that homicide rates among Mexican males fell between those of native whites and native-born blacks and that homicide remained concentrated in poor areas of the city, regardless of whether the residents were black or Mexican over the 1940 through 1980 period (Bradshaw et al. 1998). Another study found that immigration was not related to youth violence in California, while alcohol availability was an important influence on serious crime among young males in three cities with a heavy Latino population (Alaniz, Cartmill, and Parker 1998). Finally, a study of Puerto Rican newcomers found that those living in New York City had high rates of homicide, while Puerto Ricans living elsewhere had rates comparable to native whites (Rosenwaike and Hempstead 1990).

A number of studies have examined homicide among several prominent ethnic groups in Miami. Although Mariel refugees were often portrayed by the media as high-rate killers, the empirical evidence demonstrated that they were rarely overrepresented as either victims or offenders, and in fact, after a short time, were much less likely to offend than Miami's established Cubans (Martinez 1997a). In addition, despite a constant influx of Latino immigrants in the 1980s, Miami's homicide rates continued to decline (Martinez 1997b). Finally, Martinez and Lee (1998) found that Miami's Haitians and Latinos were underrepresented in homicide relative to group size, while African-Americans were over-represented, and in some cases the rate of homicide among the two immigrant groups was *lower* than that of non-Latino whites (Anglos).

Consistent with earlier studies, the criminal involvement of immigrant groups varies considerably in different cities. A good example of this variation is provided in a study of Latino homicide among El Paso's Mexicans and Miami's Cubans (Lee, Martinez, and Rodriguez 2000). Despite the two cities' similar structural characteristics (e.g., employment, poverty), Miami's Latino homicide rate was almost three times that of El Paso. In addition to city-specific characteristics such as Miami's older population, greater income inequality (see Martinez 1996 for a discussion of absolute deprivation versus relative deprivation among Latinos), and possibly greater availability of guns, other local conditions shaped the comparatively high Cuban homicide rate. For example, Cubans settled in a more violent area of the country (south Florida) than did Latinos in El Paso, and this regional context may shape each group's involvement in homicide. Wilbanks (1984; see also Epstein and Greene 1993), demonstrated that Miami's homicide trends mirror those for south Florida generally, and that this area experienced a sharp rise in homicides *prior to* the arrival of thousands of Cuban refugees in the Mariel boatlift of 1980. Thus, Miami's Latinos lived in a location experiencing higher levels of violence than El Paso's Latinos.

Just as important differences were revealed by the experience of two groups of Latinos described in the preceding research, other studies have also examined within-group differences among ethnic groups (see Hawkins 1999 for a similar strategy). Martinez and Lee (2000) investigated Afro-Caribbean homicides in Miami and found that Mariel Cuban, Haitian, and Jamaican immigrants were generally less involved in homicide than natives. Comparing the early 1980s, when these groups first began arriving in Miami in large numbers, to the late 1990s, the authors noted a strong pattern of declining violence, especially for Jamaicans and Mariels, while Haitians continuously maintained a low overall rate. As these immigrant groups grew in size and had a lower proportion of young males, homicide rates rapidly declined. This finding suggests that, contrary to key propositions of social disorganization theory, rapid immigration may not create disorganized communities but may instead stabilize neighborhoods through the creation of new social and economic institutions (see also Portes and Stepick 1993).

Public Opinion on Immigration and Crime

Rita Simon (1985, 1987, 1993) points out that, regardless of the time period, public opinion has almost always been negative on the issue of whether additional immigrants should be permitted to enter this country (see also Espenshade and Belanger 1998). In addition, the most recent immigrants are almost always viewed unfavorably, although public opinion eventually improves with the passage of time (Roper Reports 1995). According to Simon (1987, 47), older ethnic communities are viewed more positively than recent arrivals, even if the earlier communities were initially disliked.

For example, the Chinese and Japanese are viewed more favorably today in public opinion polls than they were in the 1920s, although they were once widely subjected to discriminatory legislation and prejudicial public attitudes (Abbott 1931). Similarly, opinion was decidedly against Irish, Italians, and Poles in the 1920s, but white ethnic groups are usually better regarded today, at least in some recent surveys. A 1985 survey showed that 82 eminent social scientists believe, like most Americans for the past century and a half, that the current group of immigrants (mostly Latinos) is somehow different than previous groups: They are thought less likely to assimilate and especially dangerous to cultural values and institutions (Simon 1993).

To place the current anti-immigrant sentiment in context, it is informative to examine trends in opinions about immigration and crime throughout the 20th century.[1] As Ferracuti (1968, 190; see also Short 1997; Abbott 1931) points out, in the first half of the 20th century, "popular opinion often expressed the view that migrants were responsible for a large fraction of the crime rate," despite considerable empirical evidence that they were not. Statements like the following from a turn-of-the-century New York City police commissioner were typical: "[S]omething like 85 out of one hundred of our criminals should be found to be of exotic origin" (Simon 1985, 70–71). This commissioner viewed Italians as particularly dangerous "malefactors" (Simon 1985, 71) and promoted the view that the French and Belgians organized white slavery rackets.

The idea of criminal immigrants was not a product of the 20th century; a series of articles in the *New York Times* published in 1880 was also concerned with criminal Italians, a particularly "clannish race," and the prototypical "bad Irish boy [who was] about as unwholesome a product as was ever reared in any body politic" (Simon 1985, 186). Note also that the 1892 Democratic Party platform nodded approvingly at legislation designed to keep the United States from "being used as a dumping ground for known criminals" from Europe and China (Simon 1985, 18). Such views had long been reflected in scholarly writings as well. For example, an article by William Jeffrey in an 1893 issue of the *Journal of Political Economy* also blamed immigrants for increasing crime rates (Simon 1985).

This image appeared in prominent periodicals throughout the first wave of immigration. A 1915 editorial in *North American Review* called for a restriction of immigration on the grounds of the "criminal and economic worthlessness" of southern European immigrants (Simon 1985, 71). Articles in other popular magazines also expressed the low public opinion in which immigrants were held. One 1923 issue of the *Saturday Evening Post* viewed immigrants from southeastern Europe (e.g., Italy, Greece) as the "dullest and dumbest people in

Europe," while another from the same year quoted eugenicist Harry Laughlin as saying "If America doesn't keep out the queer alien mongrelized people of Southern and Eastern Europe, her crop of citizens will eventually be dwarfed and mongrelized in turn" (Simon 1985, 85). The assumed criminal nature of immigrants is a common theme in these writings, with authors claiming that immigrants were filling penitentiaries and insane asylums faster than the native born. During the 1920s, Italians, Jews, Poles, Russians, Greeks, and others were commonly portrayed as criminals.

Contemporary anti-immigrant sentiment is often promoted by organized interest groups that accuse Third World nations of exporting their excessive numbers to the United States (Simon 1993, 69). And as in the past (see Sellin 1938), current legislation—such as California's Proposition 187 and the U.S. Congress' 1996 Immigration Reform bill—has not relied on scholarly research, even though it has been justified on the grounds that it will stem the tide of "criminal aliens," who are a growing presence in the criminal justice system (U.S. Commission on Immigration Reform 1994; Scalia 1996). This imagery has profound consequences for recent immigrants who must confront these enduring negative stereotypes, are singled out for discrimination, and are consistently viewed in public opinion polls as burdens to society (Simon 1987; Roper Reports 1995).

Public Opinion and Immigrant Homicide in Three Cities

As a point of departure, we focus on homicide victim rates, not offending rates, in the following section. Although much of our discussion has centered on offender motivation, the immigration-crime link should be evident in the following analyses of homicide victim rates given the closeness of the victim and offender relationship in most cases. The Federal Bureau of Investigation's 1995 Uniform Crime Report (UCR) notes that in 75 percent of homicide cases cleared with an arrest, the victim and offender had *some* type of prior relationship (spouse, family member, lover, friend, neighbor) or previous contact such as an acquaintance or coworker (U.S. Department of Justice, Federal Bureau of Investigation 1997, table 2.12). Thus, in most cases, the "stranger element" is absent even after considering the proportion of unknown offenders, which could fall in any category of familiarity or individual characteristic (age, race, gender). Furthermore, the vast majority of all homicides were intraracial (white on white, black on black) and speaks to neighborhood residential patterns and segregation that have long been part of American society. Most persons tend to live in areas in which other residents have similar attributes, including race and ethnicity.

In addition, historical and contemporary studies also report that many killings were victim precipitated and that the event initially arose out of

an argument (as one example) that turned lethal (Wolfgang 1958; Martinez and Lee 1998). The closeness of this relationship is further illustrated in a recent city-level homicide study of black and white victim rates. Ousey (1999, 410) reports that the effects of structural conditions on homicide victim and arrest rates are substantially similar and provide the same conclusions. This is not surprising given the spatial proximity between victims and offenders, most of whom reside in the same neighborhood and share points of economic comparison (Anderson 1990). In fact, both are also products of communities weakened by a host of social problems that impede the ability of institutions to maintain order and provide opportunities

Figure 15.1 Total and Latino immigration counts with the national Latino homicide victim rate

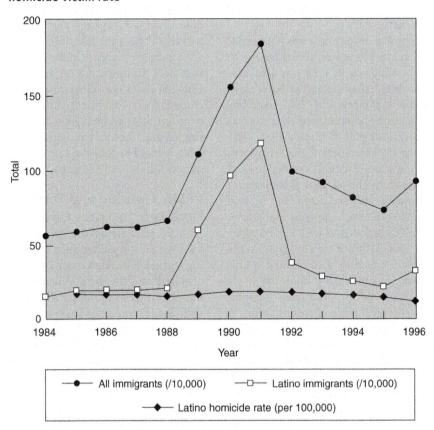

Sources: Immigration figures are reported by the U.S. Department of Justice, Immigration and Naturalization Service (1997, 1987); homicide rates are based on data from the U.S. Department of Health and Human Services, National Center for Health Statistics (1998).

to those most in need and typically more active in crime in general and violence specifically.

Finally, data issues also encourage us to focus on victim data. Homicides are rare events relative to any other type of violent crime (e.g., armed robbery, aggravated assault). Disaggregating these already scarce cases by ethnicity thins an already shallow pool even more, encouraging researchers to use all available homicide victim incidents. Furthermore, to the best of our knowledge, no large-scale datasets are available or, if available, are not fully complete that break down offending behavior for Latinos. Critics might suggest that our findings in the following section are city specific. We admit there is a chance that our findings might differ from those of others, but again, most of our cases involve members of the same group, and in all instances, the contours of victim

and offender data followed each other closely. Therefore, victimization rates represent a valuable, albeit not entirely satisfactory, proxy for group-specific offending behavior.

Despite claims by pundits and writers that high levels of crime are an unavoidable product of immigration, scholars rarely produce any systematic evidence of this recently reemerging social problem (Beck 1996; Hagan and Palloni 1998; Sampson and Lauritsen 1997). As Hagan and Palloni note, because immigration adds to the country's total population—and especially the population of young, unattached males—it will also likely increase the absolute volume of crime. The key question is whether immigrants contribute a disproportionate amount of crime beyond what we would expect from native populations with similar demographic characteristics. As Figure 15.1 shows,

Figure 15.2 Percent of U.S. population sample who believe selected immigrant groups have been a "good thing for the country"

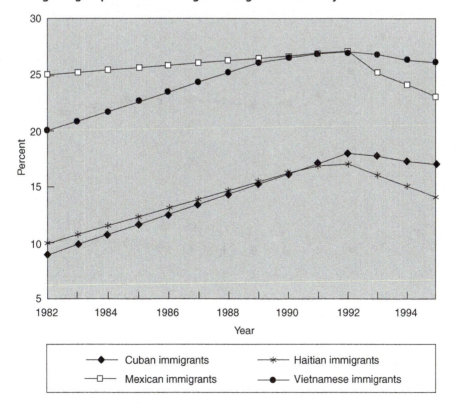

Source: Roper Reports, 1995. 113-114.

the recent wave of immigrants (predominantly Latino) appears not to have affected rates of Latino homicide.[2]

Although theory and popular wisdom suggest that immigrants should be disproportionately involved in crime, the trends reported in Figure 15.1 show that Latino homicide rates remained remarkably stable despite a massive increase in Latino immigrants in the early 1990s. Similar findings showing no systematic relationship between immigration and crime rates have been reported for the early 20th-century wave of immigration as well (Hagan and Palloni 1998, 369). In the final section of this essay, we explore the relationship between public opinion, local context, and immigrant crime by reporting previously unpublished group-specific homicide victim data.

Before turning to an examination of group-specific homicide rates, as these might be influenced by unfavorable public attitudes, we first present total homicide rates for the three cities involved. We have commented throughout this essay on the importance of local conditions in shaping immigrant crime, and it is important to place the homicide involvement of immigrant groups in their local context. Since victim data are more fully complete than offender information,

Figure 15.3 Total homicide victim rates for three cities

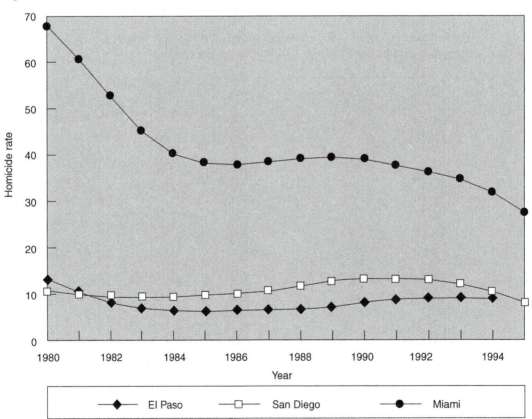

Sources: City of E1 Paso Police Department homicide investigations records 1980–95; City of Miami Police Department homicide investigations records 1980–95; City of San Diego Police Department homicide investigations records 1980–95. Population estimates are based on data from the U.S. Bureau of the Census (1990).

and given that roughly 20 to 25 percent of homicide cases are neither cleared with an arrest nor have an identified assailant, victim rates are used as proxies for homicides. Offender rates, at least in these cities, follow the same racial and ethnic contours of victimization data, allowing us to remain reasonably confident that our argument applies to all homicide cases.

As Figure 15.3 shows, homicide rates per 100,000 persons in Miami are much higher than in San Diego and El Paso, so we would expect that this finding would shape immigrant homicide.

Therefore, in the figures that follow, the homicide rates of immigrant groups will be compared with relevant local and national rates. In many of the exhibits, immigrant rates mirror both city-specific and national trends.[3]

There are probably some unique instances for Latinos and others in which changes in public attitudes and victimization rates shift over time. Take, for example, the highly publicized 1980 Mariel boatlift in which almost 125,000 people fled Cuba, with most ending up in south Florida (see Portes and Stepick 1993). The popular media

Figure 15.4 Miami's Mariel homicide victim rates in local and national context

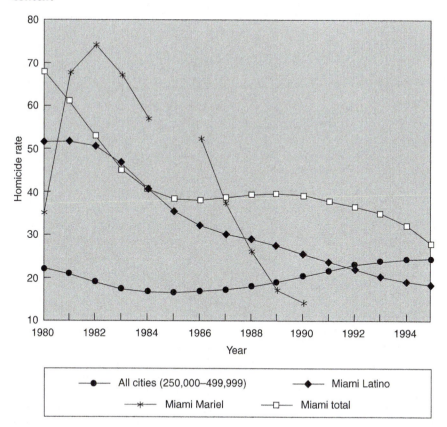

Sources: City of Miami Police Department homicide investigations records 1980–95. Population estimates are based on data from the U.S. Bureau of the Census (1990); population estimates for Mariels are based on data discussed in Portes, Clark, and Manning (1985); homicide rates for all cities are based on data from the U.S. Department of Justice, Federal Bureau of Investigation (1980–95).

linked these refugees to already record-high crime rates in Miami, labeled them as escorias, or scum, released from Cuban prisons, and generated a great deal of negative publicity about the group as a whole (see Aguirre, Saenz, and James 1997). As we see in Figure 15.4 the Mariel homicide victim rate did exceed the Miami city total from 1980 to 1986. However, the Mariel Cubans never surpassed the African-American level of victimization and apparently landed in Miami during an overall period of urban strife (see Martinez 1997 for data collection material). This is not to suggest that the Mariels were *not* overinvolved in crime.

In fact, they did contribute, like others, to the high crime levels in Miami, but at the same time they were not the persistent and high-crime-prone immigrants portrayed in the media. The Mariel contribution to local homicide was concentrated for a few years and then greatly declined, dropping below Miami's total and Latino rates and even below national rates for cities of Miami's size.

The negative attitudes toward Cubans persisted much longer than the initial negative publicity. Using the work of Portes and Stepick (1993) as a starting point, we note that the percentage of the national population agreeing that "Cubans were a

Figure 15.5 El Paso's Latino homicide victim rates in local and national context

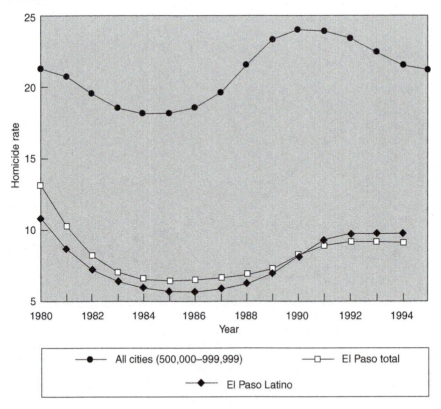

Sources: City of El Paso Police Department homicide investigations records 1980–95. Population estimates are based on data from the U.S. Bureau of the Census (1990); homicide rates for all cities are based on data from the U.S. Department of Justice, Federal Bureau of Investigation (1980–95).

good thing for the United States" was below 10 percent and rose only to about 17 percent for Cubans in 1995, according to the latest available Roper Reports (see Figure 15.2). This was despite the substantial decline of Mariel violence in Miami, where most of the refugees settled.

The same negative attitudes hold true in cities on the U.S.-Mexico border. Public opinion toward Mexicans never reflects the persistently low Latino (Mexican) victim rates in the two largest border cities—El Paso and San Diego. The homicide rate in these two cities never approached that of other cities of similar size (see Figures 15.5 and 15.6).

Figure 15.2 shows how national attitudes toward Mexicans remained flat, then actually declined, notwithstanding the low Mexican-origin homicide rates.

The connection between low victim rates and public perception becomes most apparent in the case of Miami's Haitians, as shown in Figure 15.7. Miami is not only a major destination for Afro-Caribbeans, it is home to the second largest Haitian community in the United States. Yet, again, public attitudes toward Haitians have rarely been favorable (see Figure 15.2) and are actually worsening, despite Haitians having homicide rates lower than

Figure 15.6 San Diego's Latino homicide victim rates in local and national context

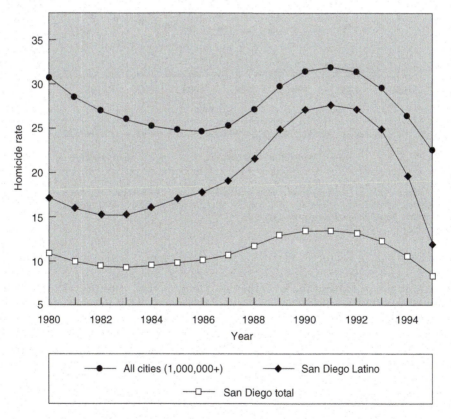

Sources: City of San Diego Police Department homicide investigations records 1980–95. Population estimates are based on data from the U.S. Bureau of the Census (1990); homicide rates for all cities are based on data from the U.S. Department of Justice, Federal Bureau of Investigation (1980–95).

Figure 15.7 Miami's Haitian homicide victim rates in local and national context

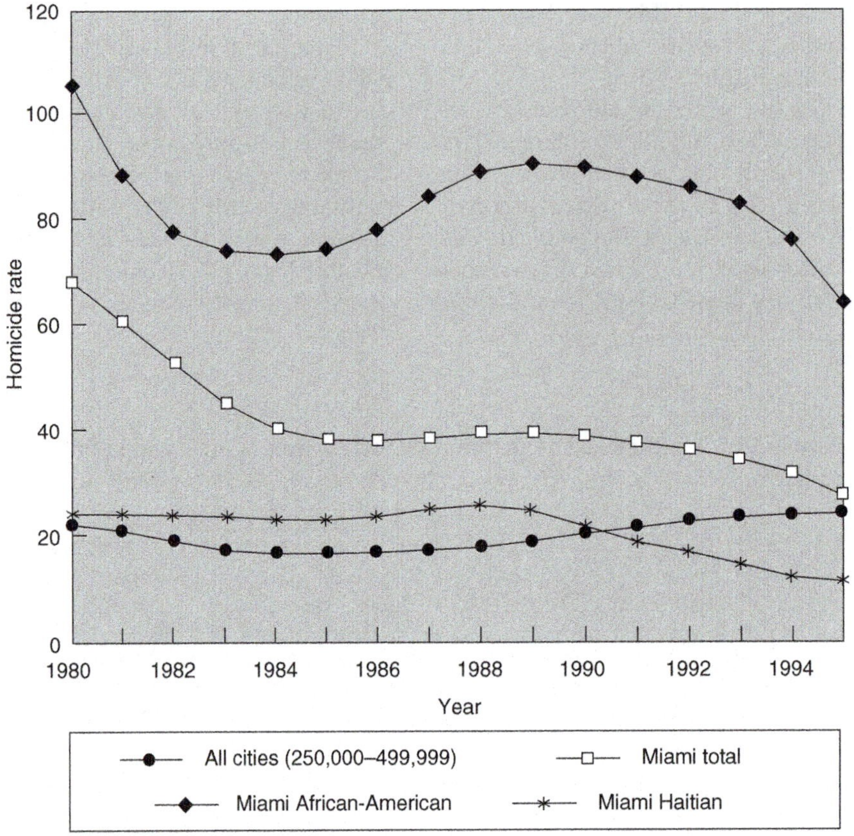

Sources: City of Miami Police Department homicide investigations records 1980–95. Population estimates are based on data from the U.S. Bureau of the Census (1990); homicide rates for all cities are based on data from the U.S. Department of Justice, Federal Bureau of Investigation (1980–95).

those of *any* ethnic group in Miami and lower than the average in all small cities in the 1990s.

Finally, we examine homicide rates among San Diego's Asian immigrants (predominantly Vietnamese) in Figure 15.8 and compare these rates with public attitudes about Vietnamese. At first glance, the level of homicide among Asians appears to ebb and flow; however, the rate never rises above single digits (7.5 to 8.0 per 100,000 Asians in San Diego). In fact, Asian rates fall below San Diego's total rate and well below the rates of cities with more than 1 million residents.

Despite this, positive attitudes toward the Vietnamese have not materialized to any appreciable degree over the period of this study (see Figure 15.2). Like the other immigrant groups, Asians continue to be viewed unfavorably despite their comparatively low involvement in crime, at least as measured by homicide rates. Apparently, national attitudes toward ethnic groups are not in line with crime rates (if we assume a favorable attitude to low crime groups) but are instead probably shaped by ethnic or racial stereotypes, not empirical data.

Figure 15.8 San Diego's Asian homicide victim rates in local and national context

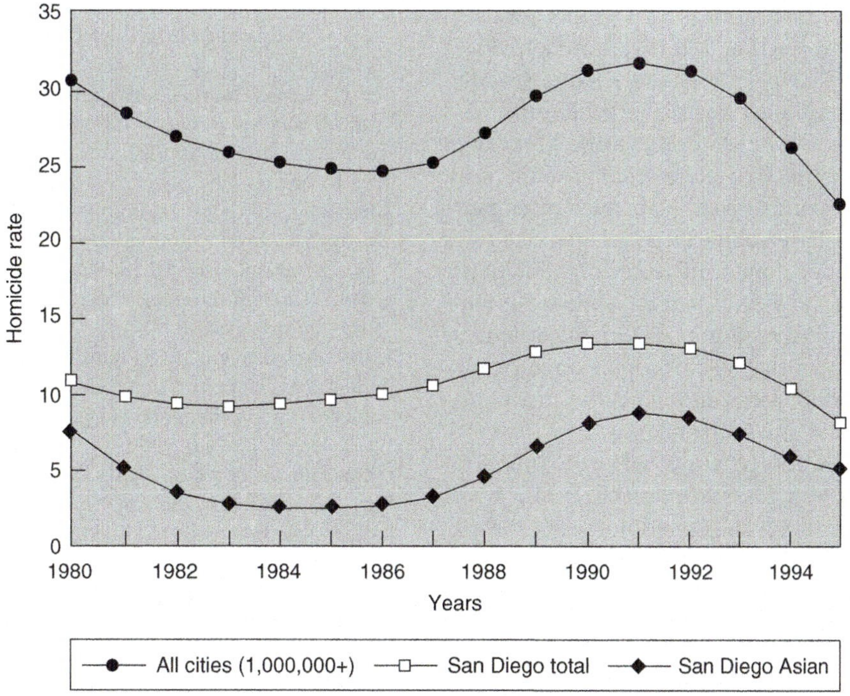

Sources: City of San Diego Police Department Homicide Investigations records 1980–95. Population estimates are based on data from the U.S. Bureau of the Census (1990); homicide rates for all cities are based on data from the U.S. Department of Justice, Federal Bureau of Investigation (1980–95).

Conclusion

We can draw a number of broad conclusions from this review of immigration and crime in 20th-century America. First, there are good theoretical reasons to believe that immigrants should be involved in crime to a greater degree than natives. For example, immigrants face acculturation problems that natives do not, and immigrants tend to settle in disorganized neighborhoods characterized by deleterious structural conditions such as poverty, ethnic heterogeneity, a preponderance of young males, and possibly more criminal opportunities in the form of gangs. Also, the cultural codes of immigrants may conflict with the legal codes constructed by native groups. Despite these and other reasons to expect high levels of immigrant crime,

the bulk of empirical studies conducted over the past century have found that immigrants are usually underrepresented in criminal statistics. There are variations to this general finding, but these appear to be linked more to differences in structural conditions across areas where immigrants settle than to the cultural traditions of the immigrant groups. Local context appears to be the central influence shaping the criminal involvement of both immigrants and natives, although in many cases, immigrants seem more able to withstand crime-facilitating conditions than native groups.

We offer some plausible explanations for why immigrant crime rates are lower than expected. Contrary to a tradition of social science research on urban violence dating back to the pioneering work of Thomas and Znaniecki (1920), contemporary immigration might not create disorganized communities but instead stabilize neighborhoods through the creation of new social and economic institutions. Immigrants reside in highly impoverished communities but provide a buffer to further neighborhood decline through higher levels of intact and extended families and regular contact with the world of work. Moore and Pinderhughes (1993) note that immigrant Latinos, as a whole, have relatively high rates of employment, but in lower blue-collar occupations (e.g., operators, fabricators, and laborers) and in the informal economy (e.g., street vendors, domestics). Thus, immigrants are characterized more as the working poor than as chronically unemployed, and they work in areas dominated by small business owners and the self-employed.

Much more research is needed on immigration and crime, particularly on the latest wave of immigration, to advance our knowledge beyond the general conclusions provided by this essay. Like others, we suggest that future research should be more open to the idea that immigration can be a positive influence on communities to suppress crime. We agree with Hagan and Palloni (1998, 382) that researchers should:

> place the priority on finding ways to preserve, protect, and promote the social capital that…immigrants bring to their experience in the United States, rather than overemphasize issues of crime and punishment.

Academic study of immigrants that is limited to gangs and crime can serve only to promote the impression that immigrants are a crime-prone group—an image that the empirical research of the past 100 years does not support. In sum, this review suggests that native groups would profit from a better understanding of how immigrant groups faced with adverse social conditions maintain relatively low levels of crime.

Notes

1. The fear that too many crime-prone immigrants are entering the United States is a contemporary concern, in addition to other reasons for anti-immigrant sentiment. In a national bestselling book promising "common sense about America's immigration disaster," a writer at *Forbes* and *National Review* magazines states: "[I]mmigration is not the *only* cause of crime. It may not even be the major cause of crime. But it is a *factor*" (Brimelow 1996, 182; emphasis in original).

   Hailed as a "non-fiction horror story of a nation that is willfully but blindly pursuing a course of national suicide" (Jesse E. Todd, Jr., cited in the front matter of Brimelow 1996), such alarmist writings assume a strong link between immigrants and crime while providing little empirical data. In fact, Brimelow (p. 182) claims that "there has been no serious academic study of the impact on crime" of the post-1965 wave of immigration.

2. Although not evident in Figure 15.5, the Latino homicide rates fluctuated from slightly more than 16 per 100,000 in 1985 to a high of 18.6 in 1991, and declined to a low of 12.4 in 1996 (U.S. Department of Health and Human Services 1998). The massive increase in legal immigration did not increase Latino homicide rates, which actually declined somewhat throughout the 1990s. Homicide rates for blacks and whites also declined after the peak years of immigration. Black rates fell from a high of 41.6 per 100,000 in 1991 to 29.9 in 1996, while white rates over a similar period dropped from 4.4 to 3.5. Thus, homicide rates declined for all groups after the arrival of large numbers of immigrants.

3. All rates are per 100,000 group-specific persons as measured by the 1990 census.

References

Abbott, Edith. 1931. The problem of crime and the foreign born. In *Report on crime and the foreign born*. National Commission on Law Observance and Enforcement Report no. 10. Washington, D.C.: U.S. Government Printing Office.

Abbott, G. 1915. Immigration and crime. *Journal of Criminal Law and Criminology* 6:522–532.

Alaniz, Maria Luisa, Randi S. Cartmill, and Robert Nash Parker. 1998. Immigrants and violence: The importance of neighborhood context. *Hispanic Journal of Behavioral Sciences* 20 (May):155–174.

Aguirre, B.E., Rogelio Saenz, and Brian Sinclair James. 1997. Marielitos ten years later: The Scarface legacy. *Social Science Quarterly* 78 (June):487–507.

Anderson, Elijah. 1990. *Streetwise: Race, class, and change in an urban community*. Chicago: University of Chicago Press.

Aponte, Robert. 1996. Urban unemployment and the mismatch dilemma: Accounting for the immigration exception. *Social Problems* 43 (August): 268–283.

Baker, Susan Gonzalez, Frank D. Bean, Augustin Escobar Latapi, and Sidney Weintraub. 1998. U.S. immigration policies and trends: The growing importance of migration from Mexico. In *Crossings: Mexican immigration in interdisciplinary perspectives,* edited by M.M. Suarez-Orozco. Cambridge: Harvard University Press.

Bankston, Carl L., III. 1998. Youth gangs and the new second generation: A review essay. *Aggression and Violent Behavior* 3 (1):35–45.

Beck, Roy. 1996. *The case against immigration.* New York: W.W. Norton.

Bowler, Alida C. 1931. Recent statistics on crime and the foreign born. In *Report on crime and the foreign born.* National Commission on Law Observance and Enforcement Report no. 10. Washington, D.C.: U.S. Government Printing Office.

Bradshaw, Benjamin, David R. Johnson, Derral Cheatwood, and Stephen Blanchard. 1998. A historical geographical study of lethal violence in San Antonio. *Social Science Quarterly* 79 (December): 863–878.

Brimelow, Peter J. 1996. *Alien nation.* New York: HarperPerennial.

Bursik, Robert J. 1988. Social disorganization and theories of crime and delinquency: Problems and prospects. *Criminology* 26 (November): 519–551.

Chin, Ko-lin. 1990. *Chinese subculture and criminality: Non-traditional crime groups in America.* Westport, Connecticut: Greenwood Press.

Cloward, Richard, and Lloyd Ohlin. 1960. *Delinquency and opportunity: A theory of delinquent gangs.* New York: Free Press.

Du Phuoc Long, Patrick. 1996. *The dream shattered: Vietnamese gangs in America.* Boston: Northeastern University Press.

Epstein, Gail, and Ronnie Greene. 1993. Dade's crime rate is highest in U.S., Florida is 1st among States. *Miami Herald,* 3 October.

Espenshade, Thomas J., and Maryanne Belanger. 1998. Immigration and public opinion. In *Crossings: Mexican immigration in interdisciplinary perspectives,* edited by M.M. Suarez-Orozco. Cambridge: Harvard University Press.

Ferracuti, Franco. 1968. European migration and crime. In *Crime and culture: Essays in honor of Thorsten Sellin,* edited by M.E. Wolfgang. New York: John Wiley & Sons.

Gans, Herbert J. 1992. Second generation decline: Scenarios for the economic and ethnic futures of the post-1965 American immigrants. *Ethnic and Racial Studies* 15:173–192.

Glueck, Sheldon, and Eleanor Glueck. 1930. *Five hundred criminal careers.* New York: Alfred A. Knopf.

Gurr, Ted Robert. 1989. The history of violent crime in America. In *Violence in America,* edited by T.R. Gurr. Vol. 1. Newbury Park, California: Sage Publications.

Hagan, John, and Alberto Palloni. 1998. Immigration and crime in the United States. In *The immigration debate,* edited by J.P. Smith and B. Edmonston. Washington, D.C.: National Academy Press.

Handlin, Oscar. 1959. *The newcomers: Negroes and Puerto Ricans in a changing metropolis.* Cambridge: Harvard University Press.

Hawkins, Darnell F. 1999. African Americans and homicide. In *Issues in the study and prevention of homicide,* edited by M.D. Smith and M. Zahn. Thousand Oaks, California: Sage Publications.

Hayner, Norman S. 1933. Delinquency areas in the Puget Sound region. *American Journal of Sociology* 39 (November): 314–328.

Jonassen, Christen T. 1949. A re-evaluation and critique of the logic and some methods of Shaw and McKay. *American Sociological Review* 14 (October): 608–614.

Kobrin, Solomon. 1959. The Chicago Area Project: A 25 year assessment. *Annals of the American Academy of Political and Social Science* 322 (March): 19–29.

Lambert, John R. 1970. *Crime, police, and race relations: A study in Birmingham.* London: Oxford University Press.

Lane, Roger. 1997. *Murder in America: A history.* Columbus: Ohio State University Press.

Laughlin, Harry H. 1939. *Immigration and conquest.* New York: Special Committee on Immigration and Naturalization of the Chamber of Commerce of the State of New York.

Lee, Matthew T., Ramiro Martinez, Jr., and S. Fernando Rodriguez. 2000. Contrasting Latinos in homicide research: The victim and offender relationship in El Paso and Miami. *Social Science Quarterly* 81 (1): 375–388.

Lee, Yoon Ho. 1998. Acculturation and delinquent behavior: The case of Korean American youths.

International Journal of Comparative and Applied Criminal Justice 22 (Fall): 273–292.

Lewis, Oscar. 1965. *La vida: A Puerto Rican family in the culture of poverty.* New York: Random House.

Lind, Andrew W. 1930a. The ghetto and the slum. *Social Forces* 9 (December): 206–215.

——. 1930b. Some ecological patterns of community disorganization in Honolulu. *American Journal of Sociology* 36 (September): 206–220.

Marshall, Ineke Haen. 1997. *Minorities, migrants, and crime: Diversity and similarity across Europe and the United States.* Thousand Oaks, California: Sage Publications.

Martinez, Ramiro, Jr. 1997a. Homicide among the 1980 Mariel refugees in Miami: Victims and offenders. *Hispanic Journal of Behavioral Sciences* 19 (May): 107–122.

——. 1997b. Homicide among Miami's ethnic groups: Anglos, blacks, and Latinos in the 1990s. *Homicide Studies* 1 (May): 17–34.

——. 1996. Latinos and lethal violence: The impact of poverty and inequality. *Social Problems* 43 (May): 131–146.

Martinez, Ramiro, Jr., and Matthew T. Lee. Forthcoming. Comparing the context of immigrant homicides in Miami: Haitians, Jamaicans, and Mariels. *International Migration Review.*

——. 1999. Extending ethnicity in homicide research: The case of Latinos. In *Homicide: A sourcebook of social research,* edited by M.D. Smith and M. Zahn. Newbury Park, California: Sage Publications.

——. 1998. Immigration and the ethnic distribution of homicide in Miami, 1985–1995. *Homicide Studies* 2 (August): 291–304.

McCord, Joan. 1995. Ethnicity, acculturation, and opportunities: A study of two generations. In *Ethnicity, race, and crime,* edited by D.F. Hawkins. Albany: State University of New York Press.

Merton, Robert K. 1938. Social structure and anomie. *American Sociological Review* 3 (October): 672–682.

Monkkonen, Eric H. 1989. Diverging homicide rates: England and the United States, 1850–1875. In *Violence in America,* edited by T.R. Gurr. Vol. 1. Newbury Park, California: Sage Publications.

Moore, Joan, and Raquel Pinderhughes. 1993. *In the barrios: Latinos and the underclass debate.* New York: Russell Sage Foundation.

Ousey, Graham C. 1999. Homicide, structural factors, and the racial invariance assumption. *Criminology* 37 (May): 405–426.

Padilla, Amado M. 1980. *Acculturation: Theory, models, and some new findings.* Boulder, Colorado: Westview Press.

Portes, Alejandro. 1996. *The new second generation.* New York: Russell Sage Foundation.

Portes, Alejandro, Juan M. Clark, and R.D. Manning. 1985. After Mariel: A survey of the resettlement experiences of 1980 Cuban refugees in Miami. *Cuban Studies* 15: 37–59.

Portes, Alejandro, and Alex Stepick. 1993. *City on the edge: The transformation of Miami.* Berkeley: University of California Press.

Roper Reports. 1995. *Roper Report 95–4.* New York: Roper Starch Worldwide, June.

Rosenwaike, Ira, and Katherine Hempstead. 1990. Mortality among three Puerto Rican populations: Residents of Puerto Rico and migrants in New York City and in the balance of the United States, 1979–81. *International Migration Review* 24 (Winter): 684–702.

Ross, Harold. 1937. Crime and the native born sons of European immigrants. *Journal of Criminal Law and Criminology* 28 (July–August): 202–209.

Sampson, Robert J. 1987. Urban black violence: The effect of male joblessness and family disruption. *American Journal of Sociology* 93 (September): 348–382.

Sampson, Robert J., and Janet L. Lauritsen. 1997. Racial and ethnic disparities in crime and criminal justice in the United States. In *Ethnicity, crime, and immigration.* Vol. 21 of *Crime and justice: A review of research,* edited by M. Tonry. Chicago: University of Chicago Press.

Sampson, Robert J., and William Julius Wilson. 1995. Toward a theory of race, crime, and urban inequality. In *Crime and inequality,* edited by J. Hagan and R. Peterson. Stanford, California: Stanford University Press.

Sanchez-Jankowski, Martin. 1991. *Islands in the street: Gangs and American urban society.* Berkeley: University of California Press.

Scalia, John. 1996. *Noncitizens in the Federal criminal justice system, 1984–1994.* Special Report, NCJ 160934. Washington, D.C.: U.S. Department of Justice, Bureau of Justice Statistics.

Schneider, Hans Joachim. 1995. Foreigners as perpetrators and as victims in Germany. *EuroCriminology* 8–9:95–108.

Sellin, Thorsten. 1938. *Culture conflict and crime.* New York: Social Science Research Council.

Shaw, Clifford R., and Henry D. McKay. [1942] 1969. *Juvenile delinquency and urban areas.* Chicago: University of Chicago Press.

——. 1931. Social factors in juvenile delinquency. In *Report on the causes of crime.* National Commission on Law Observance and Enforcement Report no. 13. Washington, D.C.: U.S. Government Printing Office.

Short, James F. 1997. *Poverty, ethnicity, and violent crime.* Boulder, Colorado: Westview Press.

Simon, Rita J. 1993. Old minorities, new immigrants: Aspirations, hopes, and fears. *Annals of the American Academy of Political and Social Science* 30 (November): 61–73.

——. 1987. Immigration and American attitudes. *Public Opinion* 10 (July–August): 47–50.

——. 1985. *Public opinion and the immigrant: Print media coverage, 1880–1980.* Lexington, Massachusetts: Lexington Books.

Stepick, Alex. 1998. *Pride against prejudice: Haitians in the United States.* Boston: Allyn and Bacon.

Suarez-Orozco, Marcelo M. 1998. Introduction to *Crossings: Mexican immigration in interdisciplinary perspectives,* edited by M.M. Suarez-Orozco. Cambridge: Harvard University Press.

Sutherland, Edwin H. 1947. *Principles of criminology.* 4th ed. Chicago: J.B. Lippincott.

——. 1934. *Principles of criminology.* Chicago: J.B. Lippincott.

Sutherland, Edwin H., and Donald R. Cressey. 1960. *Principles of criminology.* 6th ed. Chicago: J.B. Lippincott.

Taft, Donald R. 1936. Nationality and crime. *American Sociological Review* 1 (October): 724–736.

Taylor, Paul S. 1931. Crime and the foreign born: The problem of the Mexican. In *Report on crime and the foreign born.* National Commission on Law Observance and Enforcement Report no. 10. Washington, D.C.: U.S. Government Printing Office.

Thomas, William I., and Florian Znaniecki. [1920] 1984. *The Polish peasant in Europe and America: Edited and abridged.* Chicago: University of Illinois Press.

——. 1920. *The Polish peasant in Europe and America: Volume IV, disorganization and reorganization in Poland.* Boston: Gorham Press.

Tonry, Michael. 1997. Ethnicity, crime, and immigration. In *Ethnicity, crime, and immigration.* Vol. 21 of *Crime and justice: A review of research,* edited by M. Tonry. Chicago: University of Chicago Press.

U.S. Bureau of the Census. 1990. 1990 census of population and housing. Summary tape file 3A. Retrieved 30 March 2000 from the World Wide Web: http://venus.census. gov/cdrom/lookup.

U.S. Commission on Immigration Reform. 1994. *Restoring credibility.* Washington, D.C.: U.S. Commission on Immigration Reform.

U.S. Department of Health and Human Services, National Center for Health Statistics. 1998. *Health, United States, 1998: With socioeconomic status and health chartbook.* Hyattsville, Maryland.

U.S. Department of Justice, Federal Bureau of Investigation. 1997. *Crime in the United States—1996.* Retrieved 12 January 2000 from the World Wide Web: http://www.fbi.gov/ucr/ Cius_97/96CRIME/96crime2.pdf.

——. 1980–95. *Crime in the United States.* Uniform Crime Reports. Washington, D.C.

U.S. Department of Justice, Immigration and Naturalization Service. 1997. *Statistical yearbook of the Immigration and Naturalization Service, 1996.* Washington, D.C.

——. 1987. *Statistical yearbook of the Immigration and Naturalization Service, 1986.* Washington, D.C.

Vidal, Gore. 1986. The empire lovers strike back. *Nation,* 22 March, 350. Quoted in Karl Zinsmeister, Asians: Prejudice from top and bottom, *Public Opinion* 10 (July-August 1987): 10.

Vigil, James D., and J.M. Long. 1990. Emic and etic perspectives of gang culture: The Chicano case. In *Gangs in America,* edited by C.R. Huff. Newbury Park: Sage Publications.

Von Hentig, Hans. 1945. The first generation and a half: Notes on the delinquency of the native white of mixed parentage. *American Sociological Review* 10 (December): 792–798.

Warnshuis, Paul Livingstone. 1931. Crime and criminal justice among the Mexicans of Illinois. In *Report on crime and the foreign born.* National Commission on Law Observance and Enforcement Report no. 10. Washington, D.C.: U.S. Government Printing Office.

Whyte, William Foote. 1943. Social organization in the slums. *American Sociological Review* 8 (February): 34–39.

Wilbanks, William. 1984. *Murder in Miami: An analysis of homicide patterns and trends in Dade County (Miami) Florida, 1917–1983.* Lanham, Maryland: University Press of America.

Wilson, William J. 1996. *When work disappears: The world of the new urban poor.* New York: Alfred A. Knopf.

——. 1987. *The truly disadvantaged.* Chicago: University of Chicago Press.

Wolfgang, Marvin E. 1958. *Patterns in criminal homicide.* Philadelphia: University of Pennsylvania Press.

Wolfgang, Marvin, and Franco Ferracuti. 1967. *The subculture of violence: Towards an integrated theory in criminology.* London: Tavistock.

Yeager, Matthew G. 1997. Immigrants and criminality: A review. *Criminal Justice Abstracts* 29 (March): 143–171.

Young, Pauline V. 1936. Social problems in the education of the immigrant child. *American Sociological Review* 1 (June): 419–429.

Zinsmeister, Karl. 1987. Asians: Prejudice from top and bottom. *Public Opinion* 10 (July-August): 8–10, 59.

Theories of Crime

Crime does not occur in a vacuum. Although to the untrained eye, crime may appear to be random or haphazard, numerous consistent patterns or regularities have been identified with regard to crime. For example, as revealed in Section III, certain factors or correlates are associated with crime. How can we account for such regularities and patterns? Why do they exist? To attempt to answer these questions, criminologists rely on theories.

Criminological theories are systematic, consistent sets of ideas that provide comprehensive frameworks in an attempt to understand and explain crime. To be considered a theory, a set of ideas must include testable propositions. As such, a theory can be found to be untrue or it can be supported through empirical research; however, a theory can never be definitively proven to be true and applicable under all conditions. Theories not only provide a framework for understanding crime, but they can also have important policy implications for its prevention and control. For example, if policy makers believe that crime is the result of genetic causes, the approach they would take to control and prevent crime would be very different from the approach others would take if they attributed crime to socially disorganized neighborhoods.

Criminologists have produced numerous theories to explain crime and criminal behavior. Although most theories attempt to explain "street crimes," some try to explain all types of criminal and antisocial behavior. Theories vary in terms of the factors and processes they consider important for understanding crime. Some theories attempt to explain why particular individuals engage in crime; to do so, they focus on factors at the individual level (the microlevel), such as biological or psychological abnormalities of offenders. Some sociological theories are also interested in explaining the behavior of individuals, but rather than emphasize characteristics of individuals, they tend to focus on social processes, such as interactions with peers, that influence people's behavior. Other theories attempt to explain crime rates, rather than individual behavior. Such theories thus focus on structural factors (the macrolevel), such as poverty rates or social disorganization in an area.

With few exceptions, however, theories are not strictly individualist (microlevel) or structural (macrolevel) approaches. Instead, they form a continuum, ranging from more individualistic to more structural. For example, Sutherland's theory of differential association (Reading 20) focuses on individuals and the processes involved in learning to commit crime. He also includes, however, a macrolevel component (differential social organization) in describing the role of the larger social group in this learning process. In addition, different theories overlap in the types of social processes they emphasize. As an example, both differential association theory and social control theory (Reading 26) consider peers and other intimates to be important for explaining an individual's criminal behavior; the theories, however, provide different explanations concerning how and why such people influence offending. The overlaps are also apparent with regard to a relatively recent trend in criminology to attempt to integrate similar theories rather than examining them as competing approaches, such as the integrated theory of Delbert S. Elliott, Susan S. Ageton, and Rachelle J. Canter and the "control balance" theory of Charles Tittle.

Criminological theories can be broadly categorized in terms of the disciplines and their respective foci. That is, the three major areas of criminological theories are biological, psychological, and sociological. Both within and across these areas there are many different approaches to understanding crime. This section provides an overview of the major traditions within each of the three broad areas.

Biological Approaches

Biological approaches posit that crime is attributable to genetic and other biological factors at the level of the individual. In general, scholars who work in this area are interested in identifying a biological basis for behavior, and they attempt to differentiate criminals and noncriminals on the basis of such factors as brain damage or genetic abnormalities. The biological factors implicated in criminal behavior may result from genetic mutations inherited from parents, from mutations occurring after conception or while the fetus is developing, or from environmental factors, such as injury or exposure to toxins, that increase the likelihood of engaging in crime (Vold, Bernard, and Snipes, 1998).

Researchers interested in identifying a genetic basis for criminal behavior conduct family, twin, or adoption studies. In family studies, the criminality of family members is examined; similarity in crime involvement may be attributable to genetic factors. Studies of twins involve comparing the similarity, or concordance, of criminality of genetically identical twins (who are genetically identical) and that of fraternal twins (who share about 50 percent of the same genes, the same as nontwin siblings). To the extent that concordance rates are higher for identical twins than for fraternal twins, this fact should support a genetic basis for criminality. For both family and twin studies, however, the similarity in offending may be

the result of shared environment (and therefore social factors), and even of being treated the same (particularly identical twins), rather than reflecting a genetic basis. Adoption studies, by contrast, involve comparing the criminal offending of an adoptee with the behavior of both the adoptive parents and the biological parents. The extent of similarity in the adoptee's offending with that of the adopting parents is attributable to environmental factors; similarity in offending with biological parents is attributable to genetic factors. Reading 18 examines the link between biological characteristics and criminality.

Other types of biological factors have also been examined in relation to crime. Differences in responses to and levels of neurotransmitters, chemicals that play a key role in allowing electrical impulses to be transmitted in the brain, may be associated with antisocial and violent behavior. Similarly, differences in levels and responses to hormones, particularly the male androgen, testosterone (Booth and Osgood 1993), as well as hormonal changes associated with the menstrual cycle in women, may be associated with criminal and aggressive behavior. Brain irregularities, whether due to biological abnormalities or caused by injury, may also be associated with criminal behavior (Vold, Bernard, and Snipes 1998). Neuropsychological deficits, resulting from some type of brain dysfunction and manifested in terms of low verbal ability and other problems, are associated with offending behavior in adolescence (Moffitt, Lyman, and Silva 1994). In addition, the autonomic nervous system (ANS), the part of the central nervous system that controls involuntary bodily functions such as the heart rate, may play a role in crime, with some criminals having slower than average ANS responses (Vold, Bernard, and Snipes 1998).

Other biological factors may be implicated in crime. Consumption of alcohol and/or drugs may result in irrational behavior, either due directly to consumption and its effects on behavior or to irritability associated with withdrawal symptoms (Goldstein 1985). The effects of alcohol, a legal and widely used drug in the United States, may include increased aggressiveness and disinhibition, which increase the likelihood of criminal, particularly violent, behavior (Collins 1981). Other biological factors may also promote criminal behavior. Poor diet, exposure to lead, and head injury may all result in brain damage and may increase the chances of an individual's engaging in violence, or in crime more generally (Vold, Bernard, and Snipes, 1998).

Overall, the research seems to indicate that there may be a genetic or other biological basis for some criminal behavior. Such approaches are becoming more prevalent in mainstream criminology (e.g., Ellis and Walsh 1997). However, most biological approaches, and scholars who adhere to them, recognize at some level the important role of psychological and social factors in determining whether biological "vulnerabilities," or predispositions for offending actually lead to crime.

Psychological Approaches

Psychological approaches, like biological approaches, tend to focus on processes at the individual level. Psychological approaches take a variety of forms but generally are interested in differentiating offenders from nonoffenders on psychological dimensions. The major approaches in psychology have been in the areas of psychoanalysis, personality characteristics, and psychological pathologies (such as antisocial personality disorder and psychoses). Reading 19 explores the question of whether certain personality types are crime-prone.

Psychoanalytic theory provides one explanation for crime. Although Sigmund Freud did not focus on criminals specifically, much of the theorizing in this area is based on his work. The psychoanalytic tradition regards crime as the result of an imbalance in the workings of the three components of the self: the id, the ego, and the superego. The id is comprised of instincts and drives that seek immediate gratification; the superego is the conscience or social authority; and the ego attempts to balance the id's drives and the demands of the superego. From this perspective, crime may result from either the overdevelopment or underdevelopment of the ego or superego. Some suggest that such overdevelopment of the ego or superego produces excess feelings of guilt; crime provides a potential source of punishment that will alleviate feelings of guilt and restore balance to the individual. Other psychoanalysts argue that underdevelopment of these components produces crime because there is inadequate regulation or control of the id; involvement in crime provides a means to satisfy the desires, drives, and instincts located in the id. Later psychoanalysts have further developed some of these ideas; psychoanalytic approaches, however, suffer from several limitations, including the criticism that it is impossible to test their essential hypotheses. As a whole, then, psychoanalytic approaches have not been very useful for criminologists (Vold, Bernard, and Snipes 1998).

Another psychological approach attempts to identify personality characteristics that differentiate offenders from nonoffenders. Such efforts have been ongoing for several decades. Although a review of the literature in 1950 by Karl F. Schuessler and Donald R. Cressey suggested that no personality characteristics specifically differentiate criminals and noncriminals, other criminologists suggest that there are differences. For example, in the same year Sheldon Glueck and Eleanor Glueck differentiated a group of 500 delinquents from a matched group of 500 nondelinquents on the basis of such characteristics as extroversion, hostility, and impulsiveness. More recent efforts suggest that personality characteristics may be important. "Lifestyle criminals," offenders with long-term involvement in crime, are characterized by "faulty, irrational thinking" and possession of eight cognitive traits, such as mollification (justification of criminal activity in terms of external forces operating on the criminal), entitlement (a sense of privilege; the world exists to benefit and pleasure criminals), and superoptimism (an extreme sense of self-confidence in one's ability to get away with most things) (Walters 1990). The personality characteristics of "negative emotionality" (a combination of aggression, alienation, and stress reaction) and "constraint" (a combination of harm avoidance, traditionalism, and control) are consistently associated with offending and other antisocial behaviors across countries, genders, and races (Caspi et al. 1994).

Research on personality disorders is another psychological approach to crime. Of particular interest for criminologists are people with anti-social or psychopathic personalities. Psychopaths (or sociopaths) are thought to be more likely than other people to engage in criminal and antisocial behavior, and even the definition of "antisocial personality disorder" used by the American Psychiatric Association includes law violations and aggressive behavior as two of several diagnostic criteria. Such people are asocial, aggressive, highly impulsive, feel little or no guilt for antisocial behavior, and cannot form lasting bonds of affection with others. They are present oriented, impulsive, and do not plan their crimes. It must be noted, however, that not all criminals are sociopaths, nor do all sociopaths commit crimes (Vold, Bernard, and Snipes 1998).

Two recent approaches that may be considered psychological because of their emphasis on stable individual differences have had an important impact on criminology. One approach, posited by Wilson and Herrnstein, argues that people who engage in crime are impulsive and present oriented, often paying little attention to long-term consequences or rewards. These scholars argue that "constitutional factors," such as low IQ and personality characteristics, as well as social factors, such as family and peers, play a role in the development of impulsiveness and present orientedness. A somewhat similar approach is the "general theory" of crime proposed by Michael R. Gottfredson and Travis Hirschi (Reading 27). They argue that all criminals, regardless of the types of crime they commit, have little self-control. Lack of self-control is characterized by impulsiveness, risk taking, present orientedness, and other similar characteristics. Gottfredson and Hirschi argue that self-control is established early in life and is a stable trait over time; however, they posit that lack of self-control results from the family's providing the child with inadequate socialization, rather than from psychological or biological factors. The "general theory," and particularly the concept of low self-control, is currently undergoing intensive empirical testing by criminologists. As a whole, the literature suggests that lack of self-control may, in fact, be associated with criminal behavior, although this association is not unequivocal (e.g., Arneklev et al. 1993).

Sociological Approaches

With sociological theories, the focus is on social processes that affect crime, either at the individual level (microlevel theories) or at the level of the group, neighborhood, or society (macrolevel theories). As noted earlier, theories rarely fit neatly into either a micro or macro category, but instead often rely on processes ongoing at both levels. This section will consider several different sociological theories of crime, including social control theory, differential association theory, strain theory, and social disorganization theory.

Social Control Theory

Social control theories differ from most other approaches with regard to the basic question they seek to address. Although most theories attempt to determine why some people engage in crime, social control theories are interested in explaining why it is that more people do not engage in crime or, more specifically, what keeps people from committing crimes. The foundation for social control theories was provided by Walter Reckless, through his early work on containment theory, and Albert Reiss, who argued that both personal controls (factors internal to the individual) and social controls (forces external to the individual, such as the social institution of school) keep individuals from engaging in crime. The most prominent of such approaches, however, is Hirschi's social control theory; Reading 26 is an excerpt from his classic statement of the theory.

Hirschi argues that social bonds between the individual and conventional institutions and conventional persons explain why people do not engage in delinquency or crime. Strong bonds induce conformity and inhibit people from engaging in crime; weak bonds enable them to engage in crime. The four bonds are attachment (affective ties to other people), commitment (commitment to conventional goals and actions that provide a "stake in conformity"), involvement (time spent engaged in conventional activities), and belief (the extent to which an individual believes he or she should obey the norms and rules of society) (see Reading 26).

The bonds that are formed vary over the life course in terms of the individuals and institutions to which one is bonded. In childhood, strong bonds to family are key (Cernkovich and Giordano 1986; Sampson and Laub 1993; Rankin and Kern 1994); in adolescence, bonds to peers and school are important for explaining delinquency (Giordano, Cernkovich, and Pugh 1986; Cernkovich and Giordano 1992; Sampson and Laub 1993). Although Hirschi originally argued that delinquents have no friends and that friends exert pressure to conform, his own and subsequent research has convincingly demonstrated that being bonded to delinquent peers is associated with offending. In addition, social control theory has recently been extended by Robert J. Sampson and John H. Laub (1993) to explain crime and deviance over the lifecourse, with spousal attachments and jobs in adulthood found by these and other scholars (Nagin, Farrington, and Moffitt 1995; Horney, Osgood, and Marshall 1995) to be important inhibitors of offending by adults.

Differential Association

The differential association tradition stems largely from the work of Edwin Sutherland and is generally categorized as a learning theory. Sutherland was interested in developing a general statement of how all types of crime are learned (Vold, Bernard, and Snipes 1998), and he later applied his theory to explain white-collar crime (Sutherland, 1983; Reading 20).

Sutherland's theory has two components: differential association and differential social organization. As discussed in Reading 20, differential association is delineated in a set of nine propositions that provide an explanation for how individuals learn to engage in delinquency and crime. According to Sutherland, this learning involves all of the same processes that are involved in learning conventional behavior. One learns the specific techniques for committing the crime, as well as drives, motivations, and rationalizations for behavior. The learning of both the method and the meaning occurs in the context of intimate personal groups; in most cases, these groups involve one's friends. The drives, motives, and rationalizations

that an individual learns provide ways of defining the law that may support upholding it or violating it. The "principle of differential association" posits that an individual will engage in offending when the number of definitions that support violating the law is greater than the number that support conforming to the law. Differential associations (generally considered to mean contact with intimate personal groups that provide definitions concerning violation of the law) differ in terms of their priority, duration, intensity, and frequency, which helps explain why definitions provided by some people are more important than those provided by others.

Sutherland also attempted to address the question of where the definitions that support violating the law originate. He suggested that "differential social organization," a more structural element, may provide an answer. Sutherland held that groups in society are organized differently in terms of whether they support conformity to laws and law-abiding behavior or violation of the law and criminal behavior under some circumstances. In groups organized in favor of violation, delinquent traditions are initiated and perpetuated over time, providing a ready set of definitions supporting violation. According to Sutherland, those people who have contact with, or who are members of, groups organized in support of violation have the highest crime rates because of their exposure to these definitions.

Although criticized as difficult to test because of a lack of precise definitions, empirical research has generally upheld Sutherland's theory of differential association. Much of this research has focused on the role of peers in offending; having delinquent peers is one of the most consistent correlates of engaging in crime and delinquency. Further, tests of the theory's components, usually involving examination of the concepts of priority, intensity, frequency, and duration of differential associations, generally support the theory (e.g., Warr 1993). Other studies suggest, however, that engaging in crime may involve simply learning to commit the offending behavior without necessarily learning; the drives, motives, and rationalizations for it; that is, individuals may commit offenses primarily because their friends do so.

Other criminologists have sought to more fully articulate the processes involved in learning criminal behavior, attempting to expand on Sutherland's differential association theory. Most notable is the work of Robert L. Burgess and Ronald L. Akers (see also Akers 1985, and Reading 21), which combines and extends some elements of differential association with those in the psychological tradition of social learning theory. Their theory, also known in criminology as social learning theory, integrates elements such as conditioning and reinforcement, with the latter considered the most important process involved in learning delinquent (as well as other types of) behavior. When engaging in delinquency results in some form of reinforcement for the behavior, it increases the likelihood of repeating the behavior in the future. Empirical tests of Burgess and Akers's social learning theory are generally supportive of this approach (Akers et al. 1979).

Strain Theory

Strain theory was developed by Robert K. Merton (1968). Building on the notion of anomie (or normlessness) from Emile Durkheim's earlier work, Merton focused on conditions in American society that created "social structural strain" and thereby produced high crime rates. Merton argued that American society holds up certain goals for all individuals to aspire to, primarily monetary success. Although this goal is widely held, if not universal, in the United States, society is organized in such a way that the legitimate means—education, hard work, deferred gratification, and conventional jobs—used to attain this goal are not universally available. In fact, the opportunities to achieve financial success are unequally distributed, with members of the lower classes having few chances to accumulate wealth through legitimate means in comparison to members of the middle and upper classes. Even if one works hard and defers gratification, it is the result—monetary success—that counts, not simply working hard. The disjunction between monetary wealth as a cultural goal and the fact that the social structure limits access to the legitimate means to attain the goal,

typically for the lower classes, results in "strain" (Vold, Bernard, and Snipes 1998).

Merton delineated five behavioral adaptations that individuals may use in an attempt to deal with strain: conformity, innovation, ritualism, retreatism, and rebellion. The type of adaptation used depends on the person's reaction to the cultural goal (money) and to legitimate ways to achieve it (hard work). Individuals who conform accept both the cultural goal and the legitimate means for achieving it; they continue to attempt to achieve the goal through legitimate means. Innovation is of much interest to criminologists; it involves acceptance of the cultural goal and rejection of the legitimate means. As such, innovators rely on illegal means in an attempt to achieve monetary success. The third adaptation, ritualism, entails rejection of the cultural goal and acceptance of the means; that is, ritualists work hard but do not aspire to accumulate wealth. Retreatism, the fourth adaptation, involves rejection of both the cultural goals and legitimate means; these individuals, who include a variety of people such as the mentally ill or homeless, "drop out" of society and may turn to drugs or alcohol. The fifth adaptation, rebellion, not only rejects the cultural goal and legitimate means but seeks to change or replace them (Merton 1968).

In part because of criticisms and mixed empirical support, there have been several attempts to extend Merton's theory. Albert Cohen examined the delinquency of lowerclass boys, positing that they fail to achieve status (especially in school), which is defined by middle-class standards. Such boys seek to deal with the strain ("status frustration") that this situation creates for them. For some, the solution is "reaction formation," or complete rejection of middle-class values and acceptance of the values of the delinquent gang, which offer an alternative avenue to achieve status.

Another extension to strain theory was put forward in 1960 by Richard Cloward and Lloyd Ohlin. They argue that on the one hand the adaptation to strain is structured by illegitimate opportunities. Boys faced with strain will become criminal, for example, if there are criminal role models available to teach them how to be criminal, and if in their neighborhood there is an integration of offenders of different ages and of criminal and conventional values. On the other hand, boys without such opportunities for illegitimate behavior will adapt in other ways. Such boys who live in disorganized neighborhoods may become involved in a conflict gang, whose focus is on using violence as a means to attain status. Youths who do not have access to illegitimate opportunity structures or who cannot achieve status through violence are essentially "double failures." Some of them turn to drugs and alcohol, in conjunction with belonging to retreatist gangs, as a means to adapt to strain.

Merton's approach was extended again by Steven Messner and Richard Rosenfeld in 1992. They examine how crime is produced by the structural and cultural arrangements in society and the emphasis on the pursuit of the "American Dream" (Reading 29). A more social psychological extension that is currently having an important impact in criminology is offered by Robert Agnew, who suggests several additional sources of strain beyond a disjunction between the cultural goals and legitimate means to achieve them. Agnew also discusses nondelinquent coping responses and factors associated with choosing a delinquent rather than a nondelinquent response to strain. This extension of strain theory is currently being examined empirically, with the results of these studies generally supportive of its tenets (Agnew and White 1992; Brezina 1996; Reading 28).

Social Disorganization Theory

The social disorganization (or social ecology) perspective developed during the 1920s out of the work of several scholars at the University of Chicago. It focuses on explaining crime rates in various ecological areas, or neighborhoods, of cities. The work in this area relied on the earlier research of Robert Park and Ernest W. Burgess (cf. Burgess 1925). They developed the model of "The City," which depicted the processes of growth and change in the populations of various Chicago neighborhoods. In this model, there were five concentric zones, with the center located in the center of Chicago. Zone I was the "industrial area"; zone II was the "zone of transition," where new residents generally moved because of the cheap housing and

access to industrial areas; zone III contained the "workingmen's homes"; zone IV contained "better residences"; and, zone V, the greatest distance from the center of Chicago, was the "commuter's zone."

Clifford Shaw and Henry D. McKay applied the concentric-zone model to the study of crime and delinquency rates in Chicago (and subsequently in other cities; see Reading 24 and Shaw and McKay 1969). They found that delinquency rates varied largely by zone, with the zone of transition (II) having the highest delinquency rates. Delinquency rates declined sequentially as one moved out from zone II to zone V, which had the lowest rates.

Shaw and McKay attributed their findings to varying levels of social disorganization found in the different zones. The high-delinquency area, zone II, was characterized by a heterogeneous population, population turnover, bad housing, poverty, family disintegration, and a host of other problems. The heterogeneity and turnover undermined the strength of social institutions, such as churches, which are instrumental in maintaining the organization of the neighborhood. As a result, this zone was characterized by social disorganization, that is, a breakdown in a sense of community, or identification, among residents. Neighbors did not know one another; they may have spoken different languages and so did not communicate, had little or no interest in events that happened in the neighborhood, and were unable or unwilling to intervene in potentially troublesome situations. Under these circumstances, people living in the neighborhood were unable to exert informal social control over the behavior of other residents. As one moved toward the outer zones, the level of social disorganization declined. Neighborhoods were more stable, social institutions were stronger, and greater social control could be exerted over the behavior of residents, thereby producing lower delinquency rates.

In addition, Shaw and McKay demonstrated that zone II had the highest delinquency rates over an extended period of time. This finding held regardless of the nativity or the racial or ethnic composition of the people who lived there. During the time when a particular group lived in the zone of transition, it had very high delinquency rates. When members of this group moved out to zone III and beyond because they were financially able to do so (and because they were pushed out by new incoming groups), their delinquency rates declined. This fact led Shaw and McKay to conclude that delinquent behavior is due to the disorganized setting, produced by processes related to invasion and succession of different population groups, rather than to disorganized individuals (see Reading 24).

The social disorganization theory fell out of favor for a number of years, due in part to failed delinquency-prevention policies that were based on it, although research on crime and neighborhoods continued. In the 1980s and into the 1990s, there was renewed interest in the social disorganization perspective, both theoretically and empirically (Reiss and Tonry 1986). A number of changes have occurred in society, however, that have had a large impact on the growth and residential patterns of cities, such as economic restructuring (resulting in the loss of blue-collar industrial and manufacturing jobs and the creation of low-paying service jobs), the increasing pattern of racial and economic segregation, and the development of the underclass, a "truly disadvantaged" group characterized by extremely high rates of joblessness, unemployment, and isolation, among other problems (Massey and Denton 1993; Wilson 1987, 1996).

Such changes and their effects on the structure of cities have led to a dismissal of the concentric-zone component of early social disorganization theories. Instead, different efforts to "modernize" the theory have been made to account for the changes and address their implications for crime. For example, Rodney Stark delineated a series of propositions that suggest why poor, overcrowded neighborhoods marked by high rates of population turnover should also have high crime and delinquency rates. Others, such as Robert J. Bursik and Harold G. Grasmick, have emphasized the importance of considering the impact of different levels of social controls, associated with the economic and political power of neighborhoods, on crime rates. At present, the empirical work in social disorganization reflects both traditional and new foci, with research examining factors associated with social disorganization, demographic transitions, social-control mechanisms, and economic conditions in different neighborhoods in various cities, such as New York (Messner and Tardiff 1986), Chicago (Morenoff and Sampson 1997), and Miami (Martinez 1997), and their impact on crime rates.

Other Approaches

In addition to the traditional criminological theories already discussed, there are several other important approaches, including labeling theory, conflict or Marxist approaches, and feminist theories. A brief description of some of these is provided, although they are not discussed in detail here.

Labeling theory emerged in the 1950s and 1960s. Particularly important to this approach was the work of Edwin Lemert, John Kitsuse, and Howard Becker, among other scholars. This approach argues that crime and delinquency result from the very processes designed to control them; that is, once someone is identified and labeled by the police and the criminal justice system as a delinquent or a criminal, the label becomes a self-fulfilling prophecy. The label results in the individual's being isolated from conventional people and pushed to associate with similarly labeled people. In addition, the individual internalizes the label and delinquent or criminal becomes his or her master (or primary) status. As a result of coming to view oneself as delinquent, the individual comes, as other people already do, to expect such behavior from him or herself and eventually begins to engage in it again. Offending that produces the initial identification by the system is "primary deviance"; offending that occurs subsequent to the labeling process is "secondary deviance."

The similar conflict and Marxist perspectives are considered together here for the sake of brevity. Unlike other approaches, which see society based on consensus, conflict and Marxist theories see society as comprised of competing groups, the powerful and the powerless. Very simply, the difference between the conflict and the Marxist approaches is that conflict theorists are interested in power relations without specifying the source of power, whereas Marxist scholars are interested in power derived from the economic system, specifically from ownership of the means of production. According to the early conflict and Marxist scholars, such as Thorsten Sellin, Richard Quinney, William Chambliss, and Robert Seidman, among others, those with the power in society make the laws. The behaviors that are criminalized are those that threaten the interests (particularly economic and political) of the powerful, typically behaviors engaged in by the powerless, whereas the behaviors that the powerful groups engage in tend to not be criminalized (see also Reading 4 and the discussion in the introduction to Section I). Therefore, the less powerful groups in society are those with the highest crime rates, and the most powerful have low crime rates. In the last ten years, this approach has been re-conceptualized by several scholars, including Edmund McGarrell and Thomas Castellano and John Hagan, although they continue to focus on the role of power in determining what constitutes crime and who is punished as criminals (Vold, Bernard, and Snipes 1998).

Feminist theories are similar to conflict and Marxist theories in that they consider the role of power in relation to crime. For feminist theories, however, the source of power is patriarchy. Research and theorizing in this area began vigorously in the 1960s and 1970s, as documented in Section III, Prior to this time there was little research on the role of females in crime. In the 1970s, two books, one by Freda Adler (1975) and the other by Rita Simon (1975), were published that both represented, and led to interest in, the issue of women and crime. After these initial works, feminist scholarship in criminology evolved along several different lines (liberal, radical, socialist, and others; see Vold, Bernard, and Snipes 1998). Overall, however, feminist scholars paid attention principally to the roles of patriarchy and male dominance in society as they relate to crime, both in terms of the effect they have on the kinds of crimes females commit (those that tend to be powerless, such as shoplifting), as well as the crimes perpetrated against them, primarily by males, such as rape and spousal assault (Lilly, Cullen, and Ball 1995; Vold, Bernard, and Snipes 1998).

The readings that follow include both classic and contemporary statements of the major theoretical approaches in criminology in the three disciplines of biology, psychology, and sociology.

References

Adler, Freda. 1975. *Sisters in Crime: The Rise of the New Female Criminal*. New York: McGraw-Hill.

Agnew, Robert and Helene Raskin White. 1992. "An Empirical Test of General Strain Theory," *Criminology* 30: 475-499.

Akers, Ronald L. 1985. *Deviant Behavior: A Social Learning Approach* (3rd ed.). Belmont, CA: Wadsworth.

Akers, Ronald L., Marvin D. Krohn, Lonn Lanza-Kaduce, and Marcia Radosevich. 1979. "Social Learning and Deviant Behavior: A General Test of a Specific Theory," *American Sociological Review* 44: 635-655.

Arneklev, Bruce J., Harold G. Grasmick, Charles R. Tittle, and Robert J. Bursik, Jr. 1993. "Low Self-Control and Imprudent Behavior," *Journal of Quantitative Criminology* 9: 225-247.

Becker, Howard S. 1963. *Outsiders: Studies in the Sociology of Deviance*. New York: The Free Press.

Booth, Alan and D. Wayne Osgood. 1993. "The Influence of Testerone on Deviance in Adulthood: Assessing and Explaining the Relationship," *Criminology* 31: 93-117.

Brezina, Timothy. 1996. "Adapting to Strain: An Examination of Delinquent Coping Responses," *Criminology* 34: 39-60.

Burgess, Ernest W. 1925. "The Growth of the City: An Introduction to a Research Project." In R.E. Park, E.W. Burgess, and R.D. McKenzie (eds.), *The City*. Chicago: University of Chicago Press.

Burgess, Robert L. and Ronald L. Akers. 1966. "A Differential Association-Reinforcement Theory of Criminal Behavior," *Social Problems* 14: 128-147.

Bursik, Robert J. Jr. and Harold G. Grasmick. 1993. *Neighborhoods and Crime*. New York: Lexington Books.

Caspi, Avshalom, Terrie E. Moffitt, Phil A. Silva, Magda Stouthamer-Loeber, Robert F. Krueger, and Pamela S. Schmutte. 1994. "Are Some People Crime-Prone? Replications of the Personality-Crime Relationship Across Countries, Genders, Race and Methods," *Criminology* 32: 163-195.

Cernkovich, Stephen A. and Peggy C. Giordano. 1986. "Family Relationships and Delinquency," *Criminology* 25: 295-319.

Cernkovich, Stephen A. and Peggy C. Giordano. 1992. "School Bonding, Race, and Delinquency," *Criminology* 30: 261-291.

Chambliss, William and Robert Seidman. 1971. *Law, Order, and Power*. Reading, MA: Addison-Wesley.

Cloward, Richard A. and Lloyd E. Ohlin. 1960. *Delinquency and Opportunity: A Theory of Delinquent Gangs*. New York: The Free Press.

Cohen, Albert K. 1955. *Delinquent Boys: The Culture of the Gang*. New York: The Free Press.

Collins, James J. 1981. "Alcohol Use and Criminal Behavior: An Empirical, Theoretical, and Methodological Overview." In J.J. Collins Jr. (ed.), *Drinking and Crime*. New York: The Guilford Press.

Elliott, Delbert S., Suzanne S. Ageton, and Rachelle J. Canter. 1979. "An Integrated Theoretical Perspective on Delinquent Behavior," *Journal of Research in Crime and Delinquency* 16: 3-27.

Ellis, Lee and Anthony Walsh. 1997. "Gene-Based Evolutionary Theories in Criminology," *Criminology* 35: 229-276.

Giordano, Peggy C., Stephen A. Cernkovich, and M.D. Pugh. 1986. "Friendships and Delinquency," *American Journal of Sociology* 91: 1170-1202.

Glueck, Sheldon and Eleanor Glueck. 1950. *Unraveling Juvenile Delinquency*. New York: Commonwealth Fund.

Goldstein, Paul J. 1985. "The Drugs/Violence Nexus: A Tripartite Conceptual Framework," *Journal of Drugs Issues* 15: 493-506.

Gottfredson, Michael R. and Travis Hirschi. 1990. *A General Theory of Crime*. Stanford, CA: Stanford University Press.

Hagan, John. 1989. *Structural Criminology*. New Brunswick: Rutgers University Press.

Horney, Julie D., D. Wayne Osgood, and Ineke Haen Marshall. 1995. "Criminal Careers in the Short-Term: Intra-Individual Variability in Crime and Its Relation to Local Life Circumstances," *American Sociological Review*, 60: 655-673.

Kitsuse, John. 1962. "Societal Reaction to Deviance: Problems of Theory and Method," *Social Problems* 9: 247-256.

Lemert, E.M. 1951. *Social Pathology*. New York: McGraw Hill.

Lilly, J. Robert, Francis T. Cullen, and Richard A. Ball. 1995. *Criminological Theory: Context and Consequences*. Thousand Oaks, CA: Sage Publications.

Martinez, Ramiro Jr. 1997. "Homicide Among Miami's Ethnic Groups: Anglos, Blacks and Latinos in the 1990s," *Homicide Studies* 1: 17-34.

Massey, Douglas S. and Nancy A. Denton. 1993. *American Apartheid: Segregation and the Making of the Underclass*. Cambridge: Harvard University Press.

McGarrell, Edmund and Thomas Castellano. 1991. "An Integrative Conflict Model of the Criminal Law Formulation Process," *Journal of Research in Crime and Delinquency* 28: 174-96.

Merton, Robert K. 1968. *Social Theory and Social Structure*. Glencoe, IL: The Free Press.

Messner, Steven F. and Richard Rosenfeld. 1992. *Crime and the American Dream*. Belmont, CA: Wadsworth.

Messner, Steven F. and Kenneth Tardiff. 1986. "Economic Inequality and Levels of Homicide: An Analysis of Urban Neighborhoods," *Criminology* 24: 297-316.

Moffitt, Terrie E., Donald R. Lyman, and Phil A. Silva. 1994. "Neuropsychological Tests Predicting Persistent Male Delinquency," *Criminology* 32: 277-300.

Morenoff, Jeffrey D. and Robert J. Sampson. 1997. "Violent Crime and the Spatial Dynamics of Neighborhood Transition," *Social Forces* 76: 31-64.

Nagin, Daniel S., David P. Farrington, and Terrie E. Moffitt. 1995. "Life-Course Trajectories of Different Types of Offenders," *Criminology* 33: 111-139.

Quinney, Richard. 1977. *Class, State and Crime*. New York: David McKay Co.

Rankin, Joseph H. and Roger Kern. 1994. "Parental Attachments and Delinquency," *Criminology* 32: 495-515.

Reckless, Walter C. 1961. *The Crime Problem* (3rd Ed.). New York: Appleton-Century-Crofts.

Reiss, Albert J. 1951. "Delinquency as the Failure of Personal and Social Controls," *American Sociological Review* 16: 196-207.

Reiss, Albert J. and Michael Tonry (eds.). 1986. *Communities and Crime*. Volume 8. Chicago: University of Chicago Press.

Sampson, Robert J. and John H. Laub. 1993. *Crime in the Making*. Cambridge: Harvard University Press.

Schuessler, Karl F. and Donald R. Cressey. 1950. "Personality Characteristics of Criminals," *American Journal of Sociology* 55: 476-484.

Sellin, Thorsten. 1938. *Culture Conflict and Crime*. New York: Social Science Research Council.

Shaw, Clifford R. and Henry D. McKay. 1969. *Juvenile Delinquency and Urban Areas* (revised ed.). Chicago: University of Chicago Press.

Simon, Rita J. 1975. *Women and Crime*. Lexington, MA: Lexington.

Stark, Rodney. 1987. "Deviant Places: A Theory of the Ecology of Crime," *Criminology* 25: 893-909.

Sutherland, Edwin H. 1983. *White Collar Crime: The Uncut Version*. New Haven, CT: Yale University Press.

Tittle, Charles R. 1995. *Control Balance: Toward a General Theory of Deviance*. Boulder, CO: Westview Press.

Vold, George B., Thomas J. Bernard, and Jeffrey B. Snipes. 1998. *Theoretical Criminology* (4th ed.). New York: Oxford.

Walters, Glenn D. 1990. *The Criminal Lifestyle: Patterns of Serious Criminal Conduct*. Newbury Park, CA: Sage.

Warr, Mark. 1993. "Age, Peers, and Delinquency," *Criminology* 31: 17-40.

Wilson, James Q. and Richard J. Herrnstein. 1985. *Crime & Human Nature*. New York: Simon and Schuster.

Wilson, William Julius. 1987. *The Truly Disadvantaged*. Chicago: University of Chicago Press.

——. 1996. *When Work Disappears*. New York: Knopf.

CHAPTER 16

Formal and Informal Sanctions: A Comparison of Deterrent Effects

Linda S. Anderson ■ Theodore G. Chiricos ■ Gordon P. Waldo

Deterrence theory is among the oldest explanations for criminal offending, even predating the academic discipline of criminology itself. This perspective remains one of the most important and relevant in that much of the American legal system is based on its premises, whether explicitly or implicitly. Sanctioning in the criminal justice system is based in large part on the assumption that offenders and potential offenders are free-willed, rational individuals capable of calculating the costs and benefits associated with crime. Although this and other elements of the theory have been shown to be problematic, the influence of the deterrence perspective cannot be understated.

What was first an Enlightenment idea about the essential nature of man has emerged as a fruitful area for modern criminological research. In the following selection, Anderson, Chiricos, and Waldo consider how marijuana use among college students is related to the perception of formal and informal sanctions. Their results suggested that although the severity of "official" punishment is generally unrelated to marijuana use, the perception that informal sanctions are certain does serve as a deterrent.

Most deterrence research has been limited to one simple question: "Is deviant behavior reduced under conditions of greater severity and/or certainty of formal sanctions?" However useful the question, it is predicated upon a model of social control which understates the complexity of any "complete" deterrence paradigm. In many instances, the simplicity of this model may have been dictated by the constraints of available data either for homicide or for other "Index" crimes measure by official sources.[1] Although several researchers have broadened the deterrence model to encompass alternative measures of deviance or sanction (e.g. Schwartz and Orleans, 1967; Waldo and Chiricos, 1972) as well as "contextual" variables that might specify the relationship between severity of sanction and deviance (e.g. Bowers and Salem, 1972; Tittle and Rowe 1973), a thorough review of existing deterrence research by Tittle and Logan (1973:385) has concluded that many gaps in our knowledge persist:

> At this point we can safely say only that sanctions apparently have some deterrent effect under *some* circumstances. It is now necessary to undertake careful research in an attempt to specify the *conditions* under which sanctions are likely to be important influences on behavior [italics added].

In short, we need to ask a more complex question, or series of questions, addressing the variability of conditions and circumstances under which formal sanctions are presumed to exert deterrent influence. This need, frequently affirmed at a *conceptual* level (e.g., Tittle and Logan, 1973, Zimring and Hawkins, 1973), is rarely addressed in the *empirical* work of deterrence researchers.

While the range of additional variables considered relevant for deterrence has been fairly broad,[2] none has elicited more consistent mentions than

From "Formal and Informal Sanctions: A comparison of Deterrent Effects" Social Problems, 25, pp 103–114 the informal sanctions that impinge upon an actor by virtue of peer, family, or reference group memberships. This point is underscored by Clark and Gibb's (1965:402) effort to clarify the concept of social control:

Social control...is intended as the study of *social* reaction to deviant behavior rather than *societal* reaction. The distinction is important in two respects. First a concern with sanctions. And second while the term social reactions includes formal sanctions it also encompasses informal and non-legal reactions as they occur both in societies and smaller social units.

The theoretical relevance of informal sanctions has been specified. At the general level Andenaes (1966) and Ball (1955) noted that informal sanctions cannot be ignored in the study of deterrence. The logic of such a position is supported by a variety of perspectives (e.g., social learning and reference group theory) with relevance for the study of social control. Others however indicate a more specific deterrent relevance for informal sanctions. Salem and Bower (1970) as well as Zimring and Hawkins (1973) argue that formal sanctions are principally effective to the degree that they activate or reinforce sanctioning mechanisms operating at informal levels. In this regard, the position taken by Salem and Bower (1970:22) reflects a Durkheimian emphasis more appropriate to situations of mechanical solidarity:

The formal sanctions' primary effect through their capacity to strengthen the normative climate of the community—to reinforce and mobilize the informal social disapproval.

A third, more common position, argues that formal sanctions will be more or less effective given alternative conditions of informal sanction (e.g., Clark and Gibbs, 1965; Zimring and Hawkins, 1973). From this perspective it is generally argued that "the motivating influences of the penal law may become more or less neutralized by group norms working in the opposite direction" (Andenaes, 1966:959). A similar hypothesis was earlier promulgated by Ball (1955:350):

...it seems likely that laws which reinforce existing mores are apt to be more effective than those which prohibit behavior not regulated by group sentiment.

Despite the theoretical insights, how informal sanctions interact with formal sanctions in the deterrence process is an open question. It will undoubtedly become a more common question as deterrence research progresses. The present research offers a few modest answers. We shall consider the *relative* and *cumulative* impact of perception of both formal and informal sanctions of one type of deviant behavior—marijuana use among college students. We shall also present data addressing the question of how perceived formal sanctions act as deterrents under variable conditions of perceived informal sanction for marijuana use.

Clearly marijuana use by college students provides an excellent empirical setting for the study of formal and informal sanctions. Few deviant behaviors involve such strong formal penalties in conjunction with such widespread, if variable, informal support. In this regard, marijuana use reflects the condition of "conflicting group norms," which Andenaes (1966:949) saw as potentially neutralizing the effects of penal law:

In such cases, the result is a conflict between the formalized community laws, which are expressed through the criminal law, and the counteracting norms dominating the group. Against the moral effects of the penal law stands the moral influence of the group; against the fear of legal sanction stands the fear of group sanction....

Prior Research

Empirical answers to the questions we ask are in short supply, as most deterrence researchers focus on formal sanctions alone.[3] Salem and Bowers (1970), however, examine the relationship between severity of university regulations (formal sanctions) and self-reported violations of those rules, for universities with varying degrees of "normative support" (informal sanction for those regulations). They concluded:

...the effect of formal sanctions on cheating behavior varies by college context. There is generally an increase in the deterrent effect as the (informal) context of disapproval becomes stronger. Apparently, the weight of severe sanctions is more clearly brought home to potential offenders where informal disapproval is more intense [1970:28].

In their subsequent research, however, Bowers and Salem (1972) were forced to modify the earlier conclusions with the observation that formal sanctions for drinking behavior appeared to be a consequence of the normative climate and the level of drinking behavior at a college, "rather than a determinant of both as we had previously assumed" (1972:440). To our knowledge, no other deterrence studies have considered the issues of combined formal and informal sanction.

Available evidence concerning *formal* sanctions with regard to marijuana use is limited. Grupp and Lucas (1970) noted that marijuana use in California increased at the same time that courts show greater reluctance to impose prison sentences for the offense. They inferred that the leniency of the courts may have reduced the deterrent effect of statutory penalties for marijuana use. Grupp, et al., (1971) further observed that among self-reported "users" and "non-users" at a small Midwest college, there were no significant differences in the perceived risk from legal sanctions.

Waldo and Chiricos (1972) found that the proportion of admitted marijuana users was highest among those who perceived likelihood of arrest for marijuana possession or of maximum penalties upon conviction. Similarly, Teevan (1974) has observed that the likelihood of self-reported marijuana use among Canadian college and secondary school students is highest among those perceiving a low certainty of arrest, while the proportion of admitted users was much less responsive to variations in perceived severity of punishment.

A number of studies have tried to link marijuana use to variable involvement in family or peer groups with *informal* sanction power. With the presumption that drug use is part of a general rejection of parents and their values, several researchers have found that drug users are more likely than non-users to express disagreement and attenuated relationships with their parents (e.g., Blaum, 1969; Brotman, et al., 1970). Others have reported comparatively greater conflict and less solidarity within the families of drug users (e.g., Blum, 1969, Matchett, 1971). In a recent study, Tec (1970) reported a negative association between marijuana use and four presumed "independent variables." (1) availability and quality of parental

models for behavior; (2) availability of positive evaluations and recognition within family units; (3) perception of family relationships as "warm;" (4) expressions of satisfaction with, involvement in, and reliance upon the family unit (Tec, 1970:656).

The relevance of these findings for the present research is limited, of course, because little is known about the specific sanctions for drug use within the families studied. We can do little more than presume—with several of the researchers—that parents generally disapprove of drug use. Whether perceptions of family approval or disapproval related to marijuana use is a question that has not been adequately addressed by prior research. Consequently we examine it in the present study.

With regard to peer influence, a number of authors (e.g., Akers, 1970, Chapel and Taylor, 1970) have built upon Becker's (1963:41-53) description of "becoming a marijuana user," to argue that peer involvement and pressure (informal sanction) is central to the understanding of drug using behavior. Several studies have emphasized the essentially social character of marijuana use (e.g., Blum, 1969, Good, 1969) while others (Johnson, 1973; Tec, 1972) have found that marijuana use is related to associations with drug-using peers. Again the *presumption* is that drug-using peers provide positive sanction for drug use, but the validity of the assumption remains to be demonstrated.

The Present Research

We here consider how far marijuana use among college students is related to *perception* of formal and informal sanctions. The importance of perception for deterrence research has been widely acknowledged since Bentham (cf. Zimring and Hawkins, 1973:142), but generally ignored by researchers.[4] Andenaes appeared to be speaking for several deterrence theorists when he observed:

> The decisive factor in creating the deterrent effect is, of course not the objective risk of detection, but the risk as it is calculated by the potential criminal [1966:963].

Summary and Conclusion

1. The perceived severity of formal punishment is generally unrelated to reported marijuana use. However, the deterrent effectiveness of perceived severity is substantially increased for respondents perceiving certainty of punishment as high. The existing deterrence literature has shown that severe punishment—measured objectively and officially—is generally not as strong a deterrent as certain punishment (see, for example, Tittle and Logan, 1973; Gibbs, 1975). In this respect our findings come as no surprise. Of greater interest may be the finding that severe punishment is a more effective deterrent among those perceiving a high probability of arrest for marijuana use. Though consistent with the common assumption that severe punishment will be of consequence only when certainly applied, this finding runs counter to Logan's (1972:71) observation that "the effect of severity on crime rate…appears somewhat stronger under conditions of *low* certainty" [emphasis added]. Such a discrepancy could be explained by the fact that the present data employ perceptions of sanctions and a self-reported measure of deviance, where-as Logan's data are obtained from official sources. Future research should focus on the issue of how severe punishment interacts with additional sanctions in deterring deviance.[5]

2. The perception of certain punishment and the perception of informal sanctions are strongly and independently associated with marijuana use.

3. The relative deterrent impact of perceived informal sanctions, especially peer use of marijuana, is slightly greater than the impact of perceived certainty of punishment. While the relationship between perceived certainty of punishment and admitted marijuana use is consistent with most existing deterrence research, the finding that the perception of *informal* sanctions has exerted an apparent influence upon marijuana use that is strong, independent of, and possibly greater than the effects of perceived certainty of punishment is perhaps more interesting. Marijuana use is strongly peer-involved behavior, and peer sanctions may be presumed to be highly salient. However the balance of formal and informal sanction effects upon deviant behavior may vary with different types of deviance. Similarly, while the present data show peer influence to be stronger than parental influence, such a finding could obviously vary for other populations and offenses.

4. The cumulative impact of perceived certainty and perceived informal sanctions is greater than the separate impact of either certainty or the perceived informal sanctions alone. This finding lends further credence to the plausibility of employing models of deterrence that examine more than the simple effects of formal legal sanctions, and which include a variety of additional informal sanctions whose interaction with one another and with formal sanctions can be empirically ascertained.

5. The deterrent impact of the perception of both formal and informal sanctions is slightly greater for males than for females. The fact that this finding is inconsistent with the finding of Tittle and Rowe (1973) simply underscores the need for deterrence research beyond the simple question of whether sanctions deter deviance. Deterrence literature is full of suggestion about which variables would be relevant for more inclusive research designs, and those suggestion are augmented by several theoretical perspectives—notably control theory and social learning theory—whose explanatory schemes include sanctions and other dimensions of interest to deterrence researchers. In order to implement more inclusive designs, however, researchers may be forced to abandon the traditional approach to deterrence, which limits one to analyses of official, available data. These data are too far removed from human behavior, too limited in the range of deviance examined or the sanctions available for study, too constrained with regard to additional relevant variables, and too presumptive of the fact that potential deviants perceive and

respond to formal sanction, to warrant continued application by deterrence researchers.

Notes

1. Space limitations preclude the traditional listing and bibliographic reference to these studies. For good bibliographies and critiques of this literature, see Tittle and Logan (1973) and Gibbs (1975).

2. In general, reviews such as those by Tittle and Logan, (1973), and Zimring and Hawkins (1973) have called for consideration of the following: (1) the characteristics of potential rule breakers, (such as sex, age, race); (2) additional characteristics of the formal sanctions (e.g., celerity of application); (3) variation in types of behavior that can be deterred by sanction threat; (4) perceptions of sanctions by potential deviants; (5) informal sanctions; (6) the relative importance of sanctions and other deterrents such as moral commitments and investment in conventional activities.

3. Tittle and Rowe's work (1973) has compared the deterrent effectiveness of "Moral appeal" versus "sanction threats" in a classroom cheating experiment. Possibly the latter may be considered a more formal sanction than the moral appeal, but the authors were not concerned with developing this issue.

4. Among those who have specifically addressed the issue of perceived sanction are Claster (1967), Jensen (1969), Waldo and Chiricos (1972). The need for deterrence researchers to concern themselves with perceptions of sanctions is underscored by Tittle and Logan (1973:387): "But more important than the actual character of sanctions may be beliefs or perceptions about the characteristics of sanctions."

5. Several additional researchers have examined the possibility that relationships between official crime rates and severity of punishment are contingent upon the certainty of punishment. Specifically, Antunes and Hunt concluded that: "…increasing severity in a condition of low certainty will have little effect on crime rates" (1973:443); while Erickson and Gibbs have shown that "…the relation between the severity of imprisonment and criminal homicide rates is contingent on variation in the certainty of imprisonment" (1973:551). It should be noted that Erickson and Gibbs were *not* concerned with the absolute levels or magnitude of certainty, but rather with the extent of *variation* in certainty.

CHAPTER 17

The Criminal Man

Cesare Lombroso ■ As Summarized by Gina Lombroso Ferrero

Cesare Lombroso's biological theory provided an alternative to classical criminological theory and helped establish positivistic thinking with respect to criminal behavior. Lombroso developed this theory during his time as a doctor for the army and at an asylum where he became convinced the roots of criminality were biologically based. Drawing from his own experiences and influenced by Charles Darwin's newly published theory of evolution, Lombroso concluded that the antisocial tendencies of criminals were the result of unevolved "savages." Contrary to the classical perspective, positivist theories such as Lombroso's propose that criminal behavior could be cured rather than simply punished.

The method in which Lombroso developed his biological theory is presented in the following selection. Various atavistic, or criminal, traits such as strong canines, diminished number of lines in the palm of the hand, and a flattened nose are offered in support of his typology. The inability to classify all criminals into one category is also discussed with the advancement of a brief argument that nearly one-third of all law violators are born criminals.

The Classical School based its doctrines on the assumption that all criminals, except in a few extreme cases, are endowed with intelligence and feelings like normal individuals, and that they commit misdeeds consciously, being prompted thereto by their unrestrained desire for evil. The offence alone was considered, and on it the whole existing penal system has been founded, the severity of the sentence meted out to the offender being regulated by the gravity of his misdeed.

The Modern, or Positive, School of Penal Jurisprudence, on the contrary, maintains that the anti-social tendencies of criminals are the result of their physical and psychic organisation, which differs essentially from that of normal individuals; and it aims at studying the morphology and various functional phenomena of the criminal with the object of curing, instead of punishing him....

If we examine a number of criminals, we shall find that they exhibit numerous anomalies in the face, skeleton, and various psychic and sensitive functions, so that they strongly resemble primitive races. It was these anomalies that first drew my father's attention to the close relationship between the criminal and the savage and made him suspect that criminal tendencies are of atavistic origin.

When a young doctor at the Asylum in Pavia, he was requested to make a postmortem examination on a criminal named Vilella, an Italian Jack the Ripper, who by atrocious crimes had spread terror in the Province of Lombardy...."At the sight of that skull," says my father, "I seemed to see all at once, standing out clearly illumined as in a vast plain under a flaming sky, the problem of the nature of the criminal, who reproduces in civilised times characteristics, not only of primitive savages, but of still lower types as far back as the carnivora."

Thus was explained the origin of the enormous jaws, strong canines, prominent zygomae, and strongly developed orbital arches which he had so frequently remarked in criminals, for these peculiarities are common to carnivores and savages, who tear and devour raw flesh. Thus also it was easy to understand why the span of the arms in criminals so often exceeds the height, for this is a characteristic of apes, whose fore-limbs are used in walking and climbing. The other anomalies exhibited by criminals—the scanty beard as opposed to the general hairiness of the body, prehensile foot, diminished number of lines in the palm of the hand, cheek-pouches, enormous development of the middle incisors and frequent absence of the lateral ones, flattened nose and angular or sugar-loaf form of the skull, common to criminals and apes; the excessive size of the orbits, which, combined with hooked nose, so often imparts to criminals the aspect of birds of prey, the projection of the lower part of the face and jaws (prognathism) found in negroes and animals, and supernumerary teeth (amounting in some cases to a double row as in snakes) and cranial bones (epactal bone as in the Peruvian Indians): all these characteristics pointed to one conclusion, the atavistic origin of the criminal, who reproduces physical, psychic, and functional qualities of remote ancestors.

Subsequent research on the part of my father and his disciples showed that other factors besides atavism come into play in determining the criminal type. These are: disease and environment. Later on, the study of innumerable offenders led them to the conclusion that all law-breakers cannot be classed in a single species, for their ranks include very diversified types, who differ not only in their bent towards a particular form of crime, but also in the degree of tenacity and intensity displayed by them in their perverse propensities, so that, in reality, they form a graduated scale leading from the born criminal to the normal individual.

Born criminals form about one third of the mass of offenders, but, though inferior in numbers, they constitute the most important part of the whole criminal army, partly because they are constantly appearing before the public and also because the crimes committed by them are of a peculiarly monstrous character; the other two thirds are composed of criminaloids (minor offenders), occasional and habitual criminals, etc., who do not show such a marked degree of diversity from normal persons....

Discussion Questions

1. The positive school of criminology, which Lombroso helped found, argues that crime is not the result of free will; rather, it is due to factors over which the individual often has little or no control. As such, this school focuses less on the punishment of the offender and more on "curing" the offending. To what extent do you think crime is an act of free will or one caused by forces beyond the individual's control?

2. What policy recommendations might an adherent of Lombroso's theory make for controlling crime? (A consideration of these recommendations will help you understand one of the reasons why the theory was later attacked.)

3. List those factors said to distinguish "born criminals" from others. How would one go about providing a good test of Lombroso's theory?

CHAPTER 18

Does the Body Tell? Biological Characteristics and Criminal Disposition

David Rowe

Biological explanations of crime have evolved considerably over the past century and a half, moving beyond the descriptive and often scientifically flawed theories of the late nineteenth and early twentieth centuries toward highly sophisticated biosocial paradigms. Biological theories today attempt to explain how genetics and other biological factors affect personality traits that lead to criminality and other negative behavior. Some research focuses on the neurotransmitters (such as serotonin) responsible for transmitting signals from the brain and other studies have examined indicators of nervous system activity. The following selection by David Rowe summarizes the extant literature related to the search for a physiological basis of criminal disposition. Major areas of research covered include the role of testosterone, serotonin levels, heart rate, skin conductance, and brain anatomy and function.

Two medical cases have been studied by the neurologist Antonio Damasio and his colleagues that illustrate a possible neurological underpinning for psychopathy (Anderson et al. 1999). Their subjects, a man and a woman, had both suffered injuries to the prefrontal cortex during infancy. The prefrontal cortex, located just behind the eye sockets and above the bridge of the nose, is involved in planning a sequence of actions and in anticipating the future. The female subject was run over by a car when she was 15 months old. The male subject had a brain tumor removed from his

prefrontal area when he was 3 months old. Both subjects grew up in stable, middle-class families with college-educated parents and had normal biological siblings, but neither made a satisfactory social adjustment; neither had friends and both were dependent on support from their parents. Neither subject had any plans for the future. The woman was a compulsive liar; she stole from her parents and shoplifted; her early and risky sexual behavior led to a pregnancy by age 18. By age 9, the male subject had committed minor theft and aggressive delinquent acts; he had no empathy for others.

The researchers tested the two subjects on a computerized gambling test used to detect how people respond to the uncertainty of rewards and punishments. The task is designed so that payoffs to the "bad" card deck are high and immediate while payoffs to the "good" card deck are low immediately but better in the long term. Most people quickly learn to draw cards from the "good" deck that offers the better long-term payoff. Neither subject was able to learn to use the long-term payoff deck.

Most surprisingly, these brain-injured victims failed to understand the difference between right and wrong; they lacked a sense of social norms and of how to act in social situations. Their moral blindness contrasts with the thought processes of adults who have brain damage in the same region and who display symptoms of psychopathy but understand without any difficulty the moral difference between right and wrong.

Finding the Physiological Basis of Criminal Disposition

The prefrontal cortex could mediate genetic influence on criminal dispositions if genes affect the functioning of this brain region. In a prominent theory of attention deficit hyperactivity disorder, the same brain region has been implicated (Barkley 1997). Deficits in the prefrontal cortex may reduce the executive function—that is, the ability to plan and to reflect on one's actions. Impaired executive function implies impulsive and disorganized behavior, a focus on the present rather than on the future. Tests involving specific tasks that require executive function can distinguish between psychopaths and control individuals. One is the classic delay-of-gratification task. In one version, a computer screen presents a signal for a 40 percent probability of winning a nickel; the subject can take the nickel or wait 14 seconds for an 80 percent probability of a win (and better long-term winnings). Psychopathic offenders pick the immediate reward more often than nonpsychopathic offenders (Newman, Kosson, and Patterson 1992). Notice that this task presents the same basic situation as Damasio's card deck task: to work for a long-term payoff in the presence of immediate payoffs....

Blood and Saliva Tests of Criminal Disposition

Could we detect criminal disposition with a simple saliva or blood test? There is some positive evidence that a test can be done for some hormones and metabolites of neurotransmitters that circulate in the blood.

Testosterone is the hormone that is responsible for the fetus carrying a Y chromosome to develop into a male. It is a biochemical that is simple in structure and that is derived from a substance feared by dieters: cholesterol. T attaches to receptors on the surface of specific cells and triggers a cascade of biological events within these cells that ultimately change gene expression in the cell's nucleus; that is, it can turn genes off and on. Testosterone circulates in the blood, a portion free and another portion bound to a carrier protein. Free T-levels are inexpensively detectable in saliva (Dabbs et al. 1995). With its powerful physiological effects and its strong connection to masculinity, it is no wonder that men revel in the power of testosterone.

Two studies have reported on interactions between social integration and the strength of the association between testosterone level and crime in Vietnam veterans; this association was stronger when men's social integration was weaker—that is, when they were of lower social class, were unmarried, or had an unstable work history (Booth and Osgood 1993; Dabbs and Morris 1990). To illustrate, Dabbs and Morris used data on crime and testosterone level in 4,462 Vietnam-era veterans. In their study, higher T-level predicted a variety of antisocial behaviors, including aggressive ones. The association was stronger in lower-class men than in middle-class men. Table 18.1 shows the percentage of high-testosterone (upper 10 percent, N = 202) versus low-testosterone (90th percentile and below; N = 1,294) men who were classified as delinquent. Among lower-class men, a higher testosterone level almost doubled the risk of crime, but among the upper-class men, it hardly changed their already low rate of crime. Dabbs and Morris's finding suggests that T-level interacts with the social context; it may be a more potent cause of criminal disposition in a lower-class environment. Another possibility is that men who become lower class carry additional genetic risk factors that amplify the effects of testosterone. This second theory gains some credence because the men's

Table 18.1 Percentage of Sample Exhibiting Delinquent Behavior in World War II

	Veterans by Testosterone Level	
	Normal T % Delinq.	High T % Delinq.
Low Social Class	14.7	30.7
High Social Class	4.5	4.1

Note: T = Testosterone. 90 percent of the sample fell into the normal T category; 10 percent into the high T category.

class attainment was used, not the social class of their parents.

Other studies of the link between testosterone and crime have been reviewed by Jacobson and Rowe (2000). They noted that the association between testosterone and aggression was more consistent for adults than for adolescents, possibly because of the profound influence of puberty on hormone levels. One study also found the hormone estradiol, a close chemical relative, to be related to females' aggression. Only one research group has examined the association of hormones and female crime, a part of the general neglect of females in studies of crime.

In adult men, testosterone concentration in saliva has another quite different association that is more appealing than delinquency: a bass voice (Dabbs and Mallinger 1999). The strength of relationship of testosterone level to criminal disposition is about the same as it is to possessing a deep voice. A choir director would not, of course, take blood or saliva samples to find a man ready to sing the bass line in Handel's *Messiah*—the director would audition men to sing instead. Many biological risk factors do not have the specificity to allow them to be used in a strong predictive way to forecast whether a particular individual will in the future commit delinquent acts.

Serotonin Levels

Serotonin is a chemical involved in neurotransmission in the brain. When nerve signals are relayed between sending and receiving nerve cells, serotonin crosses a small gap (the synapse) between one cell and the other and binds to receptor proteins on the surface of the receiving cell. This binding process sets off a biochemical chain reaction that modulates the receiving cell's ability to send further nerve impulses to its target cells. Another molecule, the serotonin transporter protein, has the job of recycling serotonin back into a sending cell for reuse. Serotonin is made from one of the essential amino acids, tryptophan, which is abundant in the American diet, especially in meat. Serotonin originates in cells in a particular region deep in the brain. Like long wires in an electrical circuit, axons from the serotonin-producing nerve

cells extend widely throughout the brain, including into the frontal cortex, where they may modulate higher thought processes (Spoont 1992).

Serotonin levels cannot be measured directly by biological test without risking brain damage to the subject. Two indirect methods are thus used; the first involves measuring the level of a serotonin metabolite (SM) in a biochemical pathway that breaks down serotonin in cerebral spinal fluid; the second measures the level of serotonin itself inside blood platelet cells.

A consistent association has been found between low cerebral spinal fluid SM levels and suicidal impulses, suicide attempts, and completed suicides (Asberg 1997). Spinal fluid SM levels are also lower in violent criminals (Fuller 1996). Furthermore, people with suicidal ideation are sometimes impulsively aggressive, and their aggression is associated with lower SM levels.

The serotonin system is the target of a class of antidepressant drugs first discovered about 1975: the serotonin reuptake inhibitors. The most famous of these drugs, fluoxetine, goes under the trade name Prozac. The ability of the drug to relieve major depressive disorder, and seemingly to modify many other personality problems, led to the publication of a best-selling book, *Listening to Prozac* (Kramer 1997). The mechanism of Prozac's action lends further support to the hypothesis linking psychopathology with low serotonin levels. Prozac binds to and thereby blocks the action of the serotonin transporter protein; it is therefore likely that Prozac relieves depression partly by increasing the availability of serotonin in the synapses between cells. On the other hand, this account is certainly an oversimplification of how Prozac works. Prozac also binds to and thereby activates one class of serotonin receptor proteins, and it may have many unknown metabolic effects.

Unlike most previous researchers, Moffitt and her colleagues (1998) used a general population sample instead of a sample of psychiatric patients. They also measured serotonin levels in blood platelet cells. The sample consisted of 781 21-year-old men and women, all born in the same year in New Zealand. Violence was measured by using criminal convictions and self-reports of violence. In males, higher levels of platelet serotonin were found to be associated with violence. This effect also held up to statistical controls for possibly related factors such as drug use, platelet count, body mass, psychiatric disorder, social class, nonviolent crime, and family relations.

The two measures of serotonin levels, (in spinal fluid versus in platelets) have opposite relationships to behavior disorders. However, the studies of spinal fluid measure the amount of metabolite after serotonin has been released into the synapse between nerve cells and then used. If the metabolite is low, it means that less serotonin has been available for communicating between nerve cells. The platelet serotonin studies measure the amount of serotonin still stored inside the platelet—the amount that has not yet been released for communication. Thus, if communication between cells is poor, this effect would theoretically result in *high* concentrations of serotonin stored (in neurones or platelet cells) and *low* concentrations released to be converted into a serotonin metabolite (by synapse or muscle), conceptually resolving the opposite direction of the associations found with the two assays.

Heart Rate Tests of Criminal Disposition

Heart rate is a physiological activity that is exquisitely sensitive to many environmental demands. Although the heart is a peripheral organ from the brain, the activity of the brain, including a psychological appraisal of situations, determines heart rate through the nervous system. Heart rate depends on the balance of the activity of the sympathetic and parasympathetic nervous systems; the former increases heart rate while the latter decreases it. Stimuli that grab one's attention first accelerate heart rate in an orienting response. The mental exertion of a game of chess makes the heart beat more rapidly—perhaps chess qualifies as a sport after all. Imagine that you are stepping into a doctor's office or are about to receive a medical exam from a survey interviewer. Unconsciously you will appraise the situation; if it seems mildly threatening, your heart rate may increase—but not by much, if you are someone with a greater criminal disposition than the average person.

In his book on crime as a clinical disorder, Raine (1993) summarized 14 studies of the relationship between resting heart rate and crime. All 14 studies found a lower resting heart rate to be associated with a greater rate of crime. Heart rate was measured from simple pulse counting to sophisticated electrical measurements. Definitions of crime included criminal records, teacher ratings, self-reports on personality tests, and a psychiatric diagnosis of conduct disorder. The association between low heart rate and criminal disposition was found in both American and English samples and in both males and females. The statistical association was also upheld in subsequent studies (Raine et al. 1997). In sum, this finding was particularly robust because it held across samples drawn from different populations and over the various types of heart rate measures.

This association has also been found in studies that follow the same individuals through their lives, with a low heart rate measured well before the onset of criminal behaviors (Farrington 1997; Raine, Venables, and Mednick 1997). Raine et al. examined the association between heart rate when children were age 3 and the same children's antisocial behaviors when they were 11. The study took place on an island of Mauritius in the Indian Ocean, known for its excellent scuba diving. An amazing 100 percent cooperation rate was gained with the local Indian, Creole, and other descent populations by offering mothers two bags of flour, a candy for their children, and a free health screening. Heart rate was measured with a one-minute recording of the pulse. Aggressive and nonviolent antisociality were assessed by parental reports when the children were 11 years old. Those children with lower heart rates were rated as more aggressive than those with higher rates.... Children with low heart rates at age 3 had about twice the prevalence of aggression at age 11, versus those children with high heart rates at age 3. Considered from another vantage, the high-aggression group averaged about seven fewer heartbeats per minute than the low aggression group. Heart rate predicted aggressive acts more strongly than nonaggressive forms of delinquency, and this association also held when statistical controls were introduced for body size and social class.

Farrington's Cambridge Study in Delinquent Development also found a prospective association between low resting heart rate at age 18 and criminal convictions from ages 19 to 40. Among men with very low heart rates (fewer than 60 beats per minute), 17 percent had convictions, versus 5 percent of the men with very high heart rates (81 beats or more per minute). This association held when other variables were statistically controlled, including low verbal IQ, unstable job record, risk taking between the ages of 8 and 10, and parental convictions. Thus, this biological measure improved the prediction of crime.

Skin Conductance Tests of Criminal Disposition

Unlike heart rate, which assesses the interaction between the excitatory sympathetic nervous system and the inhibitory parasympathetic nervous system, skin conductance (SC) reflects only the central nervous system's stimulation of the sympathetic nervous system. In the central nervous system, skin conductance can reflect the diversion of attentional resources to a particular stimuli, as when orienting to that stimuli.

Skin conductance is measured by recording how much the fingers sweat. As fluids leak from pores in the skin, they carry ions (charged particles) of chloride and sodium that permit an electrical current to flow; skin conductance is then measured by testing the electrical resistance across wires attached to two fingers.

Associations have been found between a weak skin conductance response and criminal disposition (Raine 1993). However, the research literature on SC response is more mixed than that on resting heart rate. Psychopaths and antisocial individuals tend to be characterized by a weaker resting skin conductance response—measured in the absence of any provoking stimuli, such as a loud noise or speech. Not every study finds this relationship, and the exact reason that some studies are failures and others successful may depend on subtle changes in the test conditions. Criminally disposed individuals also show a stronger skin conductance half-recovery time. The half-recovery time is the time it takes for skin conductance to return halfway to

baseline after a stimulus, but its physiological basis is not well understood.

One underlying factor for both a weaker skin conductance and lower resting heart rate may be a lower state of arousal in the brain. This idea, that lower brain arousal leads to crime, was one of the first physiological hypotheses for criminal behavior (Eysenck and Gudjonsson 1989). Because individuals with a criminal disposition would be in a state of low mental arousal, the mildly threatening situation of a medical test would fail to raise their heart rates. This theory holds that to compensate for a low level of arousal, these individuals seek out activities that are intrinsically arousing. Crimes, such as getting into a bruising fight or threatening someone in a robbery, are physically arousing acts. For a person with a normal level of brain arousal, such acts would increase mental arousal to such an intolerable level that the acts would become psychologically aversive. But for a person with a low level of arousal, the same increase of arousal would be pleasantly stimulating and rewarding. In this case, crime is a self-medication for a chronically under aroused brain.

Another interpretation of these physiological findings is an underlying personality characteristic of fearlessness. A lack of fear may account for heart rate and resting skin conductance remaining low in a mildly threatening situation. A lack of fear could also predispose toward crime because fearless children would be more difficult to socialize than fearful ones—punishment would arouse a less intense emotion, and the lesson inadequately learned. It is also better not to be afraid when breaking into a house or threatening violence. As Clint Eastwood intoned in the movie The Unforgiven, it is fearlessness that lets the gunslinger shoot straight, not his speed of draw.

Of these two explanations. I favor low arousal over fearlessness. One of my graduate students, Bo Cleveland (1998), included both measures of fearlessness and stimulation seeking in a study of delinquency and sexual coercion. The measure of fearlessness gave uniformly disappointing findings; it correlated neither with crime nor with other measures of criminal disposition. In contrast, the measures that best fit the under arousal theory, scales of impulsiveness and sensation seeking, correlated with crime. My reading of the overall research literature is that impulsivity and sensation seeking are more strongly associated with crime than either anxiety or fearlessness.

On the other hand, the low arousal theory has its limitations. It is hardly an argument for linking physiology specifically to criminal disposition. Low arousal can be relieved through many socially acceptable activities. The NASCAR racer, the high-altitude mountain climber, and the diver exploring an undersea canyon, all have sensation-seeking traits. The low arousal theory is incomplete because it does not indicate why a particular individual turns to crime rather than to adventure. Ideally, a physiological basis of crime would distinguish between these two groups, a level of specificity that has yet to be achieved.

Tests of Brain Anatomy and Function

A technological revolution has made it possible to view the anatomy and function of the living brain with tremendous precision. A variety of brain imaging techniques have opened a whole new window on the mind. One form of brain imaging is *positron emission tomography* (PET) scanning. These scans show which part of the brain is most active during cognitive tasks.

To be PET scanned, you must first be injected with a form of sugar with a radioactive label attached to it. Sugar fuels the brain. The most active regions of the brain draw the most sugar-fuel from the bloodstream, while the less active areas draw in less sugar. This process is dynamic, with sugar utilization rapidly following changes in the level of brain metabolic activity. After receiving your injection of radioactive-labeled sugar, in the typical experiment you would be asked to work on a cognitive task for about half an hour. During this task, the most active brain regions, down to volumes a few millimeters square, would absorb the greatest amount of radioactive sugar.

After completing the task, you would lie down with your head placed in a PET scanner. The radioactively labeled sugar molecules would now be in your brain cells. Their released high-energy positrons can then be detected by the PET scanner

and these data would be used by a sophisticated computer program to create a picture of your brain regions according to the intensity of their sugar uptake; this picture thus shows which sections of the brain were most physiologically active. This method of imaging the brain, because it uses a radioactive-labeled sugar and complex equipment, is quite expensive for research use.

In comparison to a PET scan, a *magnetic resonance imaging* (MRI) scan shows brain anatomy more than brain function. As with the PET scanner, the subject lies down inside a large MRI machine and holds his head steady. A powerful magnetic field then rushes through the subject's head, causing hydrogen nuclei, like small spinning tops, to spin in one orientation. The MRI most strongly affects protrons in hydrogen atoms. Hydrogen is one of the most abundant elements in the brain, a component of water (H_2O) and of most organic molecules. Once the magnetic field is switched off, the protrons immediately reorient and give off energy in the radio spectrum that is picked up by coils in the MRI machine and translated by a computer program into an exquisitely detailed three-dimensional picture of brain anatomy—one that can be sliced along any plane, as though the brain were cut by a sharp knife and the sections held up for viewing. A modification of the MRI machine, called functional MRI, also provides information about brain activity. These marvelous technologies have greatly aided medical diagnosis and have opened to research the relationship between the mind—mental activity—and the brain, its physical organ.

Raine and his colleagues have explored the relationship between brain images and criminal disposition for more than a decade. Their general finding is that the prefrontal lobes—the brain region most involved in higher thought processes and in the integration of emotions and thought—may malfunction in the brain of criminally disposed individuals. Their earliest work was conducted with PET scanning technology. In their 1993 study, the subjects were 22 California murderers, 20 men and two women; 19 controls were normal subjects matched to the murderers on age and sex. In the murderer group, three individuals were schizophrenic; their matched controls were schizophrenic patients without a history of violence. All subjects completed a PET scan to detect their brain's sugar metabolism and thus its active regions. In the half-hour testing procedure, the subjects identified numerical targets on a computer screen. After the test was completed, they were placed into the PET scanner, and high-energy positrons were used to locate the brain areas of strongest sugar metabolism.

Results from the PET scan are relative ones. Activity in one brain area is expressed relative to activity in all other brain areas. The deficit in murderers, such that their brain activity was lower than the control group's, was relatively specific to the most forward prefrontal areas of the brain, the region behind the forehead. Schizophrenics showed lower than normal activity in the parietal lobe (upper half of the brain above the ear) and temporal lobe (behind the ear). Unlike them, the murderers were no different from controls in their parietal and temporal lobe activity levels. One murderer did not fit the overall pattern. This man was a serial killer with approximately 45 victims over the years. Raine and his colleague speculated that this man planned his crimes—otherwise, he would have been caught long before the 45th victim—and hence he needed normal prefrontal activity for planning and foresight. Raine, Buchsbaum, and LaCasse (1997) extended and replicated these PET scan findings with about twice the number of murderers and controls. They again found a reduced activity level in the prefrontal cortex, as well as abnormal activity levels in deeper brain structures related to aggression.

Why would sugar metabolism be lower in the prefrontal lobes of murderers? One possibility is that the nerve cells themselves differ in the prefrontal region. Perhaps they are less efficient metabolizers of sugar. An alternative hypothesis is that there are fewer nerve cells to uptake sugar, so lower metabolism of sugar would occur in the prefrontal region than in other brain regions. Raine and his colleagues conducted an MRI study that supported this second hypothesis that individuals with criminal disposition differed from controls in their brain anatomy.

In the MRI study, Raine and his colleagues recruited subjects through temporary employment agencies in Los Angeles (Raine et al. 2000). Some employment seekers were diagnosed with antisocial personality disorder (APD) on the basis of a psychiatric interview and a self-report violence scale. Three control groups were constructed from other employment seekers. Subjects in the normal control group had an absence of drug use or psychiatric illness. Those in the drug use control group abused illegal drugs and alcohol but were not antisocial. This control group was included to deal with the high frequency of substance use in the APD group, as Raine wanted to eliminate the possibility that drug abuse had caused brain abnormalities in the APD group. A third control group was created of individuals diagnosed with other psychiatric disorders. In this first brain-imaging study of a nonimprisoned sample of offenders, the subjects were all scanned in an MRI machine.

…At the surface of the brain, a thin layer of gray matter surrounds a larger layer of white matter. The gray layer consists of nerve cell bodies; the white area, of axons from those nerve cells that, like wires, carry signals to other parts of the brain and body. The MRI findings were extremely specific: The antisocial personality disorder group had lower prefrontal gray matter volumes than any of the three control groups. There was no difference in the volume of the prefrontal white matter. Relative to the normal controls, the APD group had an 11 percent reduction in gray-matter volume. Although this anatomical difference is too subtle to be observed in a cursory radiological examination—only a thickness difference of .5 mm—it is still a substantial statistical effect. The correlation of the ratio, prefrontal gray matter volume to whole brain volume, with APD was about .40.

Conclusions About Biological Tests of Crime

This short chapter can only sample from the many advances in the physiological testing of criminal disposition. Among the omitted topics were the association between crime and electrical activity in the brain (as measured with the electroencephalogram, or EEG); brain evoked potentials; cortisol; and other measures (Fishbein et al. 1989;

Susman, Dorn, and Chrousos 1991; see reviews in Raine 1993).

This work on the biological basis of crime differs from that of the nineteenth-century phrenologists. Those scientists sought distinctive physical stigmata that could be used to unequivocally identify criminal individuals and distinguish them from noncriminal ones. The phrenologists looked to physical features, such as large jaws and protrusions on the skull, that would absolutely classify a person as criminal. Their chosen physical markers of criminality turned out not to be associated with criminal disposition. The biologically oriented scientists in this chapter would readily admit that the goal of the phrenologists was an unrealistic one. The criminal mind, and its biology, falls on a continuum with the minds of normal, law-abiding individuals. Some noncriminals will have low resting heart rates, nonsweating hands, and thin gray matter in their prefrontal cortexes, along with other biological markers of criminal disposition. With any single biological test, the identification of criminally disposed individuals is likely to be poor. With a set of biological measures, identification can be improved, but it will still be imperfect. In their MRI study, Raine and his colleagues (2000) also tested their subjects' resting heart rate and skin conductance levels. They could predict whether someone had antisocial personality disorder with 77 percent accuracy, a 27 percent improvement over guessing.

Although much less than the phrenologists had hoped for, this level of accuracy is still a considerable accomplishment with biological tests. Biological tests predict criminal disposition with about the same strength as the best measures of individuals' environmental circumstances—correlations on the order of .20 to .40. Indeed, the biological tests perform considerably better than some environmental indicators, such as social class. Combining biological and social measures may further improve our understanding about who is at risk of becoming criminal.

A more fascinating outcome of biological research, though, is that it pinpoints a type of biological deficit that is involved in criminal dispositions. The deficit appears to lie in impaired functioning of the frontal cortex. This conclusion is consistent with Damasio's stroke victims, Raine's brain imaging, Barkley's theories of hyperactivity, and skin conductance and heart rate findings. Perhaps the nineteenth-century phrenologists were right in one sense. An enlargement of the prefrontal cortex is one of the most distinctive anatomical differences between *Homo sapiens* and our evolutionary kissing cousin, the chimpanzee. The prefrontal cortex may create our knowledge of mind—that other people are themselves thinking about us—and allow us to adjust our behavior to the needs and concerns of others. The prefrontal cortex is also the physiological basis of the executive functions of planning, of delaying the enticing impulses of the present for better outcomes in the future, and of evaluating many behavioral choices instead of just one. The phrenologists may be approximately right: What is disrupted in a criminal disposition are those abilities of the mind that make us most distinctively human.

Discussion Questions

1. List one of the biological factors discussed by Rowe (e.g., serotonin level, heart rate, skin conductance) and describe how it might increase the likelihood of crime.

2. High levels of testosterone are more likely to lead to crime in some types of environments than others. Describe the types of environments where testosterone is most likely to lead to crime.

3. Are there are any circumstances where it would be appropriate to use biological factors, such as testosterone levels and resting heart rate, to predict whether people will commit criminal acts in the future? Defend your response.

4. How do PET and MRI scans work and what do they tell us about the brain activity and anatomy of criminals and noncriminals?

CHAPTER 19

Personality and Crime: Are Some People Crime Prone?

Avshalom Caspi ■ Terrie E. Moffitt ■ Phil A. Silva ■
Magda Stouthamer-Loeber ■ Robert F. Krueger ■ Pamela S. Schmutte

The link between personality and crime has been explored in a number of studies over the past half-century, often employing varying methodologies. As the title of this selection suggests, the existence of a criminal personality is examined using data from multiple sources. Recent psychological research has shown that certain personality traits (e.g., extroversion, neuroticism, psychoticism, impulsivity, aggressiveness) are associated with criminal behavior. Despite these findings, criminological theorists have traditionally examined sociological predictors of crime in lieu of personality traits. However, as Caspi and his colleagues suggest, personality traits are receiving increased attention in criminological research.

Based on current trends in psychological research, the following selection analyzes the link between three "supertraits" and criminal involvement. Caspi and colleagues report that negative emotionality and constraint have robust correlations with crime in the expected directions. More specifically, as negative emotionality increases, crime levels also increase. Conversely, as levels of constraint increase, crime involvement decreases. These results support the argument that a criminal personality type may exist. Finally, mediating variables such as environmental factors and possible causal links are offered for discussion.

Are some people crime-prone? Is there a criminal personality? Psychologists and criminologists have long been intrigued by the connection between personality and crime....

We have studied personality and crime by using a two-pronged approach. First, we have studied individuals in different developmental contexts. Second, we have used multiple and independent measures of their personality and their criminal involvement. In New Zealand we have studied 18-year-olds from an entire birth cohort; the New Zealand study permits us to make detailed comparisons between males and females. In the United States we have studied an ethnically diverse group of 12- and 13-year-old boys; the American study permits us to make detailed comparisons between blacks and whites. By studying different age cohorts in different nations, boys and girls, blacks and whites, and by collecting in each of our studies multiple and independent measures of behavior, we can ascertain with relative confidence the extent to which personality differences are linked to crime.

Personality and Crime

Personality psychologists have proposed numerous well-articulated theories linking personality to crime and other antisocial outcomes. For example, Eysenck (1977) associates crime with extreme individual values on three personality

Excerpted from "Personality and Crime: Are Some People Crime Prone? Replications of the Personality-Crime Relationship Across Countries, Genders, Races, and Methods," by Avshalom Caspi, Terrie E. Moffitt, Phil A. Silva, Magda Stouthamer-Loeber, Robert F. Krueger, and Pamela S. Schmutte, *Criminology* 32(2), May 1994. Reprinted by permission of the American Society of Criminology.

factors: extroversion, neuroticism, and psychoticism. Zuckerman (1989) regards criminality as the sine qua non of individuals high on a factor he calls P-ImpUSS, which is characterized by impulsivity, aggressiveness, and lack of social responsibility. Cloninger (1987), using his three-factor biosocial model of personality, suggests that persons high in novelty seeking and low in harm avoidance and reward dependence are likely to be today's delinquents and tomorrow's violent, antisocial adults. In addition, a group of psychologists have proposed a link between antisocial behavior and theoretical physiological systems within the brain that are presumed to modulate impulse expression (Gray, 1977). Deficiencies in these neural systems have been suggested as the source for aggression in adults (Fowles, 1980; Gorenstein and Newman, 1980), as well as for conduct problems in children (Quay, 1986).

Many of these theories rely on trait-based personality models. In the past, the existence of traits was viewed as controversial (Mischel, 1968). In the last 20 years, however, researchers have amassed solid evidence documenting the cross-situational consistency (Epstein and O'Brien, 1985) and the longitudinal stability (Caspi and Bem, 1990) of traits, and psychology has witnessed a renaissance of the trait as an essential personality construct (Kenrick and Funder, 1988; Tellegen, 1991). Traits represent consistent characteristics of individuals that are relevant to a wide variety of behavioral domains, including criminality (see Eysenck, 1991).

Advances in personality theory and assessment, however, have had little influence on research conducted by criminologists (Gottfredson and Hirschi, 1990). Reviews of research on personality and crime appearing in mainstream criminology have identified numerous methodological problems with previous research (e.g., Schuessler and Cressey, 1950; Tennenbaum, 1977; Waldo and Dinitz, 1967), leading most criminologists to dismiss personality as a fruitless area of inquiry....

Methodological Problems in Linking Personality to Crime

Although some researchers already are convinced that personality variables are essential to understanding crime (e.g., Eysenck and Gudjonsson, 1989), the criminological reviews cited above suggest that this belief is far from universal. In particular, critics of empirical efforts to link personality to crime have pointed to problems in *measurement of personality, measurement of delinquency,* and *sampling*. In our research we have attempted to redress each of these problems.

Measurement of Personality

...In our studies of personality and crime we have used assessment instruments... that measure a comprehensive variety of personality traits; they were designed to blanket the human personality. These instruments allowed us to identify a constellation of personality traits, not merely a single trait, that might be linked to criminal involvement.

Previous studies of personality and delinquency also have been criticized for employing delinquency and personality questionnaires that included virtually identical items (Tennenbaum, 1977). For example, both the MMPI and the CPI include such items as "I have never been in trouble with the law" and "Sometimes when I was young I stole things." Similarities between legally defined offenses and the wording of items on personality inventories may inflate correlations between these two theoretically distinct constructs. In our studies we maintained sensitivity to this issue by evaluating each personality item in terms of its potential semantic overlap with any actual illegal acts.

Measurement of Delinquency

In previous studies of personality and crime, the most commonly used delinquency measure was the subject's conviction record or his presence in a correctional facility. A fundamental problem with official measures, however, is that "hidden criminals," offenders who commit crimes but are not caught, escape empirical attention and may slip into "control" samples (Schuessler and Cressey, 1950). Because only the tip of the deviance iceberg is reflected by official statistics (Hood and Sparks, 1970), many criminologists have turned to less strongly biased measures—specifically, self-reported delinquency questionnaires (Hindelang et al., 1979, 1981; Hirschi et al., 1980).

Yet self-report measures are not faultless. They have been criticized for including trivial items that query about acts which are unlikely to result in official intervention, such as skipping school or defying parental authority (Hindelang et al., 1979; Hirschi et al., 1980). Similarly, infrequent offenders may tend to report trivial events such as sibling fisticuffs in response to questions about "assault," or taking the family car without permission in response to questions about "auto theft" (Elliott and Huizinga, 1989). In contrast, frequent offenders may tend to underreport their delinquent behavior because the individual acts are so commonplace that they are not salient in the offenders' memories (Hirschi et al., 1980). Because both official records and self-report delinquency questionnaires have unique benefits and shortcomings, the use of the two measures in tandem is the most effective empirical strategy (Hirschi et al., 1980).

In our studies of personality and crime, we have collected multiple and independent measures of delinquent behavior: police records of contact, court records of conviction, self-reports, and reports from independent informants, parents, and teachers. These multiple measures have allowed us to identify robust personality correlates of crime that replicate across different measurement strategies.

Sampling

In previous studies of personality and crime, the most commonly used samples were drawn from incarcerated populations. These samples are not representative of offenders as a whole; they represent only the subset of offenders who actually are caught and subsequently are sent to jail (Hood and Sparks, 1970; Klein, 1987). Moreover, adjudicated offenders may differ systematically from non-adjudicated offenders; offenders who are white, middle class, or female may be overlooked inadvertently (e.g., Taylor and Watt, 1977). In addition, the offenders' personal characteristics may influence official responses to their aberrant behavior; for example, some offenders may have enough poise to talk their way out of an arrest. Finally, incarceration itself may contribute to personality

aberrations (Schuessler and Cressey, 1950; Wilson and Herrnstein, 1985). Thus, non-representative sampling has clouded interpretation of observed differences between captive offenders and comparison groups.

In our studies of personality and crime, we have surveyed two different age cohorts whose members' level of involvement in illegal behaviors ranges from complete abstinence to a wide variety of delinquent violations. Therefore, our results are not limited to a selected minority of adolescent offenders who have been caught and convicted of their crimes.

The results of our studies are presented in two parts. Study 1 explores the personality-crime relationship in a birth cohort of 18-year-old males and females living in New Zealand. Study 2 attempts to replicate these findings among 12- and 13-year-olds living in a large American city.

Study 1: Personality and Crime Among Males and Females: Evidence from a New Zealand Birth Cohort

Study 1 explores the personality-crime relationship in a longitudinal-epidemiological sample (Krueger et al., in press). Members of this sample have been studied since birth. At age 18 they were administered an omnibus self-report personality inventory that assesses individual differences in several focal personality dimensions. In addition to this personality assessment, we gathered information about their delinquency using multiple and independent data sources: self-reports, informant reports, and official records....

Measurement of Personality

As part of the age-18 assessment, 862 subjects completed a modified version (Form NZ) of the Multidimensional Personality Questionnaire (MPQ; Tellegen, 1982). The MPQ is a self-report personality instrument designed to assess a broad range of individual differences in affective and behavioral style. The 177-item version of the MPQ (Form NZ) yields 10 different personality scales (Tellegen, 1982: 7-8)....

The 10 scales constituting the MPQ can be viewed at the higher-order level as defining three superfactors: Constraint, Negative Emotionality, and Positive Emotionality (Tellegen, 1985; Tellegen and Waller, in press). *Constraint* is a combination of the Traditionalism, Harm Avoidance, and Control scales. Individuals high on this factor tend to endorse conventional social norms, to avoid thrills, and to act in a cautious and restrained manner. *Negative Emotionality* is a combination of the Aggression, Alienation, and Stress Reaction scales. Individuals high on this dimension have a low general threshold for the experience of negative emotions such as fear, anxiety, and anger, and tend to break down under stress (Tellegen et al., 1988). *Positive Emotionality* is a combination of the Achievement, Social Potency, Well-Being, and Social Closeness scales. Individuals high on

Positive Emotionality have a lower threshold for the experience of positive emotions and for positive engagement with their social and work environments, and tend to view life as essentially a pleasurable experience (Tellegen et al., 1988)....

Results

Higher-Order Personality Factors and Delinquency

To summarize the personality correlates of delinquent behavior across the three independent data sources, we examined correlations between the MPQ's three higher-order factors and each measure of delinquent activity....

Among both males and females, Constraint and Negative Emotionality emerged as robust correlates of delinquent behavior across the three

Table 19.1 MPQ Scale Descriptions and Internal Consistency Coefficients

MPQ Scale	Alpha	Description of a High Scorer
Constraint		
Traditionalism	.63	Desires a conservative social environment; endorses high moral standards.
Harm Avoidance	.71	Avoids excitement and danger; prefers safe activities even if they are tedious.
Control	.79	Is reflective, cautious, careful, rational, planful.
Negative Emotionality		
Aggression	.78	Hurts others for own advantage; will frighten and cause discomfort for others.
Alienation	.76	Feels mistreated, victimized, betrayed, and the target of false rumors.
Stress Reaction	.80	Is nervous, vulnerable, sensitive, prone to worry.
Positive Emotionality		
Achievement	.69	Works hard; enjoys demanding projects and working long hours.
Social Potency	.76	Is forceful and decisive; fond of influencing others; fond of leadership roles.
Well-Being	.67	Has a happy, cheerful disposition; feels good about self and sees a bright future.
Social Closeness	.75	Is sociable; likes people and turns to others for comfort.

different data sources. *Positive Emotionality* was not associated significantly with any measure of delinquent behavior.... [M]ale and female delinquents exhibited convergent personality profiles characterized by impulsivity, danger seeking, a rejection of traditional values, aggressive attitudes, feelings of alienation, and an adversarial interpersonal attitude....

Criminologists would be persuaded more fully by evidence linking personality traits to crime if personality traits could be shown to relate to serious criminal behavior. To address this issue, we examined the higher-order personality scores of three groups of persons: (1) persons who self-reported having committed multiple (two or more) index offenses in the past year, (2) persons who were identified through court conviction records as repeat offenders, and (3) persons who had been convicted for a violent offense. We restricted this examination to males because relatively few females were involved in serious criminal acts, as defined above....

Persons involved in serious criminal behavior scored significantly lower on MPQ Constraint and significantly higher on Negative Emotionality....

In sum, the results from our analyses of the personality correlates of serious crime are very similar to the results from our analyses of the personality correlates of other antisocial activities. Apparently the same personality traits are implicated in antisocial acts of varying severity.

The results have revealed robust personality correlates of delinquency. Among both males and females, three personality scales were correlated with all three independent sources of delinquency data (self-reports, informant reports, and official reports): Delinquency was associated negatively with the MPQ scales' Traditionalism and Control, and positively with Aggression. These results suggest that young men and women who engaged in delinquency preferred rebelliousness to conventionality, behaved impulsively rather than cautiously, and were likely to take advantage of others.

Two additional personality scales showed consistent patterns. Among males, all three data sources correlated with the MPQ scale Alienation, and two data sources correlated with the MPQ scale Stress Reaction; among females, two data sources correlated with both Alienation and Stress Reaction. These results suggest that young men and women who engaged in delinquency were also likely to feel betrayed and used by their friends and to become easily upset and irritable. At the higher-order factor level, greater delinquent participation was associated with a unique trait configuration: greater negative emotionality *and* less constraint.

These findings were not compromised by problems inherent in measuring delinquency; the personality correlates were robust across different methods of measuring delinquency. Moreover, the interpretation of these data was not compromised by predictor-criterion overlap because we eliminated any content overlap between the personality items and the delinquency measures. These findings, however, were observed in a single sample. We now turn to a replication of these findings in a different context.

Study 2: Personality and Crime Among Blacks and Whites: Evidence from an American Metropolis

Study 1 reported on mostly white adolescents who live in a mid-sized city with little social decay in comparison with America's largest cities. It is possible that the racial or ecological composition of this sample may have distorted the relation between personality and crime. For example, it may be that relations between personality characteristics and crime may be attenuated among inner-city youths who experience many contextual pressures to engage in illegal behavior. Will negative emotionality and constraint predict delinquent behavior in individuals from different environments and during different developmental stages?

We address these generalizability issues in Study 2 by exploring the personality-crime relationship in a separate sample of American inner-city youths age 12 and 13. At that age, caregivers provided extensive personality descriptions of the youths. In addition, we gathered information about the youths' delinquency using multiple and independent data sources: self-reports, teachers' reports, and parents' reports.

Method

Measurement of Personality

Because the MPQ is not appropriate for younger adolescents, we used a different personality assessment instrument to describe the personalities of the boys in Pittsburgh. Specifically, the caregivers completed the "Common-Language" version of the California Child Q-sort (CCQ), a language-simplified personality assessment procedure intended for use with lay observers (Caspi et al., 1992).... The CCQ contains 100 statements written on individual cards that describe a wide range of personality attributes (e.g., "He plans ahead; he thinks before he does something," "He is determined in what he does; he does not give up easily," "He tries to see what and how much he can get away with"). The caregiver's task was to sort these item cards into a forced nine-category distribution along a continuum ranging from "most like this boy" to "most *un*like this boy."...

Results

To assess the relation between personality characteristics and delinquency, we computed correlations between the CCQ measures of Constraint, Negative Emotionality, and Positive Emotionality with measures of delinquency drawn from the three independent data sources: self-reports, teachers' reports, and parents' reports....

Across all three data sources, Constraint and Negative Emotionality emerged as robust correlates of delinquency among both black and white adolescents. The positive correlations with Negative Emotionality suggested that delinquent adolescents were prone to respond to frustrating events with strong negative emotions, to feel stressed or harassed, and to approach interpersonal relationships with an adversarial attitude. The negative correlations with Constraint suggested that delinquent adolescents were likely

to be impulsive, danger-seeking, and rejecting of conventional values. Positive emotionality was not associated robustly with delinquent behavior....

Discussion

Our studies have revealed that individual differences in personality are correlated consistently with delinquency. Although we performed many analyses, the significant correlations were not scattered randomly across variables; rather, the same pattern of personality correlations was repeated consistently. We obtained these correlations in different countries, in different age cohorts, across gender, and across race. We also obtained these correlations when we measured delinquent involvement with self-reports, teachers' reports, parents' reports, informants' reports, and official records, and when we measured serious crime and less serious delinquency. Finally, we obtained these correlations when we measured personality both with self-reports and with parents' reports. The personality correlates of delinquency were robust: Greater delinquent participation was associated with greater negative emotionality and less constraint.

Gottfredson and Hirschi (1990) have suggested that individual differences in "self-control" predispose some people to criminal behavior; this single stable individual difference is said to define a propensity or proneness to crime. Our findings support this theory somewhat, but they also suggest that it is simplistic psychologically. Crime proneness is defined not by a single tendency (such as self-control or impulsivity) but by multiple psychological components. Across different samples and different methods, our studies of personality and crime suggest that crime-proneness is defined both by high negative emotionality and by low constraint.

How Might Negative Emotionality and Constraint Lead to Crime?

Negative emotionality is a tendency to experience aversive affective states such as anger, anxiety, and irritability (Watson and Clark, 1984). It is likely that individuals with chronically high levels of such negative emotions perceive interpersonal events differently than other people. They may be predisposed to construe events in a biased way, perceiving threat in the acts of others and menace in the vicissitudes of everyday life.

This situation may be aggravated when negative emotionality is accompanied by weak constraint—that is, great difficulty in modulating impulses. In low-constraint individuals, negative emotions may be translated more readily into action. Such volatile individuals should be, in the vernacular of the Wild West, "quick on the draw." Theoretically, antisocial behavior should be likely among individuals who are high in negative emotionality and low in constraint.

What Are the Origins of Negative Emotionality and Constraint?

Our findings may be placed into a developmental context by considering theories about the environmental and biological origins of negative emotionality and constraint.

The family environment has a pervasive influence on children's lives and personality development, particularly on the development of antisocial behavior (e.g., Patterson, 1982). Harsh, inconsistent disciplinary practices and a chaotic home environment have been shown to predict later aggression (Loeber and Stouthamer-Loeber, 1986). Living under the constant threat of emotional or physical harm makes negative affect more than simply a perceptual bias for these youths; negative affect is rooted in the realities of their everyday lives. Constraint also may be affected by family dynamics. For example, parental conflict has been found to predict children's scores on constraint at age 18 (Vaughn et al., 1988). Thus, a personality configuration involving high levels of negative affect and low levels of constraint may develop when children grow and learn in a discordant family environment where parent-child interactions are harsh or inconsistent.

Negative affectivity and constraint also are considered to have specific neurobiological under-pinnings. Recent research has pointed to a possible connection between the rate at which the brain expends its neurotransmitter substances and dimensions of personality (Cloninger, 1987). For example, abnormally low levels of a metabolite by-product from the neurotransmitter called serotonin have been found in the cerebrospinal fluid of prison inmates whose offense history is habitually violent and impulsive (Linnoila et al., 1983; Virkunnen et al., 1987). This finding has led theorists to outline the neural mechanisms by which low serotonin levels in the brain could simultaneously produce impulsivity *and* greater negative affectivity (Depue and Spoont, 1986; Spoont, 1992).

Theories linking personality traits to the primary neurotransmitters also may have important implications for research on the link between crime and genetics. Some adoption and twin studies have demonstrated a significant heritability for criminal behavior (see DiLalla and Gottesman, 1989; Mednick et al., 1986; Plomin et al., 1990), but these findings remain controversial in criminology (Walters and White, 1989). If future behavior genetic studies should document significant heritability for criminal behavior, how should we interpret this finding? Clearly, behavior itself cannot be inherited. Low serotonin levels, however, may be a heritable diathesis for a personality style involving high levels of negative affect and low levels of constraint, which generates in turn a vulnerability to criminal behavior. Indeed, negative affect and constraint themselves appear to be highly heritable; a study of twins reared together versus twins reared apart (Tellegen et al., 1988) found that more than 50% of the observed variance in both Negative Emotionality and Constraint (assessed by the MPQ) could be attributed to genetic factors....

Discussion Questions

1. Caspi et al. state that many criminologists have been critical of previous research linking personality traits to crime, citing certain methodological problems with such research.

What are these problems? How do Caspi et al. overcome them?

2. A researcher finds that certain personality traits are more common among prison inmates than among people in the general population. Does this mean that such traits *cause* crime? If not, why not?

3. Describe the super-traits of negative emotionality and constraint. List two questions you might ask respondents in a survey to measure each trait (or dimensions of each trait).

4. Why did Caspi et al. explore the relationship between personality traits and crime using two samples?

5. Describe all the ways that negative emotionality and low constraint might increase the likelihood of crime.

CHAPTER 20

A Sociological Theory of Criminal Behavior

Edwin H. Sutherland

Differential association, sometimes referred to as learning theory, considers the issue of how criminal or delinquent behavior is acquired. Edwin H. Sutherland's 1947 classic statement of differential association is the source of this selection.

According to Sutherland, criminal behavior is learned the same way other behaviors are learned. He delineates nine propositions that outline the process of learning criminal behavior. The process involves learning both the techniques and drives necessary for committing the offense. The drives and motives for offending are learned from the definitions concerning whether legal codes are to be obeyed or whether it is acceptable to violate them. The "principle of differential association" indicates that it is when there is an excess of definitions favorable to law violation relative to those unfavorable to law violation that crime occurs. Learning to view laws as favorable or unfavorable to violate is determined by the definitions of the law provided by people with whom an individual associates, which in turn is impacted by the community in which one lives. As Sutherland notes, some groups in society provide more definitions in favor to law violation than other groups do. Variations in crime rates across communities reflect this differential social organization.

The average citizen is confronted by a confusing and conflicting complex of popular beliefs and

Reprinted from: Edwin H. Sutherland, "A Sociological Theory of Criminal Behavior." In *Criminology*, 4th Edition, pp. 3, 6-9. Copyright © 1947 by New York: J. B. Lippincott. Reprinted by permission from the Cressey Estate.

programs in regard to crime. Some of these are traditions from eighteenth-century philosophy; some are promulgations of special interest groups; and some are blind emotional reactions. Organized and critical thinking in this field is therefore peculiarly difficult and also peculiarly necessary....

... The following statement refers to the process by which a particular person comes to engage in criminal behavior.

1. Criminal behavior is learned. Negatively, this means that criminal behavior is not inherited, as such; also, the person who is not already trained in crime does not invent criminal behavior, just as a person does not make mechanical inventions unless he has had training in mechanics.

2. Criminal behavior is learned in interaction with other persons in a process of communication. This communication is verbal in many respects but includes also "the communication of gestures."

3. The principal part of the learning of criminal behavior occurs within intimate personal groups. Negatively, this means that the impersonal agencies of communication, such as picture shows and newspapers, play a relatively unimportant part in the genesis of criminal behavior.

4. When criminal behavior is learned, the learning includes (a) techniques of committing the crime, which are sometimes very complicated, sometimes very simple; (b) the specific direction of motives, drives, rationalizations, and attitudes.

5. The specific direction of motives and drives is learned from definitions of the legal codes as favorable or unfavorable. In some societies an individual is surrounded by persons who invariably define the legal codes as rules to be observed, while in others he is surrounded by persons whose definitions are favorable to the violation of the legal codes. In our American society these definitions are almost always mixed and consequently we have culture conflict in relation to the legal codes.

6. A person becomes delinquent because of an excess of definitions favorable to violation of law over definitions unfavorable to violation of law. This is the principle of differential association. It refers to both criminal and anti-criminal associations and has to do with counteracting forces. When persons become criminal, they do so because of contacts with criminal patterns and also because of isolation from anti-criminal patterns. Any person inevitably assimilates the surrounding culture unless other patterns are in conflict; a Southerner does not pronounce "r" because other Southerners do not pronounce "r." Negatively, this proposition of differential association means that associations which are neutral so far as crime is concerned have little or no effect on the genesis of criminal behavior. Much of the experience of a person is neutral in this sense, e.g., learning to brush one's teeth. This behavior has no negative or positive effect on criminal behavior except as it may be related to associations which are concerned with the legal codes. This neutral behavior is important especially as an occupier of the time of a child so that he is not in contact with criminal behavior during the time he is so engaged in the neutral behavior.

7. Differential associations may vary in frequency, duration, priority, and intensity. This means that associations with criminal behavior and also associations with anti-criminal behavior vary in those respects. "Frequency" and "duration" as modalities of associations are obvious and need no explanation. "Priority" is assumed to be important in the sense that lawful behavior developed in early childhood may persist throughout life, and also that delinquent behavior developed in early childhood may persist

throughout life. This tendency, however, has not been adequately demonstrated, and priority seems to be important principally through its selective influence. "Intensity" is not precisely defined but it has to do with such things as prestige of the source of a criminal or anti-criminal pattern and with emotional reactions related to the associations. In a precise description of the criminal behavior of a person these modalities would be stated in quantitative form and a mathematical ratio can be reached. A formula in this sense has not been developed and the development of such a formula would be extremely difficult.

8. The process of learning criminal behavior by association with criminal and anti-criminal patterns involves all of the mechanisms that are involved in any other learning. Negatively, this means that the learning of criminal behavior is not restricted to the process of imitation. A person who is seduced, for instance, learns criminal behavior by association but this process would not ordinarily be described as imitation.

9. While criminal behavior is an expression of general needs and values, it is not explained by those general needs and values since non-criminal behavior is an expression of the same needs and values. Thieves generally steal in order to secure money, but likewise honest laborers work in order to secure money. The attempts by many scholars to explain criminal behavior by general drives and values, such as the happiness principle, striving for social status, the money motive, or frustration, have been and must continue to be futile since they explain lawful behavior as completely as they explain criminal behavior. They are similar to respiration, which is necessary for any behavior but which does not differentiate criminal from non-criminal behavior.

It is not necessary, at this level of explanation, to explain why a person has the associations which he has; this certainly involves a complex of many things. In an area where the delinquency rate is high a boy who is sociable, gregarious, active, and athletic is very likely to come in contact with the other boys in the neighborhood, learn delinquent behavior from them, and become a gangster; in the same neighborhood the psychopathic boy who is isolated, introvert, and inert may remain at home, not become acquainted with the other boys in the neighborhood, and not become delinquent. In another situation, the sociable, athletic, aggressive boy may become a member of a scout troop and not become involved in delinquent behavior. The person's associations are determined in a general context of social organization. A child is ordinarily reared in a family; the place of residence of the family is determined largely by family income; and the delinquency rate is in many respects related to the rental value of the houses. Many other factors enter into this social organization, including many of the small personal group relationships.

The preceding explanation of criminal behavior was stated from the point of view of the person who engages in criminal behavior. It is possible, also, to state theories of criminal behavior from the point of view of the community, nation, or other group. The problem, when thus stated, is generally concerned with crime rates and involves a comparison of the crime rates of various groups or the crime rates of a particular group at different times. One of the best explanations of crime rates from this point of view is that a high crime rate is due to social disorganization. The term "social disorganization" is not entirely satisfactory and

it seems preferable to substitute for it the term "differential social organization." The postulate on which this theory is based, regardless of the name, is that crime is rooted in the social organization and is an expression of that social organization. A group may be organized for criminal behavior or organized against criminal behavior. Most communities are organized both for criminal and anti-criminal behavior and in that sense the crime rate is an expression of the differential group organization....

Discussion Questions

1. Discuss Sutherland's nine propositions and describe the processes through which he suggests criminal behavior is learned.
2. According to Sutherland's framework, what specifically is meant by the term "differential association"? When does criminal behavior occur? From whom are the definitions favorable to law violation learned? Why are peers an important part of this process?
3. What is differential social organization? What role does it play with regard to learning definitions favorable to law violation?

CHAPTER 21

A Social Learning Theory of Crime

Ronald L. Akers

Edwin Sutherland, in one of the earliest sociological theories of crime, argued that criminal behavior, like all behavior, is learned in a social environment. Crime, therefore, is not the result of defective people, but rather the result of differential association with those who exhibit deviant behavior. Social learning theory, intended to be a reformulation and extension of Sutherland's differential association theory, posits that differential association with delinquent peer groups, along with additional factors such as imitation and reinforcement, causes individual delinquency.

In the following section, Ronald L. Akers explains the four major concepts of social learning theory: differential association, definitions, differential reinforcement, and imitation. Of the four concepts, Akers argues that differential association has the largest impact on behavior and subsequent delinquency. These associations accelerate the learning process by offering models for one to observe and imitate. Akers also discusses how differential association with delinquent peers introduces a person to new definitions about crime that make delinquent acts seem justifiable (neutralizing definitions) or necessary (positive definitions). Finally, criminal behavior is supported by delinquent peers through social reinforcement. Akers also considers the validity of social learning theory, which has received strong empirical support, in addition to highlighting some important critiques.

Development of the Theory

Sutherland asserted in the eighth statement of his theory that all the mechanisms of learning are involved in criminal behavior. However, beyond a brief comment that more is involved than direct imitation (Tarde, 1912), he did not explain what the mechanisms of learning are. These learning mechanisms were specified by Burgess and Akers (1966b) in their "differential association-reinforcement" theory of criminal behavior. Burgess and Akers produced a full reformulation that retained the principles of differential association, combining them with, and restating them in terms of, the learning principles of operant and respondent conditioning that had been developed by behavioral psychologists. Akers followed up his early work with Burgess to develop social learning theory, applying it to criminal, delinquent, and deviant behavior in general. He has modified the theory, provided a fully explicated presentation of its concepts, examined it in light of the critiques and research by others, and carried out his own research to test its central propositions (Akers, 1973; 1977; 1985; 1998).

Social learning theory is not competitive with differential association theory. Instead, it is a broader theory that retains all the differential association processes in Sutherland's theory (albeit clarified and somewhat modified) and integrates it with differential reinforcement and other principles of behavioral acquisition, continuation, and cessation (Akers, 1985:41). Thus, research findings supportive of differential association also support the integrated theory. But social learning theory explains criminal and delinquent behavior more thoroughly than does the original differential association theory (see, for instance, Akers et al., 1979; Warr and Stafford, 1991).

Burgess and Akers (1966b) explicitly identified the learning mechanisms as those found in modern behavioral theory. They retained the concepts of differential association and definitions from Sutherland's theory, but conceptualized them in more behavioral terms and added concepts from behavioral learning theory. These concepts include differential reinforcement, whereby "operant" behavior (the voluntary actions of the individual) is conditioned or shaped by rewards and punishments. They also contain classical or "respondent" conditioning (the conditioning of involuntary reflex behavior); discriminative stimuli (the environmental and internal stimuli that provide cues or signals for behavior), schedules of reinforcement (the rate and ratio in which rewards and punishments follow behavioral responses), and other principles of behavior modification.

Social learning theory retains a strong element of the symbolic interactionism found in the concepts of differential association and definitions from Sutherland's theory (Akers, 1985:39–70). Symbolic interactionism is the theory that social interaction is mainly the exchange of meaning and symbols; individuals have the cognitive capacity to imagine themselves in the role of others and incorporate this into their conceptions of themselves (Ritzer, 1992). This, and the explicit inclusion of such concepts as imitation, anticipated reinforcement, and self-reinforcement, makes social learning "soft behaviorism" (Akers, 1985:65). As a result, the theory is closer to cognitive learning theories, such as Albert Bandura's (1973; 1977; 1986; Bandura and Walters, 1963), than to the radical or orthodox operant behaviorism of B. F. Skinner (1953; 1959) with which Burgess and Akers began.

The Central Concepts and Propositions of Social Learning Theory

The word *learning* should not be taken to mean that the theory is only about how novel criminal behavior is acquired. "Behavioral principles are not limited to learning but are fundamental principles of performance [that account for]...the acquisition, maintenance, and modification of human behavior" (Andrews and Bonta, 1998: 150). Social learning theory offers an explanation of crime and deviance which embraces variables that operate both to motivate and control criminal behavior, both to promote and undermine conformity. The probability of criminal or conforming behavior occurring is a function of the balance of these influences on behavior.

> The basic assumption in social learning theory is that the same learning process in a context of social structure, interaction, and situation, produces both conforming and deviant behavior. The difference lies in the direction...[of] the balance of influences on behavior.
>
> The probability that persons will engage in criminal and deviant behavior is increased and the probability of their conforming to the norm is decreased when they differentially associate with others who commit criminal behavior and espouse definitions favorable to it, are relatively more exposed in-person or symbolically to salient criminal deviant models, define it as desirable or justified in a situation discriminative for the behavior, and have received in the past and anticipate in the current or future situation relatively greater reward than punishment for the behavior. (Akers, 1998: 50)

As these quotations show, while referring to all aspects of the learning process, Akers' development of the theory has relied principally on four major concepts: *differential association, definitions, differential reinforcement,* and *imitation* (Akers et al., 1979; Akers, 1985; Akers, 1998).

Differential association. Differential association refers to the process whereby one is exposed to normative definitions favorable or unfavorable to illegal or law-abiding behavior. Differential association has both behavioral interactional and normative dimensions. The interactional dimension is the direct association and interaction with others who engage in certain kinds of behavior, as well as the indirect association and identification with more distant reference groups. The normative dimension is the different patterns of norms and values to which an individual is exposed through this association.

The groups with which one is in differential association provide the major social contexts in which all the mechanisms of social learning operate. They not only expose one to definitions, they also present them with models to imitate and with differential reinforcement (source, schedule, value, and amount) for criminal or conforming behavior. The most important of these groups are the primary ones of family and friends, though they may also be secondary and reference groups. Neighbors, churches, school teachers, physicians, the law and authority figures, and other individuals and groups in the community (as well as mass media and other more remote sources of attitudes and models) have varying degrees of effect on the individual's propensity to commit criminal and delinquent behavior. Those associations that occur earlier (priority), last longer and occupy more of one's time (duration), take place most often (frequency), and involve others with whom one has the more important or closer relationship (intensity) will have the greater effect on behavior.

Definitions. Definitions are one's own attitudes or meanings that one attaches to given behavior. That is, they are orientations, rationalizations, definitions of the situation, and other evaluative and moral attitudes that define the commission of an act as right or wrong, good or bad, desirable or undesirable, justified or unjustified.

In social learning theory, these definitions are both general and specific. General beliefs include religious, moral, and other conventional values and norms that are favorable to conforming behavior and unfavorable to committing any deviant or criminal acts. Specific definitions orient the person to particular acts or series of acts. Thus, one may believe that it is morally wrong to steal and that laws against theft should be obeyed, but at the same time one may see little wrong with smoking marijuana and rationalize that it is all right to violate laws against drug possession.

The greater the extent to which one holds attitudes that disapprove of certain acts, the less one is likely to engage in them. Conventional beliefs are negative toward criminal behavior. Conversely, the more one's own attitudes approve of a behavior, the greater the chances are that one will do it. Approving definitions favorable to the commission of criminal or deviant behavior are basically positive or neutralizing. Positive definitions are beliefs or attitudes which make the behavior morally desirable or wholly permissible. Neutralizing definitions favor the commission of crime by justifying or excusing it. They view the act as something that is probably undesirable but, given the situation, is nonetheless all right, justified, excusable, necessary, or not really bad to do. The concept of neutralizing definitions in social learning theory incorporates the notions of verbalizations, rationalizations, techniques of neutralizations, accounts, disclaimers, and moral disengagement (Cressey, 1953; Sykes and Matza, 1957; Lyman and Scott, 1970; Hewitt and Stokes, 1975; Bandura, 1990). Neutralizing attitudes include such beliefs as, "Everybody has a racket," "I can't help myself, I was born this way," "I am not at fault," "I am not responsible," "I was drunk and didn't know what I was doing," "I just blew my top," "They can afford it," "He deserved it," and other excuses and justification for committing deviant acts and victimizing others. These definitions favorable and unfavorable to criminal and delinquent behavior are developed through imitation and differential reinforcement. Cognitively, they provide a mind-set that makes one more willing to commit the act when the opportunity occurs. Behaviorally, they affect the commission of deviant or criminal behavior by acting as internal discriminative stimuli. Discriminative stimuli operate as cues or signals to the individual as to what responses are appropriate or expected in a given situation.

Some of the definitions favorable to deviance are so intensely held that they almost "require" one to violate the law. For instance, the radical ideologies of revolutionary groups provide strong motivation for terrorist acts, just as the fervent moral stance of some anti-abortion groups justifies in their minds the need to engage in civil disobedience. For the most part, however, definitions favorable to crime and delinquency do not "require" or strongly motivate action in this sense. Rather, they are conventional beliefs so weakly held that they provide no restraint or are positive or neutralizing attitudes that facilitate law violation in the right set of circumstances.

Differential reinforcement. Differential reinforcement refers to the balance of anticipated or actual rewards and punishments that follow or are consequences of behavior. Whether individuals will refrain from or commit a crime at any given time (and whether they will continue or desist from doing so in the future) depends on the past, present, and anticipated future rewards and punishments for their actions. The probability that an act will be committed or repeated is increased by rewarding outcomes or reactions to it, e.g., obtaining approval, money, food, or pleasant feelings—positive reinforcement. The likelihood that an action will be taken is also enhanced when it allows the person to avoid or escape aversive or unpleasant events—negative reinforcement. Punishment may also be direct (positive), in which painful or unpleasant consequences are attached to a behavior; or indirect (negative), in which a reward or pleasant consequence is removed. Just as there are modalities of association, there are modalities of reinforcement—amount, frequency, and probability. The greater the value or amount of reinforcement for the person's behavior, the more frequently it is reinforced, and the higher the probability that it will be reinforced (as balanced against alternative behavior), the greater the likelihood that it will occur and be repeated. The reinforcement process does not operate in the social environment in a simple either/or fashion. Rather, it operates according to a "matching function" in which the occurrence of, and changes in, each of several different behaviors correlate with the probability and amount of, and changes in, the balance of reward and punishment attached to each behavior (Herrnstein, 1961; Hamblin, 1979; Conger and Simons, 1995).

Reinforcers and punishers can be non-social; for example, the direct physical effects of drugs and alcohol. However, whether or not these effects are experienced positively or negatively is contingent upon previously learned expectations. Through social reinforcement, one learns to interpret the effects as pleasurable and enjoyable or as frightening and unpleasant. Individuals can learn without contact, directly or indirectly, with social reinforcers and punishers. There may be a physiological basis for the tendency of some individuals (such as those prone to sensation-seeking) more than others to find certain forms of deviant behavior intrinsically rewarding (Wood et al., 1995). However, the theory proposes that most of the learning in criminal and deviant behavior is the result of social exchange in which the words, responses, presence, and behavior of other persons directly reinforce behavior, provide the setting for reinforcement (discriminative stimuli), or serve as the conduit through which other social rewards and punishers are delivered or made available.

The concept of social reinforcement (and punishment) goes beyond the direct reactions of others present while an act is committed. It also includes the whole range of actual and anticipated, tangible and intangible rewards valued in society or subgroups. Social rewards can be highly symbolic. Their reinforcing effects can come from their fulfilling ideological, religious, political, or other goals. Even those rewards which we consider to be very tangible, such as money and material possessions, gain their reinforcing value from the prestige and approval value they have in society. Nonsocial reinforcement, therefore, is more narrowly confined to unconditioned physiological and physical stimuli. In self-reinforcement the individual exercises self-control, reinforcing or punishing one's own behavior by taking the role of others, even when alone.

Imitation. Imitation refers to the engagement in behavior after the observation of similar behavior in others. Whether or not the behavior modeled by others will be imitated is affected by the characteristics of the models, the behavior observed, and the observed consequences of the behavior (Bandura, 1977). The observation of salient models in primary groups and in the media affects both pro-social and deviant behavior (Donnerstein and Linz, 1995). It is more important in the initial acquisition and performance of novel behavior than in the maintenance or cessation of behavioral patterns once established, but it continues to have some effect in maintaining behavior.

The Social Learning Process: Sequence and Feedback Effects

These social learning variables are all part of an underlying process that is operative in each individual's learning history and in the immediate situation in which an opportunity for a crime occurs. Akers stresses that social learning is a complex process with reciprocal and feedback effects. The reciprocal effects are not seen as equal, however. Akers hypothesizes a typical temporal sequence or process by which persons come to the point of violating the law or engaging in other deviant acts (Akers, 1998).

This process is one in which the balance of learned definitions, imitation of criminal or deviant models, and the anticipated balance of reinforcement produces the initial delinquent or deviant act. The facilitative effects of these variables continue in the repetition of acts, although imitation becomes less important than it was in the first commission of the act. After initiation, the actual social and non-social reinforcers and punishers affect whether or not the acts will be repeated and at what level of frequency. Not only the behavior itself, but also the definitions are affected by the consequences of the initial act. Whether a deviant act will be committed in a situation that presents the opportunity depends on the learning history of the individual and the set of reinforcement contingencies in that situation.

> The actual social sanctions and other effects of engaging in the behavior may be perceived differently, but to the extent that they are more rewarding than alternative behavior, then the deviant behavior will be repeated under similar circumstances. Progression into more frequent or sustained patterns of deviant behavior is promoted [to the extent] that reinforcement, exposure to deviant models, and definitions are not offset by negative formal and informal sanctions and definitions. (Akers, 1985:60)

The theory does not hypothesize that definitions favorable to law violation only precede and are unaffected by the initiation of criminal acts. Acts in violation of the law can occur in the absence of any thought given to right and wrong. Furthermore, definitions may be applied by the individual retroactively to excuse or justify an act already committed. To the extent that such excuses successfully mitigate others' negative sanctions or one's self-punishment, however, they become cues for the repetition of deviant acts. At that point they precede the future commission of the acts.

Differential association with conforming and non-conforming others typically precedes the individual's committing the acts. Families are included in the differential association process, and it is obvious that association, reinforcement of conforming or deviant behavior, deviant or conforming modeling, and exposure to definitions favorable or unfavorable to deviance occurs within the family prior to the onset of delinquency. On the other hand, it can never be true that the onset of delinquency initiates interaction in the family (except in the unlikely case of the late-stage adoption of a child who is already delinquent who is drawn to and chosen by deviant parents). This is also hypothesized as the typical process within peer groups. While one may be attracted to deviant peer groups prior to becoming involved in delinquency, associations with peers and others are most often formed initially around attractions, friendships, and circumstances, such as neighborhood proximity, that have little to do directly with co-involvement in some deviant behavior. However, after the associations have been established and the reinforcing or punishing consequences of the deviant behavior are experienced, both the continuation of old and the seeking of new associations (over which one has any choice) will themselves be affected. One may choose further interaction with others based, in part, on whether they too are involved in similar deviant or criminal behavior. But the theory proposes that the sequence of events, in which deviant associations precede the onset of delinquent behavior, will occur more frequently than the sequence of events in which the onset of delinquency precedes the beginning of deviant associations.

Social Structure and Social Learning

Akers has proposed a SSSL (social structure and social learning) model in which social structural factors are hypothesized to have an indirect effect on the individual's conduct. They affect the social learning variables of differential association, differential reinforcement, definitions, and imitation which, in turn, have a direct impact on the individual's conduct. The social learning variables are proposed as the main ones in the process by which various aspects of the social structure influence individual behavior (see Figure 21.1).

> The social structural variables are indicators of the primary distal macro-level and meso-level causes of crime, while the social learning variables reflect the primary proximate causes of criminal behavior that mediate the relationship between social structure and crime rates. Some structural variables are not related to crime and do not explain the crime rate because they do not have a crime-relevant effect on the social learning variables. (Akers, 1998:322)

As shown in Figure 21.1, Akers (1998) identifies four dimensions of social structure that provide the contexts within which social learning variables operate:

(I) *Differential Social Organization* refers to the structural correlates of crime in the community or society that affect the rates of crime and delinquency including age composition, population density, and other attributes that lean societies, communities, and other social systems "toward relatively high or relatively low crime rates" (Akers, 1998:332).

(II) *Differential Location in the Social Structure* refers to sociodemographic characteristics of individuals and social groups that indicate their niches within the larger social structure. Class, gender, race and ethnicity, marital status, and age locate the positions and standing of persons and their roles, groups, or social categories in the overall social structure.

(III) *Theoretically Defined Structural Variables* refer to anomie, class oppression, social disorganization, group conflict, patriarchy, and other concepts that have been used in one or more theories to identify criminogenic conditions of societies, communities, or groups (see Chapters 7–10).

Figure 21.1 Social Structure and Social Learning

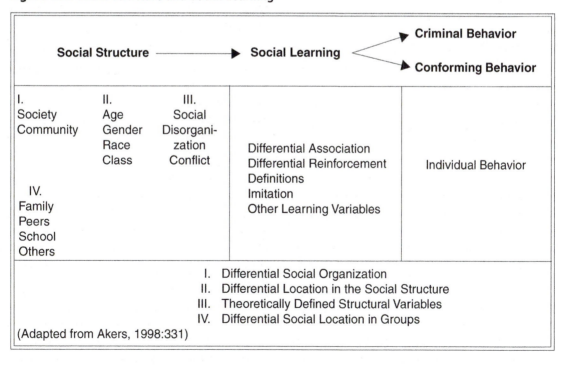

(Adapted from Akers, 1998:331)

(IV) *Differential Social Location* refers to individuals' membership in and relationship to primary, secondary, and reference groups such as the family, friendship/peer groups, leisure groups, colleagues, and work groups.

The differential social organization of society and community, as well as the differential location of persons in the social class, race, gender, religion, and other structures in society, provides the general learning contexts for individuals that increase or decrease the likelihood of their committing crime. The differential location in family, peer, school, church, and other groups provides the more immediate contexts that promote or discourage the criminal behavior of the individual. Differences in the societal or group rates of criminal behavior are a function of the extent to which their cultural traditions, norms, and social control systems provide socialization, learning environments, and immediate situations conducive to conformity or deviance. The structural conditions identified in macro-level theories can affect one's exposure to criminal associations, models, definitions, and reinforcement to induce or retard criminal actions in individuals. It is possible, therefore, to integrate these structural theories with social learning. Although this has not yet been accomplished, the SSSL model is a step in that direction.

Empirical Validity of Social Learning Theory

Critiques and Research on Social Learning Variables

The testability of the basic behavioral learning principles incorporated in social learning theory has been challenged because they may be tautological. The way in which the principle of reinforcement is often stated by behavioral psychologists makes the proposition true by definition. That is, they define reinforcement by stating that it occurs when behavior has been strengthened, that is, its rate of commission has been increased. If reinforcement is defined this way, then the statement "If behavior is reinforced, it will be strengthened"

is tautological. If reinforcement means that behavior has been strengthened, then the hypothesis states simply. "If behavior is reinforced, it is reinforced." If the behavior is not strengthened, then by definition it has not been reinforced; therefore, no instance of behavior that is not being strengthened can be used to falsify the hypothesis.

Another criticism of social learning has to do with the temporal sequence of differential peer association and delinquency. Some have argued that youths become delinquent first then seek out other delinquent youths. Rather than delinquent associations causing delinquency, delinquency causes delinquent associations. If there is a relationship between one's own delinquency and one's association with delinquent peers, then it is simply a case of "birds of a feather flocking together" rather than a bird joining a flock and changing its feathers. Differential peer associations with delinquent friends is almost always a consequence rather than a cause of one's own behavior. Association with delinquent peers takes place only or mainly after peers have already independently established patterns of delinquent involvement. No deviance-relevant learning takes place in peer groups. From this point of view, any association with delinquent youths has no direct effect on an adolescent's delinquent behavior. Therefore, association with delinquent friends has an effect on neither the onset nor acceleration, the continuation nor cessation, of delinquent behavior (Hirschi, 1969; Gottfredson and Hirschi, 1990; Sampson and Laub, 1993).

These criticisms, however, may be off the mark. Burgess and Akers (1966a) identified this tautology problem and offered one solution to it. They separated the definitions of reinforcement and other behavioral concepts from non-tautological, testable propositions in social learning theory and proposed criteria for falsifying those propositions. Others as well have proposed somewhat different solutions (Liska, 1969; Chadwick-Jones, 1976). Moreover, the variables in the process of reinforcement are always measured separately (and hence non-tautologically) from measures of crime and deviance in research on social learning theory. The theory would be falsified if it is typically the case that positive social approval or other rewards for delinquency (that are not offset by punishment) more often reduce than increase its recurrence. Also, as shown above, feedback effects are built into the reinforcement concept with both prior and anticipated reward/punishment influencing present behavior.

Furthermore, the reciprocal relationship between one's own conduct and one's definitions and association with friends is clearly recognized in social learning theory. Therefore, the fact that delinquent behavior may precede the association with delinquent peers does not contradict this theory. "Social learning admits that birds of a feather do flock together, but it also admits that if the birds are humans, they also will influence one another's behavior, in both conforming and deviant directions" (Akers, 1991:210). It would contradict the theory if research demonstrated that the onset of delinquency always or most often predates interaction with peers who have engaged in delinquent acts and/or have adhered to delinquency-favorable definitions. It would not support the theory if the research evidence showed that whatever level of delinquent behavioral involvement preceded association with delinquent peers stayed the same or decreased rather than increased after the association. Research has not yet found this to be the case. Instead, the findings from several studies favor the process proposed by social learning theory, which recognizes both direct and reciprocal effects. That is, a youngster associates differentially with peers who are deviant or tolerant of deviance, learns definitions favorable to delinquent behavior, is exposed to deviant models that reinforce delinquency, then initiates or increases involvement in that behavior, which then is expected to influence further associations and definitions (Kandel, 1978; Andrews and Kandel, 1979; Krohn et al., 1985; Sellers and Winfree, 1990; Empey and Stafford, 1991; Elliott and Menard, 1991; 1996; Kandel and Davies, 1991; Warr, 1993b; Esbensen and Huizinga, 1993; Thornberry et al., 1994; Menard and Elliott, 1994; Winfree et al., 1994a; Akers and Lee, 1996; Esbensen and Deschenes, 1998; Battin et al., 1998).

Kandel and Davies (1991: 442) note that

> although assortive pairing plays a role in similarity among friends observed at a single point in time,

longitudinal research that we and others have carried out clearly documents the etiological importance of peers in the initiation and persistence of substance use.

Warr (1993b) also refers to the considerable amount of research evidence showing that peer associations precede the development of deviant patterns (or increase the frequency and seriousness of deviant behavior once it has begun) more often than involvement in deviant behavior precedes associations with deviant peers. The reverse sequence also occurs and Warr proposes that the process is

> ...a more complex, sequential, reciprocal process: Adolescents are commonly introduced to delinquency by their friends and subsequently become more selective in their choices of friends. The "feathering" and "flocking"...are not mutually exclusive and may instead be part of a unified process. (Warr, 1993b: 39)

This is, of course, completely consistent with the sequential and feedback effects in the social learning process spelled out above. Menard and Elliott (1990; 1994; Elliott and Menard, 1996) also support the process as predicted by social learning theory. Reciprocal effects were found in their research, but:

> [I]n the typical sequence of initiation of delinquent bonding and illegal behavior, delinquent bonding (again, more specifically, association with delinquent friends) usually precedes illegal behavior for those individuals for whom one can ascertain the temporal order.... [S]imilarly...weakening of belief typically preceded the initiation of illegal behavior. (Elliott and Menard, 1994: 174)

> These results are strong enough to indicate that serious forms of delinquent behavior such as index offending rarely, if ever, precede exposure to delinquent friends. Instead, in the vast majority of cases, exposure precedes index offending. (Elliott and Menard, 1996: 43)

> We were *not* able to reject the learning theory hypothesis that the onset of exposure to delinquent others typically precedes the onset of delinquent behavior. Instead, we found that exposure to delinquent peers preceded minor delinquent behavior in a majority of cases, and serious delinquency in nearly all cases where some order could be determined.... Having delinquent friends and being

involved in delinquent behavior may influence one another, but the influence is not symmetric; the influence of exposure on delinquency begins earlier in the sequence, and remains stronger throughout the sequence, than the influence of delinquency on exposure. (Elliott and Menard, 1996: 61-62)

The preponderance of findings thus far shows a stronger effect of peer associations on the individual's delinquent behavior. However, some research finds stronger effects running in the other direction and some shows the relationship to be about equal depending on the measures and methods employed (Kandel, 1996; Krohn et al., 1996; Matsueda and Anderson, 1998).

Another criticism of the theory is that the strong relationship between self-reported delinquency and peer associations is entirely due to the fact that associations are often measured by the individual's report of the delinquency of his or her peers; they are the same thing measured twice. One is measuring the same underlying delinquent tendency, whether youngsters are asked about the delinquency of their friends or about their own delinquency. But research shows that the two are not the same and that the respondent's reports of friends' behavior is not simply a reflection of one's own delinquent behavior (Menard and Elliott, 1990; 1991; Agnew, 1991b; Warr, 1993b; Thornberry et al., 1994; Elliott and Menard, 1996; Bartusch et al., 1997).

Almost all research conducted on social learning theory has found strong relationships in the theoretically expected direction between social learning variables and criminal, delinquent, and deviant behavior. When social learning theory is tested against other theories using the same data collected from the same samples, it is usually found to account for more variance in the dependent variables or have greater support than the theories with which it is being compared (for instance, see Akers and Cochran, 1985; Matsueda and Heimer, 1987; White et al., 1986; Kandel and Davies, 1991; McGee, 1992; Benda, 1994; Burton et al., 1994). When social learning variables are included in integrated or combined models that incorporate variables from different theories, it is the measures of social learning concepts that have the strongest main and net effects (Elliott et al.,

1985; Kaplan et al., 1987; Thornberry et al., 1994; Kaplan, 1996; Catalano et al., 1996).

There is abundant evidence to show the significant impact on criminal and deviant behavior of differential association in primary groups such as family and peers. The role of the family is usually as a conventional socializer against delinquency and crime. It provides anti-criminal definitions, conforming models, and the reinforcement of conformity through parental discipline; it promotes the development of self-control. But deviant behavior may be the outcome of internal family interaction (McCord, 1991b). It is directly affected by deviant parental models, ineffective and erratic parental supervision and discipline in the use of positive and negative sanctions, and the endorsement of values and attitudes favorable to deviance. Patterson has shown that the operation of social learning mechanisms in parent-child interaction is a strong predictor of conforming/deviant behavior (Patterson, 1975; 1995; Snyder and Patterson, 1995). Ineffective disciplinary strategies by parents increase the chances that a child will learn behavior in the early years that is a precursor to his or her later delinquency. Children learn conforming responses when parents consistently make use of positive reward for proper behavior and impose moderately negative consequences for misbehavior (Capaldi et al., 1997). In some cases, parents directly train their children to commit deviant behavior (Adler and Adler, 1978). And in general, parental deviance and criminality is predictive of the children's future delinquency and crime (McCord, 1991a). Moreover, youngsters with delinquent siblings in the family are more likely to be delinquent, even when parental and other family characteristics are taken into account (Rowe and Gulley, 1992; Lauritsen, 1993; Rowe and Farrington, 1997).

Delinquent tendencies learned in the family may be exacerbated by differential peer association (Simons et al., 1994; Lauritsen, 1993). Other than one's own prior deviant behavior, the best single predictor of the onset, continuance, or desistance of crime and delinquency is differential association with conforming or law-violating peers (Loeber and Dishion, 1987; Loeber and Stouthamer-Loeber, 1986). More frequent, longer-term, and closer association with peers who do not support deviant behavior is strongly correlated with conformity, while greater association with peers who commit and approve of delinquency is predictive of one's own delinquent behavior. It is in peer groups that the first availability and opportunity for delinquent acts are typically provided. Virtually every study that includes a peer association variable finds it to be significantly and usually most strongly related to delinquency, alcohol and drug use and abuse, adult crime, and other forms of deviant behavior. There is a sizable body of research literature that shows the importance of differential associations and definitions in explaining crime and delinquency. The impact of differential peer association on delinquent behavior is among the most fully substantiated and replicated findings in criminology. Only the well-known relationships of crime rates to basic sociodemographic variables like age and sex are as consistently reported in the literature.

One special context of peer association is participation in delinquent gangs. Delinquent gangs and subcultures have received a great deal of attention in criminology for a long time. And research continues to find the strong influence of gang membership on serious delinquency. Battin et al. (1998) found that, controlling for prior delinquency, adolescents with delinquent friends are more likely to engage in delinquent conduct and come before the juvenile court on delinquency charges, even if they are not part of a gang. But they are even more likely to do so if they and their friends are members of an identified delinquent gang. Whatever the frequency and seriousness of one's previous delinquency, joining a gang promotes an even higher level of his or her delinquent involvement, in large part because

> group processes and norms favorable to violence and other delinquency within gangs subsequently encourage and reinforce participation in violent and delinquent behavior. (Battin et al., 1998: 108)

These findings suggest that, compared to having one or more non-gang delinquent friends, gang membership produces more frequent, intense, and enduring association with delinquent friends, exposure to delinquent models and definitions,

and reinforcement for delinquent behavior. Other research from the GREAT (Gang Resistance Education And Training) project by Winfree et al. (1994a; 1994b) shows that both gang membership itself and delinquency (gang-related as well as non-gang delinquency) are explained by social learning variables (attitudes, social reinforcers/punishers, and differential association). This is true even controlling for "personal-biographical characteristics, including ethnicity, gender, and place of residence" (Winfree et al., 1994a: 167). The processes specified in social learning theory are

> nearly identical to those provided by qualitative gang research. Gang members reward certain behavior in their peers and punish others, employing goals and processes that are indistinguishable from those described by Akers. (Winfree et al., 1994a:149)

Later research from the GREAT project by Esbensen and Deschenes (1998) found that while neither is especially strong, social learning models do a better job than social bonding models of distinguishing between gang and non-gang members among both boys and girls in the eighth grade.

Many studies using direct measures of one or more of the social learning variables of differential association, imitation, definitions, and differential reinforcement find that the theory's hypotheses are upheld (Elliott et al., 1985; Dembo et al., 1986; White et al., 1986; Sellers and Winfree, 1990; McGee, 1992; Winfree et al., 1993; 1994a; 1994b; Mihalic and Elliott, 1997; Skinner and Fream, 1997; Esbensen and Deschenes, 1998). The relationships between the social learning variables and delinquent, criminal, and deviant behavior found in the research are typically strong to moderate, and there has been very little negative evidence reported in the literature.

Akers' Research on Social Learning Theory

In addition to the consistently positive findings by other researchers, support for the theory comes from research conducted by Akers and his associates in which all of the key social learning variables are measured (Akers, 1998). These include tests of social learning theory by itself and tests that directly compare its empirical validity with other theories. The first of these, conducted with Marvin D. Krohn, Lonn Lanza-Kaduce, and Marcia J. Radosevich, was a self-report questionnaire survey of adolescent substance abuse involving 3000 students in grades 7 through 12 in eight communities in three Midwestern states (Akers et al., 1979; Krohn et al., 1982; Krohn et al., 1984; Lanza-Kaduce et al., 1984; Akers and Cochran, 1985; Akers and Lee, 1999). The second, conducted with Marvin Krohn, Ronald Lauer, James Massey, William Skinner, and Sherilyn Spear, was a five-year longitudinal study of smoking among 2000 students in junior and senior high school in one midwest community (Lauer et al., 1982; Krohn et al., 1985; Spear and Akers, 1988; Akers, 1992a; Akers and Lee, 1996). The third project, conducted with Anthony La Greca, John Cochran, and Christine Sellers, was a four-year longitudinal study of conforming and deviant drinking among elderly populations (1400 respondents) in four communities in Florida and New Jersey (Akers et al., 1989; Akers and La Greca, 1991; Akers, 1992a). The fourth and fifth studies were the master's and doctoral research of Scot Boeringer, conducted under Akers' supervision, on rape and sexual coercion among samples of 200 and 500 college males (Boeringer et al., 1991; Boeringer, 1992). The dependent variables in these studies ranged from minor deviance to serious criminal behavior.

The findings in each of these studies demonstrated that the social learning variables of differential association, differential reinforcement, imitation, and definitions, singly and in combination, are strongly related to the various forms of deviant, delinquent, and criminal behavior studied. The social learning model produced high levels of explained variance, much more than other theoretical models with which it was compared.

The combined effects of the social learning variables on adolescent alcohol and drug use and abuse are very strong. High amounts (from 31 to 68 percent) of the variance in these variables are accounted for by the social learning variables. Social bonding models account for about 15 percent and anomie models account for less than 5 percent of the variance.

Similarly, adolescent cigarette smoking is highly correlated with the social learning variables. These variables also predict quite well the maintenance of smoking over a three-year period. They fare less well, however, when predicting which of the initially abstinent youngsters will begin smoking in that same period. The social learning variables do a slightly better job of predicting the onset of smoking over a five-year period. The sequencing and reciprocal effects of social learning variables and smoking behavior over the five-year period are as predicted by the theory. The onset, frequency, and quantity of elderly drinking is highly correlated with social learning, and the theory also successfully accounts for problem drinking among the elderly.

The social learning variables of association, reinforcement, definitions, and imitation explain the self-perceived likelihood of using force to gain sexual contact or committing rape by college men (55 percent explained variance). They also account for the actual use of drugs or alcohol, non-physical coercion, and physical force by males to obtain sex (20 percent explained variance). Social bonding, self-control, and relative deprivation (strain) models account for less than 10 percent of the variance in these variables.

The research by Akers and others has also included some evidence on the hypothesized relationship between social structure and social learning. This research has found that the correlations of adolescent drug use and smoking, elderly alcohol abuse, and rape to socio-demographic variables of age, sex, race, and class are reduced toward zero when the social learning variables are taken into account. Also, differences in levels of marijuana and alcohol use among adolescents in four types of communities (farm, rural-nonfarm, suburban, and urban), and the differences in overall levels of drinking behavior among the elderly in four types of communities, are mediated by the social learning process. These and other findings from other research show some support for the SSSL theory (Warr, 1998; Mears et al., 1998; Akers and Lee, 1999). However, at this time there has not been enough research to confirm that social learning is the principal process mediating the relationship of social structure and crime as expected by the theory.

Summary

Akers' social learning theory combines Sutherland's original differential association theory of criminal behavior with general behavioral learning principles. The theory proposes that criminal and delinquent behavior is acquired, repeated, and changed by the same process as conforming behavior. While referring to all parts of the learning process, Akers's social learning theory in criminology has focused on the four major concepts of differential association, definitions, differential reinforcement, and imitation. That process will more likely produce behavior that violates social and legal norms than conforming behavior when persons differentially associate with those who expose them to deviant patterns, when the deviant behavior is differentially reinforced over conforming behavior, when individuals are more exposed to deviant than conforming models, and when their own definitions favorably dispose them to commit deviant acts.

This social learning explanation of crime and delinquency has been strongly supported by the research evidence. Research conducted over many years, including that by Akers and associates, has consistently found that social learning is empirically supported as an explanation of individual differences in delinquent and criminal behavior. The hypothesis that social learning processes mediate the effects of socio-demographic and community variables on behavior has been infrequently studied, but the evidence so far suggests that it will also be upheld.

Discussion Questions

1. Much data indicate that associating with delinquents increases one's own level of delinquency. According to social learning theory, why might this be so?
2. Drawing on social learning theory, describe and give an example of the major types of "definitions" favorable to crime.
3. How does positive reinforcement differ from negative reinforcement?
4. Describe the social learning *process*—note how this process changes after the initiation into deviance and describe the feedback effects in this process.
5. How might Akers explain the fact that males have higher rates of crime than females?

CHAPTER 22

Lower Class Culture as a Generating Milieu of Gang Delinquency

Walter B. Miller

Subcultural theories postulate that crime is largely the outcome of criminogenic value systems that pass from one generation to another through social learning, imitation, and, most important, internalization of values that either encourage or at least condone criminal behavior. These "cultural transmission" theories essentially affix the cause or responsibility for crime to groups that adopt atypical attitudes, outlooks, and behavioral patterns that noticeably contrast and often are in direct conflict with the values and conventional behavior of the mainstream culture.

The following article by Walter B. Miller, one of the most cited works throughout the history of criminology, describes the nature of lower-class culture and how its multiple components rather naturally lead to delinquency and crime. These "components" of lower class-culture, actually values that are termed "focal concerns," are specified and defined in terms of their relation to involvement in delinquency.

The etiology of delinquency has long been a controversial issue, and is particularly so at present. As new frames of reference for explaining human behavior have been added to traditional theories, some authors have adopted the practice of citing the major postulates of each school of thought as they pertain to delinquency, and

Miller, W.B. 1958 "Lower Class Culture as a Generating Milieu of Gang Deliquency" Journal of Social Issues, 14, pp. 517

going on to state that causality must be conceived in terms of the dynamic interaction of a complex combination of variables on many levels. The major sets of etiological factors currently adduced to explain delinquency are, in simplified terms, the physiological (delinquency results from organic pathology), the psychodynamic (delinquency is a "behavioral disorder" resulting primarily from emotional disturbance generated by a defective mother-child relationship), and the environmental (delinquency is the product of disruptive forces, "disorganization," in the actor's physical or social environment).

This paper selects one particular kind of "delinquency"[1]—law-violating acts committed by members of adolescent street corner groups in lower class communities—and attempts to show that the dominant component of motivation underlying these acts consists in a directed attempt by the actor to adhere to forms of behavior, and to achieve standards of value as they are defined within that community. It takes as a premise that the motivation of behavior in this situation can be approached most productively by attempting to understand the nature of cultural forces impinging on the acting individual as they are perceived *by the actor himself*—although by no means only that segment of these forces of which the actor is consciously aware—rather than as they are perceived and evaluated from the reference position of another cultural system. In the case of "gang" delinquency, the cultural system which exerts the most direct influence on behavior is that of the lower class community itself—a long-established, distinctively patterned tradition with an integrity of its own—rather than a so-called "delinquent subculture" which has arisen through conflict with middle class culture and is oriented to the deliberate violation of middle class norms.

The bulk of the substantive data on which the following material is based was collected in connection with a service-research project in the control of gang delinquency. During the service aspect of the project, which lasted for three years, seven trained social workers maintained contact with twenty-one corner group units in a "slum" district of a large eastern city for periods of time ranging from ten to thirty months. Groups were Negro and white, male and female, and in early, middle, and late adolescence. Over eight thousand pages of direct observational data on behavior patterns of group members and other community residents were collected; almost daily contact was maintained for a total time period of about thirteen worker years. Data include workers' contact reports, participant observation reports by the writer—a cultural anthropologist—and direct tape recordings of group activities and discussions.[2]

Focal Concerns of Lower Class Culture

There is a substantial segment of present-day American society whose way of life, values, and characteristic patterns of behavior are the product of a distinctive cultural system which may be termed "lower class." Evidence indicates that this cultural system is becoming increasingly distinctive, and that the size of the group which shares this tradition is increasing.[3] The lower class way of life, in common with that of all distinctive cultural groups, is characterized by a set of focal concerns—areas or issues which command widespread and persistent attention and a high degree of emotional involvement. The specific concerns cited here, while by no means confined to the American lower classes, constitute a distinctive *patterning* of concerns which differs significantly, both in rank order and weighting from that of American middle class culture. The following chart [Table 22.1] presents a

highly schematic and simplified listing of six of the major concerns of lower class culture. Each is conceived as a "dimension" within which a fairly wide and varied range of alternative behavior patterns may be followed by different individuals under different situations. They are listed roughly in order of the degree of *explicit* attention accorded each, and, in this sense represent a weighted ranking of concerns. The "perceived alternatives" represent polar positions which define certain parameters within each dimension. As will be explained in more detail, it is necessary in relating the influence of these "concerns" to the motivation of delinquent behavior to specify *which* of its aspects is oriented to, whether orientation is *overt* or *covert, positive* (conforming to or seeking the aspect), or *negative* (rejecting or seeking to avoid the aspect).

The concept "focal concern" is used here in preference to the concept "value" for several interrelated reasons: (1) It is more readily derivable from direct field observation. (2) It is descriptively neutral—permitting independent consideration of positive and negative valences as varying under different conditions, whereas "value" carries a built-in positive valence. (3) It makes possible more refined analysis of subcultural differences, since it reflects actual behavior, whereas "value" tends to wash out intracultural differences since it is colored by notions of the "official" ideal.

Trouble

Concern over "trouble" is a dominant feature of lower class culture. The concept has various shades of meaning; "trouble" in one of its aspects represents a situation or a kind of behavior which results in unwelcome or complicating involvement with official authorities or agencies of middle class society. "Getting into trouble" and "staying out of trouble" represent major issues for male and female, adults and children. For men, "trouble" frequently involves fighting or sexual adventures while drinking; for women, sexual involvement with disadvantageous consequences. Expressed desire to avoid behavior which violates moral or legal norms is often based less on an explicit commitment to "official" moral or legal standards than on a desire to avoid "getting into trouble," e.g., the complicating consequences of the action.

Table 22.1 Focal Concerns of Lower Class Culture

Area	Perceived Alternatives (state, quality, condition)	
1. *Trouble:*	law-abiding behavior	law-violating behavior
2. *Toughness:*	physical prowess, skill; "masculinity"; fearlessness, bravery, daring	weakness, ineptitude; effeminacy; timidity, cowardice, caution
3. *Smartness:*	ability to outsmart, dupe, "con"; gaining money by "wits"; shrewdness, adroitness in repartee	gullibility, "con-ability"; gaining money by hard work; slowness, dull-wittedness, verbal maladroitness
4. *Excitement:*	thrill; risk, danger; change, activity	boredom; "deadness," safeness; sameness, passivity
5. *Fate:*	favored by fortune, being "lucky"	ill-omened, being "unlucky"
6. *Autonomy:*	freedom from external constraint; freedom from superordinate authority; independence	presence of external constraint; presence of strong authority; dependency, being "cared for"

The dominant concern over "trouble" involves a distinction of critical importance for the lower class community—that between "law-abiding" and "non-law-abiding" behavior. There is a high degree of sensitivity as to where each person stands in relation to these two classes of activity. Whereas in the middle class community a major dimension for evaluating a person's status is "achievement" and its external symbols, in the lower class, personal status is very frequently gauged along the law-abiding-non-law-abiding dimension. A mother will evaluate the suitability of her daughter's boyfriend less on the basis of his achievement potential than on the basis of his innate "trouble" potential. This sensitive awareness of the opposition of "trouble-producing" and "non-trouble-producing" behavior represents both a major basis for deriving status distinctions, and an internalized conflict potential for the individual.

As in the case of other focal concerns, which of two perceived alternatives—"law-abiding" or "non-law-abiding"—is valued varies according to the individual and the circumstances; in many instances there is an overt commitment to the "law-abiding" alternative, but a covert commitment to the "non-law-abiding." In certain situations, "getting into trouble" is overtly recognized as prestige-conferring; for example, membership in certain adult and adolescent primary groupings ("gangs") is contingent on having demonstrated an explicit commitment to the law-violating alternative. It is most important to note that the choice between "law-abiding" and "non-law-abiding" behavior is still a choice *within* lower class culture; the distinction between the policeman and the criminal, the outlaw and the sheriff, involves primarily this one dimension; in other respects they have a high community of interests. Not infrequently brothers raised in an identical cultural milieu will become police and criminals respectively.

For a substantial segment of the lower class population "getting into trouble" is not in itself overtly defined as prestige-conferring, but is implicitly recognized as a means to other valued ends, e.g., the covertly valued desire to be "cared for" and subject to external constraint, or the overtly valued state of excitement or risk. Very frequently "getting into trouble" is multi-functional, and achieves several sets of valued ends.

Toughness

The concept of "toughness" in lower class culture represents a compound combination of qualities or states. Among its most important components are physical prowess, evidenced both by demonstrated possession of strength and endurance and athletic skill; "masculinity," symbolized by a distinctive complex of acts and avoidances (bodily tatooing; absence of sentimentality; non-concern with "art," "literature," conceptualization of women as conquest objects, etc.); and bravery in the face of physical threat. The model for the "tough guy"— hard, fearless, undemonstrative, skilled in physical combat—is represented by the movie gangster of the thirties, the "private eye," and the movie cowboy.

The genesis of the intense concern over "toughness" in lower class culture is probably related to the fact that a significant proportion of lower class males are reared in a predominantly female household, and lack a consistently present male figure with whom to identify and from whom to learn essential components of a "male" role. Since women serve as a primary object of identification during pre-adolescent years, the almost obsessive lower class concern with "masculinity" probably resembles a type of compulsive reaction-formation. A concern over homosexuality runs like a persistent thread through lower class culture. This is manifested by the institutionalized practice of baiting "queers," often accompanied by violent physical attacks, an expressed contempt for "softness" or frills, and the use of the local term for "homosexual" as a generalized pejorative epithet (e.g., higher class individuals or upwardly mobile peers are frequently characterized as "fags" or "queers"). The distinction between "overt" and "covert" orientation to aspects of an area of concern is especially important in regard to "toughness." A positive overt evaluation of behavior defined as "effeminate" would be out of the question for a lower class male; however, built into lower class culture is a range of devices which permit men to adopt behaviors and concerns which in other cultural milieux fall within the province of women, and at the same time to be defined as "tough" and manly. For example, lower class men can be professional short-order cooks in a diner and still be regarded as "tough." The highly intimate circumstances of the street corner gang involve the recurrent expression of strongly affectionate feelings towards other men. Such expressions, however, are disguised as their opposite, taking the form of ostensibly aggressive verbal and physical interaction (kidding, "ranking," roughhousing, etc.).

Smartness

"Smartness," as conceptualized in lower class culture, involves the capacity to outsmart, outfox, outwit, dupe, "take," "con" another or others, and the concomitant capacity to avoid being outwitted, "taken," or duped oneself. In its essence, smartness involves the capacity to achieve a valued entity— material goods, personal status—through a maximum use of mental agility and a minimum use of physical effort. This capacity has an extremely long tradition in lower class culture, and is highly valued. Lower class culture can be characterized as "non-intellectual" only if intellectualism is defined specifically in terms of control over a particular body of formally learned knowledge involving "culture" (art, literature, "good" music, etc.), a generalized perspective on the past and present conditions of our own and other societies, and other areas of knowledge imparted by formal educational institutions. This particular type of mental attainment is, in general, overtly disvalued and frequently associated with effeminancy; "smartness" in the lower class sense, however, is highly valued.

The lower class child learns and practices the use of this skill in the street corner situation. Individuals continually practice duping and outwitting one another through recurrent card games and other forms of gambling, mutual exchanges of insults, and "testing" for mutual "con-ability." Those who demonstrate competence in this skill are accorded considerable prestige. Leadership roles in the corner group are frequently allocated according to demonstrated capacity in the two areas of "smartness" and "toughness"; the ideal leader combines both, but the "smart" leader is often accorded more prestige than the "tough" one—reflecting a general lower class respect for "brains" in the "smartness" sense.[4]

The model of the "smart" person is represented in popular media by the card shark, the professional gambler, the "con" artist, the promoter. A conceptual distinction is made between two kinds of people: "suckers," easy marks, "lushes," dupes, who work for their money and are legitimate targets of exploitation; and sharp operators, the "brainy" ones, who live by their wits and "getting" from the suckers by mental adroitness.

Involved in the syndrome of capacities related to "smartness" is a dominant emphasis in lower class culture on ingenious aggressive repartee. This skill, learned and practiced in the context of the corner group, ranges in form from the widely prevalent semi-ritualized teasing, kidding, razzing, "ranking," so characteristic of male peer group interaction, to the highly ritualized type of mutual insult interchange known as "the dirty dozens," "the dozens," "playing house," and other terms. This highly patterned cultural form is practiced on its most advanced level in adult male Negro society, but less polished variants are found throughout lower class culture—practiced, for example, by white children, male and female, as young as four or five. In essence, "doin' the dozens" involves two antagonists who vie with each other in the exchange of increasingly inflammatory insults, with incestuous and perverted sexual relations with the mother a dominant theme. In this form of insult interchange, as well as on other less ritualized occasions for joking, semi-serious, and serious mutual invective, a very high premium is placed on ingenuity, hair-trigger responsiveness, inventiveness, and the acute exercise of mental faculties.

Excitement

For many lower class individuals the rhythm of life fluctuates between periods of relatively routine or repetitive activity and sought situations of great emotional stimulation. Many of the most characteristic features of lower class life are related to the search for excitement or "thrill." Involved here are the highly prevalent use of alcohol by both sexes and the widespread use of gambling of all kinds—playing the numbers, betting on horse races, dice,

cards. The quest for excitement finds what is perhaps its most vivid expression in the highly patterned practice of the recurrent "night on the town." This practice, designated by various terms in different areas ("honky-tonkin'"; "goin' out on the town"; "bar hoppin'"), involves a patterned set of activities in which alcohol, music, and sexual adventuring are major components. A group or individual sets out to "make the rounds" of various bars or night clubs. Drinking continues progressively throughout the evening. Men seek to "pick up" women, and women play the risky game of entertaining sexual advances. Fights between men involving women, gambling, and claims of physical prowess, in various combinations, are frequent consequences of a night of making the rounds. The explosive potential of this type of adventuring with sex and aggression, frequently leading to "trouble," is semi-explicitly sought by the individual. Since there is always a good likelihood that being out on the town will eventuate in fights, etc., the practice involves elements of sought risk and desired danger.

Counterbalancing the "flirting with danger" aspect of the "excitement" concern is the prevalence in lower class culture of other well established patterns of activity which involve long periods of relative inaction, or passivity. The term "hanging out" in lower class culture refers to extended periods of standing around, often with peer mates, doing what is defined as "nothing," "shooting the breeze," etc. A definite periodicity exists in the pattern of activity relating to the two aspects of the "excitement" dimension. For many lower class individuals the venture into the high risk world of alcohol, sex, and fighting occurs regularly once a week, with interim periods devoted to accommodating to possible consequences of these periods, along with recurrent resolves not to become so involved again.

Fate

Related to the quest for excitement is the concern with fate, fortune, or luck. Here also a distinction is made between two states—being "lucky" or "in luck," and being unlucky or jinxed. Many lower class individuals feel that their lives are subject to a set of forces over which they have relatively little control. These are not directly equated with the supernatural forces of formally organized religion, but relate more to a concept of "destiny," or man as a pawn of magical powers. Not infrequently this often implicit world view is associated with a conception of the ultimate futility of directed effort towards a goal: if the cards are right, or the dice good to you, or if your lucky number comes up, things will go your way; if luck is against you, it's not worth trying. The concept of performing semimagical rituals so that one's "luck will change" is prevalent; one hopes that as a result he will move from the state of being "unlucky" to that of being "lucky." The element of fantasy plays an important part in this area. Related to and complementing the notion that "only suckers work" (Smartness) is the idea that once things start going your way, relatively independent of your own effort, all good things will come to you. Achieving great material rewards (big cars, big houses, a roll of cash to flash in a fancy night club), valued in lower class as well as in other parts of American culture, is a recurrent theme in lower class fantasy and folk lore; the cocaine dreams of Willie the Weeper or Minnie the Moocher present the components of this fantasy in vivid detail.

The prevalence in the lower class community of many forms of gambling, mentioned in connection with the "excitement" dimension, is also relevant here. Through cards and pool which involve skill, and thus both "toughness" and "smartness"; or through race horse betting, involving "smartness"; or through playing the numbers, involving predominantly "luck," one may make a big killing with a minimum of directed and persistent effort within conventional occupational channels. Gambling in its many forms illustrates the fact that many of the persistent features of lower class culture are multifunctional—serving a range of desired ends at the same time. Describing some of the incentives behind gambling has involved mention of all of the focal concerns cited so far—Toughness, Smartness, and Excitement, in addition to Fate.

Autonomy

The extent and nature of control over the behavior of the individual—an important concern in most cultures—has a special significance and is distinctively patterned in lower class culture. The discrepancy between what is overtly valued and what is covertly sought is particularly striking in this area. On the overt level there is a strong and frequently expressed resentment of the idea of external controls, restrictions on behavior, and unjust or coercive authority. "No one's gonna push *me* around," or "I'm gonna tell him he can take the job and shove it...." are commonly expressed sentiments. Similar explicit attitudes are maintained to systems of behavior-restricting rules, insofar as these are perceived as representing the injunctions, and bearing the sanctions of superordinate authority. In addition, in lower class culture a close conceptual connection is made between "authority" and "nurturance." To be restrictively or firmly controlled is to be cared for. Thus the overtly negative evaluation of superordinate authority frequently extends as well to nurturance, care, or protection. The desire for personal independence is often expressed in such terms as "I don't need *nobody* to take care of me. I can take care of myself!" Actual patterns of behavior, however, reveal a marked discrepancy between expressed sentiment and what is covertly valued. Many lower class people appear to seek out highly restrictive social environments wherein stringent external controls are maintained over their behavior. Such institutions as the armed forces, the mental hospital, the disciplinary school, the prison or correctional institution, provide environments which incorporate a strict and detailed set of rules defining and limiting behavior, and enforced by an authority system which controls and applies coercive sanctions for deviance from these rules. While under the jurisdiction of such systems, the lower class person generally expresses to his peers continual resentment of the coercive, unjust, and arbitrary exercise of authority. Having been released, or having escaped from these milieux, however, he will often act in such a way as to insure recommitment, or choose recommitment voluntarily after a temporary period of "freedom."

Lower class patients in mental hospitals will exercise considerable ingenuity to insure continued commitment while voicing the desire to get out; delinquent boys will frequently "run" from a correctional institution to activate efforts to return them; to be caught and returned means that one is cared for. Since "being controlled" is equated with "being cared for," attempts are frequently made to "test" the severity or strictness of superordinate authority to see if it remains firm. If intended or executed rebellion produces swift and firm punitive sanctions, the individual is reassured, at the same time that he is complaining bitterly at the injustice of being caught and punished. Some environmental milieux, having been tested in this fashion for the "firmness" of their coercive sanctions, are rejected, ostensibly for being too strict, actually for not being strict enough. This is frequently so in the case of "problematic" behavior by lower class youngsters in the public schools, which generally cannot command the coercive controls implicitly sought by the individual.

A similar discrepancy between what is overtly and covertly desired is found in the area of dependence-independence. The pose of tough rebellious independence often assumed by the lower class person frequently conceals powerful dependency cravings. These are manifested primarily by obliquely expressed resentment when "care" is not forthcoming rather than by expressed satisfaction when it is. The concern over autonomy-dependency is related both to "trouble" and "fate." Insofar as the lower class individual feels that his behavior is controlled by forces which often propel him into "trouble" in the face of an explicit determination to avoid it, there is an implied appeal to "save me from myself." A solution appears to lie in arranging things so that his behavior will be coercively restricted by an externally imposed set of controls strong enough to forcibly restrain his inexplicable inclination to get in trouble. The periodicity observed in connection with the "excitement" dimension is also relevant here; after involvement in trouble-producing behavior (assault, sexual adventure, a "drunk"), the individual will actively seek a locus of imposed control (his wife, prison, a restrictive job); after a given period of subjection to this control, resentment against it mounts, leading to a "break away" and a search for involvement in further "trouble."

Focal Concerns of the Lower Class Adolescent Street Corner Group

The one-sex peer group is a highly prevalent and significant structural form in the lower class community. There is a strong probability that the prevalence and stability of this type of unit is directly related to the prevalence of a stabilized type of lower class child-rearing unit—the "female-based" household. This is a nuclear kin unit in which a male parent is either absent from the household, present only sporadically, or, when present, only minimally or inconsistently involved in the support and rearing of children. This unit usually consists of one or more females of child-bearing age and their offspring. The females are frequently related to one another by blood or marriage ties, and the unit often includes two or more generations of women, e.g., the mother and/or aunt of the principal child-bearing female.

The nature of social groupings in the lower class community may be clarified if we make the assumption that it is the *one-sex peer unit* rather than the two-parent family unit which represents the most significant relational unit for both sexes in lower class communities. Lower class society may be pictured as comprising a set of age-graded one-sex groups which constitute the major psychic focus and reference group for those over twelve or thirteen. Men and women of mating age leave these groups periodically to form temporary marital alliances, but these lack stability, and after varying periods of "trying out" the two-sex family arrangement, gravitate back to the more "comfortable" one-sex grouping, whose members exert strong pressure on the individual *not* to disrupt the group by adopting a two-sex household pattern of life.[5] Membership in a stable and solidary peer unit is vital to the lower class individual precisely to the extent to which a range of essential functions—psychological, educational, and others, are not provided by the "family" unit.

The adolescent street corner group represents the adolescent variant of this lower class structural form. What has been called the "delinquent gang" is one subtype of this form, defined on the basis of frequency of participation in law-violating activity; this subtype should not be considered a legitimate unit of study per se, but rather as one particular variant of the adolescent street corner group. The "hanging" peer group is a unit of particular importance for the adolescent male. In many cases it is the most stable and solidary primary group he has ever belonged to; for boys reared in female-based households the corner group provides the first real opportunity to learn essential aspects of the male role in the context of peers facing similar problems of sex-role identification.

The form and functions of the adolescent corner group operate as a selective mechanism in recruiting members. The activity patterns of the group require a high level of intra-group solidarity; individual members must possess a good capacity for subordinating individual desires to general group interests as well as the capacity for intimate and persisting interaction. Thus highly "disturbed" individuals, or those who cannot tolerate consistently imposed sanctions on "deviant" behavior cannot remain accepted members; the group itself will extrude those whose behavior exceeds limits defined as "normal." This selective process produces a type of group whose members possess to an unusually high degree both the *capacity* and *motivation* to conform to perceived cultural norms, so that the nature of the system of norms and values oriented to is a particularly influential component of motivation.

Focal concerns of the male adolescent corner group are those of the general cultural milieu in which it functions. As would be expected, the relative weighting and importance of these concerns pattern somewhat differently for adolescents than for adults. The nature of this patterning centers around two additional "concerns" of particular importance to this group—concern with "belonging," and with "status." These may be conceptualized as being on a higher level of abstraction than concerns previously cited, since "status" and "belonging" are achieved *via* cited concern areas of Toughness, etc.

Belonging: Since the corner group fulfills essential functions for the individual, being a member in good standing of the group is of vital importance for its members. A continuing concern over who is "in" and who is not involves the citation and detailed discussion of highly refined criteria for "in-group" membership. The phrase "he hangs with us" means "he is accepted as a member in good standing by current consensus"; conversely, "he don't hang with us" means he is not so accepted. One achieves "belonging" primarily by demonstrating knowledge of and a determination to adhere to the system of standards and valued qualities defined by the group. One maintains membership by acting in conformity with valued aspects of Toughness, Smartness, Autonomy, etc. In those instances where conforming to norms of this reference group at the same time violates norms of other reference groups (e.g., middle class adults, institutional "officials"), immediate reference group norms are much more compelling since violation risks invoking the group's most powerful sanction: exclusion.

Status: In common with most adolescents in American society, the lower class corner group manifests a dominant concern with "status." What differentiates this type of group from others, however, is the particular set of criteria and weighting thereof by which "status" is defined. In general, status is achieved and maintained by demonstrated possession of the valued qualities of lower class culture—Toughness, Smartness, expressed resistance to authority, daring, etc. It is important to stress once more that the individual orients to these concerns *as they are defined within lower class society*; e.g., the status-conferring potential of "smartness" in the sense of scholastic achievement generally ranges from negligible to negative.

The concern with "status" is manifested in a variety of ways. Intra-group status is a continued concern, and is derived and tested constantly by means of a set of status-ranking activities; the intra-group "pecking order" is constantly at issue. One gains status within the group by demonstrated superiority in Toughness (physical prowess, bravery, skill in athletics and games such as pool and cards), Smartness (skill in repartee, capacity to "dupe" fellow group members), and the like. The term "ranking," used to refer to the pattern of intra-group aggressive repartee, indicates awareness of the fact that this is one device for establishing the intra-group status hierarchy.

The concern over status in the adolescent corner group involves in particular the component of "adultness," the intense desire to be seen as "grown up," and a corresponding aversion to "kid stuff." "Adult" status is defined less in terms of the assumption of "adult" responsibility than in terms of certain external symbols of adult status—a car, ready cash, and, in particular, a perceived "freedom" to drink, smoke, and gamble as one wishes and to come and go without external restrictions. The desire to be seen as "adult" is often a more significant component of much involvement in illegal drinking, gambling, and automobile driving than the explicit enjoyment of these acts as such.

The intensity of the corner group member's desire to be seen as "adult" is sufficiently great that he feels called upon to demonstrate qualities associated with adultness (Toughness, Smartness, Autonomy) to a much greater degree than a lower class adult. This means that he will seek out and utilize those avenues to these qualities which he perceives as available with greater intensity than an adult and less regard for their "legitimacy." In this sense the adolescent variant of lower class culture represents a maximization or an intensified manifestation of many of its most characteristic features.

Concern over status is also manifested in reference to other street corner groups. The term "rep" used in this regard is especially significant, and has broad connotations. In its most frequent and explicit connotation, "rep" refers to the "toughness" of the corner group as a whole relative to that of other groups; a "pecking order" also exists among the several corner groups in a given interactional area, and there is a common perception that the safety or security of the group and all its members depends on maintaining a solid "rep" for toughness vis-à-vis other groups. This motive is most frequently advanced as a reason for involvement in gang fights: "We *can't* chicken out on this fight; our rep would be shot!"; this implies that the group would be relegated to the bottom of the status ladder and become a helpless and recurrent target of external attack.

On the other hand, there is implicit in the concept of "rep" the recognition that "rep" has or may have a dual basis—corresponding to the two aspects of the "trouble" dimension. It is recognized that group as well as individual status can be based on both "law-abiding" and "law-violating" behavior. The situational resolution of the persisting conflict between the "law-abiding" and "law-violating" bases of status comprises a vital set of dynamics in determining whether a "delinquent" mode of behavior will be adopted by a group, under what circumstances, and how persistently. The determinants of this choice are evidently highly complex and fluid, and rest on a range of factors including the presence and perceptual immediacy of different community reference-group loci (e.g., professional criminals, police, clergy, teachers, settlement house workers), the personality structures and "needs" of group members, the presence in the community of social work, recreation, or educational programs which can facilitate utilization of the "law-abiding" basis of status, and so on.

What remains constant is the critical importance of "status" both for the members of the group as individuals and for the group as a whole insofar as members perceive their individual destinies as linked to the destiny of the group, and the fact that action geared to attain status is much more acutely oriented to the fact of status itself than to the legality or illegality, morality or immorality of the means used to achieve it.

Lower Class Culture and the Motivation of Delinquent Behavior

The customary set of activities of the adolescent street corner group includes activities which are in violation of laws and ordinances of the legal code. Most of these center around assault and theft of various types (the gang fight; auto theft; assault on an individual; petty pilfering and shoplifting; "mugging"; pocketbook theft). Members of street corner gangs are well aware of the law-violating nature of these acts; they are not psychopaths, nor physically or mentally "defective"; in fact, since the corner group supports and enforces a rigorous set of standards which demand a high degree of fitness and personal competence, it tends to recruit from the most "able" members of the community.

Why, then, is the commission of crimes a customary feature of gang activity? The most general answer is that the commission of crimes by members of adolescent street corner groups is motivated primarily by the attempt to achieve ends, states, or conditions which are valued, and to avoid those that are disvalued within their most meaningful cultural milieu, through those culturally available avenues which appear as the most feasible means of attaining those ends.

The operation of these influences is well illustrated by the gang fight—a prevalent and characteristic type of corner group delinquency. This type of activity comprises a highly stylized and culturally patterned set of sequences. Although details vary under different circumstances, the following events are generally included. A member or several members of group A "trespass" on the claimed territory of group B. While there they commit an act or acts which group B defines as a violation of its rightful privileges, an affront to their honor, or a challenge to their "rep." Frequently this act involves advances to a girl associated with group B; it may occur at a dance or party; sometimes the mere act of "trespass" is seen as deliberate provocation. Members of group B then assault members of group A, if they are caught while still in B's territory. Assaulted members of group A return to their "home" territory and recount to members of their group details of the incident, stressing the insufficient nature of the provocation ("I just *looked* at her! Hardly even said anything!"), and the unfair circumstances of the assault ("About *twenty* guys jumped just the *two* of us!"). The highly colored account is acutely inflammatory; group A, perceiving its honor violated and its "rep" threatened, feels obligated to retaliate in force. Sessions of detailed planning now occur; allies are recruited if the size of group A and its potential allies appears to necessitate larger numbers; strategy is plotted, and messengers dispatched. Since the prospect of a gang fight is frightening to even the "toughest" group members, a constant rehearsal of the provocative incident or incidents and the essentially evil nature of the opponents accompanies the planning process to bolster possibly weakening motivation to fight. The excursion into "enemy" territory sometimes results in a full scale fight;

more often group B cannot be found, or the police appear and stop the fight, "tipped off" by an anonymous informant. When this occurs, group members express disgust and disappointment; secretly there is much relief; their honor has been avenged without incurring injury; often the anonymous tipster is a member of one of the involved groups.

The basic elements of this type of delinquency are sufficiently stabilized and recurrent as to constitute an essentially ritualized pattern, resembling both in structure and expressed motives for action classic forms such as the European "duel," the American Indian tribal war, and the Celtic clan feud. Although the arousing and "acting out" of individual aggressive emotions are inevitably involved in the gang fight, neither its form nor motivational dynamics can be adequately handled within a predominantly personality-focused frame of reference.

It would be possible to develop in considerable detail the processes by which the commission of a range of illegal acts is either explicitly supported by, implicitly demanded by, or not materially inhibited by factors relating to the focal concerns of lower class culture. In place of such a development, the following three statements condense in general terms the operation of these processes:

1. Following cultural practices which comprise essential elements of the total life pattern of lower class culture automatically violates certain legal norms.
2. In instances where alternate avenues to similar objectives are available, the non-law-abiding avenue frequently provides a relatively greater and more immediate return for a relatively smaller investment of energy.
3. The "demanded" response to certain situations recurrently engendered within lower class culture involves the commission of illegal acts.

The primary thesis of this paper is that the dominant component of the motivation of "delinquent" behavior engaged in by members of lower class corner groups involves a positive effort to achieve states, conditions, or qualities valued within the actor's most significant cultural milieu.

If "conformity to immediate reference group values" is the major component of motivation of "delinquent" behavior by gang members, why is such behavior frequently referred to as negativistic, malicious, or rebellious? Albert Cohen, for example, in *Delinquent Boys* (Glencoe: Free Press, 1955) describes behavior which violates school rules as comprising elements of "active spite and malice, contempt and ridicule, challenge and defiance." He ascribes to the gang "keen delight in terrorizing 'good' children, and in general making themselves obnoxious to the virtuous." A recent national conference on social work with "hard-to-reach" groups characterized lower class corner groups as "youth groups in conflict with the culture of their *(sic)* communities." Such characterizations are obviously the result of taking the middle class community and its institutions as an implicit point of reference.

A large body of systematically interrelated attitudes, practices, behaviors, and values characteristic of lower class culture are designed to support and maintain the basic features of the lower class way of life. In areas where these differ from features of middle class culture, action oriented to the achievement and maintenance of the lower class system may violate norms of middle class culture and be perceived as deliberately non-conforming or malicious by an observer strongly cathected to middle class norms. This does not mean, however, that violation of the middle class norm is the dominant component of motivation; it is a by-product of action primarily oriented to the lower class system. The standards of lower class culture cannot be seen merely as a reverse function of middle class culture—as middle class standards "turned upside down"; lower class culture is a distinctive tradition many centuries old with an integrity of its own.

From the viewpoint of the acting individual, functioning within a field of well-structured cultural forces, the relative impact of "conforming" and "rejective" elements in the motivation of gang delinquency is weighted preponderantly on the conforming side. Rejective or rebellious elements are inevitably involved, but their influence during the actual commission of delinquent acts is relatively small compared to the influence of pressures to achieve what is valued by the actor's most immediate reference groups. Expressed awareness by the actor of the element of rebellion often represents only that aspect of motivation of which he is explicitly conscious; the deepest and most compelling components of motivation—adherence to highly meaningful group standards of Toughness, Smartness, Excitement, etc.—are often unconsciously patterned. No cultural pattern as well-established as the practice of illegal acts by members of lower class corner groups could persist if buttressed primarily by negative, hostile, or rejective motives; its principal motivational support, as in the case of any persisting cultural tradition, derives from a positive effort to achieve what is valued within that tradition, and to conform to its explicit and implicit norms.

Notes

1. The complex issues involved in deriving a definition of "delinquency" cannot be discussed here. The term "delinquent" is used in this paper to characterize behavior or acts committed by individuals within specified age limits which if known to official authorities could result in legal action. The concept of a "delinquent" individual has little or no utility in the approach used here; rather, specified types of *acts* which may be committed rarely or frequently by few or many individuals are characterized as "delinquent."

2. A three year research project is being financed under National Institutes of Health Grant M–1414, and administered through the Boston University School of Social Work. The primary research effort has subjected all collected material to a uniform data-coding process. All information bearing on some seventy areas of behavior (behavior in reference to school, police, theft, assault, sex, collective athletics, etc.) is extracted from the records, recorded on coded data cards, and filed under relevant categories. Analysis of these data aims to ascertain the actual nature of customary behavior in these areas, and the extent to which the social work effort was able to effect behavioral changes.

3. Between 40 and 60 per cent of all Americans are directly influenced by lower class culture, with about 15 per cent, or twenty-five million, comprising the "hard core" lower class group—defined primarily by its use of the "female-based" household as the basic form of child-rearing unit and of the "serial monogamy" mating pattern as the primary form of marriage. The term "lower class culture" as used here refers most

specifically to the way of life of the "hard core" group; systematic research in this area would probably reveal at least four to six major subtypes of lower class culture, for some of which the "concerns" presented here would be differently weighted, especially for those subtypes in which "law-abiding" behavior has a high overt valuation. It is impossible within the compass of this short paper to make the finer intracultural distinctions which a more accurate presentation would require.

4. The "brains-brawn" set of capacities are often paired in lower class folk lore or accounts of lower class life, e.g., "Brer Fox" and "Brer Bear" in the Uncle Remus stories, or George and Lennie in "Of Mice and Men."

5. Further data on the female-based household unit (estimated as comprising about 15 per cent of all American "families") and the role of one-sex groupings in lower class culture are contained in Walter B. Miller, Implications of Urban Lower Class Culture for Social Work. *Social Service Review,* 1959, *33,* No. 3.

CHAPTER 23

The Code of the Street

Elijah Anderson

Subcultural theories of crime and delinquency, put forth by notable criminologists such as Walter B. Miller, Albert K. Cohen, and Marvin Wolfgang, were at the forefront of social scientific thinking about crime during the 1950s. Historical events during the 1960s, however, such as the civil rights movement and the Vietnam conflict, heightened a collective concern with equality and problems attributable to misuses of authority. Accordingly, the subculture perspective became unpopular with its attention to group values, which was seen as classist and sometimes racist. State facilitation of crime and discriminatory practices of criminal justice replaced the delinquency epidemic of the previous decade and were supported by critical and conflict perspectives that focused on crime as a manifestation of social inequality.

The following selection by Elijah Anderson, "The Code of the Street," offers a contemporary explanation of violent and criminal subcultures that has again brought the significance of cultural forces to the attention of criminological thought. Modern inner city African American life is portrayed as being shaped by a set of pervasive values or rules known as "street codes" that determine social order, normative behavior, and crime within disadvantaged neighborhoods.

Reprinted from: Elijah Anderson, "The Code of the Streets" in *Code of the Street*. Originally in the *Atlantic Monthly* 273, no. 5 (May 1994). Copyright © 1994 by Elijah Anderson. Reprinted with the permission of Elijah Anderson.

Of all the problems besetting the poor inner-city black community, none is more pressing than that of interpersonal violence and aggression. It wreaks havoc daily with the lives of community residents and increasingly spills over into downtown and residential middle-class areas. Muggings, burglaries, carjackings, and drug-related shootings, all of which may leave their victims or innocent bystanders dead, are now common enough to concern all urban and many suburban residents. The inclination to violence springs from the circumstances of life among the ghetto poor—the lack of jobs that pay a living wage, the stigma of race, the fallout from rampant drug use and drug trafficking, and the resulting alienation and lack of hope for the future.

Simply living in such an environment places young people at special risk of falling victim to aggressive behavior. Although there are often forces in the community which can counteract the negative influences, by far the most powerful being a strong, loving, "decent" (as inner-city residents put it) family committed to middle-class values, the despair is pervasive enough to have spawned an oppositional culture, that of "the streets," whose norms are often consciously opposed to those of mainstream society. These two orientations—decent and street—socially organize the community, and their coexistence has important consequences for residents, particularly children growing up in the inner city. Above all, this environment means that even youngsters whose home lives reflect mainstream values—and the majority of homes in the community do—must be able to handle themselves in a street-oriented environment.

This is because the street culture has evolved what may be called a code of the streets, which amounts to a set of informal rules governing interpersonal public behavior, including violence. The rules prescribe both a proper comportment and a proper way to respond if challenged. They regulate the use of violence and so allow those who are inclined to aggression to precipitate violent encounters in an approved way. The rules have been established and are enforced mainly by the street-oriented, but on the streets the distinction between street and decent is often irrelevant; everybody knows that if the rules are violated, there are penalties. Knowledge of the code is thus largely defensive; it is literally necessary for operating in public. Therefore, even though families with a decency orientation are usually opposed to the values of the code, they often reluctantly encourage their children's familiarity with it to enable them to negotiate the inner-city environment.

At the heart of the code is the issue of respect—loosely defined as being treated "right," or granted the deference one deserves. However, in the troublesome public environment of the inner city, as people increasingly feel buffeted by forces beyond their control, what one deserves in the way of respect becomes more and more problematic and uncertain. This in turn further opens the issue of respect to sometimes intense interpersonal negotiation. In the street culture, especially among young people, respect is viewed as almost an external entity that is hard-won but easily lost, and so must constantly be guarded. The rules of the code in fact provide a framework for negotiating respect. The person whose very appearance—including his clothing, demeanor, and way of moving—deters transgressions feels that he possesses, and may be considered by others to possess, a measure of respect. With the right amount of respect, for instance, he can avoid "being bothered" in public. If he is bothered, not only may he be in physical danger but he has been disgraced or "dissed" (disrespected). Many of the forms that dissing can take might seem petty to middle-class people (maintaining eye contact for too long, for

example), but to those invested in the street code, these actions become serious indications of the other person's intentions. Consequently, such people become very sensitive to advances and slights, which could well serve as warnings of imminent physical confrontation.

This hard reality can be traced to the profound sense of alienation from mainstream society and its institutions felt by many poor inner-city black people, particularly the young. The code of the streets is actually a cultural adaptation to a profound lack of faith in the police and the judicial system. The police are most often seen as representing the dominant white society and not caring to protect inner-city residents. When called, they may not respond, which is one reason many residents feel they must be prepared to take extraordinary measures to defend themselves and their loved ones against those who are inclined to aggression. Lack of police accountability has in fact been incorporated into the status system: the person who is believed capable of "taking care of himself" is accorded a certain deference, which translates into a sense of physical and psychological control. Thus the street code emerges where the influence of the police ends and personal responsibility for one's safety is felt to begin. Exacerbated by the proliferation of drugs and easy access to guns, this volatile situation results in the ability of the street-oriented minority (or those who effectively "go for bad") to dominate the public spaces.

Decent and Street Families

Although almost everyone in poor inner-city neighborhoods is struggling financially and therefore feels a certain distance from the rest of America, the decent and the street family in a real sense represent two poles of value orientation, two contrasting conceptual categories. The labels "decent" and "street," which the residents themselves use, amount to evaluative judgments that confer status on local residents. The labeling is often the result of a social contest among individuals and families of the neighborhood. Individuals of the two orientations often coexist in the same extended family. Decent residents judge themselves to be so while judging others to be of the street, and street individuals often present themselves as decent, drawing distinctions between themselves and other people. In addition, there is quite a bit of circumstantial behavior—that is, one person may at different times exhibit both decent and street orientations, depending on the circumstances. Although these designations result from so much social jockeying, there do exist concrete features that define each conceptual category.

Generally, so-called decent families tend to accept mainstream values more fully and attempt to instill them in their children. Whether married couples with children or single-parent (usually female) households, they are generally "working poor" and so tend to be better off financially than their street-oriented neighbors. They value hard work and self-reliance and are willing to sacrifice for their children. Because they have a certain amount of faith in mainstream society, they harbor hopes for a better future for their children, if not for themselves. Many of them go to church and take a strong interest in their children's schooling. Rather than dwelling on the real hardships and inequities facing them, many such decent people, particularly the increasing number of grandmothers raising grandchildren, see their difficult situation as a test from God and derive great support from their faith and from the church community.

Extremely aware of the problematic and often dangerous environment in which they reside, decent parents tend to be strict in their child-rearing practices, encouraging children to respect authority and walk a straight moral line. They have an almost obsessive concern about trouble of any kind and remind their children to be on the lookout for people and situations that might lead to it. At the same time, they are themselves polite and considerate of others, and teach their children to be the same way. At home, at work, and in church, they strive hard to maintain a positive mental attitude and a spirit of cooperation.

So-called street parents, in contrast, often show a lack of consideration for other people and have a rather superficial sense of family and community. Though they may love their children, many of them are unable to cope with the physical and emotional demands of parenthood, and find it difficult to reconcile their needs with those of

their children. These families, who are more fully invested in the code of the streets than the decent people are, may aggressively socialize their children into it in a normative way. They believe in the code and judge themselves and others according to its values.

In fact the overwhelming majority of families in the inner-city community try to approximate the decent-family model, but there are many others who clearly represent the worst fears of the decent family. Not only are their financial resources extremely limited, but what little they have may easily be misused. The lives of the street-oriented are often marked by disorganization. In the most desperate circumstances people frequently have a limited understanding of priorities and consequences, and so frustrations mount over bills, food, and at times, drink, cigarettes, and drugs. Some tend toward self-destructive behavior; many street-oriented women are crack-addicted ("on the pipe"), alcoholic, or involved in complicated relationships with men who abuse them. In addition, the seeming intractability of their situation, caused in large part by the lack of well-paying jobs and the persistence of racial discrimination, has engendered deep-seated bitterness and anger in many of the most desperate and poorest blacks, especially young people. The need both to exercise a measure of control and to lash out at somebody is often reflected in the adults' relations with their children. At the least, the frustrations of persistent poverty shorten the fuse in such people contributing to a lack of patience with anyone, child or adult, who imitates them.

In these circumstances a woman—or a man, although men are less consistently present in children's lives—can be quite aggressive with children, yelling at and striking them for the least little infraction of the rules she has set down. Often little if any serious explanation follows the verbal and physical punishment. This response teaches children a particular lesson. They learn that to solve any kind of interpersonal problem one must quickly resort to hitting or other violent behavior. Actual peace and quiet, and also the appearance of calm, respectful children conveyed to her neighbors and friends, are often what the young mother most desires, but at times she will be very aggressive in trying to get them. Thus she may be quick to beat her children, especially if they defy her law, not because she hates them but because this is the way she knows to control them. In fact, many street-oriented women love their children dearly. Many mothers in the community subscribe to the notion that there is a "devil in the boy" that must be beaten out of him or that socially "fast girls need to be whupped." Thus much of what borders on child abuse in the view of social authorities is acceptable parental punishment in the view of these mothers.

Many street-oriented women are sporadic mothers whose children learn to fend for themselves when necessary, foraging for food and money any way they can get it. The children are sometimes employed by drug dealers or become addicted themselves. These children of the street, growing up with little supervision, are said to "come up hard." They often learn to fight at an early age, sometimes using short-tempered adults around them as role models. The street-oriented home may be fraught with anger, verbal disputes, physical aggression, and even mayhem. The children observe these goings-on, learning the lesson that might makes right. They quickly learn to hit those who cross them, and the dog-eat-dog mentality prevails. In order to survive, to protect oneself, it is necessary to marshal inner resources and be ready to deal with adversity in a hands-on way. In these circumstances physical prowess takes on great significance.

In some of the most desperate cases, a street-oriented mother may simply leave her young children alone and unattended while she goes out. The most irresponsible women can be found at local bars and crack houses, getting high and socializing with other adults. Sometimes a troubled woman will leave very young children alone for days at a time. Reports of crack addicts abandoning their children have become common in drug-infested inner-city communities. Neighbors or relatives discover the abandoned children, often hungry and distraught over the absence of their mother. After repeated absences, a friend or relative, particularly a grandmother, will often step in to care for the young children, sometimes petitioning the authorities to send her, as guardian of the children, the mother's welfare check, if the mother gets one. By this time, however, the children may well have

learned the first lesson of the streets: survival itself, let alone respect, cannot be taken for granted; you have to fight for your place in the world.

Campaigning for Respect

These realities of inner-city life are largely absorbed on the streets. At an early age, often even before they start school, children from street-oriented homes gravitate to the streets, where they "hang"—socialize with their peers. Children from these generally permissive homes have a great deal of latitude and are allowed to "rip and run" up and down the street. They often come home from school, put their books down, and go right back out the door. On school nights eight- and nine-year-olds remain out until nine or ten o'clock (and teenagers typically come in whenever they want to). On the streets they play in groups that often become the source of their primary social bonds. Children from decent homes tend to be more carefully supervised and are thus likely to have curfews and to be taught how to stay out of trouble.

When decent and street kids come together, a kind of social shuffle occurs in which children have a chance to go either way. Tension builds as a child comes to realize that he must choose an orientation. The kind of home he comes from influences but does not determine the way he will ultimately turn out—although it is unlikely that a child from a thoroughly street-oriented family will easily absorb decent values on the streets. Youths who emerge from street-oriented families but develop a decency orientation almost always learn those values in another setting—in school, in a youth group, in church. Often it is the result of their involvement with a caring "old head" (adult role model).

In the street, through their play, children pour their individual life experiences into a common knowledge pool, affirming, confirming, and elaborating on what they have observed in the home and matching their skills against those of others. And they learn to fight. Even small children test one another, pushing and shoving, and are ready to hit other children over circumstances not to their liking. In turn, they are readily hit by other children, and the child who is toughest prevails.

Thus the violent resolution of disputes, the hitting and cursing, gains social reinforcement. The child in effect is initiated into a system that is really a way of campaigning for respect.

In addition, younger children witness the disputes of older children, which are often resolved through cursing and abusive talk, if not aggression or outright violence. They see that one child succumbs to the greater physical and mental abilities of the other. They are also alert and attentive witnesses to the verbal and physical fights of adults, after which they compare notes and share their interpretations of the event. In almost every case the victor is the person who physically won the altercation, and this person often enjoys the esteem and respect of onlookers. These experiences reinforce the lessons the children have learned at home: might makes right, and toughness is a virtue, while humility is not. In effect they learn the social meaning of fighting. When it is left virtually unchallenged, this understanding becomes an ever more important part of the child's working conception of the world. Over time the code of the streets becomes refined.

Those street-oriented adults with whom children come in contact—including mothers, fathers, brothers, sisters, boyfriends, cousins, neighbors, and friends—help them along in forming this understanding by verbalizing the messages they are getting through experience: "Watch your back." "Protect yourself." "Don't punk out." "If somebody messes with you, you got to pay them back." "If someone disses you, you got to straighten them out." Many parents actually impose sanctions if a child is not sufficiently aggressive. For example, if a child loses a fight and comes home upset, the parent might respond,

> Don't you come in here crying that somebody beat you up; you better get back out there and whup his ass. I didn't raise no punks! Get back out there and whup his ass. If you don't whup his ass, I'll whup your ass when you come home.

Thus the child obtains reinforcement for being tough and showing nerve.

While fighting, some children cry as though they are doing something they are ambivalent about. The fight may be against their wishes,

yet they may feel constrained to fight or face the consequences—not just from peers but also from caretakers or parents, who may administer another beating if they back down. Some adults recall receiving such lessons from their own parents and justify repeating them to their children as a way to toughen them up. Looking capable of taking care of oneself as a form of self-defense is a dominant theme among both street-oriented and decent adults who worry about the safety of their children. There is thus at times a convergence in their child-rearing practices, although the rationales behind them may differ.

Self-Image Based on "Juice"

By the time they are teenagers, most youths have either internalized the code of the streets or at least learned the need to comport themselves in accordance with its rules, which chiefly have to do with interpersonal communication. The code revolves around the presentation of self. Its basic requirement is the display of a certain predisposition to violence. Accordingly, one's bearing must send the unmistakable if sometimes subtle message to "the next person" in public that one is capable of violence and mayhem when the situation requires it, that one can take care of oneself. The nature of this communication is largely determined by the demands of the circumstances but can include facial expressions, gait, and verbal expressions—all of which are geared mainly to deterring aggression. Physical appearance, including clothes, jewelry, and grooming, also plays an important part in how a person is viewed; to be respected, it is important to have the right look.

Even so, there are no guarantees against challenges, because there are always people around looking for a fight to increase their share of respect—or "juice," as it is sometimes called on the street. Moreover, if a person is assaulted, it is important, not only in the eyes of his opponent but also in the eyes of his "running buddies," for him to avenge himself. Otherwise he risks being "tried" (challenged) or "moved on" by any number of others. To maintain his honor he must show he is not someone to be "messed with" or "dissed." In general, the person must "keep himself straight" by managing his position of respect among others; this involves in part his self-image, which is shaped by what he thinks others are thinking of him in relation to his peers.

Objects play an important and complicated role in establishing self-image. Jackets, sneakers, gold jewelry, reflect not just a person's taste, which tends to be tightly regulated among adolescents of all social classes, but also a willingness to possess things that may require defending. A boy wearing a fashionable, expensive jacket, for example, is vulnerable to attack by another who covets the jacket and either cannot afford to buy one or wants the added satisfaction of depriving someone else of his. However, if the boy forgoes the desirable jacket and wears one that isn't "hip," he runs the risk of being teased and possibly even assaulted as an unworthy person. To be allowed to hang with certain prestigious crowds, a boy must wear a different set of expensive clothes—sneakers and athletic suit—every day. Not to be able to do so might make him appear socially deficient. The youth comes to covet such items especially when he sees easy prey wearing them.

In acquiring valued things, therefore, a person shores up his identity—but since it is an identity based on having things, it is highly precarious. This very precariousness gives a heightened sense of urgency to staying even with peers, with whom the person is actually competing. Young men and women who are able to command respect through their presentation of self—by allowing their possessions and their body language to speak for them—may not have to campaign for regard but may, rather, gain it by the force of their manner. Those who are unable to command respect in this way must actively campaign for it—and are thus particularly alive to slights.

One way of campaigning for status is by taking the possessions of others. In this context, seemingly ordinary objects can become trophies imbued with symbolic value that far exceeds their monetary worth. Possession of the trophy can symbolize the ability to violate somebody—to "get in his face," to take something of value from him, to "dis" him, and thus to enhance one's own worth by stealing someone else's. The trophy does not have to be something material. It can be another person's sense of honor, snatched away with a derogatory remark. It can be the outcome of a fight. It can be the imposition of a certain standard, such as a girl's getting herself recognized as the most beautiful. Material things, however, fit easily into the pattern. Sneakers, a pistol, even somebody else's girlfriend, can become a trophy. When a person can take something from another and then flaunt it, he gains a certain regard by being the owner, or the controller, of that thing. But this display of ownership can then provoke other people to challenge him. This game of who controls what is thus constantly being played out on inner-city streets, and the trophy—extrinsic or intrinsic, tangible or intangible—identifies the current winner.

An important aspect of this often violent give-and-take is its zero-sum quality. That is, the extent to which one person can raise himself up depends on his ability to put another person down. This underscores the alienation that permeates the inner-city ghetto community. There is a generalized sense that very little respect is to be had, and therefore everyone competes to get what affirmation he can of the little that is available. The craving for respect that results gives people thin skins. Shows of deference by others can be highly soothing, contributing to a sense of security, comfort, self-confidence, and self-respect. Transgressions by others which go unanswered diminish these feelings and are believed to encourage further transgressions. Hence one must be ever vigilant against the transgressions of others or even *appearing* as if transgressions will be tolerated. Among young people, whose sense of self-esteem is particularly vulnerable, there is an especially heightened concern with being disrespected. Many inner-city young men in particular crave respect to such a degree that they will risk their lives to attain and maintain it.

The issue of respect is thus closely tied to whether a person has an inclination to be violent, even as a victim. In the wider society people may not feel required to retaliate physically after an attack, even though they are aware that they have been degraded or taken advantage of. They may feel a great need to defend themselves during an attack, or to behave in such a way as to deter aggression (middle-class people certainly can and do become victims of street-oriented youths), but they are much more likely than street-oriented people to feel that they can walk away from a possible altercation with their self-esteem intact. Some people may even have the strength of character to flee, without any thought that their self-respect or esteem will be diminished.

In impoverished inner-city black communities, however, particularly among young males and perhaps increasingly among females, such flight would be extremely difficult. To run away would likely leave one's self-esteem in tatters. Hence people often feel constrained not only to stand up and at least attempt to resist during an assault but also to "pay back"—to seek revenge—after a successful assault on their person. This may include going to get a weapon or even getting relatives involved. Their very identity and self-respect, their honor, is often intricately tied up with the way they perform on the streets during and after such encounters. This outlook reflects the circumscribed opportunities of the inner-city poor. Generally people outside the ghetto have other ways of gaining status and regard, and thus do not feel so dependent on such physical displays.

By Trial of Manhood

On the street, among males these concerns about things and identity have come to be expressed in the concept of "manhood." Manhood in the inner city means taking the prerogatives of men with respect to strangers, other men, and women—being distinguished as a man. It implies physicality and a certain ruthlessness. Regard and respect are associated with this concept in large part because of its practical application: if others have little or no regard for a person's manhood, his very life and those of his loved ones could be in jeopardy. But there is a chicken-and-egg aspect to this situation: one's physical safety is more likely to be jeopardized in public *because* manhood is associated with respect. In other words, an existential link has been created between the idea of manhood and one's self-esteem, so that it has become hard to say which is primary. For many inner-city youths, manhood and respect are flip sides of the same coin; physical and psychological well-being are

inseparable, and both require a sense of control, of being in charge.

The operating assumption is that a man, especially a real man, knows what other men know—the code of the streets. And if one is not a real man, one is somehow diminished as a person, and there are certain valued things one simply does not deserve. There is thus believed to be a certain justice to the code, since it is considered that everyone has the opportunity to know it. Implicit in this is that everybody is held responsible for being familiar with the code. If the victim of a mugging, for example, does not know the code and so responds "wrong," the perpetrator may feel justified even in killing him and may feel no remorse. He may think, "Too bad, but it's his fault. He should have known better."

So when a person ventures outside, he must adopt the code—a kind of shield, really—to prevent others from "messing with" him. In these circumstances it is easy for people to think they are being tried or tested by others even when this is not the case. For it is sensed that something extremely valuable is at stake in every interaction, and people are encouraged to rise to the occasion, particularly with strangers. For people who are unfamiliar with the code—generally people who live outside the inner city—the concern with respect in the most ordinary interactions can be frightening and incomprehensible. But for those who are invested in the code, the clear object of their demeanor is to discourage strangers from even thinking about testing their manhood. And the sense of power that attends the ability to deter others can be alluring even to those who know the code without being heavily invested in it—the decent inner-city youths. Thus a boy who has been leading a basically decent life can, in trying circumstances, suddenly resort to deadly force.

Central to the issue of manhood is the widespread belief that one of the most effective ways of gaining respect is to manifest "nerve." Nerve is shown when one takes another person's possessions (the more valuable the better), "messes with" someone's woman, throws the first punch, "gets in someone's face," or pulls a trigger. Its proper display helps on the spot to check others who would violate one's person and also helps to build a reputation that works to prevent future challenges. But since such a show of nerve is a forceful expression of disrespect toward the person on the receiving end, the victim may be greatly offended and seek to retaliate with equal or greater force. A display of nerve, therefore, can easily provoke a life-threatening response, and the background knowledge of that possibility has often been incorporated into the concept of nerve.

True nerve exposes a lack of fear of dying. Many feel that it is acceptable to risk dying over the principle of respect. In fact, among the hardcore street-oriented, the clear risk of violent death may be preferable to being "dissed" by another. The youths who have internalized this attitude and convincingly display it in their public bearing are among the most threatening people of all, for it is commonly assumed that they fear no man. As the people of the community say, "They are the baddest dudes on the street." They often lead an existential life that may acquire meaning only when they are faced with the possibility of imminent death. Not to be afraid to die is by implication to have few compunctions about taking another's life. Not to be afraid to die is the quid pro quo of being able to take somebody else's life—for the right reasons, if the situation demands it. When others believe this is one's position, it gives one a real sense of power on the streets. Such credibility is what many inner-city youths strive to achieve, whether they are decent or street-oriented, both because of its practical defensive value and because of the positive way it makes them feel about themselves. The difference between the decent and the street-oriented youth is often that the decent youth makes a conscious decision to appear tough and manly; in another setting—with teachers, say, or at his part-time job—he can be polite and deferential. The street-oriented youth, on the other hand, has made the concept of manhood a part of his very identity; he has difficulty manipulating it—it often controls him.

Girls and Boys

Increasingly, teenage girls are mimicking the boys and trying to have their own version of "manhood." Their goal is the same—to get respect, to be recognized as capable of setting or maintaining a certain standard. They try to achieve this end in the ways that have been established by the boys, including posturing, abusive language, and the use of violence to resolve disputes, but the issues for the girls are different. Although conflicts over turf and status exist among the girls, the majority of disputes seem rooted in assessments of beauty (which girl in a group is "the cutest"), competition over boyfriends, and attempts to regulate other people's knowledge of and opinions about a girl's behavior or that of someone close to her, especially her mother.

A major cause of conflicts among girls is "he say, she say." This practice begins in the early school years and continues through high school. It occurs when "people," particularly girls, talk about others, thus putting their "business in the streets." Usually one girl will say something negative about another in the group, most often behind the person's back. The remark will then get back to the person talked about. She may retaliate or her friends may feel required to "take up for" her. In essence this is a form of group gossiping in which individuals are negatively assessed and evaluated. As with much gossip, the things said may or may not be true, but the point is that such imputations can cast aspersions on a person's good name. The accused is required to defend herself against the slander, which can result in arguments and fights, often over little of real substance. Here again is the problem of low self-esteem, which encourages youngsters to be highly sensitive to slights and to be vulnerable to feeling easily "dissed." To avenge the dissing, a fight is usually necessary.

Because boys are believed to control violence, girls tend to defer to them in situations of conflict. Often if a girl is attacked or feels slighted, she will get a brother, uncle, or cousin to do her fighting for her. Increasingly, however, girls are doing their own fighting and are even asking their male relatives to teach them how to fight. Some girls form groups that attack other girls or take things from them. A hard-core segment of inner-city girls inclined toward violence seems to be developing. As one thirteen-year-old girl in a detention center for youths who have committed violent acts told me, "To get people to leave you alone, you gotta fight. Talking don't always get you out of stuff." One major difference between girls and boys: girls rarely use guns. Their fights are therefore not life-or-death struggles. Girls are not often willing to put their lives on the line for "manhood." The ultimate form of respect on the male-dominated inner-city street is thus reserved for men.

"Going for Bad"

In the most fearsome youths such a cavalier attitude toward death grows out of a very limited view of life. Many are uncertain about how long they are going to live and believe they could die violently at any time. They accept this fate; they live on the edge. Their manner conveys the message that nothing intimidates them, whatever turn the encounter takes, they maintain their attack—rather like a pit bull, whose spirit many such boys admire. The demonstration of such tenacity "shows heart" and earns their respect.

This fearlessness has implications for law enforcement. Many street-oriented boys are much more concerned about the threat of "justice" at the hands of a peer than at the hands of the police. Moreover, many feel not only that they have little to lose by going to prison but that they have something to gain. The toughening-up one experiences in prison can actually enhance one's reputation on the streets. Hence the system loses influence over the hard core who are without jobs, with little perceptible stake in the system. If mainstream society has done nothing *for them,* they counter by making sure it can do nothing to them.

At the same time, however, a competing view maintains that true nerve consists in backing down, walking away from a fight, and going on with one's business. One fights only in self-defense. This view emerges from the decent philosophy that life is precious, and it is an important part of the socialization process common in decent homes. It discourages violence as the primary means of resolving disputes and encourages youngsters to accept nonviolence and talk as confrontational strategies. But "if the deal goes down," self-defense is greatly encouraged. When there is enough positive support for this orientation, either in the home or among one's peers, then nonviolence has

a chance to prevail. But it prevails at the cost of relinquishing a claim to being bad and tough, and therefore sets a young person up as at the very least alienated from street-oriented peers and quite possibly a target of derision or even violence.

Although the nonviolent orientation rarely overcomes the impulse to strike back in an encounter, it does introduce a certain confusion and so can prompt a measure of soul-searching, or even profound ambivalence. Did the person back down with his respect intact or did he back down only to be judged a "punk"—a person lacking manhood? Should he or she have acted? Should he or she have hit the other person in the mouth? These questions beset many young men and women during public confrontations. What is the "right" thing to do? In the quest for honor, respect, and local status—which few young people are uninterested in—common sense most often prevails, which leads many to opt for the tough approach, enacting their own particular versions of the display of nerve. The presentation of oneself as rough and tough is very often quite acceptable until one is tested. And then that presentation may help the person pass the test, because it will cause fewer questions to be asked about what he did and why. It is hard for a person to explain why he lost the fight or why he backed down. Hence many will strive to appear to "go for bad," while hoping they will never be tested. But when they are tested, the outcome of the situation may quickly be out of their hands, as they become wrapped up in the circumstances of the moment.

An Oppositional Culture

The attitudes of the wider society are deeply implicated in the code of the streets. Most people in inner-city communities are not totally invested in the code, but the significant minority of hard-core street youths who are have to maintain the code in order to establish reputations, because they have—or feel they have—few other ways to assert themselves. For these young people the standards of the street code are the only game in town. The extent to which some children—particularly those who through upbringing have become most alienated and those lacking in strong and conventional social support—experience, feel, and internalize racist rejection and contempt from mainstream society may strongly encourage them to express contempt for the more conventional society in turn. In dealing with this contempt and rejection, some youngsters will consciously invest themselves and their considerable mental resources in what amounts to an oppositional culture to preserve themselves and their self-respect. Once they do, any respect they might be able to garner in the wider system pales in comparison with the respect available in the local system; thus they often lose interest in even attempting to negotiate the mainstream system.

At the same time, many less alienated young blacks have assumed a street-oriented demeanor as a way of expressing their blackness while really embracing a much more moderate way of life; they, too, want a nonviolent setting in which to live and raise a family. These decent people are trying hard to be part of the mainstream culture, but the racism, real and perceived, that they encounter helps to legitimate the oppositional culture. And so on occasion they adopt street behavior. In fact, depending on the demands of the situation, many people in the community slip back and forth between decent and street behavior.

A vicious cycle has thus been formed. The hopelessness and alienation many young inner-city black men and women feel, largely as a result of endemic joblessness and persistent racism, fuels the violence they engage in. This violence serves to confirm the negative feelings many whites and some middle-class blacks harbor toward the ghetto poor, further legitimating the oppositional culture and the code of the streets in the eyes of many poor young blacks. Unless this cycle is broken, attitudes on both sides will become increasingly entrenched, and the violence, which claims victims black and white, poor and affluent, will only escalate.

Discussion Questions

1. Describe the central values and norms (or rules) that form the "code of the streets."
2. How does Anderson explain the origin of the code of the streets?
3. Describe the socialization of "street kids," noting how this socialization increases the likelihood that they will resort to violence in various situations. In your description, draw on both Sutherland's differential association and Akers's social learning theory.
4. Why do individuals who oppose the code of the streets nevertheless conform to its rules on occasion?
5. To what extent does the code of the streets affect the behavior of girls?

CHAPTER 24

Formal Characteristics of Delinquency Areas

Clifford R. Shaw ▪ Henry D. McKay

Neighborhoods have long been important for the study of sociological processes. It is little wonder, then, that they have also played a key role in criminology. The theory that focuses on the role of neighborhoods and neighborhood organization on crime is the social-disorganization (or social-ecology) perspective. This perspective developed largely from the work of Clifford R. Shaw and Henry D. McKay in Chicago in the 1920s, 1930s, and 1940s. This selection is an excerpt from their work.

Shaw and McKay show that delinquency rates remained fairly stable over time (between 1900 to 1920) in different areas of Chicago. Applying Park and Burgess's model of "The City" to delinquency, Shaw and McKay demonstrated that the highest delinquency rates were found in neighborhoods in the "zone of transition," an area located immediately outside the industrial area. The zone of transition was characterized by severe economic hardships as evidenced by physical deterioration, changes in population size, high poverty, economic dependency, and a host of other social ills. The low rent and easy access to industrial areas (and therefore jobs) attracted poor newcomers to the zone of transition; many were either first-generation or second-generation immigrants or African Americans. When people living in these areas were financially able, they moved out to zone Three and beyond.

Because of continuous in-and-out migration and the heterogeneity of people, the zone of transition was socially disorganized, that is, lacking strong informal social-control mechanisms, such as strong churches and interested neighbors, which are important for controlling crime and delinquency.

The lack of social controls in disorganized areas allowed the development and perpetuation of delinquent traditions, which resulted in continuously high rates of delinquency, even when the former residents moved out and new people moved in. Further, the delinquency rates of each group declined as its members gradually moved away from zone Two and into more organized and stable neighborhoods. This fact demonstrates that it is not the nativity or race/ethnicity of the residents that is associated with high crime and delinquency rates, but rather the lack of social organization in some neighborhoods.

The study of the distribution of juvenile delinquents...revealed wide variations in the rates of delinquents in the 113 areas of the city. Likewise it was found that the areas of low and high rates of delinquents assume a typical configuration with regard to the center of the city and also that this configuration of low and high rate areas has remained relatively unchanged over a long period of time. In attempting to interpret these findings, certain questions invariably arise: (1) What are the characteristics of these areas of high rates and how may they be differentiated from the areas with low rates? (2) Why do the low and high rate areas

Reprinted from: Clifford R. Shaw and Henry D. McKay, "Formal Characteristics of Delinquency Areas." In *National Commission on Law Observance and Enforcement, Report on the Causes of Crime, Vol. II,* pp 60-108. United States Government Printing Office, 1931.

assume this configuration in relation to the center of the city? (3) Why have the rates in most of the areas of the city remained relatively constant over a long period of time? Any attempt to answer these questions must take into consideration the organic nature of the city and the processes of segregation and differentiation that take place in its growth and expansion.

Students of social problems have repeatedly pointed out that there are marked differences between areas within the city. The business center, the foreign districts, the slum, the industrial centers, and many other districts have been differentiated. Of these, the slum has probably received the most attention. This term has been used in a general way to designate areas where such conditions as physical deterioration, bad housing, overcrowding, poverty, and crime are prevalent. Attempts have been made to explain these conditions in terms of the other conditions existing in the same area and in terms of the local situation. Upon further analysis, however, it appears that all of these conditions of the local situation are products of the more general processes of expansion and segregation within the city.

The nature of these processes has been the subject of considerable study during recent years. Students of the city, comprehending its unity and noting its organic nature, have described these processes in natural science terms by suggesting that every American city of the same class tends to reproduce, in the course of its expansion, all the different types of areas. The areas produced by this process are natural in the sense that they are not planned; they are typical in the sense that they tend to exhibit, from city to city, the same physical, social, and cultural characteristics. The natural process involved in the creation of these natural areas within the city is summarized in the following quotation from Robert E. Park:

The city plan establishes metes and bounds, fixes in a general way the location and character of the city's constructions, and imposes an orderly arrangement with the city area, upon the buildings which are erected by private initiative as well as by public authority. Within the limitations prescribed, however, the inevitable processes of human nature proceed to give these regions and these buildings a character which it is less easy to control.... Personal tastes and convenience, vocational and economic interests, infallibly tend to segregate and thus to classify the populations of great cities. In this way the city acquires an organization and distribution of population which is neither designed nor controlled....

Physical geography, natural advantages and disadvantages, including means of transportation, determine in advance the general outlines of the urban plan. As the city increases the population, the subtler influences of sympathy, rivalry, and economic necessity tend to control the distribution of population. Business and industry seek advantageous locations and draw around them certain portions of the population. There spring up fashionable residence quarters from which the poorer classes are excluded because of the increased value of the land. Then there grow up slums which are inhabited by great numbers of the poorer classes who are unable to defend themselves from associations with the derelict and vicious.

In the course of time every section and quarter of the city takes on something of the character and qualities of its inhabitants. Each separate part of the city is inevitably stained with the peculiar sentiments of its population. The effect of this is to convert what was at first a mere geographical expression into a neighborhood, that is to say, a locality with sentiments, traditions, and a history of its own. Within this neighborhood the continuity of the historical processes is somehow maintained. The past imposes itself upon the present, and the life of every locality moves on with a certain momentum of its own, more or less independent of the larger circle of life and interests about it.[1]

In his description of the processes of radial expansion, Prof. E. W. Burgess has advanced the thesis that, in the absence of counteracting factors, the modern American city takes the form of five concentric urban zones. This ideal construction, applied to the city of Chicago, is presented graphically in Figure 24.1. Burgess characterized in the following manner the areas which are differentiated in the process of radial expansion from the center of the city:

Zone I: *The central business district.*—At the center of the city as the focus of its commercial, social, and civic life is situated the central business district. The heart of this district is the downtown retail district

Figure 24.1 Urban Zones and Areas

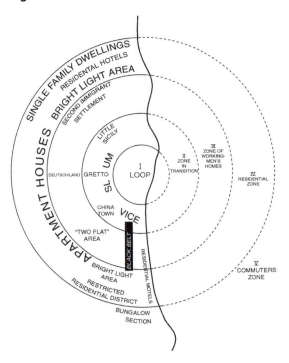

Zone III: *The zone of independent workingmen's homes.*—This third broad urban ring in Chicago, as well as in northern industrial cities, largely constituted by neighborhoods of second immigrant settlement. Its residents are those who desire to live near but not too close to their work.

Zone IV: *The zone of better residences.*—Extending beyond the neighborhoods of second immigrant settlements, we come to the zone of better residences in which the great middle classes of native-born Americans live, small business men, professional people, clerks, and the salesmen. Once communities of single homes, these are becoming in Chicago apartment-house residential-hotel areas. Within these areas at strategic points are found local businesses called satellite Loops. The typical constellation of business and recreational units includes a bank, one or more United Cigar Stores, a drug store, a high-class restaurant, an automobile display row, and a so-called "wonder" motion-picture theater....

Zone V: *The commuters' zone.*—Out beyond the areas of better residence is a ring of encircling small cities, towns, hamlets, which, taken together, constitute the suburbs, because the majority of men residing there spend the day at work in the Loop (central business district), returning only for the night. The communities in this commuters' zone are probably the most highly segregated of any in the entire gamut from an incorporated village run in the interests of crime and vice, such as Burnham, to Lake Forest, with its wealth, culture, and public spirit.[2]

The actual situation in any given city is, of course, somewhat different from this ideal presentation of city growth. In every city there are disturbing factors, such as lake fronts, rivers, elevations, railroads, and other barriers which affect the actual configuration that the city takes in its growth. Nevertheless, such an ideal construction furnishes a frame of reference from which the processes of city growth may be studied. It presents not only a general picture of the location of types of areas in a city at any given time, but it draws attention to one of the most significant characteristics of expansion, namely, succession, or the tendency of each inner zone to extend its area by invading the next outer zone.

It is the purpose of this chapter to present a picture of the structure of Chicago and to locate and characterize, by means of indices of organization and disorganization, the areas which have been

with its department stores, its smart shops, its office buildings, its clubs, its banks, its hotels, its theaters, its museums, and its headquarters of economic, social, civic and political life. Encircling this area of work and play is the less well-known wholesale business district with its market, its warehouses, and storage buildings.

Zone II: *The zone in transition.*—Surrounding the central business district are areas of residential deterioration caused by the encroaching of business and industry from Zone I.

Thus it may therefore be called a zone in transition, with a factory district for its inner belt and an outer ring of retrogressing neighborhoods, of first-settlement immigrant colonies, of rooming-house districts, of homeless men areas, of resorts of gambling, bootlegging, sexual vice, and breeding places of crime. In this area of physical deterioration and social disorganization our studies show the greatest concentration of cases of poverty, bad housing, juvenile delinquency, family disintegration, physical and mental disease. As families and individuals prosper, they escape from this area into Zone III beyond, leaving behind as marooned a residuum of defeated, leaderless, and helpless.

produced by these processes of expansion and succession acting within this structure. These indices, it is hoped, will afford a basis for differentiating between the areas of low and high rates of delinquents, and will serve as a partial explanation of the location of the high-rate areas and the constancy of the rates in these areas over a long period of time.

The effect of Lake Michigan on the configuration of Chicago is seen in the fact that the business district, which has remained at the point of original settlement, is on the lake shore and not in the center of the city. The study of the growth of Chicago in terms of concentric circles is at once modified to a study in terms of semicircles.

As elevation is a negligible factor in Chicago, the only other natural barrier which has interfered significantly with the free movement of population according to the radial pattern of expansion is the Chicago River. Although not a large river, its two branches, which extend almost diagonally out from the center of the city, have rather effectively divided Chicago into three divisions, each one of which may be thought of as being somewhat distinct from the others. These two branches of the river have also complicated the transportation problem and thus affected the movement of population in near-by areas.

Very early in the history of Chicago industry was attracted to the areas along both branches of the river. This development was accompanied by settlements of early immigrants in the surrounding areas, while high-class residential districts developed north, south, and west of the central business district....

In the course of the growth of Chicago marked changes in the character of the areas around the central business district have taken place. Residential districts close to the center of the city were forced to give away to industrial and commercial developments, while other areas of single-family dwellings along the main transportation lines have become apartment-house districts. The high-class residential districts formerly located on the near west side and near south side have disappeared, but it is interesting to note that a high-class residential district on the near north side, locally known as the Gold Coast, has as yet withstood the invasion of industry.

South Chicago, an outlying business center on the Lake front, which developed almost as early as Chicago proper, was at the time of its founding, and still is, the center of a large industrial development. Likewise the district of Pullman, located just west of Lake Calumet, has always been an industrial center. Outer districts such as Lake View on the North Shore and Hyde Park on the South Shore, which also became a part of Chicago through annexation, have largely retained their strictly residential character.

Distribution of Industrial and Commercial Centers

One index which may be used to distinguish the types of areas that have been differentiated in the process of the growth of Chicago is the configuration of its major industrial and commercial developments. Figure 24.2, gives an outline of the areas zoned for industry and commerce by the Chicago zoning ordinance of 1923. The central commercial and light industrial district is indicated by the cross-hatched sections of this figure. The Loop is almost entirely occupied by commercial houses. In the zoned areas adjacent to the Loop, but not occupied by heavy industry, are slight industrial plants, warehouses, and similar buildings. Some of this area is still used for residential purposes but it is subject to occupancy by industry and commerce as the central district expands.

In contrast with the commercial and light industrial developments in and adjacent to the center of a city, heavy industry tends to be located where there are natural advantages such as rivers, along the trunk lines of railroads, or on the Lake front.

Thus the heavy industrial districts in Chicago, which are indicated in solid black on Figure 24.2, are quite widely dispersed throughout the city. The largest developments are along the banks of the Chicago River and extend outward from the point where the first industries were established. The north extension follows the north branch about three miles from the central district, while the southern extension follows the south branch of the river to the city limits and includes a large portion of the Union Stock Yards and the central

Figure 24.2 Zoning Map of Chicago (Adapted)

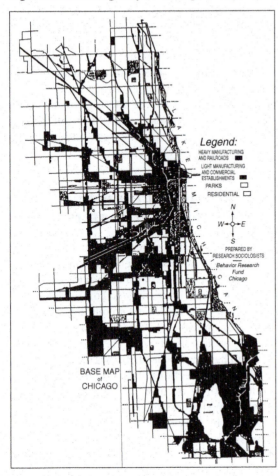

Legend:
HEAVY MANUFACTURING
AND RAILROADS
LIGHT MANUFACTURING
AND COMMERCIAL
ESTABLISHMENTS
PARKS
RESIDENTIAL

N
W—◆—E
S
PREPARED BY
RESEARCH SOCIOLOGISTS
Behavior Research
Fund
Chicago

BASE MAP
of
CHICAGO

manufacturing district. The other major industrial areas outlined on this figure are in the South Chicago and Calumet district where, as previously indicated, more or less independent industrial communities developed early in the history of Chicago.

When the maps showing the distribution of delinquents in Chicago are compared with this industrial map, it will be noted that most of the concentrations of delinquents and most of the high-rate areas of delinquents are either included in or are adjacent to the districts zoned for industry and commerce. The high-rate areas along the two branches of the Chicago River on the west side, on the south side, in the stockyard district, and in South Chicago are either completely or in part included in the shaded areas. On the other hand, the areas with low rates of delinquents are, generally speaking, quite far removed from the major industrial developments.

From the foregoing it may be said that, in general, proximity to industry and commerce is an index of the areas of Chicago in which high rates of delinquents are found. It is not assumed that this relationship exists because industry and commerce are in themselves causes of delinquency. But it is assumed that the areas adjacent to industry and commerce have certain characteristics which result from this proximity and which serve to differentiate them from the areas with low rates of delinquents. An effort will be made, therefore, to show how these areas are affected by industry and commerce and to present some of their more significant characteristics.

Physical Deterioration

As the city grows, the areas of light industry and commerce near the center of the city expand and encroach upon the areas used for residential purposes. The dwellings in such areas, already undesirable because of age, are allowed to deteriorate under the threat of invasion, because further investment in them is unprofitable. Others are junked to make way for new industrial or commercial structures. The effect of the changes is that the areas become increasingly undesirable through general depreciation.…

Likewise, the areas adjacent to heavy industrial centers, but not yet occupied by industry, are subject to invasion. While the threat of invasion is not so great as in the areas close to the center of the city, first-class residences are not constructed in these areas and there is a definite tendency toward physical deterioration. Furthermore, the areas that are near heavy industrial developments are often rendered more undesirable for residential purposes because of noise, smoke, odors, or the general unattractiveness of the surroundings. The total result is, therefore, that both the areas adjacent to commercial and light industrial properties near the center of the city and those adjacent to centers of heavy industrial development in the outlying sections are in general almost equally unattractive and undesirable for residential areas.

Areas of Increasing and Decreasing Population

Further evidence of the process of deterioration and rapid change in the areas adjacent to commerce and industry is seen…in the percentage increase and decrease of the population in each of the 113 areas during the period from 1910 to 1920…. Twelve areas, all of them near the center of the city, decreased more than 20 percent in this 10-year period; and a total of 23 areas, either near the central business district of the heavy industrial sections, showed some decrease….

Most of the heavy concentrations of delinquents and most of the high-rate areas are included in those sections of the city which show a decreasing population. Likewise, the areas that are slowly increasing in population tend to be the areas with medium rates of delinquents, while the areas of more rapid increases tend to be the low-rate areas….

The reader is cautioned against attaching causal significance to the correspondence between rates of delinquents and percentage increase and decrease of population…or to any of the variables considered in relation to rates of delinquents in this chapter. All the variables considered in this chapter are used solely to indicate differences between community backgrounds. The facts concerning increasing and decreasing population serve as a basis for differentiating between the areas of high rates and those of low rates. It is probable that decreasing population, rather than contributing to delinquency, is a symptom of the more basic changes that are taking place in those areas of the city that are subject to invasion by industry and commerce….

Despite the fact that the districts near the center of the city show a decreasing population, the net density of population, as measured by the number of inhabitants per acre in the area not occupied by industry, is greatest in the areas within 2 miles of the central district and tends to decrease with

considerable regularity out from the inner zone. In general the areas with the highest rates of delinquents fall within those sections of the city having the greatest density of population. The notable exceptions to this tendency are found in the high-class apartment districts, where the density is relatively high but the rates of delinquents are low, and in a few outlying areas where the rates of delinquency are comparatively high but the density is low because of the presence of considerable unoccupied waste land.

Economic Dependency

The areas adjacent to industry and commerce are also characterized by low rents and low family income. These are complementary characteristics. The rents in old, dilapidated buildings in deteriorated neighborhood are naturally low and these low rents attract the population group of the lowest economic status.

…These rates of dependency are based upon the total number of families which received financial aid from the United Charities and the Jewish Charities during 1921.[3] The rates represent the percentage of the families in each area that received financial aid from these two agencies during the year. While it is not assumed that this series of dependency cases furnishes an ideal index of the economic status of all of the families in these areas, it is probably that, with the exception of some Negro communities, it outlines the poverty areas quite accurately.

The areas of highest rates of dependency, are concentrated…around the central business and industrial section and in the stockyards district. The second class of areas—that is, those with rates of dependency ranging from 1.5 to 2—are concentrated just outside the highest-rate areas in the center of the city, in the "back-of-the-yards" district, and in the South Chicago industrial district. On the other hand, the areas of lowest rates are in the outlying residential communities….

It will be observed that the variation in rates of delinquents as between the areas with highest rates of dependency and those with the lowest rates of dependency is 11 to 2.2 in the police series, 9.2 to 2.9 in the juvenile court series, and

3.2 to 0.8 in the juvenile court commitment series. These facts indicate that there is a marked similarity in the variation of rates of family dependency and rates of juvenile delinquents, since for each decrease in rates of dependency there is a corresponding decrease in rates of delinquency for each of the three series of delinquents....

Distribution of Foreign and Negro Population

Another characteristic of the areas of decreasing population, physical deterioration, and economic dependency is the high percentage of foreign and Negro population. The process of selection and segregation, operating on both economic and cultural bases, attract into these areas the population groups of the lowest economic status. These groups, include, for the most part, the newest immigrants and the Negroes.... [T]he Negroes and the immigrants are of somewhat comparable economic status; both are unaccustomed to the conditions of a modern urban community and are faced with the problem of making an adjustment in a situation with which they are not familiar. The cultural backgrounds of both groups are largely rural....

[T]he highest percentages of foreign and Negro population are in the areas around the center of the city, in the stockyards district, and in South Chicago.... [T]hese are the areas of high rates of delinquents.

A further analysis of the population by square-mile areas revealed that the percentage of aliens among the foreign born was disproportionately large in the areas where the percentage of foreign born in the total population was highest.... [N]ear the center of the city, the percentage of aliens in the foreign-born population was 40.0.... Thus it is clear that in the areas of high rates of delinquents a much smaller proportion of the foreign born are naturalized than in the outlying areas where the rates are low. This fact suggests that the newest immigrants are concentrated, for the most part, in the areas of highest rates of delinquents.

As distinguished from the other indices of community organization and disorganization, the variation in the percentage of the combined foreign and Negro groups in the total population is of additional interest since the children of these two groups have, for a long period of time, constituted a disproportionate percentage of the delinquents in the juvenile court. This is indicated when the 8,141 delinquents included in our 1917-1923 juvenile court series are classified on the basis of the nativity of the father and compared either with the nativity distribution of the male adults in the total population or the nationality distribution of the total aged 10 to 16 male population as recorded in the 1920 census. Of the total number of delinquents classified in the 1917-1923 juvenile court series, 9.1 percent were Negroes, and of the total number of white delinquents. 24.4 percent had native-born fathers and 75.6 percent had foreign-born fathers. The distribution of the male adults in Chicago shows quite different proportions in each of these groups. Of the total population in 1920, 4.9 percent of the male adults (21 years and over) were Negroes, and of the total male white population, 48.3 percent were foreign born and 51.7 percent were native born. Thus, although 75.6 percent of the white delinquents had foreign-born fathers, only 48.3 percent of the total male white population were foreign born.

A comparison of the nationality distribution of the boys in the juvenile court series with that of the aged 10 to 16 male population for the city as a whole also revealed certain significant differences between these two groups. Of the total 10 to 16 white male population. 64.6 percent had foreign-born fathers[4] as against 75.6 percent of the white boys in the 1917-1923 juvenile court series. Interesting differences between the extent of delinquency among the children of native parentage and foreign parentage are revealed when actual rates are computed for each of these groups. The rate for the delinquents with native fathers was 2.9 against 5.0 for the delinquents with foreign-born fathers. Thus the rate for the children with foreign-born fathers is 72 percent greater than that for the delinquents with native-born fathers. The rate in the native group for the single year 1920 was 0.8 and for the native white of foreign parentage 1.3. Thus for this single year the rate of the delinquents of foreign parentage was 62 percent greater than that for the native white of native parentage.

The Negro group shows a somewhat higher rate of delinquents than either the native white of native parentage or the native white of foreign parentage. While the aged 10 to 16 male Negro population was only 2.5 percent of the total aged 10 to 16 male population, 9.9 percent of the delinquents in the 1917-1923 series were Negroes. For this series as a whole the rate for the Negro group was 15.6 and for the single year 1920 the rate was 4.6.

It is significant to note that the presence of a large Negro and foreign-born population in the areas having high rates of delinquents was not a unique situation in 1920. A study of the distribution of racial and national groups in both the school census of 1898 and the Federal census of 1910 showed that the highest percentage of the Negro and foreign born was in the areas having the highest rates of delinquents in the 1900–1906 juvenile court series....

Succession of Cultural Groups in Delinquent Areas

Before attempting to interpret the fact that a disproportionately large number of boys brought before the juvenile court are of foreign born and Negro parentage, or that the highest percentage of foreign born and Negro population is found in the areas having the highest rates of delinquents, it is necessary to consider two complementary changes that have taken place in the history of Chicago. In the first place, during the period between 1900 and 1920 marked changes took place in the racial and national composition of the population which inhabited the areas with the highest rates of delinquents. In the second place, this change in the composition of the population was paralleled by a corresponding change in the racial and nationality groupings among children brought before the juvenile court of Cook County during the 20-year period.

...[T]he relative magnitude of the rates of delinquent boys in 1920 has changed relatively little since 1900. In view of this fact, the above-mentioned changes in the composition of the population in these areas are of great significance in the study of juvenile delinquency and will therefore be considered in greater detail....

The movement of the immigrant groups from the areas of the first immigrant settlement to the areas of the second and third settlement, and the succession of nationalities in the areas adjacent to the center of the city, are matters of great significance when considered in relation to the process of city growth and the distribution of juvenile delinquents. Attracted by the low rents and accessibility to employment, the newer immigrants settle in the areas adjacent to industry and commerce, force out the older immigrants, and then in turn give way to still newer immigrant groups. It is in these deteriorated areas, therefore, that the members of each nationality have been forced to make their first adjustments to the new world and to rear their children.

The rate of movement of immigrants out of the areas of first settlement depends, among other things upon the rapidity of growth of the city. In cities that are growing very slowly this movement is less marked both because there is less pressure from incoming groups and because the areas of first settlement are not seriously threatened by the invasion of industry and commerce. In Chicago, because of the vary rapid increase of the population through immigration and the tremendous industrial development, the older groups have been under constant pressure to move out of the areas of first settlement to make way for the newer immigrant groups.

The result has been a continuous change in the composition of the population in the areas of first immigrant settlement, which have been shown to be the areas of highest delinquency rates....

The changes in the distribution of racial and national groups both in the population and the delinquents...are paralleled by very similar changes in all of the areas of first immigrant settlement, as well as those that have been invaded by the Negroes. An analysis of the changes in all of the areas in which there has been a succession of foreign groups reveals that, with few exceptions, the older immigrant groups have replaced the newer immigrant groups, and that these changes have been accompanied by little variation in the rates of delinquents.

Changes in the Nationality Distribution Among Juvenile Court Delinquents for the City as a Whole

The movement of the German, Irish, English, and Scandinavian groups out of the areas of first settlement into the areas of second settlement has been paralleled by a corresponding decrease in the percentage of delinquent boys in these nationalities in the Cook County Juvenile Court. Likewise, the increase of Italians, Polish, Russians, Lithuanians, and Negroes in the areas of first settlement has been paralleled by an increase in the percentage of boys in these groups in the juvenile court. This fact is indicated both in the nationality classification of the delinquents in our two series of court delinquents and in the nationality classification published in the annual reports of the juvenile court.[5] For the purpose of making the present comparisons, the classifications in the reports of the court will be used, since they give the nationality distribution by single years for a period of 30 years. The nationality distribution of the delinquents in the juvenile court, as shown by the annual reports, is presented for each fifth year from 1900 to 1930 in Table 24.1.

Only the cases classified by nationality or race were included in the computations of the percentages. This table indicates that of the 1,035 cases of male delinquents brought to the court during 1900, the German and Irish groups showed the highest percentage, the former 20.4 and the latter 18.7. The percentages in these two groups had decreased to 1.9 and 1.3, respectively, by 1930. Of equal consistency, but opposite in tendency, is the increase in the percentage of Italians and Poles, the former having increased from 5.1 percent in 1900 to 11.7 percent in 1930, and the latter from 15.1 percent to 21.0 percent in 1930.

While these changes were taking place in the foreign group, the percentage of cases in the white

Table 24.1 Nationality of Delinquent Boys Based on the Nativity of Their Parents Expressed in Percentages of the Total Number of Cases Classified by Race and Nationality for Each Fifth Year Since 1900

Nationality	1900	1905	1910	1915	1920	1925	1930
Total number of cases classified	1,035	1,828	1,123	2,215	1,829	1,910	2,307
American:							
White	16.0	19.0	16.5	16.5	23.0	21.7	19.5
Negro	4.7	5.1	5.5	6.2	9.9	17.1	21.7
German	20.4	18.5	15.5	11.0	6.3	3.5	1.9
Irish	18.7	15.4	12.3	10.7	6.1	3.1	1.3
Italian	5.1	8.3	7.9	10.1	12.7	12.8	11.7
Polish	15.1	15.7	18.6	22.1	24.5	21.9	21.0
English-Scotch	3.4	3.0	2.5	2.6	.9	.7	.6
Scandinavian	3.8	5.6	2.9	2.8	2.3	.5	.8
Austrian	.1	.3	.9	1.3	.8	2.2	1.7
Lithuanian	.1	.3	1.1	2.9	2.2	3.9	3.8
Czechoslovakian	4.6	4.3	5.5	3.0	2.2	2.8	4.2
All others	8.0	4.5	11.8	10.8	9.1	9.8	11.8
Total	100.0	100.0	100.0	100.0	100.0	100.0	100.0

American group show relatively little increase. The percentage of American Negroes, on the other hand, increased from 4.7 percent in 1900 to 9.9 percent in 1920, and to 21.7 percent in 1930.

In order to interpret the changes in the percentage of juvenile court delinquents among the various racial and national groups, it is necessary to take into consideration the changes in the proportion of each group in the total population of the city. The extent to which population change is responsible for the decrease in the percentage of the early immigrant groups among the juvenile court delinquents, may be illustrated by a special analysis of the German and Irish groups.

When the percentages of persons of Irish and German nativity in the total population in 1900 and 1920 were compared with the percentages of these nationalities in the juvenile court delinquents for the same years, it was found that the relative decrease in these two nationalities in the total population accounted for 51.8 percent of the decrease in the Irish, and 43.3 percent of the decrease in the German group. In other words, it was found that there was a 48.3 percent decrease in the relative number of delinquents of Irish parentage, and 56.7 decrease in the relative number of delinquents of German parentage in the juvenile court cases after corrections were made for the changes in the ratio of each of these nationalities to the total population. On the other hand, calculations revealed that the increase in the percentages of Italian and Polish delinquents in the juvenile court was greater than the increase in the proportion of these groups in the total population.

The above facts indicate that without question the decrease from 1900 to 1920 in the proportion of the German and Irish in the delinquent group is much greater than the decrease in the proportion of these groups in the total population of the city. It is probable that this disproportionate decrease in the percentage of German and Irish delinquents in the juvenile court from 1900 to 1920 is due to the movement of these groups out of the area of first immigrant settlement and of high rates of delinquents during the 20-year period.

It is important to observe that the descendants of the early immigrant groups that have moved out of the areas of highest rates are not appearing in the juvenile court in great numbers. This fact is clearly indicated in the German and Irish groups when the probable number of their descendants in the population is considered. For while the absolute number of persons in Chicago of German and Irish nativity decreased between 1900 and 1920, the actual number of persons of German and Irish nationality, when defined to include the members of the third and fourth generations, probably grew through natural increase at a rate almost in proportion to the growth of the population of the city as a whole. If these descendants were appearing in the juvenile court in the same proportion in 1920 as did the children of German and Irish parentage in 1900, the percentage of delinquents among the white Americans would have increased between 1900 and 1920 in proportion to the decrease of the German and Irish group, since the descendants of these groups would be classified as Americans in 1920. Table 24.1 shows that, while the percentage of Germans and Irish decreased from almost 40 percent of the total number of delinquents in 1900 to 3.2 percent in 1930, the percentage of white Americans failed to show any consistent increase. This indicates that the rate of delinquency among the descendants of the German and Irish in 1920 was relatively insignificant as compared with the rate of delinquents in these two groups when they resided in the high-rate areas near the center of this city.

This same difference is indicated by the aforementioned fact that the rate of delinquents is more than 70 percent greater among the boys of foreign-born parents. All of the children of immigrants would be included in the first group, while all of the descendants after the second generation would be included in the latter.

The decrease in the rates of delinquents in the nationality groups that moved out of the areas of high rates during the period is established quite apart from the nationality classification of cases in the juvenile court by the fact that the rates of delinquents in the areas of second and third settlement are much lower than the rates in the areas of first settlement....

It has been pointed out in this section that there has been a succession of nationalities in the areas of the first settlement near the central business district and the important industrial centers in Chicago, and that while this change was taking place there were few significant changes in the relative rates of delinquents in the same areas. In other words, the composition of the population changed; the relative rates of delinquents remained unchanged.

It was found also that as the older immigrant group moved out of the areas of first settlement there was a decrease in the percentage of these nationalities among the cases in the juvenile court. This fact, which suggests that the high rate of delinquents in these national groups was at least in part due to residence in these areas of high rates, is substantiated by the fact that the rates of delinquents are much lower in the areas of second and third immigrant settlement.

Similarly, it was pointed out in this section that for a long period of time there had been a disproportionate number of delinquents of foreign-born parents in the juvenile court in Chicago. This fact has attracted attention to the foreign-born population in the study of delinquency. One reason for this disproportion, as suggested by these materials, is that a disproportionate percentage of the foreign-born live in the areas of high rates of delinquents. These high rates of delinquents can not be explained in terms of population, for as has been shown in this section the population has changed in many of these areas while the rates of delinquents remained relatively unchanged. All of this material, therefore, suggests, the need for further analysis of the neighborhood situation in these areas of high rates of delinquents.

Disintegration of Neighborhood Organization

Thus far in this chapter we have presented certain formal indices of community organization and disorganization which serve to differentiate the areas of high and low rates of delinquents. When considered collectively these indices imply certain important variations in the community life in the areas adjacent to the central business district and the large industrial centers as compared to the outlying residential neighborhoods. They suggest that certain areas are characterized by great mobility, change, disintegration of the social structure and lack of stability, while in other areas, the neighborhood is more settled, stable, and highly integrated. Decreasing population implies that the security of the neighborhood is threatened; poverty implies bad housing, lack of sanitation, and a dearth of facilities for maintaining adequate neighborhood agencies and institutions; while the presence of a high percentage of foreign-born populations, comprising many divergent cultures and types of background, implies a confusion of moral standards and lack of social solidarity. Where such conditions prevail, the community is rendered relatively ineffective as an agency of control. There is little effective public opinion, community spirit, and collective effort to meet the local problems of the neighborhood.

…Under the disintegrative forces of city life many of the traditional institutions of the community are weakened or destroyed. While this tendency is to be observed in the city as a whole, it is particularly accentuated in certain sections of the city. It is obvious that there are tremendous differences between sections of the city in the extent to which the community is vital and effective and concerns itself with the solution of its local problems.

As suggested by Thomas, an effective community life is dependent upon the solidarity and stability of the social organization. In the areas close to the central business district, and to a less extent in the areas close to industrial developments, the neighborhood organization tends to disintegrate. For in these areas the mobility of population is so great that there is little opportunity for the development of common attitudes and interests. This fact is suggested by the difference between the percentage of families owning their homes in the areas close to the center of the city and in the outlying districts. For example, along Radial II the percentages of home ownership by square-mile areas from the Loop outward show the following variation: 6, 13, 25, 34, 44, 47, and 60. The low percentage of home ownership in the areas near the center of the city indicates, among other things, that there is not sufficient permanence to encourage the buying of homes, while the high percentage in the outlying areas indicates that a much larger proportion of the families are settled and permanently established.

It is a significant fact that many of the traditional institutions of society disintegrate under the influence of the rapidly changing conditions that prevail in the deteriorated areas of the large city.... If the institution attempts to perpetuate itself in the area, it becomes dependent upon subsidy or endowments from persons or organizations outside of the local area; it ceases to be a spontaneous and self-supporting agency of the neighborhood life....

The inability of the inhabitants of the "slum" to act collectively with reference to their local problems has long been recognized. For example, the settlement movement was a response to the recognized need for establishing in these disintegrated sections of the city, neighborhood agencies and institutions.

A study of the distribution of social settlements and similar agencies in Chicago in 1925 revealed that of the 59 such institutions, 19 or 32.2 percent were located within two miles of the heart of the Loop, and a total of 50 or 84.8 percent were located within four miles of the center of the central business district. Of the remaining eight, three were in the Negro district and two were in South Chicago. Presumably, the concentration of settlements indicate those areas in which the local neighborhood organization is least effective and where there is the greatest need for assistance from other communities.

Apart from the social institutions which are supported and controlled by persons from more prosperous communities, there are few agencies in delinquency areas for dealing with the problems of delinquent behavior. The absence of common community ideals and standards prevents cooperative social action either to prevent or suppress delinquency. In some of the more stable integrated communities in the outlying districts any increase in the amount of delinquency is responded to by mass meetings and other indications of collective action among women's clubs, business men's organizations, church societies, and fraternal orders. On the other hand there is little such spontaneous and concerted action on the part of the inhabitants of the areas of high rates of delinquents to deal with the delinquent.

The neighborhood disorganization in the areas outside of the central business district is probably common to all rapidly growing American cities. However, in northern industrial cities, such as Chicago, the disorganization is intensified by the fact that the population in these areas is made up largely of foreign immigrants who are making their first adjustment to the complex life of the modern city. This adjustment involves profound and far-reaching modification of the whole structure of the cultural organization of the immigrant group....

The problem of assimilation among them differs as regards the extent to which national attitudes are involved and the extent to which cultural backgrounds differ from our own; it involves a more or less complete change from a stable rural life to a rapidly changing and complex industrial urban community. In this situation, as Thomas and Znaniecki point out, demoralization takes place in both the first and the second generation:

> In order to reorganize his life on a new basis he needs a primary group as strong and coherent as the one he left in the old country. The Polish-American society gives him a few new schemes of life, but not enough to cover all of his activities. A certain lowering of his moral level is thus inevitable. Though it does not always lead to active demoralization, to anti-social behavior, it manifests itself at least in what we may call passive demoralization, a partial or a general weakening of social interests, a growing narrowness or shallowness of the individual's social life.
>
> Of course the second generation, unless brought in direct and continuous contact with the better aspects of American life than those with which the immigrant community is usually acquainted, degenerates further still, both because the parents have less to give than they had received themselves in the line of social principles and emotions, and because the children brought up in American cities have more freedom and less respect for their parents. The second generation is better adapted intellectually to the practical conditions of American life, but their moral horizon grows still narrower on the average

and their social interests still shallower. One might expect to find fewer cases of active demoralization of antisocial behavior, than in the first generation, which has to pass through the crisis of adaptation to new conditions. And yet it is a well-known fact that even the number of crimes is proportionately much larger among the children of immigrants than among the immigrants themselves.[6]

The disorganization among the foreign immigrants is paralleled by a similar disorganization among the Negroes. More than one-half of the Negroes in Chicago in 1920 were born outside of the State of Illinois; probably most of them in the rural districts in the Southern States. In any event, like the peasants from Europe, they are largely unaccustomed to the life in a large urban community.

But in one respect the background of the Negro is different from that of the foreign immigrant as described by Thomas and Znaniecki. Unlike the immigrant, the Negro has relatively few stabilizing traditions extending back over "hundreds of years." Neither does he have as a background a stable community organization which has remained unchanged over a long period of time. His institutions are very new and inadequately developed. Consequently they break down completely as agencies of social control in the process of adjustment to the complex life on an urban community. This social disorganization is accompanied by a large amount of personal disorganization and demoralization among Negro adults as well as among Negro children.[7]

No doubt this absence of stabilizing tradition in the Negro group is a very important factor underlying the high rates of delinquents already noted among Negro boys. As a whole their situation is much less constructive than that of the children of foreign immigrants, both because there is less tradition in their own group, and because a larger proportion of them live in areas of high rates of delinquents. These conditions are probably important factors in determining the disproportionate number of Negro delinquents in the juvenile court.

Adult Offenders

In concluding this study of the formal characteristics of the delinquency areas of Chicago, it is important to point out that these areas also show the greatest concentration and highest rates of adult offenders.

In the absence of an effective neighborhood organization delinquency gains a foothold in the disorganized areas, despite the efforts of settlements and other social agencies to combat and suppress it. In this situation large numbers of the juvenile delinquents from these areas continue in adult crime....

Summary

In this chapter an attempt has been made to locate and characterize the areas which have been differentiated in the process of the growth of the city and to indicate the variation in the rate of juvenile delinquents among these areas. Particular effort has been made to show the differences between the areas with the highest rates and those with the lowest rates of delinquents. These types of areas represent the two extremes of a continuum between which there are areas with all the intermediate grades of variation.

It was found that the areas of high rates of delinquents are adjacent to the central business district and the major industrial developments. Generally speaking, these areas were found to be characterized by physical deterioration, decreasing population, high rates of dependency, high percentage of foreign-born and Negro population, and high rates of adult offenders.

One of the most significant findings in this part of the study is the fact that, while the relative rates of delinquents in these high-rate areas remained more or less constant over a period of 20 years, the nationality composition of the population changed almost completely in the interval. As the older national groups moved out of these areas of first immigrant settlement, the percentage of juvenile delinquents in these groups showed a consistent decrease.

It was indicated, also, that the areas of high rates of delinquents are characterized by marked disintegration of the traditional institutions and neighborhood organization. In this type of area, the community fails to function effectively as an agency of social control....

Discussion Questions

1. What does "social disorganization" mean? According to Shaw and McKay, why is it important for the study of crime and delinquency?

2. Why do socially disorganized areas remain disorganized over time? Why does the zone of transition have the highest rates of crime and delinquency regardless of the nativity or race/ethnicity of the group living there? Based on this information, what conclusion do Shaw and McKay make concerning the importance of nativity and race/ethnicity for explaining crime and delinquency rates?

3. What are some of the characteristics, identified by Shaw and McKay, of the zone of transition? Are these characteristics directly related to crime and delinquency rates or do they reflect the social and economic circumstances of the neighborhood's residents? What are the implications of the characteristics of the zone of transition for developing strong social controls?

Notes

1. Park, R. E.: "Human Behavior in Urban Environment;" in *The City*, by R. E. Park, E. W. Burgess et al., Chicago, the University of Chicago Press, 1925, pp. 4-6.

2. Burgess, E. W.: *Urban Areas in Chicago: An Experiment in Social Science Research.* Edited by T. V. Smith and L. D. White, Chicago, University of Chicago Press, 1929, pp. 114-117.

3. This series of dependency cases was secured by Prof. Earle Fisk Young and Faye B. Karpf under the direction of Prof. Robert E. Park.

4. The total aged 10 to 16 white male population with foreign-born fathers for the city was secured by combining the native white of foreign parentage, the foreign born, and one-half of the native white of mixed parentage (the latter division was made on the assumption that one-half of the parents were native born and one-half foreign born). While this population is available for the city as a whole it could not be secured for local areas within the city.

5. In the Cook County Juvenile Court Reports through 1920 the delinquents were classified on the basis of the nationality of the parents. It is impossible to ascertain exactly the extent to which nationality represents nativity. Probably in some instances foreign-born parents give their nationality as American, while others who were native born give as their nationality the country from which their ancestors came. In our study of the court records we attempted to make all classification on the basis of the nativity of the father. When our results are compared with the published records of the court the percentage distribution for nationalities are quite similar.

6. Thomas, William I., and Znaniecki, Florian: *The Polish Peasant in Europe and America.* New York, Alfred A. Knopf, 1927, Vol. II, p. 1650.

7. This point of view is quite fully developed by Prof. E. Franklin Frazier, of Fisk University, in an excellent study. This study was prepared as a doctor's dissertation in the Department of Sociology at the University of Chicago and is as yet unpublished.

CHAPTER 25

Routine Activity Theory

Lawrence E. Cohen ■ Marcus Felson

The routine activity approach explains criminal victimization as the convergence of a motivated offender, a suitable target, and the lack of a capable guardian. Contrary to typical criminological theories of victimization, the routine activity approach assumes the existence of motivated offenders and instead focuses on the importance of suitable targets and capable guardians. In short, routine activities theory posits that a crime can only occur if a motivated offender is aware of a suitable target that is lacking proper guardianship. Crime, then, is made possible primarily by opportunity.

In the following selection, Cohen and Felson suggest that changes in everyday routine activities (increased mobility and time spent away from home) by the average American after World War II led to a significant expansion of criminal opportunities. Given the assumed existence of motivated offenders, Cohen and Felson argue that increased opportunities are the only element necessary to cause an increase in crime rates. Because the theory states that changes in a single factor (motivated offender, suitable target, lack of capable guardian) can result in subsequent changes in victimization, Cohen and Felson explain the heightened crime rates following World War II as the product of increased numbers of suitable targets with decreased levels of guardianship. Therefore, the explanatory burden need

not focus on the offender, but instead on societal changes in routine daily activities.

We argue that structural changes in routine activity patterns can influence crime rates by affecting the convergence in space and time of the three minimal elements of direct-contact predatory violations: (1) motivated offenders, (2) suitable targets, and (3) the absence of capable guardians against a violation. We further argue that the lack of any one of these elements is sufficient to prevent the successful completion of a direct-contact predatory crime, and that the convergence in time and space of suitable targets and the absence of capable guardians may even lead to large increases in crime rates without necessarily requiring any increase in the structural conditions that motivate individuals to engage in crime. That is, if the proportion of motivated offenders or even suitable targets were to remain stable in a community, changes in routine activities could nonetheless alter the likelihood of their convergence in space and time, thereby creating more opportunities for crimes to occur. Control therefore becomes critical. If controls through routine activities were to decrease, illegal predatory activities could then be likely to increase....

Unlike many criminological inquiries, we do not examine why individuals or groups are inclined criminally, but rather we take criminal inclination as given and examine the manner in which the spatiotemporal organization of social activities helps people to translate their criminal inclinations into action. Criminal violations are treated here as routine activities which share many attributes of, and are interdependent with, other routine activities....

The Minimal Elements of Direct-Contact Predatory Violations

As we previously stated, despite their great diversity, direct-contact predatory violations share some important requirements which facilitate analysis of their structure. Each successfully completed violation minimally requires an *offender* with both criminal inclinations and the ability to carry out those inclinations, a person or object providing a *suitable target* for the offender, and *absence of guardians* capable of preventing violations. We emphasize that the lack of any one of these elements normally is sufficient to prevent such violations from occurring. Though guardianship is implicit in everyday life, it usually is marked by the absence of violations, hence it is easy to overlook. While police action is analyzed widely, guardianship by ordinary citizens of one another and property as they go about routine activities may be one of the most neglected elements in sociological research on crime, especially since it links seemingly unrelated social roles and relationships to the occurrence or absence of illegal acts.

The conjunction of these minimal elements can be used to assess how social structure may affect the tempo of each type of violation. That is, the probability that a violation will occur at any specific time and place might be taken as a function of the convergence of likely offenders and suitable targets in the absence of capable guardians. Through consideration of how trends and fluctuations in social conditions affect the frequency of this convergence of criminogenic circumstances, an explanation of temporal trends in crime rates can be constructed....

The Ecological Nature of Illegal Acts

Since illegal activities must feed upon other activities, the spatial and temporal structure of routine legal activities should play an important role in determining the location, type and quantity of illegal acts occurring in a given community or society. Moreover, one can analyze how the structure of community organization as well as the level of technology in a society provide the circumstances under which crime can thrive. For example, technology and organization affect the capacity of persons with criminal inclinations to overcome their targets, as well as affecting the ability of guardians to contend with potential offenders by using whatever protective tools, weapons and skills they have at their disposal. Many technological advances designed for legitimate purposes—including the automobile, small power tools, hunting weapons, highways, telephones, etc.—may enable offenders to carry out their own work more effectively or may assist people in protecting their own or someone else's person or property.

Not only do routine legitimate activities often provide the wherewithal to commit offenses or to guard against others who do so, but they also provide offenders with suitable targets. Target suitability is likely to reflect such things as value (i.e., the material or symbolic desirability of a personal or property target for offenders), physical visibility, access, and the inertia of a target against illegal treatment by offenders (including the weight, size, and attached or locked features of property inhibiting its illegal removal and the physical capacity of personal victims to resist attackers with or without weapons). Routine production activities probably affect the suitability of consumer goods for illegal removal by determining their value and weight. Daily activities may affect the location of property and personal targets in visible and accessible places at particular times. These activities also may cause people to have on hand objects that can be used as weapons for criminal acts or self-protection or to be preoccupied with tasks which reduce their capacity to discourage or resist offenders.

While little is known about conditions that affect the convergence of potential offenders, targets and guardians, this is a potentially rich source of propositions about crime rates. For example, daily work activities separate many people from those they trust and the property they value. Routine activities also bring together at various times of day or night persons of different background, sometimes in the presence of facilities, tools or weapons which influence the commission or avoidance of illegal acts. Hence, the timing of work, schooling and leisure may be of central importance for explaining crime rates....

Microlevel Assumptions of the Routine Activity Approach

The theoretical approach taken here specifies that crime rate trends in the post-World War II United States are related to patterns of what we have called routine activities. We define these as any recurrent and prevalent activities which provide for basic population and individual needs, whatever their biological or cultural origins. Thus routine activities would include formalized work, as well as the provision of standard food, shelter, sexual outlet, leisure, social interaction, learning and child-rearing. These activities may go well beyond the minimal levels needed to prevent a population's extinction, so long as their prevalence and recurrence makes them a part of everyday life.

Routine activities may occur (1) at home, (2) in jobs away from home, and (3) in other activities away from home. The latter may involve primarily household members or others. We shall argue that, since World War II, the United States has experienced a major shift of routine activities away from the first category into the remaining ones, especially those nonhousehold activities involving nonhousehold members. In particular, we shall argue that this shift in the structure of routine activities increases the probability that motivated offenders will converge in space and time with suitable targets in the absence of capable guardians, hence contributing to significant increases in the points in the direct-contact predatory crime rates over these years.

If the routine activity approach is valid, then we should expect to find evidence for a number of empirical relationships regarding the nature and distribution of predatory violations. For example, we would expect routine activities performed within or near the home and among family or other primary groups to entail lower risk of criminal victimization because they enhance guardianship capabilities. We should also expect that routine daily activities affect the location of property and personal targets in visible and accessible places at particular times, thereby influencing their risk of victimization. Furthermore, by determining their size and weight and in some cases their value, routine production activities should affect the suitability of consumer goods for illegal removal. Finally, if the routine activity approach is useful for explaining the paradox presented earlier, we should find that the circulation of people and property, the size and weight of consumer items etc., will parallel changes in crime rate trends for the post-World War II United States.

The veracity of the routine activity approach can be assessed by analyses of both microlevel and macrolevel interdependencies of human activities. While consistency at the former level may appear noncontroversial, or even obvious, one nonetheless needs to show that the approach does not contradict existing data before proceeding to investigate the latter level.

Empirical Assessment

Circumstances and Location of Offenses

The routine activity approach specifies that household and family activities entail lower risk of criminal victimization than nonhousehold-nonfamily activities, despite the problems in measuring the former.

National estimates from large-scale government victimization surveys in 1973 and 1974 support this generalization (see methodological information in Hindelang et al., 1976: Appendix 6). Table 25.1 presents several incident-victimization rates per 100,000 population ages 12 and older. Clearly, the rates in Panels A and B are far lower at or near home than elsewhere and far lower among relatives than others. The data indicate that risk of victimization varies directly with social distance between offender and victim. Panel C of this table indicates, furthermore, that risk of lone victimization far exceeds the risk of victimization for groups. These relationships are strengthened by considering time budget evidence that, on the

Table 25.1 Offense Analysis Trends for Robbery, Burglary, Larceny and Murder; United States, 1960–1975

A. ROBBERIES[a]	1960	1965	1970	
Highway Robbery	52.6	57.0	59.8	
Residential Robbery	8.0	10.1	13.1	
Commercial Robbery	39.4	32.9	27.1	
Totals	100.0	100.0	100.0	
B. BURGLARIES	**1960**	**1965**	**1970**	**1975**
Residential	15.6	24.5	31.7	33.2
Residential Nightime	24.4	25.2	25.8	30.5
Commercial	60.0	50.2	42.5	36.3
Totals	100.0	99.9	100.0	100.0
C. LARCENIES	**1960**	**1965**	**1970**	**1975**
Shoplifting	6.0	7.8	9.2	11.3
Other	94.0	92.2	90.8	88.7
Totals	100.0	100.0	100.0	100.0
D. MURDERS	**1963**	**1965**	**1970**	**1975**
Relative Killings	31.0	31.0	23.3	22.4
Romance, Arguments[b]	51.0	48.0	47.9	45.2
Felon Types[c]	17.0	21.0	28.8	32.4
Totals	100.0	100.0	100.0	100.0

Source: Offense Analysis from UCR, various years.
[a]Excluding miscellaneous robberies. The 1975 distribution omitted due to apparent instability of post-1970 data.
[b]Includes romantic triangles, lovers' quarrels, and arguments.
[c]Includes both known and suspected felon acts.

average, Americans spend 16.26 hours per day at home, 1.38 hours on streets, in parks, etc., and 6.36 hours in other places (Szalai, 1972:795). Panel D of Table 25.1 presents our estimates of victimization per billion person-hours spent in such locations. For example, personal larceny rates (with contact) are 350 times higher at the hands of strangers in streets than at the hands of nonstrangers at home. Separate computations from 1973 victimization data (USDJ, 1976: Table 48) indicate that there were two motor vehicle thefts per million

vehicle-hours parked at or near home, 55 per million vehicle-hours in streets, parks, playgrounds, school grounds or parking lots, and 12 per million vehicle-hours elsewhere. While the direction of these relationships is not surprising, their magnitudes should be noted. It appears that risk of criminal victimization varies dramatically among the circumstances and locations in which people place themselves and their property.

Target Suitability

Another assumption of the routine activity approach is that target suitability influences the occurrence of direct-contact predatory violations. Though we lack data to disaggregate all major components of target suitability (i.e., value, visibility, accessibility and inertia), together they imply that expensive and movable durables, such as vehicles and electronic appliances, have the highest risk of illegal removal.

As a specific case in point, we compared the 1975 composition of stolen property reported in the Uniform Crime Report (FBI, 1976: Tables 26-7) with national data on personal consumer expenditures for goods (CEA, 1976: Tables 13-16) and to appliance industry estimates of the value of shipments the same year (*Merchandising Week*, 1976). We calculated that $26.44 in motor vehicles and parts were stolen for each $100 of these goods consumed in 1975, while $6.81 worth of electronic appliances were stolen per $100 consumed. Though these estimates are subject to error in citizen and police estimation, what is important here is their size relative to other rates. For example, only 8¢ worth of nondurables and 12¢ worth of furniture and nonelectronic household durables were stolen per $100 of each category consumed, the motor vehicle risk being, respectively, 330 and 220 times as great. Though we lack data on the "stocks" of goods subject to risk, these "flow" data clearly support our assumption that vehicles and electronic appliances are greatly overrepresented in thefts.

The 1976 Buying Guide issue of *Consumer Reports* (1975) indicates why electronic appliances are an excellent retail value for a thief. For example, a Panasonic car tape player is worth $30 per lb., and a Phillips phonograph cartridge is valued at over $5,000 per lb., while large appliances such as refrigerators and washing machines are only worth $1 to $3 per lb. Not surprisingly, burglary data for the District of Columbia in 1969 (Scarr, 1972: Table 9) indicate that home entertainment items alone constituted nearly four times as many stolen items as clothing, food, drugs, liquor, and tobacco combined and nearly eight times as many stolen items as office supplies and equipment. In addition, 69% of national thefts classified in 1975 (FBI, 1976: Tables 1, 26) involve automobiles, their parts or accessories, and thefts from automobiles or thefts of bicycles. Yet radio and television sets plus electronic components and accessories totaled only 0.10% of the total truckload tonnage terminated in 1973 by intercity motor carriers, while passenger cars, motor vehicle parts and accessories, motorcycles, bicycles, and their parts, totaled only 5.5% of the 410 million truckload tons terminated (ICC, 1974). Clearly, portable and movable durables are reported stolen in great disproportion to their share of the value and weight of goods circulating in the United States.

Family Activities and Crime Rates

One would expect that persons living in single-adult households and those employed outside the home are less obligated to confine their time to family activities within households. From a routine activity perspective, these persons and their households should have higher rates of predatory criminal victimization. We also expect that adolescents and young adults who are perhaps more likely to engage in peer group activities rather than family activities will have higher rates of criminal victimization. Finally, married persons should have lower rates than others.... We note that victimization rates appear to be related inversely to age and are lower for persons in "less active" statuses (e.g., keeping house, unable to work, retired) and persons in intact marriages. A notable exception is... where persons unable to work appear more likely to be victimized by rape, robbery and personal larceny with contact than are other "inactive persons." Unemployed persons also have unusually high rates of victimization. However, these rates

are consistent with the routine activity approach offered here: the high rates of victimization suffered by the unemployed may reflect their residential proximity to high concentrations of potential offenders as well as their age and racial composition, while handicapped persons have high risk of personal victimization because they are less able to resist motivated offenders. Nonetheless, persons who keep house have noticeably lower rates of victimization than those who are employed, unemployed, in school or in the armed forces....

Burglary and robbery victimization rates are about twice as high for persons living in single-adult households as for other persons in each age group examined. Other victimization data (USDJ, 1976: Table 21) indicate that, while household victimization rates tend to vary directly with household size, larger households have lower rates per person. For example, the total household victimization rates (including burglary, household larceny, and motor vehicle theft) per 1,000 households were 168 for single-person households and 326 for households containing six or more persons. Hence, six people distributed over six single-person households experience an average of 1,008 household victimizations, more than three times as many as one six-person household. Moreover, age of household head has a strong relationship to a household's victimization rate for these crimes. For households headed by persons under 20, the motor vehicle theft rate is nine times as high, and the burglary and household larceny rates four times as high as those for households headed by persons 65 and over (USDJ, 1976: Table 9).

While the data presented in this section were not collected originally for the purpose of testing the routine activity approach, our efforts to rework them for these purposes have proven fruitful. The routine activity approach is consistent with the data examined and, in addition, helps to accommodate within a rather simple and coherent analytical framework certain findings which, though not necessarily new, might otherwise be attributed only "descriptive" significance. In the next section, we examine macrosocial trends as they relate to trends in crime rates.

Changing Trends in Routine Activity Structure and Parallel Trends in Crime Rates

The main thesis presented here is that the dramatic increase in the reported crime rates in the U.S. since 1960 is linked to changes in the routine activity structure of American society and to a corresponding increase in target suitability and decrease in guardian presence. If such a thesis has validity, then we should be able to identify these social trends and show how they relate to predatory criminal victimization rates.

Trends in Human Activity Patterns

The decade 1960–1970 experienced noteworthy trends in the activities of the American population. For example, the percent of the population consisting of female college students increased 118% (USBC, 1975: Table 225). Married female labor force participant rates increased 31% (USBC, 1975: Table 563), while the percent of the population living as primary individuals increased by 34% (USBC, 1975: Table 51; see also Kobrin, 1976). We gain some further insight into changing routine activity patterns by comparing hourly data for 1960 and 1971 on households *unattended* by persons ages 14 or over when U.S. census interviewers first called…. These data suggest that the proportion of households unattended at 8 A.M. increased by almost half between 1960 and 1971. One also finds increases in rates of out-of-town travel, which provides greater opportunity for both daytime and nighttime burglary of residences. Between 1960 and 1970, there was a 72% increase in state and national park visits per capita (USBC, 1975), an 144% increase in the percent of plant workers eligible for three weeks vacation (BLS, 1975: Table 116), and an 184% increase in overseas travellers per 100,000 population (USBC, 1975: Table 366). The National Travel Survey, conducted as part of the U.S. Census Bureau's Census of Transportation, confirms the general trends, tallying an 81% increase in the number of vacations taken by Americans from 1967 to 1972, a five-year period (USBC, 1973a: Introduction).

The dispersion of activities away from households appears to be a major recent social change. Although this decade also experienced an important 31% increase in the percent of the population ages 15–24, age structure change was only one of many social trends occurring during the period, especially trends in the circulation of people and property in American society.

The importance of the changing activity structure is underscored by taking a brief look at demographic changes between the years 1970 and 1975, a period of continuing crime rate increments. Most of the recent changes in age structure relevant to crime rates already had occurred by 1970; indeed, the proportion of the population ages 15–24 increased by only 6% between 1970 and 1975, compared with a 15% increase during the five years 1965 to 1970. On the other hand, major changes in the structure of routine activities continued during these years. For example, in only five years, the estimated proportion of the population consisting of husband-present, married women in the labor force households increased by 11%, while the estimated number of non-husband-wife households per 100,000 population increased from 9,150 to 11,420, a 25% increase (USBC, 1976: Tables 50, 276, USBC, 1970–1975). At the same time, the percent of population enrolled in higher education increased 16% between 1970 and 1975.

Related Property Trends and Their Relation to Human Activity Patterns

Many of the activity trends mentioned above normally involve significant investments in durable goods. For example, the dispersion of population across relatively more households (especially non-husband-wife households) enlarges the market for durable goods such as television sets and automobiles. Women participating in the labor force and both men and women enrolled in college provide a market for automobiles. Both work and travel often involve the purchase of major movable or portable durables and their use away from home.

Considerable data are available which indicate that sales of consumer goods changed dramatically between 1960 and 1970 (as did their size and weight), hence providing more suitable property available for theft. For example, during this decade, constant-dollar personal consumer expenditures in the United States for motor vehicles and parts increased by 71%, while constant-dollar expenditures for other durables increased by 105% (calculated from CEA, 1976: Table B-16). In addition, electronic household appliances and small household shipments increased from 56.2 to 119.7 million units (*Electrical Merchandising Week*, 1964; *Merchandising Week*, 1973). During the same decade, appliance imports increased in value by 681% (USBC, 1975: Table 1368).

This same period appears to have spawned a revolution in small durable product design which further feeds the opportunity for crime to occur. Relevant data from the 1960 and 1970 Sears catalogs on the weight of many consumer durable goods were examined. Sears is the nation's largest retailer and its policy of purchasing and relabeling standard manufactured goods makes its catalogs a good source of data on widely merchandised consumer goods. The lightest television listed for sale in 1960 weighed 38 lbs., compared with 15 lbs. for 1970. Thus, the lightest televisions were 2½ times as heavy in 1960 as 1970. Similar trends are observed for dozens of other goods listed in the Sears catalog. Data from *Consumer Reports Buying Guide*, published in December of 1959 and 1969, show similar changes for radios, record players, slide projectors, tape recorders, televisions, toasters and many other goods. Hence, major declines in weight between 1960 and 1970 were quite significant for these and other goods, which suggests that the consumer goods market may be producing many more targets suitable for theft. In general, one finds rapid growth in property suitable for illegal removal and in household and individual exposure to attack during the years 1960–1975.

Related Trends in Business Establishments

Of course, as households and individuals increased their ownership of small durables, businesses also increased the value of the merchandise which they transport and sell as well as the money involved in these transactions. Yet the Census of Business conducted in 1958, 1963, 1967, and 1972 indicate that the number of wholesale, retail, service, and public warehouse establishments (including establishments owned by large organizations) was a nearly constant ratio of one for every 16 persons in the United States. Since more goods and money were distributed over a relatively fixed number of business establishments, the tempo of business activity per establishment apparently was increasing. At the same time, the percent of the population employed as sales clerks or salesmen in retail trade declined from 1.48% to 1.27% between 1960 and 1970, a 14.7% decline (USBC, 1975: Table 589).

Though both business and personal property increased, the changing pace of activities appears to have exposed the latter to greater relative risk of attack, whether at home or elsewhere, due to the dispersion of goods among many more households, while concentrating goods in business establishments. However, merchandise in retail establishments with heavy volume and few employees to guard it probably is exposed to major increments in risk of illegal removal than is most other business property.

Composition of Crime Trends

If these changes in the circulation of people and property are in fact related to crime trends, the *composition* of the latter should reflect this. We expect relatively greater increases in personal and household victimization as compared with most business victimizations, while shoplifting should increase more rapidly than other types of thefts from businesses. We expect personal offenses at the hands of strangers to manifest greater increases than such offenses at the hands of nonstrangers. Finally, residential burglary rates should increase more in daytime than nighttime.

The available time series on the composition of offenses confirm these expectations. For example, Table 25.1 shows that commercial burglaries declined from 60% to 36% of the total, while daytime residential burglaries increased from 16% to 33%. Unlike the other crimes against business, shoplifting increased its share. Though we lack trend data on the circumstances of other violent offenses, murder data confirm our expectations. Between 1963 and 1975, felon-type murders increased from 17% to 32% of the total. Compared with a 47% increase in the rate of relative killings in this period, we calculated a 294% increase in the murder rate at the hands of known or suspected felon types.

Thus the trends in the composition of recorded crime rates appear to be highly consistent with the activity structure trends noted earlier. In the next section we apply the routine activity approach in order to model crime rate trends and social change in the post-World War II United States.

The Relationship of the Household Activity Ratio to Five Annual Official Index Crime Rates in the United States, 1947–1974

In this section, we test the hypothesis that aggregate official crime rate trends in the United States vary directly over time with the dispersion of activities away from family and household. The limitations of annual time series data do not allow construction of direct measures of changes in hourly activity patterns, or quantities, qualities and movements of exact stocks of household durable goods, but the Current Population Survey does provide related time series on labor force and household structure. From these data, we calculate annually (beginning in 1947) a household activity ratio by adding the number of married, husband-present female labor force participants (source: BLS, 1975: Table 5) to the number of non-husband-wife households (source: USBC, 1947–1976), dividing this sum by the total number of households in the U.S. (source: USBC, 1947–1976). This calculation provides an estimate of the proportion of American households in year *t* expected to be most highly exposed to risk of personal and property victimization due to the dispersion of their activities away from family and household and/or their likelihood of owning extra sets of durables subject to high risk of attack. Hence, the household activity ratio should vary directly with official index crime rates.

Our empirical goal in this section is to test this relationship, with controls for those variables which other researchers have linked empirically to crime rate trends in the United States. Since various researchers have found such trends to increase with the proportion of the population in teen and young adult years (Fox, 1976; Land and Felson, 1976; Sagi and Wellford, 1968; Weliford, 1973), we include the population ages 15–24 per 100,000 resident population as our first control variable (source: USBC, various years). Others (e.g., Brenner, 1976a; 1976b) have found unemployment rates to vary directly with official crime rates over time, although this relationship elsewhere has been shown to be empirically questionable (see Mansfield et al., 1974: 463; Cohen and Felson, 1979). Thus, as our second, control variable, we take the standard annual unemployment rate (per 100 persons ages 16 and over) as a measure of the business cycle (source: BLS, 1975).

Four of the five crime rates that we utilize here (forcible rape, aggravated assault, robbery and burglary) are taken from FBI estimates of offenses per 100,000 U.S. population (as revised and reported in OMB, 1973).... For our homicide indicator we employ the homicide mortality rate taken from the vital statistics data collected by the Bureau of the Census (various years)....

Findings
Our time-series analysis for the years 1947–1974 consistently revealed positive and statistically significant relationships between the household activity ratio and each official crime rate change....

Discussion

In our judgment many conventional theories of crime (the adequacy of which usually is evaluated by cross-sectional data, or no data at all) have difficulty accounting for the annual changes in crime rate trends in the post-World War II United States. These theories may prove useful in explaining crime trends during other periods, within specific communities, or in particular subgroups of the population. Longitudinal aggregate data for the

United States, however, indicate that the trends for many of the presumed causal variables in these theoretical structures are in a direction opposite to those hypothesized to be the causes of crime. For example, during the decade 1960-1970, the percent of the population below the low-income level declined 44% and the unemployment rate declined 186%.

Central city population as a share of the whole population declined slightly, while the percent of foreign stock declined 0.1%, etc. (see USBC, 1975: 654, 19, 39).

On the other hand, the convergence in time and space of three elements (motivated offenders, suitable targets, and the absence of capable guardians) appears useful for understanding crime rate trends. The lack of any of these elements is sufficient to prevent the occurrence of a successful direct-contact predatory crime. The convergence in time and space of suitable targets and the absence of capable guardians can lead to large increases in crime rates without any increase or change in the structural conditions that motivate individuals to engage in crime. Presumably, had the social indicators of the variables hypothesized to be the causes of crime in conventional theories changed in the direction of favoring increased crime in the post-World War II United States, the increases in crime rates likely would have been even more staggering than those which were observed. In any event, it is our belief that criminologists have underemphasized the importance of the convergence of suitable targets and the absence of capable guardians in explaining recent increases in the crime rate. Furthermore, the effects of the convergence in time and space of these elements may be multiplicative rather than additive. That is, their convergence by a fixed percentage may produce increases in crime rates far greater than that fixed percentage, demonstrating how some relatively modest social trends can contribute to some relatively large changes in crime rate trends....

Without denying the importance of factors motivating offenders to engage in crime, we have focused specific attention upon violations themselves and the prerequisites for their occurrence. However, the routine activity approach might in the future be applied to the analysis of offenders and their inclinations as well. For example, the structure of primary group activity may affect the likelihood that cultural transmission or social control of criminal inclinations will occur, while the structure of the community may affect the tempo of criminogenic peer group activity. We also may expect that circumstances favorable for carrying out violations contribute to criminal inclinations in the long run by rewarding these inclinations.

We further suggest that the routine activity framework may prove useful in explaining why the criminal justice system, the community and the family have appeared so ineffective in exerting social control since 1960. Substantial increases in the opportunity to carry out predatory violations may have undermined society's mechanisms for social control. For example, it may be difficult for institutions seeking to increase the certainty, celerity and severity of punishment to compete with structural changes resulting in vast increases in the certainty, celerity and value of rewards to be gained from illegal predatory acts.

It is ironic that the very factors which increase the opportunity to enjoy the benefits of life also may increase the opportunity for predatory violations. For example, automobiles provide freedom of movement to offenders as well as average citizens and offer vulnerable targets for theft. College enrollment, female labor force participation, urbanization, suburbanization, vacations, and new electronic durables provide various opportunities to escape the confines of the household while they increase the risk of predatory victimization. Indeed, the opportunity for predatory crime appears to be enmeshed in the opportunity structure for legitimate activities to such an extent that it might be very difficult to root out substantial amounts of crime without modifying much of our way of life. Rather than assuming that predatory crime is simply an indicator of social breakdown, one might take it as a by product of freedom and prosperity as they manifest themselves in the routine activities of everyday life.

Discussion Questions

1. According to the routine activity approach, it is possible to experience large increases in the

crime rate *without* any increase in the supply of motivated offenders. How can this be?

2. What do Cohen and Felson mean by "suitable targets" and "the absence of capable guardians"? Describe how targets and guardianship have changed in the United States since World War II.

3. Describe the "routine activities" in which you engage. How might these activities increase or decrease your chance of criminal victimization?

4. Young people and males have higher rates of criminal victimization. How might the routine activities approach explain this?

CHAPTER 26

A Control Theory of Delinquency

Travis Hirschi

Most criminological theories seek to explain why some people commit crime and others do not. Control theories, sometimes referred to as social-bond theories, ask a different question. They seek to understand why more people are not offenders. To this end, they attempt to identify factors that inhibit or prevent delinquent and criminal behavior rather than factors contributing to such behavior. Travis Hirschi has provided what is perhaps the definitive statement on control theory, which is summarized in this selection.

Hirschi's popular conceptualization of control theory posits that four social bonds to conventional institutions (e.g., schools) and people (e.g., parents) serve to explain why some individuals do not engage in delinquency and crime. The four bonds are attachment, commitment, involvement, and belief. According to his perspective, possessing strong social bonds gives the individual a "stake in conformity"; engaging in delinquency or crime involves the risk of losing those things that the individual deems valuable, such as love and respect from parents or time and effort expended in school to obtain a good job. Stronger social bonds are generally associated with no or lower involvement in crime; weak or nonexistent social bonds are associated with an increased likelihood of offending.

Reprinted from: Travis Hirschi, "A Control Theory of Delinquency." In *Causes of Delinquency*, pp. 16-26, 31-34. Copyright © 1969 by Berkeley: University of California Press. Reprinted by permission of Travis Hirschi.

"The more weakened the groups to which [the individual] belongs, the less he depends on them, the more he consequently depends on himself and recognizes no other rules of conduct than what are founded on his private interests."[1]

Control theories assume that delinquent acts result when an individual's bond to society is weak or broken. Since these theories embrace two highly complex concepts, the *bond* of the individual to *society*, it is not surprising that they have at one time or another formed the basis of explanations of most forms of aberrant or unusual behavior. It is also not surprising that control theories have described the elements of the bond to society in many ways, and that they have focused on a variety of units as the point of control.

I begin with a classification and description of the elements of the bond to conventional society. I try to show how each of these elements is related to delinquent behavior and how they are related to each other. I then turn to the question of specifying the unit to which the person is presumably more or less tied, and to the question of the adequacy of the motivational force built into the explanation of delinquent behavior.

Elements of the Bond

Attachment

...Durkheim said it many years ago: "We are moral beings to the extent that we are social beings."[2] This may be interpreted to mean that we are moral beings to the extent that we have "internalized the norms" of society. But what does it mean to say that a person has internalized the norms of society? The norms of society are by definition shared by the members of society. To violate a norm is, therefore, to act contrary to the wishes and expectations of other people. If a person does not care about the wishes and expectations of other people—that is, if he is insensitive to the opinion of others—then he is to that extent not bound by the norms. He is free to deviate.

The essence of internalization of norms, conscience, or superego thus lies in the attachment of the individual to others.[3] This view has several advantages over the concept of internalization. For one, explanations of deviant behavior based on attachment do not beg the question, since the extent to which a person is attached to others can be measured independently of his deviant behavior. Furthermore, change or variation in behavior is explainable in a way that it is not when notions of internalization or superego are used. For example, the divorced man is more likely after divorce to commit a number of deviant acts, such as suicide or forgery. If we explain these acts by reference to the superego (or internal control), we are forced to say that the man "lost his conscience" when he got a divorce; and, of course, if he remarries, we have to conclude that he gets his conscience back.

This dimension of the bond to conventional society is encountered in most social control-oriented research and theory. F. Ivan Nye's "internal control" and "indirect control" refer to the same element, although we avoid the problem of explaining changes over time by locating the "conscience" in the bond to others rather than making it part of the personality.[4] Attachment to others is just one aspect of Albert J. Reiss's "personal controls"; we avoid his problems of tautological empirical *observations* by making the relationship between attachment and delinquency problematic rather than definitional.[5] Finally, Scott Briar and Irving Piliavin's "commitment" or "stake in conformity" subsumes attachment, as their discussion illustrates, although the terms they use are more closely associated with the next element to be discussed.[6]

Commitment

"Of all passions, that which inclineth men least to break the laws, is fear. Nay, excepting some generous natures, it is the only thing, when there is the appearance of profit or pleasure by breaking the laws, that makes men keep them."[7] Few would deny that men on occasion obey the rules simply from fear of the consequences. This rational component in conformity we label commitment. What does it mean to say that a person is committed to conformity? In Howard S. Becker's formulation it means the following:

> First, the individual is in a position in which his decision with regard to some particular line of action has consequences for other interests and activities not necessarily [directly] related to it. Second, he has placed himself in that position by his own prior actions. A third element is present though so obvious as not to be apparent: the committed person must be aware [of these other interests] and must recognize that his decision in this case will have ramifications beyond it.[8]

The idea, then, is that the person invests time, energy, himself, in a certain line of activity—say, getting an education, building up a business, acquiring a reputation for virtue. When or whenever he considers deviant behavior, he must consider the costs of this deviant behavior, the risk he runs of losing the investment he has made in conventional behavior.

If attachment to others is the sociological counterpart of the superego or conscience, commitment is the counterpart of the ego or common sense. To the person committed to conventional lines of action, risking one to ten years in prison for a ten-dollar holdup is stupidity, because to the committed person the costs and risks obviously exceed ten dollars in value. ...In the sociological control theory, it can be and is generally assumed that the decision to commit a criminal act may well be rationally determined—that the actor's decision was not irrational given the risks and costs he faces. Of course, as Becker points out, if the actor is capable of in some sense calculating the costs of a line of action, he is also capable of calculational errors: ignorance and error return, in the control theory, as possible explanations of deviant behavior.

The concept of commitment assumes that the organization of society is such that the interests of most persons would be endangered if they were to engage in criminal acts. Most people, simply by the process of living in an organized society, acquire goods, reputations, prospects that they do not want to risk losing....Many hypotheses about the antecedents of delinquent behavior are based on this premise. For example, Arthur L. Stinchombe's hypothesis that "high school rebellion...Occurs when future status is not clearly related to present performance"[9] suggests that one is committed to conformity not only by what one has but also by what one hopes to obtain. Thus "ambition" and/or "aspiration" play an important role in producing conformity. The person becomes committed to a conventional line of action, and he is therefore committed to conformity.

Most lines of action in a society are of course conventional. The clearest examples are educational and occupational careers. Actions thought to jeopardize one's chances in these areas are presumably avoided....

Involvement

Many persons undoubtedly owe a life of virtue to a lack of opportunity to do otherwise. Time and energy are inherently limited: "Not that I would not, if I could, be both handsome and fat and well dressed, and a great athlete, and make a million a year, be a wit, a bon vivant, and a lady killer, as well as a philosopher, a philanthropist, a statesman, warrior, and African explorer, as well as a 'tone-poet' and saint. But the thing is simply impossible."[10] The things that William James here says he would like to be or do are all, I suppose, within the realm of conventionality, but if he were to include illicit actions he would still have to eliminate some of them as simply impossible.

Involvement or engrossment in conventional activities is thus often part of a control theory. The assumption, widely shared, is that a person may be simply too busy doing conventional things to find time to engage in deviant behavior. The person involved in conventional activities is tied to appointments, deadlines, working hours, plans, and the like, so the opportunity to commit deviant acts rarely arises. To the extent that he is engrossed in conventional activities, he cannot even think about deviant acts, let alone act out his inclinations.[11]

This line of reasoning is responsible for the stress placed on recreational facilities in many programs to reduce delinquency, for much of the concern with high school dropouts, and for the idea that boys should be drafted into the Army to keep them out of trouble. So obvious and persuasive is the idea that involvement in conventional activities is a major deterrent to delinquency that it was accepted even by Sutherland: "In the general area of juvenile delinquency it is probable that the most significant difference between juveniles who engage in delinquency and those who do not is that the latter are provided abundant opportunities of a conventional type for satisfying their recreational interests, while the former lack those opportunities or facilities."[12]

The view that "idle hands are the devil's workshop" has received more sophisticated treatment in recent sociological writings on delinquency. David Matza and Gresham M. Sykes, for example, suggest that delinquents have the values of a leisure class, the same values ascribed by Veblen to *the* leisure class: a search for kicks, disdain of work, a desire for the big score, and acceptance of aggressive toughness as proof of masculinity.[13] Matza and Sykes explain delinquency by reference to this system of values, but they note that adolescents at all class levels are "to some extent" members of a leisure class, that they "move in a limbo between earlier parental domination and future integration with the social structure through the bonds of work and marriage.[14] In the end, then, the leisure of the adolescent produces a set of values, which, in turn, leads to delinquency.

Belief

Unlike the cultural deviance theory, the control theory assumes the existence of a common value system within the society or group whose norms are being violated. If the deviant is committed to a value system different from that of conventional society, there is, within the context of the theory, nothing to explain. The question is, "Why does a man violate the rules in which he believes?" It is not, "Why do men differ in their beliefs about what constitutes good and desirable conduct?" The person is assumed to have been socialized (perhaps imperfectly) into the group whose rules he is violating; deviance is not a question of one group imposing its rules on the members of another group. In other words, we not only assume the deviant *has* believed the rules, we assume he believes the rules even as he violates them.

How can a person believe it is wrong to steal at the same time he is stealing? In the strain theory, this is not a difficult problem....However, given the control theory's assumptions about motivation, if both the deviant and the nondeviant believe the deviant act is wrong, how do we account for the fact that one commits it and the other does not?

Control theories have taken two approaches to this problem. In one approach, beliefs are treated as mere words that mean little or nothing if the other forms of control are missing....In short, beliefs, at least insofar as they are expressed in words, drop out of the picture; since they do not differentiate between deviants and nondeviants, they are in the same class as "language" or any other characteristic common to all members of the group. Since they represent no real obstacle to the commission of delinquent acts, nothing need be said about how they are handled by those committing such acts. The control theories that do not mention beliefs (or values), and many do not, may be assumed to take this approach to the problem.

The second approach argues that the deviant rationalizes his behavior so that he can at once violate the rule and maintain his belief in it....In both Cressey's and Sykes and Matza's treatments, these rationalizations (Cressey calls them "verbalizations," Sykes and Matza term them "techniques of neutralization") occur prior to the commission of the deviant act. If the neutralization is successful, the person is free to commit the act(s) in question. Both in Cressey and in Sykes and Matza, the strain that prompts the effort at neutralization also provides the motive force that results in the subsequent deviant act. Their theories are thus, in this sense, strain theories. Neutralization is difficult to handle within the context of a theory that adheres closely to control theory assumptions, because

in the control theory there is no special motivational force to account for the neutralization. This difficulty is especially noticeable in Matza's later treatment of this topic, where the motivational component, the "will to delinquency" appears *after* the moral vacuum has been created by the techniques of neutralization.[15]...

In attempting to solve a strain theory problem with control theory tools, the control theorist is thus led into a trap. He cannot answer the crucial question. The concept of neutralization assumes the existence of moral obstacles to the commission of deviant acts. In order plausibly to account for a deviant act, it is necessary to generate motivation to deviance that is at least equivalent in force to the resistance provided by these moral obstacles. However, if the moral obstacles are removed, neutralization and special motivation are no longer required. We therefore follow the implicit logic of control theory and remove these moral obstacles by hypothesis. Many persons do not have an attitude of respect toward the rules of society: many persons feel no moral obligation to conform regardless of personal advantage. Insofar as the values and beliefs of these persons are consistent with their feelings, and there should be a tendency toward consistency, neutralization is unnecessary; it has already occurred.

Does this merely push the question back a step and at the same time produce conflict with the assumption of a common value system? I think not....We do not assume, in other words, that the person constructs a system of rationalizations in order to justify commission of acts he *wants* to commit. We assume, in contrast, that the beliefs that free a man to commit deviant acts are *unmotivated* in the sense that he does not construct or adopt them in order to facilitate the attainment of illicit ends. In the second place, we do not assume, as does Matza, that "delinquents concur in the conventional assessment of delinquency."[16] We assume, in contrast, that there is *variation* in the extent to which people believe they should obey the rules of society, and, furthermore, that the less a person believes he should obey the rules, the more likely he is to violate them.[17]

In chronological order, then, a person's beliefs in the moral validity of norms are, for no teleological reason, weakened. The probability that he will commit delinquent acts is therefore increased. When and if he commits a delinquent act, we may justifiably use the weakness of his beliefs in explaining it, but no special motivation is required to explain either the weakness of his beliefs or, perhaps, his delinquent act.

The keystone of this argument is of course the assumption that there is variation in belief in the moral validity of social rules. This assumption is amenable to direct empirical test and can thus survive at least until its first confrontation with data....

The idea of a common (or, perhaps better, a single) value system is consistent with the fact, or presumption, of variation in the strength of moral beliefs. We have not suggested that delinquency is based on beliefs counter to conventional morality; we have not suggested that delinquents do not believe delinquent acts are wrong. They may well believe these acts are wrong, but the meaning and efficacy of such beliefs are contingent upon other beliefs, and, indeed, on the strength of other ties to the conventional order.[18]...

Where Is the Motivation?

The most disconcerting question the control theorist faces goes something like this: "Yes, but *why* do they do it?" In the good old days, the control theorist could simply strip away the "veneer of civilization" and expose man's "animal impulses" for all to see. These impulses appeared to him (and apparently to his audience) to provide a plausible account of the motivation to crime and delinquency. His argument was *not* that delinquents and criminals alone are animals, but that we are all animals, and thus all naturally capable of committing criminal acts....

It was no longer fashionable (within sociology, at least) to refer to animal impulses. The control theorist tended more and more to deemphasize the motivational component of his theory. He might refer in the beginning to "universal human needs," or some such, but the driving force behind crime and delinquency was rarely alluded to. At the same time, his explanations of crime and delinquency increasingly left the reader uneasy. What, the reader asked, is the control theorist assuming?...

There are several additional accounts of "why they do it" that are to my mind persuasive and at the same time generally compatible with control theory.[19] But while all of these accounts may be compatible with control theory, they are by no means deducible from it. Furthermore, they rarely impute built-in, unusual motivation to the delinquent: he is attempting to satisfy the same desires, he is reacting to the same pressures as other boys (as is clear, for example, in the previous quotation from Briar and Piliavin). In other words, if included, these accounts of motivation would serve the same function in the theory that "animal impulses" traditionally served: they might add to its persuasiveness and plausibility, but they would add little else, since they do not differentiate delinquents from nondelinquents.

In the end, then, control theory remains what it has always been: a theory in which deviation is not problematic. The question "Why do they do it?" is simply not the question the theory is designed to answer. The question is, "Why don't we do it?" There is much evidence that we would if we dared.

Discussion Questions

1. Hirschi argues that four social bonds serve to inhibit or prevent involvement in delinquency and crime. Identify and define each of Hirschi's four social bonds. Why does each of the bonds inhibit or prevent involvement in delinquency?

2. Two institutions that are often examined in empirical studies involving social control theory are family and school. Given your knowledge of social control theory, why should attachment to parents limit or prevent offending? Commitment to school?

3. Hirschi makes the case that control theories differ from other criminological theories. How do they differ from other types of theories? Why is this is an important difference?

Notes

1. Emile Durkheim, *Suicide*, trans. John A. Spaulding and George Simpson (New York: The Free Press, 1951), p. 209.
2. Emile Durkheim, *Moral Education*, trans. Everett K. Wilson and Herman Schnurer (New York: The Free Press, 1961), p. 64.
3. Although attachment alone does not exhaust the meaning of internalization, attachments and beliefs combined would appear to leave only a small residue of "internal control" not susceptible in principle to direct measurement.
4. F. Ivan Nye, *Family Relationships and Delinquent Behavior* (New York: Wiley, 1958), pp. 5-7.
5. Albert J. Reiss, Jr., "Delinquency as the Failure of Personal and Social Controls," *American Sociological Review*, XVI (1951), 196-207. For example, "Our observations show…That delinquent recidivists are less often persons with mature ego ideals or nondelinquent social roles." (p. 204).
6. Scott Briar and Irving Piliavin, "Delinquency, Situational Inducements, and Commitment to Conformity," *Social Problems*, XIII (1965), 41-42. The concept "stake in conformity" was introduced by Jackson Toby in his "Social Disorganization and Stake in Conformity: Complementary Factors in the Predatory Behavior of Hoodlums," *Journal of Criminal Law, Criminology and Police Science*, XLVIII (1957), 12-17. See also his "Hoodlum or Business Man: An American Dilemma," *The Jews*, ed. Marshall Sklare (New York: The Free Press, 1958), pp. 542-550. Throughout the text, I occasionally use "stake in conformity" in speaking in general of the strength of the bond to conventional society. So used, the concept is somewhat broader than is true for either Toby or Briar and Piliavin, where the concept is roughly equivalent to what is here called "commitment."
7. Thomas Hobbes, *Leviathan* (Oxford: Basil Blackwell, 1957), p. 195.
8. Howard S. Becker, "Notes on the Concept of Commitment," *American Journal of Sociology* LXVI (1969).
9. Arthur L. Stinchcombe, *Rebellion in a High School* (Chicago: Quadrangle, 1964), p. 5.
10. William James, *Psychology* (Cleveland: World Publishing Co., 1948), p. 186.
11. Few activities appear to be so engrossing that they rule out contemplation of alternative lines of behavior, at least if estimates of the amount of time men spend plotting sexual deviations have any validity.
12. The Sutherland Papers, ed. Albert K. Cohen et al. (Bloomington: Indiana University Press, 1956), p. 37.
13. David Matza and Gresham M. Sykes, "Juvenile Delinquency and Subterranean Values," *American Sociological Review*, XXVI (1961), 712-719.
14. Ibid., p. 718.
15. David Matza, *Delinquency and Drift* (New York: Wiley, 1964), pp. 181-191.
16. *Delinquency and Drift*, p. 43.
17. This assumption is not, I think, contradicted by the evidence presented by Matza against the existence of a delinquent subculture. In comparing the attitudes and actions of delinquents with the picture painted by delinquent subculture theorists, Matza emphasizes—and perhaps exaggerates—the extent to which delinquents are tied to the conventional order. In implicitly comparing delinquents with a supermoral man, I emphasize—and perhaps exaggerate—the extent to which they are not tied to the conventional order.
18. The position taken here is therefore somewhere between the "semantic dementia" and the "neutralization" positions. Assuming variation, the delinquent is, at the extremes, freer than the neutralization argument assumes. Although the possibility of wide discrepancy between what the delinquent professes and what he practices still exists, it is presumably much rarer than is suggested by studies of articulate "psychopaths."
19. For example: Carl Wertham, "The Function of Social Definitions in the Development of Delinquent Careers," *Juvenile Delinquency and Youth Crime*, Report of the President's Commission on Law Enforcement and Administration of Justice (Washington: USGPO, 1967), pp. 155-170; Jackson Toby, "Affluence and Adolescent Crime," *ibid.*, pp. 132-144; James F. Short, Jr., and Fred L. Strodtbeck, *Group Process and Gang Delinquency* (Chicago: University of Chicago Press, 1965), pp. 248-264.

CHAPTER 27

The Nature of Criminality: Low Self-Control

Michael R. Gottfredson ■ Travis Hirschi

Most criminological theories attempt to discern the reasons why individuals commit crime. Control theories on the other hand, are unique because they explain criminality from a different perspective; why people do not commit crime. Control theories assume that, if left alone, man would naturally commit criminal acts. Therefore, crime is a natural impulse that must be controlled.

The following selection presents the most recent, and most influential of control theories, Gottfredson and Hirschi's theory of low self-control. As Gottfredson and Hirschi explain, self-control is an internal mechanism that controls antisocial impulses. Those lacking self-control are typically impulsive, insensitive to others, physical (as opposed to mental), risk-taking, shortsighted, nonverbal, and will tend to engage in criminal and analogous acts. Individuals with low self-control have been characterized as those who act without thinking of the long-term consequences of their actions. Low self-control is a behavioral characteristic that is not inherited or transmitted, but rather it is the product of ineffective parental socialization during childhood. Ineffective socialization can take on many forms (low attachment between parent and child, lack of supervision, lack of recognition of deviant behavior by parent, lack of punishment) and is more likely to occur in families where parents also have low self-control. In this way, self-control

theory explains why small proportions of individuals account for the majority of criminal acts.

Theories of crime lead naturally to interest in the propensities of individuals committing criminal acts. These propensities are often labeled "criminality." In pure classical theory, people committing criminal acts had no special propensities. They merely followed the universal tendency to enhance their own pleasure. If they differed from noncriminals, it was with respect to their location in or comprehension of relevant sanction systems. For example, the individual cut off from the community will suffer less than others from the ostracism that follows crime; the individual unaware of the natural or legal consequences of criminal behavior cannot be controlled by these consequences to the degree that people aware of them are controlled; the atheist will not be as concerned as the believer about penalties to be exacted in a life beyond death. Classical theories on the whole, then, are today called *control theories*, theories emphasizing the prevention of crime through consequences painful to the individual.

Although, for policy purposes, classical theorists emphasized legal consequences, the importance to them of moral sanctions is so obvious that their theories might well be called underdeveloped *social control* theories. In fact, Bentham's list of the major restraining motives—motives acting to prevent mischievous acts—begins with goodwill, love of reputation, and the desire for amity (1970: 134–36). He goes on to say that fear of detection prevents crime in large part because of detection's consequences for "reputation, and the desire for amity" (p. 138). Put another way, in Bentham's view, the restraining power of legal sanctions in large part stems from their connection to social sanctions.

If crime is evidence of the weakness of social motives, it follows that criminals are less social than noncriminals and that the extent of their asociality may be determined by the nature and number of their crimes. Calculation of the extent of an individual's mischievousness is a complex affair, but in general the more mischievous or depraved the offenses, and the greater their number, the more mischievous or depraved the offender (Bentham 1970: 134–42). (Classical theorists thus had reason to be interested in the seriousness of the offense. The relevance of seriousness to current theories of crime is not so clear.)

Because classical or control theories infer that offenders are not restrained by social motives, it is common to think of them as emphasizing an asocial human nature. Actually, such theories make people only as asocial as their acts require. Pure or consistent control theories do not add criminality (i.e., personality concepts or attributes such as "aggressiveness" or "extraversion") to individuals beyond that found in their criminal acts. As a result, control theories are suspicious of images of an antisocial, psychopathic, or career offender, or of an offender whose motives to crime are somehow larger than those given in the crimes themselves. Indeed, control theories are compatible with the view that the balance of the total control structure favors conformity, even among offenders:

> For in every man, be his disposition ever so depraved, the social motives are those which…regulate and determine the general tenor of his life.…The general and standing bias of every man's nature is, therefore, towards that side to which the force of the social motives would determine him to adhere. This being the case, the force of the social motives tends continually to put an end to that of the dissocial ones; as, in natural bodies, the force of friction tends to put an end to that which is generated by impulse. Time, then, which wears away the force of the dissocial motives, adds to that of the social. (Bentham 1970: 141)

Positivism brought with it the idea that criminals differ from noncriminals in ways more radical than this, the idea that criminals carry within themselves properties peculiarly and positively conducive to crime. [Previously], we examined the efforts of the major disciplines to identify these properties. Being friendly to both the classical and positivist traditions, we expected to end up with a list of individual properties reliably identified by competent research as useful in the description of "criminality"—such properties as aggressiveness, body build, activity level, and intelligence. We further expected that we would be able to connect these individual-level correlates of criminality directly to the classical idea of crime. As our review progressed, however, we were forced to conclude that we had overestimated the success of positivism in establishing important differences between "criminals" and "noncriminals" beyond their tendency to commit criminal acts. Stable individual differences in the tendency to commit criminal acts were clearly evident, but many or even most of the other differences between offenders and nonoffenders were not as clear or pronounced as our reading of the literature had led us to expect.

If individual differences in the tendency to commit criminal acts (within an overall tendency for crime to decline with age) are at least potentially explicable within classical theory by reference to the social location of individuals and their comprehension of how the world works, the fact remains that classical theory cannot shed much light on the positivistic finding (denied by most positivistic theories…) that these differences *remain reasonably stable with change in the social location of individuals and change in their knowledge of the operation of sanction systems.* This is the problem of self-control, the differential tendency of people to avoid criminal acts whatever the circumstances in which they find themselves. Since this difference among people has attracted a variety of names, we begin by arguing the merits of the concept of self-control.

Self-Control and Alternative Concepts

Our decision to ascribe stable individual differences in criminal behavior to self-control was made only after considering several alternatives, one of which (criminality) we had used before (Hirschi and Gottfredson 1986). A major consideration was consistency between the classical conception of crime and our conception of the criminal. It seemed unwise to try to integrate a choice theory of crime with a deterministic image of the offender, especially when such integration was unnecessary. In fact, the compatibility of the classical view of crime and the idea that people differ in self-control is, in our view, remarkable. As we have seen, classical theory is a theory of social or external control, a theory based on the idea that the costs of crime depend on the individual's current location in or bond to society. What classical theory lacks is an explicit idea of self-control, the idea that people also differ in the extent to which they are vulnerable to the temptations of the moment. Combining the two ideas thus merely recognizes the simultaneous existence of social and individual restraints on behavior.

An obvious alternative is the concept of criminality. The disadvantages of that concept, however, are numerous. First, it connotes causation or determinism, a positive tendency to crime that is contrary to the classical model and, in our view, contrary to the facts. Whereas self-control suggests that people differ in the extent to which they are restrained from criminal acts, criminality suggests that people differ in the extent to which they are compelled to crime. The concept of self-control is thus consistent with the observation that criminals do not require or need crime, and the concept of criminality is inconsistent with this observation. By the same token, the idea of low self-control is compatible with the observation that criminal acts require no special capabilities, needs, or motivation; they are, in this sense, available to everyone. In contrast, the idea of criminality as a special tendency suggests that criminal acts require special people for their performance and enjoyment. Finally, lack of restraint or low self-control allows almost any deviant, criminal, exciting, or dangerous act; in contrast, the idea of criminality covers only a narrow portion of the apparently diverse acts engaged in by people at one end of the dimension we are now discussing.

The concept of conscience comes closer than criminality to self-control, and is harder to distinguish from it. Unfortunately, that concept has connotations of compulsion (to conformity) not, strictly speaking, consistent with a choice model (or with the operation of conscience). It does not seem to cover the behaviors analogous to crime that appear to be controlled by natural sanctions rather than social or moral sanctions, and in the end it typically refers to how people feel about their acts rather than to the likelihood that they will or will not commit them. Thus accidents and employment instability are not usually seen as produced by failures of conscience, and writers in the conscience tradition do not typically make the connection between moral and prudent behavior. Finally, conscience is used primarily to summarize the results of learning via negative reinforcement, and even those favorably disposed to its use leave little more to say about it (see, e.g., Eysneck 1977; Wilson and Herrnstein 1985).

We are now in position to describe the nature of self-control, the individual characteristic relevant to the commission of criminal acts. We assume that the nature of this characteristic can be derived directly from the nature of criminal acts. We thus infer from the nature of crime what people who refrain from criminal acts are like before they reach the age at which crime becomes a logical possibility. We then work back further to the factors producing their restraint, back to the causes of self-control. In our view, lack of self-control does not require crime and can be counteracted by situational conditions or other properties of the individual. At the same time, we suggest that high self-control effectively reduces the possibility of crime—that is, those possessing it will be substantially less likely at all periods of life to engage in criminal acts.

The Elements of Self-Control

Criminal acts provide *immediate* gratification of desires. A major characteristic of people with low self-control is therefore a tendency to respond to tangible stimuli in the immediate environment, to have a concrete "here and now" orientation. People with high self-control, in contrast, tend to defer gratification.

Criminal acts provide easy or simple gratification of desires. They provide money without work, sex without courtship, revenge without court delays. People lacking self-control also tend to lack diligence, tenacity, or persistence in a course of action.

Criminal acts are *exciting, risky, or thrilling.* They involve stealth, danger, speed, agility, deception, or power. People lacking self-control therefore tend to be adventuresome, active, and physical. Those with high levels of self-control tend to be cautious, cognitive, and verbal.

Crimes provide *few or meager long-term benefits.* They are not equivalent to a job or a career. On the contrary, crimes interfere with long-term commitments to jobs, marriages, family, or friends. People with low self-control thus tend to have unstable marriages, friendships, and job profiles. They tend to be little interested in and unprepared for long-term occupation pursuits.

Crimes require *little skill or planning.* The cognitive requirements for most crimes are minimal. It follows that people lacking self-control need not possess or value cognitive or academic skills. The manual skills required for most crimes are minimal. It follows that people lacking self-control need not possess manual skills that require training or apprenticeship.

Crimes often result in *pain or discomfort for the victim.* Property is lost, bodies are injured, privacy is violated, trust is broken. It follows that people with low self-control tend to be self-centered, indifferent, or insensitive to the suffering and needs of others. It does not follow, however, that people with low self-control are routinely unkind or antisocial. On the contrary, they may discover the immediate and easy rewards of charm and generosity.

Recall that crime involves the pursuit of immediate pleasure. It follows that people lacking self-control will also tend to pursue immediate pleasures that are *not* criminal: They will tend to smoke, drink, use drugs, gamble, have children out of wedlock, and engage in illicit sex.

Crimes require the interaction of an offender with people or their property. It does not follow that people lacking self-control will tend to be gregarious or social. However, it does follow that, other things being equal, gregarious or social people are more likely to be involved in criminal acts.

The major benefit of many crimes is not pleasure but relief from momentary irritation. The irritation caused by a crying child is often the stimulus for physical abuse. That caused by a taunting stranger in a bar is often the stimulus for aggravated assault. It follows that people with low self-control tend to have minimal tolerance for frustration and little ability to respond to conflict through verbal rather than physical means.

Crimes involve the risk of violence and physical injury, of pain and suffering on the part of the offender. It does not follow that people with low self-control will tend to be tolerant of physical pain or to be indifferent to physical discomfort. It does follow that people tolerant of physical pain or indifferent to physical discomfort will be more likely to engage in criminal acts whatever their level of self-control.

The risk of criminal penalty for any given criminal act is small, but this depends in part on the circumstances of the offense. Thus, for example, not all joyrides by teenagers are equally likely to result in arrest. A car stolen from a neighbor and returned unharmed before he notices its absence is less likely to result in official notice than is a car stolen from a shopping center parking lot and abandoned at the convenience of the offender. Drinking alcohol stolen from parents and consumed in the family garage is less likely to receive official notice than drinking in the parking lot outside a concert hall. It follows that offenses differ in their validity as measures of self-control: those offenses with large risk of public awareness are better measures than those with little risk.

In sum, people who lack self-control will tend to be impulsive, insensitive, physical (as opposed to mental), risk-taking, short sighted, and nonverbal, and they will tend therefore to engage in criminal and analogous acts. Since these traits can be identified prior to the age of responsibility for crime, since there is considerable tendency for these traits to come together in the same people, and since the traits tend to persist through life, it seems reasonable to consider them as comprising a stable construct useful in the explanation of crime.

The Many Manifestations of Low Self-Control

Our image of the "offender" suggests that crime is not an automatic or necessary consequence of low self-control. It suggests that many noncriminal acts analogous to crime (such as accidents, smoking, and alcohol use) are also manifestations of low self-control. Our image therefore implies that no specific act, type of crime, or form of deviance is uniquely required by the absence of self-control.

Because both crime and analogous behaviors stem from low self-control (that is, both are manifestations of low self-control), they will all be engaged in at a relatively high rate by people with low self-control. Within the domain of crime, then, there will be much versatility among offenders in the criminal acts in which they engage.

Research on the versatility of deviant acts supports these predictions in the strongest possible way. The variety of manifestations of low self-control is immense. In spite of years of tireless research motivated by a belief in specialization, no credible evidence of specialization has been reported. In fact, the evidence of offender versatility is overwhelming (Hirschi 1969; Hindelang 1971; Wolfgang, Figlio, and Sellin 1972; Petersilia 1980; Hindelang, Hirschi, and Weis 1981; Rojek and Erickson 1982; Klein 1984).

By versatility we mean that offenders commit a wide variety of criminal acts, with no strong inclination to pursue a specific criminal act or a pattern of criminal acts to the exclusion of others. Most theories suggest that offenders tend to specialize, whereby such terms as robber, burglar, drug dealer, rapist, and murderer have predictive or descriptive import. In fact, some theories create offender specialization as part of their explanation of crime. For example, Cloward and Ohlin (1960) create distinctive subcultures of delinquency around particular forms of criminal behavior, identifying subcultures specializing in theft, violence, or drugs. In a related way, books are written about white-collar crime as though it were a clearly distinct specialty requiring a unique explanation. Research projects are undertaken for the study of drug use, or vandalism, or teen pregnancy (as though every study of delinquency were not a study of drug use and vandalism and teenage sexual behavior). Entire schools of criminology emerge to pursue patterning, sequencing, progression, escalation, onset, persistence, and desistance in the career of offenses or offenders. These efforts survive largely because their proponents fail to consider or acknowledge the clear evidence to the contrary. Other reasons for survival of such ideas may be found in the interest of politicians and members of the law enforcement community who see policy potential in criminal careers or "career criminals" (see, e.g., Blumstein et al. 1986).

Occasional reports of specialization seem to contradict this point, as do everyday observations of repetitive misbehavior by particular offenders. Some offenders rob the same store repeatedly over a period of years, or an offender commits several rapes over a (brief) period of time. Such offenders may be called "robbers" or "rapists." However, it should be noted that such labels are retrospective rather than predictive and that they typically ignore a large amount of delinquent or criminal behavior by the same offenders that is inconsistent with their alleged specialty. Thus, for example, the "rapist" will tend also to use drugs, to commit robberies and burglaries (often in concert with the rape), and to have a record for violent offenses other than rape. There is a perhaps natural tendency on the part of observers (and in official accounts) to focus on the most serious crimes in a series of events, but this tendency should not be confused with a tendency on the part of the offender to specialize in one kind of crime.

Recall that one of the defining features of crime is that it is simple and easy. Some apparent specialization will therefore occur because obvious opportunities for an easy score will tend to repeat themselves. An offender who lives next to a shopping area that is approached by pedestrians will have repeat opportunities for purse snatching, and this may show in his arrest record. But even here the specific "criminal career" will tend to quickly run its course and to be followed by offenses whose content and character is likewise determined by coincidence and opportunity (which is the reason why some form of theft is always the best bet about what a person is likely to do next).

The evidence that offenders are likely to engage in noncriminal acts psychologically or theoretically equivalent to crime is, because of the relatively high rates of these "noncriminal" acts, even easier to document. Thieves are likely to smoke, drink, and skip school at considerably higher rates than nonthieves. Offenders are considerably more likely than nonoffenders to be involved in most types of accidents, including household fires, auto crashes, and unwanted pregnancies. They are also considerably more likely to die at an early age (see, e.g. Robins 1966; Eysenck 1977; Gottfredson 1984).

Good research on drug use and abuse routinely reveals that the correlates of delinquency and drug use are the same. As Akers (1984) has noted,

> compared to the abstaining teenager, the drinking, smoking and drug-taking teen is much more likely to be getting into fights, stealing, hurting other people, and committing other delinquencies.

Akers goes on to say, "but the variation in the order in which they take up these things leaves little basis for proposing the causation of one by the other." In our view, the relation between drug use and delinquency is not a causal question. The correlates are the same because drug use and delinquency are both manifestations of an underlying tendency to pursue short-term, immediate pleasure. This underlying tendency (i.e., lack of self-control) has many manifestations, as listed by Harrison Gough (1948):

> unconcern over the rights and privileges of others when recognizing them would interfere with personal satisfaction in any way; impulsive behavior, or apparent incongruity between the strength of the stimulus and the magnitude of the behavioral response; inability to form deep or persistent attachments to other persons or to identify in interpersonal relationships; poor judgment and planning in attaining defined goals; apparent lack of anxiety and distress over social maladjustment and unwillingness or inability to consider maladjustment qua maladjustment; a tendency to project blame onto others and to take no responsibility for failures; meaningless prevarication, often about trivial matters in situations where detection is inevitable; almost complete lack of dependability...and willingness to assume responsibility; and, finally, emotional poverty. [p. 362]

This combination of characteristics has been revealed in the life histories of the subjects in the famous studies by Lee Robins. Robins is one of the few researchers to focus on the varieties of deviance and the way they tend to go together in the lives of those she designates as having "antisocial personalities." In her words:

> We refer to someone who fails to maintain close personal relationships with anyone else, [who] performs poorly on the job, who is involved in illegal behaviors (whether or not apprehended), who fails to support himself and his dependents without outside aid, and who is given to sudden changes of plan and loss of temper in response to what appear to others as minor frustrations. (1978: 255)

For 30 years Robins traced 524 children referred to a guidance clinic in St. Louis, Missouri, and she compared them to a control group matched on IQ, age, sex, and area of the city. She discovered that, in comparison to the control group, those people referred at an early age were more likely to be arrested as adults (for a wide variety of offences), were less likely to get married, were more likely to be divorced, were more likely to marry a spouse with a behavior problem, were less likely to have children (but if they had children were likely to leave more children), were more likely to have children with behavior problems, were more likely to be unemployed, had considerably more frequent job changes, were more likely to be on welfare, had fewer contacts with relatives, had fewer friends, were substantially less likely to attend church, were less likely to serve in the armed forces and more likely to be dishonorably discharged if they did serve, were more likely to exhibit physical evidence of excessive alcohol use, and were more likely to be hospitalized for psychiatric problems (1966: 42–73).

Note that these outcomes are consistent with four general elements of our notion of low self-control: basic stability of individual differences over a long period of time; great variability in the kinds of criminal acts engaged in; conceptual or causal equivalence of criminal and noncriminal acts; and inability to predict the specific forms of deviance engaged in, whether criminal or noncriminal. In our view, the idea of an antisocial personality defined by certain behavioral consequences is too positivistic or deterministic, suggesting that the offender must do certain things given his antisocial personality. Thus we would say only that the subjects in question are *more likely* to commit criminal acts (as the data indicate they are). We do not make commission of criminal acts part of the definition of the individual with low self-control.

Be this as it may, Robins's retrospective research shows that predictions derived from a concept of antisocial personality are highly consistent with the results of prospective longitudinal and cross-sectional research: offenders do not specialize; they tend to be involved in accidents, illness, and death at higher rates than the general population; they tend to have difficulty persisting in a job regardless of the particular characteristics of the job (no job will turn out to be a good job); they have difficulty acquiring and retaining friends; and they have difficulty meeting the demands of long-term financial commitments (such as mortgages or car payments) and the demands of parenting.

Seen in this light, the "costs" of low self-control for the individual may far exceed the costs of his criminal acts. In fact, it appears that crime is often among the least serious consequences of a lack of self-control in terms of the quality of life of those lacking it.

The Causes of Self-Control

We know better what deficiencies in self-control lead to than where they come from. One thing is, however, clear: low self-control is not produced by training, tutelage, or socialization. As a matter of fact, all of the characteristics associated with low self-control tend to show themselves in the absence of nurturance, discipline, or training. Given the classical appreciation of the causes of human behavior, the implications of this fact are straightforward: the causes of low self-control are negative rather than positive; self-control is unlikely in the absence of effort, intended or unintended, to create it. (This assumption separates the present theory from most modern theories of crime, where the offender is automatically seen as a product of possessive forces, a creature of learning, particular pressures, or specific defect. We will return to

this comparison once our theory has been fully explicated.)

At this point it would be easy to construct a theory of crime causation, according to which characteristics of potential offenders lead them ineluctably to the commission of criminal acts. Our task at this point would simply be to identify the likely sources of impulsiveness, intelligence, risk-taking, and the like. But to do so would be to follow the path that has proven so unproductive in the past, the path according to which criminals commit crimes irrespective of the characteristics of the setting or situation.

We can avoid this pitfall by recalling the elements inherent in the decision to commit a criminal act. The object of the offense is clearly pleasurable, and universally so. Engaging in the act, however, entails some risk of social, legal, and/or natural sanctions. Whereas the pleasure attained by the act is direct, obvious, and immediate, the pains risked by it are not obvious, or direct, and are in any event at greater remove from it. It follows that, though there will be little variability among people in their ability to see the pleasures of crime, there will be considerable variability in their ability to calculate potential pains. But the problem goes further than this: whereas the pleasures of crime are reasonably equally distributed over the population, this is not true for the pains. Everyone appreciates money; not everyone dreads parental anger or disappointment upon learning that the money was stolen.

So, the dimensions of self-control are, in our view, factors affecting calculation of the consequences of one's acts. The impulsive or shortsighted person fails to consider the negative or painful consequences of his acts; the insensitive person has fewer negative consequences to consider; the less intelligent person also has fewer negative consequences to consider (has less to lose).

No known social group, whether criminal or noncriminal, actively or purposefully attempts to reduce the self-control of its members. Social life is not enhanced by low self-control and its consequences. On the contrary, the exhibition of these tendencies undermines harmonious group relations and the ability to achieve collective ends. These facts explicitly deny that a tendency to crime is a product of socialization, culture, or positive learning of any sort.

The traits composing low self-control are also not conducive to the achievement of long-term individual goals. On the contrary, they impede educational and occupational achievement, destroy interpersonal relations, and undermine physical health and economic well-being. Such facts explicitly deny the notion that criminality is an alternative route to the goals otherwise obtainable through legitimate avenues. It follows that people who care about the interpersonal skill, educational and occupational achievement, and physical and economic well-being of those in their care will seek to rid them of these traits.

Two general sources of variation are immediately apparent in this scheme. The first is the variation among children in the degree to which they manifest such traits to begin with. The second is the variation among caretakers in the degree to which they recognize low self-control and its consequences and the degree to which they are willing and able to correct it. Obviously, therefore, even at this threshold level the sources of low self-control are complex.

There is good evidence that some of the traits predicting subsequent involvement in crime appear as early as they can be reliably measured, including low intelligence, high activity level, physical strength, and adventuresomeness (Glueck and Glueck 1950; West and Farrington 1973). The evidence suggests that the connection between these traits and commission of criminal acts ranges from weak to moderate. Obviously, we do not suggest that people are born criminals, inherit a gene for criminality, or anything of the sort. In fact, we explicitly deny such notions....What we do suggest is that individual differences may have an impact on the prospects for effective socialization (or adequate control). Effective socialization is, however, always possible whatever the configuration of individual traits.

Other traits affecting crime appear later and seem to be largely products of ineffective or incomplete socialization. For example, differences in impulsivity and insensitivity become noticeable later in childhood when they are no longer common to all children. The ability and willingness to delay immediate gratification for some larger purpose may

therefore be assumed to be a consequence of training. Much parental action is in fact geared toward suppression of impulsive behavior, toward making the child consider the long-range consequences of acts. Consistent sensitivity to the needs and feelings of others may also be assumed to be a consequence of training. Indeed, much parental behavior is directed toward teaching the child about the rights and feelings of others, and of how these rights and feelings ought to constrain the child's behavior. All of these points focus our attention on child-rearing.

Child-Rearing and Self-Control: The Family

The major "cause" of low self-control thus appears to be ineffective child-rearing. Put in positive terms, several conditions appear necessary to produce a socialized child. Perhaps the place to begin looking for these conditions is the research literature on the relation between family conditions and delinquency. This research (e.g., Glueck and Glueck 1950; McCord and McCord 1959) has examined the connection between many family factors and delinquency. It reports that discipline, supervision, and affection tend to be missing in the homes of delinquents, that the behavior of the parents is often "poor" (e.g., excessive drinking and poor supervision [Glueck and Glueck 1950: 110–11]), and that the parents of delinquents are unusually likely to have criminal records themselves. Indeed, according to Michael Rutter and Henri Giller, "of the parental characteristics associated with delinquency, criminality is the most striking and most consistent" (1984: 182).

Such information undermines the many explanations of crime that ignore the family, but in this form it does not represent much of an advance over the belief of the general public (and those who deal with offenders in the criminal justice system) that "defective upbringing" or "neglect" in the home is the primary cause of crime.

To put these standard research findings in perspective, we think it necessary to define the conditions necessary for adequate child-rearing to occur. The minimum conditions seem to be these: in order to teach the child self-control, someone must

(1) monitor the child's behavior; (2) recognize deviant behavior when it occurs; and (3) punish such behavior. This seems simple and obvious enough. All that is required to activate the system is affection for *or* investment in the child. The person who cares for the child will watch his behavior, see him doing things he should not do, and correct him. The result may be a child more capable of delaying gratification, more sensitive to the interests and desires of others, more independent, more willing to accept restraints on his activity, and more unlikely to use force or violence to attain his ends.

When we seek the causes of low self-control, we ask where this system can go wrong. Obviously, parents do not prefer their children to be unsocialized in the terms described. We can therefore rule out in advance the possibility of positive socialization to unsocialized behavior (as cultural or subcultural deviance theories suggest). Still, the system can go wrong at any one of four places. First, the parents may not care for the child (in which case none of the other conditions would be met); second, the parents, even if they care, may not have the time or energy to monitor the child's behavior; third, the parents, even if they care *and* monitor, may not see anything wrong with the child's behavior; finally, even if everything else is in place, the parents may not have the inclination or the means to punish the child. So, what may appear at first glance to be nonproblematic turns out to be problematic indeed. Many things can go wrong. According to much research in crime and delinquency, in the homes of problem children many things have gone wrong: "Parents of stealers do not track ([they] do not interpret stealing…as 'deviant'); they do not punish; and they do not care" (Patterson 1980: 88–89; see also Glueck and Glueck 1950; McCord and McCord 1959; West and Farrington 1977).

Let us apply this scheme to some of the facts about the connection between child socialization and crime, beginning with the elements of the child-rearing model.

The Attachment of the Parent to the Child

Our model states that parental concern for the welfare or behavior of the child is a necessary condition for successful child-rearing. Because it is too often assumed that all parents are alike in their love for their children, the evidence directly on this point is not as good or extensive as it could be. However, what exists is clearly consistent with the model. Glueck and Glueck (1950: 125–28) report that, compared to the fathers of delinquents, fathers of nondelinquents were twice as likely to be warmly disposed toward their sons and one-fifth as likely to be hostile toward them. In the same sample, 28 percent of the mothers of delinquents were characterized as "indifferent or hostile" toward the child as compared to 4 percent of the mothers of nondelinquents. The evidence suggests that stepparents are especially unlikely to have feelings of affection toward their stepchildren (Burgess 1980), adding in contemporary society to the likelihood that children will be "reared" by people who do not especially care for them.

Parental Supervision

The connection between social control and self-control could not be more direct than in the case of parental supervision of the child. Such supervision presumably prevents criminal or analogous acts and at the same time trains the child to avoid them on his own. Consistent with this assumption, supervision tends to be a major predictor of delinquency, however supervision or delinquency is measured (Glueck and Glueck 1950; Hirschi 1969; West and Farrington 1977; Riley and Shaw 1985).

Our general theory in principle provides a method of separating supervision as external control from supervision as internal control. For one thing, offenses differ in the degree to which they can be prevented through monitoring; children at one age are monitored much more closely than children at other ages; girls are supervised more closely than boys. In some situations, monitoring is universal or nearly constant; in other situations monitoring for some offenses is virtually absent. In the present context, however, the concern is with the connection between supervision and self-control, a connection established by the stronger tendency of those poorly supervised when young to commit crimes as adults (McCord 1979).

Recognition of Deviant Behavior

In order for supervision to have an impact on self-control, the supervisor must perceive deviant behavior when it occurs. Remarkably, not all parents are adept at recognizing lack of self-control. Some parents allow the child to do pretty much as he pleases without interference. Extensive television-viewing is one modern example, as is the failure to require completion of homework, to prohibit smoking, to curtail the use of physical force, or to see to it that the child actually attends school. (As noted, truancy among second-graders presumably reflects on the adequacy of parental awareness of the child's misbehavior.) Again, the research is not as good as it should be, but evidence of "poor conduct standards" in the homes of delinquents is common.

Punishment of Deviant Acts

Control theories explicitly acknowledge the necessity of sanctions in preventing criminal behavior. They do not suggest that the major sanctions are legal or corporal. On the contrary, as we have seen, they suggest that disapproval by people one cares about is the most powerful of sanctions. Effective punishment by the parent or major caretaker therefore usually entails nothing more than explicit disapproval of unwanted behavior. The criticism of control theories that dwells on their alleged cruelty is therefore simply misguided or ill informed (see, e.g., Currie 1985).

Not all caretakers punish effectively. In fact, some are too harsh and some are too lenient (Glueck and Glueck 1950; McCord and McCord 1959; West and Farrington 1977; see generally Loeber and Stouthamer-Loeber 1986). Given our model, however, rewarding good behavior cannot compensate for failure to correct deviant behavior. (Recall that, in our view, deviant acts carry with them their own rewards....)

Given the consistency of the child-rearing model with our general theory and with the research literature, it should be possible to use it to explain other family correlates of criminal and otherwise deviant behavior.

Parental Criminality

Our theory focuses on the connection between the self-control of the parent and the subsequent self-control of the child. There is good reason to expect, and the data confirm, that people lacking self-control do not socialize their children well. According to Donald West and David Farrington, "the fact that delinquency is transmitted from one generation to the next is indisputable" (1977: 109; see also Robins 1966). Of course our theory does not allow transmission of criminality, genetic or otherwise. However, it does allow us to predict that some people are more likely than others to fail to socialize their children and that this will be a consequence of their own inadequate socialization. The extent of this connection between parent and child socialization is revealed by the fact that in the West and Farrington study fewer than 5 percent of the families accounted for almost half of the criminal convictions in the entire sample. (In our view, this finding is more important for the theory of crime, and for public policy, than the much better-known finding of Wolfgang and his colleagues [1972] that something like 6 percent of *individual* offenders account for about half of all criminal acts.) In order to achieve such concentration of crime in a small number of families, it is necessary that the parents and the brothers and sisters of offenders also be unusually likely to commit criminal acts.

Why should the children of offenders be unusually vulnerable to crime? Recall that our theory assumes that criminality is not something the parents have to work to produce; on the contrary, it assumes that criminality is something they have to work to avoid. Consistent with this view, parents with criminal records do *not* encourage crime in their children and are in fact as disapproving of it as parents with no record of criminal involvement (West and Farrington 1977). Of course, not wanting criminal behavior in one's children and being upset when it occurs do not necessarily imply that great effort has been expended to prevent it. If criminal behavior is oriented toward short-term rewards, and if child-rearing is oriented toward long-term rewards, there is little reason to expect parents themselves lacking self-control to be particularly adept at instilling self-control in their children.

Consistent with this expectation, research consistently indicates that the supervision of delinquents in families where parents have criminal records tends to be "lax," "inadequate," or "poor." Punishment in these families also tends to be easy, short-term, and insensitive—that is, yelling and screaming, slapping and hitting, with threats that are not carried out.

Such facts do not, however, completely account for the concentration of criminality among some families. A major reason for this failure is probably that the most subtle element of child-rearing is not included in the analysis. This is the element of *recognition* of deviant behavior. According to Gerald Patterson (1980), many parents do not even recognize *criminal* behavior in their children, let alone the minor forms of deviance whose punishment is necessary for effective child-rearing. For example, when children steal outside the home, some parents discount reports that they have done so on the grounds that the charges are unproved and cannot therefore be used to justify punishment. By the same token, when children are suspended for misbehavior at school, some parents side with

the child and blame the episode on prejudicial mistreatment by teachers. Obviously, parents who cannot see the misbehavior of their children are in no position to correct it, even if they are inclined to do so....

Discussion Questions

1. What is low self-control? What are its main elements?
2. Give examples of acts that are "analogous" to crime? Why do Gottfredson and Hirschi believe that low self-control explains both crime and these analogous acts?
3. How does Gottfredson and Hirschi's self-control theory differ from Hirschi's earlier social bond theory?
4. What is the main reason that people have low self-control? In turn, based on Gottfredson and Hirschi's theory, what would be the best way to try to reduce crime?

CHAPTER 28

Foundation for a General Strain Theory of Crime and Delinquency

Robert Agnew

Strain theories posit that crime results from attempts to deal with stressful situations, that is, "strain." Although the source of strain varies according to different theorists in this tradition, strain often is considered to be the result of factors or conditions in the larger social structure, such as a disjunction between culturally acceptable goals (e.g., financial success) and socially approved means of achieving these goals (e.g., hard work). It is the individual's responses to such a strain that may result in crime. Robert Agnew, author of this selection, has recently reconceptualized strain theory in social psychological terms.

The extensions of strain theory delineated by Agnew may allow this approach to be a more successful explanation of individual-level criminal and delinquent behavior than earlier versions of strain theory. Agnew's theory goes beyond earlier versions by including a more comprehensive set of strains that may lead to crime or delinquency. Indeed, he argues that there are three major sources of strain. The first is "failure to achieve positively valued goals," which may involve a disjunction between one's aspirations and expectations or actual achievements or a disjunction between just or fair outcomes and actual outcomes. The second is "the removal of positively valued stimuli," such as job loss. The third is "the presentation of negative stimuli," such as adverse situations. In Agnew's framework, the emotion of anger plays a key role. However, criminal behavior does not automatically result when strain is experienced. Instead, Agnew discusses various coping mechanisms—cognitive, behavioral, and emotional—that may be used when strain is experienced so that it does not result in crime. The likelihood of an individual responding to strain by delinquency is related to individual-level factors, such as a person's goals, values or identities, coping resources, and social support.

After dominating deviance research in the 1960s, strain theory came under heavy attack in the 1970s (Bernard, 1984; Cole, 1975), with several prominent researchers suggesting that the theory be abandoned (Hirschi, 1969; Kornhauser, 1978). Strain theory has survived those attacks, but its influence is much diminished (see Agnew, 1985a; Bernard, 1984; Farnworth and Leiber, 1989). In particular, variables derived from strain theory now play a very limited role in explanations of crime/delinquency. Several recent causal models of delinquency, in fact, either entirely exclude strain variables or assign them a small role (e.g., Elliott et al., 1985; Johnson, 1979; Massey and Krohn, 1986; Thornberry, 1987; Tonry et al., 1991). Causal models of crime/delinquency are dominated, instead, by variables derived from differential association/social learning theory and social control theory.

This paper argues that strain theory has a central role to play in explanations of crime/delinquency, but that the theory has to be substantially

Reprinted from: Robert S. Agnew, "Foundation for a General Strain Theory of Crime and Delinquency." In *Criminology* 30, pp. 47-87. Copyright © 1992 by The American Society of Criminology. Reprinted by permission.

revised to play this role. Most empirical studies of strain theory continue to rely on the strain models developed by Merton (1938), A. Cohen (1955), and Cloward and Ohlin (1960). In recent years, however, a wealth of research in several fields has questioned certain of the assumptions underlying those theories and pointed to new directions for the development of strain theory.... This paper draws on the above literatures, as well as the recent revisions in strain theory, to present the outlines of a general strain theory of crime/delinquency.

The theory is written at the social-psychological level: It focuses on the individual and his or her immediate social environment—although the macroimplications of the theory are explored at various points.... This general theory, it will be argued, is capable of overcoming the theoretical and empirical criticisms of previous strain theories and of complementing the crime/delinquency theories that currently dominate the field....

Strain Theory as Distinguished From Control and Differential Association/Social Learning Theory

Strain, social control, and differential association theory are all sociological theories: They explain delinquency in terms of the individual's social relationships. Strain theory is distinguished from social control and social learning theory in its specification of (1) the type of social relationship that leads to delinquency and (2) the motivation for delinquency. First, strain theory focuses explicitly on *negative relationships with others*: relationships in which the individual is not treated as he or she wants to be treated. Strain theory has typically focused on relationships in which others prevent the individual from achieving positively valued goals. Agnew (1985a), however, broadened the focus of strain theory to include relationships in which others present the individual with noxious or negative stimuli. Social control theory, by contrast, focuses on the *absence of significant relationships with conventional others and institutions*. In particular, delinquency is most likely when (1) the adolescent is not attached to parents, school,

or other institutions; (2) parents and others fail to monitor and effectively sanction deviance; (3) the adolescent's actual or anticipated investment in conventional society is minimal; and (4) the adolescent has not internalized conventional beliefs. Social learning theory is distinguished from strain and control theory by its focus on *positive relationships with deviant others*. In particular, delinquency results from association with others who (1) differentially reinforce the adolescent's delinquency, (2) model delinquent behavior, and/or (3) transmit delinquent values.

Second, strain theory argues that adolescents *are pressured into delinquency by the negative affective states—most notably anger and related emotions—that often result from negative relationships* (see Kemper, 1978, and Morgan and Heise, 1988, for typologies of negative affective states). This negative affect creates pressure for corrective action and *may* lead adolescents to (1) make use of illegitimate channels of goal achievement, (2) attack or escape from the source of their adversity, and/or (3) manage their negative affect through the use of illicit drugs. Control theory, by contrast, denies that outside forces pressure the adolescent into delinquency. Rather, the absence of significant relationships with other individuals and *groups frees the adolescent to engage in delinquency*. The freed adolescent either drifts into delinquency or, in some versions of control theory, turns to delinquency in response to inner forces or situational inducements (see Hirschi, 1969:31-34). In differential association/social learning theory, the adolescent commits delinquent acts because group forces lead the adolescent to *view delinquency as a desirable or at least justifiable form of behavior* under certain circumstances.

Strain theory, then, is distinguished by its focus on negative relationships with others and its insistence that such relationships lead to delinquency through the negative affect—specially anger—they sometimes engender....

Phrased in the above manner, it is easy to see that strain theory complements the other major theories of delinquency in a fundamental way. While these other theories focus on the absence of relationships or on positive relationships, strain theory is the only theory to focus explicitly on negative relationships. And while these other theories view delinquency as the result of drift or of desire, strain theory views it as the result of pressure.

The Major Types of Strain

Negative relationships with others are, quite simply, relationships in which others are not treating the individual as he or she would like to be treated. The classic strain theories of Merton (1938), A. Cohen (1955), and Cloward and Ohlin (1960) focus on only one type of negative relationship: relationships in which others prevent the individual from achieving positively valued goals. In particular, they focus on the goal blockage experienced by lowerclass individuals trying to achieve monetary success or middle-class status. More recent versions of strain theory have argued that adolescents are not only concerned about the future goals of monetary success/middle-class status, but are also concerned about the achievement of more immediate goals such as good grades, popularity with the opposite sex, and doing well in athletics (Agnew, 1984; Elliott and Voss, 1974; Elliott et al., 1985; Empey, 1982; Greenberg, 1977; Quicker, 1974). The focus, however, is still on the achievement of positively valued goals. Most recently, Agnew (1985a) has argued that strain may result not only from the failure to achieve positively valued goals, but also from the inability to escape legally from painful situations....

Three major types of strain are described—each referring to a different type of negative relationship with others. Other individuals may (1) prevent one from achieving positively valued goals, (2) remove or threaten to remove positively valued stimuli that one possesses, or (3) present or threaten to present one with noxious or negatively valued stimuli. These categories of strain are presented as ideal types....

Strain as the Failure to Achieve Positively Valued Goals

At least three types of strain fall under this category. The first type encompasses most of the major strain theories in criminology, including the classic strain theories of Merton, A. Cohen, and Cloward and Ohlin, as well as those modem strain theories focusing on the achievement of immediate goals. The other two types of strain in this category are derived from the justice/equity literature and have not been examined in criminology.

Strain As the Disjunction Between Aspirations and Expectations/Actual Achievements. The classic strain theories of Merton, A. Cohen, and Cloward and Ohlin argue that the cultural system encourages everyone to pursue the ideal goals of monetary success and/or middle-class status. Lower-class individuals, however, are often prevented from achieving such goals through legitimate channels. In line with such theories, adolescent strain is typically measured in terms of the disjunction between *aspirations* (or ideal goals) and *expectations* (or expected levels of goal achievement). These theories, however, have been criticized for several reasons (see Agnew, 1986, 1991b; Clinard, 1964; Hirschi, 1969; Kornhauser, 1978; Liska, 1987; also see Bernard, 1984; Farnworth and Leiber, 1989)....

As a consequence of these criticisms, several researchers have revised the above theories. The most popular revision argues that there is a youth subculture that emphasizes a variety of immediate goals.... This version of strain theory, however, continues to argue that strain stems from the inability to achieve certain ideal goals emphasized by the (sub)cultural system. As a consequence, strain continues to be measured in terms of the disjunction between *aspirations and actual achievements* (since we are dealing with immediate rather than future goals, actual achievements rather than expected achievements may be examined)....

Strain As the Disjunction Between Expectations and Actual Achievements. ....Here the focus is on the disjunction between *expectations and actual achievements* (rewards), and it is commonly argued that such expectations are existentially based. In particular, it has been argued that such expectations derive from the individual's past experience and/or from comparisons with referential (or generalized) others who are similar to the individual (see Berger et al., 1972, 1983; Blau, 1964; Homans, 1961; Jasso and Rossi, 1977; Mickelson, 1990; Ross et al., 1971; Thibaut and Kelley, 1959). Much of the research in this area has focused on income expectations, although the above theories apply to expectations regarding all manner of positive stimuli. The justice literature argues that the failure to achieve such expectations may lead to such emotions as anger, resentment, rage, dissatisfaction, disappointment, and unhappiness—that is, all the emotions customarily associated with strain in criminology. Further, it is argued that individuals will be strongly motivated to reduce the gap between expectations and achievements—with deviance being commonly mentioned as one possible option.

Strain as the Disjunction Between Just/Fair Outcomes and Actual Outcomes. ...A third conception of strain, also derived from the justice/equity literature, makes a rather different argument. It claims that individuals do not necessarily enter interactions with specific outcomes in mind. Rather, they enter interactions expecting that certain distributive justice rules will be followed, rules specifying how resources should be allocated. The rule that has received the most attention in the literature is that of equity. An equitable relationship is one in which the outcome/input ratios of the actors involved in an exchange/allocation relationship are equivalent (see Adams, 1963, 1965; Cook and Hegtvedt, 1983; Walster et al., 1978). Outcomes encompass a broad range of positive and negative consequences, while inputs encompass the individual's positive and negative contributions to the exchange. Individuals in a relationship will compare the ratio of their outcomes and inputs to the ratio(s) of specific others in the relationship. If the ratios are equal to one another, they feel that the outcomes are fair or just. This is true, according to equity theorists, even if the outcomes are low. If outcome/input ratios are not equal, actors will feel that the outcomes are unjust and they will experience distress as a result. Such distress is especially likely when individuals feel they have been underrewarded rather than overrewarded (Hegtvedt, 1990).

The equity literature has described the possible reactions to this distress, some of which involve deviance (see Adams, 1963, 1965; Austin, 1977; Walster et al., 1973, 1978; see Stephenson and White, 1968, for an attempt to recast A. Cohen's strain theory in terms of equity theory). In particular, inequity may lead to delinquency for several reasons—all having to do with the restoration of equity. Individuals in inequitable relationships may engage in delinquency in order to (1) increase their outcomes (e.g., by theft); (2) lower their inputs (e.g., truancy from school); (3) lower the outcomes of others (e.g., vandalism, theft, assault); and/or (4) increase the inputs of others (e.g., by being incorrigible or disorderly). In highly inequitable situations, individuals may leave the field (e.g., run away from home) or force others to leave the field.[1]

Summary: Strain As the Failure to Achieve Positively Valued Goals. ...Three types of strain in this category have been listed: strain as the disjunction between (1) aspirations and expectations/actual achievements, (2) expectations and actual achievements, and (3) just/fair outcomes and actual outcomes. Strain theory in criminology has focused on the first type of strain, arguing that it is most responsible for the delinquency in our society. Major research traditions in the justice/equity field, however, argue that anger and frustration derive primarily from the second two types of strain. To complicate matters further, one can list still additional types of strain in this category. Certain of the literature, for example, has talked of the disjunction between "satisfying outcomes" and reality, between "deserved" outcomes and reality, and between "tolerance levels" or minimally acceptable outcomes and reality....

Given these multiple sources of strain, one might ask which is the most relevant to the explanation of delinquency. This is a difficult question to answer given current research. The most fruitful strategy at the present time may be to assume that all of the above sources are relevant—that there are several sources of frustration.... One would expect strain to be greatest when several standards were not being met, with perhaps greatest weight being given to expectations and just/fair outcomes.[2]

Strain As the Removal of Positively Valued Stimuli From the Individual

Drawing on the stress literature, then, one may state that a second type of strain or negative relationship involves the actual or anticipated removal (loss) of positively valued stimuli from the individual.... The actual or anticipated loss of positively valued stimuli may lead to delinquency as the individual tries to prevent the loss of the positive stimuli, retrieve the lost stimuli or obtain substitute stimuli, seek revenge against those responsible for the loss, or manage the negative affect caused by the loss by taking illicit drugs....

Strain as the Presentation of Negative Stimuli

The literature on stress and the recent psychological literature on aggression also focus on the actual or anticipated presentation of negative or noxious stimuli.[3]...Noxious stimuli may lead to delinquency as the adolescent tries to (1) escape from or avoid the negative stimuli; (2) terminate or alleviate the negative stimuli; (3) seek revenge against the source of the negative stimuli or related targets, although the evidence on displaced aggression is somewhat mixed (see Berkowitz, 1982; Bernard, 1990; Van Houten, 1983; Zillman, 1979); and/or (4) manage the resultant negative affect by taking illicit drugs.

A wide range of noxious stimuli have been examined in the literature, and experimental, survey, and participant observation studies have linked such stimuli to both general and specific measures of delinquency—with the experimental studies focusing on aggression. Delinquency/ aggression, in particular, has been linked to such noxious stimuli as child abuse and neglect (Rivera and Widom, 1990), criminal victimization (Lauritsen et al., 1991), physical punishment (Straus, 1991), negative relations with parents (Healy and Bonner, 1969), negative relations with peers (Short and Strodtbeck, 1965), adverse or negative school experiences (Hawkins and Lishner, 1987), a wide range of stressful life events (Gersten et al., 1974; Kaplan et al., 1983; Linsky and Straus, 1986; Mawson, 1987; Novy and Donohue, 1985; Vaux and Ruggiero, 1983), verbal threats and insults, physical pain, unpleasant odors, disgusting scenes, noise, heat, air pollution, personal space violations, and high density (see Anderson and Anderson, 1984; Bandura, 1973, 1983; Berkowitz, 1982, 1986; Mueller, 1983)....

The Links Between Strain and Delinquency

Three sources of strain have been presented: strain as the actual or anticipated failure to achieve positively valued goals, strain as the actual or anticipated removal of positively valued stimuli, and strain as the actual or anticipated presentation of negative stimuli. While these types are theoretically distinct from one another, they may sometimes overlap in practice. So, for example, the insults of a teacher may be experienced as adverse because they (1) interfere with the adolescent's aspirations for academic success, (2) result in the violation of a distributive justice rule such as equity, and (3) are conditioned negative stimuli and so are experienced as noxious in and of themselves. Other examples of overlap can be given, and it may sometimes be difficult to disentangle the different types of strain in practice. Once again, however, these categories are ideal types and are presented only to ensure that all events with the potential for creating strain are considered in empirical research.

Each type of strain increases the likelihood that individuals will experience one or more of a range of negative emotions. Those emotions include disappointment, depression, and fear. Anger, however, is the most critical emotional reaction for the purposes of the general strain theory. Anger results when individuals blame their adversity on others, and anger is a key emotion because it increases the individual's level of felt injury, creates a desire for retaliation/revenge, energizes the individual for action, and lowers inhibitions, in part because individuals believe that others will feel their aggression is justified (see Averill, 1982; Berkowitz, 1982; Kemper, 1978; Kluegel and Smith, 1986: Ch. 10; Zillman, 1979). Anger, then, affects the individual in several ways that are conducive to delinquency. Anger is distinct from many of the other types of negative affect in this respect, and this is the reason that anger occupies a special place in the general strain theory.[4] It is important to note, however, that delinquency may still occur in response to other types of negative affect—such as despair, although delinquency is less likely in such cases.[5] The experience of negative affect, especially anger, typically creates a desire to take corrective steps, with delinquency being one possible response. Delinquency may be a method for alleviating strain, that is, for achieving positively valued goals, for protecting or retrieving positive stimuli, or for terminating or escaping from negative stimuli. Delinquency may be used to seek revenge; data suggest that vengeful behavior often occurs even when there is no possibility of eliminating the adversity that stimulated it (Berkowitz, 1982). And delinquency may occur as adolescents try to manage their negative affect through illicit drug use (see Newcomb and Harlow, 1986). The general strain theory, then, has the potential to explain a broad range of delinquency, including theft, aggression, and drug use.

Each type of strain may create a *predisposition* for delinquency or function as a *situational event* that instigates a particular delinquent act.... Strain creates a predisposition for delinquency in those cases in which it is chronic or repetitive. Examples include a continuing gap between expectations and achievements and a continuing pattern of ridicule and insults from teachers. Adolescents subject to such strain are predisposed to delinquency because (1) nondelinquent strategies for coping with strain are likely to be taxed; (2) the threshold for adversity may be lowered by chronic strains (see Averill, 1982:289); (3) repeated or chronic strain may lead to a hostile attitude—a general dislike and suspicion of others and an associated tendency to respond in an aggressive manner (see Edmunds and Kendrick, 1980:21); and (4) chronic strains increase the likelihood that individuals will be high in negative affect/arousal at any given time (see Bandura, 1983; Bernard, 1990). A particular instance of strain may also function as the situational event that ignites a delinquent act, especially among adolescents predisposed to delinquency....

Adaptations to (Coping Strategies for) Strain

The discussion thus far has focused on the types of strain that might promote delinquency. Virtually all strain theories, however, acknowledge that only *some* strained individuals turn to delinquency. Some effort has been made to identify those factors that determine whether one adapts to strain through delinquency. The most attention has been focused on the adolescent's commitment to legitimate means and association with other strained/delinquent individuals (see Agnew, 1991b)....

Adaptations to Strain

What follows is a typology of the major cognitive, emotional, and behavioral adaptations to strain, including delinquency.

Cognitive Coping Strategies. Several literatures suggest that individuals sometimes cognitively reinterpret objective stressors in ways that minimize their subjective adversity. Three general strategies of cognitive coping are described below; each strategy has several forms. These strategies for coping with adversity may be summarized in the following phrases: "It's not important," "It's not that bad," and "I deserve it."...

Ignore/Minimize the Importance of Adversity. The subjective impact of objective strain depends on the extent to which the strain is related to the central goals, values, and/or identities of the individual. As Pearlin and Schooler (1978:7) state, individuals may avoid subjective strain "to the extent that they are able to keep the most strainful experiences within the least valued areas of their life." Individuals, therefore, may minimize the strain they experience by reducing the absolute and/or relative importance assigned to goals/values and identities (see Agnew, 1983; Thoits, 1991a)....

Maximize Positive Outcomes/Minimize Negative Outcomes. In the above adaptation, individuals acknowledge the existence of adversity but relegate such adversity to an unimportant area of their life. In a second adaptation, individuals attempt to deny the existence of adversity by maximizing their positive outcomes and/or minimizing their negative outcomes. This may be done in two ways: lowering the standards used to evaluate outcomes or distorting one's estimate of current and/or expected outcomes.

Lowering one's standards basically involves lowering one's goals or raising one's threshold for negative stimuli (see Suls, 1977). Such action, of course, makes one's current situation seem less adverse than it otherwise would be....

In addition to lowering their standards, individuals may also cognitively distort their estimate of outcomes. As Agnew and Jones (1988) demonstrate, many individuals exaggerate their actual and expected levels of goal achievement. In addition to exaggerating positive outcomes, individuals may also minimize negative outcomes—claiming that their losses are small and their noxious experiences are mild.

The self-concept literature discusses the many strategies individuals employ to accomplish such distortions (see Agnew and Jones, 1988; Rosenberg, 1979). Two common strategies, identified across several literatures, are worth noting. In "downward comparisons," individuals claim that their situation is less worse or at least no worse than that of similar others (e.g., Brickman and Bulman, 1977; Gruder, 1977; Pearlin and Schooler, 1978; Suls, 1977)....In a second strategy, "compensatory benefits," individuals cast "about for some positive attribute or circumstance within a troublesome situation...the person is aided in ignoring that which is noxious by anchoring his attention to what he considers the more worthwhile and rewarding aspects of experience" (Pearlin and Schooler, 1978:6-7). Crime victims, for example, often argue that their victimization benefitted them in certain ways, such as causing them to grow as a person (Agnew, 1985b).

Accept Responsibility for Adversity. Third, individuals may *minimize* the subjective adversity of objective strain by convincing themselves that they *deserve* the adversity they have experienced. There are several possible reasons why *deserved* strain is less adverse than undeserved strain. Undeserved strain may violate the equity principle, challenge one's "belief in a just world" (see Lerner, 1977), and—if attributed to the malicious behavior of another—lead one to fear that it will be repeated in the future. Such reasons may help explain why individuals who make internal attributions for adversity are less distressed than others (Kluegel and Smith, 1986; Mirowsky and Ross, 1990).

Behavioral Coping Strategies. ...There are two major types of behavioral coping: those that seek to minimize or eliminate the source of strain and those that seek to satisfy the need for revenge.

Maximizing Positive Outcomes/Minimizing Negative Outcomes. Behavioral coping may assume several forms, paralleling each of the major types of strain. Individuals, then, may seek to achieve positively valued goals, protect or retrieve positively valued stimuli, or terminate or escape from negative stimuli. Their actions in these areas may involve conventional or delinquent behavior....

Vengeful Behavior. Data indicate that when adversity is blamed on others it creates a desire for revenge that is distinct from the desire to end the adversity. A second method of behavioral coping, then, involves the taking of revenge. Vengeful behavior may also assume conventional or delinquent forms, although the potential for delinquency is obviously high. Such behavior may involve efforts to minimize the positive outcomes, increase the negative outcomes, and/or increase the inputs of others (as when adolescents cause teachers and parents to work harder through their incorrigible behavior).

Emotional Coping Strategies. Finally, individuals may cope by acting directly on the negative emotions that result from adversity. Rosenberg (1990), Thoits (1984, 1989, 1990, 1991b), and others list several strategies of emotional coping. They include the use of drugs such as stimulants and depressants, physical exercise and deep-breathing techniques, meditation, biofeedback and progressive relaxation, and the behavioral manipulation of expressive gestures through playacting or "expression work." In all of these examples, the focus is on alleviating negative emotions rather than cognitively reinterpreting or behaviorally altering the situation that produced those emotions....Emotional coping is especially likely when behavioral and cognitive coping are unavailable or unsuccessful.

It should be noted that individuals may employ more than one of the above coping strategies (see Folkman, 1991).

Predicting the Use of Delinquent Versus Nondelinquent Adaptations

The above typology suggests that there are many ways to cope with strain—only some of which involve delinquency. And data from the stress literature suggest that individuals vary in the extent to which they use the different strategies (Compas et al., 1988; Menaghan, 1983; Pearlin and Schooler, 1978). These facts go a long way toward explaining the weak support for strain theory....

The existence of the above coping strategies poses a serious problem for strain theory. If strain theory is to have any value, it must be able to explain the selection of delinquent versus nondelinquent adaptations....

Constraints to Nondelinquent and Delinquent Coping.

While there are many adaptations to objective strain, those adaptations are not equally available to everyone. Individuals are constrained in their choice of adaptation(s) by a variety of internal and external factors. The following is a partial list of such factors.

Initial Goals/Values/Identities of the Individual. If the objective strain affects goals/values/identities that are high in absolute and relative importance, and if the individual has few alternative goals/values/identities in which to seek refuge, it will be more difficult to relegate strain to an unimportant area of one's life (see Agnew, 1986; Thoits, 1991a). This is especially the case if the goals/values/identities receive strong social and cultural support (see below). As a result, strain will be more likely to lead to delinquency in such cases.

Individual Coping Resources. A wide range of traits can be listed in this area, including temperament, intelligence, creativity, problem-solving skills, interpersonal skills, self-efficacy, and self-esteem. These traits affect the selection of coping strategies by influencing the individual's sensitivity to objective strains and ability to engage in cognitive, emotional, and behavioral coping (Agnew, 1991a; Averill, 1982; Bernard, 1990; Compas, 1987; Edmunds and Kendrick, 1980; Slaby and Guerra, 1988; Tavris, 1984)....

Conventional Social Support. The major types of social support, in fact, correspond to the major types of coping listed above. Thus, there is informational support, instrumental support, and emotional support (House, 1981). Adolescents with conventional social supports, then, should be better able to respond to objective strains in a nondelinquent manner.

Constraints to Delinquent Coping. The crime/delinquency literature has focused on certain variables that constrain delinquent coping. They include (1) the costs and benefits of engaging in delinquency in a particular situation (Clarke and Comish, 1985), (2) the individual's level of social control (see Hirschi, 1969), and (3) the possession of those "illegitimate means" necessary for many delinquent acts (see Agnew, 1991a, for a full discussion).

Macro-Level Variables. The larger social environment may affect the probability of delinquent versus nondelinquent coping by affecting all of the above factors. First, the social environment may affect coping by influencing the importance attached to selected goals/values/identities. For example, certain ethnographic accounts suggest that there is a strong social and cultural emphasis on the goals of money/status among certain segments of the urban poor....

Second, the larger social environment may affect the individual's sensitivity to particular strains by influencing the individual's beliefs regarding what is and is not adverse. The subculture of violence thesis, for example, is predicated on the assumption that young black males in urban slums are taught that a wide range of provocations and insults are highly adverse. Third, the social environment may influence the individual's ability to minimize cognitively the severity of objective strain. Individuals in some environments are regularly provided with external information about their accomplishments and failings (see Faunce, 1989), and their attempts at cognitively distorting such information are quickly challenged. Such a situation may exist among many adolescents and among those who inhabit the "street-corner world" of the urban poor. Adolescents and those on the street corner live in a very "public world"; one's accomplishments and failings typically occur before a large audience or they quickly become known to such an audience. Further, accounts suggest that this audience regularly reminds individuals of their accomplishments and failings and challenges attempts at cognitive distortion.

Fourth, certain social environments may make it difficult to engage in behavioral coping of a nondelinquent nature. Agnew (1985a) has argued that adolescents often find it difficult to escape legally from negative stimuli, especially negative stimuli encountered in the school, family, and neighborhood. Also, adolescents often lack the resources to negotiate successfully with adults, such as parents and teachers (although see Agnew, 1991a). Similar arguments might be made for others, and they often find it difficult to escape legally from adverse environments—by, for example, quitting their job (if they have a job) or moving to another neighborhood.

The larger social environment, then, may affect individual coping in a variety of ways. And certain groups, such as adolescents and the urban underclass, may face special constraints that make nondelinquent coping more difficult. This may explain the higher rate of deviance among these groups.

Factors Affecting the Disposition to Delinquency. The selection of delinquent versus nondelinquent coping strategies is not only dependent on the constraints to coping, but also on the adolescent's disposition to engage in delinquent versus nondelinquent coping. This disposition is a function of (1) certain temperamental variables (see Tonry et al., 1991), (2) the prior learning history of the adolescent, particularly the extent to which delinquency was reinforced in the past (Bandura, 1973; Berkowitz, 1982), (3) the adolescent's beliefs, particularly the rules defining the appropriate response to provocations (Bernard's, 1990, "regulative rules"), and (4) the adolescent's attributions regarding the causes of his or her adversity. Adolescents who attribute their adversity to others are much more likely to become angry, and as argued earlier, that anger creates a strong predisposition to delinquency....

A key variable affecting several of the above factors is association with delinquent peers. It has been argued that adolescents who associate with delinquent peers are more likely to be exposed to delinquent models and beliefs and to receive reinforcement for delinquency (see especially, Akers, 1985). It may also be the case that delinquent peers increase the likelihood that adolescents will attribute their adversity to others.

The individual's disposition to delinquency, then, may condition the impact of adversity on delinquency. At the same time, it is important to note that continued experience with adversity may create a disposition for delinquency. This argument has been made by Bernard (1990), Cloward and Ohlin (1960), A. Cohen (1955), Elliott et al. (1979), and others. In particular, it has been argued that under certain conditions the experience of adversity may lead to beliefs favorable to delinquency, lead adolescents to join or form delinquent peer groups, and lead adolescents to blame others for their misfortune....

Conclusion

...The general strain theory builds upon traditional strain theory in criminology in several ways. First, the general strain theory points to several new sources of strain. In particular, it focuses on three categories of strain or negative relationships with others: (1) the actual or anticipated failure to achieve positively valued goals, (2) the actual or anticipated removal of positively valued stimuli, and (3) the actual or anticipated presentation of negative stimuli. Most current strain theories in criminology only focus on strain as the failure to achieve positively valued goals, and even then the focus is only on the disjunction between aspirations and expectations/actual achievements. The disjunctions between expectations and achievements and just/fair outcomes and achievements are ignored. The general strain theory, then, significantly expands the focus of strain theory to include all types of negative relations between the individual and others.

Second, the general strain theory more precisely specifies the relationship between strain and delinquency, pointing out that strain is likely to have a cumulative effect on delinquency after a certain threshold level is reached. The theory also points to certain relevant dimensions of strain that should be considered in empirical research, including the magnitude, recency, duration, and clustering of strainful events.

Third, the general strain theory provides a more comprehensive account of the cognitive, behavioral, and emotional adaptations to strain. This account sheds additional light on the reasons why many strained individuals do *not* turn to delinquency, and it may prove useful in devising strategies to prevent and control delinquency. Individuals, in particular, may be taught those nondelinquent coping strategies found to be most effective in preventing delinquency.

Fourth, the general strain theory more fully describes those factors affecting the choice of delinquent versus nondelinquent adaptations. The failure to consider such factors is a fundamental reason for the weak empirical support for strain theory....

Strain theory is the only major theory to focus explicitly on negative relations with others and to argue that delinquency results from the negative affect caused by such relations. As such, it complements social control and differential association/social learning theory in a fundamental way. It is hoped that the general strain theory will revive interest in negative relations and cause criminologists to "bring the bad back in."

Discussion Questions

1. According to Agnew's framework, what are the three major sources of strain? Why is each a potential source of strain?
2. According to Agnew, why may strain lead to crime or delinquency? What are some of the noncriminal responses to strain?
3. What are some of the factors involved in determining whether one's response to strain will be non-criminal or criminal? Why might one choose criminal responses over non-criminal responses and vice versa?

Notes

1. Theorists have recently argued that efforts to restore equity need not involve the specific others in the inequitable relationship. If one cannot restore equity with such specific others, there may be an effort to restore "equity with the world" (Austin, 1977; Stephenson and White, 1968; Walster et al., 1978). That is, individuals who feel they have been inequitably treated may respond by inequitably treating peers. The concept of "equity with the world" has not been the subject of much empirical research, but it is intriguing because it provides a novel explanation for displayed aggression.

It has also been argued that individuals may be distressed not only by their own inequitable treatment, but also by the inequitable treatment of others (see Crosby and Gonzales-Intal, 1984; Walster et al., 1978.) We may have, then, a sort of vicarious strain, a type little investigated in the literature.

2. This strategy assumes that all standards are relevant in a given situation, which may not always be the case. In certain situations, for example, one may make local comparisons but not referential comparisons (see Brickman and Bulman, 1977; Crosby and Gonzales-Intal, 1984). In other situations, social comparison processes may not come into play at all; outcomes may be evaluated in terms of culturally derived standards (see Folger, 1986).

3. Some researchers have argued that it is often difficult to distinguish the presentation of negative stimuli from the removal of positive stimuli (Michael, 1973; Van Houten, 1983; Zillman, 1979). Suppose, for example, that an adolescent argues with parents. Does this represent the presentation of negative stimuli, (the arguing) or the removal of positive stimuli (harmonious relations with one's parents)? The point is a valid one, yet the distinction between the two types of strain still seems useful since it helps ensure that all major types of strain are considered by researchers.

4. The focus on blame/anger represents a major distinction between the general strain theory and the stress literature. The stress literature simply focuses on adversity, regardless of whether it is blamed on another. This is perhaps appropriate because the major outcome variables of the stress literature are inner-directed states, like depression and poor health. When the focus shifts to outer-directed behavior, like much delinquency, a concern with blame/anger becomes important.

5. Delinquency may still occur in the absence of blame and anger (see Berkowitz, 1986; Zillman, 1979). Individuals who accept responsibility for their adversity are still subject to negative affect, such as depression, despair, and disappointment (see Kemper, 1978; Kluegel and Smith, 1986). As a result, such individuals will still feel pressure to take corrective action, although the absence of anger places them under less pressure and makes vengeful behavior much less likely. Such individuals, however, may engage in inner-directed delinquency, such as drug use, and if suitably disposed, they may turn to other forms of delinquency as well. Since these individuals lack the strong motivation for revenge and the lowered inhibitions that anger provides, it is assumed that they must have some minimal disposition for deviance before they respond

to their adversity with outer-directed delinquency (see the discussion of the disposition to delinquency).

References

Adams, J. Stacy. 1963. "Toward an understanding of inequity." *Journal of Abnormal and Social Psychology*, 67:422-436.

——. "Inequity in social exchange". In Leonard Berkowitz (ed.), *Advances in Experimental Social Psychology*. New York: Academic Press.

Agnew, Robert. 1983. "Social class and success goals: An examination of relative and absolute aspirations." *Sociological Quarterly*, 24:435-452.

——. 1984. "Goal achievement and delinquency." *Sociology and Social Research,*" 68:435-451.

——. 1985a. "A revised strain theory of delinquency." *Social Forces,* 64:151-167.

——. 1985b. "Neutralizing the impact of crime." *Criminal Justice and Behavior*, 12:221-239.

——. 1986. "Challenging strain theory: An examination of goals and goal-blockage." Paper presented at the annual meeting of the American Society of Criminology, Atlanta.

——. 1989. "A longitudinal test of the revised strain theory." *Journal of Quantitative Criminology,* 5:373-387.

——. 1990. "The origins of delinquent events: An examination of offender accounts." *Journal of Research in Crime and Delinquency*, 27:267-294.

——. 1991a. "Adolescent resources and delinquency." *Criminology,* 28:535-566.

——. 1991b. "Strain and subculture crime theory." In Joseph Sheley (ed.), *Criminology: A Contemporary Handbook*. Belmont, Calif.: Wadsworth.

Agnew, Robert and Diane Jones. 1988. "Adapting to deprivation: An examination of inflated educational expectations." *Sociological Quarterly*, 29:315-337.

Aiken, Leona S. and Stephen G. West. 1991. *Multiple Regression: Testing and Interpreting Interactions*. Newbury Park, Calif.: Sage.

Akers, Ronald L. 1985. *Deviant Behavior: A Social Learning Approach*. Belmont, Calif.: Wadsworth.

Alves, Wayne M. and Peter H. Rossi. 1978. "Who should get what? Fairness judgments of the distribution of earnings." *American Journal of Sociology*, 84:541-564.

Alwin, Duane F. 1987. "Distributive justice and satisfaction with material well-being." *American Sociological Review*, 52:83-95.

Anderson, Elijah. 1978. *A Place on the Corner*. Chicago: University of Chicago Press.

Anderson, Craig A. and Dona C. Anderson. 1984. "Ambient temperature and violent crime: Tests of the linear and curvilinear hypotheses." *Journal of Personality and Social Psychology*, 46:91-97.

Austin, William. 1977. "Equity theory and social comparison processes." In Jerry M. Suls and Richard L. Miller (eds.), *Social Comparison Processes*. New York: Hemisphere.

Averill, James R. 1982. *Anger and Aggression*. New York: Springer-Verlag.

Avison, William R. and R. Jay Turner. 1988. "Stressful life events and depressive symptoms: Disaggregating the effects of acute stressors and chronic strains." *Journal of Health and Social Behavior,* 29:253 -264.

Bandura, Albert. 1973. *Aggression: A Social Learning Analysis*. Englewood Cliffs, N.J.: Prentice-Hall.

——. 1983. "Psychological mechanisms of aggression." In Russell G. Geen and Edward Donnerstein (eds.), *Aggression: Theoretical and Empirical Reviews*. New York: Academic Press.

——. 1989. "Human agency and social cognitive theory." *American Psychologist*, 44:1175-1184.

Berger, Joseph, Morris Zelditch, Jr., Bo Anderson, and Bernard Cohen. 1972. "Structural aspects of distributive justice: A status-value formulation." In Joseph Berger, Morris Zelditch, Jr., and Bo Anderson (eds.), *Sociological Theories in Progress*. New York: Houghton Mifflin.

Berger, Joseph, M. Hamit Fisck, Robert Z. Norman, and David G. Wagner. 1983. "The formation of reward expectations in status situations." In David M. Messick and Karen S. Cook (eds.), *Equity Theory: Psychological and Sociological Perspectives*. New York: Praeger.

Berkowitz, Leonard. 1978. "Whatever happened to the frustration-aggression hypothesis?" *American Behavioral Scientist*, 21:691-708.

——. 1982. "Aversive conditions as stimuli to aggression." In Leonard Berkowitz (ed.), *Advances in Experimental Social Psychology. Vol. 15*. New York: Academic Press.

——. 1986. *A Survey of Social Psychology*. New York: Holt, Rinehart & Winston.

Bernard, Thomas J. 1984. "Control criticisms of strain theories: An assessment of theoretical and empirical adequacy." *Journal of Research in Crime and Delinquency*, 21:353-372.

Bernard, Thomas J.. 1987. "Testing structural strain theories." *Journal of Research in Crime and Delinquency*, 24:262-280.

——. 1990. "Angry aggression among the 'truly disadvantaged'." *Criminology*, 28:73-96.

Blau, Peter. 1964. *Exchange and Power in Social Life.* New York: John Wiley & Sons.

Brewin, Chris R. 1988. "Explanation and adaptation in adversity." In Shirley Fisher and James Reason (eds.), *Handbook of Life Stress, Cognition and Health.* Chichester, England: John Wiley & Sons.

Brickman, Philip and Ronnie Janoff Bulman. 1977. "Pleasure and pain in social comparison." In Jerry M. Suis and Richard L. Miller (eds.), *Social Comparison Processes.* New York: Hemisphere.

Clarke, Ronald V. and Derek B. Cornish. 1985. "Modeling offenders' decisions: A framework for research and policy." In Michael Tonry and Norval Morris (eds.), *Crime and Justice: An Annual Review of Research.* Vol. 6. Chicago: University of Chicago Press.

Clinard, Marshall B. 1964. *Anomie and Deviant Behavior.* New York: Free Press.

Cloward, Richard A. and Lloyd E. Ohlin. 1960. *Delinquency and Opportunity.* New York: Free Press.

Cohen, Albert K. 1955. *Delinquent Boys.* New York: Free Press.

——. 1965. "The sociology of the deviant act: Anomie theory and beyond." *American Sociological Review*, 30:5-14.

Cohen, Ronald L. 1982. "Perceiving justice: An attributional perspective." In Jerald Greenberg and Ronald L. Cohen (eds.), *Equity and Justice in Social Behavior.* New York: Academic Press.

Cole, Stephen. 1975. "The growth of scientific knowledge: Theories of deviance as a case study." In Lewis A. Coser (ed.), *The Idea of Social Structure: Papers in Honor of Robert K. Merton.* New York: Harcourt Brace Jovanovich.

Compas, Bruce E. 1987. "Coping with stress during childhood and adolescence." *Psychological Bulletin*, 101:393-403.

Compas, Bruce E., Vanessa L. Maicame, and Karen M. Fondacaro. 1988. "Coping with stressful events in older children and young adolescents." *Journal of Consulting and Clinical Psychology*, 56:405-411.

Compas, Bruce E. and Vicky Phares. 1991. "Stress during childhood and adolescence: Sources of risk and vulnerability." In E. Mark Cummings, Anita L. Greene, and Katherine H. Karraker (eds.), *Life-Span Developmental Psychology: Perspectives on Stress and Coping.* Hillsdale, N.J.: Lawrence Eribaum.

Cook, Karen S., and Karen A. Hegtvedt. 1983. "Distributive justice, equity, and equality." *Annual Review of Sociology*, 9:217-241.

——. 1991. "Empirical evidence of the sense of justice." In Margaret Gruter, Roger D. Masters, Michael T. McGuire (eds.), *The Sense of Justice: An Inquiry into the Biological Foundations of Law.* New York: Greenwood Press.

Cook, Karen S. and David Messick. 1983. "Psychological and sociological perspectives on distributive justice: Convergent, divergent, and parallel lines." In David M. Messick and Karen S. Cook (eds.), *Equity Theory: Psychological and Sociological Perspectives.* New York: Praeger.

Cook, Karen S. and Toshio Yamagishi. 1983. "Social determinants of equity judgments: The problem of multidimensional input." In David M. Messick and Karen S. Cook (eds.), *Equity Theory: Psychological and Sociological Perspectives.* New York: Praeger.

Crittenden, Kathleen S. 1983. "Sociological aspects of attribution." *Annual Review of Sociology*, 9:425-446.

——. 1989. "Causal attribution in sociocultural context: Toward a self-presentational theory of attribution processes." *Sociological Quarterly*, 30:1-14.

Crosby, Faye and A. Miren Gonzales-Intal. 1984. "Relative deprivation and equity theories: Felt injustice and the undeserved benefits of others." In Robert Folger (ed.), *The Sense on Injustice: Social Psychological Perspectives.* New York: Plenum.

Cummings, E. Mark and Mona El-Sheikh. 1991. "Children's coping with angry environments: A process-oriented approach." In E. Mark Cummings, Anita L. Greene, and Katherine H. Karraker (eds.), *Life-Span Developmental Psychology: Perspectives on Stress and Coping.* Hillsdale, N.J.: Lawrence Eribaum.

Della Fave, L. Richard. 1974. "Success values: Are they universal or class-differentiated?" *American Journal of Sociology*, 80:153-169.

——. 1980. "The meek shall not inherit the earth: Self-evaluations and the legitimacy of stratification." *American Sociological Review*, 45:955-971.

Della Fave, L. Richard and Patricia Klobus. 1976. "Success values and the value stretch: A biracial comparison." *Sociological Quarterly*, 17:491-502.

Deutsch, Morton. 1975. "Equity, equality, and need: What determines which value will be used as the basis of distributive justice." *Journal of Social Issues*, 31:137-149.

Dohrenwend, Bruce P. 1974. "Problems in defining and sampling the relevant population of stressful life events." In Barbara Snell Dohrenwend and Bruce P. Dohrenwend (eds.), *Stressful Life Events: Their Nature and Effects*. New York: John Wiley & Sons.

Dohrenwend, Barbara Snell and Bruce P. Dohrenwend. 1974. "Overview and prospects for research on stressful life events." In Barbara Snell Dohrenwend and Bruce P. Dohrenwend (eds.), *Stressful Life Events: Their Nature and Effects*. New York: John Wiley & Sons.

Donnerstein, Edward and Elaine Hatfield. 1982. "Aggression and equity." In Jerald Greenberg and Ronald L. Cohen (eds.), *Equity and Justice in Social Behavior*. New York: Academic Press.

Edmunds, G. and D.C. Kendrick. 1980. *The Measurement of Human Aggressiveness*. New York: John Wiley & Sons.

Elliott, Delbert and Harwin Voss. 1974. *Delinquency and Dropout*. Lexington, Mass.: Lexington Books.

Elliott, Delbert, Suzanne Ageton, and Rachel Canter. 1979. "An integrated theoretical perspective on delinquent behavior." *Journal of Research in Crime and Delinquency*, 16:3-27.

Elliott, Delbert, David Huizinga, and Suzanne Ageton. 1985. *Explaining Delinquency and Drug Use*. Beverly Hills, Calif.: Sage.

Empey, LaMar. 1956. "Social class and occupational aspiration: A comparison of absolute and relative measurement." *American Sociological Review*, 21:703-709.

——. 1982. *American Delinquency: Its Meaning and Construction*. Homewood, Ill.: Dorsey.

Farnworth, Margaret and Michael J. Leiber. 1989. "Strain theory revisited: Economic goals, educational means, and delinquency." *American Sociological Review*, 54:263-274.

Faunce, William A. 1989. "Occupational status-assignment systems: The effect of status on self-esteem." *American Journal of Sociology*, 95:378-400.

Folger, Robert. 1984. "Emerging issues in the social psychology of justice." In Robert Folger (ed.), *The Sense of Injustice: Social Psychological Perspectives*. New York: Plenum.

——. 1986. "Rethinking equity theory: A referent cognitions model." In Hans Wemer Bierhoff, Ronald L. Cohen, and Jerald Greenberg (eds.), *Justice in Social Relations*. New York: Plenum.

Folkman, Susan. 1991. "Coping across the life-span: Theoretical issues." In E. Mark Cummings, Anita L. Greene, and Katherine H. Karraker (eds.), *Life-Span Developmental Psychology: Perspectives on Stress and Coping*. Hillsdale, N.J.: Lawrence Eribaum.

Garrett, James and William L. Libby, Jr. 1973. "Role of intentionality in mediating responses to inequity in the dyad." *Journal of Personality and Social Psychology*, 28:21-27.

Gersten, Joanne C., Thomas S. Langer, Jeanne G. Eisenberg, and Lida Ozek. 1974. "Child behavior and life events: Undesirable change or change per se." In Barbara Snell Dohrenwend and Bruce P. Dohrenwend (eds.), *Stressful Life Events: Their Nature and Effects*. New York: John Wiley & Sons.

Gersten, Joanne C., Thomas S. Langer, Jeanne G. Eisenberg, and Ora Smith-Fagon. 1977. "An evaluation of the etiological role of stressful life-change events in psychological disorders." *Journal of Health and Social Behavior*, 18:228-244.

Greenberg, David F. 1977. "Delinquency and the age structure of society." *Contemporary Crises*, 1:189-223.

Gruder, Charles L. 1977. "Choice of comparison persons in evaluating oneself." In Jerry M. Suis and Richard L. Miller (eds.), *Social Comparison Processes*. New York: Hemisphere.

Hawkins, J. David and Denise M. Lishner. 1987. "Schooling and delinquency." In Elmer H. Johnson (ed.), *Handbook on Crime and Delinquency Prevention*. New York: Greenwood.

Healy, William and Augusta F. Bonner. 1969. *New Light on Delinquency and Its Treatment*. New Haven, Conn.: Yale University Press.

Hegtvedt, Karen A. 1987. "When rewards are scarce: Equal or equitable distributions." *Social Forces*, 66:183-207.

——. 1990. "The effects of relationship structure on emotional responses to inequity." *Social Psychology Quarterly*, 53:214-228.

——. 1991a. "Justice processes." In Martha Foschi and Edward J. Lawler (eds.), *Group Processes: Sociological Analyses*. Chicago: Nelson-Hall.

1991b. "Social comparison processes." In Edgar F. Borgotta and Marie E. Borgotta (eds.), *Encyclopedia of Sociology*. New York: Macmillan.

Hirschi, Travis. 1969. *Causes of Delinquency*. Berkeley: University of California Press.

——. 1979. "Separate and unequal is better." *Journal of Research in Crime and Delinquency*, 16:34-38.

Hirschi, Travis and Michael Gottfredson. 1986. "The distinction between crime and criminality." In Timothy F. Hartnagel and Robert A. Silverman (eds.), *Critique and Explanation*. New Brunswick, N.J.: Transaction Books.

Hochschild, Jennifer L. 1981. *What's Fair: American Beliefs about Distributive Justice*. Cambridge, Mass.: Harvard University Press.

Homans, George C. 1961. *Social Behavior: Its Elementary Forms*. New York: Harcourt, Brace and World.

House, James S. 1981. *Work Stress and Social Support*. Reading, Mass.: Addison-Wesley.

Hyman, Herbert. 1953. "The value systems of the different classes: A social-psychological contribution to the analysis of stratification." In Reinhard Bendix and Seymour Martin Lipset (eds.), *Class, Status, and Power*. New York: Free Press.

Jasso, Guillermina. 1980. "A new theory of distributive justice." *American Sociological Review,* 45:3-32.

Jasso, Guillermina and Peter H. Rossi. 1977. "Distributive justice and earned income." *American Sociological Review,* 42:639-651.

Jensen, Gary. 1986. "Dis-integrating integrated theory: A critical analysis of attempts to save strain theory." Paper presented at the annual meeting of the American Society of Criminology, Atlanta.

Johnson, Richard E. 1979. "Juvenile Delinquency and Its Origins." London: Cambridge University Press.

Kaplan, Howard B. 1980. *Deviant Behavior in Defense of Self*. New York: Academic Press.

Kaplan, Howard B., Cynthia Robbins, and Steven S. Martin. 1983. "Toward the testing of a general theory of deviant behavior in longitudinal perspective: Patterns of psychopathology." In James R. Greenley and Roberta G. Simmons (eds.), *Research in Community and Mental Health*. Greenwich, Conn.: Jai Press.

Kemper, Theodore D. 1978. *A Social Interactional Tleory of Emotions*. New York: John Wiley & Sons.

Kluegel, James R. and Eliot R. Smith. 1986. *Beliefs about Inequality*. New York: Aldine De Gruyter.

Kornhauser, Ruth Rosner. 1978. *Social Sources of Delinquency*. Chicago: University of Chicago Press.

Labouvie, Erich W. 1986a. "Alcohol and marijuana use in relation to adolescent stress." *International Journal of the Addictions*, 21:333-345.

———. 1986b. "The coping function of adolescent alcohol and drug use." In Rainer K. Silbereisen, Klaus Eyfeth and Georg Rudinger (eds.), *Development as Action in Context."* New York: Springer.

Lauritsen, Janet L., Robert J. Sampson, and John Laub. 1991. "The link between offending and victimization among adolescents." *Criminology,* 29:265-292.

Lerner, Melvin J. 1977. "The justice motive: Some hypotheses as to its origins and forms." *Journal of Personality,* 45:1-52.

Leventhal, Gerald S. 1976. "The distribution of rewards and resources in groups and organizations." In Leonard Berkowitz and Elaine Walster (eds.), *Advances in Experimental Social Psychology: Equity Theory: Toward a General Theory of Social Interaction*. New York: Academic Press.

Leventhal, Gerald S., Jurgis Karuzajar, and William Rick Fry. 1980. "Beyond fairness: A theory of allocation preferences." In Gerald Mikula (ed.), *Justice and Social Interaction*. New York: Springer-Veriag.

Lind, E. Allan and Tom R. Tyler. 1988. *The Social Psychology of Procedural Justice*. New York: Plenum.

Linsky, Arnold S. and Murray A. Straus. 1986. *Social Stress in the United States*. Dover, Mass.: Auburn House.

Liska, Allen E. 1987. *Perspectives on Deviance*. Englewood Cliffs, N.J.: Prentice-Hall.

McClelland, Katherine. 1990. "The social management of ambition." *Sociological Quarterly,* 31:225-251.

MacLeod, Jay. 1987. *Ain't No Makin' It*. Boulder, Colo.: Westview Press.

Mark, Melvin M. and Robert Folger. 1984. "Responses to relative deprivation: A conceptual framework." In Philip Shaver (ed.), *Review of Personality and Social Psychology. Vol. 5*. Beverly Hills, Calif.: Sage.

Martin, Joanne. 1986. "When expectations and justice do not coincide: Blue collar visions of a just world." In Hans Weiner Bierhoff, Ronald L. Cohen, and Jerald Greenberg (eds.), *Justice in Social Relations*. New York: Plenum.

Martin, Joanne and Alan Murray. 1983. "Distributive injustice and unfair exchange." In David M. Messick and Karen S. Cook (eds.), *Equity Theory: Psychological and Social Perspectives*. New York: Praeger.

———. 1984. "Catalysts for collective violence: The importance of a psychological approach." In Robert Folger (ed.), *The Sense of Injustice: Social Psychological Perspectives*. New York: Plenum.

Massey, James L. and Marvin Krohn. 1986. "A longitudinal examination of an integrated social process model of deviant behavior." *Social Forces*, 65:106-134.

Mawson, Anthony R. 1987. *Criminality: A Model of Stress-Induced Crime*. New York: Praeger.

Menaghan, Elizabeth. 1982. "Measuring coping effectiveness: A panel analysis of marital problems and coping efforts." *Journal of Health and Social Behavior*, 23:220-234.

——. 1983. "Individual coping efforts: Moderators of the relationship between life stress and mental health outcomes." In Howard B. Kaplan (ed.), *Psychosocial Stress: Trends in Theory and Research*. New York: Academic Press.

Merton, Robert. 1938. "Social structure and anomie." *American Sociological Review*, 3:672-682.

Messick, David M. and Keith Sentis. 1979. "Fairness and preference." *Journal of Experimental Social Psychology*, 15:418-434.

——. 1983. "Fairness, preference, and fairness biases." In David M. Messick and Karen S. Cook (eds.), *Equity Theory: Psychological and Sociological Perspectives*. New York: Praeger.

Michael, Jack. 1973. "Positive and negative reinforcement, a distinction that is no longer necessary; or a better way to talk about bad things." In Eugene Ramp and George Semb (eds.), *Behavior Analysis: Areas of Research and Application*. Englewood Cliffs, N.J.: Prentice-Hall.

Mickelson, Roslyn Arlin. 1990. "The attitude-achievement paradox among black adolescents." *Sociology of Education*, 63:44-61.

Mikula, Gerold. 1980. *Justice and Social Interaction*. New York: Springer-Veriag.

——. 1986. "The experience of injustice: Toward a better understanding of its phenomenology." In Hans Wemer Bierhoff, Ronald L. Cohen, and Jerald Greenberg (eds.), *Justice in Social Relations*. New York: Plenum.

Mirowsky, John and Catherine E. Ross. 1990. "The consolation-prize theory of alienation." *American Journal of Sociology*, 95:1505-1535.

Morgan, Rick L. and David Heise. 1988. "Structure of emotions." *Social Psychology Quarterly*, 51:19-31.

Mueller, Charles W. 1983. "Environmental stressors and aggressive behavior." In Russell G. Geen and Edward I. Donnerstein (eds.), *Aggression: Theoretical and Empirical Reviews. Vol. 2*. New York: Academic Press.

Newcomb, Michael D. and L. L. Harlow. 1986. "Life events and substance use among adolescents:

Mediating effects of perceived loss of control and meaninglessness in life." *Journal of Personality and Social Psychology*, 51:564-577.

Novy, Diane M. and Stephen Donohue. 1985. "The relationship between adolescent life stress events and delinquent conduct including conduct indicating a need for super-vision." *Adolescence*, 78:313-321.

Pearlin, Leonard I. 1982. "The social contexts of stress." In Leo Goldberger and Shlomo Berznitz (eds.), *Handbook of Stress*. New York: Free Press.

——. 1983. "Role strains and personal stress." In Howard Kaplan (ed.), *Psychosocial Stress: Trends in Theory and Research*. New York: Academic Press.

Pearlin, Leonard I. and Carmi Schooler. 1978. "The structure of coping." *Journal of Health and Social Behavior*, 19:2-21.

Pearlin, Leonard I. and Morton A. Lieberman. 1979. "Social sources of emotional distress." In Roberta G. Simmons (cd.), *Research in Community and Mental Health. Vol. I*. Greenwich, Conn.: Jai Press.

Pearlin, Leonard I., Elizabeth G. Menaghan, Morton A. Lieberman, and Joseph T. Mullan. 1981. "The stress process." *Journal of Health and Social Behavior*, 22:337-356.

Quicker, John. 1974. "The effect of goal discrepancy on delinquency." *Social Problems*, 22:76-86.

Rivera, Beverly and Cathy Spatz Widom. 1990. "Childhood victimization and violent offending." *Violence and Victims*, 5:19-35.

Rosenberg, Morris. 1979. *Conceiving the Self*. New York: Basic.

——. 1990. "Reflexivity and emotions." *Social Psychology Quarterly*, 53:3-12.

Ross, Michael, John Thibaut, and Scott Evenback. 1971. "Some determinants of the intensity of social protest." *Journal of Experimental Social Psychology*, 7:401-418.

Schwinger, Thomas. 1980. "Just allocations of goods: Decisions among three principles." In Gerald Mikula (ed.), *Justice and Social Interaction*. New York: Springer-Verlag.

Shepelak, Norma J. 1987. "The role of self-explanations and self-evaluations in legitimating inequality." *American Sociological Review*, 52:495-503.

Shepelak, Norma J. and Duane Alwin. 1986. "Beliefs about inequality and perceptions of distributive justice." *American Sociological Review*, 51:30-46.

Short, James F. and Fred L. Strodtbeck. 1965. *Group Process and Gang Delinquency*. Chicago: University of Chicago Press.

Slaby, Ronald G. and Nancy G. Guerra. 1988. "Cognitive mediators of aggression in adolescent offenders: 1." *Developmental Psychology*, 24: 580-588.

Sprecher, Susan. 1986. "The relationship between inequity and emotions in close relationships." *Social Psychology Quarterly*, 49:309-321.

Stephenson, G.M. and J.H. White. 1968. "An experimental study of some effects of injustice on children's moral behavior." *Journal of Experimental Social Psychology*, 4:460-469.

Straus, Murray. 1991. "Discipline and deviance: Physical punishment of children and violence and other crimes in adulthood." *Social Problems*, 38:133-154.

Sullivan, Mercer L. 1989. *Getting Paid*. Ithaca, N.Y.: Cornell University Press.

Suls, Jerry M. 1977. "Social comparison theory and research: An overview from 1954." In Jerry M. Suls and Richard L. Miller (eds.), *Social Comparison Processes*. New York: Hemisphere.

Suls, Jerry M. and Thomas Ashby Wills. 1991. *Social Comparison: Contemporary Theory and Research*. Hillsdale, N.J.: Lawrence Erlbaum.

Tavris, Carol. 1984. "On the wisdom of counting to ten." In Philip Shaver (ed.), *Review of Personality and Social Psychology: 5*. Beverly Hills, Calif.: Sage.

Thibaut, John W. and Harold H. Kelley. 1959. "The Social Psychology of Groups." New York: John Wiley & Sons.

Thoits, Peggy. 1983. "Dimensions of life events that influence psychological distress: An evaluation and synthesis of the literature." In Howard B. Kaplan (ed.), *Psychosocial Stress: Trends in Theory and Research*. New York: Academic Press.

——. 1984. "Coping, social support, and psychological outcomes: The central role of emotion." In Philip Shaver (ed.), *Review of Personality and Social Psychology*: 5. Beverly Hills, Calif.: Sage.

——. 1989. "The sociology of emotions." In W. Richard Scott and Judith Blake (eds.), *Annual Review of Sociology. Vol. 15*. Palo Alto, Calif.: Annual Reviews.

——. 1990. "Emotional deviance research." In Theodore D. Kemper (ed.), *Research Agendas in the Sociology of Emotions*. Albany: State University of New York Press.

——. 1991a. "On merging identity theory and stress research." *Social Psychology Quarterly*, 54:101-112.

——. 1991b. "Patterns of coping with controllable and uncontrollable events." In E. Mark Cummings, Anita L. Greene, and Katherine H. Karraker (eds.), *Life-Span Developmental Psychology: Perspectives on Stress and Coping*. Hillsdale, N.J.: Lawrence Erlbaum.

Thornberry, Terence P. 1987. "Toward an Interactional Theory of Delinquency." *Criminology*, 25:863-891.

Tonry, Michael, Lloyd E. Ohlin, and David P. Farrington. 1991. *Human Development and Criminal Behavior*. New York: Springer-Verlag.

Tornblum, Kjell Y. 1977. "Distributive justice: Typology and propositions." *Human Relations*, 30:1-24.

Utne, Mary, Kristine and Robert Kidd. 1980. "Equity and attribution." In Gerald Mikula (ed.), *Justice and Social Interaction*. New York: Springer-Verlag.

Van Houten, Ron. 1983. "Punishment: From the animal laboratory to the applied setting." In Saul Axelrod and Jack Apsche (eds.), *The Effects of Punishment on Human Behavior*. New York: Academic Press.

Vaux, Alan. 1988. *Social support: Theory, Research, and Intervention*. New York: Praeger.

Vaux, Alan and Mary Ruggiero. 1983. "Stressful life change and delinquent behavior." *American Journal of Community Psychology*, 11:169-183.

Walster, Elaine, Ellen Berscheid, and G. William Waister. 1973. "New directions in equity research." *Journal of Personality and Social Psychology*, 25:151-176.

Walster, Elaine, G. William Waister, and Ellen Berscheid. 1978. *Equity: Theory and Research*. Boston: Allyn & Bacon.

Wang, Alvin Y. and R. Stephen Richarde. 1988. "Global versus task-specific measures of self-efficacy." *Psychological Record*, 38:533-541.

Weiner, Bernard. 1982. "The emotional consequences of causal attributions." In Margaret S. Clark and Susan T. Fiske (eds.), *Affect and Cognition: The Seventeenth Annual Carnegie Symposium on Cognition*. Hillsdale, N.J.: Lawrence Erlbaum.

Williams, Carolyn L. and Craige Uchiyama. 1989. "Assessment of life events during adolescence: The use of self-report inventories." *Adolescence*, 24:95-118.

Wylie, Ruth. 1979. *The Self-Concept. Vol. 2*. Lincoln: University of Nebraska Press.

Zillman, Dolf. 1979. *Hostility and Aggression*. Hillsdale, N.J.: Lawrence Erlbaum.

CHAPTER 29

Crime and the American Dream

Richard Rosenfeld ■ Steven F. Messner

Robert Merton's (1938) anomie theory posits that variation in crime rates within and between societies can be explained by differential cultural emphasis of means and goals. Specifically, Merton explained that American society has elevated the goal of achieving wealth far above legitimate means necessary toward realization of that end. For this reason, legitimate means are devalued while acceptance of the goal remains largely universal. The disproportionate distribution of legitimate opportunities (educational and employment opportunities) places added strain on those in the lower class. Merton argued that these strains can lead to several different coping strategies, or adaptations, some of which involve criminal offending.

Rosenfeld and Messner extend Merton's theory by emphasizing the role that the economy has played in altering the importance and value of noneconomic institutions (school, family, polity). More specifically, Rosenfeld and Messner argue that the interrelationship among the economy, family, school, and polity has negatively influenced commitment to legitimate means due to the imbalance of power afforded the economy. Rosenfeld and Messner believe that this devaluation of noneconomic institutions has led to insufficient socialization and a reduction in the influence of legitimate means. Conversely, most have sustained their commitment to wealth. As a result, many disadvantaged individuals experience

strain, which often leads to criminal involvement. Rosenfeld and Messner suggest that to effectively diminish crime, "fundamental social transformations and a rethinking of the dream" are necessary.

The obsession with crime in the United States cannot be dismissed as an irrational feature of the American character or as a peculiarly American penchant for inventing crime waves or using crime as a stage for enacting other social dramas. Rather, the American obsession with crime is rooted in an objective social reality. Levels of crime in the United States, and more specifically levels of serious crime, are in fact very high in comparative perspective....

We maintain that the comparatively high level of serious criminal behavior in the United States is one of the more important facts about crime to be explained by criminological theory (cf. Braithwaite 1989). Curiously, however, criminologists have devoted relatively little attention to this issue for at least two interrelated reasons: the dominance of individual-level perspectives in contemporary criminology and a corresponding deemphasis on serious forms of criminal behavior. Nonetheless, we propose that the foundations for an explanation of the distinctively high levels of crime in the United States can be found in the arguments advanced by Robert Merton in his classic essay "Social Structure and Anomie" (1938, 1968; hereafter SS&A).

Merton proposes that the sources of crime in the United States lie in the same cultural commitments and social arrangements that are conventionally regarded as part of the American success story. High rates of crime are thus not simply the "sick" outcome of individual pathologies, such as defective personalities or aberrant biological structures. Nor are they the "evil consequence" of individual moral failings. Instead, crime in America derives in significant measure from highly prized cultural and social conditions—indeed, from the American Dream itself.

In this chapter, we offer an explanation of American crime rates that is based on an expanded version of Merton's theory. We amplify the theory in two ways. First, we restore the original macrolevel intent and orientation to SS&A that were removed in the conversion of "anomie theory" into "strain theory." We then extend anomie theory by considering the connections between core elements of the American Dream, which Merton discussed in some detail, and an aspect of social structure to which he devoted little attention: the interrelationships among social institutions. Our basic thesis is that the anomic tendencies inherent in the American Dream both produce and are reproduced by an *institutional balance of power* dominated by the economy. The result of the interplay between the basic cultural commitments of the American Dream and the companion institutional arrangements is widespread anomie, weak social controls, and high levels of crime....

The Anomie Tendencies of the American Dream

In SS&A, Merton advances the provocative argument that there are inherent features of American culture, of the American Dream itself, that ultimately contribute to the high rates of crime and deviance observed in the United States. Although Merton does not provide a formal definition of "the American Dream," it is possible to formulate a reasonably concise characterization of this cultural orientation on the basis of his discussion of American culture in general and his scattered references to the American Dream. The American Dream refers to a commitment to the goal of material success, to be pursued by everyone in society, under conditions of open, individual competition.

Merton proposes that the American Dream has been highly functional for society in certain respects. This cultural ethos is particularly effective in satisfying motivational requirements because it encourages high levels of "ambition" (Merton 1968: 200). At the same time, there is a dark side to the American Dream. It tends to promote an anomic imbalance wherein the importance of using the legitimate means is deemphasized relative to the importance of attaining the desired cultural goals.

Merton explains that this anomic tendency derives ultimately from the very same basic value commitments upon which the American Dream rests. One such commitment is a strong *achievement orientation*. In American society, personal worth tends to be evaluated on the basis of what people have achieved rather than who they are or how they relate to others in social networks. "Success" is to a large extent the ultimate measure of social worth. Quite understandably, then, there are pervasive cultural pressures to achieve at any cost. A strong achievement orientation, at the level of basic cultural values, thus cultivates and sustains a mentality that "it's not how you play the game; it's whether you win or lose."

A second basic value orientation that contributes to the anomic imbalance in American culture is *individualism*. In the pursuit of success, people are encouraged to "make it" on their own. Fellow members of society are thus competitors in the struggle for achievement and the ultimate validation of personal worth. This intense, individual competition to succeed further encourages a tendency to disregard normative restraints on behavior when these restraints interfere with the realization of goals. Andrew Hacker (1992: 29) offers a cogent description of this distinctive feature of American culture:

> America has always been the most competitive of societies. It poises its citizens against one another, with the warning that they must make it on their own. Hence the stress on moving past others, driven by a fear of falling behind. No other nation so rates its residents as winners or losers.

A third component of American culture that is conducive to anomic imbalance is its *universalism*.

Everyone is encouraged to aspire to social ascent, and everyone is susceptible to evaluation on the basis of individual achievements. As a consequence, the pressures to "win" are pervasive; no one is exempt from the pursuit of success (Merton 1968: 200; Orru 1990: 234).

Finally, in American culture, success is signified in a special way: by the accumulation of *monetary rewards*. Merton is keenly aware of the high priority awarded to money in American culture. He observes that

> in some large measure, money has been consecrated as a value in itself, over and above its expenditure for articles of consumption or its use for the enhancement of power. (1968: 190)

Merton's key point is not that Americans are uniquely materialistic; a strong interest in material well-being can be found in most societies. Rather, the distinctive feature of American culture is the preeminent role of money as the "metric" of success. As Orru puts it, "money is literally, in this context, a *currency* for measuring achievement" (1990: 235).

Merton points to an important implication of the signification of achievement with reference to monetary rewards. Monetary success is inherently open-ended. Because it is always possible in principle to have more money, "in the American Dream there is no final stopping point" (1968: 190). Cultural prescriptions thus mandate "never-ending achievement" (Passas 1990: 159). Relentless pressures to accumulate money, in turn, encourage people to disregard normative restraints when they impede the pursuit of personal goals.

In sum, dominant value patterns of American culture, specifically its achievement orientation, its competitive individualism, its universalism in goal orientations and evaluative standards—when harnessed to the preeminent goal of monetary success—give rise to a distinctive cultural ethos: the American Dream. The American Dream, in turn, encourages members of society to pursue ends, in Merton's words, "limited only by considerations of technical expediency" (1968: 189). One consequence of this open, wide-spread competitive, and anomic quest for success by any means necessary is high levels of crime....

Merton's cultural critique represents only a partial explanation of the high levels of crime in the United States considered in comparative perspective. A complete explanation requires identification of the social structural underpinnings of American culture and its associated strains toward anomie. Merton's analysis stops short of an explication of the ways in which specific features of the institutional structure—beyond the class system—interrelate to generate the anomic pressures that are held to be responsible for crime (cf. Cohen 1985: 233). As a consequence, the anomie perspective is best regarded as a "work in progress." In Cohen's words, Merton

> has laid the groundwork for an explanation of deviance [and crime] on the sociological level, but the task, for the most part, still lies ahead. (1985: 233)

The Institutional Dynamics of Crime

The Normal Functions of Social Institutions

Social institutions are the building blocks of whole societies. As such, they constitute the fundamental units of macro-level analysis. Institutions are "relatively stable sets of norms and values, statuses and roles, and groups and organizations" that regulate human conduct to meet the basic needs of a society (Bassis, Gelles, and Levine 1991: 142). These social needs include the need to adapt to the environment, to mobilize and deploy resources for the achievement of collective goals, and to socialize members in the society's fundamental normative patterns.

Adaptation to the environment is the primary responsibility of economic institutions, which organize the production and distribution of goods and services to satisfy the basic material requirements for human existence. The political system, or "polity," mobilizes and distributes power to attain collective goals. One collective purpose of special importance is the maintenance of public safety. Political institutions are responsible for

> protecting members of society from invasions from without, controlling crime and disorder within, and

providing channels for resolving conflicts of interest. (Bassis, Gelles, and Levine 1991: 142)

The institution of the family has primary responsibility for the maintenance and replacement of members of society. These tasks involve setting the limits of legitimate sexual relations among adults; the physical care and nurturing of children; and the socialization of children into the values, goals, and beliefs of the dominant culture. In addition, a particularly important function of the family in modern societies is to provide emotional support for its members. To a significant degree, the family serves as a refuge from the tensions and stresses generated in other institutional domains. In this idea of the family as a "haven" from the rigors of the public world lies the implicit recognition of the need to counterbalance and temper the harsh, competitive conditions of public life (Lasch 1977).

The institution of education shares many of the socialization functions of the family. Like the family, schools are given responsibility for transmitting basic cultural standards to new generations. In modern industrial societies, schools are also oriented toward the specific task of preparing youth for the demands of adult occupational roles. In addition, education is intended to enhance personal adjustment, facilitate the development of individual human potential, and advance the general "knowledge base" of the culture.

These four social institutions—the economy, polity, family, and education—are the focus of our explanation of crime. They do not, of course, exhaust the institutional structure of modern societies, nor are they the only institutions with relevance to crime. However, the interconnections among these four institutions are central to an institutional analysis of crime in modern societies, in general, and of the exceptionally high levels of crime in the United States, in particular.

Social institutions are to some extent distinct with respect to the primary activities around which they are organized. At the same time, however, the functions of institutions are overlapping and interdependent. For example, the performance of the economy is dependent on the quality of the "human capital" (i.e., the motivations, knowledge, and skills) cultivated in the schools. The capacity of the schools to develop human capital is circumscribed by the individual backgrounds, what Pierre Bourdieu refers to as the "cultural capital," that students bring with them from their families (MacLeod 1987: 11–14). The effective functioning of all three of these institutions—the economy, education, and the family—presupposes an environment with at least a modicum of social order, for which the polity is largely responsible. Finally, the capacity of the polity to promote the collective good depends on the nature and quality of economic and human resources supplied by the other institutions.

The interdependence of major social institutions implies that some coordination and cooperation among institutions is required for societies to "work" at all. The requirements for the effective functioning of any given institution, however, may conflict with the requirements of another. This potential for conflict is illustrated by the particularly stark contrast between the dominant values embodied in two institutions: the economy and the family.

Economic life and family life are supposed to be governed by fundamentally different standards in modern industrial societies. Family relationships are expected to be regulated by the norm of particularism, and positions and roles in the family are allocated, in large measure, on the basis of ascribed characteristics. Each member is entitled to special considerations by virtue of his or her unique identity and position in the family. In contrast, economic relationships, such as transactions in the marketplace, are supposed to entail universalistic orientations, and economic positions are supposed to be filled according to achievement criteria. Persons who occupy the same or functionally equivalent statuses are to be treated similarly, and access to these statuses is supposed to be gained by demonstrating the capacity to successfully perform their duties and responsibilities. There is thus an inevitable tension between the kinds of normative orientations required for the effective functioning of the family and those required for the efficient operation of a market economy.

Any given society will therefore be characterized by a distinctive arrangement of social institutions that reflects a balancing of the sometimes competing claims and requisites of the different institutions, yielding a distinctive institutional balance of power. Further, the nature of the resulting configuration of institutions is itself intimately related to the larger culture. Indeed, our basic premise about social organization is that culture and the institutional balance of power are mutually reinforcing. On the one hand, culture influences the character of institutions and their positions relative to one another. Culture is in a sense "given life" in the institutional structure of society. On the other hand, the patterns of social relationships constituting institutions, which Parsons (1964: 239) terms the "backbone" of the social system, reproduce and sustain cultural commitments. This is, ultimately, where culture "comes from."

In the macrocriminological analysis of a concrete social system, then, the task is to describe the interpenetration of cultural and institutional patterns, to trace the resulting interconnections among institutions that constitute the institutional balance of power, and finally, to show how the institutional balance of power influences levels of crime. In the following sections, we apply this kind of analysis to the relationships among culture, institutional functioning, and crime in the United States.

The American Dream and the Institutional Balance of Power

... The core elements of the American Dream—a strong achievement orientation, a commitment to competitive individualism, universalism, and most important, the glorification of material success—have their institutional underpinnings in the economy. The most important feature of the economy of the United States is its capitalist nature. The defining characteristics of any capitalist economy are private ownership and control of property, and free market mechanisms for the production and distribution of goods and services.

These structural arrangements are conducive to, and presuppose, certain cultural orientations. For the economy to operate efficiently, the private owners of property must be profit-oriented

and eager to invest, and workers must be willing to exchange their labor for wages. The motivational mechanism underlying these conditions is the promise of financial returns. The internal logic of a capitalist economy thus presumes that an attraction to monetary rewards as a result of achievement in the marketplace is widely diffused throughout the population (cf. Passas 1990: 159).

A capitalist economy is also highly competitive for all those involved, property owners and workers alike. Firms that are unable to adapt to shifting consumer demands or to fluctuations in the business cycle are likely to fail. Workers who are unable to keep up with changing skill requirements or who are unproductive in comparison with others are likely to be fired. This intense competition discourages economic actors from being wedded to conventional ways of doing things and instead encourages them to substitute new techniques for traditional ones if they offer advantages in meeting economic goals. In short, a capitalist economy naturally cultivates a competitive, innovative spirit.

These structural and cultural conditions are common to all capitalist societies. What is distinctive about the United States, however, is the *exaggerated* emphasis on monetary success and the *unrestrained* receptivity to innovation. The goal of monetary success overwhelms other goals and becomes the principal measuring rod for achievements. The resulting proclivity and pressures to innovate resist any regulation that is not justified by purely technical considerations. The obvious question that arises is why cultural orientations that express the inherent logic of capitalism have evolved to a particularly extreme degree in American society. The answer, we submit, lies in the inability of other social institutions to tame economic imperatives. In short, the institutional balance of power is tilted toward the economy....

Capitalism developed in the United States without the institutional restraints found in other societies. As a consequence, the economy assumed an unusual dominance in the institutional structure of society from the very beginning of the nation's history. This economic dominance, we argue, has continued to the present and is manifested in three somewhat different ways: (1) in the *devaluation* of noneconomic institutional functions and roles; (2) in the *accommodation* to economic requirements by other institutions; and (3) in the *penetration* of economic norms into other institutional domains.

Consider the relative devaluation of the distinctive functions of education and of the social roles that fulfill these functions. Education is regarded largely as a means to occupational attainment, which in turn is valued primarily insofar as it promises economic rewards. The acquisition of knowledge and learning for its own sake is not highly valued. Effective performance of the roles involved with education, accordingly, do not confer particularly high status. The "good student" is not looked up to by his or her peers; the "master teacher" receives meager financial rewards and public esteem in comparison with those to be gained by success in business.

Similar processes are observed in the context of the family, although the tendency toward devaluation is perhaps not as pronounced as in other institutional arenas. There is indeed a paradox here because "family values" are typically extolled in public rhetoric. Nevertheless, the lack of appreciation for tasks such as parenting, nurturing, and providing emotional support to others is manifested in actual social relationships. It is the home owner rather than the homemaker who is widely admired and envied—and whose image is reflected in the American Dream. Indeed, perhaps the most telling evidence of the relative devaluation of family functions is the inferior status in our society of those persons most extensively involved in these activities: women.

The relative devaluation of the family in comparison with the economy is not an inevitable consequence of the emergence of a modern, industrial society, whether capitalist or socialist. Adler (1983: 131) points to nations such as Bulgaria, the (then) German Democratic Republic, Japan, Saudi Arabia, and Switzerland to illustrate the possibilities for maintaining a strong commitment to the family despite the profound social changes that accompany the transformation from agriculturally based economies to industrial economies. Each of these countries has made extensive, and sometimes costly, efforts to preserve the vitality of the family. Furthermore, these are precisely the kinds of societies that exhibit low crime rates and are not, in Adler's words, "obsessed with crime."

The distinctive function of the polity, providing for the collective good, also tends to be devalued in comparison with economic functions. The general public has little regard for politics as an intrinsically valuable activity and confers little social honor on the role of the politician. Perhaps as a result, average citizens are not expected to be actively engaged in public service, which is left to the "career" politician. The contrast with economic activity is illuminating. The citizen who refuses to vote may experience mild social disapproval; the "able-bodied" adult who refuses to work is socially degraded. Economic participation is obligatory for most adults. In contrast, even the minimal form of political participation entailed in voting (which has more in common with shopping than with work) is considered discretionary, and useful primarily to the extent that it leads to tangible economic rewards (e.g., lower taxes).

Moreover, the very purpose of government tends to be conceptualized in terms of its capacity to facilitate the individual pursuit of economic prosperity. A good illustration is the advice given to the Democratic ticket in the 1992 presidential campaign by the conservative columnist, George Will. Will chastised liberal Democrats for allegedly becoming preoccupied with issues of rights based on ethnicity and sexuality and advised the Democratic presidential candidates to remember the following point that two popular presidents—Franklin Roosevelt and Ronald Reagan—understood very well:

> Americans are happiest when pursuing happiness, happiness understood as material advancement, pursued with government's help but not as a government entitlement. (Will 1992: E5)

Will's advice to liberal Democrats is revealing, not only of the core content of the American Dream and its effect on popular views of government, but of a particular kind of collective "right" to which Americans *are* entitled: the right to consume (cf. Edsall 1992: 7). Both of the major political parties celebrate the right to acquire material possessions; they differ mainly with respect to the proper degree of governmental involvement in expanding access to the means of consumption. No matter which party is in power, the function of government, at least in the domestic sphere, remains subsidiary to individual economic considerations.

Interestingly, one distinctive function of the polity does not appear to be generally devalued, namely, crime control. There is widespread agreement among the American public that government should undertake vigorous efforts to deal with the crime problem. If anything, Americans want government to do more to control crime. Yet, this apparent exception is quite compatible with the claim of economic dominance. Americans' "obsession" with crime is rooted in fears that crime threatens, according to political analyst Thomas Edsall (1992: 9) "their security, their values, their rights, and their livelihoods and the competitive prospects of their children." In other words, because crime control bears directly on the pursuit of the American Dream, this particular function of the polity receives high priority.

A second way in which the dominance of the economy is manifested is in the *accommodations* that emerge in those situations in which institutional claims are in competition. Economic conditions and requirements typically exert a much stronger influence on the operation of other institutions than vice versa. For example, family routines are dominated by the schedules, rewards, and penalties of the labor market. Consider the resistance of employers (and their representatives in government) to proposals for maternity leaves, flexible hours, or on-the-job child care. The contrast between the United States and another capitalist society with very low crime rates—Japan—is striking in this regard. In Japan, business enterprises are accommodated to the needs of the family, becoming in some respects a "surrogate family," with services ranging from child rearing to burial (Adler 1983: 132).

The most important way that family life is influenced by the economy, however, is through the necessity for paid employment to support a family. Joblessness makes it difficult for families to remain intact and to form in the first place. In the urban underclass, where rates of joblessness are chronically high, so too are rates of separation, divorce, single-parent households, and births to unmarried women (Wilson 1987).

Educational institutions are also more likely to accommodate to the demands of the economy than is the economy to respond to the requirements of education. The timing of schooling reflects occupational demands rather than intrinsic features of the learning process or personal interest in the pursuit of knowledge. People go to school largely to prepare for "good" jobs, and once in the labor market, there is little opportunity to pursue further education for its own sake. When workers do return to school, it is almost always to upgrade skills or credentials to keep pace with job demands, to seek higher paying jobs, or to "retool" during spells of unemployment. At the organizational level, schools are dependent on the economy for financial resources, and thus it becomes important for school officials to convince business leaders that education is suitably responsive to business needs.

The polity likewise is dependent on the economy for financial support. Governments must accordingly take care to cultivate and maintain an environment hospitable to investment. If they do not, they run the risk of being literally "downgraded" by financial markets, as happened to Detroit in 1992 when Moody's Investors Service dropped the city's credit rating to noninvestment grade. Cities have little choice but to accommodate to market demands in such situations. "A city proposes, Moody's disposes. There is no appeals court or court of last ratings resort" (*New York Times*, 1992: C1). The pursuit of the collective good is thus circumscribed by economic imperatives.

A final way in which the dominance of the economy in the institutional balance of power is manifested is in the *penetration* of economic norms into other institutional areas. Schools rely on grading as a system of extrinsic rewards, like wages, to insure compliance with goals. Learning takes place within the context of individualized competition for these external rewards, and teaching inevitably tends to become oriented toward testing. Economic terminology permeates the very language of education, as in the recent emphasis in higher education on "accountability" conceptualized in terms of the "value-added" to students in the educational production process.

Within the polity, a "bottom-line" mentality develops. Effective politicians are those who deliver the goods. Moreover, the notion that the government would work better if it were run more like a business continues to be an article of faith among large segments of the American public.

The family has probably been most resistant to the intrusion of economic norms. Yet even here, pressures toward penetration are apparent. Contributions to family life tend to be measured against the all-important "breadwinner" role, which has been extended to include women who work in the paid labor force. No corresponding movement of men into the role of "homemaker" has occurred, and a declining number of women desire or can afford to occupy this role on a full-time basis. Here again, shifts in popular terminology are instructive. Husbands and wives are "partners" who "manage" the household "division of labor." We can detect no comparable shifts in kin-based terminology, or primary group norms, from the family to the workplace.

In sum, the social organization of the United States is characterized by a striking dominance of the economy in the institutional balance of power. As a result of this economic dominance, the inherent tendencies of a capitalist economy to orient the members of society toward an unrestrained pursuit of economic achievements are developed to an extreme degree. These tendencies are expressed at the cultural level in the preeminence of monetary success as the overriding goal—the American Dream—and in the relative deemphasis placed on the importance of using normative means to reach this goal—anomie. The anomic nature of the American Dream and the institutional structure of American society are thus mutually supportive and reinforcing. The key remaining question is the impact of this type of social organization on crime.

Anomie, Weak Social Controls, and Crime

The American Dream contributes to high levels of crime in two important ways, one direct and the other indirect. It has a direct effect on crime through the creation of an anomic normative order, that is, an environment in which social norms are unable to exert a strong regulatory force on the members of society. It has an indirect effect on crime by contributing to an institutional balance of power that inhibits the development of strong mechanisms of external social control. The criminogenic tendencies of the American Dream are thus due in part to the distinctive content of the cultural values and beliefs that comprise it and in part to the institutional consequences of these values and beliefs.

One criminogenic aspect of the specific content of the American Dream is the expression of the primary success goal in monetary terms. Because monetary success is inherently open-ended and elusive, the adequacy of the legitimate means for achieving this particular cultural goal is necessarily suspect. No matter how much money someone is able to make by staying within legal boundaries, illegal means will always offer further advantages in pursuit of the ultimate goal. There is thus a perpetual attractiveness associated with illegal activity that is an inevitable corollary of the goal of monetary success.

This culturally induced pressure to "innovate" by using illegitimate means is exacerbated by the dominance of the economy in the institutional balance of power. There are, of course, important noneconomic tasks carried out in other institutional arenas, tasks associated with goals that might in fact be readily attainable within the confines of the legal order. However, as we have suggested, roles effectively performed in the capacity of being a parent or spouse, a student or scholar, an engaged citizen or public servant are simply not the primary bases upon which success and failure are defined in American society. The dominance of the economy continuously erodes the structural supports for functional alternatives to the goal of economic success.

Nor does the ethos of the American Dream contain within it strong counterbalancing injunctions against substituting more effective illegitimate means for less effective legitimate means. To the contrary, the distinctive cultural "value" accompanying the monetary success goal in the American Dream is the *devaluation* of all but the most technically efficient means.

The American Dream does not completely subsume culture. There are other elements of culture that define socially acceptable modes of behavior and that affirm the legitimacy of social norms, including legal norms. In principle, these other cultural elements could counterbalance the anomic pressures that emanate from the American Dream. However, the very same institutional dynamics that contribute to the pressures to innovate in the pursuit of economic goals also make it less likely that the anomic pressures inherent in the American Dream will in fact be counterbalanced by other social forces.

As noneconomic institutions are relatively devalued, are forced to accommodate to economic needs, and are penetrated by economic standards, they are less able to fulfill their distinctive functions effectively. These functions include socialization into acceptance of the social norms. Weak families and poor schools are handicapped in their efforts to promote allegiance to social rules, including legal prohibitions. As a result, the pressures to disregard normative constraints in the pursuit of the goal of monetary success also tend to undermine social norms more generally. In the absence of the cultivation of strong commitments to social norms, the selection of the means for realizing goals *of any type* is guided mainly by instrumental considerations.

In addition, the relative impotence of noneconomic institutions is manifested in a reduced capacity to exert external social control. The government is constrained in its capacity to provide public goods that would make crime less attractive and in its efforts to mobilize collective resources—including moral resources—to effectively deter criminal choices. Single-parent families or those in which both parents have full-time jobs, all else equal, are less able to provide extensive supervision over children. All families must rely to some extent on other institutions, usually the schools, for assistance in social control. Yet poorly funded or crowded schools also find it difficult to exert effective supervision, especially when students see little or no connection between what is taught in the classroom and what is valued outside of it.

Finally, weak institutions invite challenge. Under conditions of extreme competitive individualism,

people actively resist institutional control. They not only fall from the insecure grasp of powerless institutions, sometimes they deliberately, even proudly, push themselves away. The problem of "external" social control, then, is inseparable from the problem of the "internal" regulatory force of social norms, or anomie. Anomic societies will inevitably find it difficult and costly to exert social control over the behavior of people who feel free to use whatever means that prove most effective in reaching personal goals. Hence the very sociocultural dynamics that make American institutions weak also enable and entitle Americans to defy institutional controls. If Americans are exceptionally resistant to social control—and therefore exceptionally vulnerable to criminal temptations—it is because they live in a society that enshrines the unfettered pursuit of individual material success above all other values. In the United States, anomie is a virtue.

Conclusion

This reformulation of Merton's classic theory of social structure and anomie is intended to challenge criminologists and policymakers alike to think about crime in America as a macrolevel product of widely admired cultural and social structures with deep historical roots. Criminological theories that neglect the ironic interdependence between crime and the normal functioning of the American social system will be unable to explain the preoccupation with crime that so dramatically separates the United States from other developed societies. Significant reductions in crime will not result from reforms limited to the criminal justice system, which is itself shaped in important ways by the same cultural and social forces—the same desperate emphasis on ends over means—that produce high rates of crime. Nor will social reforms, whatever their other merits, that widen access to legitimate opportunities for persons "locked out" of the American Dream bring relief from the crimes of those who are "locked in" the American Dream, exposed to its limitless imperatives in the absence of moderating social forces. Reducing these crimes will require fundamental social transformations that few Americans desire, and a rethinking of a dream that is the envy of the world.

Discussion Questions

1. What are the core features of the American Dream? Do you agree with Rosenfeld and Messner's characterization of the American Dream?

2. Describe *how* the dominance of the economy interferes with the effective functioning of other institutions (family, school, polity) in the United States.

3. What policy recommendations would Rosenfeld and Messner make for controlling crime? Would they recommend increasing the opportunities for monetary success, as do many strain theorists?

4. Rosenfeld and Messner argue that the American Dream and the dominance of the economy promote crime by reducing social control (see Part V). Do you think that the American Dream and the dominance of the economy also promote the types of strain described by Merton and Agnew?

CHAPTER 30

Causes of Crime: A Radical View

Michael J. Lynch ■ W. Byron Groves

Criminology, rooted deep in various sociological theoretical traditions, is often dichotomized into consensus and conflict camps. Although this categorization tends to oversimplify explanations of crime and its control (criminal processes and criminal justice system activity, for example, are often better addressed from an interactionist perspective), this distinction is useful for illustrating definitional and ideological differences. Whereas consensus models view civil society as a function of majority endorsement of social institutions and customs (e.g., the criminal law reflects normative consensus), conflict theory, per its namesake, views social order as a function class stratification and resource inequality across groups in society. Implications for crime control from the consensus model are simply enforcement of existing laws considered legitimate by democratic process. Conflict theorists provide a sharply contrasting view that criminal law and its enforcement is not representative of the majority of society, rather the function of upper-class interests.

The following selection discusses crime causation from a radical (i.e., conflict) perspective. A case is made for the import of social inequality in the origination and continuation of crime among various groups disenfranchised and labeled by current consensus-oriented justice policy.

Critiques of early radical theories of crime causation offer the following observations: first, radicals, like conflict and labelling theorists, have seen crime simply as the mirror image of control, thus ruling out questions of causation, or succumbing to tautological reasoning where the only cause of crime is law (Spitzer 1980,180; Akers 1980; Quinney 1970b, 123). A second criticism is that radicals have limited themselves to an oversimplified, "uni-causal" approach where the only source of crime is capitalism (Shichor 1980). And third, many have argued that avoiding the issue of causation has resulted in a neglect of empirical research among radicals (Sparks 1980; Shichor 1980; Taylor et al. 1975).

In recent years radicals have addressed each of these criticisms. Specifically, they have added to the insights drawn from conflict and labelling theories (Greenberg 1981); have qualified the depiction of capitalism as the "source of all evil" without deemphasizing the structuring power of capitalism's political economy (Mankoff, 1978); and have undertaken a number of important empirical studies (Hagan and Bernstein 1979; Hagan and Albonetti 1982; Hagan and Leon 1977; Lizotte 1978; Lizotte et al. 1982; Humphries and Wallace 1980; Jacobs 1979a, 1979b; Liska et al. 1981; Greenberg 1981; Groves and Corrado 1983; Hagan et al. 1987, 1985, 1979; Box and Hale 1983a, 1983b; Lynch 1988a; Lynch et al. 1988). Thus, the criticisms listed above may have been legitimate in 1975. They no longer apply today.

From *Primer in Radical Criminology: Critical Perspectives on Crime, Power, and Identity.* Michael J Lynch & Raymond J Michaelowski (Eds) 2006 Monsey, Ny: CJ Press

When discussing Marx we referred to his views on class conflict, materialism, and the dialectic. The following four propositions relate those materials to the issue of causation:

1. The capitalist system has at its core a conflict between labor and capital, which means that capitalism is one in a long sequence of historical systems based on inequalities between those who own and those who work.
2. Through this fundamental structural inequality between labor and capital, society becomes stratified into social classes characterized by tremendous differences in wealth, status, power, and authority.
3. Taken together, these differences constitute variable material conditions of life which offer persons in different social classes vastly different opportunities in terms of life chances and life choices.
4. Among these opportunities are the chance or choice of becoming criminal.

Class…is an important category for radicals. Social stratification accounts for the unequal distribution of chances and choices available to persons at different locations in the class structure. It also accounts for the differential allocation of incentives and motivations for both criminal and non-criminal behavior. To support these claims radicals emphasize the causal connection between political economy, inequality, and crime.

Social Class, Stratification, and Inequality

…Marx defined social classes in terms of their relation to the means of production, and since then social theorists (e.g. Max Weber) have expanded Marx's conception to include unequal distributions of socially valued items such as power, prestige, wealth, or income. By focusing on how class position affects life chances, political power, and socialization patterns, radicals reaffirm the causal influence of economic factors on social life.

The most dramatic and decisive factor in social stratification is wealth, which "is extraordinarily concentrated in the United States" (Gilbert and Kahn 1982, 105). Federal Reserve Board figures indicate that the top 20 percent of consumers own over 76 percent of the total wealth, while the bottom 20 percent hold only 0.2 percent (Gilbert and Kahn 1982, 106). More dramatically, the top 1 percent of the wealthy in the U.S. own 42 percent of all wealth (Perlow 1988, 52).

Income is also unequally distributed. The U.S. Bureau of the Census reports that nearly half of all income is received by 20 percent of families and individuals, while the bottom 20 percent receive only 4 percent of the total income. Putting aside political rhetoric concerning progress and equality, the fact is that distributions of income and wealth have remained fairly constant in the U.S. over the past 50 years (Currie and Skolnick 1984:100-107). Contrary to the you-can-make-it-if-you-try ideology, this suggests that there is little chance that a significant number of lower class persons will advance in the American class structure.

In addition, recent data on occupational stratification point to a decline in both the quality and rewards associated with white collar work, a drop in blue collar employment, an increase in menial labor, and permanent levels of unemployment. These trends suggest "an increased hardening of class lines" (Gilbert and Kahn 1982, 83), which particularly affect women and blacks in terms of wealth, income and occupation. For example, women on average earn only 66 percent of what men take home in wages (Currie and Skolnick 1984), and many households below the official poverty level established by the U.S. government are female headed households. Blacks are also at a disadvantage. In 1981 the median family income for whites was $23,517, while the median family income for blacks was only $13,266 (Currie and Skolnick 1984, 147). Unemployment rates for black males are twice those of white males (U.S. Commission on Civil Rights), and blacks who have jobs are paid less on average for the same work, or are restricted to minimum wage and poorly paid service sector employment (Currie and Skolnick 1984, 162-181).

To supplement our discussion of inequality, we present a few "quality of life" indicators for persons in disadvantaged socioeconomic positions.

Though many such indicators exist (e.g. pertaining to illness, mental health, housing, perceived deficiencies in self-concept and happiness, etc.), we limit discussion to those which help us understand ways in which stratification and inequality bear on criminal behavior patterns.

Compared with the middle and upper classes, the American poor have far less access to quality education and, as a consequence, have lower educational levels. They are also more likely to be unemployed, or employed in secondary labor markets which offer undesirable work and inferior wages. Their families are more likely to be large, and they are less likely to remain cohesive. And last but not least, poor persons are more likely to be victims of violent crime (Vanfossen 1979; Bradburn and Caplovitz, 1965; Gurin et al. 1960; Gilbert and Kahn 1982; Kohn and Schooler 1969).

Turning to the top of the class structure, it comes as no surprise that those holding positions of relative advantage are able to gain additional leverage by translating economic strength into political power. As Mills (1956) demonstrates in his *Power Elite,* wealthy people are able to lobby for their interests, purchase political power with campaign contributions, secure important positions in both the public and private sectors, involve themselves in corporate and government decisions at the highest levels, and generally use their political and economic power to shape national policy in accordance with their interests.

All of this helps explain why radicals see political economy and inequality as such important contributors to crime causation. From a radical perspective, stratification and inequality are in large part due to political and economic factors as these relate to the antagonism between capital and labor—itself a defining characteristic of capitalism. If Marx was right, if productive relationships condition social relationships, and if the relations of production vary such that different social classes relate to the system of production in different ways, then class standing should have a significant impact on social relationships, i.e. familial and educational relationships. As we shall see, many social relationships are directly related to criminal behavior. Thus, the extent to which capitalism adversely influences these relationships

is the extent to which it shares responsibility for generating crime.

Political Economy, Inequality, and Crime

We begin with a question: What do social class, menstruation, broken homes, race, unemployment, and lunar cycles have in common? The answer: each has been specified as a cause of crime. This tells us two things: first, criminologists have traveled far and wide in their quest to discover the causes of crime (even to the moon!). And second, that causation is no simple matter. But where does this leave the student? What allows one to choose between causes as dissimilar as I.Q. and capitalism?

To answer these questions let us review an issue.... that dialectical thinking broadened causal inquiry to include the effects of political and economic institutions as these bear on the crime problem. In practical terms this means that radical criminologists attempt to make sense of causation by placing micro-causal explanations in a wider socio-political context. By broadening the scope of criminological inquiry to include significant social, political, and economic institutions, radical criminologists simultaneously expanded the arena in which we search for causes. The goal of radical inquiry is to expand and integrate causal levels, to try and see how micro-level variables such as broken homes or defective educational institutions are "shaped by larger social structures" (Greenberg 1981, 86; Sparks 1982).

With this strategy in mind three British criminologists (Taylor, Walton, and Young 1973) wrote a now famous book entitled *The New Criminology,* in which they argued that models of crime causation must include a macro-level analysis which incorporates a *political economy of crime.* Central to their argument are ways in which crime is affected by "the overall social context of inequalities of power, wealth and authority in the developed industrial society" (Taylor et al. 1973, 270). In addition to their emphasis on political economy, which they see as constituting the "wider origins" of the deviant act, Taylor, Walton, and Young argue that radical criminology must also explain the "immediate origins" of criminal behavior (Taylor et al. 1973, 271). Reduced to its simplest terms, Taylor et al. (1973) suggest that the wider arena of political economy will condition more immediate social milieus, and that these two levels together cause crime. What follows is a review of several studies which emphasize political economy and inequality as these bear on both the wider and immediate origins of criminal behavior.

Political Economy, Inequality, and Crime: The Evidence

In specifying ways in which economic institutions and structures cause crime, Blau and Blau (1982) published an empirical study that relies explicitly on Marxian predictions. After demonstrating that socio-economic inequalities increase rates of violence, they conclude that inequality is the root cause of both social disorganization and crime. In their view inequality increases alienation and undermines social cohesion

> by creating multiple parallel social differences which widen the separations between ethnic groups and between social classes, and it creates a situation characterized by much social disorganization and prevalent latent animosities (Blau and Blau 1982, 119).

Michalowski (1985, 410) makes this same point in simpler terms when he notes that "inequality tends to increase crime by weakening the social bond." Both the Blaus and Michalowski argue that it is inequality rather than simple poverty which produces crime (see Michalowski 1985, 406-409 for further discussion).

The emphasis on inequality may put some of the recent controversy regarding social class and crime into perspective. Recent statistical studies suggest a weak direct effect of social class on crime (Tittle et al. 1978; Messner, 1982). But this does not mean that social class is unimportant. On the contrary, radical theory suggests that inequality affects other processes which in turn impact directly on crime. Thus, for instance, Blau and Blau (1982) suggest that family disorganization (e.g. percent divorced, percent female headed families) mediates the effect of inequality. Indeed, they

found that percent divorced was positively related to inequality, and that percent divorced had the strongest direct effects on crime.

Lee Rainwater has also offered a causal framework which combines wider and immediate origins by relating crime and family disorganization to inequality and racial oppression. Adding race to his discussion of social class, Rainwater (1970) argues that the economic marginality of black men leads to tense and conflicting role relationships, which increases marital instability and ultimately leads to a pattern of female-based households and matrifocal family structure. Like Blau and Blau, he concludes that inequality, low economic status, and race interact to produce crime through social disorganization. Simply put, both studies suggest that those who are economically disadvantaged are more likely to suffer disorganized or "segregated" family structures, and that strains experienced in these types of families provide a fertile precondition for increased rates of crime and delinquency.

Inequality, Family Disorganization, and Crime

Family measures such as percent divorced and percent headed by women have long been powerful correlates of delinquency, and many have suggested that family disorganization is an important cause of crime (Nye 1958; Hirschi 1983). However, in line with their preference for contextual explanations, radicals view family structure as an intervening rather than an independent variable. This is the strategy adopted by both Blau and Blau (1982) and Rainwater (1970). Others have suggested that inconsistent family socialization patterns can be traced to experiences in the workplace (see Hagan et al. 1979, 1985, 1987; Hill and Atkinson 1989). Inconsistent socialization patterns have been firmly established as a cause of delinquency (Glueck and Glueck 1950; McCord, McCord, and Zola 1959; Hirschi 1969).

Drawing on the works of Kohn (1969, 1976, 1977), Edwards (1979), and Etzioni (1970), Colvin and Pauly (1983) argue that socialization experiences in the workplace spill into socialization experiences in the home, and that negative experiences in either setting increase the likelihood that children will "engage in serious, patterned delinquency" (Colvin and Pauly 1983, 515).

In pursuing this claim Colvin and Pauly conclude that stable socialization experiences in desirable white-collar professions promote internalized moral commitments to the workplace. Parents in these occupations encourage family socialization experiences which rely on *internalized control structures,* a type of control which promotes a child's attachment to the socialization sequence. As a result, socialization experiences are "positive" in that children have "initial bonds of high intensity" to the family unit.

Blue collar employees, on the other hand, work under *utilitarian control structures,* which means that their bond to the organization depends on a calculation of extrinsic material rewards (e.g. pay increases, seniority, job security). Workers socialized in this way tend to reproduce that structure in the family, producing "calculative bonds of intermediate intensity in their children" (Colvin and Pauly 1982, 536).

And finally, parents holding low skill, low pay, dead-end jobs are exposed to *inconsistent coercive control structures* that are externally enforced. Such parents are likely to impose inconsistent controls on their children, oscillating between punitiveness to permissiveness. In this section of the working class we can expect "more alienated initial bonds to be produced in children who experience such arbitrary, inconsistent, and coercive family control structures" (Colvin and Pauly 1982, 536). One drawback in Colvin and Pauly's model is that it does not examine unemployed families. Parents in these families are not exposed to consistent socialization patterns that can be replicated within the home, and the controls employed in this type of family (especially the chronically unemployed) are likely to be very unstable, differing from one family to the next, and within the same family over time. Given Colvin and Pauly's other assertions, it follows that chronically unemployed parents are least able to employ social control methods which minimize criminal behavior among their children. As a result, those children are more likely to violate the law and to be arrested for those violations.

In sum, Colvin and Pauly (1983, 535-536) suggest that persons socialized under coercive control structures at work will employ similar socialization methods in the home or, more generally, that different parental attitudes toward child rearing will be produced in different work-related contexts. By combining sound sociological research with secure empirical findings in criminology concerning the relationship between inconsistent socialization patterns and delinquency, Colvin and Pauly broaden causal inquiry and conclude that (1) socialization patterns in both workplace and family settings are distributed along class lines, (2) that these patterns are defined by the relations of production underlying capitalism, and (3) that these differential socialization sequences determine "the patterned processes of development of both delinquent and non-delinquent behavior" (Colvin and Pauly 1982, 525). Their consistent Marxist approach breathes new life into the traditional emphasis on family structure as an "independent" variable. Again, this is the strategy preferred by radicals, who always try to place micro-level variables within a more encompassing causal context.

Economic Conditions and Criminal Behavior

The emphasis on linking crime with the economic structure of society is logically appealing given empirical distributions of criminal behavior. For example, 93 percent of Index Crimes involve property offenses (Sourcebook 1986, 319—we include robbery in this estimate since it is performed for economic gain). And surely the primary motivation behind white-collar and corporate crime is economic. Thus, both crimes of the powerful and powerless are closely linked with economic motivations.

There are a number of ways to establish an empirical connection between the economic system and criminal behavior. For example, radical theorists have examined how perceived and real economic inequality causes crime (e.g. Blau and Blau 1982). Others have suggested that capitalist class structures limit the ability of certain individuals to make non-criminal choices (Groves and Frank 1987). In terms of street crime, the concern with social class gives rise to the observation that those in marginal economic positions are most likely to become involved in street crime, or to be labelled as street criminals (Spitzer 1975; Quinney 1980; Platt 1978). To test this assertion, let us review the connection between unemployment and crime.

Unemployment and Criminal Behavior

A number of radical theorists claim to have established a relationship between crime and unemployment (Quinney 1980, 1979; Reiman 1984; Box 1981, 1984, 1987; Box and Hale 1983a, 1983b; Greenberg 1977a; Chiricos 1987; Platt 1978; Currie 1985; Bohm 1985; Gordon 1973, 1971). While traditional criminologists are also concerned with this issue, their approach fails to address the economic sources of unemployment. Radicals, by contrast, are concerned with the structural sources of unemployment, how increases or decreases in the rate of unemployment affect rates of criminal activity, and how the economy can be restructured to reduce unemployment.

Unemployment is a consequence of the normal operation of capitalist economies. To increase profit and produce more value (especially surplus value), capitalists are forced to pursue technological innovations which increase productivity. When more technology is employed in the production process, there is a high probability that human labor will be replaced. As a result, many technological innovations (e.g. machines that perform work formerly done by wage workers) remove workers from the production process. Thus, in its normal development, capitalism's increasing reliance on machine technology creates a surplus or economically marginal population, and this includes both unemployed and underemployed workers (Marx 1974, 631-648).

While unemployment is a fact of life associated with American capitalism, it can be controlled to a certain extent. But using the Phillips Curve, economists have demonstrated that inflation is the price for maintaining low levels of unemployment (Dolan 1977, 258-262). Further, there is general agreement that this trade-off between inflation and unemployment cannot be solved within the structural confines of capitalism (Applebaum

1979). This is an example of what Marx meant when he accused capitalism of harboring internal and irreconcilable contradictions.

Whether one uses radical or traditional economic approaches, it is agreed that unemployment is an intractable feature of capitalism. Having established this, we turn to the connection between unemployment and crime. Addressing this issue Greenberg (1977a, 648) notes that:

> persons who are unemployed can be assumed to have a greater incentive to steal than those who are not. In addition, they may risk less when they engage in crime, for they cannot lose their jobs if caught. If this reasoning is correct, crime rates will increase during periods of unemployment.

In this view crime becomes a rational response to a structural constraint (in this case, unemployment) associated with capitalism (Quinney 1980; Gordon 1971, 1973). Unemployed individuals have fewer choices available to them (Groves and Frank 1987; Box 1987, 29). As a result of the limited choices, crime may become an attractive alternative. In addition, given the pressure to succeed—which in the U.S. is measured by material possessions—even those who are not absolutely impoverished feel that they have failed if they cannot purchase more than food and shelter. Crime is one way both the absolutely and relatively impoverished can obtain material evidence of "success."

In a recent review of the literature on unemployment and crime, Chiricos (1987) concluded that there was a non-spurious correlation between the rate of unemployment and levels of property crime. Given that capitalism is unable to avoid generating unemployment, and the logical and empirical connections between unemployment and crime, there is ample justification for the claim that capitalism sets causal parameters for crime production. This contention will be addressed later in this chapter. First, we examine arguments which go beyond the unemployment-crime connection.

Beyond Unemployment and Crime

It certainly makes sense to suggest that unemployment causes crime. The empirical relation between crime and unemployment, however, is not over-whelmingly strong, and unemployment cannot explain the general upward trend in crime over the past thirty years (Freeman, 1983). Furthermore, there is scant evidence linking unemployment with violent crime. This latter finding is not at all surprising to a number of traditional criminologists, who claim that unemployment should have little if any effect on the crime rate (Wilson and Herrnstein 1985; Wilson and Cook 1985; Fox 1978). This finding would, however, appear to contradict the expectations of a radical model of crime.

But radical criminologists seem unconcerned by the modest empirical relationship between crime and unemployment. Bohm, for example, using a broader contextual model, has argued that radical theorists should assume that "the relationship between unemployment and most criminal behavior in the United States is spurious and is due to the influence ... [of] the social relations peculiar to a capitalist mode of production" (1985, 213). Bohm suggests that radicals should not link crime to unemployment, but should examine the broader social relationships which might cause both crime and unemployment. Capitalism, for instance, fosters competition, self-interest, and subordination of the working class. In this view crime is not simply the result of unemployment, it is the result of competition over scarce resources (including jobs) and the promotion of self-interest. In Bonger's (1916) terms, capitalism promotes egoism, which in turn generates crime in all classes.

This approach is more consistent with observable crime trends. The white-collar or corporate criminal, for example, is employed, yet still commits crime. Competitive pressures to cut the costs of production often merge with an egoistic pursuit of capital accumulation, and these concerns supply ample motivation for violating the law. In Bohm's view, self-interest and competition influence all members of a capitalist society, and this sets up conditions conducive to criminal behavior among all classes (see also Engels, 1981, 1978, for a similar argument).

While Bohm's approach downplays the significance of unemployment as a primary cause of crime, he remains sensitive to the idea that unemployment creates additional strains which may lead individuals to criminality. Unemployment is particularly high among young minority males, who constitute a large at risk crime population (1985, 215). Bohm acknowledges the idea that unemployment is caused by the natural progression of capitalism, yet sensitizes us to forces beyond unemployment which affect all classes and also act as causes of crime.

Addressing the issue of social policy, Bohm argues that we must transcend capitalism in order to solve the crime problem. In his view creating jobs will not reduce crime, since the overall experience of capitalism still leaves the majority of the population alienated and vulnerable to criminal incentives. Other radicals have argued that if there is a connection between unemployment and crime, creating more jobs will reduce the property crime rate here and now (Currie 1985; Quinney 1980; Chiricos 1987). Thus, there is tension in the policy recommendations suggested by radical theorists. Short term policies which can be instituted under the current system clash with the long-term policies for altering the social order.

Box (1987) has also suggested that radicals downplay the significance of unemployment, and focus instead on broader economic conditions that affect all social classes. Like Bohm, Box argues that the unemployment explanation fails to account for crimes of the powerful. He suggests that radicals examine the connection between recession and crime.

In Box's view, recessions create conditions conducive to crime which affect both the powerless and the powerful. The powerful are under additional pressure to maintain or increase profits during recessions. Faced with a recession, white-collar workers confront a constellation of organizational motivations and incentives which can easily lead to violations of law. On the other hand recessions drive the lower class further into poverty, block legitimate means to success, and reduce commitment to the conventional social order. All of this makes increases in crime more likely among the lower class.

Recessions also affect the way powerful persons view the powerless. Recessions bring with them unemployment and an enlarged surplus population. This surplus population is "viewed more suspiciously by the governing elite, not because it actually does become disruptive and rebellious, but because it might" (Box 1987, 62). This increased fear results in increased state coercion of the powerless in the form of rising arrest and incarceration rates (Box 1987, 62-63). Recessionary trends also affect the way police enforce the law, and Box claims that recessions can be linked to an increased number of police crimes, including fabricating evidence, police brutality, and the killing of offenders perceived as threats to the social order (Box 1987, 63-65).

Surplus Value and Crime

A recent trend in radical theory has been to examine the relationship between crime rates and the rate of surplus value (Lynch 1988a; Lynch, Groves and Lizotte 1988). This research attempts to link the driving productive forces of capitalism to the production of criminal behavior.

Marx's clearest illustration of surplus value describes it as the ratio of paid to unpaid labor, which implies that workers produce value far in excess of what they receive in wages. This excess is appropriated by the capitalist, who uses it for capital expansion and profit. There are two primary ways to increase the rate of surplus value. First, the working day may be extended with no commensurate increase in wages (absolute surplus value). And second, more efficient machines may replace people in the production process (relative surplus value). Either of these strategies allows owners to achieve their desired goal, which is to squeeze more production from the labor process. Given that capitalists derive profit from high rates of surplus value, it is in their interest to keep that rate as high as possible.

Marx went on to argue that increases in the rate of surplus value were directly related to the economic marginalization of the labor force. For its part the extraction of absolute surplus value means that employed laborers receive a smaller share of the surplus they produce. The extraction of relative surplus value, on the other hand, creates unemployment and underemployment as a result of workers being technologically displaced. In effect,

a rising rate of surplus value affects both employed and unemployed laborers (Perlow 1988).

As the rate of surplus value rises, more and more people become economically marginal. This decreases commitment to the conventional order, and increases the probability that persons will engage in crime. Lynch (1988a) and Lynch, Groves and Lizotte (1988) have uncovered a statistically significant relationship between the rate of surplus value and property crime arrest rates in the U.S. from 1950-1975. This research demonstrates that Marx's key economic concept—the extraction of surplus value—is useful for explaining how capitalist economic systems generate conditions conducive to street crime—especially property crime, the most prevalent type of crime in our society.

Does Capitalism Cause Crime?

Several theorists use Marxist arguments to suggest that capitalism stimulates a significant proportion of all criminal behavior. They are indebted, though in different ways, to theorists such as Engels (1973, 1978, 1981, 1983) and Bonger (1916), who argued that criminal behavior is a direct reflection of the strains associated with life under capitalism.

Engels' point is twofold. First, he points out that many technological advances associated with capitalism expel workers from production, generate unemployed populations, and result in "want, wretchedness, and crime" (1973, 173). This theme reappears in the contemporary writings of Quinney (1979, 1980) and Gordon (1971, 1973), who suggest that crime is a rational response to systems of inequitable distribution characteristic of capitalism. Spitzer (1975) also argues that capitalism excludes certain groups from meaningful attachment to economic and social institutions. For Spitzer, those with a reduced stake in conformity—which includes those who are economically marginal—are more likely to engage in criminal behavior.

Engels' second point is that capitalism generates competitive structural and psychological orientations which are both beneficial and harmful to society. Competition benefits capitalists when it functions to keep wages low and productivity high. On the other hand Marx noted that in their competitive scramble to control and monopolize markets, it is often the case that "one capitalist kills many." Similarly, competition can benefit the working class when labor is scarce and owners must pay high wages to attract workers. But competition can also injure the working class; not only must they compete with owners for better working conditions, they are often forced to compete with one another for a limited number of jobs and resources. Consequently, Engels views crime as the result of competition over scarce resources, and sees competition engendered by capitalism as the cause of crime by the masses (1964, 224; 1973, 168-173), the businessman (1964, 201-202, 209), and middle classes (1981, 49). Further, he sees a collective psychological component to competition, which he describes as follows (1964, 224):

> Competition has penetrated all the relationships of our life and completed the reciprocal bondage in which men now hold themselves. Competition is the great mainspring which...jerks into activity our aging and withering social order, or rather disorder...Competition governs the numerical advances of mankind; it likewise governs its moral advance...[S]tatistics of crime...[show] the peculiar regularity with which crime advances year by year...The extension of the factory system is followed everywhere by an increase in crime...This regularity proves that crime, too, is governed by competition; that society creates a demand for crime which is met by a corresponding supply...

In *Criminality and Economic Conditions* (1916), Bonger makes a similar argument. For Bonger, however, the competitiveness created by capitalism manifests itself as egoism in individuals—and it is egoism which generates crime among all classes. While Bonger believed egoism was evenly distributed throughout the class structure, he noted that the political strength of the ruling class enabled it to perform exploitative acts without having those acts defined as crimes. This explains why more lower class persons are processed by the criminal justice system.

Engels (1964, 224) and Marx (1981, 52-53) also claim that capitalism "creates a demand for crime which is met by a corresponding supply..." (Engels 1964, 224). Expanding on this theme, Colvin and Pauly (1983) and the Schwendingers

(1976a) suggest that the inequality and stratification which accompany capitalism affect educational opportunities, which in turn structure an individual's propensity to crime. Greenberg (1985) explains variations in delinquency rates in terms of the structural demands of capitalism; Barnett (1981a) has analyzed criminal opportunity as it relates to capital accumulation; and Wallace and Humphries (1981) have reinterpreted the criminogenic effects of urbanization and industrialization by placing these processes within a broader Marxist perspective on investment and capital accumulation. Each of these studies employs a broad contextual approach to crime, and each is a solid contribution to the radical perspective on crime causation.

Women and Crime: The Traditional Approach

The 1975 publication of Freda Adler's *Sisters in Crime* and Rita Simon's *Women and Crime* marked a turning point in the study of female criminality. Prior to 1975, female criminality was rarely addressed. When it was, criminologists focused on biological differences between men and women to explain lower rates of female crime (Lombroso and Ferrero 1894; Warker 1875; Adam 1914; Bishop 1931; Glueck and Glueck 1935; Pollak 1950). Lombroso, for example, thought female criminals were "born criminals" who exhibited masculine and atavistic (primitive) characteristics. Since most women did not possess masculine or atavistic characteristics, they were less likely than men to commit crimes. Others, like Pollak, rejected the idea that women committed fewer crimes than men. Female crimes, he argued, had a "masked" character (Pollak 1950,5); they were difficult to detect and were easily hidden (e.g. shoplifting, abortion, poisoning, domestic thefts). Pollak also argued that the masked character of female criminality was related to women's deceitful nature. This deceitfulness resulted from the interaction of social and biological factors unique to females.

Simon and Adler rejected these claims. By placing greater emphasis on female social roles, they moved away from individual and biological explanations towards explanations that were at once sociological and contextual.

Simon and Adler argued that increased liberation generated by the women's movement expanded female social roles, which in turn increased criminal opportunities for women. Both theorists support "gender convergence" rationale with regard to explanations of male and female criminality. That is, as females became equivalent to males in terms of their social and economic roles, the criminal behaviors of males and females would begin to converge as well. This, however, is where Adler and Simon part company.

For her part, Adler argued that the increase in female criminality was concentrated in violent crimes. In Adler's approach, the women's movement led to the masculinization of female behavior. This increased aggressiveness among women, leading them to commit more violent crimes. Simon, however, argued that the increase in female criminality was restricted to property crimes, particularly occupationally related thefts and "pink-collar crimes." Both supported their contentions by analyzing increases in the number of UCR arrests for women. When the dust settled, it supported the view that increases in female crime have been nonviolent in nature (see Messerschmidt 1986, 79-81; Steffensmeier 1981).

A Radical Approach to Understanding Female Criminality

In general, radical theorists have objected to Simon and Adler's work, claiming that the women's movement is not criminogenic (Klein 1979; Klein and Kress 1976; Box and Hale 1983a, 1983b). Rather, the forces which influence female criminality are broader than the women's movement—they are embedded in the social and economic fabric of American society (Daly and Chesney-Lind, 1988). In their rejection of Simon and Adler's hypotheses, some radicals have suggested that female emancipation will lead to reductions rather than increases in female criminality (Box and Hale 1983b, 477, 1983a).

The central concern in the study of female criminality is why women commit significantly fewer crimes than men. Several radical theorists have taken up this challenge by employing Marxist-feminist theory (Klein 1982, 1979; Klein and Kress 1976; Weiss 1978; Box 1984, 3; Box and Hale 1983a, 1983b; Balkan et al, 1980). Balkan, Berger and Schmidt, for example, argue that women commit certain types of crimes because gender-specific socialization limits their opportunities under capitalism. Simply put, women's socialization experiences, and the opportunities available to them in terms of economic activities, define both the types and amounts of crime they are able to commit. Since the traditional place for women in American society is "in the home," they have few opportunities to commit white-collar and corporate crimes. The crimes they do commit (e.g. shoplifting, forgery, fraud, abortion) are related to their roles as wives, mothers or homemakers (Balkan et al., 1980, 211-217). These crimes reflect the powerless position of women in American society. Even female violence is directed by their social roles. When women engage in violence it is aimed primarily at family members (Messerschmidt 1986, 14), and is likely to involve household items rather than guns (Messerschmidt 1986, 14).

Balkan, Berger and Schmidt also argue that crimes committed *against* women are the result of socialization patterns fostered by capitalism (on rape, see Schwendinger and Schwendinger 1976, 1981, 1983). Crimes against women are acts which replicate the types of gender and class domination characteristic of patriarchal capitalism.

In Schur's (1984, 34-37) view, women in America occupy a devalued status because they are viewed as commodities or objects: women are thought of as things to be owned or admired for their beauty, and are treated as sexual objects. Many women internalize this stereotypical view of themselves. They behave as men expect them to behave, and are inclined to become submissive. Thus, they commit crimes which fit the stereotype—nonviolent, powerless, self-destructive, and sex-related crimes (e.g. prostitution, adultery, abortion, infanticide, drug abuse). This devalued view of women cannot be understood apart from the types of social and economic roles women fulfill in American society.

Hagan and his associates (see Hagan et al. 1979, 1985, 1987) have argued that the relationship between gender and delinquency can be linked to the forms of power and control exerted by the family, which in turn are related to the economic roles filled by parents (see also Singer and Levine 1988; Hill and Atkinson 1988). This theory is closely related to Colvin and Pauly's work. The resulting power-control theory implies that "dominance and control in the household organizes delinquent conduct by gender" (Singer and Levine 1988, 627). In this view gender socialization is related to family patterns of control, which varies according to the family's social class. Parents, in effect, reaffirm their own power relationships by the way they control their children (Hagan et al. 1987, 792). For example, mothers locked into traditional roles attempt to raise daughters with similar values by socializing their children to accept traditional expectations (Hagan et al 1987, 791). This means keeping the daughter close to home, teaching domestic chores, and reaffirming domestic consumption patterns, all of which promotes conformity and submission to stereotypical role expectations among young women.

In traditional households fathers are the authority figures, while mothers remain powerless except in relation to their daughters. In these *unbalanced households* fathers are in a position of authority due to their economic status, while mothers are unemployed or are employed in a low status occupation. Operating in these occupational and gender structures a mother's control over her male offspring is minimal, giving sons in male dominated households greater freedom to deviate than daughters.

In *balanced households,* mothers and fathers are both in positions of prestige and authority in the workplace, and workplace equality tends to translate into household equality in terms of parental authority. This creates egalitarian attitudes toward the control of male and female children, which decreases differences in criminality among male and female offspring.

Empirical analyses of this hypothesis (Hagan et al. 1987, 1985; Singer and Levine 1988; Hill and Atkinson 1988) support many of the contentions of power-control theory. An exception is found by Singer and Levine, who discovered that boys in balanced households were more likely than boys in unbalanced households to become involved in delinquency (1988, 640). They were, however, able to confirm a number of other hypotheses associated with power-control theory (1988, 640-645). The major thrust of this research suggests that control of juveniles is strongly related to economic positions occupied by parents because social control techniques employed within the family "reflect gender divisions found in the workplace..." (Hill and Atkinson 1988, 144; Colvin and Pauly 1983). Thus, the production of delinquency, and the differences between male and female delinquency, can be traced to three interrelated factors: first is the economic context and workplace position of parents; second is the way in which equality (or inequality) in the workplace translates into gender equality (or inequality) in the home; and third is the effect gender equality (or inequality) has on fortifying (or undermining) parental authority over children.

Messerschmidt (1986) has employed a broader theory to interpret female criminality by suggesting that Marxism, which places primary emphasis on the mode of production, suffers theoretical limitations. His suggestion is that social theorists also include modes of reproduction in their analyses (Harris, 1986). This approach assumes that social life is shaped and determined by both economic and biological reproduction. The implication is that an individual's place in society is not merely a consequence of class, but is a consequence of the interaction between class and gender.

Messerschmidt expands on the economic explanation radicals normally employ by incorporating a discussion of the economic, social and gender contexts which condition both male and female criminality. In certain respects Messerschmidt's argument is more radical than a conventional Marxist critique because it (literally) hits closer to home. After all, most criminologists are males, and they do not live with the impoverished proletariat. They do, however, live with spouses. Given its ability to re-direct our critical gaze, let us pursue the argument presented in *Capitalism, Patriarchy, and Crime* in more detail.

Citing anthropological evidence, Messerschmidt argues that the sexual division of labor emerged prior to the division of society into classes. In early societies the division of labor was based on physical strength and was inclined towards patriarchy (male domination). Because earlier forms of male domination persist, Messerschmidt concludes that American society is characterized by patriarchal as well as capitalistic social relationships.

From this perspective capitalists control the labor of workers, while men control the economic and biological labor of women. Thus, society contains both class and gender mechanisms of subordination and control. This double subordination of women to both gender and class control explains why women commit fewer and less serious crimes then men.

> Individuals are enmeshed in class and gender structures that organize the way people think about their circumstances and devise solutions to act upon them. Gender and class shape one's possibilities... Criminality is related, then, to the interaction of patriarchy and capitalism and the structural possibilities this interaction creates (Messerschmidt 1986, 41).

Women in patriarchal capitalist society commit fewer crimes then men because women are less powerful socially, economically and biologically. Women are isolated within the family, and have fewer opportunities to commit crimes requiring power (e.g. white-collar and corporate crime). Furthermore, women are denied access to many illegitimate sources of success (e.g. street crime) since illegitimate opportunities, like legitimate opportunities, are controlled by men (Messerschmidt 1986, 42-45). In sum, Messerschmidt argues that "oppression and powerlessness in both the home and the labor market...generate specific forms of criminality on the part of women" (1986, 72). Since women are powerless, they tend to commit less serious crimes, nonviolent crimes, and crimes of self-destruction (e.g. drug abuse) [for a critique see Schwendinger and Schwendinger 1988, and Messerschmidt's reply, 1988].

In Sum...

Thus far we have reviewed the causal contributions of criminologists explicitly aligned with a radical or Marxist perspective. All of the theories discussed above explain the production of crime with reference to its social and economic context. For radical theorists sensitive to developments in the areas of feminism and patriarchy, criminality is explained with reference to a broader array of social, economic, and gender contexts facing men and women....

Types of Crime

Although the question "What is crime?" appears to be a simple one, it has a very complex answer. Crime is not only a social construction, varying and changing across jurisdictions and time; it is also a legal concept, defined by the laws of a state or jurisdiction. Once an action is legally defined as a crime, it becomes more precise, specific, tangible, and measurable, and is therefore generally more amenable to the scrutiny of research. The study of crime is aided by the use of crime typologies, or groupings of similar types of offenses. Although there is no single list of typologies with which every scholar agrees, there are a number of broad categories, such as violent crime and property crime, and a number of specific typologies, such as murder and burglary, about which there is a general, if not detailed, consensus. For example, most if not all scholars would agree that there is a category of crime referred to as rape, although some would define the action much more broadly than others.

Marshall B. Clinard and Richard Quinney (1973) attempt to define or distinguish types of criminal behavior because, as they observe, placing events into categories allows us to reduce them to a level of commonality in which they can be compared and studied systematically. Types, they say, help us create hypotheses and give direction to our research, based on the similar characteristics of all the actions that fall into a particular category. According to Clinard and Quinney, typologies can be based on many different variables or assumptions. Legalistic typologies, for example, are based

on the seriousness of the crime (felonies, misdemeanors) or the type of punishment received. Individualistic typologies, by contrast, are based on characteristics of individual offenders, such as genetics, personality, or psychological traits. Social typologies classify criminals by such characteristics as whether they are occasional, infrequent offenders or habitual, repeat offenders, or whether they are professional offenders who make their living from crime or accidental offenders who seem to stumble into criminal behavior. The reason for the great number of typologies, according to Clinard and Quinney, is that they are based on the "purposes they are to serve" and are needed to accommodate crime definitions and criminological theories, both of which change over time. Six commonly agreed-upon types of crimes will be considered here: violent crime, property crime, public-order crime, professional crime, organized crime, and white-collar crime.

Violent Crime

Violent crimes are only a small portion of the nation's total crime. They are murder, forcible rape, robbery, and assault. Some criminologists believe that the term should also include automobile gas tanks that explode upon impact; factory accidents occurring as a result of employers' blatant disregard for worker safety, often in violation of laws regulating working conditions; or the foreign marketing of pharmaceuticals that have been banned domestically because of known serious side effects. But there is no consensus on that point. Violence on the streets is given more publicity and is more widely feared than violence created in corporate suites. Indeed, street violence is more widely feared than violence in the home, although people are more likely to be murdered or assaulted in their own homes or the homes of someone they know than they are to be on the street (Hagan 1998). Thus, "violent crimes" typically refers to the four "street" violent crimes.

The United States has always experienced violence; indeed, violence is an integral part of our heritage. As a nation, we gained our independence through a revolution. We fought Native Americans, foreign foes, and even against one another in a bloody civil war. We have seen violence expressed in slavery, in such groups as the Ku Klux Klan, in labor protests, and in Old West vigilante groups. We are fascinated by it in the newspapers and even pay to see it on the silver screen. So much violence is portrayed on television and in the theaters that it is feared that we as a society are becoming desensitized.

Violence, like other crime, experiences trends (see Reading 31). Homicide, for example, has peaked and declined several times throughout the past century (Reiss and Roth 1993). During the 1960s, urban rioting and looting, seizure of campus and government buildings by militant students, and assassinations were of primary concern (Moynihan 1969). At the present time special attention seems to focus on drug-related violence, gang-related violence, spousal and child abuse, serial murders, domestic terrorists, workplace violence, juvenile violence, and acquaintance rape.

Violent crime is predominantly, though not always, an urban problem. It is typically committed by males, aged fifteen to twenty-four, from lower socioeconomic levels, in minority inner-city areas. Traits of the victims are similar to those of the offenders, except in the case of robbery, whose victims tend to be older and white (Gabor et al. 1988). With the exception of robbery, crimes of violence are likely to be motivated by passion and other emotions among people who know each other, even intimately. It is not unusual for violent offenders to have a history of previous violence.

Homicides, though relatively small in number, capture the attention of the public perhaps more than any other crime. Homicide includes a wide range of categories, from vehicular homicide to manslaughter, and from single crimes of passion to various types of multiple murder. It often involves the use of alcohol, precipitation by the victim, and some level of social interaction. For example, James Bourdouis (1974) has identified a number of common social interactions in which murder is quite likely to occur. Among them are domestic relations, circles of friends and acquaintances (roommates, neighbors, coworkers), love affairs (couples, triangles), business relations (doctor-patient, professor-student, landlord-tenant), criminal transactions, and suicide-murder.

Multiple homicides do not occur often, but when they do they capture a great deal of media attention and public concern. Serial killings seem to be the most frequent type of multiple homicides. A serial killer murders three or more victims, usually unknown to him or her, in separate instances separated by long intervals, sometimes even years. Serial killers are generally white, middle-aged men from all social classes, who maintain a low profile and are usually employed. Their victims tend to be females with whom they are not or are only slightly acquainted, and they kill for reasons that would not make sense to a normal person (Voigt et al. 1994). Unlike other types of murder, serial killings have a very low clearance rate. Often in cases where serial killings are suspected, FBI agents construct a profile of the killer, in which they attempt to determine the personality, age, occupation, and pattern of killing, to increase the chances of identifying the killer and stopping him or her.

Forcible rape is another dreaded but common form of violence. Victims of rape often know their assailants. According to research findings (Hagan 1998), half of rape victims are under eighteen years of age; the younger the victim, the more likely it is that he or she knows the rapist. When the victim knows the rapist, the crime is less likely to be reported to the police. For many years, forced sexual relations involving spouses were not regarded as rape (Russell 1982), although that has now changed. In instances of date or acquaintance rape, the victim was often viewed by the courts as a willing participant or was thought to have led the man on through provocative dress or behavior, by going to a bar, or by entering his apartment, room, or vehicle. Victims, when they pressed charges, were often treated as if they were on trial, as their past sexual experiences were used to discredit their character and their account of the incident. Some people have suggested that this treatment resulted in the victim's being victimized a second time by the criminal justice system. Much of this attitude has now changed, however, with the implementation of laws and policies designed to protect victims of rape, such as rape-shield laws. Nevertheless, Susan Estrich (1987) has characterized the general attitude toward rape with the terms "real rape" (rape involving violence) and "simple rape" (which does not involve violence). Real rape is taken seriously by the courts, whereas simple rape is not.

Three types of rapists have been described in the literature on rape, giving some insight into why it is considered a violent crime rather than a sex crime (Voigt et al. 1994). The angry rapist shows displaced aggression, expressing anger toward a wife or woman friend by hurting someone else. The power rapist uses rape to assert his manhood. The sadistic rapist, the worst type, becomes sexually excited by hurting his victim. Feminists contend that dominant attitudes toward rape are extensions of a paternalistic society's differential socialization for males and females, in which males are taught to dominate and be aggressive, and females are taught to be submissive and subservient. This pattern of gender socialization is the result of historical capitalistic notions of women being the property of men (Brownmiller 1975).

Another area, according to feminists, that reflects the cultural mores of male dominance, control, aggression, and intimidation is domestic abuse. Domestic abuse consists of spousal abuse, child abuse and neglect, and abuse of parents and siblings. Recent data conclude that as many as 2,500 people are killed annually as a result of domestic abuse (Federal Bureau of Investigation 1997). Partly because of changing attitudes and partly because of laws requiring certain professionals such as doctors and schoolteachers to report suspected cases of child abuse, many more cases are reported now than in the past. Based on known cases, men are usually the abusers in cases of spousal abuse. Although some criminologists contend that women are abusive nearly as often as men, it is women who sustain the most serious and life-threatening injuries, because of men's superior physical strength. Children who have experienced or witnessed abuse have a greater chance of growing up to be abusers themselves, as well as having an adult criminal record.

People often wonder why abused wives do not leave their abusers. There are many reasons, from economic dependence, learned dependence (in which the wife is emotionally battered into thinking it is her fault and she deserves no better), to the cycle of violence. In the cycle of violence, there is an escalation period in which stress and pressure build, finally culminating in the violent act. The abuser then becomes very repentant, begging forgiveness, and swearing never to do it again; a sort of honeymoon period ensues, in which he tries to compensate for his behavior. A woman who still loves her husband or partner has high hopes that he means it this time. As stress and pressures mount, however, the partner, with his poor self-concept, his dependence on his wife, and his traditional view of male and female roles, does batter again, and each incident becomes more violent than the last. Some wives, afraid to leave but unable to take any more abuse, may resort to killing their battering spouse, usually when he is vulnerable and weak, such as when he is sleeping. Battered-wife syndrome is sometimes used in court as a defense similar to self-defense (Monahan and Walker 1994).

Robbery, which may seem to be a property offense, is considered a violent offense because it involves a confrontation and the use or threat of violence, causing victims to fear for their safety. Although most crimes are predominantly intraracial, robbery is often interracial, because many robbers are poor, young, African American males, and many of their victims are older white males perceived to be more affluent. A small portion of robbers are professionals who depend on robbery to make a living. The majority, however, are opportunistic, unskilled, with no advanced plan for the offense. Many adult robbers indicate that financial need is their motivation (Petersilia 1980).

Assaults can be differentiated into two types: aggravated, which involves serious bodily injury and usually involves a weapon, and simple, which does not involve a weapon. Albert J. Reiss and Jeffrey A. Roth (1993) point out that in 1990, 67 percent of assaults were attempts, almost half of reported assaults were simple (involving no weapon and no injury), and the least common assaults were those involving injuries. They conclude, however, that the costs of violence involve more than just physical injury. There are psychological effects on the victim, the family, and the neighborhood, such as fear, decreased cohesion, and impaired ability to live one's life as before. There are also economic consequences, such as medical and rehabilitation costs, loss of income for the victim, and economic costs for society, such as law enforcement and corrections expenses.

Property Crime

The largest proportion of street crimes in the United States are property crimes committed for monetary gain (see Reading 32 and Section II). These crimes involve the illegal acquisition of, and sometimes the destruction of, various types of property, including money, tangible goods, other property, and, more recently, data. Property index crimes listed in the Uniform Crime Reports are burglary, motor vehicle theft, larceny-theft, and arson. Advances in technology, such as automated banking, widespread use of credit and debit cards, and computer-accessed databases have provided new opportunities for both professional and unskilled property offenders, although the latter are in the majority. It is not uncommon for both amateur and professional thieves to assume the identity of others by entering computer databases and using that information to obtain access to bank accounts and credit cards.

Motor vehicle theft includes the theft of automobiles, trucks, buses, and vans. Many states also include the theft of motorcycles, snowmobiles, and motorscooters (Voigt et al. 1994). There are a number of possible motives for vehicle theft, which range from teenage joyriding, in which the offenders intend only to take the vehicle temporarily, to stealing the vehicle for resale, stripping it for parts, or using it in the commission of a crime. With hundreds of millions of automobiles available in the United States and deterrence devices unreliable, the rate of motor vehicle theft is rising, and clearance rates remain low. Most stolen vehicles are eventually recovered, however.

Burglary involves the unlawful entry of a structure (residences, businesses, even boats and trailers) for the purpose of committing a felony. Most burglars are male, and the majority are under the age of twenty-five (Voigt et al. 1994). Some burglars are inexperienced, whereas others plan their crimes carefully and have been committing them for a number of years. More than half of all burglaries occur during the daytime, and two-thirds occur in residences; about 21 percent are cleared by arrest (Hagan 1998). Those more likely to become victims of burglaries include African Americans, younger people, those in lower socioeconomic levels, and renters (Voigt et al. 1994). Suburban burglaries have increased because suburbs are more affluent than cities, homes are unoccupied during the day, police forces are smaller, and urban dwellers are moving to the suburbs. This increase is consistent with a routine-activities explanation of crime, which views offenses as resulting from everyday behavior (Felson 1998). In other words, those motivated to commit crime (e.g., persons in need of money) find suitable targets (e.g., homes or businesses believed to contain things of value) that are vulnerable (e.g., not well protected).

Larceny-thefts are perhaps the most common property crimes in the nation. Larceny is the wrongful taking of another's property by physically removing it or by means of fraud or deceit. This broad category includes employee theft, shoplifting, purse snatching, bicycle theft, credit card theft, picking pockets, and a host of other thefts that do not involve force or intimidation. Shoplifting is one of few crimes in which females are substantially represented, constituting as much as 58 percent of those arrested (Lindquist 1988). In addition, it is a crime that more and more senior citizens are committing (Alston 1986). Although most shoplifters are amateurs, there are a number of professional rings that shoplift for great profit, often working in teams and using sophisticated methods and devices.

It has been estimated that one-third of all employees commit employee theft (Voigt et al. 1994), taking items for personal use, robbing the employer of company time by taking long breaks, making personal phone calls, using computers and other equipment for personal reasons, and so on. Some criminologists believe the biggest problems come from lower-level, young, disgruntled employees, but others think they occur among management-level employees. James Tucker (1989) suggests that employee theft is the result of employees seeking "justice" against what they perceive to be a deviant employer, a way of evening the score, of getting what they think they deserve.

Some types of property crimes are destructive. Arson, the willful or malicious burning of property, is one example. There are a number of types of arson based on the arsonist's underlying motives (Voigt et al. 1994). There is profit-motivated or insurance-claim arson, often committed by professionals, wherein property is burned to collect the insurance. Excitement arson is committed by pyromaniacs, who derive some excitement or pleasure from setting and watching fires. Revenge arson is committed to get even with someone. Vandalism arson refers to setting fires for fun, and crime-concealment arson is committed to hide another crime.

Vandalism is another destructive form of property crime. It is a willful destruction of property and includes such things as graffiti, the destruction of library materials, the trashing of buildings, breaking of windows, and so forth. It can be vindictive, predatory, or wanton (Hagan 1998). Vindictive vandalism is fueled by hatred of some group, such as people of another race. Predatory vandalism is for gain, such as the destruction of vending machines to steal the contents. Finally, wanton vandalism is committed for no purpose other than to have fun.

Public-Order Crime

Public-order crimes differ from all the others because they are the so-called "victimless crimes." Public-order crimes include (among others) prostitution, pornography, sex offenses (flashing, voyeurism, fetishism), drug offenses, gambling, drunkenness, disorderly conduct, and vagrancy. They are the *mala prohibita* crimes in which it appears that the state is attempting to legislate morality, the morality that binds us together as a society. As Victoria Swigert (1984) points out, these are the crimes in which people willingly engage, the crimes without complainants. They are the crimes about which a society has mixed feelings. Although laws prohibiting sin look good on the books, many people do not hesitate to indulge in the prohibited behavior; law enforcement officials often hesitate to make arrests for such actions, and judicial systems typically deal lightly with them (with the exception of many drug offenses, which now carry mandatory sentences).

On the one hand, some people argue that these are not really victimless crimes. For example, prostitutes are brutalized and women and children are exploited by pornography (Swigert 1984). The children of prostitutes, alcoholics, and drug addicts suffer from a diminished quality of life. Society pays for drug rehabilitation and law enforcement, and individuals become victims of robberies, burglaries, and other crimes committed to support drug and alcohol habits. On the other hand, other people point out that without prostitution, for example, some women would lead lives that were economically even more marginal, because they have no other way to support themselves or their children (Reynolds 1986).

Some public-order laws, such as those prohibiting prostitution, are enforced selectively, often based on political decisions. In any given city, prostitutes may be left alone for a period of time and then arrested when neighbors complain or when the mayor is running for reelection. Public-order offenses by their very nature and the ambiguity with which we regard them are a breeding ground for police corruption. Because there are few complainants, police officers must be proactive instead of reactive in their handling of such offenses (Swigert 1984). Individual officers may take payoffs to ignore behavior such as illegal gambling, for example. Because many members of the neighborhood frequent gambling establishments, they are not concerned that the police are turning their backs instead of enforcing law. During Prohibition, even FBI Director J. Edgar Hoover was known to frequent establishments serving illegal liquor.

Prostitution is a good example of society's mixed feelings toward public-order crimes, and it also serves as an example of a double standard between males and females in terms of law enforcement. As already noted, prostitution laws are sometimes enforced rigorously and at other times they are ignored or prostitutes are given only a slap on the wrist, depending on the political climate. Because most (but not all) prostitutes are women, selective enforcement of the law has a greater impact on women than on men. In addition, although there are two parties involved in the act itself, the prostitute and the john (customer), it is usually only the prostitute who is arrested. Johns, by contrast, particularly when they are considered upstanding members of the community, are often allowed to slip away with no embarrassing arrest. Periodically, cities arrest johns or publish their names in newspapers, but these campaigns are usually short-lived.

Prostitutes (both female and male) are often underage runaways, attempting to survive on the streets. Some young girls have been ensnared by street pimps, who sexually abuse them, control them, and get them hooked on drugs and alcohol. Prostitutes are at great risk of contracting AIDS and other sexually transmitted diseases and are often targets of serial killers and men with various psychological problems (Lane and Gregg 1992; Diana 1985).

Before the Harrison Act of 1914, drug use and sale were not considered to be crimes. Narcotic drugs were commonly found in elixirs and patent medicines, and the original Coca-Cola even contained cocaine. This situation was far different from the current "law and order" campaign against possession, use, and sale of drugs. With the 1980s' "war on drugs," federal drug-related convictions increased by 134 percent (Voigt et al. 1994: 420). Many current convictions are for possession of drugs, with no intent to use. A number of states have mandatory sentences for those convicted of drug possession. These sentences have been a major cause of prison overcrowding and the growing cost of maintaining correctional facilities. In this regard, society may be the biggest victim of enforcing laws against the possession and use of drugs.

There is a great racial disparity in drug arrests and in the perception of drug use. Though drug use is more prevalent among white suburban teenagers than among African American urban teenagers, suburban use occurs in the privacy of homes, clubs, and cars, whereas urban use is often in-your-face, street-corner transactions that make the six o'clock news, thus giving the perception that drug abuse is a particularly African American problem. Laws governing the use of crack, a drug used predominantly by African Americans, are more stringent than laws governing cocaine, a similar drug used predominantly by whites. Federal guidelines stipulate a sentence as severe for 1 gram of crack as for 100 grams of cocaine. Such disparities in the law and its enforcement lead some people to charge that public-order laws are less concerned with what is being done than with who is doing it.

Professional Crime

Professional crime can be defined as much by the characteristics of its perpetrators as by the types of crime involved. Professional criminals, unlike amateurs, choose crime as their livelihood, and engage in it purely for economic gain (Inciardi 1987). They identify themselves as criminals, regard themselves as professionals, and become highly skilled in their trades (Staats 1977). Often having been selected and taught by other criminals, they tend to associate with others of similar status, avoiding and looking down on amateurs. Because of their high level of skill, they are less likely to be arrested or incarcerated and thus enjoy relatively long criminal careers. They may come from many social classes and are often drawn from legitimate peripheral occupations, rather than working their way up through a hierarchy of petty crimes. Where amateur criminals may still subscribe to societal values, professional criminals often hold values different from those of the rest of society; they believe people deserve to be victimized (Staats 1977). Within their culture, there are expected standards of behavior (such as not informing on a peer), typically reinforced by their own argot, or language, which enhances group identity and status and provides a measure of protection (Nash 1985). Professional criminals may work alone or in teams and tend to engage in nonviolent crimes (Staats 1977). They often specialize in one type of offense, although there are those who contend that professionals are not as likely to specialize now as much as they have in the past. To be successful and avoid apprehension, shoplifters, pickpockets, and confidence swindlers must also be transient, working new territory where they are not known and staying ahead of the law (Inciardi 1987).

Of the many types of professional crime, one of the most intriguing is the confidence game. Confidence swindles, big and small, depend on the ability of the criminal to gain the confidence of the victim, a matter of great skill. Anyone, even savvy investors, can be caught up in a fraudulent scheme. Victims are often motivated by greed; they forget that if it sounds too good to be true, then it probably is. Because they have been duped and may suffer from both embarrassment and guilt, victims are reluctant to report these crimes to the authorities.

Ponzi schemes, named after the infamous con artist Charles Ponzi, involve inducing people to invest their money by promising them big returns. The first investors do receive big returns, and they tell their friends, who also invest. Early investors are paid with the money of later investors ("robbing Peter to pay Paul"), and the con artist keeps large amounts of money for himself or herself. Eventually, there is no money left and the investors have lost everything. Such a Ponzi scheme was perpetrated in Philadelphia, by the foundation for New Era Philanthropy. John G. Bennett, Jr. duped universities, museums, philanthropists, and others (Hagan 1998). These individuals and organizations would generally be more knowledgeable and cautious about investing than most ordinary citizens, clearly illustrating the fact than anyone can be duped.

Professional pickpockets work in teams of two or three people. The first person distracts the victim; the second one lifts the wallet or other item; and may pass it off to a third person, who is nowhere around by the time the police are summoned. A training "school" in Colombia, called the School of the Seven Bells, trains pickpockets, who must lift an item from a coat without ringing any of the bells (Hagan 1998).

Other forms of professional crime include shoplifting, burglary, sneak theft, extortion, forgery, and counterfeiting (Inciardi 1977). Professional burglars generally work in teams, although the composition of teams may change from job to job. Such burglars may operate in residences, warehouses, hotel rooms, or other locations. They generally receive tips from hotel employees, household help, and other insiders regarding good targets. Many burglars are experienced at picking locks; some are licensed locksmiths. Stolen merchandise is then passed to another type of professional criminal, a fence, to be sold.

Organized Crime

One of the most enduring beliefs regarding organized crime, both on the part of the media and on the part of many law enforcement agencies (Morash 1984), is what is commonly referred to as the alien-conspiracy theory. According to this theory, a group of foreigners, Italians, or Sicilians to be exact, emigrated to the United States and brought with them an organized crime syndicate. Further, this syndicate has conspired to control most if not all of the organized crime in this country. The problem with this theory is that it is in direct contradiction with the evidence.

Examining organized crime allows us to see that it has existed for a long time and has involved people from many different ethnic backgrounds (see Reading 33). Organized crime is a profit-motivated crime that provides illegal goods and services that the public wants. It involves a number of people who are associated for a long period in a hierarchy and who conspire together to commit illegal acts. This type of crime occasionally involves violence and coercion and relies on political corruption for protection from investigation and prosecution (Voigt et al. 1994).

Throughout most of this nation's history, urban gangs, often formed along ethnic lines, have attempted to improve their political status and financial well-being. Gangs have been composed of German, Irish, Italian, Jewish, Greek, African

American, Hispanic, Asian, Russian, and a host of other ethnic groups (Morash 1984; Potter 1994). During the late 1890s and early 1900s, at about the same time that corporations began to see the value of mergers, urban gangs did, too. During Prohibition, from 1920 to 1933, due to the great market for illegal alcohol, gangs merged and organized further and expanded into syndicates. After the end of Prohibition, these syndicates moved into providing other illegal goods, including narcotics. Many of these organized-crime gangs have continued to operate since then, adapting to changing conditions and product demands.

One explanation for organized crime is ethnic-succession theory (Potter 1994). This theory holds that different ethnic groups dominated organized crime at different times. As new ethnic groups arrived in the country or migrated to urban areas, they utilized marginalized means (such as crime) to gain a foothold in the economy. As new groups came in, they replaced old groups, which were now better equipped to achieve success legitimately. From this perspective, Italian Americans dominated organized crime longer than most groups because restrictive immigration policies prevented new groups from quickly taking their place. So many groups now participate in organized crime that the word *Mafia*, once used to refer to Italian organized-crime groups, has become a generic label, and one now hears of the Russian mafia, the Colombian mafia, the Vietnamese mafia, and so forth.

Another theory of organized crime is the market-model, or enterprise, theory, in which organized crime is compared to legitimate business operations. Crime syndicates create markets, work to retain them, and try to extend their markets in much the same way that large corporations selling cars or toothpaste do (Potter 1994). In fact, scholars have drawn attention not only to organized crime's similarities to legitimate business but also to its relationships with legal enterprises. Merry Morash (1984) describes organized crime as relationships between the underworld and the upper world that involve criminal activities, violence and extortion at both levels, and infiltration into legitimate businesses. It is not unusual for organized-crime racketeers to join with seemingly legitimate business

and corporate leaders to engage in enterprises that are mutually beneficial (see Reading 34).

Efforts by federal and state law enforcement agencies to attack organized crime have occurred throughout the twentieth century, with only modest success. Recently, however, the federal government has been more successful in prosecuting traditional organized crime because of the Racketeer Influenced and Corrupt Organizations Act, or RICO (Kenney and Finckenauer 1994). Created in 1970, this law subjects to prosecution any enterprise that shows a pattern of racketeering, as well as members of the enterprise committing two or more crimes related to the organization's work. Further, membership in such criminal organizations is defined as a crime. Conviction of any of the specified violations of the RICO law may result in the forfeiture of assets and a long prison term. Using this law, prosecutors have convicted a significant number of the leaders of the older, established crime groups and have undermined the operations of their illegal syndicates. It has yet to be seen if these tactics will be equally successful against the newly emerging organized-crime syndicates.

White-Collar Crime

Developed as a concept by Sutherland in 1939, white-collar crime describes crimes committed by middle-class and upper-class people during the normal course of their business life. These crimes involve some violation of the implicit trust that is placed in the offenders and their positions. Sutherland developed this concept in conjunction with his differential association theory, a theory based on social learning and therefore able to account for both street crime and upper-level crimes (Geis 1984) (see Reading 20).

Some common types of white-collar crime include insider stock trading, advertising fraud, violations of antitrust law, environmental pollution, restraint of trade, misuse of trademarks, and the manufacture of unsafe foods and drugs (Clinard and Quinney 1973). According to Gilbert Geis, these types of crimes, being "an extension of regular practices," involve less risk than street crimes. Unlike burglars, who have no excuse to be prowling where they do not belong, white-collar criminals are operating where they belong (at work) and are engaging in the general type of activities one expects of them due to their positions (Geis 1984: 137).

Emile Durkheim said in the 1890s that a certain amount of crime is functional for a society. Crimes committed by a few strengthen the group solidarity of the rest, pulling society together and defining its boundaries of right and wrong. White-collar crime, on the other hand, has just the opposite effect. Because it breaks down the implicit trust necessary for a society to function and undermines social solidarity, it causes anomie, or normlessness, and threatens our solidarity. Instead of scorning white-collar criminals, however, many people in society tend to emulate them. The collective "we" tends to think the white-collar criminal is shrewd and wonders if we can get away with similar acts. Prosecutors, judges, and others often think of white-collar criminals as just like them, "respectable" people from the middle and upper classes.

Part of the reason white-collar crimes are often not considered to be "crimes" is that few people are aware of the harms to society they cause, nor do they necessarily feel directly affected or victimized by such crimes, as they would by an assault, for example. And yet, white-collar crime is the most expensive kind of crime, costing society many times more each year than street crime possibly could, because white-collar crime is committed on such a large scale. Imagine the far-reaching harm that could result if a community's drinking water were contaminated with toxic wastes (Geis 1984). A number of years ago, some Ford Pinto automobiles exploded in rear end collisions, a dangerous situation the manufacturer knew about before selling the vehicle. Death and destruction resulting from these collisions caused a great deal more harm to society than petty crimes committed by a number of street criminals. Unsafe work conditions and failure to comply with occupational health and safety standards causes widespread harm and even death. Brown lung disease has been contracted by 85,000 cotton textile mill workers; 100,000 miners have been killed and another 265,000 disabled by black lung disease; there are

8,000 deaths per year in this country from asbestos-related cancer, and over the next 30 years, another 240,000 are expected to die (Mokhiber 1989). James W. Coleman (1989) attributes half of all asbestos-caused deaths to direct workplace exposure. Although the personal harm and financial costs of such actions by corporations and their executives are evident, they are typically treated as normal business practices rather than violations of criminal statutes.

Two types of white-collar crimes can be distinguished: occupational and corporate. Occupational crimes involve an act of deceit or fraud against one's own company or employer. Perhaps the most common crime of this type is embezzlement. A chief executive officer who violates the trust placed in him or her by stockholders by embezzling from the company is guilty of occupational crime. So is the employee who steals from the company, whether it is a clerk pilfering office supplies or an executive stealing thousands of dollars in raw materials. Crime of this type is solely for personal gain. Corporate crime is that committed for the benefit of the corporation. Although there may well be some personal gain for the offender, it is indirect and not the main purpose of the misdeed. Workers may lie, cheat, violate safety standards, or otherwise break the law to give the company a competitive edge or enhance corporate profits. These types of violations seldom bring criminal charges against corporate officers. Instead, the corporation itself is likely to be charged or, more likely, sued in civil court or brought before a regulatory agency rather than face criminal charges. Why is this so?

In 1890 the Sherman Antitrust Act was passed to prevent industries from merging into monopolies. The act also bestowed on the corporation the legal rights of an individual; the corporation became a legal entity, which could be held responsible for illegal action. This provision tends to absolve those who run the corporation from being charged with wrongdoing, instead allowing the corporation to be charged and taken to court. It is very rare that a chief executive or manager goes to trial for a corporate crime. Therefore, when a corporation is charged and convicted of some infraction, it is usually fined, and the fine is included in the cost of doing business and passed on to its customers.

Corporations are so complex that it is difficult to place the blame for a decision or action on any particular individuals. Susan P. Shapiro (1990) discusses the interworkings of organizations and how they (purposefully and otherwise) hinder the processes of law enforcement. In complex corporate structures, paper or electronic trails can be easily hidden, altered, or falsified, making it easy to commit illegal acts but difficult to detect them. The structure of the organization, the internal networks, the hierarchy, the specialization, the internal diversification, and the task segregation all tend to work together to disguise illicit acts and block the flow of information from both insiders and outsiders. Illicit activities can be divided among many workers or divisions, widely separated by time and place, and may appear to be part of the ordinary routine. Therefore, it is hard to determine who is guilty and hard to put together a prosecution case.

From crimes of violence to white-collar crimes, it has been shown that criminal typologies are helpful in allowing us to understand the nature of criminal offenses. Although this section has reviewed only a few types of major crimes, it is apparent that crime is more than a violation of the legal code. It is a social phenomenon that has many nuances and extensive ramifications. The following readings were selected to shed more light on the types of crimes discussed in this section.

References

Alston, Letitia T. 1986. *Crime and Older Americans.* Springfield, IL: Charles C. Thomas.

Bourdouis, James. 1974. "A Classification of Homicide." *Criminology* 11: 525-540.

Brownmiller, Susan. 1975. *Against Our Will: Men, Women, and Rape.* New York: Simon and Sohuster.

Clinard, Marshall B. and Richard Quinney. 1973. *Criminal Behavior Systems: A Typology* (2nd ed.). New York: Holt, Rinehart and Winston.

Coleman, James W. 1989. *The Criminal Elite: The Sociology of White Collar Crime* (2nd ed.). New York: St. Martins.

Diana, Lewis. 1985. *The Prostitute and Her Clients: Your Pleasure Is Her Business.* Springfield, IL: Charles C. Thomas.

Durkheim, Emile. 1893. *The Division of Labor in Society.* New York: Free Press.

Estrich, Susan. 1987. *Real Rape.* Cambridge: Harvard University Press.

Federal Bureau of Investigation. 1997. *Uniform Crime Reports–1996.* Washington, DC: U.S. Government Printing Office, p. 19.

Felson, Marcus. 1998. *Crime and Everyday Life.* Thousand Oaks, CA: Pine Forge.

Gabor, Thomas, Micheline Baril, Maurice Cusson, Daniel Elie, Marc LaBlanc, and Andre Normandeau. 1988. *Armed Robbery: Cops, Robbers, and Victims.* Springfield, IL: Thomas.

Geis, Gilbert. 1984. "White-Collar and Corporate Crime," in R. S. Meier (ed.), *Major Forms of Crime.* Beverly Hills: Sage.

Hagan, Frank E. 1998. *Introduction to Criminology: Theories, Methods, and Criminal Behavior* (4th ed.). Chicago: Nelson-Hall.

Inciardi, James. 1987. "In Search of the Class Cannon: A Field Study of Professional Pickpockets." In R. Weppner (ed.), *Street Ethnography.* Beverly Hills: Sage.

Kenney, Dennis J. and James O. Finckenauer. 1994. *Organized Crime in America.* New York: Wadsworth.

Lane, Brian and Wilfred Gregg. 1992. *The Encyclopedia of Serial Killers.* London: Headline Book Publishing.

Lindquist, J. 1988. *Misdemeanor Crime.* Newbury Park, CA: Sage.

Mokhiber, Russell. 1989. *Corporate Crime and Violence: Big Business Power and the Abuse of the Public Trust.* San Francisco: Sierra Club Books.

Monahan, John and Laurens Walker. 1994. *Social Science in Law: Cases and Materials.* Westbury, NY: Foundation Press.

Morash, Merry. 1984. "Organized Crime," in R. S. Meier (ed.), *Major Forms of Crime.* Beverly Hills: Sage.

Moynihan, Daniel P. 1969. *Violent Crime: Homicide, Assault, Rape, Robbery: The Report of the National Commission on The Causes and Prevention of Violence.* New York: George Braziller.

Nash, Jeffrey. 1985. *Social Psychology: Society and Self.* St. Paul: West Publishing Company.

Petersilia, Joan. 1980. "Criminal Career Research: A Review of Recent Evidence." *Crime and Justice* 2: 321-379.

Potter, Gary W. 1994. *Criminal Organizations: Vice, Racketeering, and Politics in an American City.* Prospect Heights, IL: Waveland Press.

Reiss, Albert J. Jr. and Jeffrey A. Roth. 1993. *Understanding and Preventing Violence.* Washington, DC: National Academy Press.

Reynolds, Helen. 1986. *The Economics of Prostitution.* Springfield, IL: Charles C. Thomas.

Russell, Diana E. H. 1982. *Rape in Marriage.* New York: Macmillan.

Shapiro, Susan P. 1990. "Collaring the Crime, Not the Criminal: Reconsidering the Concept of White-Collar Crime," *American Sociological Review* 55: 346-365.

Staats, Gregory R. 1977. "Changing Conceptualizations of Professional Criminals: Implications for Criminology Theory," *Criminology* 15: 49-65.

Swigert, Victoria. 1984. "Public-Order Crime," in R. S. Meier (ed.), *Major Forms of Crime.* Beverly Hills: Sage.

Tucker, James. 1989. "Employee Theft as Social Control," *Deviant Behavior* 10: 319-334.

Voigt, Lydia, William E. Thornton, Jr., Leo Barrile, and Jerrol M. Seaman. 1994. *Criminology and Justice.* New York: McGraw-Hill.

CHAPTER 31

Violent Crime in the United States

Albert J. Reiss, Jr. ■ Jeffrey A. Roth

Anyone watching the evening news on television in any American city must conclude that violence is rampant in our nation. Stories abound of shootings, stabbings, murders, rapes, abuse, and other forms of injury or death. Is this a true representation of American criminal violence or a distorted interpretation by the mass media to attract viewers or readers? What is the extent of violence in our society and what patterns of such behavior can be discovered from systematic study? These questions and others are addressed by Albert J. Reiss and Jeffrey A. Roth in the following excerpt taken from an exhaustive study of violence sponsored by the National Academy of Science. Using all available data sources, these authors present the most comprehensive study of violent crime ever undertaken in the United States.

Many of the findings of this study confirm what we have learned from other research. Both victims of homicide and their killers tend to be young men of the same ethnic group living in urban areas. In fact, age is the characteristic most likely to predict one's being a victim of violence. Minorities, especially African Americans, are overrepresented among those arrested for all violent crimes, and men far outnumber women as violent offenders. It is quite difficult to predict an act of violence, although persons with long criminal careers usually commit at least one such act.

Among the relevant information on violent crimes presented in this selection is a discussion of violent bias, or "hate," crimes. The authors note the increased concern for such crimes as manifested in new federal and state statutes, and the requirement that the Uniform Crime Reports collect and publish statistics on such crimes. It is often difficult to discern the motive of many violent crimes, however. Such knowledge is a necessary prerequisite to classifying an act of violence as a "hate" crime or one motivated by other emotions.

How much crime is violent? The technical problems discussed above preclude any precise estimate of how much of all crime in the United States is violent. We report below some crude estimates, which are useful mainly to establish relative magnitudes among the types of crime and to discern overall trends. Comparisons focus primarily on the 1990 reporting year, the latest available at this writing.

National Estimates

In 1990 the National Crime Survey reported an estimated 34,403,610 personal and household crime victimizations.[1] Of these, 17 percent were attempted or completed violent crimes—8 percent if one excludes simple assault.[2] In considering only the 18,984,120 attempted or completed personal victimizations reported, about 32 percent were violent—just over 6 million. Of these, just over half were simple assaults, the least serious violent offense (Bureau of Justice Statistics, 1992:Table 1a).

The bulk of personal victimizations reported are theft from persons, which includes larceny with and without contact with the victim.[3] Together with the violent act of simple assault,[4] these nonviolent thefts constitute the large majority of personal victimizations.

In 1990 UCR estimated that the nation's police departments received reports of 14,475,600 index crimes, excluding arson; of these, about 1.8 million, or 13 percent, were attempted or completed violent crimes.[5] Police departments reports a smaller proportion of all offenses as violent than the NCS reports, excluding simple assault (13 compared with 15 percent). This is in part due to the fact that victims were somewhat more likely to report property crimes than crimes of violence to the police. In 1988 victims reported a higher fraction of household victimizations of burglary, household larceny, and motor vehicle theft (40 percent) than violent personal victimizations (36 percent) to the police (Bureau of Justice Statistics, 1990:Table 92).[6]

Prototype Pattern

The NCS program reported 6,008,790 violent victimizations in 1990, and the UCR program counted 1,820,127 violent index crimes reported to police agencies. Despite their differences, the prototype violent event that emerges from the two systems is an assault, either aggravated or simple. Of the violent victimizations, aggravated and simple assault account for nearly 8 of every 10. By excluding homicide from the UCR and simple assault from the NCS counts to achieve rough comparability, aggravated assaults account for almost 6 of 10 violent crimes reported in both systems. Robbery, which is an assault or threat of assault for the purposes of taking valuables, accounts for most of the rest—which means that at least 9 of every 10 acts reported as violent crimes or victimizations in the United States are either assaults or robberies. Sexual assaults account for most of the remaining violent offenses, and homicides account for just over 1 percent—23,438 of the violent crimes counted by the UCR....

The various types of assault show the expected inverse relationship between frequency and seriousness. In 1990, 67 percent of assaults were attempts. Of all aggravated and simple assaults, 46 percent were attempted simple assaults without a weapon and without injury; 21 percent were attempted aggravated assaults with a weapon, but without injury; 20 percent were simple assaults with injury; and 13 percent were aggravated assaults with injury (Bureau of Justice Statistics, 1992: Table 1a). Assaults with injury are least frequently reported; attempted simple assaults without a weapon and without injury constitute almost half of all reported assaults.

Violent victimizations are more likely than nonviolent ones to involve multiple simultaneous victims. Therefore, on average, every 100 aggravated assault victimizations occurred in 80 events and every 100 simple assaults in about 90 events.

Victims of Violence

Although the rhetoric of campaigns against violence suggests that victims and offenders are distinct populations, in fact there is great similarity in their demographic profiles. Generally, both groups—those at the highest risk of violent offending as well as those at highest risk of violent victimization—tend to be young, black males of low socioeconomic status who live in the nation's central cities.... Victim characteristics are discussed in this section, and offender characteristics in the next.

Risks of Violent Victimization

... The annual risk of becoming a victim of personal violence—of homicide, forcible rape, robbery, or assault—is well below that of victimization from property crimes. As judged by victim reports to NCS, the risk of becoming a victim of personal violence in 1990 was 1 in 34 for people age 12 and older. That risk is less than half the risk of becoming a victim of a personal theft, which was 1 in 16 in 1990 for people age 12 and older (Bureau of Justice Statistics, 1992: Table 1a). In 1990 the risk of household victimization through burglary, household larceny, or motor vehicle theft was 1 in

6 households (Bureau of Justice Statistics, 1992: Table 1a).

For many purposes, the lifetime risk of violent victimization would be a more informative description than the annual risk for any single age range. The Bureau of Justice Statistics, drawing on the annual prevalence rates from the National Crime Survey, estimated that about 83 percent of the people now age 12 will be violently victimized in their lifetimes (Koppel, 1987). There is good methodological reason to conclude that this is a substantial overestimate (Lynch, 1989). However, because information is unavailable on the proportion of victims in any year who have also been victimized in previous years, we were unable to determine the degree to which it is overestimated....

Homicide. Usable estimates of lifetime risk have been calculated for homicide (Loftin and Wiersma, 1991). In 1987 and 1988, the *annual* risk of becoming a victim of a homicide was about 1 in 12,000, although by 1990 it had risen close to 1 in 10,600. The *lifetime* risk of being a homicide victim is of course much greater (Figure 31.1). Of the six demographic subgroups shown in the figure—male and female whites, blacks, and American

Indians—black males are at the highest lifetime risk: 4.16 per 100 black males, which is equivalent to a 1 chance in 24.1 of dying by homicide. American Indian males are also at high risk (1.75 per 100 American Indian males, 1 chance in 57), as are black females (1.02 per 100 black females, 1 in 98.1). For white males and females and for American Indian females, chances of dying by homicide are substantially less than 1 in 100.[7]

This figure also makes clear that, despite media attention to the killings of adolescents and young adults, *less than one-fourth of one's lifetime homicide risk is experienced before the twenty-fifth birthday.* For five of the six subgroups (the exception is American Indian males), the ratio of homicide risk by age 24 to lifetime risk lies in a narrow range, between 0.21 and 0.26. Murders of American Indian males occur later in life on average; the corresponding ratio is only 0.14.

Recent media attention has focused on homicides of young black males. The rate for black males ages 15-24 rose during the late 1980s, approaching levels not observed since a previous peak around 1970 (see Figure 31.2). However, Figure 31.1 makes clear that, although a sizable fraction of black

Figure 31.1 Cumulative Homicide Rate in Five-Year Age Intervals by Race and Gender, 1987

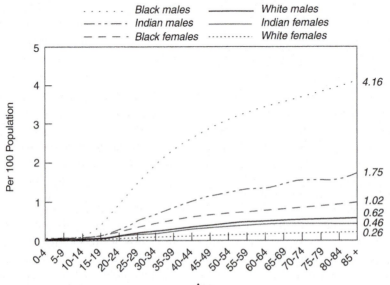

Figure 31.2 Homicide Rates, Persons Ages 15-24 Years, by Race and Sex, 1940–1988

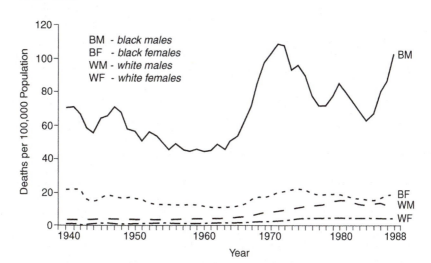

males die of murder by age 24, the high homicide rate for young black males must be viewed in light of the high homicide rate for black males at *all* ages. One major unresolved question is why the homicide death rate is so high for blacks at all ages, especially black males (see Griffin and Bell, 1989). Another is to understand why, for this age category, the trends for black and white males have moved in different directions during several periods since 1940, as Figure 31.2 shows....

There is considerable variation in homicide mortality by gender and age. In 1988, for example, the homicide mortality rate ranged from 4.2 for females to 14.2 for males, and from 5.3 for whites to 34.4 for blacks. The variation by age and sex within these groups was, for example, from 2.7 for black males age 5 to 9 to 128.2 for black males age 20-24. The range for white males was from 0.8 for age 5 to 9 to 14.6 for white males 20-24 (National Center for Health Statistics, 1991).

The UCR Supplementary Homicide Report discloses that most victims in single offender-single victim homicides are slain by an offender of the same ethnic status:[8] 86 percent of white victims and 93 percent of black victims in 1990. In this kind of homicide, only 6 percent of white victims

were slain by black offenders (calculated from Federal Bureau of Investigation, 1992:11).

Multiple homicides by one offender in a single event (so-called mass murders) account for only a very small proportion of all homicides. Similarly, in projecting from data on homicides by known offenders, instances of serial homicide by one offender also appear to be quite infrequent—on the order of 1 percent of all homicides, according to estimates prepared by Fox and Levin for the panel (J. Fox and J. Levin, personal communication, 1990)....

Individual Risks of Nonfatal Violent Victimizations

In this section we examine how the risks of violent victimization differ according to people's age, gender, ethnic status, marital status, and socioeconomic status. Two- and three-way associations for age, gender, and ethnic status suggest that the relationships among these factors are generally additive.... For some subgroups of the population, the relative risk of violent victimization is higher than expected because of interaction effects. Age has the largest independent effect, followed by gender; ethnic status has the smallest effect of the three.

The rates reported are based on statistical information for the 1990 National Crime Survey (Bureau of Justice Statistics, 1992) unless another source is specified.

Age. Age is one of the most important single predictors of an individual's risk of violent victimization (Hindelang et al., 1978). The annual risk of victimization by violent crime peaks at age 16 to 19 for both men (95 per 1,000 population) and women (54 per 1,000) and declines substantially with age, to 3-4 per 1,000 at age 65 and older. This declining risk of victimization by age holds for the major violent crimes of forcible rape, robbery, aggravated assault, and simple assault, with substantially higher rates below than above age 25. Although the risk of violent victimization is highest at the younger ages, there is evidence that juvenile victimization is less likely to involve serious injury (Garofalo et al., 1987).

Gender. Except for forcible rapes and partner assaults, the risk of a woman becoming a victim of a violent crime is lower than that of a man. Among all female murder victims in 1990, however, 30 percent were slain by husbands or male friends compared with 4 percent of male victims killed by wives or women friends (Federal Bureau of Investigation, 1992:13). The lifetime risk of homicide is three to four times greater for men than for women. Gender differences are much smaller for robbery (Bureau of Justice Statistics, 1992: Table 3).

Women are substantially less likely than men to report being victims of aggravated or simple assault or attempted assault with a weapon. The risk of injury for assault victims is somewhat greater for women than men (38 per 1,000 for women and 30 for men). Women have a higher rate of both simple and aggravated assault by relatives than do men. Their vulnerability to assault by relatives is greater for simple than aggravated assault: the 1990 rate of simple assault by relatives was six times greater for women than men; the rate for aggravated assault was only roughly twice that for men (Bureau of Justice Statistics, 1992: Appendix V).

The reported forcible rape rate for women[9] in 1990 was 1.0 for every 1,000 women age 12 and over (Bureau of Justice Statistics, 1992: Table 3), well below their rates of aggravated assault (4.5) and simple assault (12.7). Female children are

three times more likely than male children to be sexually abused (Sedlak, 1991:5-7).

Ethnic Status. Americans of minority status are at greater risk of victimization by violent crime than are those of majority status. The overall 1990 violent victimization rate reported by the NCS was 39.7 for blacks and 37.3 for Hispanics compared with a rate of 28.2 for whites (Bureau of Justice Statistics, 1992: Tables 6 and 8). Simple assaults are a substantially larger proportion of all violent crimes for whites (56%) than for blacks or Hispanics (35%), but the risk of simple assault is about the same for these ethnic groups (16 per thousand whites, 14 for blacks, 13 for Hispanics). Excluding simple assaults from the violent crime rate, the rate of violent crime (forcible rape, robbery, and aggravated assault) for blacks and Hispanics is roughly twice that of whites—13 for whites, 26 for blacks, 24 for Hispanics. For reasons discussed early in this chapter, it is not possible to report victimization rates for other ethnic groups.

As noted above, blacks, especially black males, are disproportionately the victims of homicide. Although variations have occurred over time in rates by ethnic status and sex, black rates of homicide have exceeded white rates since at least 1910. In 1990 half of all homicide victims were black, and blacks were homicide victims at a rate six times that of whites (Federal Bureau of Investigation, 1992). Several studies using subnational data have found that the black-white homicide differential is attenuated substantially at high income levels....

American Indians and Alaska natives are also at greater risk of homicide than are white Americans, though exact comparisons are lacking. In a recent special report, the Indian Health Service (1991) placed their age-adjusted rate at 14.1 per 100,000 in 1988—above that for the total population at 9.0 but half the 28.2 rate for all groups other than white. According to the Indian Health Service (1988:Chart 4.21) the rate for Native Americans has substantially exceeded the white rate, but has not exceeded the rate for the entire nonwhite population, since at least 1955.

Socioeconomic Status. Family income,[10] the primary indicator of socioeconomic status measured by the NCS, is inversely related to the risk of violent victimization. In 1988 the risk of victimization was 2.5 times greater for individuals in families with the lowest income (under $7,500) as the highest ($50,000 and over). Of all violent crimes, this negative relation is strongest for robbery.

The net effect of family income is less than that for age, gender, race, and marital status (Sampson and Lauritsen, Volume 3). Its contribution relative to these other factors may be negligible; consequently it remains unclear just how much and in what ways poverty contributes to the risk of violent victimization....

Violent Offenders

There is more uncertainty about the perpetrators of violent crimes than about their victims because of measurement errors in arrest records and sampling errors in surveys of offenders' self-reports. Because the two data sources are subject to different sources of error, one can be fairly confident about the conclusions on which they converge. The panel cautions readers against interpreting annual statistics on arrestees as an indicator of the distribution of the people actually committing crimes: because persons arrested more than once in any year are disproportionally represented in arrest statistics, there are doubts that the arrest population is representative of the offender population.

Personal Characteristics

Ethnic Status. Blacks are disproportionately represented in all arrests, and more so in those for violent crimes than for property crimes. In terms of violent crimes, blacks constitute 45 percent of all arrestees. They are most overrepresented in the most serious violent crimes of homicide, forcible rape, and robbery (Table 31.1). Particularly striking is their substantial overrepresentation in the crime of robbery, a crime that is both a person and a property crime.

Other minorities are also overrepresented among all arrestees and among those arrested for violent crimes. Particularly striking is the relatively high representation of American Indians and Alaska natives, especially for aggravated and other assaults, given their proportions in the U.S. population (Federal Bureau of Investigation, 1990: Table 38).

It is not possible to calculate annual arrest rates for violent crimes for most demographic categories; however, rates of arrest can be calculated separately for whites, blacks, and others.[11] Thus: 1 white was arrested for every 576 whites in the population; 1 black for every 94 blacks; and 1 "other"

Table 31.1 Percentage Distributions of All Persons Arrested for Violent Crimes, by Ethnic Status, 1990

Offense Charged	Ethnic Status				
	White American	Black American	American Indian or Alaskan Native	Asian or Pacific Islander	Total
Murder and nonnegligent manslaughter	43.7	54.7	0.7	0.9	100.0
Forcible rape	55.1	43.2	0.8	0.9	100.0
Robbery	37.7	61.2	0.4	0.8	100.0
Aggravated assault	59.9	38.4	0.9	0.8	100.0
Other assaults	64.1	33.9	1.2	0.8	100.0

Source: Federal Bureau of Investigation (1991: Table 38).

for every 739 "others." This arrest rate for violent crimes is about six times greater for blacks than whites. However, because data are not available on repeat arrests during the year, these arrest incidence figures do *not* reflect the annual prevalences of arrest for the different subgroups.

Gender and Age. Men make up 89 percent of all people arrested for violent crimes (Federal Bureau of Investigation, 1991: Table 37). Women accounted for only 10 percent of all arrestees for murder and nonnegligent manslaughter, 8 percent of those for robbery, and 1 percent of arrestees for forcible rape. They accounted for a higher proportion of those arrested for assaults: 13 percent for aggravated assault and 16 percent for simple assaults.

In 1990, arrestees for violent crimes were somewhat older on average than victims, with more falling in the age range of 25-29 than in any other. The age distribution for female arrestees is similar to that of males. Males under age 18, who constituted 16 percent of the U.S. population in 1988, represented roughly comparable portions of male arrestees for murder and nonnegligent manslaughter (14%), forcible rape (15%), aggravated assault (14%), and other assault (15%); they were overrepresented among arrestees for robbery at 24 percent (Federal Bureau of Investigation, 1990: Table 34).

The only major gender-age interaction of note is that the male arrest rate declines beginning at ages 45-49, while the female arrest rate remains fairly constant after age 45. After age 65, the female arrest rate approaches half that of males with both rates at their lowest for any age—comparable to their arrest rate for murder at age 14 and under....

Patterns of Offending

Violent Co-offending. Nearly three-fourths of all violent crimes are committed by lone offenders. Forcible rape was most likely to be committed alone: in 1990 only 12 of every 100 forcible rapes involved co-offenders. Robbery was most likely to be committed with others: in 1990 about 48 of every 100 completed robberies involved co-offenders.

Although the majority of violent crimes involve a single offender, co-offending substantially increases the number of people involved in violent victimizations. For example (using Figure 31.3 and Bureau of Justice Statistics, 1992: Table 70), for every 100 completed robberies, there will be a minimum

Figure 31.3 Violent Crimes: Percentage Distribution of Co-Offenders by Type of Violence, 1990

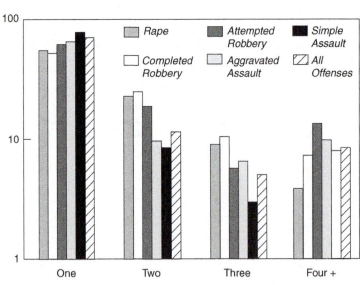

of 182 offenders. That means that 182 people would have to be apprehended to clear all 100 robberies by arrest. Because a fair number of these offenders are also involved in other robberies or/and in other offenses with other co-offenders, they are linked in a much larger offending network that recruits and selects offenders (Reiss and Farrington, 1991).

Criminal Careers. A question asked by policy makers and others is whether criminals specialize in committing violent crimes or if "careers" in crime show a pattern of escalation from nonviolent to violent crimes. If either of these situations were the case, it would have implications for the effectiveness of selective incarceration strategies to reduce levels of violence. The evidence, however, shows otherwise.

Studies of various American and European cohorts have found that no more than 1 in 5 persons ever arrested had an arrest for a violent crime. Furthermore, such arrests were likely to be embedded in long careers dominated by arrests for nonviolent crimes, so that arrests for violence accounted for no more than 1 in 8 of all arrests in the group studied (see for example Farrington, 1991). There is a clear tendency for adult criminals to specialize in various kinds of property crimes or in various kinds of violent crimes rather than to switch between the two types (Blumstein et al., 1986; Farrington et al., 1988).

Although few criminal careers begin with a violent crime, most lengthy careers contain at least one. This pattern is sometimes erroneously interpreted as evidence of escalation from nonviolent to violent crime, or as a demonstration that certain arrest patterns predict subsequent violent crimes. In fact, by most measures, predictions of future violent behavior from arrest records have proven highly inaccurate (Monahan, 1988; Piper, 1985). This is true in part because officially recorded violent crimes are committed largely in the course of lengthy, versatile criminal careers rather than by specialized violent career criminals who could be easily targeted in a strategy of incarceration.

Victim-Offender Relationships
Overlap Between Offenders and Victims. National-level estimates are available on social and personal relationships between victims and offenders that may affect the distribution and consequences of violent events. By social relationship, we mean whether the offender and victim are of the same or different categories—defined in such terms as gender, ethnic status, and sexual preference. By personal relationship we mean the connections between victim and offender as *individuals*—strangers, drinking partners, lovers, spouses, custodian and inmate, and others.

Social Relationships. Clear-cut statements can be made about social relationships defined in terms of characteristics such as gender and ethnic status, which are easily observable and traditionally recorded in counting systems. When characteristics are more ambiguous, there is greater error in classification. As an example of the latter, violent bias crimes, which have recently attracted substantial public attention, are subject to greater error in reporting.

Gender. Violence frequently crosses gender lines. Sexual assaults are disproportionally committed by males against females. Homicides by both men and women are more likely to involve male victims. Assaults, in contrast, are more likely to involve an offender and a victim of the same gender. Like assaults against women generally, cross-gender violence has more serious consequences for female victims....

Ethnic Status. For violent crimes that involve blacks and whites, one can construct a "chance-encounter" race mix by assuming that each individual's chances of violent offending and victimization are independent of race, so that the probability of any offender-victim race combination depends only on the prevalence of each race in the U.S. population. In these hypothetical circumstances, 78 percent of all violent events would involve a white offender and victim, 21 percent would cross racial lines, and only 1 percent would involve a black offender and victim.

According to the 1987 National Crime Survey (calculated from Bureau of Justice Statistics, 1989b: Table 43), in single-offender victimizations, whites assault whites at about the chance-encounter rate, blacks assault whites at about 72 percent of that rate, and whites assault blacks at about 56 percent of the chance-encounter rate. In contrast, blacks assault blacks at about 800 percent of the chance-encounter rate.

Violent Bias Crimes. One type of violent behavior that has been recently defined in the criminal law is referred to as *hate* or *bias* crimes. Bias crimes are distinguished from other crimes by the presumed role of social relationships in their motivation. The Hate Crime Statistics Act of 1990 requires the UCR program to begin counting bias crimes and specifies that violent attacks, intimidation, arson, and property damage "that manifest evidence of prejudice based on race, religion, sexual orientation, or ethnicity" are all considered to be violent bias crimes. New state and local statutes that prescribe enhanced sentences for bias crimes define them in fairly similar terms.

Documenting and analyzing patterns of violent bias crimes is difficult, because these crimes are sometimes hard to recognize. Absent such signals as graffiti, organizational identity, or lifestyle of victims, classifying some violent act as a bias crime makes it necessary to determine the perpetrator's motivation—a difficult task subject to uncertainty, especially when the prejudice serves only to aggravate a conventional robbery with a gratuitous shooting, beating, or mutilation, for example.

The available statistics have generally been developed by advocacy organizations. Such organizations often lack the resources and infrastructure for regularly counting incidents and classifying them according to rigorous criteria but, by increasing awareness of bias crimes, they may encourage the designation of ambiguous events as bias crimes. Thus, for example, Montgomery County, Maryland, reported 196 bias crimes during 1989. This count constitutes between 14 and 81 percent of various advocacy groups' recent *national* counts (compiled by Ellis, 1990, for the panel), a share that is severely disproportionate to Montgomery County's 0.2 percent share of the U.S. population.

Most of the available data do not distinguish between violent and nonviolent bias crimes. An exception is a synthesis of 10 available victimization surveys of gay men and lesbians (Berrill, 1990). Between 24 and 48 percent of the gay men and lesbians surveyed reported having been threatened by violence related to their sexual orientation at some time in their lives. Similarly, between 9 and 23 percent reported having been punched, hit, or kicked, and between 4 and 10 percent reported having been assaulted with a weapon. In most of the surveys, the victimization rates for gay men exceed the rates for lesbians by factors of 2–4 to 1—slightly greater than the difference by gender for assault victimization in the general population, according to the National Crime Survey (Aurand et al., 1985; Gross et al., 1988).

Personal Relationships. About half of all homicide victims are murdered by neither intimate family members nor total strangers, but rather by people with some kind of preexisting relationship; friends, neighbors, casual acquaintances, workplace associates, associates in illegal activities, or members of their own or a rival gang.... The high prevalence of such preexisting relationships between victims and their killers suggests that most people's fears of being killed by strangers overestimate the risk; by the same token, people underestimate the probability of being killed by someone with a close or a known relationship to them.

As discussed earlier in this chapter, women face only about one-third the homicide risk faced by men (4.2 and 14.2 per 100,000, respectively). However, among homicide victims, women are about four times as likely as men to have been killed by intimate partners, and 50 percent more likely to be killed by other family members.

For violent crimes that do not end in death, a preexisting relationship between victim and offender is less likely, yet there is variation by type of crime. Of all nonfatal violent crime types, forcible rapes are most likely to involve intimates or acquaintances (61%), and attempted robbery is least likely (14%)....

Discussion Questions

1. With regard to race/ethnicity, gender, age, and other demographic characteristics, who is more at risk of becoming the victim of a violent crime? What crimes is a person more likely to be a victim of? Is violent crime likely to be interracial or intraracial?
2. What are the characteristics of violent offenders? What are the patterns of offending? What can be said about the "criminal careers" of violent offenders?

3. What are the most common victim-offender relationships? What is a bias crime? What are its characteristics? Is there a relationship between the victims and offenders of bias crimes?

Notes

1. The NCS classifies all victimizations as either personal- or household-sector victimizations. Burglary, household larceny, and motor vehicle theft are household-sector victimizations. Personal-sector victimizations are classified as crimes of violence (rape, robbery, and assault) or crimes of theft (personal larceny with contact and personal larceny without contact). NCS violent victimizations are only roughly comparable to UCR index crimes of violence, for reasons discussed earlier in this chapter.

2. The calculation excludes an estimated 3,128,130 simple assaults for crude comparisons with UCR. Their exclusion reduces the number of violent victimizations from 6,008,790 to 2,880,660.

   Aggravated assaults are attacks by one person on another for the purpose of inflicting severe or aggravated bodily injury. Attempts are included since it is not necessary that an injury result when a gun, a knife, or another weapon, including hands, fists, and feet, are used that could, and probably would, result in serious personal injury were the crime successfully completed. Both UCR and NCS classify injuries as serious when they result in broken bones, lost teeth, internal injuries, and loss of consciousness. The NCS also classifies any injury as serious if it requires two or more days of hospitalization.

3. Personal larcenies or personal crimes of theft include two subgroups. *Personal larceny with contact* involves personal contact between the victim and the offender and includes such crimes as purse snatching and pocket picking. *Personal larceny without contact* is theft of property of the victim without personal contact from any place other than the home or its immediate vicinity. The crime differs from household larceny only in the location in which the theft occurs.

4. The panel recognizes that the division between simple and aggravated assault involves considerable classification error and also that there are valid reasons for including simple assault as a violent crime, especially given its prevalence in domestic violence.

5. UCR violent index crimes are offenses of murder, forcible rape, robbery, and aggravated assault (Federal Bureau of Investigation, 1990: Table 1).

6. The inclusion of commercial and nonresidential offenses in the UCR but not the NCS also accounts for some of the difference, as it disproportionally increases the base for property crimes....

7. Loftin and Wiersma (1991) could not calculate risks for Hispanics because, at the time their data were collected, death certificates in only five states provided for that demographic category.

8. Single victim-single offender homicides account for only 54 percent of all homicides in which the ethnic status of victims was reported in 1990 (calculated from Federal Bureau of Investigation, 1990:11)....

9. Until 1990, the NCS had reports of fewer than 10 sample cases of sexual assaults on males classified as forcible rape. The 1990 rate was reported as 0.2 per 1,000 males. There is a substantial underreporting of sexual assault on both males and females, but especially so for males at younger ages. Efforts should be made to secure more reliable measures of sexual assaults for both men and women at all ages.

10. Family income in the NCS includes the income of the household head and all other related persons residing in the same housing unit. The income of persons unrelated to the head of household is excluded (Bureau of Justice Statistics, 1990: Glossary).

11. Numerators are counts of violent crime arrests in Federal Bureau of Investigation (1992: Table 38). Denominators are estimated populations, 12 years of age and over by race in Bureau of Justice Statistics (1992: Table 6).

References

Aurand, S. K., R. Adessa, and C. Bush. 1985. "Violence and Discrimination Against Philadelphia Lesbian and Gay People." (Available from Philadelphia Lesbian and Gay Task Force, 1501 Cherry Street, Philadelphia, PA 19102).

Berrill, K. T. 1990. "Anti-gay Violence and Victimization in the United States: An Overview." *Journal of Interpersonal Violence* 5(3, September):274-294.

Blumstein, A., J. Cohen, J. A. Roth, and C. A. Visher. 1986. *Criminal Careers and 'Career Criminals.'* Vol. I. Washington, D.C.: National Academy Press.

Bureau of the Census. 1990. *Statistical Abstract of the United States: 1990.* Washington, D.C.: U.S. Government Printing Office.

Bureau of Justice Statistics. 1989a. *Injuries From Crime: Special Report.* Washington, D.C.: U.S. Government Printing Office.

Bureau of Justice Statistics. 1989b. *Criminal Victimization in the United States, 1987.* Washington, D.C.: U.S. Government Printing Office.

Bureau of Justice Statistics. 1990. *Criminal Victimization in the United States, 1988.* A National Crime Survey Report, December 1990, NCJ-122024.

———. 1992. *Criminal Victimization in the United States, 1990.* Washington, D.C.: U.S. Government Printing Office.

Ellis, W. W. 1990. "Bias Crime." Commissioned paper for the Committee on Research on Law Enforcement and the Administration of Justice, National Research Council.

Farrington, D. P. 1991. "Childhood Aggression and Adult Violence: Early Precursors and Later-life Outcomes." Pp. 5-29 in D. J. Pepler and K. H. Rubin, eds., *The Development and Treatment of Childhood Aggression.* Hillsdale, N.J.: Erlbaum.

Farrington, D., H. Snyder, and T. Finnegan. 1988. "Specialization in Juvenile Court Careers." *Criminology* 26:461-488.

Federal Bureau of Investigation. 1969. *Uniform Crime Reports: Crime in the United States, 1968.* Washington, D.C.: U.S. Government Printing Office.

———. 1974. *Uniform Crime Reporting Handbook.* Washington, D.C.: U.S. Government Printing Office.

———. 1990. *Uniform Crime Reports: Crime in the United States, 1989.* Washington, D.C.: U.S. Government Printing Office.

———. 1991. *Uniform Crime Reports: Crime in the United States, 1990.* Washington, D.C.: U.S. Government Printing Office.

———. 1992. *Uniform Crime Reports: Crime in the United States, 1991.* Washington, D.C.: U.S. Government Printing Office.

Garofalo, J., L. Siegel, and J. Laub. 1987. "School-Related Victimizations Among Adolescents: An Analysis of National Crime Survey Narratives." *Journal of Quantitative Criminology* 3:321-338.

Griffin, Ezra E. H., and Carl C. Bell. 1989. "Recent Trends in Suicide and Homicide Among Blacks." Special Communication. *Journal of the American Medical Association* 282(16):2265-2269.

Gross, L., S. Aurand, and R. Adessa. 1988. "Violence and Discrimination Against Lesbian and Gay People in Philadelphia and the Commonwealth of Pennsylvania." (Available from Philadelphia Lesbian and Gay Task Force, 1501 Cherry Street, Philadelphia, PA 19102).

Gurr, T. R. 1989. "Historical Trends in Violent Crime: Europe and the United States." In T. R. Gurr, ed., *Violence in America. Vol. 1: The History of Crime.* Newbury Park, CA: Sage Publications.

Haenazel, W. 1950. "A Standardized Rate for Mortality Defined in Units of Lost Years of Life." *American Journal of Public Health* 40:17-26.

Hindelang, M., M. Gottfredson, and J. Garofalo. 1978. *Victims of Personal Crime: An Empirical Foundation for a Theory of Personal Victimization.* Cambridge, MA: Ballinger.

Holinger, Paul C. 1987. *Violent Deaths in the United States: An Epidemiologic Study of Suicide, Homicide, and Accidents.* New York: Guilford Press.

Indian Health Service. 1988. *Regional Differences in Indian Health.* Washington, D.C.: U.S. Department of Health and Human Services.

———. 1991. *Regional Differences in Indian Health.* Washington, D.C.: U.S. Department of Health and Human Services.

Jencks, Christopher, and Susan E. Mayer. 1990. "The Social Consequences of Growing Up in A Poor Neighborhood." Pp. 111-186 in Laurence E. Lynn, Jr. and Michael G.H. McGeary, eds., *Inner-City Poverty in the United States.* Washington, D.C.: National Academy Press.

Koppel, Herbert. 1987. "Lifetime Likelihood of Victimization." Bureau of Justice Statistics Technical Report NCJ-104274. U.S. Department of Justice.

Lane, Roger. 1979. *Violent Death in the City: Suicide, Accident, and Murder in Nineteenth Century Philadelphia.* Cambridge, MA: Harvard University Press.

Loftin, Colin, and Ellen J. MacKenzie. 1990. "Building National Estimates of Violent Victimization." Draft paper presented at the Symposium on the Understanding and Control of Violent Behavior. Destin, FL. April 1-4.

Loftin, Colin, and Brian Wiersma. 1991. "Lifetime Risk of Violent Victimization from Homicide." Unpublished memo to the Panel on the Understanding and Control of Violent Behavior.

Lynch, James P. 1989. "An Evaluation of Lifetime Likelihood of Victimization." *Public Opinion Quarterly* 53:262-264.

Maxfield, M. G. 1989. "Circumstances in Supplementary Homicide Reports: Variety and Validity." *Criminology* 27(4):671-695.

Monahan, J. 1988. "Risk Assessment of Violence Among the Mentally Disordered: Generating

Useful Knowledge." *International Journal of Law and Psychiatry* 11:249-257.

Monkkonen, Eric H. 1989. "Diverging Homicide Rates: England and the United States, 1850-1875." Pp. 80-101 in T. R. Gurr, ed., *Violence in America. Vol. 1: The History of Crime*. Newbury Park, CA: Sage Publications.

National Center for Health Statistics. 1991. *Vital Statistics of the United States 1988. Volume II: Mortality*. Washington, D.C.: U.S. Government Printing Office.

Piper, E. 1985. "Violent Recidivism and Chronicity in the 1958 Philadelphia Cohort." *Journal of Quantitative Criminology* 1:319-344.

Pyle, G .F. 1980. "Systematic Sociospatial Variation in Perceptions of Crime Location and Severity." Pg. 226 in D. Georges-Abeyie and K. D. Harries, eds., *Crime: A Spatial Perspective*. New York: Columbia University Press.

Reiss, A. J., Jr. 1985. "Some Failures in Designing Data Collection that Distort Results." pp. 161-177 in L. Burstein, H. E. Freeman, and P. H. Rossi, eds., *Collecting Evaluation Data: Problems and Solutions*. Beverly Hills, CA: Sage Publications.

Reiss, A. J., Jr., and D. P. Farrington. 1991. "Advancing Knowledge About Co-offending: Results From a Prospective Longitudinal Survey of London Males." *Journal of Criminal Law and Criminology* 82(2):360-395.

Sedlak, Andra J. 1991. *National Incidence and Prevalence of Child Abuse and Neglect: 1988*. Washington, D.C.: Westat, Inc. (Revised September 5, 1991).

U.S. Department of Health and Human Services. 1990. *Health United States, 1989*. Hyattsville, MD: Public Health Service.

van Dijk, Jan J. M., Pat Mayhew, and Martin Killias. 1990. *Experiences of Crime Across the World: Key Findings From the 1989 International Crime Survey*. Deventer, The Netherlands: Kluwer Law and Taxation Publishers.

CHAPTER 32

The Motivation to Commit Property Crime

Kenneth D. Tunnell

Why do criminals break the law? What motivates them to violate norms protecting the security of one's person and property? These are the questions that Kenneth D. Tunnell asks in his study of sixty "repetitive property criminals." Through in-depth interviews with convicted felons, Tunnell probes their motives and rationalizations for various property offenses. Often using their own words, he demonstrates that property offenders are not all alike in what motivates their crime. They are, however, articulate in explaining their motives.

Tunnell is not the first scholar to attempt to understand common property criminals. Other researchers have attributed their crimes to economic motives, a search for thrills and excitement, or revenge. Because there are literally millions of property offenders among the criminal population, finding some common motivating factor could be an important step toward developing an effective crime prevention strategy. Tunnell's work demonstrates that will not be easy.

Eighty-eight percent of the interviewed offenders committed a property crime because they "just wanted money." They perceived that stealing was an easier way of obtaining money for their needs than working. With relatively little effort they could finance their drugs, alcohol, partying, and generally having a good time with relatively little risk of

detection. Some study participants did attribute their crime to a sense of accomplishment, sport, vengeance, or power, but in most cases these motivations were secondary to the criminal's desire for quick and easy money.

Although these findings should not be surprising, as stealing what one wants has always been a viable if illegal alternative to earning it, they show the necessity of providing everyone with employment opportunities and the skills needed to earn a living. With a skill and a real job, it is possible that many property offenders would fulfill their needs in a legitimate way.

Rational choice theorists assume that individual decision makers analytically resolve decision problems through a logically calculated series of steps that culminate in a rational decision. As a way of situating this research within a larger theoretical tradition, this study relied on social-psychological variables indicative of these steps that lead to rational decisions. The process of deciding and the various steps involved constitute the focus of this study and the components of such processes served as lines of inquiry.

During the in-depth interviews, I had each of the 60 participants reconstruct specific criminal decision problems and their resolutions. To this end, each participant was asked to recall the most recent typical crime he had committed and could remember clearly.[1] Once they had selected the most recent crime, all of the daily events, conversations, and thoughts which occurred during the decision to commit the crime were reconstructed through conversation. The conversations produced 60 crime-specific decision problems, and the way they were framed and resolved.

One of the earliest factors in the temporal process of deciding to commit a crime is the dimension of motivation. During the interviews, I occasionally posed the question simply as, "Why did you break into that house that day?" Sometimes I arrived at the information in less direct ways, by deducing motivation from the various topics of conversation about the day of the crime and its events.

As I describe the motivations to commit crime among this sample of repetitive property criminals in this chapter, decision-making theorists might be rather disappointed that the accounts offered by these prisoners are neither complex nor analytically sophisticated. But, these criminals may not be the most reflective individuals, who rational choice theorists may desire studying. They may have given little thought to motivational forces in their lives, and in this way are not unlike "normal," law-abiding individuals, who might also be hard-pressed to explain the reasons for their actions and the choices they have made. Nonetheless, with this type of self-reporting retrospective research, we are left with little choice but to rely on the respondents for enlightening us as to motivation.

Motivations: Framing the Decision Problem

Social psychologists inform us that motivation is inseparable from goal attainment. Motivation research focuses primarily on the various factors that determine what psychologists call "goal-directed behavior," which is of central importance in understanding motivated behavior. "Motivated behavior can perhaps best be described by its purposefulness and persistence until the goal is reached" (Van Doren, 1972: 369) and such behavior usually will continue if the results are beneficial or positive. An attempt at goal attainment generally is preceded by the expectation of an end product—the perception of expected benefits from a particular act—and is the motivation for engaging in such an act. However, to analytically understand

individuals' motivations is difficult, for motivation cannot be observed directly and must be inferred from either observed behavior or individuals' self-reporting of prebehavioral thoughts and perceptions of goals.

Motive is considered an essential component of criminality by both jurists and investigators of criminal decision making. Jurists are interested in motivation because to them it represents an integral part of intent or *mens rea*. Decision-making researchers are interested in motivation because it represents a component of the decision problem: the benefits and calculable results the decision maker anticipates from engaging in a particular act.

It's Money That Matters

The motivating force among this sample of repetitive property criminals was nearly uniform—money—"quick, easy money," which they believed they would obtain from committing crimes. Table 32.1 illustrates the motivations to commit crime among this sample.

In fact, 53 of the 60 (88 percent) reported that money was their primary motivating force for committing property crimes, as the following conversation with a twenty seven-year-old high-rate burglar illustrates.[2]

Q: Why do think you did the armed robbery?

A: For the money.

Q: Any other reason?

A: I just wanted money.

Table 32.1 Motivations to Commit Crime

Motivation Type	Number	Percent
Money	53	88
A sense of accomplishment	3	5
Crime as sport	2	3
Vengeance	2	3
Crime as power	2	5

The total number is greater than the N of 60 and the total percent is greater than 100 due to some overlap among the members' reporting.

The financial payoff from crime was defined as especially attractive when compared to the wages they would have expected, perhaps from past experience, to legally earn. The following brief excerpts from conversations with three of the 60 participants are illustrative of this primary motivation. I asked the following of a 31-year-old high-rate burglar who was quite aware of the possibility of his earning a decent legitimate wage.

Q: What about crime is attractive to you or appealing?

A: It doesn't take very long, the profit is quick. If I worked construction I would make a week what I could make in fifteen minutes. That's pretty much why it's appealing.

The following dialogue with a 29-year-old burglar illustrates how money acted as the only benefit that he and others like him believed they would obtain from committing crimes.

Q: So, when you were doing these burglaries then, what benefits did you see coming from them?

A: The money to make it from day to day, to pay me gas, pot, party money. To have a good time.

Q: Some people say they break into places for the thrill of it or the excitement or the accomplishment of it.

A: It never gave me no thrill and I really wasn't accomplishing nothing but putting money in my pocket. So, I didn't get no thrill because of it.

The attractive benefits of criminality are illustrated in the following conversation with a high-rate burglar.

Q: So it sounds like you're saying that the money you've made illegally far outweighs the money you can make—

A: Far outweighs. I don't mind working, but it's hard to work all day and kill yourself for really nothing.

And the following conversation with a 38-year-old armed robber who began his criminal activities with shoplifting also illustrates the benefits of earning money through crime.

Q: What benefit did you see coming from shoplifting and committing other crimes?

A: Just getting money to run around on the weekends with and buy some beer and whiskey and shit like that.

The financial attractiveness, coupled with the perception that threats of formal sanction were not serious, explains a significant part of the decision-making processes found among many of these respondents, particularly the high-rate persistent offenders.

Benefits identified other than money included the excitement of committing crime, the enjoyment of "getting over on" the powers that be, respect from peers for committing crime, and the control over crime situations and crime victims.[3] These anticipated benefits, however, represent *latent* benefits and not the prime objective considered as these men resolved criminal decision problems. The following dialogue with a 28-year-old high school dropout who had committed dozens of burglaries and auto thefts illustrates this point.

Q: What was the reason you did the burglary?

A: Well, for the money, for the money. That's the only reason I did any burglaries. Really, any crime at all would be for the money. And the excitement, you know, it was always there, but it was for the money, more or less.

Q: Did you see any other benefits coming from doing burglaries or was it just the money?

A: Just the money.

Q: You didn't do it because it was exciting or—

A: It was fun, I guess it was kind of exciting in a way.

We can see from the above dialogue that money represented the primary motivation and expected benefit from this crime. Excitement was present but only as a latent benefit—a byproduct of the criminal act.

Although excitement did contribute to the motivation for some of these offenders, the burglar in the following dialogue claimed that for him excitement was not an issue.

Q: Why did you do it, for the money, or excitement, or—

A: Oh, for the money and no, I don't think it was for the excitement, it was just for the money.

Although some of these criminals had very few living expenses (they lived either at home with their parents, with a spouse or a lover who worked, or with a series of lovers), they wanted "easy money" to spend on leisure and recreational activities. This 29-year-old burglar, who rarely worked a legitimate job, reported this when I questioned him about motivation:

Q: Why did you do the burglary?

A: Broke and needed money and wasn't working. And just needed money to drink and party. It wasn't for bills.

As previous research has likewise shown (e.g., Petersilia et al., 1978), money represents the most common motivation. In fact, 53 reported that money was nearly the only element that motivated them to commit crimes. However, nearly a third of the sample (N = 17 or 32 percent) sought money because they had severe physical drug addictions. Their motive was to obtain money to purchase a drug to which they were literally physically addicted (or they defined their situation as such) and they committed crimes to sustain an addiction to a very expensive drug, not necessarily as a "way of life." The following conversation with a 33-year-old individual who committed a wide variety of crimes, but tended to specialize in a particular crime type for a period of time, sheds light on the motivating power of money for drugs.

Q: Why did you commit forgeries at that time?

A: The reason was to get money to buy the drugs with.

Q: That was the main reason?

A: That was the only reason.

Q: Did you use a lot of drugs?

A: Constantly. It was money for drugs. Now I know if I didn't have that drug habit I wouldn't be in this prison. It had got to the point that I

really wasn't out there for nothing but just to do drugs.

And the following conversation with a 30-year old high-rate armed robber illustrates how a drug-addiction propelled him to commit crimes.

Q: Why did you do it, at that time?

A: I was doing drugs real heavy, powerful drugs, and I liked it and by me liking that I took them chances. I really didn't think about the risks period then hardly. All I though about was just getting dope and I'd go to any lengths to get it. The urge for that dope is stronger than getting caught so I'd go ahead and do it. I was doing it just to get money and it was for that damn dope. I didn't really think about all the trouble I'd end up in or anything. I was just wanting to get the money for dope.

Clearly, money for 53 of these participants represents the most significant motivating factor in their criminal calculus. Two-thirds needed money for either living expenses or miscellaneous expenses and considered crime a relatively easy way to maintain their lifestyles. A third, however, were driven to commit crimes because they needed money to regularly obtain physically addictive drugs (e.g., cocaine, heroin, and Dilaudid.)[4]

A Sense of Accomplishment

A second and less-often-stated motivation for committing crimes was for the sense of accomplishment. From the respondents' self-reporting, this was the primary motivation only rarely. In fact, only three of the 60 reported "sense of accomplishment" rather than "easy money" as their motivation. The following dialogue with Floyd, a high-rate shoplifter and later a high-rate armed robber, well illustrates this motivation in the case of shoplifting.

Q: Why would you do it?

A: Because I enjoyed it and the people with me enjoyed it. I'm the type of person, man, if I could steal something from way in the back row or if the store manager is standing here and I could take something right under his nose, that's what I'd get.

Q: Why would you prefer that?

A: Because it was more of an accomplishment.

Although for some this motivation was primary, it nearly always was coupled with the desire for easily obtainable money or a sense of enjoyment, as the following comments from Floyd illustrate.

Q: What do you think the major motivations were to commit shoplifting?

A: Because it's easy money, it's exciting to do it, it ain't never hard to sell the stuff. But wanting to do it man, wanting to do it. Love to do it. *Love* to do it would be the word.

Those who committed crimes for the sense of accomplishment represent the segment that was very committed to a criminal lifestyle. They reported to me that crime was their job, their profession, and a way of obtaining both pecuniary and nonpecuniary benefits that they could not have earned from a "square-john" lifestyle. Although the sense of accomplishment was not a widespread motivational force among this sample, it did represent a significant factor in a few cases.

Crime as Sport

Two sample members reported in vivid detail a motivation for their crimes unlike those of others. Both individuals committed burglaries at a very high frequency and considered crime a fun and exciting game. The game-like rewards served as motivation to commit crimes. The easy money, which was motivating, paled in significance to beating the opponent of the game, or as they called it, "getting over on the law," which they considered a risky, yet psychologically fulfilling, act. I asked a 29-year-old, rather flamboyant, and very high-rate burglar why he committed the particular burglary he described to me. He described his motivation to commit burglaries in general.

A: If I had to write a damn paper on the reason I steal, there would be one sentence—it was for the game. It's a high, now, I mean it's exhilarating. I mean, some people like racquetball and some people like tennis, but I get off going through doors.

Successfully completing a crime provided them with a sense of accomplishment and purpose, and reinforced their belief that they had "won the game." They functioned with the knowledge that in this game, like others, there emerges a winner and a loser. And whenever they were arrested and convicted, they simply admitted to having lost the game, but only temporarily.

The following dialogue with a 28-year-old high-rate offender clearly illustrates this motivation. This particular individual was a burglar who went on "burglary binges" much like drunks go on drinking binges. During those times he would burglarize nonstop in a rather blatant way, with the belief that he was untouchable. He fancied himself an outlaw, a modern day John Dillinger. Coming from a small town where law enforcement officers were few in number and lagged behind in investigative and detective skills, he considered himself beyond the law, as his willingness to boast about just how good he thought he was proves.

A: It got to be a game. I've been locked up since I was sixteen. I've wasted the best years of my life. I can never get them back because I've played this game of 'I'm going to beat them.' And then you get to that stage, you wonder, 'Who in the hell is it I'm trying to beat?' But it got to be a game. I played the game and lost. You got me. Let's go ahead and run it and start it over.

Q: Did you feel like you were winning the game?

A: Well, it starts, it's just like the trumpets at a horse race. I mean that sounds a silly way to sum it up, but now, that's the damn, that's just about it. It's like a starting gun at a swim meet that starts the game. And it's not ended until you stand before that judge or you beat it. It's just like a chess game. I'm trying to stay a step ahead. I mean, fuck, it's a challenge. I mean, by God, it gets down to where it's just me against them and that's the way it is. To me, getting over on him or beating him at this game is 90 percent of it. The fucking money ain't nothing. Getting over on them is what it is. It got to where I just liked it.

Q: What did you like about it?

A: The excitement and the feeling of, you know, I fucked them, I mean, I had got over on them. They put their best investigators on me and I fucked them, man. I sit back and laugh thinking. Really. Basically, and you know yourself, it's a sorry mother-fucking thing, but I mean it provides that damn challenge. Crime was a game…with a whole lot of reality to it.

Thus, we can see from the two individuals who felt this motivation for committing crimes that the financial payoffs were rather insignificant compared to the psychologically fulfilling rewards of beating the opponent of the criminal game, a game with "a whole lot of reality to it." Ironically, they considered the years they spent incarcerated punishment for losing the game and not necessarily for breaking the law. One of the two individuals made the statement that going to prison was analogous to violating a rule in the board game Monopoly—go directly to jail, do not pass go, do not collect two hundred dollars. Again, this motivation was rare among this sample of repeat offenders but a very real factor in explaining why these few individuals committed crimes repetitively and what types of benefits they believed they would obtain from committing crimes.

Vengeance Is Mine

The fourth type of motivation found among this sample, and only used by two armed robbers, was the desire for retaliation and vengeance. These armed robbers claimed to have suffered severely due to official governmental decision making, or lack of it. Both claimed to have lost legitimate earnings, both believed the government had done them an injustice, and one was homeless at the time that he committed his most serious crime of armed robbery. They acted criminally for revenge, generalizing and striking out at others as a representation of government and legitimate society. Although their crimes were individualistic, expressive acts and had no anti-systemic impact, they believed they were getting even with the status quo and the state that had caused them such harm.

Such motivation has been described by previous researchers. Becker, for example, wrote of revenge as both motivation and rationalization for committing crimes for individuals who believe they have been wronged and are entitled to such revenge. Revenge can also motivate individuals who believe their lives are out of control or that they are in the grips of "an uncontrollable force" (Becker, 1970: 332). Thus, individuals who commit crimes out of vengeance often define their situation as one imposed on them, over which they have little control.

The motivation of one of the two armed robbers clearly was shaped by his definition of his situation. He believed that some of his legal earnings from early in life had been wrongfully collected from him by the Internal Revenue Service. He claimed to have lost nearly all of his legally earned capital due to the collection of back taxes and legal fees. It was then that he decided to enter crime as a way of life to retaliate against the system and legitimate society. Crime as work also became a matter of principle to him since he had come to define legitimate work, where individual workers end up with little to show for their labor, as unfair. I had the following conversation with him about when he first began committing crimes in the early 1950s. He was 58 years old and serving his third prison sentence.

Q: Did you try and find a job?

A: I was determined then that I wasn't going to work and make a living. I wasn't going to go out and work all day and week after week and pay the government for working. I mean this is the way I felt then. I felt that if I went out and got a job and they took federal tax out, they took state tax out, they took medicare out, they took Social Security out and by the time I got my check they had already took out 30 dollars or 40 dollars. So why would I work to pay the government for working? That's the way I felt.

The second armed robber expressed similar rebellion against a government that he believed had done him an injustice by refusing to assist him with his physical and emotional problems in a time of serious need. During the interview he certainly looked the part of a man in questionable health. He looked much older than his 42 years, favored his bent back, and had some difficulty breathing. Although serving his third prison sentence, he claimed that he had committed relatively few crimes. He had committed the most serious, armed robbery, only twice and admitted he was motivated by frustration and a desire for vengeance. His words provide an inside view of his world.

A: The government did this somewhat to me too by denying me benefits.

Q: Your Social Security?

A: Yeah. I mean I was desperate. I didn't know what the hell I was going to do because I couldn't even keep the roof over my head. I moved into my car and I didn't have much of a car, but I slept in my car for a long time. I've had three back surgeries and now I've got heart trouble on top of the back surgery, so how in the hell am I going to get a job? My wife took me to _____ Mental Hospital because I did have an alcoholic problem and drugs and I asked her to take me there. And she did and I got turned away from over there, saying they didn't have the funds or money to help me and there was no room for me. No place for me there.

Q: And it was before that that you had gotten turned down for Social Security?

A: Right. I had many problems, mental problems. It got to the point where I knew I needed help and I couldn't get it. And that whole chain of events got me right in prison. I was on my Social Security and they cut it out and when they cut it out it like to cut my life off. I lost my Social Security, I lost my truck and I didn't know what the hell I was going to do. I done it out of desperation and frustration at life, no help, no money, living in a car. I couldn't even take a bath. Nowhere to take a bath. I felt less than worthless.

Those who committed crimes out of vengeance calculated their crimes emotionally rather than logically, as the following comment from the 58-year-old robber illustrates.

A: When you're mad like that and a person did something to you, you be in a mental state of mind, you don't give a damn about no police, or being locked up, or a judge, or no damn nobody else.

This vengeance motivation was rare among this sample. These two individuals made their decisions and then committed their crimes using emotionally charged reasoning processes and modes of behavior. They were not that methodical in their planning, understandings of benefits and risks, or target selections. They typically robbed spontaneously and selected targets without rhyme or reason.

Crime as Power

A fifth and particularly important latent motivation found among armed robbers was the exertion of power and the control of victims and of the crime situation. The following conversation with a 30-year-old, very experienced and seasoned armed robber illustrates how control and power were important elements to him, although money was obviously the primary benefit from the crime.

Q: Is that a pretty scary experience when you walk in with a gun pulled asking for money?

A: No, it's not really scary because you know you've got control of the situation, you know? It's a surprise, an element of surprise. You go in and you throw a gun on the table and everybody flips out. But it never did scare me because I always just put myself in their position. But it's just getting in that door. After you get through that door it ain't nothing, it's like you're running, like you own that place.

Q: You said like you own the place?

A: Yeah, you are ruling everything because everybody, whoever is in there is going to pay attention to you, I didn't want to hurt nobody. The only thing I wanted was the money. If you go in there you've got to play that act all the way out whether you get hurt or not.

Q: I think you're saying you were also prepared to do whatever to get the money?

A: Right. It wouldn't be that they'd try to harm me, it would be that they wouldn't give up the money. Because, you see, if you go in there and then let them tell you what to do, then there ain't no sense in you going in there at all.

Armed robbers who expressed this type of psychological benefit from and motivation for armed robbery were few in number (N = 3). The armed robbers almost universally reported the desire for quick cash as the single motivating factor in their decisions to commit crime. And even the very few who reported this expressive benefit of power and control indicated that it was not as significant in motivating them as the desire or necessity of money.

Conclusion

Although the majority of these repetitive criminals reported one primary motivation, many reported one primary and other less important or latent motivations. But, not surprisingly, the goal-directed behavior among this sample was nearly entirely for monetary gain. The other motivational forces found among this group of chronic offenders pale in significance to money. Monetary gain, for whatever reason (e.g., for drugs, for living expenses, for pleasurable commodities) represents the most significant and most widely reported source of motivation among this sample of repetitive property criminals. The benefits that these offenders believed they would obtain by committing crimes was a significant component of the process of deciding to commit a crime.

Such findings from this sample of repetitive offenders are both similar and dissimilar to those from previous research. For example, this study differs from that of Frazier and Meisenhelder (1985), who reported that many of their 95 property offenders found crime to be exciting and believed they were "getting over on" someone or away with something. Many respondents in my sample reported the same. In fact, nearly all 60 found it exciting. But, excitement was a latent benefit neither primarily nor objectively sought after. Very few respondents reported excitement as a reason for committing crime. Rather, "quick, easy money" was the most common reason for doing crime. If committing crime was also exciting, then

that added more pleasure to a financially rewarding activity. But, few entered crime motivated primarily by a desire for excitement.

These findings are similar to those of Reppetto (1974), who interviewed 97 burglars and found money to be the primary benefit of crime. Excitement was mentioned most often among the young and least often among the old. This age-related difference is similar for the 60 men of my research. Motivation responses were measured across three different age periods of these men's lives.[5] These data show that excitement was often a primary motivator among the young, but its importance lessened with age until it typically became, at most, a latent benefit and motivating force.

Discussion Questions

1. What are the motivations for committing crime, as expressed in this article? Are some motivations stronger than others? Do you think these same motivations would be present in most crimes committed by females? Why or why not?
2. For those who regard "crime as sport," what are the rewards of crime? What does incarceration mean to them? What is their attitude toward the law? Do you think this motivation would ever be present in the commission of white collar/corporate crimes?
3. After reading their responses, would you say that criminals use the same rational choice, logical decision-making process that non-criminals use? Why or why not? What is a jury's interest in an offender's decision-making process?

Notes

1. The respondents typically would recall and begin to describe an exceptional crime that stood out in their minds for one reason or another. Knowing the types of crimes they committed and something about their frequency, I would remind them that I was interested in a typical crime that they had committed. They would then discontinue their description of the outstanding crime and begin describing a more typical crime for them. In this way, I was able to learn about the various events, conversations, and thoughts

(as they reconstructed them) for a crime that they most frequently committed and the type most often committed by serious repetitive property criminals.

2. "High rate" as used in this work refers to those individuals in this sample who committed the most property crimes of the 60. As an arbitrary cutoff point, high-rate criminals are those who committed more than 100 property felonies during their lives in the "free world" and low-rate criminals, among this sample, are those who committed fewer than 100 felony crimes during their lives in the "free world." These high-rate felons are classified as persistent decision makers....High-rate criminals represent those criminals who are very committed to a criminal way of life and criminal profession. Such high-rate criminals clearly make decisions differently than low-rate repetitive criminals, who are classified as sporadic criminals in the taxonomy of decision makers among this sample.

3. "Getting over on" the law is a phrase used by criminals to describe successfully committing a crime and often refers to committing a crime with law enforcement officials nearby. "Getting over on" gives criminals satisfaction and is an expressive benefit derived from crime commission.

4. According to the *Physicians Desk Reference*,, Dilaudid is a "hydrogenated ketone of morphine...a narcotic analgesic." The PDR has this to say about this widely used and very addictive drug:

> Small doses of Dilaudid produce effective and prompt relief of pain usually with minimal disturbance from nausea and vomiting. Generally, the analgesic action of Dilaudid is apparent within 15 minutes and remains in effect for more than five hours. May be habit forming. The relative addiction

potential does not exceed that of morphine with equi-analgesic doses (Physicians Desk Reference, 1977: 871).

Dilaudid was certainly a drug of choice among the very serious drug users and addicts among this sample. Dilaudid was preferred over heroin because the users claimed that they felt safe with Dilaudid, knowing that it was clean, laboratory produced and had not been "stepped on" (i.e., cut with an additive).

5. Each of the 60 was asked about motivation and benefit perceptions for three different age periods—juvenile (under age 18), young adult (ages 18 to 26), and adult (age 27 and older). Their responses reveal that excitement as a motivational force and as a perceived benefit lessened with age.

References

Becker, Howard S. 1970. "Conventional crime: Rationalizations and punishments." pp. 329-39 in *Sociological Work: Method and Substance*. Chicago: Aldine.

Frazier, Charles E. and Thomas Meisenhelder. 1985. "Criminality and emotional ambivalence: Exploratory notes on an overlooked dimension." *Qualitative Sociology* 8:266-84.

Petersilia, Joan, Peter Greenwood, and Marvin Lavin. 1978. *Criminal Careers of Habitual Felons*. Washington, DC: U.S. Department of Justice.

Reppetto, T. A. 1974. *Residential Crime*. Cambridge, MA: Ballinger.

Van Doren, Bob. 1972. *Psychology Today*. 2d ed. Del Mar, CA: CRM Books.

CHAPTER 33

Organized Crime

Frank R. Scarpitti

What American has not heard of organized crime? From tales of Prohibition-era gangsters to the Godfather books and movies, organized crime has become part of the nation's folk legends. It has been romanticized unlike any other type of criminality but remains an enigma to many people. Organized crime is another form of career crime to which participants become committed and around which a unique lifestyle develops. Understanding organized crime allows us to see the often intricate relationships that exist among law, morality, vice, ethnicity, social mobility, and politics. No other form of criminality blends so many social dynamics; perhaps that is what makes it such an intriguing and romantic subject.

In this selection, Frank R. Scarpitti presents a short history of organized crime in the United States and its current nature. Beginning with the pirates of the seventeenth and eighteenth centuries, there have always been groups of criminals willing to provide the public with goods and services that were desired but forbidden by law. Although the groups changed over the centuries, their mission did not. In the twentieth century organized crime groups were identified with immigrant groups searching for the American dream but using illegal means to attain it. Although this pattern has led some observers to speculate that an alien conspiracy controls U.S. organized crime, most scholars see ethnic succession

and enterprise theory as more reasonable explanations of its origin and permanence.

As this selection makes clear, controlling organized crime has been difficult. Because law enforcement has traditionally seen this type of crime as the product of evil persons or groups, emphasis has been placed on prosecuting individuals rather than on systemic change. Denying organized crime access to illegal profits by legalizing some of the goods and services it provides would be one alternative. The likelihood of such change, however, is not very great. So, as individuals and groups are successfully prosecuted, they are replaced by others, and illegal goods and services continue to be provided to willing consumers.

Any consumer of popular culture is exposed to a great deal of information about organized crime. Books, articles, news reports, movies, television shows, all feature numerous stories about this form of criminal behavior and those who engage in it. These fictional and nonfictional accounts of crime syndicates and their operators have, unfortunately, created a number of myths about organized crime and made some organized criminals virtual folk heroes. Despite this public and media attention, there remains significant disagreement about the exact nature of organized crime, its etiology, and the role it plays in contemporary American society.

Defining Organized Crime

Controversy begins with attempting to define organized crime. Although criminologists have

Reprinted from: Frank R. Scarpitti, "Organized Crime." In *Social Problems*, pp. 145-157. Copyright © 1993 by McGraw-Hill. Reprinted by permission.

offered numerous definitions, several common features are noted in most. Organized crime is profit-motivated,[1] provides illegal goods and services,[2] involves planning and conspiracies among group members,[3] uses violence and coercion,[4] and relies on political corruption to protect itself.[5] It is violation of the law that involves more than one person, a group that intends to remain associated with one another in an identifiable hierarchy of authority in order to commit additional crimes.[6]

These attributes of organized crime groups allow us to see that they are *organized* because they are hierarchically arranged conspiracies of like individuals designed to provide goods and services to buyers at substantial profits. They are prone to using violence and corruption to maintain monopolistic control of markets and to achieve their illegal goals. In addition, organized crime groups are self-perpetuating and engage in ongoing criminal activity.

Although this definition of organized crime is generally accepted by law enforcement agencies, they have placed greater emphasis on several key characteristics than most criminologists believe to be accurate. The model of organized crime perpetuated by the U.S. Justice Department and its enforcement agencies suggests that a single national syndicate (Cosa Nostra), sometimes working with other national or international groups, controls most organized criminal activities.[7] Such groups, it is believed, are highly structured and tightly controlled by ruthless bosses who have great power. As two investigators have commented:

> They [the government] picture a secret organization of ruthless and violent men bound by a common interest in illicit gain, ordered by a rigid code of rules, rights, and obligations, and maintained by the constant threat of death to informers or defectors.[8]

While this conception of organized crime and criminals has been questioned by numerous scholars, it is still popular among social control agents and continues to shape the public image.

History of Organized Crime

Although some believe that American organized crime began to emerge early in the twentieth century, others contend that its origin can be traced to the pirates of the seventeenth and eighteenth centuries.[9] Highly organized and subscribing to hierarchical authority, these bandits of the seas earned their livings from crime. Their loot was sold to otherwise lawful consumers who valued the bargains, and their wealth ingratiated them with government officials. In nearly every way, these early criminal organizations possessed the attributes of organized crime groups as defined earlier.

Pirates were not the only organized criminal groups in the colonies, however. In all of the major port cities, gangs stole from docked ships, raided warehouses, smuggled, and provided sex and liquor to sailors and others willing to pay. Following the American Revolution, huge land frauds were perpetrated by officials in high office and their henchmen, setting the stage for the great "robber barons" of the nineteenth century. Called "financial pirates"[10] by one writer, they were determined to make their fortunes by whatever means necessary, often using illegal methods of the most callous type. These early crooks, Anglo-Saxon and Protestant, served as role models for immigrants who arrived later and also bent upon making their fortunes in the new land. It has been pointed out that:

> ...with the wealth of the "robber barons" now institutionalized and their progeny firmly in control of the economy, there...[was] little opportunity for the poor but ambitious adventurers of our urban frontiers. These later immigrants, Irish, Jewish, Italian, sought to innovate, not on the grand scale of the Vanderbilts, the Rockefellers, and the Morgans, but in a manner more consistent with available opportunity.[11]

Largely German and Irish before the Civil War and Italian and Jewish after, these later immigrants settled in the cities of the new country, usually in ethnic neighborhoods with others like themselves. Poor and uneducated, but fiercely ambitious, they searched for ways to achieve the promises of their adopted society. The young formed gangs which frequently saw crime as a means to attain the riches promised by their new life. Their crimes, of course, were those, with their limited skills, to which they had access, typically providing countrymen with the vices forbidden by the law. Urban political machines, usually corrupt, appealed to the immigrants for their support, often by giving tacit approval and protection to the gangs and their illegal activities. The collaboration between local gangs engaged in organized criminality and political operatives offering support in exchange for payoffs was simply an extension of the system that originated with the Colonial pirates.

The magnitude and nature of the problem changed after 1920, however, with the advent of Prohibition.[12] Although outlawed, Americans still wanted to drink liquor, and organized crime groups were ready to provide for their needs. Anticipating huge revenues, local gangs expanded their bootlegging activities by importing liquor, financing clandestine breweries and distilleries, and establishing speakeasies and other places where liquor could be purchased. Profits from such operations provided capital for expansion as well as for the financing of other illegal enterprises. Local, neighborhood crime groups soon began to grow well beyond their original boundaries.

In New York City, the most influential organized crime groups were dominated by Jewish and Italian gangsters. Often the groups cooperated, but just as frequently they fought for control of territory and enterprises. In Chicago, the second hub of organized crime activity, most gangs were controlled by Irish and Italian criminals, although here as in other places groups of various ethnic and racial origins were also involved in organized criminal activities. After bitter conflict, however, the group led by Al Capone eventually dominated organized criminality in Chicago.

By the time World War II ended, the prevalence of Italian-Americans in organized crime activities was attracting increased attention. Many experts attributed this to an international conspiracy known as the Mafia (later to be called La Cosa Nostra), manned by Italian immigrants from Sicily and now in control of organized crime activities across the nation.[13] Others disputed the notion of an Italian-dominated conspiracy, pointing out there was scant evidence of such a scheme and that the belief was based largely on myth often supplied by low-level syndicate members. In addition, little attention was paid during this period to the organized crime activities of other ethnic and racial group members, creating a false notion of ethnic and racial homogeneity among all organized crime groups. To both law enforcement and the public, however, organized crime in America was controlled by Italian-Americans.

Whatever the extent of Italian-American control and domination of organized crime, it began to diminish in the late 1960s.[14] Members of the old crime "families" were targeted by law enforcement, especially at the federal level, with intense scrutiny, investigation, and prosecution, resulting in the imprisonment of many. As members of the ethnic group attained middle class status, fewer of the young saw organized crime as a legitimate avenue for mobility, and leadership roles were not being filled with new recruits as vacancies occurred. Other groups became more brazen in challenging the old "families" for a share of the illegal markets. Clearly, changes began to take place that have continued since, with the old Italian-American gangs or "families" having very limited power in organized crime today.[15]

Since the 1970s, new organized crime groups have assumed power in certain geographical areas or over specific types of criminal activities. Many are identified by their ethnic affiliation, and, like the Irish, Jews, and Italians before them, usually representing the nation's newest immigrants. Thus, there are now recognized Mexican, Jamaican, Colombian, Asian, Israeli, and Russian crime groups, as well as those held together by other loyalties, like motorcycle gangs.[16] While most of these groups engage in a variety of crimes, the illegal drug business seems to be one criminal enterprise shared by many. Importing and distributing drugs has become so profitable that it attracts numerous groups to organized crime activity, making them rich and powerful very quickly, as well as increasingly violent as they fight to establish and retain their share of the market.

Role of Organized Crime in Society

Organized crime is a business, and like any business its objective is to maximize profits. It is different than legitimate businesses in that it operates in the illegal market which imposes certain conditions that do not pertain to legal enterprises. Nevertheless, organized crime is motivated by the same fundamental assumptions that control conventional business activities, namely, the need to create, retain, and extend a share of the market.[17] Organized crime becomes more understandable when it is seen as entrepreneurship that is defined as illegal.

Since no business survives without customers, it is obvious that a considerable market exists for the goods and services that organized crime provides. These goods and services—drugs, gambling, sex, usurous loans, waste dumping, to name a few—are in demand by a significant portion of the population but are not provided by legitimate businesses. In most cases they are forbidden by law because they are contrary to moral principles to which a substantial number of us subscribe, although in practice both principle and law are violated with enough frequency to create a lucrative market for illicit suppliers. Without public demand, organized crime would have little or no function.

Providing goods and services that are wanted by consumers but are illegal allows crime groups to make substantial profits. The amount of profit is determined by the risk involved for the provider and the fact that the commodity is in short supply. Such profit has been referred to as "the crime tariff,"[18] or the cost consumers pay for illegal goods or services which are unavailable in the legitimate market and which may cause the supplier to be arrested and prosecuted. The crime tariff assures profitability and makes the business of organized crime worthwhile. Because risk varies by activity, however, the tariff is greater for some activities than for others. Heroin importation and distribution is better policed and more heavily sanctioned than growing and selling marijuana, for example; therefore, it is more profitable. While the cost of each substance reflects the risk involved to the supplier, the market for each is assured since there are no legal alternative sources for the drugs.

Organized crime groups devote considerable time and attention to minimizing risk. One way to do this is to operate within a limited area in order to control the operating environment.[19] Because new risks are encountered with growth, organized crime groups tend not to expand too widely nor to acquire new markets, as profitable as this might be. The transportation of illegal goods, communication among accomplices, protection from the law, all become more difficult and riskier with growth and territorial expansion. As one observer states, this "helps to explain why most organized crime groups operate in a small and limited area.... Effective and efficient organization guarantees a continuation of significant profits; greed and over-expansion may well spell the end of the enterprise all together."[20]

Risk is also diminished through the corruption of public officials. Without such corruption, organized crime would have a difficult time carrying on its illegal activities. Because there is considerable public ambivalence about the illegal nature of some organized crime activities forbidden by law (gambling, for example), social control agents are often able to justify lax enforcement and even outright bribery. In addition, the availability of huge amounts of money to offer public officials makes it very difficult for them to resist requests from organized criminals to assist their enterprises in various subtle ways. Police officers may selectively enforce laws to favor an organized crime group, or deliberately overlook criminal activity on the part of syndicate operators. Politicians may use their political clout to assist criminals in the courts, before zoning boards, or in legislatures. All this, of course, is in exchange for direct payoffs, campaign contributions, or even the delivery of votes.

Collusion among organized criminals, the police, and politicians appears to be as old as such crime itself and essential to its strength and profitability.[21] As we have seen, organized crime has endured over a long period of time despite repeated efforts by law enforcement and congressional committees to eradicate it. It has survived by being a part of the political establishment and by continuing to provide goods and services wanted by a willing public. Although some commodities have changed over time, those that exist today continue to make organized crime a powerful force in our society.

Experts agree that the illegal drug trade is organized crime's most profitable business. Revenues from drug sales have been estimated to be between $81[22] and $100[23] billion each year. Processing and importing drugs, especially heroin and cocaine, are done by large crime groups, usually with international connections. The distribution of drugs on the streets is typically controlled by local, neighborhood groups which operate as retailers in the marketing process. Law enforcement attempts to curb the drug trade have been largely unsuccessful, since the crime bosses are virtually immune from arrest and prosecution and street pushers are easily replaced if arrested.

Organized crime has been supplying illegal drugs to consumers since the implementation of the Harrison Act in 1914, the original federal law outlawing narcotic drugs. Criminalizing drug use created a black market which organized crime quickly satisfied. Later, in 1937, when marijuana was added to the list of prohibited substances, the market enlarged, as it did again in 1970 when synthetic drugs (amphetamines and barbiturates, for example) were included. Ironically, legal attempts to deter use have expanded organized crime's market and make the drug trade more profitable.

Another lucrative service provided by organized crime groups is gambling. A Presidential Commission has estimated that Americans spend more than $59 billion a year on illegal gambling.[24] While this may appear surprising when legal gambling is increasingly available, it is understandable when one remembers that illegal gains are not taxed, telephoned bets are accepted, and credit may be extended to the gambler. The most popular forms of illegal gambling are betting on sporting events (bookmaking) and playing the numbers (a form of lottery). Each of these appeals to working class people who tend to believe that winning will make their lives easier.

Since the 1940s, organized crime groups have been involved in Las Vegas gambling, often as the hidden owners of large casinos.[25] In addition to making legal profits from casino gambling, they also engage in "skimming," the practice of stealing part of the money spent by patrons before it is tallied for tax purposes. While the presence of organized crime groups in Atlantic City is not debated, their relationship to that city's casino industry is unclear.[26] It is known that they are involved with many of the industries that support and service the hotels and casinos, and in that way exert an unhealthy influence on the gambling industry.

It is estimated that organized crime groups earn between $2 and $3 billion each year from interest on loans for which they charge very high and illegal rates of interest.[27] Known as loansharking, this activity caters to those who are unable to secure a legitimate loan and are desperate for cash. Customers include those with bad credit records, or persons in need of quick cash, perhaps to cover a failing business or a gambling debt. The services of the loanshark are popular because they are secret, informal, and convenient.[28] Transactions are not subject to public scrutiny or credit checks, no applications need be completed, and cash is available immediately. For this, borrowers may pay as much as 20 percent a week in interest on the principal. Although failure to pay may lead to violence, that consequence is quite rare and exists more in stereotype than in reality. Loansharks tend to deal with customers who pay off their loans and often return to borrow again.[29]

Another commodity provided by organized crime groups is illicit sex. According to one study, "Sex services run the gamut from prostitution, after-hours clubs catering to solicitation of various sexual preferences, and pornography outlets, to the production of pornographic films."[30] Providing sex to willing customers is nothing new for organized crime, although its nature and organization has changed. At one time, large and profitable prostitution rings were operated under the direction of organized criminals and their associates. Brothel prostitutes, streetwalkers, and call girls were often recruited and employed by crime groups which ran the business and offered the women protection. More recently, with changing sexual mores and the decline of organized prostitution, other sex services have become more profitable, and now seem to occupy more of the attention of organized crime groups. Clubs featuring exotic dancers, sex shops with live shows sometimes viewed through peepholes, pornographic book and film stores, and the production of pornographic films are now more profitable ventures, and may even be legal.

When American labor unions were attempting to organize workers, they sometimes turned to crime groups for help in combatting the hired thugs of management. Thus marked the entry of organized crime into what has come to be called "labor racketeering." By controlling certain unions, organized criminals have placed themselves in a position to have a powerful impact on the economy and on the lives of thousands of working men and women. They have negotiated "sweetheart contracts" that benefit themselves more than their union members, accepted kickbacks, drained union pension funds for their own enrichment, and driven up the cost of many goods and services essential to the national economy. Often, legitimate union members have been killed or beaten when they have opposed their corrupt leadership. While this pattern of labor crime has been found in several industries and the unions associated with them, the worst case may well be the Teamsters Union, one of the country's largest and most powerful. Until recently, a pattern of illegality involving organized criminals has existed in the national Teamsters Union and its locals that have been the subject of countless investigations and indictments.

Just as organized crime groups have infiltrated legitimate trade unions, they have also entered many legal businesses, often bringing their illegal tactics with them. A good example of this is the waste industry.[31] In many areas of the country, especially the large metropolitan regions of the Northeast, trash hauling has been controlled by organized crime since the 1940s. During that time, this essential business was marked by unfair trade practices, rigged bids, kickbacks to officials, and even violence among competitors. Profits are huge for company owners and their protectors in the mob, with consumers paying inflated prices for garbage removal. But the illegality of many of these companies has gotten even worse. They have recently moved into the collection and disposal of toxic wastes, bringing with them the same tactics used for years in the solid waste business. In addition, the difficulty associated with the disposal of toxic waste has led to their dumping it in sanitary landfills, sewers, waterways, fields, and on highways from the back of tanker trucks. While some have argued that there are few "victims" of organized crime since most of the consumers of

their goods and services are willing participants, this cannot be said for those innocent persons adversely affected by the contamination of the land and water around them.

In addition to waste disposal, organized crime has entered numerous other legitimate businesses, using the huge profits made from illegal activities to gain entry. This not only helps clean their "dirty" money, it gives them vast new opportunities to use illegal techniques to gain market advantage and increase profits. One commentator has indicated that organized crime groups have already entered many areas of big business, including banking, construction, credit cards, entertainment, real estate, securities, and various others.[32] Sometimes, a reciprocal relationship develops between the legitimate and illegitimate participants in a business, with their coming to rely on each other for services and favors. In this way, organized crime becomes integrated into a community's business structure and criminals assume a powerful role in its economic and political life.

Explanations of Organized Crime

At least three explanations of the origins and perpetuation of organized crime have been offered: alien conspiracy theory, ethnic succession theory, and enterprise theory. While each recognizes the existence of organized crime in American society, they differ greatly in their interpretations of its meaning and function.

The alien conspiracy theory views organized crime as an evil imposed on our society by a foreign conspiracy.[33] According to this theory, these foreigners, usually Italians of Sicilian extraction, have infiltrated our society and created a secret organization, the Mafia, that is undermining the American way of life; the Mafia, controlling all organized crime in the United States, is governed by a national commission of gang leaders who coordinate a well-orchestrated attack on our traditional values. This explanation of organized crime seems to have arisen in the 1950s and was quickly adopted by law enforcement agencies, especially at the federal level. It provided a simple explanation by creating a conspicuous scapegoat who transplanted this type of criminality from another culture. This concept of organized crime gained popularity in the media as well as with the public.

Often referred to as the "Mafia myth,"[34] this explanation is no longer accepted by either law enforcement officials or social scientists. In addition to being unable to explain organized crime before the arrival of the ominous foreigners, this idea fails to recognize that organized crime groups simply respond to the needs or desires of customers who want the goods or services that are for sale. Before the arrival of the Italians other groups furnished them, and in recent years, non-Italian groups and independent entrepreneurs have played a larger role in such activities. This is not to say, of course, that many organized crime groups have not been ethnically similar. They have, but more for reasons having to do with kinship, friendship, patterns of recruitment, and trust than with an alien conspiracy.

The ethnic nature of many organized crime groups has also supported the notion that disadvantaged minorities have used such criminality to achieve upward social mobility.[35] Francis Ianni states, "How do you escape poverty through socially approved routes when such routes are often foreign to the ghetto life? Crime resolves the dilemma because it provides a quick if perilous route out."[36] He notes that every major ethnic group has faced the problem and has chosen organized crime as one solution. While each group quickly assimilates the goals of the new society, it takes some time for it to achieve the legitimate means to attain those goals. In the meantime, groups must "innovate" or devise whatever means work to share the rewards of the new society.[37] Organized crime may be considered to be one such innovation.

As the assimilation process progresses and legitimate means to attain society's goals are achieved, later generations of each group find less need to use organized crime as a vehicle for upward mobility. Just as one ethnic group has succeeded the other in its involvement in crime groups, so too one has followed the other in its attainment of education, legitimate jobs, and respectability. While this theory cannot account for those who experience the deprivations of ethnic groups but do not become

criminals, or those who become organized criminals although they are not members of deprived ethnic groups, it does demonstrate that deprived social status may contribute to crime causation.

Clearly, neither conspiracy nor ethnic succession theories appear to be adequate in explaining the etiology of organized crime. Instead, modern scholars have turned increasingly to enterprise theory,[38] or some modification of it. In fact, the basic tenets of that perspective had been used throughout this discussion of organized crime. Enterprise theorists maintain that there is no evidence of a nationwide conspiracy to control organized crime activities, that such activities are not limited to members of certain ethnic groups, and that the use of violence by organized crime groups is exaggerated. Instead, organized crime groups are local in nature, typically have shifting and overlapping memberships, and can often achieve their goals because they are believed to be violent and benefit from their bad reputation.[39]

The essence of enterprise theory, however, is that organized crime groups and legitimate business groups are engaged in similar activities, providing goods and services to consumers. Organized crime exists because the legitimate market does not meet the needs of a substantial number of buyers. While one type of business deals with legal products, the other deals with illegal products. The behaviors, ideas, beliefs and values that motivate the legitimate business person are the same as those that motivate the organized criminal. Markets must be found and maintained, goods and services provided, risk reduced, and competition controlled, all good business objectives whether the product is textbooks or illegal drugs. Organized crime, then, is like any other business.

Combatting Organized Crime

Because law enforcement and political leaders have traditionally viewed organized crime as the product of evil persons or groups imposing their criminality on a law-abiding society, typical control techniques have focused on the prosecution of individuals.[40] Assuming that the crimes would disappear if the criminals were removed from society, local and federal law enforcement agencies have launched countless investigations over the years, often resulting in the arrest, prosecution, and imprisonment of organized crime figures. These efforts have been aided by special congressional hearings, federal strike forces, a witness protection program, local crime commissions, investigative grand juries, the use of informants, and a variety of other methods and programs designed to attack organized crime.[41]

Among the most comprehensive efforts directed at organized crime groups was the 1970 Organized Crime Control Act, in particular its provision creating the Racketeer Influence and Corrupt Organizations Act (RICO).[42] RICO imposes stiff penalties on those convicted in federal court of various racketeering offenses, requires those convicted to forfeit any property acquired by or used in criminal activity, and allows the federal government to bring civil action against suspected criminals. The latter provision of the Act is important because the standard of proof is not as great in civil court as it is in criminal court, and allows the opportunity to extract large monetary judgments from defendants. Since the inception of RICO, a large number of reputed crime bosses and their underlings, principally members of the old Italian-American gangs, have been convicted under its provisions, but the activities of other organized crime groups have not been diminished.

Some critics have suggested that the only effective way to control organized crime is to take away its access to illegal profits.[43] This could be done by legalizing many of the illegal goods and services that are in demand but legally unavailable. This is particularly true of gambling and drugs, both of which could be legalized, taxed, and controlled by the government, thereby divesting crime groups of those markets. Deprived of the revenue from its two chief money makers, organized crime would have less capital to fund other illegal activities and to corrupt public officials. Since organized crime has become an integral part of our social structure, as proponents charge, only real change in the definition of victimless or consensual crimes will be effective in controlling it. Opponents argue, however, that organized crime would continue to offer advantages that the legitimate market could

not match and that it would continue to operate. In addition, legalizing the so-called victimless crimes would legitimize them and encourage their use by some who would otherwise not consider them.

At the present time, major social policy reform appears unlikely, and controlling organized crime groups will remain a law enforcement function. Even though this approach has not proven to be very effective, that seems to be how Americans want it.

Conclusion

Organized crime groups have operated in America since Colonial days, filling a market niche by providing certain goods and services defined by law as illegal but coveted by consumers nevertheless. Whatever the illegal goods and services, the fact that they are outlawed means that lucrative profits can be attached to making them available. Driven by the profit motive, groups of criminals have organized to satisfy consumer demand and protect their markets from competitors as well as from social control agents. Violence, or at least its threat, and political corruption are common mechanisms used by these groups to achieve their goals. Seen in this way, there is nothing very mysterious about organized crime. The stratified and heterogenous nature of our society encourages socially marginal groups to use organized crime activities as a means of achieving material goals and even some social standing within the community. The makeup of organized crime groups has changed over time, however, and continues to change today, as legitimate opportunities for social mobility become available and replace organized crime as a ladder toward upward mobility.

Because organized crime is built into our social, economic, and political structures, it has survived repeated attempts to eradicate it. As local gang leaders and even entire gangs fall, others replace them, and control shifts to a new group of organized criminals. Illegal goods and services continue to be provided, needs of otherwise good citizens continue to be met, and corruption continues to be part of the legal and political systems.

In this sense, organized crime appears to be "an American way of life."[44]

Discussion Questions

1. What are the characteristics of organized crime? Which model of organized crime is perpetuated by the U.S. Justice Department and remains popular among the public, but is questioned by criminologists?

2. Trace the history of organized crime. How did it begin in the seventeenth and eighteenth centuries? What caused small gangs to grow, then solidify into large crime groups? What part did race and ethnicity play in this process? What ethnic groups are involved in organized crime today?

3. In what ways is organized crime similar to large organizations or businesses? What goods/services does it provide? How is the amount of profit determined? What is a crime tariff?

Notes

1. Howard Abadinsky, *Organized Crime*, Chicago, Nelson-Hall, 1985; Joseph L. Albini, *The American Mafia: Genesis of a Legend*, New York, Appleton-Century-Crofts, 1971.

2. Gary W. Potter, *Criminal Organizations: Vice, Racketeering, and Politics in an American City*, Prospect Heights, IL, Waveland, 1994.

3. National Advisory Committee on Criminal Justice Standards and Goals, *Organized Crime: Report of the Task Force on Organized Crime*, Washington, D.C., U.S. Department of Justice, 1976.

4. Abadinsky, op. cit.; Albini, op. cit.

5. Ibid.

6. Michael Maltz, "On Defining 'Organized Crime': The Development of a Definition and a Typology," *Crime and Delinquency* 22: 336-348, 1976.

7. Potter, op. cit., p. 173.

8. Francis A. J. Ianni and E. Reuss-Ianni, *A Family Business: Kinship and Social Control in Organized Crime*, New York, Russell Sage Foundation, 1972, p. 5.

9. Dennis J. Kenney and James O. Finckenauer, *Organized Crime in America*, New York, Wadsworth, 1994, chap. 3.

10. Abadinsky, op. cit., p. 53.

11. Ibid.

12. Kenney and Finckenauer, op. cit., chap. 6.

13. Ibid., chap. 9.

14. Humbert S. Nelli, "A Brief History of American Syndicate Crime," in T. Bynum, ed., *Organized Crime in America: Concepts and Controversies*, Monsey, N.Y., Criminal Justice Press, pp. 15-29.

15. Ibid.; Kenney and Finckenauer, op. cit., pp. 252-255.

16. President's Commission on Organized Crime, *Organized Crime Today*, Washington, D.C., U.S. Government Printing Office, 1985, pp. 58-128.

17. Dwight C. Smith, Jr., "Paragons, Pariahs, and Pirates: A Spectrum-Based Theory of Enterprise," *Crime and Delinquency*, 26: 358-386, 1980.

18. Stuart Hills, *Crime, Power and Morality: The Criminal Law Process in the United States*, Scranton, PA, Chandler, 1971.

19. Potter, op. cit., pp. 130-131.

20. Ibid., p. 131.

21. Mark Haller, *History of Organized Crime: 1920-1945*, Washington, D.C., National Institute on Law Enforcement and Criminal Justice, U.S. Government Printing Office, 1976.

22. Alan A. Block and William Chambliss, *Organizing Crime*, New York, Elsevier, 1981.

23. Erich Goode, *Drugs in American Society*, New York, McGraw-Hill, 1989.

24. President's Commission on Organized Crime, *Organized Crime and Gambling*, Washington, D.C., U.S. Government Printing Office, 1985.

25. Humbert S. Nelli, *The Business of Crime*, New York, Oxford, 1976.

26. Ovid Demaris, *The Boardwalk Jungle*, New York, Bantam, 1986.

27. James Cook, "The Invisible Enterprise," *Forbes*, September 29, 1980.

28. John Seidl, "Loan-sharking," in L. Savitz and N. Johnson, eds., *Crime in Society*, New York, Wiley, 1978.

29. Jonathan Rubenstein and Peter Reuter, *Bookmaking in New York*, New York, Policy Sciences Center, Inc., 1978.

30. Potter, op. cit., p. 91.

31. Alan A. Block and Frank R. Scarpitti, *Poisoning for Profit: The Mafia and Toxic Waste in America*, New York, Morrow, 1985.

32. Ralph Salerno, as cited in Alan A. Block, "Thoughts on the History of Organized Crime: In Praise of Revisionist Criminology," paper presented at the annual meeting of the American Society of Criminology, 1990, p. 16.

33. Dwight C. Smith, Jr., *The Mafia Mystique*, New York, Basic Books, 1975; and "Mafia: The Prototypical Alien

Conspiracy," *The Annals of the American Academy of Political and Social Science* 423: 75-88, January 1976.

34. Gordon Hawkins, "God and the Mafia," *The Public Interest* 14: 24-51, 1969; Kenney and Finckenauer, op. cit., pp. 230-250.

35. Ianni and Reuss-Ianni, op. cit.; Francis A.J. Ianni, *Ethnic Succession in Organized Crime*, Washington, D.C., U.S. Department of Justice, Law Enforcement Assistance Administration, December 1973.

36. Ianni, Ibid., p. 13.

37. Robert K. Merton, "Social Structure and Anomie," *American Sociological Review* 3: 672-682, 1938.

38. Smith, op. cit., 1980; Dwight C. Smith, Jr., "Organized Crime and Entrepreneurship," *International Journal of Criminology and Penology* 6: 161-177, 1978.

39. Peter Reuter, "The Value of a Bad Reputation," Santa Monica, CA, Rand Corporation, 1982.

40. Smith, op. cit., 1978.

41. Kenney and Finckenauer, op. cit., pp. 324-341.

42. Ibid., pp. 317-323.

43. Ibid., pp. 364-369.

44. Daniel Bell, *The End of Ideology*, Glencoe, IL, Free Press, 1964.

CHAPTER 34

Casinos and Banking: Organized Crime in the Bahamas

Alan A. Block ▪ Frank R. Scarpitti

Revenues derived by organized crime from its many illegal enterprises total billions of dollars each year. In many instances it is necessary to "clean" the "dirty" money by laundering it through a legitimate enterprise. Money laundering may be accomplished in a number of ways, but perhaps the most common technique is to invest in legitimate enterprises. Using its tainted money from drugs, prostitution, pornography, gambling, and other criminal activities, organized crime has invested in real estate, construction, entertainment, the food industry, and other areas of commerce. Often bringing their usual business tactics to these endeavors, crime syndicates gain an unfair advantage while corrupting entire markets.

In this selection Alan A. Block and Frank R. Scarpitti examine the relationship between offshore banks and gambling casinos in the Bahamas. Caribbean casinos have been used by U.S. organized crime figures to launder money since the 1940s, while being a source of new profits as well. Because many countries in that area have strict bank secrecy laws, local banks have also been established for the purpose of tax evasion. In the Bahamas, these interests merged as local developers and politicians worked to attract casinos through favorable legislation, especially regarding gambling and banking. The resort town of Freeport, for example, was developed

largely through the efforts of organized criminals and their business and government supporters.

The influence of organized crime on the Bahamas has been dramatic and long lasting. Government corruption has been noted by many commentators, and the islands of that nation continue to be used as a transshipment point for drug money from South to North America. Numerous investigations of the offshore banks have turned up cases of tax fraud and evasion by U.S. citizens. No island paradise is exempt from the effects of organized crime.

Within the past few years, both the President's Commission on Organized Crime and the U.S. Senate's Permanent Subcommittee on Investigations have reported on the extensive use of offshore banks and businesses by American criminal interests to launder money and evade taxes (Permanent Subcommittee on Investigations, 1983; President's Commission on Organized Crime, 1984). A recent government report "concludes that the use of so-called 'secret' offshore facilities has become so pervasive that it challenges basic assumptions regarding the ability of federal and state authorities to enforce the laws" (Permanent Subcommittee on Investigations, 1983:1). Such enterprises are established in tax haven countries around the world, but for a number of reasons, those in the Caribbean have grown fastest in recent years and now appear to control billions of dollars of illegally gained and untaxed money. Although the Caribbean's proximity to the United States makes it especially attractive to

Reprinted from: Alan A. Block and Frank R. Scarpitti, "Casinos and Banking: Organized Crime in the Bahamas." In *Deviant Behavior*, vol. 7, pp. 301–312. Copyright © 1986 by Taylor & Francis, Washington D.C. Reprinted by permission.

Americans wanting to hide money, its development as an important stop in the South American drug traffic and the fact that some countries have stringent bank secrecy laws also contribute to its contemporary popularity. In fact, a few Caribbean nations have been so corrupted by illegal foreign dollars that they have virtually offered themselves as crime havens (Permanent Subcommittee on Investigations, 1983:49-95).

Among the Caribbean nations active in hosting offshore enterprises owned by Americans have been the Bahamas. Like all tax havens, the Bahamas are characterized by the essential elements of strict rules of bank secrecy and little or no taxes. Since 1965 bank secrecy has been based on legislation which prohibits and punishes the disclosure by a bank employee of an account holder's name or financial situation (the 1965 legislation increased the severity of the crime of disclosure). The strict secrecy associated with banks also applies to the activities and ownership of corporations. In addition, there are no income, profit, capital gains, gift, inheritance, estate or withholding taxes in the Bahamas. Although the nation does tax imports and some real property, this has little effect on those who own or use its many banks and corporations. Hence, for a small initial cost and annual fee, one may own a bank or company that can receive and disburse large sums of money in complete secrecy and without the threat of taxation. These advantages, of course, are available to bank depositors as well.

Even though offshore tax havens may provide legitimate investment opportunities for American citizens wishing to avoid taxes, a practice recognized as lawful by U.S. courts, it is the evasion of taxes by using tax haven services that now concerns law enforcement authorities. "Tax evasion...involves acts intended to misrepresent or to conceal facts in an effort to escape lawful tax liability" (Workman, 1982:667). Tax havens may be used to hide income or to misrepresent the nature of transactions in order to put the taxpayer in a more favorable tax position. A corollary problem concerns the "laundering" of illegal money gained from strictly criminal activity. This "is the process by which one conceals the existence, illegal source, or illegal application of income, and then

disguises that income to make it appear legitimate" (President's Commission on Organized Crime, 1984:1). Off-shore tax havens, with their strict secrecy laws, dependence on foreign deposits, and disregard for the sources of overseas cash, provide ideal vehicles for assorted racketeers, drug dealers and financial manipulators to hide "dirty" money while it is being cleaned for further use. For both the tax evader and money launderer, the offshore haven guarantees that any paper trail will be blocked.

The popularity of the Bahamas as an offshore tax haven may be seen in the amount of corporate and bank activity which it hosts. This small island nation of just over 200,000 inhabitants has some 15,000 active companies and 330 chartered banks, or one bank for ever 600 residents (Lernoux, 1984: 85). Nevertheless, Bahamian banks held over $95 billion of foreign assets in 1978 (Workman, 1982:680) and a 1979 Ford Foundation study estimated that the flow of U.S. criminal and tax evasion money into the Bahamas was $20 billion per year (Blum and Kaplan, 1979).

Even though the accuracy of these figures may be questioned, due largely to the Bahamian government's and banking industry's reluctance to provide reliable data, it seems obvious that the American contribution to these questionable assets constitutes a considerable resource for the Bahamas and a substantial loss in taxes for the United States.

The Bahamas evolved into an offshore haven for tax evaders and money launderers in a very short period of time. The process included receptive public officials, international entrepreneurs and American racketeers entering into formal and informal relationships designed to serve their respective financial positions. A partial examination of the history of the Bahamas reveals the extent of the collusion among political, business, and criminal interests to serve their illicit purposes.

This history also demonstrates the important relationship between offshore banks and gambling casinos. In fact, key Bahamian offshore banks were formed by or for individuals deeply involved in Nevada casinos and who subsequently played big roles in developing the first large-scale, modern casinos in the Bahamas. Most likely, the relationship between the casinos and banks emerged in order to hide the casinos' "skim," that portion of casino profits unreported to taxing authorities. The historical material which follows discusses those individuals whose mutual interests embraced both casino gambling and haven banking and who were instrumental in providing organized criminal elements with both an economic bonanza and sanctuary.

The Making of Freeport

The process started on Grand Bahama Island located about 60 miles from the Florida coast. The prime mover on Grand Bahama was an American named Wallace Groves who first came to the Bahamas in the 1930's. Groves' background had been in investment trusts administered through a firm called Equity Corporation which he sold for $750,000. Following this, he became affiliated with a company known as the General Investment Corporation. After these deals were in place, Groves sailed to the Bahamas, started two Bahamian companies (Nassau Securities Ltd. and North American Ltd.), and purchased an island, Little Whale Cay, about 35 miles from Nassau, the capital of the country. During this first, eventful trip, Groves met Stafford Sands, a member of the local political elite known as the Bay Street Boys. This elite was composed of certain merchants and attorneys who met on a regular basis after work in a club located on Bay and Charlotte Streets in Nassau. They were invariably white and, by the standards of the Bahamas, wealthy and influential. The Bay Street Boys controlled Bahamian development, both the licit and illicit, until 1967 when the first black Prime Minister was elected (United Kingdom, 1971).

Unfortunately for Groves, in the late fall of 1938 he was indicted on numerous counts of mail fraud and looting the General Investment Corporation of almost one million dollars. Eventually, Groves was convicted and sentenced to two years in prison. He was released in 1944 and returned to the Bahamas. During Groves' time of troubles, his associate, Stafford Sands, was busy arranging a way for casinos to operate legally. Sands successfully

sponsored a bill in the Assembly which allowed casinos under certain circumstances. By securing a Certificate of Exemption from the local government, a gambling casino could operate with what amounted to a government license. The bill passed in 1939 and certificates of exemption were granted to two small casinos which had been operating illegally for years.[1]

It was in the 1950's that Groves, Sands, and others to be discussed shortly put their talents together on Grand Bahama Island. They created a new city, Freeport, which soon had a casino and several significant "haven" banks. Stafford Sands, who had become Chairman of the Bahamas Development Board (equivalent to Minister of Tourism) in the 1950's, crafted legislation "to establish a port and an industrial complex" on Grand Bahama Island (United Kingdom, 1971:6). The Hawksbill Creek Act, as the legislation was entitled, was signed on August 4, 1955. The deal called for Groves to "organize a company, to be called the Grand Bahama Port Authority Limited, which would undertake to dredge and construct a deep water harbour and turning basin at Hawksbill Creek as a preliminary aid for factories and other industrial undertakings to be set up there" (United Kingdom, 1971:6). In return, the government made available thousands of acres of Crown Land to the Port Authority for one pound per acre (equivalent then to around $2.80 an acre). In fact, by 1960 Groves' company had acquired a total of 138,296 acres which was officially "designated as a town (Freeport) in Grand Bahama" (United Kingdom, 1971:6).

The terms of the initial Hawksbill Creek Act allowed "that the whole of Freeport was to be the private property of the Port Authority in whom was vested the supreme right to its administration and control" (United Kingdom, 1971:16). An analysis of the legislation by a Royal Commission in 1971 commented on this extraordinary transfer of authority noting that the company had "exclusive responsibility" for traditional governmental services such as education, health, communications, energy "and all other public utilities and services and the performance of all aviation activities." The Commission also wrote that no one was allowed to interfere with the Port Authority's decisions, especially in awarding licenses or otherwise controlling firms doing business in Freeport.

The major shareholders of The Grand Bahama Port Authority in 1959 included Wallace Groves and his wife, Georgette, who individually held a small amount of shares but whose company, Abaco Lumber, held almost one million. Other significant owners were Variant Industries which represented the interests of Charles W. Hayward, an English entrepreneur, and held just over one half million shares; Charles Allen, whose family's financial interests in New York and Hollywood (especially motion picture companies) were very extensive and who held over a quarter million shares; Arthur Rubloff, a Chicago real estate agent, who had over 70,000 shares; and Charles C. Goldsmith, who owned about 100,000 shares and listed his affiliation in 1959 as the New York Cosmos Bank. Wallace Groves was the company's Director and Charles Hayward and his son, Jack, were other important officers (Grand Bahama Port Authority, 1959). Although Allen and Goldsmith appeared to play no managerial role in the company, they "were well aware that the major partner in the enterprise…was…a convicted stock manipulator who had served time in federal prison for mail fraud and conspiracy" (McClintick, 1982:89).

Even with his new financiers, Groves' project was barely limping along in 1960. Because the industrial development of Freeport was extremely far off, perhaps far-fetched, Groves and others decided that Freeport could best be developed around tourism. Hence, an amendment to the original Hawksbill Creek Act was enacted which, among other things, allowed the Port Authority to build a "first-class deluxe resort hotel" (United Kingdom, 1971:7). By the time the hotel was completed in 1963, it had the added attraction of a casino, and the Bahamas had become the new Caribbean headquarters of Meyer Lansky's underworld gambling enterprise.

Lansky had operated in the Caribbean for quite some time, of course, running casinos in Cuba with the full cooperation of that country's government. With the overthrow of Battista, however, American organized crime figures and their gambling operations were no longer welcomed and were soon thrown out of the country by Fidel Castro. Even

before that actually happened, Lansky was looking around for another site in the Caribbean, a place where tourists from the United States would come for the sun and the gambling, where local officials would be cooperative, and where he could establish a worldwide gambling empire (Messick, 1971: 225). The Bahamas appeared to be the ideal spot.

According to Lansky biographer, Hank Messick, the gambling czar moved quickly once he decided to seek additional fortunes in the Bahamas. Early in 1960 he dispatched an associate, Louis Chesler, to the islands to meet with Groves and Sands, presumably to discuss plans by which the Port Authority would be salvaged and gambling established in Freeport (Messick, 1971:228). In order to accomplish the first part of the plan, the Port Authority formed a company called Grand Bahama Development Corporation (known as DEVCO). DEVCO immediately placed Chesler on its Board of Directors, giving him an official position in the Bahamas from which he could supervise the development of casino gambling. Another Lansky associate, Max Orovitz, was also placed on the DEVCO board (Grand Bahama Development Corporation, 1964). But it was Chesler who would protect Lansky's interests and serve as a dominant force in the early development of Bahamian gambling.

Chesler's earliest known contacts with organized crime began in 1942 when he had as partners in several businesses John Pullman and Pullman's brother-in-law. A.C. Cowan (McClintick, 1982: 87–93). Pullman, an important associate of Meyer Lansky for a number of decades, had served a prison term for bootlegging in the early 1930's. By the mid-1950's, Pullman had moved to Canada and been granted Canadian citizenship (Charbonneau, 1976). Chesler, also Canadian, had a series of dealings with Lansky and Lansky's associates prior to the formation of DEVCO which are revealing. He hired, for instance, a key Lansky operative, Mike McLaney, as the manager of a Miami Beach dinner club which Chesler owned.

In 1958, Chesler's association with Lansky became more visible through the financial machinations of Maxwell Golhar, another of his partners. Golhar became Chairman of the Board of an enterprise called New Mylamaque Explorations

Ltd. A well-known Lansky associate, Sam Garfield, purchased 100,000 shares of New Mylamaque which he divided in the following manner: Edward Levinson, 50,000 shares; Moe Dalitz, former Cleveland racketeer, 25,000; and Allard Roen, 25,000. Roen's shares were then divided further with Ben Siegelbaum receiving 15,000 and Meyer Lansky 10,000. Finally, 50,000 more shares of New Mylamaque were parceled out, with 10,000 going to Dalitz, 15,000 to Siegelbaum, and 25,000 to Lansky. This same group of investors also provided capital for Miami's new international airport hotel in 1958. Other investors in the hotel (brought in by Lansky and Chesler) were Bryant B. Burton, connected to the Sands and Freemont Hotels in Las Vegas, and Jack Cooper, who owned a highly successful dog track in Miami (New York State Senate, n.d.a.).

With the formation of DEVCO there was only one hurdle left to transform Freeport into a center for casino gambling run by organized crime. That hurdle was acquiring the necessary Certificate of Exemption. The second Certificate ever granted in the Bahamas was offered on March 27, 1963, to a new company called Bahamas Amusement Ltd., which had been formed only the previous week. The Certificate allowed Bahamas Amusement to operate a casino at the Lucayan Beach Hotel in Freeport. In order to secure the Certificate a considerable amount of money had been passed to key members of the government by DEVCO. Stafford Sands acted as the financial intermediary between DEVCO and Sands' political cronies who were hired as "consultants" and paid very handsome fees (United Kingdom, 1967). The original directors of Bahamas Amusement included Chesler, Georgette Groves, and a member of the Hayward family.

Less than a week after the Certificate was granted, there were meetings attended by Meyer Lansky and his brother, Jake, Lou Chesler, Max Orovitz, and others to discuss issues concerning both the hotel and the casino, called the Monte Carlo. A number of important Lansky racketeers were hired to work in the casino, including Dino Cellini, George Saldo, Charles Brudner, Max Courtney, and Frank Ritter. Other subjects discussed at this time included the purchase of casino equipment from Las Vegas and probably the Beverly Hills Club in Newport, Kentucky, and the establishing of a casino training school in London, England (United Kingdom, 1967; Messick, 1971; Block and Klausner, 1985-86). About ten months after the Certificate was granted, the hotel and casino formally opened with the Lansky men firmly entrenched in casino management as well as overseers of all credit arrangements.

Bahamian Banks

Let us now turn to those banks formed by or for individuals with multi-million dollar investments in Nevada casinos and deeply involved in the Freeport development. John Pullman, mentioned above as a Chesler associate since 1942 and, in effect, an important member of Meyer Lansky's organized crime syndicate, was responsible for putting the banks and casinos together. Pullman, recently identified as a "Canadian organized crime figure" (Pennsylvania Crime Commission, 1980: 195), was instrumental in forming two banks (with subsequent numerous off-shoots) created to handle the skim from the Monte Carlo and most likely the Sands and Frontier casinos in Nevada (New York State Senate, n.d.a).

The bank connected to the Monte Carlo was the International Credit Bank (ICB) which was formed by John Pullman in partnership with Dr. Tibor Rosenbaum (New York State Senate, n.d.c). The bank was located in Geneva, Switzerland, with branches in the Bahamas. The major shareholder was a trust (international Credit Trust) resident in Vaduz, Lichtenstein. At least part of the Monte Carlo skim undoubtedly traveled from the casino to the Bahamian branch of Pullman's ICB, then to Switzerland, and ultimately to the obscurity of Lichtenstein. Other more direct but clumsy avenues for the skim no doubt existed. For instance, a Royal Commission reported that "large quantities of cash up to $60,000, and in one case $120,000, were being despatched by the Amusements Company to the Marine Midland Grace Trust Co., of New York. They were being parceled up in Pauli Girl beer cartons" (United Kingdom, 1967:19).

Although formed as a conduit for unreported casino profits, the ICB quickly developed additional interests. One of the early major clients for ICB Geneva, for example, was Investor Overseas Services, the infamous mutual fund operation run by Bernard Cornfeld and later looted by Robert Vesco. The relationship between the fund and the bank became exceptionally close when ICB people were used to smuggle money out of various countries into Switzerland on behalf of mutual fund clients. One of the principal ICB money couriers, Sylvain Ferdman, was identified as an organized crime money mover by Life magazine in 1967. Ferdman performed the same function for another Bahamian bank called Atlas Bank. Actually, Ferdman and Dr. Rosenbaum were two of the directors of Atlas. A close scrutiny of both Atlas and ICB indicates they were virtually identical in ownership, management and function. Furthermore, there is some evidence to suggest that ICB and Atlas, which both had several branches or permutations, were also linked to another bank located in Beirut, Lebanon, which, in turn, appeared to own a major Lebanese casino (*Fortune*, 1966:93).

The ICB and Atlas banks are two primary examples of the links between organized crime gamblers and the offshore banking industry put together in the Bahamas. Another major example involving the same cast was the Bank of World Commerce, formed on September 21, 1961, most likely to launder the skim from Nevada casinos (New York State Senate, n.d.c; Wall Street Journal, 1976). John Pullman was the president and director, while the former Lieutenant Governor of Nevada, Clifford A. Jones, was one of the larger shareholders, holding about 8% of the total. The other directors included Alvin I. Malnik and Philip J. Matthews who owned about 32 percent of the shares.

Malnik was believed to have been one of Meyer Lansky's closest associates and, when Lansky died in 1982, some speculated that Malnik may have inherited much of Lansky's action (New York State Senate, n.d.a). In 1980, the Pennsylvania Crime Commission detailed a series of shady transactions involving Caesars World, Inc., which owned casinos in Las Vegas and Atlantic City, and "Alvin I. Malnik and Samuel Cohen, who have ties to Meyer Lansky, a major financial advisor to organized criminals" (Pennsylvania Crime Commission,

1980:252). The Crime Commission also stated that "Vincent Teresa, a former Cosa Nostra capo, said that, in the underworld, dealing with Malnik is the same as dealing with Lansky and that the purpose of Malnik's association with Lansky is to launder illegal cash by investing it in real estate" (Pennsylvania Crime Commission, 1980:252). Other reports cited by the Crime Commission had Malnick with Lansky and members of the Carlo Gambino crime syndicate discussing "the construction and/or ownership of two or three casinos in Florida if a gambling referendum passed. Some $20 million to $25 million was to be invested in the casinos and profits were to be skimmed off the top and channeled back to the investors" (Pennsylvania Crime Commission, 1980:255).

The relationships among Malnik, Pullman, and Matthews (the largest single shareholder in the bank) preceded the formation of the Bank of World Commerce (New York State Senate, n.d.c). Several years earlier, Malnik and Matthews had been involved with two closely connected firms, including one called Allied Empire, Inc. When the Bank of World Commerce started, Allied Empire showed up as a shareholder and then as the recipient of a large loan from the new bank. Furthermore, Malnik, Matthews and a former racketeer associate of Louis Buchalter (executed by the State of New York in 1944 for murder) had worked together long before the founding of the Bank of World Commerce to purchase a small, "brass plate," Bahamian bank from one of Lou Chesler's associates.

Chesler, Pullman, Lansky, Malnik, Matthews, and other gamblers and racketeers from New York, Miami, Newport, Kentucky, Montreal, Toronto, Las Vegas, and Los Angeles formed both gambling casinos and offshore Bahamian banks, the latter to solve the problem of "washing" the money generated by the former. Stock manipulators like Wallace Groves, allied with well-known financiers from the United States and the United Kingdom, organized crime figures, and, of course, important local politicians, turned Grand Bahama Island into an experimental station for money gathering and laundering. To help the scheme along, the Bahamian government actually relinquished part of its sovereign territory to this mixed group.

Some Consequences

The impact the developers had on the original inhabitants of Grand Bahama Island was hardly beneficial. Prior to the Bahamian government's enacting the Hawksbill Creek Agreement, the island was described by a Royal Commission as nothing more than "a pine barren with less than 5,000 inhabitants" (United Kingdom, 1971:5). After the Agreement and the building of Freeport, most of the island remained a pine barren with the exception of the area around Freeport which the Royal Commission found to be "predominantly non-Bahamian" (United Kingdom, 1971: 31). Bahamians made up only 34 percent of the population of Freeport in 1968, as compared with about 84 percent on New Providence Island where the capital, Nassau, is situated. And although some held DEVCO's many construction projects to be a benefactor for Bahamian labor, in fact DEVCO turned to Haiti for a supply of cheap labor whenever it could. Through 1968, the percent of Haitians in Freeport was over four times that of New Providence Island (United Kingdom, 1971:31). The Port Authority, of course, contributed to the pattern of exploitation engaged in by its creation, DEVCO. About 30 percent of the licenses granted by the Port Authority to people wishing to do business in its part of Grand Bahama went to non-Bahamians (United Kingdom, 1971:33).

The combination of Certificates of Exemption, bank secrecy laws, and the Hawksbill Creek Agreement set more than Freeport into motion. It stamped the Bahamas as a center for organized crime activities. Indeed, as we noted earlier, the Bahamas has been recognized as one of the principal transshipment points for drug traffickers moving cocaine and marijuana from South America to the U.S. and Canada (Royal Canadian Mounted Police, 1983:42-46). In one recent narcotics case, the defendants were charged with buying and using "the Darby Islands, a group of five islands in the Bahamas, as a trans-shipment point," and using Bahamian companies including banks and a major Bahamian Trust Company to launder their money (U.S. District Court, 1981). In another case, an officer of the Columbus Trust Company, Nassau, has been charged with using the trust company, a

Bahamian corporation named Dundee Securities, Barclays Bank International (The Bahamas), and the Southeast First National Bank of Miami in a complicated scheme to wash millions of dollars for a drug syndicate (U.S. District Court, 1980).

The symbiotic relationships among casinos, offshore banks and professional criminals are complex, to say the least. In numerous contemporary cases, professional criminals utilize both casinos and banks to launder money. An IRS Special Agent reporting on a major drug and tax case gave an example of this as he detailed how a financial services corporation served drug racketeers. The "laundering" method included (1) exchanging the smugglers's initial small denomination cash (mostly tens and twenties) for $100 bills in a Las Vegas casino; (2) moving the new "casino" money from the U.S. to offshore banks and depositing it in secret accounts; (3) returning the money to the U.S. "disguised as offshore loans"; and (4) investing the phony loans in businesses through blind trusts and fictitious corporate fronts (U.S. District Court, n.d.).

Even without the use of offshore banks, casinos themselves perform many clandestine banking services for professional criminals. Drug Enforcement Administrator, Gary D. Liming, testified that casinos "exchange small bills for large bills, travelers' checks or money orders; wire transfer money overseas to associate casinos; provide safety deposit boxes; and make loans…without being required to report the transactions to the Department of the Treasury" (Judiciary Committee, 1984:8-9). Casinos, therefore, are acting like offshore banks providing anonymity for depositors (players) and various "laundering" options. Consequently, there are enforcement agents who are convinced that certain casinos have been built solely to launder the proceeds of drug transactions.[2]

However, long before the full potential of casinos working either alone or with offshore banks and other shady financial institutions was realized by drug traffickers, developers in the Bahamas had started the process of bringing casinos and banks together. Within less than a decade, the groundwork for organized crime's penetration of the Bahamas was established. Networks of banks, trust companies, holding companies, casinos, hotels, marinas, mutual funds, and so on representing illicit interests all across the U.S. and many other countries were, and most importantly remain, paramount.

Discussion Questions

1. What is money laundering? How does it affect our tax base? How does it affect our government's ability to enforce the law? What characteristics of a country make it a favorable place to launder money? What makes the Caribbean such an attractive money laundering location?
2. What is the relationship between the Bahamas and Nevada casinos? How does the relationship benefit the casinos? How does the relationship benefit the Bahamas?
3. What was the Hawksbill Creek Act? What was its stated purpose? What rights of authority did it confer upon the company (the Grand Bahama Port Authority)? How did gambling begin in Freeport? Why?

Notes

1. The two illegal casinos included one opened by American Frank Reid for private membership in 1920. By 1923, Reid's club was joined by another called the Bahamian Club, run by a gambler known as Honest John Kelly. Over the course of the Prohibition Era, the Bahamian Club was managed first by Kelly, then Herbert McGuire, and then purchased by Willard McKenzie and Frank Dineen. Like all Bahamian tourist-supported establishments, it was only open during the three winter months when the wealthy arrived to escape the seasonal rigors. At least one other casino was opened during Prohibition. On a privately-owned island close by the Bahamian fishing resort of Bimini, New Yorker Louis Wasey opened a private membership casino called the Cat Cay Club. Authors' interviews conducted in the Bahamas, 1984.
2. Authors' interview with Special Agent, Department of Labor, June, 1985.

References

Block, Alan A. and Patricia Klausner. 1985-86. "Masters of Paradise Island, part 1: Organized Crime, Neo-Colonialism and the Bahamas." *Dialectical Anthropology*. Winter.

Blum, Richard and John Kaplan. 1979. "Offshore Banking: Issues With Respect to Criminal Use." Report submitted to the Ford Foundation.

Charbonneau, Jean-Pierre. 1976. *The Canadian Connection*. Montreal: Optimum Publishing Company.

Fortune. 1966. "Business Around the Globe." 77: 93-99.

Grand Bahama Development Corporation. 1964. Letter to the Registrar in the Bahama Registry.

Grand Bahama Port Authority. 1959. "Annual Report." Bahamas Registry.

Judiciary Committee. 1984. U.S. House of Representatives. "Statement of Gary D. Liming on Casino Money Laundering." Washington, D.C.: Government Printing Office.

Lernoux, Penny. 1984. *In Banks We Trust*. New York: Anchor/Doubleday.

McClintick, David. 1982. *Indecent Exposure: A True Story of Hollywood and Wall Street*. New York: Dell.

Messick, Hank. 1971. *Lansky*. New York: Putnam.

New York State Senate. n.d.a. Select Committee on Crime. Bahamian File: Lansky Folder.

——. n.d.b. Select Committee on Crime. Bahamian File: ICB Folder.

——. n.d.c. Select Committee on Crime. Bahamian File: Bank of World Commerce Folder.

Pennsylvania Crime Commission. 1980. *A Decade of Organized Crime: 1980 Report*. Commonwealth of Pennsylvania.

Permanent Subcommittee on Investigation. 1983. Committee on Government Affairs, U.S. Senate. *Crime and Secrecy: The Use of Offshore Banks and Companies*. Washington, D.C.: Government Printing Office.

President's Commission on Organized Crime. 1984. *The Cash Connection: Organized Crime, Financial Institutions, and Money Laundering*. Interim Report to the President and the Attorney General.

Royal Canadian Mounted Police. 1983. *National Drug Intelligence Estimate*, 1982. Ottawa: Minister of Supply and Services.

U.S. District Court. 1980. Western District of Pennsylvania, Indictment. *U.S. Versus Thomas E. Long*, et al.

——. n.d. Southern District of Mississippi. Affidavit for Search Warrant, *U.S. Versus Offices and Premises of Red Carpet Inns International*, Biloxi, Mississippi.

United Kingdom. 1967. Commission on Inquiry into the Operation of the Business of Casinos in Freeport and in Nassau. Report published in the Nassau Guardian.

——. 1971. Royal Commission Appointed on the Recommendation of the Bahamas Government to Review the Hawksbill Creek Agreement. Report, Volume 1. Her Majesty's Stationery Office.

Wall Street Journal. 1976. "Empire Builder." December 15.

Workman, Douglas J. 1982. "The Use of Offshore Tax Havens for the Purpose of Criminally Evading Income Taxes." *The Journal of Criminal Law and Criminology* 73:675-706.

CHAPTER 35

Denying the Guilty Mind

Michael L. Benson

Multimillion-dollar corporate scandals, such as the Enron catastrophe, have helped sway public opinion toward intensifying regulation of white-collar crime in recent years. The movement toward "getting tough" on white-collar crime, no doubt, is driven by raised awareness of massive victimization resulting from gross corporate wrongdoing. Although media-driven attention to corporate America's criminality has come to characterize contemporary notions of white-collar crime, smaller and much more frequent everyday economic workplace offenses constitute the real bulk of white-collar crime.

The following well-known study by Michael L. Benson provides an overview of the types of everyday white-collar offenders and how they, in their own words, describe and interpret their offenses. Of particular importance is Benson's attention to how offenders attempt to justify their actions through transfer of responsibility and blame to other individuals and employers (i.e., techniques of neutralization).

The present study treats the accounts given by a sample of convicted white-collar offenders, focusing specifically on the techniques they use to deny their own criminality. The emphasis is on general patterns and regularities in the data. The central research question is: How do convicted white-collar offenders account for their

Reprinted from: *Criminology* 23, No. 4, 1985, 583–607. Reprinted by permission of the American Society of Criminology and the author.

adjudication as criminals? While researchers have frequently expressed outrage at the denial of criminality that is thought to be typical of white-collar criminals, few attempts have been made to understand how this process occurs or to relate it to general deviance theory. Rather, researchers have all too often concentrated on morally condemning offenders (Clinard and Yeager 1978).

Over 30 years ago, Sutherland (1949:222, 225) wrote,

> Businessmen develop rationalizations which conceal the fact of crime.... Even when they violate the law, they do not conceive of themselves as criminals.... Businessmen fight whenever words that tend to break down this rationalization are used.

This view of white-collar offenders has continued to the present day (Geis 1982; Meier and Geis 1982). Indeed, failure to confront and penetrate the rationalizations used by white-collar offenders and to get beyond a sympathetic view of the individual offender is considered by some to be one of the reasons for the continued widespread prevalence of white-collar crimes (Geis 1982: 55–57; Meier and Geis 1982:98). In addition, others have argued that the leniency with which white-collar criminals are treated by the justice system derives in part from their ability to evoke sympathy from judges (Conklin 1977).

The Study

This study is based primarily on interviews conducted with a sample of 30 convicted white-collar offenders. The interviews were supplemented by an examination of the files maintained on 80 white-collar offenders and by further interviews with federal probation officers, federal judges, Assistant U.S. Attorneys, and defense attorneys specializing in white-collar cases.

The sample of interviewed offenders was essentially self-selected. A letter which introduced the researcher and described the nature of the study was sent to most of the 80 offenders in the sample.[1] The letter indicated that the researcher was interested in the subject's impressions of the way in which his case was handled and in the effect that conviction had on his self-image and life prospects.[2] Offenders were assured that their remarks would not be attributable to them as individuals. The proposed interviews would be open-ended and unstructured.

In light of the small and nonrandom nature of the sample, the results reported here must be viewed as provisional. There are no systematic differences between the offenders who agreed to be interviewed and those who did not in terms of their social and offense characteristics, but there is some likelihood that the interviewees differed psychologically or experientially from those who refused to participate.

The letter inviting participation in the study was sent from the Probation Office, and it is possible that some offenders viewed their participation as a way of ingratiating themselves with their respective probation officers. They also may have felt under some coercion to participate in the study. While these potential sources of bias cannot be completely ruled out, it is the researcher's impression that most of the interviewees agreed to participate because they welcomed an opportunity to express their views on the criminal justice system in a confidential and nonjudgmental forum.

In the interviews no attempt was made to challenge the explanations or rationalizations given by offenders regarding their offenses. Rather, offenders were encouraged to talk of themselves and their feelings regarding the case and they were allowed to focus on the aspects they considered to be most important. This approach was followed for two reasons: first, the sensitive nature of the subject matter under discussion did not permit the use of an interrogatory or inquisitorial style. The emotional trauma wrought by conviction was, indeed, evident in many of the interviews and, considering the voluntary nature of the interviews, to challenge the subjects seemed insensitive and unnecessary. Second, the goal of the study was not to determine how strong the rationalizations were, nor was it to bring about a "rehabilitative" awareness in the offender of the criminality of past acts. Rather, it was to determine how offenders account for their actions to themselves and to significant others, who it is assumed are unlikely to challenge or refute their explanations.

The Offenders

For the purposes of this study, white-collar offenders were those convicted of economic offenses committed through the use of indirection, fraud, or collusion (Shapiro 1980). The offenses represented in the sample are those that are usually thought of as presumptively white-collar offenses, such as securities and exchange fraud, antitrust violations, embezzlement, false claims and statements, and tax violations. In terms of socioeconomic status, the sample ranges from a formerly successful practitioner of international law to a man currently self-employed as a seller of jewelry trinkets. For some offenders, particularly licensed professionals and those employed in the public sector, conviction was accompanied by loss of occupation and other major changes in life-style. For others, such as businessmen and those employed in the private sector, conviction was not accompanied by collateral disabilities other than the expense and trauma of criminal justice processing (Benson 1984).

Denying the Guilty Mind

In court, defense lawyers are fond of presenting white-collar offenders as having suffered enough by virtue of the humiliation of public adjudication as criminals. On the other hand, prosecutors present them as cavalier individuals who arrogantly ignore the law and brush off its weak efforts to stigmatize them as criminals. Neither of these stereotypes is entirely accurate. The subjective effects of conviction on white-collar offenders are varied and complex. One suspects that this is true of all offenders, not only white-collar offenders.

The emotional responses of offenders to conviction have not been the subject of extensive research. However, insofar as an individual's emotional response to adjudication may influence the deterrent or crime-reinforcing impact of punishment on him or her, further study might reveal why some offenders stop their criminal behavior while others go on to careers in crime (Casper 1978:80).

Although the offenders displayed a variety of different emotions with respect to their experiences, they were nearly unanimous in denying basic criminality. To see how white-collar offenders justify and excuse their crimes, we turn to their accounts. The small number of cases rules out the use of any elaborate classification techniques. Nonetheless, it is useful to group offenders by offense when presenting their interpretations.

Antitrust Violators

Four of the offenders had been convicted of antitrust violations, all in the same case involving the building and contracting industry. Four major themes characterized their accounts. First, antitrust offenders focused on the everyday character and historical continuity of their offenses.

> It was a way of doing business before we even got into the business. So it was like why do you brush your teeth in the morning or something.... It was part of the everyday.... It was a method of survival.

The offenders argued that they were merely following established and necessary industry practices. These practices were presented as being necessary for the well-being of the industry as a whole, not to mention their own companies. Further, they argued that cooperation among competitors was either allowed or actively promoted by the government in other industries and professions.

The second theme emphasized by the offenders was the characterization of their actions as blameless. They admitted talking to competitors and admitted submitting intentionally noncompetitive bids. However, they presented these practices as being done not for the purpose of rigging prices nor to make exorbitant profits. Rather, the everyday

practices of the industry required them to occasionally submit bids on projects they really did not want to have. To avoid the effort and expense of preparing full-fledged bids, they would call a competitor to get a price to use. Such a situation might arise, for example, when a company already had enough work for the time being, but was asked by a valued customer to submit a bid anyway.

> All you want to do is show a bid, so that in some cases it was for as small a reason as getting your deposit back on the plans and specs. So you just simply have no interest in getting the job and just call to see if you can find someone to give you a price to use, so that you didn't have to go through the expense of an entire bid preparation. Now that is looked on very unfavorably, and it is a technical violation, but it was strictly an opportunity to keep your name in front of a desired customer. Or you may find yourself in a situation where somebody is doing work for a customer, has done work for many, many years and is totally acceptable, totally fair. There is no problem. But suddenly they (the customer) get an idea that they ought to have a few tentative figures, and you're called in, and you are in a moral dilemma. There's really no reason for you to attempt to compete in that circumstance. And so there was a way to back out.

Managed in this way, an action that appears on the surface to be a straightforward and conscious violation of antitrust regulations becomes merely a harmless business practice that happens to be a "technical violation." The offender can then refer to his personal history to verify his claim that, despite technical violations, he is in reality a law-abiding person. In the words of one offender, "Having been in the business for 33 years, you don't just automatically become a criminal overnight."

Third, offenders were very critical of the motives and tactics of prosecutors. Prosecutors were accused of being motivated solely by the opportunity for personal advancement presented by winning a big case. Further, they were accused of employing prosecution selectively and using tactics that allowed the most culpable offenders to go free. The Department of Justice was painted as using antitrust prosecutions for political purposes.

The fourth theme emphasized by the antitrust offenders involved a comparison between their crimes and the crimes of street criminals. Antitrust offenses differ in their mechanics from street crimes in that they are not committed in one place and at one time. Rather, they are spatially and temporally diffuse and are intermingled with legitimate behavior. In addition, the victims of antitrust offenses tend not to be identifiable individuals, as is the case with most street crimes. These characteristics are used by antitrust violators to contrast their own behavior with that of common stereotypes of criminality. Real crimes are pictured as discrete events that have beginnings and ends and involve individuals who directly and purposely victimize someone else in a particular place and at a particular time.

> It certainly wasn't a premeditated type of thing in our cases as far as I can see…. To me it's different than —— and I sitting down and we plan, well, we're going to rob this bank tomorrow and premeditatedly go in there…. That wasn't the case at all…. It wasn't like sitting down and planning I'm going to rob this bank type of thing…. It was just a common everyday way of doing business and surviving.

A consistent thread running through all of the interviews was the necessity for antitrust-like practices, given the realities of the business world. Offenders seemed to define the situation in such a manner that two sets of rules could be seen to apply. On the one hand, there are the legislatively determined rules—laws—which govern how one is to conduct one's business affairs. On the other hand, there is a higher set of rules based on the concepts of profit and survival, which are taken to define what it means to be in business in a capitalistic society. These rules do not just regulate behavior; rather, they constitute or create the behavior in question. If one is not trying to make a profit or trying to keep one's business going, then one is not really "in business." Following Searle (1969:33-41), the former type of rule can be called a regulative rule and the latter type a constitutive rule. In certain situations, one may have to violate a regulative rule in order to conform to the more basic constitutive rule of the activity in which one is engaged.

This point can best be illustrated through the use of an analogy involving competitive games.

Trying to win is a constitutive rule of competitive games in the sense that if one is not trying to win, one is not really playing the game. In competitive games, situations may arise where a player deliberately breaks the rules even though he knows or expects he will be caught. In the game of basketball, for example, a player may deliberately foul an opponent to prevent him from making a sure basket. In this instance, one would understand that the fouler was trying to win by gambling that the opponent would not make the free throws. The player violates the rule against fouling in order to follow the higher rule of trying to win.

Trying to make a profit or survive in business can be thought of as a constitutive rule of capitalist economies. The laws that govern *how* one is allowed to make a profit are regulative rules, which can understandably be subordinated to the rules of trying to survive and profit. From the offender's point of view, he is doing what businessmen in our society are supposed to do—that is, stay in business and make a profit. Thus, an individual who violates society's laws or regulations in certain situations may actually conceive of himself as thereby acting more in accord with the central ethos of his society than if he had been a strict observer of its law. One might suggest, following Denzin (1977), that for businessmen in the building and contracting industry, an informal structure exists below the articulated legal structure, one which frequently supersedes the legal structure. The informal structure may define as moral and "legal" certain actions that the formal legal structure defines as immoral and "illegal."

Tax Violators

Six of the offenders interviewed were convicted of income tax violations. Like antitrust violators, tax violators can rely upon the complexity of the tax laws and an historical tradition in which cheating on taxes is not really criminal. Tax offenders would claim that everybody cheats somehow on their taxes and present themselves as victims of an unlucky break, because they got caught.

> Everybody cheats on their income tax, 95% of the people. Even if it's for ten dollars it's the same

principle. I didn't cheat. I just didn't know how to report it.

The widespread belief that cheating on taxes is endemic helps to lend credence to the offender's claim to have been singled out and to be no more guilty than most people.

Tax offenders were more likely to have acted as individuals rather than as part of a group and, as a result, were more prone to account for their offenses by referring to them as either mistakes or the product of special circumstances. Violations were presented as simple errors which resulted from ignorance and poor recordkeeping. Deliberate intention to steal from the government for personal benefit was denied.

> I didn't take the money. I have no bank account to show for all this money, where all this money is at that I was supposed to have. They never found the money, ever. There is no Swiss bank account, believe me.
>
> My records were strictly one big mess. That's all it was. If only I had an accountant, this wouldn't even of happened. No way in God's creation would this ever have happened.

Other offenders would justify their actions by admitting that they were wrong while painting their motives as altruistic rather than criminal. Criminality was denied because they did not set out to deliberately cheat the government for their own personal gain. Like the antitrust offenders discussed above, one tax violator distinguished between his own crime and the crimes of real criminals.

> I'm not a criminal. That is, I'm not a criminal from the standpoint of taking a gun and doing this and that. I'm a criminal from the standpoint of making a mistake, a serious mistake.... The thing that really got me involved in it is my feeling for the employees here, certain employees that are my right hand. In order to save them a certain amount of taxes and things like that, I'd extend money to them in cash, and the money came from these sources that I took it from. You know, cash sales and things of that nature, but practically all of it was turned over to the employees, because of my feeling for them.

All of the tax violators pointed out that they had no intention of deliberately victimizing the government. None of them denied the legitimacy of

the tax laws, nor did they claim that they cheated because the government is not representative of the people (Conklin 1977:99). Rather, as a result of ignorance or for altruistic reasons, they made decisions which turned out to be criminal when viewed from the perspective of the law. While they acknowledged the technical criminality of their actions, they tried to show that what they did was not criminally motivated.

Violations of Financial Trust

Four offenders were involved in violations of financial trust. Three were bank officers who embezzled or misapplied funds, and the fourth was a union official who embezzled from a union pension fund. Perhaps because embezzlement is one crime in this sample that can be considered *mala in se,* these offenders were much more forthright about their crimes. Like the other offenders, the embezzlers would not go so far as to say "I am a criminal," but they did say "What I did was wrong, was criminal, and I knew it was." Thus, the embezzlers were unusual in that they explicitly admitted responsibility for their crimes. Two of the offenders clearly fit Cressey's scheme as persons with financial problems who used their positions to convert other people's money to their own use.

Unlike tax evasion, which can be excused by reference to the complex nature of tax regulations or antitrust violations, which can be justified as for the good of the organization as a whole, embezzlement requires deliberate action on the part of the offender and is almost inevitably committed for personal reasons. The crime of embezzlement, therefore, cannot be accounted for by using the same techniques that tax violators or antitrust violators do. The act itself can only be explained by showing that one was under extraordinary circumstances which explain one's uncharacteristic behavior. Three of the offenders referred explicitly to extraordinary circumstances and presented the offense as an aberration in their life history. For example, one offender described his situation in this manner:

> As a kid, I never even—you know kids will sometimes shoplift from the dime store—I never even did that. I had never stolen a thing in my life and

that was what was so unbelieveable about the whole thing, but there were some psychological and personal questions that I wasn't dealing with very well. I wasn't terribly happily married. I was married to a very strong-willed woman and it just wasn't working out.

The offender in this instance goes on to explain how, in an effort to impress his wife, he lived beyond his means and fell into debt.

A structural characteristic of embezzlement also helps the offender demonstrate his essential lack of criminality. Embezzlement is integrated into ordinary occupational routines. The illegal action does not stand out clearly against the surrounding set of legal actions. Rather, there is a high degree of surface correspondence between legal and illegal behavior. To maintain this correspondence, the offender must exercise some restraint when committing his crime. The embezzler must be discrete in his stealing; he cannot take all of the money available to him without at the same time revealing the crime. Once exposed, the offender can point to this restraint on his part as evidence that he is not really a criminal. That is, he can compare what happened with what could have happened in order to show how much more serious the offense could have been if he was really a criminal at heart.

> What I could have done if I had truly had a devious criminal mind and perhaps if I had been a little smarter—and I am not saying that with any degree of pride or any degree of modesty whatever, [as] it's being smarter in a bad, an evil way—I could have pulled this off on a grander scale and I might still be doing it.

Even though the offender is forthright about admitting his guilt, he makes a distinction between himself and someone with a truly "devious criminal mind."

Contrary to Cressey's (1953:57–66) findings, none of the embezzlers claimed that their offenses were justified because they were underpaid or badly treated by their employers. Rather, attention was focused on the unusual circumstances surrounding the offense and its atypical character when compared to the rest of the offender's life. This strategy is for the most part determined by

the mechanics and organizational format of the offense itself. Embezzlement occurs within the organization but not for the organization. It cannot be committed accidentally or out of ignorance. It can be accounted for only by showing that the actor "was not himself" at the time of the offense or was under such extraordinary circumstances that embezzlement was an understandable response to an unfortunate situation. This may explain the finding that embezzlers tend to produce accounts that are viewed as more sufficient by the justice system than those produced by other offenders (Rothman and Gandossy 1982). The only plausible option open to a convicted embezzler trying to explain his offense is to admit responsibility while justifying the action, an approach that apparently strikes a responsive chord with judges.

Fraud and False Statements

Ten offenders were convicted of some form of fraud or false statements charge. Unlike embezzlers, tax violators, or antitrust violators, these offenders were much more likely to deny committing any crime at all. Seven of the ten claimed that they, personally, were innocent of any crime, although each admitted that fraud had occurred. Typically, they claimed to have been set up by associates and to have been wrongfully convicted by the U.S. Attorney handling the case. One might call this the scapegoat strategy. Rather than admitting technical wrongdoing and then justifying or excusing it, the offender attempts to paint himself as a victim by shifting the blame entirely to another party. Prosecutors were presented as being either ignorant or politically motivated.

The outright denial of any crime whatsoever is unusual compared to the other types of offenders studied here. It may result from the nature of the crime of fraud. By definition, fraud involves a conscious attempt on the part of one or more persons to mislead others. While it is theoretically possible to accidentally violate the antitrust and tax laws, or to violate them for altruistic reasons, it is difficult to imagine how one could accidentally mislead someone else for his or her own good. Furthermore, in many instances, fraud is an aggressively acquisitive crime. The offender develops a scheme to bilk other people out of money or property, and does this not because of some personal problem but because the scheme is an easy way to get rich. Stock swindles, fraudulent loan scams, and so on are often so large and complicated that they cannot possibly be excused as foolish and desperate solutions to personal problems. Thus, those involved in large-scale frauds do not have the option open to most embezzlers of presenting themselves as persons responding defensively to difficult personal circumstances.

Furthermore, because fraud involves a deliberate attempt to mislead another, the offender who fails to remove himself from the scheme runs the risk of being shown to have a guilty mind. That is, he is shown to possess the most essential element of modern conceptions of criminality: an intent to harm another. His inner self would in this case be exposed as something other than what it has been presented as, and all of his previous actions would be subject to reinterpretation in light of this new perspective. For this reason, defrauders are most prone to denying any crime at all. The cooperative and conspiratorial nature of many fraudulent schemes makes it possible to put the blame on someone else and to present oneself as a scapegoat. Typically, this is done by claiming to have been duped by others.

Two illustrations of this strategy are presented below.

> I figured I wasn't guilty, so it wouldn't be that hard to disprove it, until, as I say, I went to court and all of a sudden they start bringing in these guys out of the woodwork implicating me that I never saw. Lot of it could be proved that I never saw.
>
> Inwardly, I personally felt that the only crime that I committed was not telling on these guys. Not that I deliberately, intentionally committed a crime against the system. My only crime was that I should have had the guts to tell on these guys, what they were doing, rather than putting up with it and then trying to gradually get out of the system without hurting them or without them thinking I was going to snitch on them.

Of the three offenders who admitted committing crimes, two acted alone and the third acted with only one other person. Their accounts were similar to the others presented earlier and tended to focus on either the harmless nature of their violations or on the unusual circumstances that drove them to commit their crimes. One claimed that his violations were only technical and that no one besides himself had been harmed.

> First of all, no money was stolen or anything of that nature. The bank didn't lose any money.... What I did was a technical violation. I made a mistake. There's no question about that, but the bank lost no money.

Another offender who directly admitted his guilt was involved in a check-kiting scheme. In a manner similar to embezzlers, he argued that his actions were motivated by exceptional circumstances.

> I was faced with the choice of all of a sudden, and I mean now, closing the doors or doing something else to keep that business open.... I'm not going to tell you that this wouldn't have happened if I'd had time to think it over, because I think it probably would have. You're sitting there with a dying patient. You are going to try to keep him alive.

In the other fraud cases more individuals were involved, and it was possible and perhaps necessary for each offender to claim that he was not really the culprit.

The investigation, prosecution, and conviction of a white-collar offender involves him in a very undesirable status passage (Glaser and Strauss 1971). The entire process can be viewed as a long and drawn-out degradation ceremony with the prosecutor as the chief denouncer and the offender's family and friends as the chief witnesses. The offender is moved from the status of law-abiding citizen to that of convicted felon. Accounts are developed to defeat the process of identity transformation that is the object of a degradation ceremony. They represent the offender's attempt to diminish the effect of his legal transformation and to prevent its becoming a publicly validated label.

Summary and Implications

In effect, offenders attempt to adjust the normative lens through which their offenses are viewed by society.[3] Societal reaction to crimes and criminals varies according to many factors. Although there is no clear-cut consensus on the number and relative importance of factors, it can be assumed that two elements of significance are (1) the seriousness of the offense, and (2) the blameworthiness of the offender. Any offender interested in avoiding being labeled a criminal must be able to minimize the blameworthiness and seriousness of his actions to a degree such that the label "criminal" will be regarded as inappropriate.

Seriousness

The partial legitimacy of the outcomes of some white-collar crimes seems to play an important role in the offender's minimization of seriousness. Some antitrust offenses, tax violations, and false statements made to lending institutions have as their outcomes more than just illegal gain for the perpetrators. They may also shore up a failing business or provide stability in employment. While defrauding the Medicaid system, a doctor or dentist may also be providing at least some much-needed services for the poor. The harm experienced by the victim or victims is balanced against the benefits derived by other uninvolved parties, such as employees and family. The congruence of legitimacy and illegitimacy that characterizes the commission of white-collar and corporate crimes (Clinard and Quinney 1973) may be reproduced in the final products of those crimes and in the justifications presented by offenders.

A belief in widespread illegality was frequently expressed in the interviews. It seemed to be assumed that everybody is unscrupulous in one way or another. This fosters a callousness of attitude with regard to criminal behavior (Denzin 1977). Criminal behavior is seen as acceptable and necessary for survival in the business world. This belief leads to the view that certain types of law violations, since they are normal, are not really serious crimes, which provides a blanket excuse for illegal behavior.

The belief in widespread illegality extends beyond the legitimate business world to society at large, which offenders seem to assume is at the mercy of rampant and unpunished street criminality. The lack of identifiable individual victims has been suggested as one of the reasons for the lack of societal concern with white-collar criminality. This characteristic of white-collar offenses may also be used by offenders before they commit their crimes. That is, the lack of individual victims may help the offender in using the familiar neutralization techniques of denying the victim and the harm.

Blameworthiness

The complexity of the laws and regulations governing the business world seems to facilitate relieving the offender's sense of blameworthiness. Crimes committed out of ignorance or inattention to detail are less offensive to the social conscience than those deliberately committed. Unlike the common street crimes, it is possible to accidentally violate laws that govern the conduct of businesses, professions, and industries. This means that the motives underlying conduct cannot automatically be inferred from the conduct itself. An offense that would be considered blameworthy if committed knowingly may be excusable, or at least understandable, if committed out of ignorance. Complexity gives rise to an ambiguity in the connection between the act and its motive. This may allow offenders to persuade themselves and others that the motive was not really criminal, so therefore the act was not really a crime.

Such a process may even work in advance of the crime when offenders maintain a concerted ignorance of the law or of the activities of subordinates. Katz (1979) has argued that individuals involved in organizational crimes are frequently aware that there is a chance that the crime will eventually come to light. Yet, even though discovery is a possibility, offenders may nonetheless choose to participate provided that they can construct anticipatory defenses that will allow them to eventually deny blameworthiness. Many features of corporate organization facilitate the building of these "metaphysical escapes" (Katz 1979). In other words, offenders may purposely attempt to structure crimes so that the connection between act and motive remains ambiguous and deniable.

Individuals who commit crimes outside an organizational context or who act against organizations (embezzlers) may attempt to reduce their blameworthiness by setting the crime within the context of an otherwise impeccable life. If a crime can be shown to be an aberration, then its importance as an indicator of the offender's true character is dramatically reduced. His or her personality can be shown to have both good and bad points with the good outnumbering the bad. The obvious inconsistency of the offender's conviction vis-à-vis the rest of his life may be handled by family, friends, and perhaps society at large by denying the implications of the offender's actions in order to maintain a consistent and favorable attitude toward him (Geis 1982:97).

As with the use of concerted ignorance, the process of setting the crime within a context of impeccability may be used by offenders prior to the illegal act as a neutralization technique. A lifetime of socially acceptable and desirable behavior in one arena is used to excuse an occasional indiscretion in another.

What needs to be determined is how effective these strategies are in helping the offender avoid stigmatization as a criminal—that is, avoid being thought of and treated like a criminal by others. If certain classes of offenders can commit crimes, be convicted, and yet still, through the use of appropriate accounting strategies, avoid being labeled as criminals, then one of the primary functions of the criminal law and the criminal justice system—the symbolic separation of the offender from the community—is negated. A moral environment is thereby perpetuated in which the symbolic consequences of criminal behavior for some offenders can largely be ignored.

Notes

1. Some offenders whose files were examined were not available to be interviewed, because they were incarcerated at the time of the study.
2. All of the offenders who consented to being interviewed were men.
3. The idea of a "normative lens" and much of the following discussion is indebted to a paper presented at an annual meeting of the American Society of Criminology by Wheeler (1984).

References

Casper, Jonathan D. 1978. *Criminal Courts: The Defendant's Perspective.* Washington, D.C.: U.S. Department of Justice.

Clinard, Marshall B., and Richard Quinney. 1973. *Criminal Behavior Systems: A Typology.* New York: Holt, Rinehart, and Winston.

Clinard, Marshall B. and Peter C. Yeager. 1978. "Corporate crime: Issues in research." *Criminology* 16: 255–272.

Conklin, John E. 1977. *Illegal but Not Criminal: Business Crime in America.* Englewood Cliffs, NJ: Prentice Hall.

Cressey, Donald. 1953. *Other People's Money.* New York: Free Press.

Denzin, Norman K. 1977. "Notes on the criminogenic hypothesis: A case study of the American liquor industry." *American Sociological Review* 42: 905–920.

Geis, Gilbert. 1982. *On White-Collar Crime.* Lexington, MA: Lexington.

Katz, Jack. 1979. "Concerted ignorance: The social construction of cover-up." *Urban Life* 8: 295–316.

Meier, Robert, and Glbert Geis. 1982. "The psychology of the white-collar offender." In Gilbert Geis (ed.), *On White-Collar Crime.* Lexington, MA: Lexington.

Rothman, Martin, and Robert F. Gandossy. 1982. "Sad tales: The accounts of white-collar defendants and the decision to sanction." *Pacific Sociological Review* 4: 449–473.

Shapiro, Susan P. 1980. *Thinking About White-Collar Crime: Matters of Conceptualization and Research.* Washington. D.C. U.S. Government Printing Office.

Searle, John R. 1969. *Speech Acts.* Cambridge: Cambridge University Press.

Sutherland, Edwin H. 1949. *White Collar Crime.* New York: Dryden.

CHAPTER 36

Trouble in the School Yard: A Study of the Risk Factors of Victimization at School

Christopher J. Schreck ■ J. Mitchell Miller ■ Chris L. Gibson

In recent years, school crime has become a matter of grave public concern. Although property and drug offenses are common in school settings, violent crime has captured popular attention—unfortunately through a fairly lengthy series of school shootings and similar catastrophic domestic terrorist events. These terrible crises certainly capture public attention due to losses of lives and media attention; more latent forms of bullying and gang intimidation are far more common.

The following study, acknowledging the increased likelihood of school-based exposure to crime, identifies and considers both situational and personal risk factors of victimization at school. Building on the extant criminological knowledge base on the strong correlation between involvement in offending and victimization, association with delinquent others and the degree of offender presence are argued to be more consequential factors than community variables.

Media reports of crimes on school property—particularly shootings—create the impression that victimization can occur to any student at any school (e.g., Ferdinand, 2001; Tucker, 2001). This impression of school climate is not especially new. Even during the 1970s, there was widespread public and media fixation on school victimization (Gottfredson & Gottfredson, 1985). In response to this persistent concern (and aided

by the financial wherewithal of the federal government via the Safe Schools Act of 1994 [P.L. 103-227]), many schools have turned to security guards and metal detectors. Accounts taken from articles in major newspapers such as *The Washington Post* suggest that schools continue to develop a variety of protective strategies, with the intention of minimizing the consequences of the apparently random and inevitable occurrence of crime—especially serious violent crime (e.g., Cooper & Russakopf, 1999).

There is some empirical basis for this alarm over the safety of schoolchildren. Young people have a disproportionately high risk of victimization relative to other age groups (Bureau of Justice Statistics, 1999). Because juveniles often spend much of their day on school grounds, it would seem to follow that school is among the likeliest places for victimization to occur. Some victimization data, however, question this reasoning. Regoli and Hewitt (2000), for instance, reported that 3,000 children died in 1997 from gunfire off the school campus, whereas only 40 children were slain on campus grounds—an annual risk of death at school from shooting of "roughly one in a million." Other studies, in contrast, find that school is the modal context in which juvenile victimization occurs (Whitaker & Bastian, 1991). Although this may be so, the data indicate that an explosion of crime and violence has not taken place. Estimates of the annual prevalence of nonfatal assault victimization of students on school property were stable between 1989 and 1995, hovering between

CRIME & DELINQUENCY, Vol. 49 No. 3, July 2003 460-484
DOI: 10.1177/0011128703252275 © 2003 Sage Publications

7% and 8% (Kaufman et al., 1999). Apparently, victimization happens at school for very few children during any given school year. Yet victimization does occur. What factors, if any, single out individual students to become victims of crime while at school? Does everyone share equal risk? The answers to these questions can inform the design of relevant and efficient policy to protect American schoolchildren.

Previous Research

The research is clear that victimization does not happen to just anyone (e.g., Fisher, Sloan, Cullen, & Lu, 1998; Lauritsen, Sampson, & Laub, 1991; Miethe & Meier, 1994; Miethe, Stafford, & Long, 1987; Mustaine & Tewksbury, 1998; Sampson & Lauritsen, 1990). Certain variables stand out as salient predictors. With the exception of a few very recent studies (Wallace, 2001; Welsh, 2001), however, most victimization research does not specifically target schoolchildren or distinguish between victimization at school and in other settings. Nevertheless, the research literature finds that victimization occurs through the confluence of individual and situational variables. For our purposes, we believe that students possess characteristics that have some bearing on their level of vulnerability, whereas the school and community characteristics are potential situational sources of risk. In the following sections, we discuss how these three sources of risk can help identify potential victims of crime at school.

Individual Risk Factors

Our starting point for describing victimization risk at school looks at the routine daily activity of the individual student (Cohen & Felson, 1979; Cohen, Kluegel, & Land, 1981; Hindelang, Gottfredson, & Garofalo, 1978; Garofalo, 1987). The major thesis of the lifestyle/routine activity framework is that victimization is most likely to occur in situations in which likely offenders are near worthwhile and poorly defended targets. This framework leads us to examine student demographic, exposure, attractiveness, and guardianship risk factors.

We begin by discussing demographic correlates of victimization. General population studies reveal that the representative victim in the general population—besides being youthful—is Black and male (Bureau of Justice Statistics, 1999). This pattern generally persists in the context of school victimization, as well (Kaufman et al., 1999). In and of itself, however, a demographic characteristic reveals nothing about why victimization occurs. Hindelang, Gottfredson, & Garofalo (1978) designed lifestyle theory in an attempt to make sense of these demographic patterns, arguing that demographic variables indirectly influence victimization risk through their effect on lifestyle. Demographic characteristics determine risk factors, such as levels of exposure and guardianship, which in turn are responsible for demographic variation in victimization. For example, lifestyle theory might argue that Blacks, who are more likely to be victims, tend to associate with other Blacks, who tend to have a higher risk of arrest (and, presumably, represent motivated offenders).

Although this may be true, it is more desirable to also consider direct indicators of exposure. Research has consistently noted that people with delinquent friends tend to be especially vulnerable to victimization (Jensen & Brownfield, 1986; Mustaine & Tewksbury, 1998; Sampson & Lauritsen, 1990; Schreck, Wright, & Miller, 2002). There are a few reasons why this may be so. First, much of the delinquency that occurs among juveniles is group activity (Erickson & Jensen, 1977), and it is possible that juvenile victimization is simply a by-product of retaliation of other groups for the delinquent actions of the peer group (Singer, 1981). Contact with delinquent peers is also direct exposure to would-be offenders (Mustaine & Tewksbury, 1998; Sampson & Lauritsen, 1990). Because delinquent peers would be unlikely to resist any temptation offered by their friends for long, the peer group is likely to prey on itself. Consequently, students with delinquent friends should have more risk of victimization at school.

Exposure to offenders is not always enough to make victimization likely. As Felson (1998) noted, offenders also must have access to desirable targets. Offenders may use robbery and theft to reap economic benefits, or they may wish to possess something that has intrinsic or symbolic value. One might reasonably expect that the amount of cash a person carries would influence that person's attractiveness as a target, but Miethe and Meier (1994) only found mixed support for this indicator of attractiveness. In their general population study, income predicted assault victimization but not theft. Fisher et al. (1998), on the other hand, found that income predicted theft of property among college students but not violent victimization. Junior and senior high school students do not usually live at school (which would require them to bring potentially expensive possessions), although they do frequently bring valuables, such as jewelry, expensive shoes and clothes, light electronic goods, and cash onto school grounds or to school-related extracurricular activities, which could present offenders with opportunities.

Students might reduce their risk of victimization by increasing the level of guardianship around themselves and their belongings. Social guardianship is one strategy. At the school, fellow students and teachers can act as potential guardians against victimization. Strong social bonds between the individual and other teachers and students might facilitate even stronger protection (see Felson, 1986; 1998). Gottfredson and Gottfredson (1985) found that students with strong bonds of commitment to school as well as strong beliefs that school officials fairly and efficiently enforced discipline tend to experience less victimization. Schreck et al. (2002) found that—at least at the bivariate level—strong social bonds inhibited violent victimization. An alternative guardianship strategy to social protection might include target hardening. In the school setting, individual target hardening might include bringing weapons to campus. It is unclear, however, whether this strategy will promote guardianship or, as is very likely, simply reflect the delinquent tendencies of the individual carrying the weapon—something that should work to increase risk. So far, the research results (which do not focus on the school setting) offer mixed support for either physical or social protection (Miethe & Meier, 1994; Rosenbaum, 1987).

School-Related Risk Factors

The literature indicates that victimization risk can also originate from sources outside the individual.

This suggests that schools can also influence victimization risk among students. Some of the characteristics that we consider relate to social disorganization at the school level, whereas others are relevant to target hardening and the exposure of students to criminal peers.

At the individual schools, there may be variation in the number of delinquent students on the campus. Presumably, schools with a greater proportion of delinquents would expose all students to higher victimization risk. The presence of criminal youth gangs on the school campus is indicative of likely offenders, which would increase the victimization risk of other students. As noted in the earlier section, the carrying of weapons onto a school campus is a delinquent activity, and the fact that other students do so may reflect the presence of would-be offenders among the student population. Taken together, a campus with a greater proportion of delinquents should make victimization a more likely possibility for everyone, no matter what individual students do to protect themselves.

We also reason that students who attend schools in which they are a racial minority will be more vulnerable to crime because few other students will be willing to serve as their guardians. This, for example, would be the case for a White student at a predominantly Black school, and vice versa. We borrow this hypothesis from social disorganization theory, in which being a member of a different race or culture might, in turn, become a source of fear, distrust, and decreased communication (Suttles, 1968). Applied to the school, this distrust can manifest itself in the decreased willingness of the students of the racial majority to act as guardians for other students. This, in turn, should increase the risk of victimization for the minority student.

The requirement that students attend schools outside their community might also inhibit the effectiveness of social guardianship. This hypothesis is somewhat related to the notion of residential mobility in social disorganization theory (Kasarda & Janowitz, 1974). In the community, the assimilation of residents into the social networks of the community can lead to improved social control. People who are continually moving from location to location, however, face an enormous obstacle in joining the social fabric of the community because social ties take time to develop. The same situation should hold in the school. Geographic distance from the school should weaken the ability of students to develop social relationships with other students who live closer to the school itself. This, in turn, might undermine widespread friendship bonds on campus and, in turn, the willingness of these other students to act as guardians.

Schools can act to minimize the risk of victimization for their students by having key employees assume the role of guardian. Teachers and school administrators, for instance, are socially situated to act as guardians. However, a large student body, whether or not it is predominantly delinquent, might interfere with guardianship. Researchers have speculated that administrators face greater challenges exercising supervision and social control in schools with very large numbers of students (Toby, 1983). Although a large school size appears to have many harmful consequences—such as greater disorder, fear of crime, and teacher victimization—the level of student victimization appeared to have been unaffected (Gottfredson & Gottfredson, 1985; Welsh, Stokes, & Greene, 2000).

Most of these school-related antecedents of victimization reviewed here are not variables that the school is in a position to influence directly. Yet the school can actively strive to shield students from victimization by employing a variety of target-hardening strategies. The belief is that by using teachers to supervise hallways, installing metal detectors, and hiring security guards, the likely offender will have a harder time carrying out a crime. The question remains, however, whether these efforts significantly reduce the likelihood that an individual student will become a victim.

Community-Related Risk Factors

Considerable research has investigated the role of community disorder and victimization in the general population (e.g., Lauritsen, 2001; Lauritsen et al., 1991; Miethe & McDowall, 1993; Rountree, Land, & Miethe, 1994; Sampson & Lauritsen, 1990). Community characteristics might also affect victimization in the schoolyard, as schools

exist in a considerable diversity of community contexts (see Gottfredson & Gottfredson, 1985; Welsh et al., 2000). Children on their way to school may risk victimization if they have to transit (or await transportation to school) in disorganized communities. Students attending schools located in disorganized areas may also have a greater risk of victimization because the school campuses are more vulnerable to infiltration by local criminals. Shaw and McKay (1942) theorized that disorganized communities have three characteristics: low socioeconomic status, ethnic heterogeneity, and residential mobility. These characteristics, in turn, weakened community cohesion and led to greater crime. Welsh, Greene, and Jenkins (1999) and Welsh et al. (2000), in their sophisticated analysis of disorder in Philadelphia public schools, however, found that school characteristics mediated much of the direct influence of community factors, although community characteristics still exercised some influence on school disorder. The question remains as to how much community variables affect the victimization risk of individuals while at school.

Summary

The criminological literature has recently begun to give more attention to the school setting (e.g., Wallace, 2001; Welsh, 2001; Welsh et al., 1999, 2000). Although the multivariate analysis of the sources of individual risk of victimization is not new, much existing research employed general population samples and did not specifically study junior and senior high school students (e.g., Kennedy & Forde, 1990; Lauritsen, 2001; Miethe et al., 1987; Miethe, Stafford, & Sloan, 1990; Rountree et al., 1994). Several victimization studies have targeted the adolescent population (e.g., Lauritsen et al., 1991; Sampson & Lauritsen, 1990; Schreck et al., 2002), but these researchers did not have a specific interest in victimization in the school setting. The research on individual victimization in the educational setting is confined mainly to studies of college students (e.g., Fisher et al., 1998; Mustaine & Tewksbury, 1998), with measures relevant for those enrolled in higher education. There is a need for more research that can identify individual, school, and community predictors of schoolyard victimization.

Using data from the 1993 National Household and Education Survey's School Safety and Discipline component (NHES-SSD), we examine the antecedents of individual schoolyard victimization in a representative sample of American children enrolled in school. In our analysis, we employed logistic regression to account for variation in individual student victimization risk. Our study attempted to identify salient community, school, and individual antecedents of schoolyard victimization. Moreover, we attempt to discover whether school-related antecedents mediate demographic and community predictors of victimization and whether individual characteristics can reduce the influence of demographic, community, and school indicators. Our basic model thus begins with community and demographic predictors of school victimization. Our analysis then introduces school measures and, finally, individual measures. We finally investigate how these factors relate to specific forms of victimization, such as property and violent victimization.

Conclusions

Most Americans will spend a significant proportion of their childhood attending school. If the media accounts of the hysteria of policy makers and the public about school crime are accurate, efforts to understand what distinguishes victims from nonvictims is important. If researchers can identify the sources of victimization risk at school, then policy makers can more effectively focus attention on correcting risk factors that actually bear some relationship with victimization in the school setting. These were our main goals.

Our research emphasized the routine activity and lifestyles-exposure approach to understanding victimization risk. These theories consider the role of proximity and exposure to criminal offenders, the degree of target hardening and self-protection, and target attractiveness. Moreover, the literature on victimization indicates that risk can come from a variety of sources—contextual and individual. Besides school-relevant risk factors, we believed that communities where the student lives, as well as the individual students themselves, have something to do with levels of victimization risk.

We found that victimization at school does indeed reflect the confluence of community, school, and individual student characteristics. These characteristics explain at least a portion of statistically significant demographic patterns in victimization risk at school, particularly gender differences in theft victimization. Variables that most consistently affect victimization risk were the measures of exposure to criminals. Students who live in communities where they perceive a crime problem tend to have a higher risk of victimization. One reasonable interpretation might be that some school-related victimization occurs while children are walking through unsafe areas to go to or from school, or else while waiting at bus stops in areas with high crime. In fact, students are more fearful of victimization during these times than when they are actually at school (see Lab & Clark, 1997). Our conclusion is tentative because we had to rely on proxy measures of community risk; however, the results appear in line with the findings of other research. Other risk factors for exposure are also important, however. The presence of delinquents at the school—drug dealers, children with weapons, and gangs—consistently make victimization more likely, which supports the routine activities thesis that close proximity to criminals brings risk. Confirming the results of similar research (Welsh, 2001), we found that students who have delinquent friends also tend to have more risk independently of whether they share the same campus with gang members, drug dealers, and the like. This finding supports the notion that such friends have considerable opportunity to prey on each other (e.g., Schreck et al., 2002) and/or place one another at risk for retaliation after having victimized others (Singer, 1981).

Students who indicate being alienated from school and who report feeling that school rules are unfair tend to have greater risk of victimization, which is consistent with other research (Welsh, 2001). Our findings allude to a couple of interpretations. First, schools may have earned the distrust of students by being ineffective at their role of protecting the student—victimization may have preceded the development of hostile attitudes.

Second, hostile attitudes toward school may correspond with the unwillingness on the part of the student to seek help from school authorities or rely on their protection. If the latter is true, then students who are isolated from teachers and staff may have the most risk. Our data, unfortunately, do not allow us to determine the precise connection between feelings about school and victimization. Future research should attempt to establish why these attitudes correspond with more risk.

Not every aspect of routine activities theory received uniform support, however. Income did not significantly affect victimization risk, even for property crime. In addition, the attempts to augment capable guardianship through target hardening (such as with guards or metal detectors) fail to reduce the likelihood of victimization. Although this finding is, on its face, contrary to the predictions of routine activities, a couple of other explanations appear plausible. One might argue that our results indicate that the usual attempts to make schools safer may focus on factors largely irrelevant to school-related victimization. In particular, the hardening strategies measured in our study apply best to victimization during school hours. If much of the victimization that students reported to the NHES-SSD takes place immediately after school when children are on their way home, as National Incident-Based Reporting System data show (see Snyder, Sickmund, & Poe-Yamagata, 1996), then these hardening strategies merely boost security where risk is already quite small. One may also argue that the implementation of existing target hardening requires attention. Security guards, for instance, may lack numbers, training, or competence. In short, there is a clear need for a thorough programmatic evaluation of the different strategies schools employ to curb disorder and protect students from crime. Evaluation research in this area can enable school authorities to determine (a) whether implementation problems exist that might compromise the effectiveness of the program, and (b) whether the program is effective enough to justify the expense.

Effective strategies against victimization need not turn the school into a fortress, however. One program that appears to address the victimization risk factors identified in this study is an antibullying program implemented in Sweden. Dan Olweus (1993, 1996) evaluated this program and found it to be highly successful at reducing the amount of bullying that takes place at school. This program may have broader utility at reducing victimization risk. The program would include having administrators periodically survey students to determine the extent of victimization and where it tends to occur. Moreover, administrators would need to devote resources toward improving surveillance of problem areas for victimization, including cafeterias, bathrooms, playgrounds, hallways, and between buildings. Teachers and school staff can thus prevent victimization by simply maintaining a strong and active visible presence, and thus serve as gentle reminders to the delinquents who are predisposed to victimize other students (Felson, 1998). Olweus's bullying-prevention program also called for increased communication among teachers, students, and parents—all of which might reduce hostility and, potentially, the reluctance of some students to seek protection. Readers should be aware, however, the joint role of community, school, and individual risk factors suggests that the emphasis of prevention policy on the school alone is an oversimplification of a much more complex problem.

Readers should be aware of some of the limitations of this research. First, victimization research has uncovered a variety of risk factors; the NHES-SSD data do not measure all variables potentially relevant in the etiology of victimization, so clearly the low degree of explained variation is partly a function of omitted variables. Self-control theory (Gottfredson & Hirschi, 1990; see also, Schreck, 1999; Schreck et al., 2002) and control balance theory (Tittle, 1995; see also, Piquero, Hickman, & Henderson, in press) are two possible starting points for better developing individual-level indicators. Moreover, research has suggested that the size of the victim may likewise be a source of risk, at least for interpersonal violence (Felson, 1996). A second limitation lies in the crude measurement of community characteristics. If much of the school-related victimization takes place as children return home from school, then the community takes on a much more important role than policy makers or the public have yet realized. Many of the studies

APPENDIX: Description of Measures and Simple Statistics

Variable	Description (Type of Variable and Coding)	Mean	SD
Victimization			
Violence	Dichotomous variable: 1 = victim (assault and strong-arm robbery)	.05	.22
Theft	Dichotomous variable: 1 = victim	.14	.35
Overall	Dichotomous variable: 1 = victim	.17	.38
Demographic			
Male	Dichotomous variable: 1 = male	.50	.50
Grade level	Discrete variable: range 6 to 12	8.76	1.97
Black	Dichotomous variable: 1 = Black	.145	.35
Hispanic	Dichotomous variable: 1 = Hispanic	.14	.35
Other racial group	Dichotomous variable: 1 = other race	.03	.18
School characteristics			
Approximately how many students enrolled at the school?[a]	Discrete variable: 1 = less than 300, 2 = 301-599, 3 = 600-999, 4 = 1000+	2.80	1.02
Does your child go to a public or private school?[a]	Dichotomous variable: 1 = public	.91	.29
Approximately what percentage of the students are of the same race or ethnic background as your child?[a]	Discrete variable: 1 = less than 25%, 2 = 25%-75%, 3 = more than 75%	2.33	.68
Is the school located in the neighborhood where you live?	Dichotomous Variable: 1 = yes	.64	.48
Does the school have...?			
Security guards	Dichotomous variables: 1 = yes	.34	.47
Metal detectors		.06	.23
Locked doors during the day		.31	.46
A requirement that visitors sign in		.75	.43
Limits on going to the restroom		.37	.48
Teachers assigned to supervise the hallway		.67	.47
Regular locker checks		.30	.46
Hall passes required to leave class		.86	.35
Index: extensiveness of drug education	Discrete variable: 0 (*no drug education*) through 4 (*extensive drug education*)	1.74	1.23
Do you know of any other students bringing weapons to school this year?	Dichotomous variable: 1 = yes	.43	.50
Do any students at your school belong to fighting gangs?	Dichotomous variable: 1 = yes	.36	.48
Community characteristics			
Would you say your school is:	Discrete variable: 1 = safer than neighborhood, 2 = about as safe, 3 = not as safe as my neighborhood	1.68	.64
Percentage Black	Discrete variable: 1 = less than 6%, 2 = 6-15%, 3 = 16%-40%, 4 = 41% or more	2.30	1.16

(continued)

Appendix: continued

Variable	Description (Type of Variable and Coding)	Mean	SD
Individual characteristics			
Is this the first year your child attended the school?[a]	Dichotomous variable: 1 = yes	.32	.47
During the school year, did you ever bring something to school to protect yourself from being attacked or harmed?	Dichotomous variable: 1 = yes	.03	.17
Index: perception that rules are not enforced fairly	Discrete variable: 1 (most fairness)	3.75	1.82
Index: do friends smoke, drink, or use marijuana or other drugs?	Discrete variable: 1 = friends do none of these, 4 = friends do all four of these	1.20	1.38
Index: alienation toward school	Discrete variable: 2 = least alienation, 6 = most alienation	4.26	1.05

[a]Denotes information provided by parent.

that explore the role that communities play in vulnerability look at a substantially more contextual measure than is available in the NHES. Our data also do not allow us to control for such characteristics as school involvement, which Welsh (2001) found to relate to school yard victimization.

This study has other important limitations. Because the NHES-SSD is a cross-sectional data set, temporal sequencing is, for many of the victimization predictors, impossible to establish with any certainty. The study is also limited insofar as the NHES-SSD lacks school identifiers. This disadvantage is potentially important because the influence of individual-level correlates of victimization may be, in part, determined by the setting in which the individual lives or goes to school. Nevertheless, this study provides insights about which correlates of victimization among schoolchildren are most important. From an intervention perspective, the ability to identify children who are at risk of suffering from schoolyard crime is potentially useful even where causal direction is ambiguous.

Notes

1. The appendix contains a listing of all variables, and parent-provided items are noted.
2. This index contains the following question items: the school rules are fair; punishment for breaking school rules is the same no matter who you are; school rules

are strictly enforced; if a rule is broken, students know what kind of punishment will follow.
3. The number of variables is too large to report all bivariate correlations easily, so we concentrate only on the relationships of the variables with victimization. We can provide the complete correlation table on request.

References

Brick, J. M., Collins, M., & Chandler, K. (1997). *An overview of response rates in the National Household Education Survey: 1991, 1993, 1995, and 1996.* (NCES No. 97-948). Washington DC: U.S. Department of Education and National Center for Education Statistics.

Brick, J. M., Keeter, S., Waksberg, J., & Bell, B. (1996). *Adjusting for coverage bias using telephone service interruption data.* (NCES No. 97-336). Washington DC: U.S. Department of Education and National Center for Education Statistics.

Brick, J. M., Tubbs, E., Collins, M. A., & Nolin, M. J. (1997). *Unit and item response, weighting, and imputation procedures in the 1993 National Household Education Survey (NHES: 93).* (Working Paper No. 97-05). Washington DC: U.S. Department of Education and National Center for Education Statistics.

Bryk, A., & Raudenbusch, S. (1992). *Hierarchical linear models: Applications and data analysis methods.* Newbury Park, CA: Sage.

Bureau of Justice Statistics. (1999). *Criminal victimization 1998*. Washington, DC: U.S. Government Printing Office.

Cohen, L. E., & Felson, M. (1979). Social change and crime rate trends: A routine activity approach. *American Sociological Review, 52*: 170-183.

Cohen, L. E., Kluegel, J. R., & Land, K. (1981). Social inequality and predatory criminal victimization: An exposition and test of a formal theory. *American Sociological Review, 46*: 505-524.

Cooper, K. J., & Russakopf, D. (1999, May 27). Schools accused of overreacting in disciplining students. *The Washington Post*, p. Al.

Erickson, M., & Jensen, G. F. (1977). Delinquency is still group behavior!: Toward revitalizing the group premise in the sociology of deviance. *Journal of Criminal Law & Criminology, 68*: 262-273.

Felson, M. (1986). Linking criminal choices, routine activities, informal control, and criminal outcomes. In D. B. Cornish & R. V. Clarke (Eds.), *The reasoning criminal: Rational choice perspectives on offending*, (pp. 119-128). New York: Springer-Verlag.

Felson, M. (1998). *Crime and everyday life*. Thousand Oaks, CA: Pine Forge.

Felson, R. B. (1996). Big people hit little people: Sex differences in physical power and interpersonal violence. *Criminology, 34*: 433-452.

Ferdinand, P. (2001, December 27). Shaken but unharmed, Mass. school says 'the system worked.' *The Washington Post*, p. A3.

Fisher, B. S., Sloan, J. J., Cullen, F. T., & Lu, C. (1998). Crime in the ivory tower: The level and sources of student victimization. *Criminology, 36*: 671-710.

Garofalo, J. (1987). Reassessing the lifestyle model of criminal victimization. In M. Gottfredson, & T. Hirschi (Eds.), *Positive criminology* (pp. 23-42). Newbury Park, CA: Sage.

Gottfredson, G. D., & Gottfredson, D. C. (1985). *Victimization in schools*. New York: Plenum.

Gottfredson, M. R., & Hirschi, T. (1990). *A general theory of crime*. Stanford, CA: Stanford University Press.

Hindelang, M. S., Gottfredson M. R., & Garofalo, J. (1978). *Victims of personal crime*. Cambridge, MA: Ballinger.

Hirschi, T. (1969). *Causes of delinquency*. Berkeley: University of California Press.

Jensen, G. F., & Brownfield, D. M. (1986). Gender, lifestyles, and victimization: Beyond routine activity theory. *Violence & Victims, 1*: 85-99.

Kasarda, J., & Janowitz, M. (1974). Community attachment in mass society. *American Sociological Review, 39*: 328-339.

Kaufman, P., Chen, X., Choy, S. P., Ruddy, S. A., Miller, A. K., Chandler, K. A., et al. (1999). *Indicators of school crime and safety*. Washington, DC: U.S. Department of Education and U.S. Department of Justice.

Kennedy, L. W., & Forde, D. R. (1990). Routine activities and crime: An analysis of victimization in Canada. *Criminology, 28*: 137-152.

Lab, S. P., & Clark, R. D. (1997). Crime prevention in schools: Individual and collective responses. In S. P. Lab (Ed.), *Crime prevention at a crossroads* (pp. 127-140). Cincinnati, OH: Anderson.

Lauritsen, J. L. (2001). The social ecology of violent victimization: individual and contextual effects in the NCVS. *Journal of Quantitative Criminology, 17*: 3-37.

Lauritsen, J. L., Sampson, R. J., & Laub, J. H. (1991). Addressing the link between offending and victimization among adolescents. *Criminology, 29*: 265-291.

Miethe, T. D., & McDowall, D. (1993). Contextual effects in models of criminal victimization. *Social Forces, 71*: 741-749.

Miethe, T. D., & Meier, R. F. (1994). *Crime and its social context: Toward an integrated theory of offenders, victims, and situations*. Albany: State University of New York Press.

Miethe, T. D., Stafford, M. C., & Long, J. S. (1987). Social differentiation in criminal victimization: A test of routine activities/lifestyles theories. *American Sociological Review, 52*: 184-194.

Miethe, T. D., Stafford, M. C., & Sloan, D. (1990). Lifestyle changes and risk of criminal victimization. *Journal of Quantitative Criminology, 6*: 357-376.

Mustaine, E. E., & Tewksbury, R. (1998). Predicting risks of larceny theft victimization: A routine activity analysis using refined activity measures. *Criminology, 36*, 829-858.

Olweus, D. (1993). *Bullying at school: What we know and what we can do*. Oxford: Blackwell.

Olweus, D. (1996). Bully/victim problems at school: Facts and effective intervention. *Journal of Emotional & Behavioral Problems, 5*: 15-22.

Piquero, A. R., Hickman, M., & Henderson, K. (in press). Extending Tittle's control balance theory to account for victimization. *Criminal Justice & Behavior*.

Regoli, R. M., & Hewitt, J. D. (2000). *Delinquency in society*. Boston: McGraw-Hill.

Rosenbaum, D. P. (1987). Community crime prevention: A review and synthesis of the literature. *Justice Quarterly, 5:* 323-395.

Rountree, P. W., Land, K. C., & Miethe, T. D. (1994). Macro-micro integration in the study of victimization: A hierarchical logistic model analysis across Seattle neighborhoods. *Criminology, 32:* 387-414.

Sampson, R. J., & Lauritsen, J. L. (1990). Deviant lifestyles, proximity to crime, and the offender-victim link in personal violence. *Journal of Research in Crime & Delinquency, 27:* 110-139.

Schreck, C. J. (1999). Criminal victimization and low self-control: An extension and test of a general theory of crime. *Justice Quarterly, 16:* 633-654.

Schreck, C. J., Wright, R. A., & Miller, J. M. (2002). A study of the individual and situational antecedents of violent victimization. *Justice Quarterly, 19:* 159-180.

Shaw, C., & McKay, H. (1942). *Juvenile delinquency and urban areas.* Chicago: University of Chicago Press.

Singer, S. I. (1981). Homogeneous victim-offenders populations: A review and some research implications. *Journal of Criminal Law & Criminology, 72:* 779-788.

Snyder, H., Sickmund, M., & Poe-Yamagata, E. (1996). *Juvenile offenders and victims: 1996 update on violence: Statistics summary.* Pittsburgh, PA: National Center for Juvenile Justice.

Suttles, G. (1968). *The social order of the slum.* Chicago: University of Chicago.

Tittle, C. R. (1995). *Control balance: Toward a general theory of deviance.* Boulder, CO: Westview.

Toby, J. (1983). Violence in school. In M. Tonry & N. Morris (Eds.), *Crime and justice: An annual review of research* (pp. 1-47). Chicago: University of Chicago Press.

Tucker, N. (2001, April 11). Report says youth violence overplayed. *The Washington Post,* p. B2.

Wallace, L. H. (2001). Reports from rural Mississippi: A look at school violence. *Journal of Security Administration, 24:* 15-32.

Welsh, W. N. (2001). Effects of student and school factors on five measures of school disorder. *Justice Quarterly, 18:* 911-947.

Welsh, W. N., Greene, J. R., & Jenkins, P. H. (1999). School disorder: The influence of individual, institutional, and community factors. *Criminology, 37:* 73-115.

Welsh, W. N., Stokes, R., & Greene, J. R. (2000). A macro-level model of school disorder. *Journal of Research in Crime & Delinquency, 37:* 243-283.

Whitaker, C. J., & Bastian, L. D. (1991). *Teenage victims: A national crime survey report.* (Report No. NCJ-128129). Washington, DC: U.S. Department of Justice, Bureau of Justice Statistics.

CHAPTER 37

Researching Dealers and Smugglers

Patricia A. Adler

Drug ethnography is investigative fieldwork of a fascinating nature. Qualitative research on drug subcultures varies in terms of the degree of disclosure of researcher roles and agendas from traditional overt participant observation and in-depth interview approaches to covert participant observation. When considered in the context of drug ethnography, the latter is essentially undercover research on undercover foci.

The following discussion on researching active drug criminals by Patricia A. Adler identifies leading methodological challenges and ethical issues inherent to conducting fieldwork in deviant settings. The overt versus covert methodological strategy is also portrayed as somewhat of a false dichotomy, with drug research instead being somewhere on a dynamic continuum between these two defined endpoints. Clearly, the richness of the data collected and the detailed insight obtained through fieldwork furthers understanding of the nature of drug dealing in ways simply beyond the reach of surveys and quantitative research strategies.

I strongly believe that investigative field research (Douglas 1976), with emphasis on direct personal observation, interaction, and experience, is the only way to acquire accurate knowledge about deviant behavior. Investigative techniques are especially necessary for studying groups such as drug dealers

and smugglers because the highly illegal nature of their occupation makes them secretive, deceitful, mistrustful, and paranoid. To insulate themselves from the straight world, they construct multiple false fronts, offer lies and misinformation, and withdraw into their group. In fact, detailed, scientific information about upper-level drug dealers and smugglers is lacking precisely because of the difficulty sociological researchers have had in penetrating into their midst. As a result, the only way I could possibly get close enough to these individuals to discover what they were doing and to understand their world from their perspectives (Blumer 1969) was to take a membership role in the setting. While my different values and goals precluded my becoming converted to complete membership in the subculture, and my fears prevented my ever becoming "actively" involved in their trafficking activities, I was able to assume a "peripheral" membership role (Adler and Adler 1987). I became a member of the dealers' and smugglers' social world and participated in their daily activities on that basis. In this chapter, I discuss how I gained access to this group, established research relations with members, and how personally involved I became in their activities.

Getting In

When I moved to Southwest County [California] in the summer of 1974, 1 had no idea that I would soon be swept up in a subculture of vast drug trafficking and unending partying, mixed with

Reprinted from: Patricia A. Adler. *Wheeling and Dealing* (New York: Columbia University Press, 1985). © Columbia University Press. Reprinted by permission of the publisher.

occasional cloak-and-dagger subterfuge. I had moved to California with my husband, Peter, to attend graduate school in sociology. We rented a condominium townhouse near the beach and started taking classes in the fall. We had always felt that socializing exclusively with academicians left us nowhere to escape from our work, so we tried to meet people in the nearby community. One of the first friends we made was our closest neighbor, a fellow in his late twenties with a tall, hulking frame and gentle expression. Dave, as he introduced himself, was always dressed rather casually, if not sloppily, in T-shirts and jeans. He spent most of his time hanging out or walking on the beach with a variety of friends who visited his house, and taking care of his two young boys, who lived alternately with him and his estranged wife. He also went out of town a lot. We started spending much of our free time over at his house, talking, playing board games late into the night, and smoking marijuana together. We were glad to find someone from whom we could buy marijuana in this new place, since we did not know too many people. He also began treating us to a fairly regular supply of cocaine, which was a thrill because this was a drug we could rarely afford on our student budgets. We noticed right away, however, that there was something unusual about his use and knowledge of drugs: while he always had a plentiful supply and was fairly expert about marijuana and cocaine, when we tried to buy a small bag of marijuana from him he had little idea of the going price. This incongruity piqued our curiosity and raised suspicion. We wondered if he might be dealing in larger quantities. Keeping our suspicions to ourselves, we began observing Dave's activities a little more closely. Most of his friends were in their late twenties and early thirties and, judging by their lifestyles and automobiles, rather wealthy. They came and left his house at all hours, occasionally extending their parties through the night and the next day into the following night. Yet throughout this time we never saw Dave or any of his friends engage in any activity that resembled a legitimate job. In most places this might have evoked community suspicion, but few of the people we encountered in Southwest County seemed to hold traditionally structured jobs. Dave, in fact, had no visible means of financial support. When we asked him what he did for a living, he said something vague about being a real estate speculator, and we let it go at that. We never voiced our suspicions directly since he chose not to broach the subject with us.

We did discuss the subject with our mentor, Jack Douglas, however. He was excited by the prospect that we might be living among a group of big dealers, and urged us to follow our instincts and develop leads into the group. He knew that the local area was rife with drug trafficking, since he had begun a life history case study of two drug dealers with another graduate student several years previously. That earlier study was aborted when the graduate student quit school, but Jack still had many hours of taped interviews he had conducted with them, as well as an interview that he had done with an undergraduate student who had known the two dealers independently, to serve as a cross-check on their accounts. He therefore encouraged us to become friendlier with Dave and his friends. We decided that if anything did develop out of our observations of Dave, it might make a nice paper for a field methods class or independent study.

At Washington University we had participated in a nationally funded project on urban heroin use (see Cummins et al. 1972). Our role in the study involved using fieldwork techniques to investigate the extent of heroin use and distribution in St. Louis. In talking with heroin users, dealers, and rehabilitation personnel, we acquired a base of knowledge about the drug world and the subculture of drug trafficking. Second, we had a generally open view toward soft drug use, considering moderate consumption of marijuana and cocaine to be generally nondeviant. This outlook was partially etched by our 1960s-formed attitudes, as we had first been introduced to drug use in an environment of communal friendship, sharing, and counterculture ideology. It also partially reflected the widespread acceptance accorded to marijuana and cocaine use in the surrounding local culture. Third, our age (mid-twenties at the start of the study) and general appearance gave us compatibility with most of the people we were observing.

We thus watched Dave and continued to develop our friendship with him. We also watched his friends and got to know a few of his more regular visitors. We continued to build friendly relations by doing, quite naturally, what Becker (1963), Polsky (1969), and Douglas (1972) had advocated for the early stages of field research: we gave them a chance to know us and form judgments about our trustworthiness by jointly pursuing those interests and activities which we had in common.

Then one day something happened which forced a breakthrough in the research. Dave had two guys visiting him from out of town and, after snorting quite a bit of cocaine, they turned their conversation to a trip they had just made from Mexico, where they piloted a load of marijuana back across the border in a small plane. Dave made a few efforts to shift the conversation to another subject, telling them to "button their lips," but they apparently thought that he was joking. They thought that anybody as close to Dave as we seemed to be undoubtedly knew the nature of his business. They made further allusions to his involvement in the operation and discussed the outcome of the sale. We could feel the wave of tension and awkwardness from Dave when this conversation began, as he looked toward us to see if we understood the implications of what was being said, but then he just shrugged it off as done. Later, after the two guys left, he discussed with us what happened. He admitted to us that he was a member of a smuggling crew and a major marijuana dealer on the side. He said that he knew he could trust us, but that it was his practice to say as little as possible to outsiders about his activities. This inadvertent slip, and Dave's subsequent opening up, were highly significant in forging our entry into Southwest County's drug world. From then on he was open in discussing the nature of his dealing and smuggling activities with us.

He was, it turned out, a member of a smuggling crew that was importing a ton of marijuana weekly and 40 kilos of cocaine every few months. During that first winter and spring, we observed Dave at work and also got to know the other members of his crew, including Ben, the smuggler himself. Ben was also very tall and broad shouldered, but his long black hair, now flecked with gray, bespoke his earlier membership in the hippie subculture. A large physical stature, we observed, was common

to most of the male participants involved in this drug community. The women also had a unifying physical trait: they were extremely attractive and stylishly dressed. This included Dave's ex-wife, Jean, with whom he reconciled during the spring. We therefore became friendly with Jean and through her met a number of women ("dope chicks") who hung around the dealers and smugglers. As we continued to gain the friendship of Dave and Jean's associates we were progressively admitted into their inner circle and apprised of each person's dealing or smuggling role.

Once we realized the scope of Ben's and his associates' activities, we saw the enormous research potential in studying them. This scene was different from any analysis of drug trafficking that we had read in the sociological literature because of the amounts they were dealing and the fact that they were importing it themselves. We decided that, if it was at all possible, we would capitalize on this situation, to "opportunistically" (Riemer 1977) take advantage of our prior expertise and of the knowledge, entrée, and rapport we had already developed with several key people in this setting. We therefore discussed the idea of doing a study of the general subculture with Dave and several of his closest friends (now becoming our friends). We assured them of the anonymity, confidentiality, and innocuousness of our work. They were happy to reciprocate our friendship by being of help to our professional careers. In fact, they basked in the subsequent attention we gave their lives.

We began by turning first Dave, then others, into key informants and collecting their life histories in detail. We conducted a series of taped, depth interviews with an unstructured, open-ended format. We questioned them about such topics as their backgrounds, their recruitment into the occupation, the stages of their dealing careers, their relations with others, their motivations, their lifestyle, and their general impressions about the community as a whole.

We continued to do taped interviews with key informants for the next six years until 1980, when we moved away from the area. After that, we occasionally did follow-up interviews when we returned for vacation visits. These later interviews focused on recording the continuing unfolding of events and included detailed probing into specific conceptual areas, such as dealing networks, types of dealers, secrecy, trust, paranoia, reputation, the law, occupational mobility, and occupational stratification. The number of taped interviews we did with each key informant varied, ranging between 10 and 30 hours of discussion.

Our relationship with Dave and the others thus took on an added dimension—the research relationship. As Douglas (1976), Henslin (1972), and Wax (1952) have noted, research relationships involve some form of mutual exchange. In our case, we offered everything that friendship could entail. We did routine favors for them in the course of our everyday lives, offered them insights and advice about their lives from the perspective of our more respectable position, wrote letters on their behalf to the authorities when they got in trouble, testified as character witnesses at their non-drug-related trials, and loaned them money when they were down and out. When Dave was arrested and brought to trial for check-kiting, we helped Jean organize his defense and raise the money to pay his fines. We spelled her in taking care of the children so that she could work on his behalf. When he was eventually sent to the state prison we maintained close ties with her and discussed our mutual efforts to buoy Dave up and secure his release. We also visited him in jail. During Dave's incarceration, however, Jean was courted by an old boyfriend and gave up her reconciliation with Dave. This proved to be another significant turning point in our research because, desperate for money, Jean looked up Dave's old dealing connections and went into the business herself. She did not stay with these marijuana dealers and smugglers for long, but soon moved into the cocaine business. Over the next several years her experiences in the world of cocaine dealing brought us into contact with a different group of people. While these people knew Dave and his associates (this was very common in the Southwest County dealing and smuggling community), they did not deal with them directly. We were thus able to gain access to a much wider and more diverse range of subjects than we would have had she not branched out on her own.

Dave's eventual release from prison three months later brought our involvement in the research to an even deeper level. He was broke and had nowhere to go. When he showed up on our doorstep, we took him in. We offered to let him stay with us until he was back on his feet again and could afford a place of his own. He lived with us for seven months, intimately sharing his daily experiences with us. During this time we witnessed, firsthand, his transformation from a scared ex-con who would never break the law again to a hard-working legitimate employee who only dealt to get money for his children's Christmas presents, to a full-time dealer with no pretensions at legitimate work. Both his process of changing attitudes and the community's gradual reacceptance of him proved very revealing.

We socialized with Dave, Jean, and other members of Southwest County's dealing and smuggling community on a near-daily basis, especially during the first four years of the research (before we had a child). We worked in their legitimate businesses, vacationed together, attended their weddings, and cared for their children. Throughout their relationship with us, several participants became co-opted to the researcher's perspective [1] and actively sought out instances of behavior which filled holes in the conceptualizations we were developing. Dave, for one, became so intrigued by our conceptual dilemmas that he undertook a "natural experiment" entirely on his own, offering an unlimited supply of drugs to a lower-level dealer to see if he could work up to higher levels of dealing, and what factors would enhance or impinge upon his upward mobility.

In addition to helping us directly through their own experiences, our key informants aided us in widening our circle of contacts. For instance, they let us know when someone in whom we might be interested was planning on dropping by, vouching for our trustworthiness and reliability as friends who could be included in business conversations. Several times we were even awakened in the night by phone calls informing us that someone had dropped by for a visit, should we want to "casually" drop over too. We rubbed the sleep from our eyes, dressed, and walked or drove over, feeling like sleuths out of a television series. We thus were able to snowball, through the active efforts of our key informants,[2] into an expanded study population. This was supplemented by our own efforts to cast a research net and befriend other dealers, moving from contact to contact slowly and carefully through the domino effect.

The Covert Role

The highly illegal nature of dealing in illicit drugs and dealers' and smugglers' general level of suspicion made the adoption of an overt research role highly sensitive and problematic. In discussing this issue with our key informants, they all agreed that we should be extremely discreet (for both our sakes and theirs). We carefully approached new individuals before we admitted that we were studying them. With many of these people, then, we took a covert posture in the research setting. As nonparticipants in the business activities which bound members together into the group, it was difficult to become fully accepted as peers. We therefore tried to establish some sort of peripheral, social membership in the general crowd, where we could be accepted as "wise" (Goffman 1963) individuals and granted a courtesy membership. This seemed an attainable goal, since we had begun our involvement by forming such relationships with our key informants. By being introduced to others in this wise rather than overt role, we were able to interact with people who would otherwise have shied away from us. Adopting a courtesy membership caused us to bear a courtesy stigma,[3] however, and we suffered since we, at times, had to disguise the nature of our research from both lay outsiders and academicians.

In our overt posture we showed interest in dealers' and smugglers' activities, encouraged them to talk about themselves (within limits, so as to avoid acting like narcs), and ran home to write field notes. This role offered us the advantage of gaining access to unapproachable people while avoiding researcher effects, but it prevented us from asking some necessary, probing questions and from tape recording conversations.[4] We therefore sought, at all times, to build toward a conversion to the overt role. We did this by working to develop their trust.

Developing Trust

Like achieving entrée, the process of developing trust with members of unorganized deviant groups can be slow and difficult. In the absence of a formal structure separating members from outsiders, each individual must form his or her own judgment about whether new persons can be admitted to their confidence. No gatekeeper existed to smooth our path to being trusted, although our key informants acted in this role whenever they could by providing introductions and references. In addition, the unorganized nature of this group meant that we met people at different times and were constantly at different levels in our developing relationships with them. We were thus trusted more by some people than by others, in part because of their greater familiarity with us. But as Douglas (1976) has noted, just because someone knew us or even liked us did not automatically guarantee that they would trust us.

We actively tried to cultivate the trust of our respondents by tying them to us with favors. Small things, like offering the use of our phone, were followed with bigger favors, like offering the use of our car, and finally really meaningful favors, like offering the use of our home. Here we often trod a thin line, trying to ensure our personal safety while putting ourselves in enough of a risk position, along with our research subjects, so that they would trust us. While we were able to build a "web of trust" (Douglas 1976) with some members, we found that trust, in large part, was not a simple status to attain in the drug world. Johnson (1975) has pointed out that trust is not a one-time phenomenon, but an ongoing developmental process. From my experiences in this research I would add that it cannot be simply assumed to be a one-way process either, for it can be diminished, withdrawn, reinstated to varying degrees, and re-questioned at any point. Carey (1972) and Douglas (1972) have remarked on this waxing and waning process, but it was especially pronounced for us because our subjects used large amounts of cocaine over an extended period of time. This tended to make them alternately warm and cold to us. We thus lived through a series of ups and downs with the people we were trying to cultivate as research informants.

The Overt Role

After this initial covert phase, we began to feel that some new people trusted us. We tried to intuitively feel when the time was right to approach them and go overt. We used two means of approaching people to inform them that we were involved in a study of dealing and smuggling: direct and indirect. In some cases our key informants approached their friends or connections and, after vouching for our absolute trustworthiness, convinced these associates to talk to us. In other instances, we approached people directly, asking for their help with our project. We worked our way through a progression with these secondary contacts, first discussing the dealing scene overtly and later moving to taped life history interviews. Some people reacted well to us, but others responded skittishly, making appointments to do taped interviews only to break them as the day drew near, and going through fluctuating stages of being honest with us or putting up fronts about their dealing activities. This varied, for some, with their degree of active involvement in the business. During the times when they had quit dealing, they would tell us about their present and past activities, but when they became actively involved again, they would hide it from us.

This progression of covert to overt roles generated a number of tactical difficulties. The first was the problem of *coming on too fast* and blowing it. Early in the research we had a dealer's old lady (we thought) all set up for the direct approach. We knew many dealers in common and had discussed many things tangential to dealing with her without actually mentioning the subject. When we asked her to do a taped interview of her bohemian lifestyle, she agreed without hesitation. When the interview began, though, and she found out why we were interested in her, she balked, gave us a lot of incoherent jumble, and ended the session as quickly as possible. Even though she lived only three houses away we never saw her again. We tried to move more slowly after that.

A second problem involved simultaneously *juggling our overt and covert roles* with different people. This created the danger of getting our cover blown with people who did not know about our research (Henslin 1972). It was very confusing to separate the people who knew about our study from those who did not, especially in the minds of our informants. They would make occasional veiled references in front of people, especially when loosened by intoxicants, that made us extremely uncomfortable. We also frequently worried that our snooping would someday be mistaken for police tactics. Fortunately, this never happened.

Cross-Checking

The hidden and conflictual nature of the drug dealing world made me feel the need for extreme certainty about the reliability of my data. I therefore based all my conclusions on independent sources and accounts that we carefully verified. First, we tested information against our own common sense and general knowledge of the scene. We adopted a hard-nosed attitude of suspicion, assuming people were up to more than they would originally admit. We kept our attention especially riveted on "reformed" dealers and smugglers who were living better than they could outwardly afford, and were thereby able to penetrate their public fronts.

Second, we checked out information against a variety of reliable sources. Our own observations of the scene formed a primary reliable source, since we were involved with many of the principals on a daily basis and knew exactly what they were doing. Having Dave live with us was a particular advantage because we could contrast his statements to us with what we could clearly see was happening. Even after he moved out, we knew him so well that we could generally tell when he was lying to us or, more commonly, fooling himself with optimistic dreams. We also observed other dealers' and smugglers' evasions and misperceptions about themselves and their activities. These usually occurred when they broke their own rules by selling to people they did not know, or when they commingled other people's money with their own. We also cross-checked our data against independent, alternative accounts. We were lucky, for this purpose, that Jean got reinvolved in the drug world. By interviewing her, we gained additional insight into Dave's past, his early dealing and smuggling activities, and his ongoing involvement from another person's perspective. Jean (and her connections) also talked to us about Dave's associates, thereby helping us to validate or disprove their statements. We even used this pincer effect to verify information about people we had never directly interviewed. This occurred, for instance, with the tapes that Jack Douglas gave us from his earlier study. After doing our first round of taped interviews with Dave, we discovered that he knew the dealers Jack had interviewed. We were excited by the prospect of finding out what had happened to these people and if their earlier stories checked out. We therefore sent Dave to do some investigative work. Through some mutual friends he got back in touch with them and found out what they had been doing for the past several years.

Finally, wherever possible, we checked out accounts against hard facts: newspaper and magazine reports; arrest records; material possessions; and visible evidence. Throughout the research, we used all these cross-checking measures to evaluate the veracity of new information and to prod our respondents to be more accurate (by abandoning both their lies and their self-deceptions).[5]

After about four years of near-daily participant observation, we began to diminish our involvement in the research. This occurred gradually, as first pregnancy and then a child hindered our ability to follow the scene as intensely and spontaneously as we had before. In addition, after having a child, we were less willing to incur as many risks as we had before; we no longer felt free to make decisions based solely on our own welfare. We thus pulled back from what many have referred to as the "difficult hours and dangerous situations" inevitably present in field research on deviants (see Becker 1963: Carey 1972; Douglas 1972). We did, however, actively maintain close ties with research informants (those with whom we had gone overt), seeing them regularly and periodically doing follow-up interviews.

Problems and Issues

Reflecting on the research process, I have isolated a number of issues which I believe merit additional discussion. These are rooted in experiences which have the potential for greater generic applicability.

The first is the *effect of drugs on the data-gathering process.* Carey (1972) has elaborated on some of the problems he encountered when trying to interview respondents who used amphetamines, while Wax (1952. 1957) has mentioned the difficulty of trying to record field notes while drinking

for sake. I found that marijuana and cocaine had nearly opposite effects from each other. The latter helped the interview process, while the former hindered it. Our attempts to interview respondents who were stoned on marijuana were unproductive for a number of reasons. The primary obstacle was the effects of the drug. Often, people became confused, sleepy, or involved in eating to varying degrees. This distracted them from our purpose. At times, people even simulated overreactions to marijuana to hide behind the drug's supposed disorienting influence and thereby avoid divulging information. Cocaine, in contrast, proved to be a research aid. The drug's warming and sociable influence opened people up, diminished their inhibitions, and generally increased their enthusiasm for both the interview experience and us.

A second problem I encountered involved *assuming risks while doing research.* As I noted earlier, dangerous situations are often generic to research on deviant behavior. We were most afraid of the people we studied. As Carey (1972), Henslin (1972), and Whyte (1955) have stated, members of deviant groups can become hostile toward a researcher if they think that they are being treated wrongfully. This could have happened at any time from a simple occurrence, such as a misunderstanding, or from something more serious, such as our covert posture being exposed. Because of the inordinate amount of drugs they consumed, drug dealers and smugglers were particularly volatile, capable of becoming malicious toward each other or us with little warning. They were also likely to behave erratically owing to the great risks they faced from the police and other dealers. These factors made them moody, and they vacillated between trusting us and being suspicious of us.

At various times we also had to protect our research tapes. We encountered several threats to our collection of taped interviews from people who had granted us these interviews. This made us anxious, since we had taken great pains to acquire these tapes and felt strongly about maintaining confidences entrusted to us by our informants. When threatened, we became extremely frightened and shifted the tapes between different hiding places. We even ventured forth one rainy night with our tapes packed in a suitcase to meet a person who was uninvolved in the research at a secret rendezvous so that he could guard the tapes for us.

We were fearful, lastly, of the police. We often worried about local police or drug agents discovering the nature of our study and confiscating or subpoenaing our tapes and field notes. Sociologists have no privileged relationship with their subjects that would enable us legally to withhold evidence from the authorities should they subpoena it.[6] For this reason we studiously avoided any publicity about the research, even holding back on publishing articles in scholarly journals until we were nearly ready to move out of the setting. The closest we came to being publicly exposed as drug researchers came when a former sociology graduate student (turned dealer, we had heard from inside sources) was arrested at the scene of a cocaine deal. His lawyer wanted us to testify about the dangers of doing drug-related research, since he was using his research status as his defense. Fortunately, the crisis was averted when his lawyer succeeded in suppressing evidence and had the case dismissed before the trial was to have begun. Had we been exposed, however, our respondents would have acquired guilt by association through their friendship with us.

Our fear of the police went beyond our concern for protecting our research subjects, however. We risked the danger of arrest ourselves through our own violations of the law. Many sociologists (Becker 1963; Carey 1972; Polsky 1969; Whyte 1955) have remarked that field researchers studying deviance must inevitably break the law in order to acquire valid participant observation data. This occurs in its most innocuous form from having "guilty knowledge": information about crimes that are committed. Being aware of major dealing and smuggling operations made us an accessory to their commission, since we failed to notify the police. We broke the law, secondly, through our "guilty observations," by being present at the scene of a crime and witnessing its occurrence (see also Carey 1972). We knew it was possible to get caught in a bust involving others, yet buying and selling was so pervasive that to leave every time it occurred would have been unnatural and highly suspicious. Sometimes drug transactions even occurred in our home, especially when Dave was living there, but we finally had to put a stop to that because we could not handle the anxiety. Lastly, we broke the law through our "guilty actions," by taking part in illegal behavior ourselves. Although we never dealt drugs (we were too scared to be seriously tempted), we consumed drugs and possessed them in small quantities. Quite frankly, it would have been impossible for a nonuser to have gained access to this group to gather the data presented here. This was the minimum involvement necessary to obtain even the courtesy membership we achieved. Some kind of illegal action was also found to be a necessary or helpful component of the research by Becker (1963), Carey (1972). Johnson (1975), Polsky (1969), and Whyte (1955).

Another methodological issue arose from the *cultural clash between our research subjects and ourselves.* While other sociologists have alluded to these kinds of differences (Humphreys 1970, Whyte 1955), few have discussed how the research relationships affected them. Relationships with research subjects are unique because they involve a bond of intimacy between persons who might not ordinarily associate together, or who might otherwise be no more than casual friends. When fieldworkers undertake a major project, they commit themselves to maintaining a long-term relationship with the people they study. However, as researchers try to get depth involvement, they are apt to come across fundamental differences in character, values, and attitudes between their subjects and themselves. In our case, we were most strongly confronted by differences in present versus future orientations, a desire for risk versus security, and feelings of spontaneity versus self-discipline. These differences often caused us great frustration. We repeatedly saw dealers act irrationally, setting themselves up for failure. We wrestled with our desire to point out their patterns of foolhardy behavior and offer advice, feeling competing pulls between our detached, observer role which advised us not to influence the natural setting, and our involved, participant role which called for us to offer friendly help whenever possible.[7]

Each time these differences struck us anew, we gained deeper insights into our core, existential selves. We suspended our own taken-for-granted feelings and were able to reflect on our culturally formed attitudes, character, and life choices from the perspective of the other. When comparing how we might act in situations faced by our respondents, we realized where our deepest priorities lay. These revelations had the effect of changing our self-conceptions: whereas we, at one time, had thought of ourselves as what Rosenbaum (1981) has called "the hippest of non-addicts" (in this case nondealers), we were suddenly faced with being the straightest members of the crowd. Not only did we not deal, but we had a stable, long-lasting marriage and family life, and needed the security of a reliable monthly paycheck. Self-insights thus emerged as one of the unexpected outcomes of field research with members of a different cultural group.

The final issue I will discuss involved the various *ethical problems* which arose during this research. Many fieldworkers have encountered ethical dilemmas or pangs of guilt during the course of their research experiences (Carey 1972; Douglas 1976: Humphreys 1970: Johnson 1975; Klockars 1977, 1979; Rochford 1985). The researchers' role in the field makes this necessary because they can never fully align themselves with their subjects while maintaining their identity and personal commitment to the scientific community. Ethical dilemmas, then, are directly related to the amount of deception researchers use in gathering the data, and the degree to which they have accepted such acts as necessary and therefore neutralized them.

Throughout the research, we suffered from the burden of intimacies and confidences. Guarding secrets which had been told to us during taped interviews was not always easy or pleasant. Dealers occasionally revealed things about themselves or others that we had to pretend not to know when interacting with their close associates. This sometimes meant that we had to lie or build elaborate stories to cover for some people. Their fronts therefore became our fronts, and we had to weave our own web of deception to guard their performances. This became especially disturbing during the writing of the research report, as I was torn by conflicts between using details to enrich the data and glossing over description to guard confidences.[8]

Using the covert research role generated feelings of guilt, despite the fact that our key informants deemed it necessary, and thereby condoned it. Their own covert experiences were far more deeply entrenched than ours, being a part of their daily existence with non–drug world members. Despite the universal presence of covert behavior throughout the setting, we still felt a sense of betrayal every time we ran home to write research notes on observations we had made under the guise of innocent participants.

We also felt guilty about our efforts to manipulate people. While these were neither massive nor grave manipulations, they involved courting people to procure information about them. Our aggressively friendly postures were based on hidden ulterior motives: we did favors for people with the clear expectation that they could only pay us back with research assistance. Manipulation bothered us in two ways: immediately after it was done, and over the long run. At first, we felt awkward, phony, almost ashamed of ourselves, although we believed our rationalization that the end justified the means. Over the long run, though, our feelings were different. When friendship became intermingled with research goals, we feared that people would later look back on our actions and feel we were exploiting their friendship merely for the sake of our research project.

The last problem we encountered involved our feelings of whoring for data. At times, we felt that we were being exploited by others, that we were putting more into the relationship than they, that they were taking us for granted or using us. We felt that some people used a double standard in their relationship with us: they were allowed to lie to us, borrow money and not repay it, and take advantage of us, but we were at all times expected to behave honorably. This was undoubtedly an outgrowth of our initial research strategy where we did favors for people and expected little in return. But at times this led to our feeling bad. It made us feel like we were selling ourselves, our sincerity, and usually our true friendship, and not getting treated right in return.

Conclusions

The aggressive research strategy I employed was vital to this study. I could not just walk up to strangers and start hanging out with them as Liebow (1967) did, or be sponsored to a member of this group by a social service or reform organization as Whyte (1955) was, and expect to be accepted, let alone welcomed. Perhaps such a strategy might have worked with a group that had nothing to hide, but I doubt it. Our modern, pluralistic society is so filled with diverse subcultures whose interests compete or conflict with each other that each subculture has a set of knowledge which is reserved exclusively for insiders. In order to serve and prosper, they do not ordinarily show this side to just anyone. To obtain the kind of depth insight and information I needed. I had to become like the members in certain ways. They dealt only with people they knew and trusted, so I had to become known and trusted before I could reveal my true self and my research interests. Confronted with secrecy, danger. hidden alliances, misrepresentations, and unpredictable changes of intent, I had to use a delicate combination of overt and covert roles. Throughout, my deliberate cultivation of the norm of reciprocal exchange enabled me to trade my friendship for their knowledge, rather than waiting for the highly unlikely event that information would be delivered into my lap. I thus actively built a web of research contacts, used them to obtain highly sensitive data, and carefully checked them out to ensure validity.

Throughout this endeavor I profited greatly from the efforts of my husband, Peter, who served as an equal partner in this team field research project. It would have been impossible for me to examine this social world as an unattached female and not fall prey to sex role stereotyping which excluded women from business dealings. As a couple, our different genders allowed us to relate in different ways to both men and women (see Warren and Rasmussen 1977). We also protected each other when we entered the homes of dangerous characters, buoyed each other's initiative and courage, and kept the conversation going when one of us faltered. Conceptually, we helped each other keep a detached and analytical eye on the setting, provided multiperspectival insights, and corroborated, clarified, or (most revealingly) contradicted each other's observations and conclusions.

Finally, I feel strongly that to ensure accuracy, research on deviant groups must be conducted in the settings where it naturally occurs. As Polsky (1969: 115–16) has forcefully asserted:

> This means—there is no getting away from it—the study of career criminals *au natural*, in the field, the study of such criminals as they normally go about their work and play, the study of "uncaught" criminals and the study of others who in the past have been caught but are not caught at the time you study them....Obviously we can no longer afford the convenient fiction that in studying criminals in their natural habitat, we would discover nothing really important that could not be discovered from criminals behind bars.

By studying criminals in their natural habitat I was able to see them in the full variability and complexity of their surrounding subculture, rather than within the artificial environment of a prison. I was thus able to learn about otherwise inaccessible dimensions of their lives, observing and analyzing firsthand the nature of their social organization, social stratification, lifestyle, and motivation.

Notes

1. Gold (1958) discouraged this methodological strategy, cautioning against overly close friendship or intimacy with informants, lest they lose their ability to act as informants by becoming too much observers. Whyte (1955), in contrast, recommended the use of informants as research aides, not for helping in conceptualizing the data but for their assistance in locating data which supports, contradicts, or fills in the researcher's analysis of the setting.
2. See also Biernacki and Waldorf 1981: Douglas 1976; Henslin 1972: Hoffman 1980; McCall 1980; and West 1980 for discussions of "snowballing" through key informants.
3. See Kirby and Corzine 1981; Birenbaum 1970; and Henslin 1972 for more detailed discussion of the nature, problems, and strategies for dealing with courtesy stigmas.
4. We never considered secret tapings because, aside from the ethical problems involved, it always struck us as too dangerous.

5. See Douglas (1976) for a more detailed account of these procedures.

6. A recent court decision, where a federal judge ruled that a sociologist did not have to turn over his field notes to a grand jury investigating a suspicious fire at a restaurant where he worked, indicates that this situation may be changing (Fried 1984).

7. See Henslin 1972 and Douglas 1972, 1976 for further discussions of this dilemma and various solutions to it.

8. In some cases I resolved this by altering my descriptions of people and their actions as well as their names so that other members of the dealing and smuggling community would not recognize them. In doing this, however, I had to keep a primary concern for maintaining the sociological integrity of my data so that the generic conclusions I drew from them would be accurate. In places, then, where my attempts to conceal people's identities from people who know them have been inadequate. I hope that I caused them no embarrassment. See also Polsky 1969; Rainwater and Pittman 1967: and Humphreys 1970 for discussions of this problem.

References

Adler, Patricia A., and Peter Adler. 1987. *Membership Roles in Field Research.* Beverly Hills. CA: Sage.

Becker, Howard. 1963. *Outsiders.* New York: Free Press.

Biernacki, Patrick, and Dan Waldorf. 1981. "Snowball sampling." *Sociological Methods and Research* 10: 141–63.

Birenbaum, Arnold. 1970. "On managing a courtesy stigma." *Journal of Health and Social Behavior* 11: 196–206.

Blumer, Herbert. 1969. *Symbolic Interactionism.* Englewood Clifts. NJ: Prentice-Hall.

Carey, James T. 1972. "Problems of access and risk in observing drug scenes." In Jack D. Douglas, ed., *Research on Deviance,* pp. 71–92. New York: Random House.

Cummins, Marvin, et al. 1972. *Report of the Student Task Force on Heroin Use in Metropolitan Saint Louis.* Saint Louis: Washington University Social Science Institute.

Douglas, Jack D. 1972. "Observing deviance." In Jack D. Douglas, ed., *Research on Deviance,* pp. 3–34. New York: Random House.

——. 1976. *Investigative Social Research.* Beverly Hills, CA: Sage.

Fried, Joseph P. 1984. "Judge protects waiter's notes on fire inquiry." *New York Times,* April 8: 47.

Goffman, Erving. 1963. *Stigma.* Englewood Cliffs, NJ: Prentice-Hall.

Gold, Raymond. 1958. "Roles in sociological field observations." *Social Forces* 36: 217–23.

Henslin, James M. 1972. "Studying deviance in four settings: research experiences with cabbies, suicides, drug users and abortionees." In Jack D. Douglas, ed., *Research on Deviance,* pp. 35–70. New York: Random House.

Hoffman, Joan E. 1980. "Problems of access in the study of social elites and boards of directors." In William B. Shaffir, Robert A. Stebbins, and Allan Turowetz, eds., *Fieldwork Experience.* pp. 45–56. New York: St. Martin's.

Humphreys, Laud. 1970. *Tearoom Trade.* Chicago: Aldine.

Johnson, John M. 1975. *Doing Field Research.* New York: Free Press.

Kirby, Richard, and Jay Corzine. 1981. "The contagion of stigma." *Qualitative Sociology* 4: 3–20.

Klockars, Carl B. 1977. "Field ethics for the life history." In Robert Weppner, ed., *Street Ethnography,* pp. 201–26. Beverly Hills. CA: Sage.

——. 1979. "Dirty hands and deviant subjects." In Carl B. Klockars and Finnbarr W. O'Connor, eds., *Deviance and Decency,* pp. 261–82. Beverly Hills. CA: Sage.

Liebow, Elliott. 1967. *Tally's Corner.* Boston: Little, Brown.

McCall, Michal. 1980. "Who and where are the artists?" In William B. Shaffir, Robert A. Stebbins and Allan Turowetz, eds., *Fieldwork Experience,* pp. 145–58. New York: St. Martin's.

Polsky, Ned. 1969. *Hustlers, Beats, and Others.* New York: Doubleday.

Rainwater, Lee R., and David J. Pittman. 1967. "Ethical problems in studying a politically sensitive and deviant community." *Social Problems* 14: 357–66.

Riemer, Jeffrey W. 1977. "Varieties of opportunistic research." *Urban Life* 5: 467–77.

Rochford, E. Burke, Jr. 1985. *Hare Krishna in America.* New Brunswick. NJ: Rutgers University Press.

Rosenbaum, Marsha. 1981. *Women on Heroin.* New Brunswick, NJ: Rutgers University Press.

Warren, Carol A. B., and Paul K. Rasmussen. 1977. "Sex and gender in field research." *Urban Life* 6: 349–69.

Wax, Rosalie. 1952. "Reciprocity as a field technique." *Human Organization* 11: 34–37.

——. 1957. "Twelve years later: An analysis of a field experience." *American Journal of Sociology* 63: 133–42.

West, W. Gordon. 1980. "Access to adolescent deviants and deviance." In William B. Shaffir, Robert A. Stebbins, and Allan Turowetz, eds., *Fieldwork Experience*, pp. 31–44. New York: St. Martin's.

Whyte, William F. 1955. *Street Corner Society*. Chicago: University of Chicago Press.

Responses to Crime

Crime consists of those acts codified into the criminal law, and therefore thought to be potentially disruptive to the social order. They are considered threatening enough to individual and group security to call for state responses, rather than relying on private citizens to respond. When a crime is committed, the state, acting on behalf of all the citizens, reacts by mobilizing agencies of the government to assess responsibility, to apprehend, and, ultimately, to punish the guilty party. Known as the criminal justice process, this state-sponsored response to crime consists of police, court, and correctional personnel and procedures intended to control crime and make law breakers accountable for their acts. How the agents and agencies of government carry out these important responsibilities is determined by the rule of law and the interpretation of relevant laws by those charged with implementing them. Both making law and implementing them are influenced by the social context, which in the last ten years has been hostile to conventional law violators.

There are, in effect, two responses to crime, the official and the unofficial. The official response includes all of the institutionalized elements of the criminal justice process; the unofficial response includes the public's feelings and attitudes about crime, especially the fear of it. It is these unofficial sentiments that determine the context within which criminal statutes and their penalties are framed and within which the agents of the justice system carry out their responsibilities. Society's fear of crime has certainly increased by the steady rise in crime, especially violent crime, in the 1970s and 1980s: widespread drug use, drive-by shootings, and other urban dangers. Because of these conditions, city dwellers are often frightened to leave their homes, worry about the safety of their children, and feel compelled to use extraordinary security measures. In an environment of such fear and concern, the public often expresses its anger about the way crime is being addressed by the government and the way criminals are handled by the justice system. One commentator claims that "…Americans are increasingly alarmed at news stories of violent crimes committed by individuals who had received long sentences for other crimes and yet were released after serving only a small fraction of their time" (Wooten 1995: 150). Even in the 1990s, the fear of crime appeared to be rising, although the crime rate, especially for serious crime, steadily declined (Kappeler, Blumberg, and Potter 1996).

Three factors appear to be responsible for the difference between the diminishing amount of crime and the perception of the rising amount of crime: media reporting, law enforcement warnings, and the politicalization of crime (Kappeler, Blumberg, and Potter 1996). For example, the number of investigative television shows that portray sensational but atypical crimes, and the entertainment programming that provides a steady diet of violence, influence our public perception and subsequent fear of crime. In addition, the obvious financial benefit to various branches of the criminal justice system (police, courts, and prisons) of keeping crime in the public's view as a serious problem and the politicians who use the issue of crime to garner public support also contribute to the exaggerated picture the public has of the severity of the crime problem.

Of these factors, it may well be that media coverage of crime is the most important in shaping our fear and determining the public agenda. Some contend that when the media speak, the government and others listen (Mead 1994). Moreover, it is not really the content of the coverage but the extent of it that makes people think an issue is important (Johnson et al. 1994). If this logic is applied to crime and its constant portrayal in the news and in the entertainment field, it becomes clear why people are convinced that crime is a serious problem and one that needs to be dealt with effectively.

An important myth about crime is the distinction between criminals and noncriminals, a kind of us-and-them mentality that ignores the fact that many Americans have committed crimes for which they could be incarcerated at some time in their lives (Kappeler, Blumberg, and Potter 1996). When all of these factors—exaggerated exposure to crime, the resulting fear of crime and altered lifestyles, the us-and-them distinction, and public outrage at the seemingly lenient treatment of offenders—are combined, they form the basis for the public's punitive attitude toward offenders. Indeed, Victor E. Kappeler and his colleagues suggest that the public's desire for punishment outweighs its concern for fair judicial treatment of the offender. Although the philosophy of the American correctional system has vacillated among a number of goals, such as retribution (vengeance), incapacitation (the removal of an offender from society), rehabilitation (treatment for the offender), and deterrence (both specifically aimed at the offender, and generally aimed at using the offender as an example to society), the public in recent years has cried for greater vengeance. Evidence of this attitude can be seen in the growing public support for the death penalty, longer sentences, mandatory sentences, the abolition of parole in many states, and "three strikes and you're out" legislation. Both the public and its lawmakers seem to be less interested in rehabilitation or the general welfare of

inmates than in punitive sentences and scapegoats to bear the brunt of public outrage and fear.

Within this context of rising public fear of crime, the official agents of the criminal justice system work to ensure public safety and protect the established social order. How these goals are accomplished has varied over time, but at each point in history the roles of the police, the courts, and the correctional system have been debated and argued. The debate continues today.

Policing Society

For most people, our first response to knowledge of a crime is to call the police. It is the responsibility of the police to protect us from those who would break the law by enforcing codes of conduct found in criminal statutes. But the police do more than just protect us; they engage in many activities that have little to do with enforcing the law (see Reading 38). Although the police are often held responsible for rising crime rates and are accused of not being able to prevent crime, the truth is that the public has misconstrued the true nature of police work. Policing actually involves little crime control and almost no crime prevention. James A. Inciardi (1996: 196) claims that only a small percentage of police activities are related to law enforcement; other criminologists are more specific, placing the amount of law enforcement activity as low as 10 to 20 percent (Kappeler, Blumberg, and Potter, 1996). Instead, large portions of the work day are given to peacekeeping (control of disorderly crowds and individuals, directing traffic, providing directions, and so forth), and mundane activities such as filling out reports and testifying in court. A majority of police work is reactive, not proactive. Police respond when they are called, and the manner and nature of the response have often generated controversy.

Although policing society is arguably the justice system's most important function, it is also the one fraught with the gravest problems and the most sensitive issues, including police discretion, coercive force, brutality, and corruption. Interestingly, policing is one area of work in which the amount of discretion increases as one goes from the top of the organization down to patrol officers (Glaser

1972). Police discretion is the ability to make quick, on-the-spot decisions, sometimes contrary to official rules. An important discretionary decision is whether or not to make an arrest. If every instance of law violation known to the police led to an arrest, the system would be overwhelmed and paralyzed. Discretion allows some screening of whom the police react to and process officially. Some factors that influence the decision to arrest, for example, include the seriousness of the offense, how well the victim and offender know each other, department policy, and the demeanor of the offender toward the police (Voigt et al. 1994). One important problem with police discretion is the potential for institutionalized discrimination. Even with problems associated with discretion, many scholars agree that it is a necessary and integral part of police work and should be controlled (not eliminated) by formal rules created within the agencies themselves (Walker 1993).

An important detail that sets the police apart from the rest of society is that they have the "legitimate right to use [coercive] force" in situations where it may be required (Inciardi 1996: 196). Sometimes the use of force is carried too far and turns into police brutality, as in the 1991 beating of Rodney King by Los Angeles police officers. Police brutality is most likely to take place when an individual shows disrespect for the police or when the police want information.

One factor that contributes to police brutality, as well as to corruption, is the police subculture, which "provide[s] officers with a shared cognitive framework from which to view the world…the beliefs, values, definitions and manners of expression necessary to depart from society's expectation of acceptable behavior" (Kappeler, Blumberg, and Potter 1994: 124). Police officers, who are generally exposed to the negative aspects of society, feel isolated, sometimes even hostile toward much of society, and they soon learn to trust very few people except fellow officers. Not only are they dependent on one another for safety on the job, but they find that fellow officers are the only ones who can understand and relate to the stresses, strains, and alienation associated with police work. As a result, they tend to associate with one another and maintain an us-and-them attitude. One consequence is

that few officers will implicate a fellow officer in any wrongdoing, preferring instead to maintain a "code of silence."

According to Daniel Glaser, there are three types of policing: the watchman style, the legalistic style, and the service style. Officers in "watchman" departments, typically located in older cities with strong political machines, have little education, have little training, and receive low pay. Most police efforts in the watchman style are for the benefit of people of high status; lower-class people are served grudgingly. Officers in legalistic departments stress a high level of law enforcement and have somewhat more education. Most of their efforts are directed against those of lower status. Officers in the service-style departments stress courtesy and neighborhood relations; compared to outsiders, residents receive preferential treatment from the police.

In the last twenty years, efforts have been made to professionalize police departments. Many now have higher standards of admission, requiring applicants to have at least an Associate's degree. In 1988 almost 23 percent of police officers had four or more years of college; not quite 35 percent of officers had no college education, down from 80 percent in 1960 (Walker 1993). In many jurisdictions, rates of pay have been increased substantially in order to attract and keep higher-level officers on the force and to reduce temptations for corruption. Officers receive better training than in the past; training hours have almost doubled from 340 hours to 633 hours in the thirty-year period from 1952 to 1982, and training has been expanded to cover more topics. Closer attention is also being paid to police-community relationships, with community-based and problem-oriented policing becoming trendy options.

Although there is substantial agreement on the need to professionalize the police and make them more responsive to their local communities, some methods used to achieve these objectives are not well accepted by rank-and-file officers. To combat brutality and corruption, most urban police departments have internal-affairs departments, which attempt to monitor, review, and at times discipline inappropriate police behavior. These units are sometimes seen as violations of the unofficial police subculture, which expects officers to keep silent about one another's transgressions. In a number of communities, citizen review boards have been formed to hear and investigate citizen complaints against police officers. These boards have typically been opposed by the police, who see them as an unwarranted intrusion into their departmental affairs.

In response to past injustices and abuses, the behaviors of police are bound (or limited) by a number of Supreme Court rulings. In 1914 the Court found in *Weeks v. United States* that evidence seized illegally, in violation of the Fourth Amendment's unreasonable search-and-seizure clause, could not be used in federal courts. In 1961, the Supreme Court's ruling in *Mapp v. Ohio* extended the exclusionary rule to state courts as well. Unfortunately, this ruling was viewed by many as tying the hands of police officers in their fight against crime. *Escobedo v. Illinois* (1964) guaranteed a suspect the right to an attorney when police questioning becomes accusatory. The implications of *Miranda v. Arizona* (1966) included protection from self-incrimination. Suspects must be informed of their Miranda rights, a process now familiar to most of society: the right to remain silent, the right to an attorney, and the warning that any statements can be used against the accused in a court of law. In 1985 in *Tennessee v. Garner*, the Supreme Court affirmed the step that most police departments had already taken by invalidating the "fleeing felon" rule in favor of the "defense of life" standard in police decisions involving whether or not to shoot (Walker 1993). Some states have adopted laws requiring police departments to develop rules governing high-speed pursuits. There are, of course, varying opinions on whether these limitations improve or hinder policing.

The Judicial System

The judicial system in the United States is an accusatorial, or adversarial, system, unlike inquisitorial systems found elsewhere. In an adversarial system, two opposing sides (the prosecution and the defense) argue their cases before an impartial referee (the judge) and a jury of the accused's peers. In an inquisitorial system, the judge is a part

of the fact-finding mission, and all sides cooperate to bring forth the truth, regardless of whether or not it benefits the side that discloses the evidence.

Prosecutors enjoy some of the broadest discretionary powers of any criminal justice personnel (see Reading 40). They decide when and whom to prosecute, the nature and degree of the charges, and whether or not to offer a plea bargain. Their decisions are often based on such arbitrary considerations as their win-lose court record, the credibility of the victim (taking into consideration a victim's character and background), or the relationship between an offender and a victim (Voigt et al. 1994). The wishes of a victim or victim's family to avoid trial (for various reasons such as fear or inconvenience), bargains in which the defendant agrees to testify against others, the strength or absence of societal pressure to prosecute, and the ego of the prosecutor may also determine whether a deal is struck (Holten and Lamar 1991).

Although the U.S. Constitution guarantees the right to trial by a jury of one's peers, in reality, a trial is not what generally happens. Ninety percent of all cases are decided through plea bargaining, an informal procedure in which the prosecution or the state makes an offer to lower the charges or set a limit on the punishment imposed in exchange for a plea of guilty from the defendant (Inciardi 1996: 346). There are many advantages and some disadvantages to the widespread use of plea bargaining. One of the biggest advantages is that it greatly reduces the number of cases being tried on already overcrowded court dockets. Plea bargaining is particularly advantageous to prosecutors who have weak cases, poor witnesses, and small staffs; it allows them to win a case that might otherwise be lost or require too much preparation time and manpower.

Plea bargains are also advantageous for overworked defense attorneys, particularly public defenders or court-appointed attorneys, who are assigned huge workloads and who may have only a few minutes to spend with each defendant. Defense attorneys often succumb to "work group pressures," knowing that giving judges and prosecutors too much flack on one case may jeopardize the treatment of their other clients (Holten and Lamar 1991). Some public defenders may not want to rock the boat if they aspire to higher-level jobs in the system. Public defenders have been described as "double agents," giving the appearance of representing the defendant but in actuality working for the court and coming to regard guilty pleas as the most cost-effective way to run the system (Voigt et al. 1994). Public defenders often approach their cases with the assumption that their clients are guilty of something (Voigt et al. 1994), and they work from that assumption.

Plea bargaining has several disadvantages. There is always a chance that innocent persons will take a plea bargain for fear of going to prison if they are found guilty in a trial. In addition, those who plead guilty give up their constitutional rights to a trial by jury, the right to confront and cross-examine witnesses against them, and so forth. Nevertheless, the public often feels that plea bargaining lets criminals off easy with less punishment than they deserve. This effect erodes the public's confidence in the criminal justice system and may fuel a punitive, "get tough" attitude toward offenders.

Even cases that go to trial are fraught with the possibility of unfair and discriminatory treatment and outcomes. Defendants are guaranteed a right to a trial by a jury of their peers. For many years, however, African Americans and other minorities, even females, could not serve on juries, so it was highly questionable whether a defendant from one of these groups was tried by a jury of peers. Defendants and jurors often come from different social classes, further reducing the likelihood of facing a jury of one's "peers." During *voir dire*, the jury screening process, each side (defense and prosecution) may eliminate a certain number of candidates it thinks are unsuitable. But today, it is perfectly legal for those with enough money to hire professional jury consultants to help select a "winning" jury. That practice negates the idea of random jury selection and puts those who cannot afford consultants at a disadvantage. Juries are often unpredictable. In jury nullification, or jury pardons, for example, juries often refuse to convict a person they think is guilty, because they do not believe he or she deserves the punishment (Holten and Lamar 1991).

Another area in which there is disparity in treatment of defendants is that of bail. Judges set bail based on a number of factors, such as the seriousness of the crime and the likelihood that the defendant will appear in court as ordered. Little consideration is given to the defendant's ability to post bail. Therefore, upper-class and well-to-do defendants are often freed on bail, whereas poor, lower-class defendants often languish in jail or detention centers awaiting hearings or trials. Consequently, those accused of petty offenses may be jailed even as those with more serious offenses are allowed to remain free until their cases come to trial because of differing economic circumstances. Innocent people have been incarcerated (sometimes for a long period of time) while awaiting hearings or trials. Those in jail have no opportunity to participate in the preparation of their defense. Often families of lower-class and middle-class jailed defendants experience great financial hardship in their absence.

Punishment

Earlier, it was stated that all criminal laws contain a penalty, or a specification of the punishment that one deserves for breaking the law. The provision of punishment is society's way of attempting to prevent and control crime, the overall goals of the criminal justice system. Punishment is not, of course, the only objective of the correctional system (see Reading 42). Indeed, social control theorists generally identify four goals of American corrections: retribution, deterrence (general and specific), incapacitation, and rehabilitation (or treatment). Retribution is akin to vengeance, a situation in which the severity of the punishment is equal to the severity of the crime. Specific deterrence reflects the idea that offenders will find the punishment unpleasant enough that they will refrain from committing the crime again in the future. General deterrence involves the punishment of an offender serving as an example to the rest of society not to engage in a particular activity. Incapacitation simply means that an offender is not able to commit other illegal acts while incarcerated. Rehabilitation seeks to change offenders in some way that will encourage them to engage in legal activities and stay away from crime.

Deterrence, incapacitation, and rehabilitation are forward-looking goals with an eye toward preventing future crime, while retribution is backward-looking, intent only on punishment, with no thought for crime prevention (Travis, Schwartz, and Clear 1983). Looking at the goals from this perspective illuminates a flaw in the public desire for retribution at the expense of other goals, especially treatment: It offers no hope of a solution, no possibility of change or improvement in the problem of crime, and it may actually worsen the situation. The large number of recidivists seem to illustrate that our correctional facilities are doing little to facilitate change, except perhaps change for the worse.

Correctional goals should be based on the "least drastic alternative," that is, the least severe punishment necessary to obtain the desired result (Travis, Schwartz, and Clear 1983: 230). Why incarcerate those who pose no physical threat to society? This can only be answered when society has a clear idea of what its goals of punishment are. If the goal is retribution, then incarceration fulfills that goal. If the goals include the prevention of future crime, incarceration alone does not address this goal. There is a need for some form of rehabilitation, either within the process of incarceration or perhaps instead of it.

Not everyone agrees, of course, that the U.S. system incarcerates too many people for too long. For example, James Wooten discusses the costs of letting people out of prison early. They include the commission of new crimes, the cost of private protection (lights, locks, guards) against criminals, and the cost of insurance. Victims, he says, experience a loss of property and wages, and altered lifestyles. In addition, costs of crime include medical costs, business losses passed on to consumers, and urban blight. From this perspective, keeping a large number of offenders, especially chronic offenders, under state supervision might even be considered cost effective.

Although punishment is an integral and often used element of our criminal justice system, it is not always administered fairly or effectively. There is racial, class, and gender disparity in punishment. As noted previously, penalties for possession and sale of crack, a drug used primarily by

African Americans, are stiffer than penalties for possession and sale of cocaine, a very similar drug used primarily by whites. Capital punishment discriminates against minorities, males, and the lower class. One study found that over a sixty-year period, 13 percent of murders were committed by women, but they made up less than 1 percent of the executions (Lee 1995). During the same sixty-year period, almost half of those executed were people of color (Stephens 1995). It has been found that a person of any race is more likely to be executed if the victim was white (Kappeler, Blumberg, and Potter 1996). Eighty-five percent of those executed during one recent twenty-year period had white victims (Stephens 1995).

Prisons

In 1997, more than 1 million adults were incarcerated in federal and state prisons and more than 500,000 were imprisoned in local jails (Donziger 1996). By 2007, this number was up to 2.2 million for an incarceration rate of 497 per 100,000 American citizens. This is the largest number of incarcerated men and women in the history of the country, and it ranks the United States second only to Russia in number of persons locked up. In addition, several million more are under the supervision of a correctional system (on probation or parole or serving a sentence in a community facility). The rates of incarceration and correctional supervision have grown significantly since 1980 for members of all racial and ethnic groups, although African American males have experienced the largest growth.

Although they do not receive as much public attention as prisons, there are more than 3,300 local jails in the United States. Jails hold persons who are awaiting a court appearance or sentencing as well as those serving sentences of one year or less. Between 1989 and 1997, the jail population rose 43 percent (Bureau of Justice Statistics, 1998), and at midyear 2006 more than 766,000 inmates were held in the nation's local jails. The inmates of the nation's jails are typically poor men, largely of a racial minority, who were using drugs, alcohol, or both at the time of their arrest. Sometimes characterized as the "ultimate ghetto" of the criminal justice system, jails are often unsafe, brutal places where inmate services are lacking and rehabilitation programs nonexistent (Inciardi 1996).

The number of prisoners and the composition of prison populations change as a result of two factors: changes in criminal activity and changes in responses of the system (Beck and Brien 1995). Such changes in the last twenty years are well documented. One of the most striking changes has been in the number of drug-related offenses coming to the attention of authorities. The number of inmates in prison for a drug crime has risen to the point where they now make up approximately 50 percent of those in federal prisons and 23 percent of those in state prisons (Office of National Drug Control Policy 1998). As drug-related offenses have increased, legislatures have cracked down by passing laws that increase the likelihood of incarceration on conviction, impose mandatory sentences, and make early release more difficult. At the same time, several offenses not necessarily related to drugs, such as weapons possession, drunk driving, and some sexual assaults, also carry stiffer prison sentences. Although the advent of sentencing guidelines has allowed greater uniformity in sentencing, it has also increased the overall time served in prison.

Although we keep building new prisons, we fill them almost as fast as they can be built and overcrowding continues to be a major problem. In 1993 "state prisons were estimated to be operating at between 18 and 29 percent above capacity [and] the federal system...36 percent over capacity" (Crouch et al. 1995: 66). Today overcrowding represents one of the foremost challenges to the correctional system. Overcrowding and its resulting stress, coupled with the almost total loss of privacy, can lead to violence and abuse and is conducive to the spreading of illness.

The cost of prisons is great. It costs $160,000 per "bed" (not including interest paid on borrowed money) to build a maximum-security prison (Irwin and Austin 1997) and $25,000 a year to support one inmate (DiIulio and Piehl 1995). Additional costs include loss of tax revenue from inmates, loss of property taxes from prison grounds, and payment of social services to inmates' families; these costs add up to another $21,000 per inmate (Irwin and Austin 1997). Money used to build and support prisons is money taken from some other service, such as education.

There are other costs to society besides monetary, however. Because prisons are a breeding ground for crime, many first-time petty offenders who end up in prison turn into hardened criminals who commit more heinous crimes on their eventual release. A prison record and a lack of educational opportunities and job-training programs make it difficult for many prison releasees to find employment, thus increasing their chances of becoming recidivists. Society pays a steep price for their continued criminal activities.

Prisons are "total institutions," with involuntary residents; the institution controls every area of the inmates' lives. On entering prison, inmates suffer a number of losses, first and foremost the loss of liberty and personal space. They are separated from family and friends, are deprived of heterosexual relationships, and lose their sense of security. Their movements are restricted, and the goods and services that they are allowed are limited primarily to basic needs, unless obtained through prison gangs or "service providers." Inmates are not allowed to make many decisions and are reduced to a dependent state, a situation that does nothing to help them cope with common problems of living when they are released.

There are a number of less severe and less costly alternatives to prisons. Many of these fall into the category of community-based corrections, halfway houses, work-release programs, and community service (Voigt et al. 1994). Individuals may be diverted from the system by entering rehabilitation programs, counseling programs, or drug and alcohol treatment programs, or by such innovations as house arrest with electronic surveillance devices. Drug courts, an increasingly popular option, stipulate drug treatment with parole in lieu of incarceration; successful completion of this sentence results in the original charges being dropped.

Probation is another alternative to prison sentences. Probation allows an offender to be under supervision while continuing to live in the community, thus creating only minor disruptions in his or her life. The probationer is expected to follow certain rules (different for each person), such as visiting or calling the probation officer at regular intervals, avoiding the use of alcoholic beverages, or staying away from criminal acquaintances. Not only is probation less expensive than incarceration, but it allows an offender to keep his or her job, maintain family relationships, and avoid the violent and corrupt prison setting. Also, the typical probationer experiences less social stigma than a convict who has served time in prison. For many first-time or nonviolent offenders, probation is often a viable option. Taken in total, by the end of 2005, there were 7 million Americans under some form of correctional supervision, including prisons, jails, probation, and parole. This translates to 3.2 % of all U.S. residents or 1 in every 31 adults.

Decriminalization

As a result of the get-tough-on-crime policy, which now characterizes this nation's reaction to the perceived growth in law-violating behavior, U.S. prisons and jails are filled beyond capacity, and probation and parole caseloads are unmanageably large. In 1992, the latest year for which data are available, nationwide spending on corrections exceeded $31 billion (*Seeking Justice* 1997). "Between 1987 and 1993, state spending increases for corrections outpaced higher education by 41 percent nationwide" (ibid, p. 9). Since then, there have been no indications that the rate of commitment to correctional programs or the cost of such policies has slowed. How long can the nation continue to spend more on incarcerating its citizens than on educating them?

One way of reducing the burden now being shouldered by the police, courts, and correctional facilities is to eliminate some behaviors from the criminal statutes. If a behavior were no longer considered a crime, it would not be of concern to the police, and those engaging in the activity would not be sent to overcrowded prisons and jails. Decriminalization is repealing a law or laws governing some type of behavior that should no longer be labeled as criminal (see Reading 43). Admittedly applicable to a limited number of offenses, generally public-order crimes about which there is ambivalent moral consensus, decriminalization could be an important alternative response to some

criminal activity, as much of the current criminal justice crisis has resulted from the enforcement of substance-abuse laws. Decriminalization of drug offenses, for example, would drastically reduce the number of individuals incarcerated in prisons and alleviate the problem of overcrowding without building more prisons or letting serious felons out the back door as new offenders come in the front door. It would also reduce court dockets substantially.

Using drugs as an example, arguments for and against decriminalization may be analyzed. From Arnold Trebach's point of view (see Trebach and Inciardi 1993), the war against drugs has filled prisons with small-time drug offenders; invaded personal privacy and violated constitutional rights; provoked hatred of racial minorities; wasted large sums of money; encouraged violent drug traffickers and police corruption; diverted resources and attention from other pressing problems such as racial hatred, criminal violence, and AIDS; and pushed crime and violence levels higher. Furthermore, Trebach points out, there is really no scientific basis for distinguishing legal and illegal drugs as far as potential harm to users, inasmuch as annual deaths from alcohol and cigarettes far outstrip those from illicit substances. He claims that for most simple cases of drug possession (the majority of which are for marijuana), prison is an entirely inappropriate punishment, because the punishment far exceeds the crime.

It is Trebach's contention, therefore, that the legalization of drugs would help curb the problems of massive drug abuse, high levels of crime and violence (such as murders and maimings), the spread of AIDS, the collapse of cities, and vicious racial conflict. He believes we should have addict-maintenance programs in conjunction with the legalization of drugs.

Inciardi, by contrast, is against the legalization of drugs. He refutes Trebach's contention that legalization would probably not increase drug use, and he also refutes the idea that drugs such as marijuana are harmless (Trebach and Inciardi 1993). Although Inciardi is careful to point out that for most individuals criminal activities begin long before drug use, he does believe that drugs intensify criminal careers. The drug-crime interaction may be seen in each of three types of drug-related violence delineated by Paul Goldstein: the psychopharmacologic, the economically compulsive, and the systemic. The psychopharmacologic type results from drug-induced irrational behavior; cocaine psychosis fits this type. In the economically compulsive type, some users support their habit through economically oriented violent crime. Finally, the systemic type results from interactions involving drug trafficking, such as fights over turf. Inciardi believes that any decrease in systemic violence that might occur as a result of legalization would be compensated for by an increase in psychopharmacologic violence. Therefore, he does not see legalization as a means of decreasing crime and, in fact, thinks that it may create more addicts (hence, more psychopharmacologic crime), because unlike Trebach, he believes that current laws do limit access to drugs for many groups, especially teenagers. He contends that the legalization of currently illegal drugs will not discourage their use but will most likely encourage it.

Perhaps the best response to crime is to prevent it from occurring in the first place. Crime prevention is often discussed but seldom implemented. The reason for that may be the difficulty in knowing precisely what to do to prevent crime. Programs designed to improve social conditions, to deliver more effective policing, to "get tough" on violators have all claimed some success in reducing the crime rate, but empirical verification of such claims is scarce. In the meantime, responses to crime after it has occurred continue to be the principal way in which society handles crime and criminals.

The readings that follow deal in some detail with the topics discussed in this section: the police, courts, corrections, the efficacy of punishment, and the possibility of decriminalization.

References

Beck, Allen J. and Peter M. Brien. 1995. "Trends in the U.S. Correctional Populations: Recent Findings from the Bureau of Justice Statistics," in Kenneth C. Haas and Geoffrey P. Alpert (eds.), *The Dilemmas of Corrections: Contemporary Readings* (3rd ed.). Prospect Heights, IL: Waveland Press.

Bureau of Justice Statistics. 1998. *Profile of Jail Inmates 1996*. Washington, DC: U.S. Department of Justice.

Crouch, Ben M., Geoffrey P. Alpert, James W. Marquart, and Kenneth C. Haas. 1995. "The American Prison Crisis: Clashing Philosophies of Punishment and Crowded Cellblocks," in Kenneth C. Haas and Geoffrey P. Alpert (eds.), *The Dilemmas of Corrections: Contemporary Readings* (3rd ed.), Prospect Heights, IL: Waveland Press.

DiIulio, John J. Jr. and Anne Morrison Piehl. 1995. "Does Prison Pay? The Stormy National Debate Over the Cost-Effectiveness of Imprisonment," in Kenneth C. Haas and Geoffrey P. Alpert (eds.), *The Dilemmas of Corrections: Contemporary Readings* (3rd ed.). Prospect Heights, IL: Waveland Press.

Donziger, Stephen R., ed. 1996. *The Real War on Crime*. New York: Harper Perennial.

Glaser, Daniel. 1972. *Adult Crime and Social Policy*. Englewood Cliffs, NJ: Prentice-Hall.

Goldstein, Paul (1985). "The Drugs/Violence Nexus: A Tripartite Conceptual Framework," *Journal of Drug Issues* (Fall): 493-506.

Heineman, Robert A., Steven A. Peterson, and Thomas H. Rasmussen. 1995. *American Government* (2nd ed.). New York: McGraw-Hill.

Holten, N. Gary and Lawson L. Lamar. 1991. *The Criminal Courts: Structures, Personnel, and Processes*. New York: McGraw-Hill.

Inciardi, James A. 1996. *Criminal Justice* (5th ed.) San Diego: Harcourt Brace Jovanovich.

Irwin, John and James Austin. 1997. *It's About Time: America's Imprisonment Binge* (2nd ed.). Belmont, CA: Wadsworth.

Johnson, Paul E., Gary J. Miller, John H. Aldrich, David W. Rohde, and Charles W. Ostrom, Jr. 1994. *American Government: People, Institutions, and Policies* (3rd ed.). Boston: Houghton Mifflin.

Kappeler, Victor E., Mark Blumberg, and Gary W. Potter. 1996. *The Mythology of Crime and Criminal Justice* (2nd ed.). Prospect Heights, IL: Waveland Press.

Kappeler, Victor E., Richard D. Sluder, and Geoffrey P. Alpert. 1994. *Forces of Deviance: Understanding the Dark Side of Policing*. Prospect Heights, IL: Waveland Press.

Lee, Robert W. 1995. "Deserving to Die," in George McKenna and Stanley Feingold (eds.), *Taking Sides: Clashing Views on Controversial Political Issues* (9th ed.). Guilford, CT: Dushkin.

Mead, Timothy D. 1994. "The Daily Newspaper as Political Agenda Setter: The Charlotte Observer and Metropolitan Reform," *State and Local Government Review*, 26 (Winter): 27-37.

Office of National Drug Control Policy. 1998. Drug Policy Information Clearinghouse, *Fact Sheet* (March).

Seeking Justice: Crime and Punishment in America. 1997. New York: Edna McConnell Clark Foundation.

Stephens, Matthew L. 1995. "Instrument of Justice or Tool of Vengeance?" in George McKenna and Stanley Feingold (eds.), *Taking Sides: Clashing Views on Controversial Political Issues* (9th ed.). Guilford, CT: Dushkin.

Travis, Lawrence F. III, Martin D. Schwartz, and Todd R. Clear. 1983. *Corrections: An Issues Approach* (2nd ed.). Cincinnati, OH: Anderson.

Trebach, Arnold S. and James A. Inciardi. 1993. *Legalize It?: Debating American Drug Policy*. Washington, DC: The American University Press.

Voigt, Lydia, William E. Thornton, Jr., Leo Barrile, and Jerrol M. Seaman. 1994. *Criminology and Justice*. New York: McGraw-Hill.

Walker, Samuel. 1993. "Beyond the Supreme Court: Alternative Paths to the Control of Police Behavior," in Chris W. Eskridge (ed.), *Criminal Justice: Concepts and Issues*. Los Angeles: Roxbury.

Wooten, James. 1995. "Truth in Sentencing: Why States Should Make Violent Criminals Do Their Time," in George McKenna and Stanley Feingold (eds.), *Taking Sides: Clashing Views on Controversial Political Issues* (9th ed.). Guilford, CT: Dushkin.

CHAPTER 38

Police

Carl B. Klockars

Why do we have police in our society and what do they do? Are they the first line of defense against lawlessness and anarchy? Or do they serve the larger, more subtle function of protecting the status quo and those who have a vested interest in it? Questions such as these have been debated by scholars and social critics for a long time, with few clear-cut answers emerging from the discussion. What we do know, however, is that all societies have some sort of social control agency charged with enforcing laws and maintaining order. Although the nature and organization of such agencies may vary, their functions are generally similar. For most citizens, the police represent the criminal justice system, and for most law violators, the police are their first contact with the process of justice.

In this selection Carl B. Klockars examines the roles of police in modern American society. He demonstrates that the police do much more than fight crime, that their roles are so varied and complex it is difficult to offer a precise definition of their function. Nevertheless, the common element in all police roles and functions is the right to use legitimate coercive force. Such force may be used immediately in responding to one of the situations police are expected to handle. Obviously, this gives the police enormous discretionary authority that

must be supervised by government agents who are responsive to the people.

Klockars demonstrates the origins and background of some of the unique features of American police. The uniform, for example, links the police to a military model of organization, which helps account for their believing they are engaged in a "war on crime." Winning such a war cannot be done by the police, because crime results from factors over which the police have no control. The best that might be achieved is controlling crime more effectively with nontraditional tactics. Two ideas that have recently emerged as part of the reform movement of policing are community-oriented policing and problem-oriented policing. These techniques, targeting "hot spots" and working more closely with the community, may well be the models of policing for the future. But this selection shows that they, too, are not without shortcomings and potentially serious problems.

For modern sociology the core problem of police has been, and continues to be, the extrication of the concept *police* from the forms and institutions in which it has been realized and the symbols and concealments in which it has been wrapped. Doing so is essential to the interpretive understanding of the idea of police and is prerequisite to mature answers to the question of what policing means, has meant, and can mean. In one form or another it is the project that has occupied sociologists of police since the early 1960s, and although there is occasional overlap and interchange, attention to

Reprinted from: Carl B. Klockars, "Police." In Edgar F. Borgatta and Marie L. Borgatta (eds.), *Encyclopedia of Sociology*, Vol. 3, pp. 1463-1471. Copyright © 1992 by Edgar F. Borgatta and Marie L. Borgatta. Reprinted with permission of Macmillan Library Reference, a Simon & Schuster Company.

it is primarily what distinguishes contributions to the sociology of police from scholarly efforts in the study of police administration, jurisprudence, criminalistics, and police science.

The Police: A Sociological Definition

By the end of the 1960s a small number of now-classic empirical studies of police had made it apparent that conventional understandings of the idea of police were fundamentally and irreparably flawed. In the face of large-scale studies by Reiss (1971) and Black (1971) which showed that the model tour of duty of a patrol officer in the high-crime areas of the nation's largest cities did not involve the arrest of a single person, it became impossible for sociologists to continue to speak of police as "law enforcers" or of their work as "law enforcement." Likewise, both Skolnick's *Justice Without Trial* (1966) and Wilson's *Varieties of Police Behavior* (1968) illustrated dramatic differences in the way police were organized and the relationships they elected to enjoy with courts and law. Similarly, early studies of both the exercise of patrol officer discretion (Bittner 1967a, 1967b) and requests for police service (Cumming et al. 1965; Bercal 1970) cast substantial doubt on the notion that as substantial, much less a defining, activity of police was "fighting crime."

Police Role and Functions

The task of extricating the concept of police from these common misconceptions was assumed by Egon Bittner in his *The Functions of Police in Modern Society* (1970). A fundamental theme of Bittner's work was that to define police as "law enforcers," "peacekeepers," "agents of social control," "officers of the court," or, indeed, in any terms that suppose what police should do, confuses police role and function. Throughout history, in this country and in others, police have performed all sorts of functions. In fact, the functions, both manifest and latent, which police have performed are so numerous and so contradictory that any attempt to define police in terms of the functions they are supposed to perform or the ends they are supposed to achieve is doomed to failure.

Force as the Core of the Police Role

Sociologically, policing cannot be defined in terms of its ends; it must be defined in terms of its means. In *Functions* Bittner advanced an approach to understanding the role of the police that was based on the single means which was common to all police, irrespective of the ends to which they aspired or were employed. The means Bittner found to define police was a right to use coercive force. Police, said Bittner, are "a mechanism for the distribution of non-negotiable, coercive force" (1971). No police had ever existed, nor is it possible to conceive of an entity that could be called police ever existing, that did not claim the right to use coercive force.

Sociologically, Bittner's formulation has three major virtues. First, it was universal. It was applicable to police everywhere as diverse as the sheriff's posse of the old West, the London bobby, the FBI, or the police of Hitler's Third Reich or Castro's Cuba. Second, it was politically, and morally neutral. It could be used to refer to police whose behavior was exemplary as readily as it could be applied to police whose behavior was appalling. And, third, it made it possible to make explicit and to probe in systematic ways a host of questions about the role of police that could not previously be explored because they had been concealed in the confusion between role and function: Why do all modern societies, from the most totalitarian and most tyrannical to the most open and democratic, have police? What does having police make available to society that no other institution can supply? What functions are appropriate to assign to police and what are best left to other institutions?

These questions are of such enormous consequence and so fundamental to an understanding of the role of the police that it is difficult to conceive of a sociology of police existing prior to their recognition.

Why Police?

If police are a "mechanism for the distribution of non-negotiably coercive force," why should all modern societies find it necessary to create and sustain such a mechanism? What does having such a mechanism make available to modern societies that no other institution can provide?

Bittner's answer is that no other institution has the special competence required to attend to "situations which ought not to be happening and about which something ought to be done NOW!" (1974, p. 30). The critical word in Bittner's careful formulation of the role of the police is "now." What the right to distribute coercive force gives to police is the ability to resolve situations that cannot await a later resolution. The crucial element is time. Turning off a fire hydrant against the wishes of inner-city street bathers, preventing the escape of a serial murderer, halting the escalation of a domestic dispute, or moving back the curious at the scene of a fire so that emergency equipment can pass—these and hundreds of other tasks fall to police because their capacity to use force may be required to achieve them "now."

This view of police radically inverts some conventional conceptions. While popular opinion holds that police acquire their right to use coercive force from their duty to enforce the law, the sociology of police holds that police acquire the duty to enforce the law because doing so may require them to invoke their right to use coercive force. Similarly, focus by police on the crimes and misdemeanors of the poor and humble, and their relative lack of attention to white-collar and corporate offenders, is often promoted as reflecting a class or race bias in institutions of social control. While not denying that such biases can exist and do sometimes influence the direction of police attention, if such biases were eliminated entirely, the distribution of police effort and attention would undoubtedly remain unchanged. It would remain unchanged because the special competence of police, their right to use coercive force, is essential in enforcement efforts in which offenders are likely to physically resist or to flee. In white-collar and corporate crime investigations, the special competence of lawyers and accountants is essential, while the special competence of police is largely unnecessary.

Institutional Forms

Although all modern societies have found it necessary to create and maintain some form of police, it is obvious that any institution which bears the right to use coercive force is extraordinarily dangerous and highly subject to abuse and corruption. The danger of the institution of police would appear to be magnified when it gains a monopoly or a near monopoly on the right to use coercive force and those who exercise that monopoly are almost exclusively direct and full-time employees of the state. Appearances and dangers notwithstanding, these are nevertheless the major terms of the institutional arrangement of police in every modern democracy. Some comment on the sociology of this institutional uniformity may be helpful.

Avocational Policing

For most of human history most policing has been done by individuals, groups, associations, and organizations in the private sector. This type of private-sector policing, done by citizens not as a job but as an avocation, may be classified into at least three types, each of which offered a somewhat different kind of motivation to private citizens for doing it (Klockars 1985). Historically, the most common type is *obligatory avocational policing*. Under its terms private citizens are compelled to police by the threat of some kind of punishment if they fail to do so. In American police history the sheriff's posse is perhaps the most familiar variety of this type of policing. The English systems of frankpledge (Morris 1910) and parish constable (Webb and Webb 1906) were also of this type.

A second type of private-sector policing, *voluntary avocational policing,* is done by private citizens not because they are obliged by a threat of punishment but because they, for their own reasons, want to do it. The most familiar American example of this type of policing is vigilante groups, over three hundred of which are known to have operated throughout the United States up to the end of the nineteenth century (Brown 1975).

A third type, *entrepreneurial avocational policing*, includes private citizens who as English thief takers, American bounty hunters, French agents provocateurs, and miscellaneous paid informants police on a per-head, per-crime basis for money.

The institutional history of these avocational forms of policing is thoroughly disappointing, and modern societies have largely abandoned these ways of getting police work done. The central flaw in all systems of obligatory avocational policing is that as the work of policing becomes more difficult or demanding, obligatory avocational policing takes on the character of forced labor. Motivated only by the threat of punishment, those who do it become unwilling and resistant, a situation offering no one any reason to learn or cultivate the skill to do it well. All forms of voluntary avocational policing suffer from the exact opposite problem. Voluntary avocational police, vigilantes and the like, typically approach their work with passion. The problem is that because the passionate motives of voluntary avocational police are their own, it is almost impossible to control who and where and what form of police work they do and on whom they do it. Finally, the experience with entrepreneurial forms of avocational policing—thief takers, bounty hunters, and paid informants—has been the most disappointing of all. The abuse and corruption of entrepreneurial avocational police has demonstrated unequivocally that greed is too narrow a basis on which to build a police system.

Sociologically, the shortcoming of all forms of avocational policing is that none of them offers adequate means of controlling the police. This observation leads directly to the question of why one might have reason to suspect that a full-time, paid police should be easier to control than its avocational precedents. What new means of control is created by establishing a full-time, paid, police vocation?

The answer to this problem is that only when policing becomes a full-time, paid occupation is it possible to dismiss, to *fire*, any particular person who makes his or her living doing it. The state can only hire entrepreneurial avocational police, bounty hunters, paid informants, and thief takers; it cannot fire them. Vigilantes are driven by their own motives and cannot be discharged from them. Obligatory avocational police are threatened with punishment if they don't work; most would love to be sacked. Because the option to fire, to take police officers' jobs away from them, is the only essential means of controlling police work that separates the police vocation from all avocational arrangements for policing, how that option is used will, more than anything else, determine the shape and substance of the police vocation.

The Police Vocation

The English, who in 1829 created the first modern police, were intimately familiar with the shortcomings of all forms of avocational policing. They had, in fact, resisted the creation of a paid, full-time police for more than a century, out of fear that such an institution would be used as a weapon of political oppression by the administrative branch of government. To allay the fears that the "New Police" would become such a weapon, the architects of the first modern police, Home Secretary Robert Peel and the first commissioners of the New Police, Richard Mayne, and Charles Rowan, imposed three major political controls on them. Peel, Mayne, and Rowan insisted that the New Police of London would be unarmed, uniformed, and confined to preventive patrol. Each of these features shaped in profound ways the institution of the New Police and, in turn, the police of the United States and other Western democracies that explicitly copied the English model.

Unarmed

Politically, the virtue of an unarmed police is that its strength can be gauged as a rough equivalent of its numbers. Weapons serve as multipliers of the strength of individuals and can increase the coercive capacity of individuals to levels that are incalculable. One person with a rifle can dominate a dozen citizens; with a machine gun, hundreds; with a nuclear missile, thousands. One person with a police truncheon is only slightly stronger than another, and that advantage can be quickly eliminated by the other's picking up a stick or a stone. In 1829 the individual strength of the three thousand-constable, unarmed New Police offered little to fear to London's 1.3 million citizens.

While this political virtue of an unarmed police helped overcome resistance to the establishment of the institution, the long-run sociological virtue of an unarmed police proved far more important. Policing is, by definition, a coercive enterprise. Police must, on occasion, compel compliance from persons who would do otherwise. Force is, however, not the only means to compel compliance. Sociologically, at least three other bases for control are possible: authority, power, and persuasion.

Unarmed and outnumbered, the New Police "bobby" could not hope to police effectively on the basis of force. Peel, Mayne, and Rowan knew that if the New Police were to coerce successfully, they would have to do so on the basis of popular respect for the authority and power of the institution of which they were a part. The respect owed each constable was not owed to an individual but to a single, uniform temperament, code of conduct, style of work, and standard of behavior that every constable was expected to embody.

In order to achieve this uniformity of temperament, style, conduct, and behavior, the architects of the New Police employed the option to dismiss with a passion. "Between 1830 and 1838, to hold the ranks of the New Police of London at a level of 3300 men required nearly 5000 dismissals and 6000 resignations, most of the latter not being altogether voluntarily" (Lee 1971, p. 240). During the first eight years of its organization, every position on the entire force was fired or forced to resign more than three times over!

Unlike their earlier London counterparts, the new American police were undisciplined by the firing option. What prevented the effective use of the firing option by early American police administrators was that police positions were, by and large, patronage appointments of municipal politicians. In New York, for example, the first chief of police did not have the right to fire any officer under his command. So while London bobbies were being dismissed for showing up late to work or behaving discourteously toward citizens, American police were assaulting superior officers, taking bribes, refusing to go on patrol, extorting money from prisoners, and releasing prisoners from the custody of other officers.

In New York, Boston, Chicago, and other American cities the modern police began, in imitation of London's bobbies, as unarmed forces; but, being corrupt, undisciplined, and disobedient, they could not inspire respect for either their power or their authority. In controlling citizens they had no option but to rely on their capacity to use force. The difficulty with doing so unarmed is that someone armed with a multiplier of strength can always prove to be stronger. Gradually, against orders, American police armed themselves, at first with the quiet complicity of superior officers and later, as the practice became widespread, in open defiance of departmental regulations. Eventually, in an effort to control the types of weapons their officers carried, the first municipal police agencies began issuing standard service revolvers.

The long-run sociological consequence of arming the American police can be understood only by appreciating how it shaped American police officers' sense of the source of their capacity to control the citizens with whom they dealt. While the London bobbies drew their capacity for control from the profoundly social power and authority of the institution of which they were a part, American police officers understood their capacities for control to spring largely from their own personal, individual strength, multiplied if necessary by the weapon they carried on their hips. This understanding of the source of their capacity for control led American police officers to see the work they did and the choices they made in everyday policing to be largely matters of their individual discretion. Thus, the truly long-run sociological effect of the arming of the American police has been to drive discretionary decision making to the lowest and least public levels of American police agencies. Today how an American police officer handles a drunk, a domestic disturbance, an unruly juvenile, a marijuana smoker, or a belligerent motorist is largely a reflection not of law or agency policy but of that particular officer's personal style. This is not to say that law or agency policy cannot have influence over how officers handle these types of incidents. However, one of the major lessons of recent attempts by sociologists to measure the impact of changes in law or police policy in both domestic violence and drunken driving enforcement is that officers can resist those changes vigorously when the new law or policy goes against their views of proper police response (see Dunford et al. 1990; Mastrofski et al. 1988).

Uniformed

Politically, the requirement that police be uniformed is a guarantee that they will not be used as spies; that they will be given information only when their identity as police is known; that those who give them information, at least when they do so in public, are likely to be noticed doing so; and that they can be held accountable, as agents of the state, for their behavior. The English, who had long experience with uniformed employees of many types, understood these political virtues of the uniform completely. In fact, an incident in 1833 in which a police sergeant assumed an un-uniformed undercover role resulted in such a scandal that it nearly forced the abolition of the New Police.

By contrast, the early American understanding of the uniform was totally different. Initially it was seen to be a sign of undemocratic superiority. Later it was criticized by officers themselves as a demeaning costume and resisted on those grounds. For twelve years, despite regulations that required them to do so, early New York policemen successfully refused to wear uniforms. In 1856 a compromise was reached by allowing officers in each political ward to decide on the color and style they liked best.

Despite the early resistance to the uniform and the lack of appreciation for its political virtues, American police eventually became a uniformed force. But while the London bobby's uniform was explicitly designed to have a certain "homey" quality and reflect restraint, the modern American police officer's uniform is festooned with the forceful tools of the police trade. The gun, ammunition, nightstick, black-jack, handcuffs, and Mace, all tightly bolstered in shiny black leather and set off with chromium buckles, snaps, badges, stars, flags, ribbons, patches, and insignia, suggest a decidedly military bearing. The impression intended is clearly one not of restraint but of the capacity to overcome the most fearsome of enemies by force.

The Military Analogy and the War on Crime

To understand the sociology of the American police uniform, it is necessary to see in it a reflection of a major reform movement in the history of the American police. Around 1890 American police administrators began to speak about the agencies they administered as if they were domestic armies engaged in a war on crime (Fogelson 1977).

The analogy was powerful and simple. It drew upon three compelling sources. First, it sought to connect police with the victories and heroes of the military and to dissociate them from the corruption and incompetence of municipal politics. Second, it evoked a sense of urgency and emergency, in calls for additional resources. From the turn of the century to the present day, the war on crime has proved a useful device for getting municipal governments and taxpayers to part with money for police salaries and equipment. And, third and most important, the war on crime and the military analogy sought to create a relationship between police administrators and politicians at the municipal level that was similar to the relationship enjoyed by military generals and politicians at the national level. At the national level Americans have always conceded that the decision on whether to fight a war was a politicians' decision, but how that war was to be fought and the day-to-day discipline of the troops was best left to the generals. By getting the public and the politicians to accept these terms of the police-politics relationship, the early police administrators found a way to wrest from the hands of politicians the tool they needed to discipline their troops: the option to fire disobedient officers.

The uniform of the war-ready American police officer is testimony to the fact that since the 1940s, American police administrators have won the battle to conceive of police as engaged in a war on crime. And in doing so then, have gained control of the option to fire for administrative purposes. However, the cost of that victory has been enormous.

A major problem is the idea of a war on crime and the expectation police have promoted that they can, in some sense, fight or win it. In point of fact, a war on crime is something police can neither fight nor win for some fundamental sociological reasons. It is simply not within the capacity of police to change those things—unemployment, the age distribution of the population, moral education, civil liberties, ambition and the social and economic opportunities to realize it—that influence the amount and type of crime in any society. These are the major social correlates of crime, and despite presentments to the contrary, police are but a small tail on a gigantic social kite. Moreover, any kind of real "war on crime" is something that no democratic society would be prepared to let its police fight. No democratic society would be able to tolerate the kinds of abuses to the civil liberties of innocent citizens that fighting any real "war" on crime would necessarily involve. It is a major contribution of the sociology of police since the 1960s to demonstrate that almost nothing police do can be shown to have any substantial effect on reducing crime.

The problems of policing in the name of crime when one cannot do much of anything about it are enormous. It is not uncommon for patrol officers to see their employers as hypocritical promoters of a crime-fighting image that is far removed from what they know to be the reality of everyday police work. They may seek to explain what they know to be their failure to do much about crime in terms of the lack of courage of their chief, the incompetence of police administration, or sinister political forces seeking to "handcuff" the police. They often close off what they regard as the disappointing reality of what they do in cynicism, secrecy, and silence—the "blue curtain," the occupational culture of policing.

Equally problematic as a spoil of the early chiefs' victory in their war on crime is the quasi-military police administrative structure. Although once heralded as a model of efficiency, it is now regarded as an organizationally primitive mode of management. It works, to the extent that it works, by creating hundreds and sometimes even thousands of rules and by punishing departures from those rules severely. The central failing of such an administrative model is that it rests on the unwarranted assumption that employees will not discover that the best way to avoid punishment for doing something wrong is to do as little as possible. The administration can, in turn, respond by setting quotas for the minimum amount of work it will tolerate from employees before it moves to punish them, but if it does so, that minimal amount of work is, by and large, all it will get.

Preventive Patrol

The third major mechanism with which architects of the New Police sought to neutralize their political uses was to confine police to preventive patrol. This restriction was understood to have the effect of limiting the uniformed, patrolling constable to two relatively apolitical types of interventions: situations in which constables would be called upon for help by persons who approached them on the street and situations that, from the street, constables could see required their attention. These political virtues of patrol impressed the architects of the New Police, particularly Sir Richard Mayne. Mayne postponed the formation of any detective unit in the New Police until 1842, and for his 40 years as commissioner held its ranks to fewer than 15 detectives in a force of more than 3,500.

In the early American experience uniformed patrol served the principal purpose of imposing some semblance of order on unruly officers. Patrol offered some semblance of assurance that officers could be found at least sometimes near the area to which they were assigned. And while American police created detective forces almost immediately after they were organized, patrol has become in the United States, as in Britain and other modern democracies, the major means of getting police work done.

Sociologically, patrol has had tremendous consequences for the form and substance of policing. It has, for example, been extraordinarily amenable to the three most profound technological developments of the past century: the automobile, the telephone, and the wireless radio. And while there is no evidence that increasing or decreasing the amount of patrol has any influence whatsoever on the crime rate, each of these technological developments has made police patrol more convenient and attractive to citizens who wish to call for police service. It is not an exaggeration to say that the vast majority of the activity of most modern police agencies is driven by a need to manage citizen demand for patrol service.

In recent years attempts to manage this demand have taken many forms. Among the most common are the creation of computer-aided dispatch systems that prioritize the order in which patrol officers are assigned to complaints and increasingly stringent policies governing the types of problems for which police will provide assistance. Also increasingly common are attempts to handle complaints that merely require a written report, by taking that report over the telephone or having the complainant complete a mail-in form. In no small part, such efforts at eliminating unnecessary police response and making necessary police response efficient have produced some of the increasing cost for police labor.

Reorienting Policing

Despite efforts at prioritization, limitation of direct police response, and development of alternative ways of registering citizen complaints, demand for police service continues to grow. And despite the fact that individual citizens appear to want this form of police service more than any other, some contemporary approaches suggest that the entire idea of "dial-a-cop," "incident-driven" policing requires reconsideration. Two such approaches, "community-oriented policing" (Skolnick and Bayley 1986) and "problem-oriented policing" (Goldstein 1979, 1990), have been advanced as the next generation of "reform" movements in American policing (Greene and Mastrofski 1988).

As theories of police reform, both "problem-oriented" and "community-oriented" policing are grounded in the suspicion that the traditional police response of dispatching patrol officers in quick response to citizen complaints does little to correct the underlying problem that produced the complaint. To some degree at least, this suspicion is confirmed by studies which tend to show that a fairly small number of addresses tend to generate disproportionate numbers of calls for police service, and that patrol officers commonly return to such "hot spots" again and again to attend to similar problems (Sherman et al. 1989).

Both problem-oriented and community-oriented policing offer strategies to deal with such problems that go beyond merely dispatching an officer to the scene. Problem-oriented policing offers a generic, four-step, problem-solving strategy—scanning, analysis, response, and assessment—that police can use to identify problems and experiment with solutions. Community-oriented policing, by contrast, does not offer a mechanism for problem analysis and solution. It is, however, committed to a general strategy that calls for cooperative, police-community efforts in problem solving. In such efforts it encourages the employment of a variety of police tactics—foot patrol, storefront police stations, neighborhood watch programs—that tend to involve citizens directly in the police mission.

While both approaches to reorienting policing have been heralded as revolutionary in their implications for the future of policing, both confront some major obstacles to their realization. The first is that neither problem-oriented nor community-oriented police efforts have been able to reduce the demand for traditional patrol response. Unless that demand is reduced or police resources are increased to allow it to be satisfied along with nontraditional approaches, the community- and problem-oriented policing approaches will most likely be relegated, at best, to a secondary, peripheral role.

The second problem confronting both community- and problem-oriented policing stems from the definition of police and the role appropriate to it in a modern democratic society. The special competence of police is their capacity to use force, and for that reason all modern societies find it necessary and appropriate to have them attend to situations that cannot await a later resolution. Reactive, incident-driven, dial-a-cop patrol is a highly popular, extremely efficient, and, as near as possible, politically neutral means of delivering that special competence. To expand the police role to include responsibility for solving the root problems of neighborhoods and communities is an admirable aspiration. But it is a responsibility that seems to go beyond the special competence of police and to require, more appropriately, the special competence of other institutions.

Discussion Questions

1. Why do societies have police? What is the key operative word in Bittner's explanation of why we have police? Explain how this word separates policing from other methods of societal problem-resolution.

2. Define obligatory avocational policing, voluntary avocational policing, and entrepreneurial avocational policing. What are examples of each model? What are the problems with each of these models?

3. Describe the evolution of policing with regard to arms (weapons), clothing, and patrol. What was the reasoning behind the changes? What is the military analogy of policing? What strengths and weaknesses are associated with it?

References

Bercal, T. E. 1970 "Calls for Police Assistance: Consumer Demand for Governmental Service." *American Behavioral Scientist,* 13, no. 2 (May–August): 221-238.

Bittner, E. 1967a "Police Discretion in Apprehension of Mentally Ill Persons." *Social Problems,* 14 (Winter): 278-292.

———. 1967b "The Police on Skid Row: A Study of Peace Keeping." *American Sociological Review,* (October): 699-715.

———. 1970. *The Functions of Police in Modern Society.* Washington, DC: U.S. Government Printing Office.

———. 1974. "Florence Nightingale in Pursuit of Willie Sutton: A Theory of Police." In H. Jacob, ed., *The Potential for Reform of Criminal Justice.* Beverly Hills, CA: Sage.

Black, D. 1971 "The Social Organization of Arrest." *Stanford Law Review,* 23 (June): 1087-1111.

Brown, R. M. 1975 *Strain of Violence: Historical Studies of American Violence and Vigilantism.* Oxford: Oxford University Press.

Cumming, E., I. Cumming, and L. Edell. 1965. "Policeman as Philosopher, Guide, and Friend." *Social Forces,* 12, no. 3: 276-286.

Dunford, F. W., D. Huizinga, and D. S. Elliott. 1990. "The Role of Arrest in Domestic Assault: The Omaha Police Experiment." *Criminology,* 28, no. 2: 183-206.

Fogelson, R. 1977. *Big City Police.* Cambridge, MA: Harvard University Press.

Goldstein, H. 1979 "Improving Policing: A Problem-Oriented Approach." *Crime and Delinquency,* 25 (April): 236-258.

———. 1990. *Problem-Oriented Policing.* New York: McGraw-Hill.

Greene, J. and S. Mastrofski. 1988. *Community Policing: Rhetoric or Reality.* New York: Praeger.

Klockars, C. B. 1985. *The Idea of Police.* Beverly Hills, CA: Sage.

Lee, M. 1971. *A History of Police in England.* Montclair, NJ: Patterson Smith.

Mastrofski, S., R. R. Ritti, and D. Hoffmaster. 1988. "Organizational Determinants of Police Discretion: The Case of Drunk Driving." *Journal of Criminal Justice,* 15: 387-402.

Morris, W. A. 1910. *The Frankpledge System.* New York: Longmans, Green and Co.

Reiss, A. J., Jr. 1971. *Police and the Public.* New Haven, CT: Yale University Press.

Sherman, L. W., P. Gartin, and M. E. Buerger. 1989. "Hot Spots of Predatory Crime: Routine Activities and the Criminology of Place." *Criminology,* 27: 27-55.

Skolnick, J. K. 1966. *Justice Without Trial.* New York: John Wiley.

———, and D. Bayley. 1986 *The New Blue Line.* New York: Free Press.

Webb, S. and B. Webb. 1906. *English Local Government from the Revolution to the Municipal Corporations Act: The Parish and the County.* York: Longmans, Green and Co.

Wilson, J. Q. 1968. *Varieties of Police Behavior: The Management of Law and Order in Eight Communities.* Cambridge, MA: Harvard University Press.

CHAPTER 39

Racial Profiling

David A. Harris

Racial profiling has emerged as one of the foremost controversial issues in criminal justice today. It remains a problem that plagues police departments across the United States and galvanizes those who value social justice. Although the practice of racial profiling can manifest in any number of ways, it is typically discussed in the context of traffic stops. Although frequently a topic of political discussion, little empirical research has actually been conducted on the phenomenon. Those statistics that are available, however, have consistently supported the contention that blacks are stopped, searched, and arrested at a rate that exceeds both that of whites and relative to their proportion in the population.

In the following selection, David A. Harris reviews the available data on racial profiling that provides only a snapshot of the actual nature and extent of the practice within American police departments. Data from New Jersey, Maryland, and Ohio indicate a pervasive practice of racial profiling wherein blacks are seemingly targeted for no apparent reason other than skin color. The author goes on to discuss the latent consequences of this form of racial discrimination covering thought-provoking topics such as civil liberties violations, the criminalization of blackness, the rationalization of discrimination, and the expansion of police discretion.

Reprinted from: David A. Harris, "The Stories, the Statistics and the Law: Why 'Driving While Black' Matters," *Minnesota Law Review* v. 84, no. 1 (Dec. 1999): 265–326. Reprinted by permission of the author.

It has happened to actors Wesley Snipes, Will Smith, Blair Underwood, and LeVar Burton. It has also happened to football player Marcus Allen, and Olympic athletes Al Joyner and Edwin Moses. African-Americans call it "driving while black"—police officers stopping, questioning, and even searching black drivers who have committed no crime, based on the excuse of a traffic offense.

Data on this problem are not easy to come by. This is, in part, because the problem has only recently been recognized beyond the black community. It may also be because records concerning police conduct are either irregular or nonexistent. But it may also be because there is active hostility in the law enforcement community to the idea of keeping comprehensive records of traffic stops. In 1997, Representative John Conyers of Michigan introduced H.R. 118, the Traffic Stops Statistics Act, which would require the Department of Justice to collect and analyze data on all traffic stops around the country—including the race of the driver, whether a search took place, and the legal justification for the search.[1] When the bill passed the House with unanimous, bipartisan support the National Association of Police Organizations (NAPO), an umbrella group representing more than 4,000 police interest groups across the country, announced its strong opposition to the bill.[2] Officers would "resent" having to collect the data, a spokesman for the group said. Moreover, there is "no pressing need or justification" for collecting the data.[3] In other words, there is no problem, so there is no need to collect data.

NAPO's opposition was enough to kill the bill in the Senate in the 105th Congress. As a consequence, there is now no requirement at the federal level that law enforcement agencies collect data on traffic stops that include race. Thus, all of the data gathering so far has been the result of statistical inquiry in lawsuits or independent academic research.

New Jersey

The most rigorous statistical analysis of the racial distribution of traffic stops was performed in New Jersey by John Lamberth of Temple University. In the late 1980s and early 1990s, African-Americans often complained that police stopped them on the New Jersey Turnpike more frequently than their numbers on that road would have predicted. Similarly, public defenders in the area had observed that "a strikingly high proportion of cases arising from stops and searches on the New Jersey Turnpike involve black persons."[4] In 1994, the problem was brought to the state court's attention in *State v. Pedro Soto*,[5] in which the defendant alleged that he had been stopped because of his ethnicity.[6] The defendant sought to have the evidence gathered as a result of the stop suppressed as the fruit of an illegal seizure. Lamberth served as a defense expert in the case. His report is a virtual tutorial on how to apply statistical analysis to this type of problem.[7]

The goal of Lamberth's study was "to determine if the State Police stop, investigate, and arrest black travelers at rates significantly disproportionate to the percentage of blacks in the traveling population, so as to suggest the existence of an official or de facto policy of targeting blacks for investigation and arrest."[8] To do this, Lamberth designed a research methodology to determine two things: first, the rate at which blacks were being stopped, ticketed, and/or arrested on the relevant part of the highway, and second, the percentage of blacks among travelers on that same stretch of road.

To gather data concerning the rate at which blacks were stopped, ticketed and arrested, Lamberth reviewed and reconstructed three types of information received in discovery from the state: reports of all arrests that resulted from stops on the turnpike from April of 1988 through May of 1991. patrol activity logs from randomly selected days from 1988 through 1991, and police radio logs from randomly selected days from 1988 through 1991.[9] Many of these records identified the race of the driver or passenger.

Then Lamberth sought to measure the racial composition of the traveling public on the road. He did this through a turnpike population census—direct observation by teams of research assistants who counted the cars on the road and tabulated whether the driver or another occupant appeared black. During these observations, teams of observers sat at the side of the road for randomly selected periods of 75 minutes from 8:00 a.m. to 8:00 p.m.[10] To ensure further precision, Lamberth also designed another census procedure—a turnpike violation census. This was a rolling survey by teams of observers in cars moving in traffic on the highway, with the cruise control calibrated and set at five miles per hour above the speed limit. The teams observed each car that they passed or that passed them, noted the race of the driver, and also noted whether or not the driver was exceeding the speed limit.[11]

The teams recorded data on more than forty-two thousand cars.[12] With these observations, Lamberth was able to compare the percentages of African-American drivers who are stopped, ticketed, and arrested, to their relative presence on the road. This data enabled him to carefully and rigorously test whether blacks were in fact being disproportionately targeted for stops.

By any standard, the results of Lamberth's analysis are startling. First, the turnpike violator census, in which observers in moving cars recorded the races and speeds of the cars around them, showed that blacks and whites violated the traffic laws at almost exactly the same rate; there was no statistically significant difference in the way they drove.[13] Thus, driving behavior alone could not explain differences in how police might treat black and white drivers.[14] With regard to arrests, 73.2% of those stopped and arrested were black, while only 13.5% of the cars on the road had a black driver or passenger.[15] Lamberth notes that the disparity between these two numbers "is statistically vast."[16] The number of standard deviations present—54.27—means that the probability that the racial disparity is a random result "is infinitesimally small."[17] Radio and patrol logs yielded similar results. Blacks are approximately 35% of those stopped,[18] though they are only 13.5% of those on the road—19.45 standard deviations.[19] Considering all stops in all three types of records surveyed, the chance that 34.9% of the cars combined would have black drivers or occupants "is substantially less than one in one billion."[20] This led Lamberth to the following conclusion:

> Absent some other explanation for the dramatically disproportionate number of stops of blacks, it would appear that the race of the occupants and/or drivers of the cars is a decisive factor or a factor with great explanatory power. I can say to a reasonable degree of statistical probability that the disparity outlined here is strongly consistent with the existence of a discriminatory policy, official or de facto, of targeting blacks for stop and investigation.... Put bluntly, the statistics demonstrate that in a population of blacks and whites which is (legally) virtually universally subject to police stop for traffic law violation, (cf. the turnpike violator census), blacks in general are several times more likely to be stopped than non-blacks.[21]

Maryland

A short time after completing his analysis of the New Jersey data, Lamberth also conducted a study of traffic stops by the Maryland State Police on Interstate 95 between Baltimore and the Delaware border.[22] In 1993, an African-American Harvard Law School graduate named Robert Wilkins filed a federal lawsuit against the Maryland State Police. Wilkins alleged that the police stopped him as he was driving with his family, questioned them and searched the car with a drug-sniffing dog because of their race.[23] When a State Police memo surfaced during discovery instructing troopers to look for drug couriers who were described as "predominantly black males and black females,"[24] the State Police settled with Wilkins. As part of the settlement, the police agreed to give the court data on every stop followed by a search conducted with the

driver's consent or with a dog for three years. The data also were to include the race of the driver.

With this data, Lamberth used a rolling survey, similar to the one in New Jersey, to determine the racial breakdown of the driving population. Lamberth's assistants observed almost 6,000 cars over approximately 42 randomly distributed hours. As he had in New Jersey, Lamberth concluded that blacks and whites drove no differently; the percentages of blacks and whites violating the traffic code were virtually indistinguishable. More importantly, Lamberth's analysis found that although 17.5% of the population violating the traffic code on the road he studied was black, more than 72% of those stopped and searched were black. In more than 80% of the cases, the person stopped and searched was a member of some racial minority.[25] The disparity between 17.5% black and 72% stopped includes 34.6 standard deviations.[26] Such statistical significance, Lamberth said, "is literally off the charts.[27] Even while exhibiting appropriate caution, Lamberth came to a devastating conclusion:

> While no one can know the motivation of each individual trooper in conducting a traffic stop, the statistics presented herein, representing a broad and detailed sample of highly appropriate data, show without question a racially discriminatory impact on blacks...from state police behavior along I–95. The disparities are sufficiently great that taken as a whole, they are consistent and strongly support the assertion that the state police targeted the community of black motorists for stop, detention, and investigation within the Interstate 95 corridor.[28]

Ohio

In the Spring of 1998, several members of the Ohio General Assembly began to consider whether to propose legislation that would require police departments to collect data on traffic stops. But in order to sponsor such a bill, the legislators wanted some preliminary statistical evidence—a prima facie case, one could say—of the existence of the problem. This would help them persuade their colleagues to support the effort, they said. I was asked to gather this preliminary evidence. The methodology used here presents a case study in how to analyze this type of problem when the best type of data to do so is not available.

In the most fundamental ways, the task was the same as Lamberth's had been in both New Jersey and Maryland: use statistics to test whether blacks in Ohio were being stopped in numbers disproportionate to their presence in the driving population. Doing this would require data on stops broken down by race, and a comparison of those numbers to the percentage of black drivers on the roads. But if the goal was the same, two circumstances made the task considerably more difficult to accomplish in Ohio. First, Ohio does not collect statewide data on traffic stops that can be correlated with race. In fact, no police department of any sizeable city in the state keeps any data on all of its traffic stops that could be broken down by race. Second, the state legislators wanted some preliminary statistics to demonstrate that "driving while black" was a problem in all of Ohio, or at least in some significant—and different—parts of the whole state. While Lamberth's stationary and rolling survey methods worked well to ascertain the driving populations of particular stretches of individual, limited access highways, those methods were obviously resource- and labor-intensive. Applying the same methods to an entire city—even a medium-sized one—would entail duplicating the Lamberth approach on many major roads to get a complete picture. It would be impractical, not to mention prohibitively expensive, to do this in communities across an entire state. Thus, different methods had to be found.

To determine the percentage of blacks stopped, data was obtained from municipal courts in four Ohio cities.[29] Municipal courts in Ohio handle all low-level criminal cases and virtually all of the traffic citations issued in the state. Most of these courts also generate a computer file for each case, which includes the race of the defendant as part of a physical description. This data provided the basis for a breakdown of all tickets given by the race of the driver.

The downside of using the municipal court data is that it only includes stops in which citations were given. Stops resulting in no action or a warning are not included. In all likelihood, using tickets alone might underestimate any racial bias that is present because police might not ticket blacks stopped for nontraffic purposes. Since using tickets could underestimate any possible racial bias, any resulting calculations are conservative and tend to give law enforcement the benefit of the doubt. Similarly, the way the racial statistics are grouped in the analysis is also conservative because the numbers are limited to only two categories of drivers: black and nonblack. In other words, all minorities other than African-Americans are lumped together with whites, even though some of these other minorities, notably Hispanics, have also complained about targeted stops directed at them. Using conservative assumptions means that if a bias does show up in the analysis, we can be relatively confident that it actually exists.[30]

The percentage of all tickets in 1996, 1997, and the first four months of 1998[31] that were issued to blacks by the Akron, Dayton, and Toledo Police Departments and all of the police departments in Franklin County[32] are set out in Table 39.1.

With ticketing percentages used as a measure of stops, attention turns to the other number needed for the analysis: the presence of blacks in the driving population. Given the concerns about the use of Lamberth's method in a statewide, preliminary study, another approach—a less exact one than direct observation, to be sure, but one that would yield a reasonable estimate of the driving population—was devised. Data from the U.S. Census breaks down the populations of states, counties, and individual cities by race and

Table 39.1 Ticketing of African-Americans for 1996, 1997, and 1998*

City	Percentage of all Tickets in City Issued to African-Americans
Akron	37.6%
Toledo	30.8%
Dayton	50.0%
Columbus/Franklin County**	5.2%

*Through April 30, 1998.
**Data for Franklin County include 1996 and 1997, but not 1998, and include tickets issued by all law enforcement units in the county, not just the city of Columbus.

by age. This data is readily available and easy to use.[33] Using this data, a reasonable basis for comparing ticketing percentages can be constructed: blacks versus nonblacks in the *driving age population*. This was done by breaking down the general population by race and by age. By selecting a lower and upper age limit—fifteen and seventy-five, respectively for driving age, the data yield a reasonable reflection of what we would expect to find if we surveyed the roads themselves. The data on driving age population can also be sharpened by using information from the National Personal Transportation Survey.[34] a study done every five years by the Federal Highway Administration of the U.S. Department of Transportation. The 1990 survey indicates that 21% of black households do not own a vehicle.[35] If the driving age population figure is reduced by 21%, this gives us another baseline with which to make a comparison to the ticketing percentages. Both baselines—black driving age population, and black driving age population less 21%—for Akron, Dayton, Toledo, and Franklin County are set out in Table 39.2.

The ticketing percentages in Table 39.1 and the baselines in Table 39.2 can then be compared by constructing a "likelihood ratio" that will show whether blacks are receiving tickets in numbers that are out of proportion to their presence in the driving age population and the driving age population less 21%. The likelihood ratio will allow the following sentence to be completed: "If you're black,

you're—times as likely to be ticketed by this police department than if you are not black." A likelihood ratio of approximately one means that blacks received tickets in roughly the proportion one would expect, given their presence in the driving age population. A likelihood ratio of much greater than one indicates that blacks received tickets at a rate higher than would be expected. Using both baselines—the black driving age population, and the black driving age population less 21%—the likelihood ratios for Akron, Dayton, Toledo and Franklin County are presented in Table 39.3.

Table 39.4 combines population baselines from Table 39.2 and likelihood ratios from Table 39. 3.

The method used here to attempt to discover whether "driving while black" is a problem in Ohio is less exact than the observation-based method used in New Jersey and Maryland. There are assumptions built into the analysis at several points in an attempt to arrive at reasonable substitutes for observation-based data. Since better data do not exist, all of the assumptions made in the analysis involve some speculation. But all of the assumptions are conservative, calculated to err on the side of caution. According to sociologist and criminologist Joseph E. Jacoby, the numbers used here probably are flawed because blacks are probably "at an even greater risk of being stopped" than these numbers show.[36] For example, blacks are likely to drive fewer miles than whites, which suggests that police have fewer opportunities to stop blacks for

Table 39.2 Population Baselines

City	Black Driving Age Population* (Percentage of City Total)	Black Driving Age Population, Less 21% of Black Households Without Vehicles**
Akron	22.7%	17.9%
Toledo	18%	14.2%
Dayton	38%	30.0%
Columbus/Franklin County***	16%	12.6%

*Source: U.S. Census Bureau.
**Source: Federal Highway Admin., U.S. Dep't of Transp., 1995 *National Personal Transportation Survey*, (visited Sept. 27, 1999) <http://www.bts.gov/ntda/npts>; Letters from Eric Hill, Research Associate, Center for Urban Transportation, to David A. Harris (Sept. 28 & Oct. 9, 1998).
***Data for all of Franklin County, not just the city of Columbus.

Table 39.3 Likelihood Ratio "If You're Black, You're_____Times as Likely to Get a Ticket in This City Than if You Are Not Black"

City	Black Driving Age Population*	Black Driving Age Population, Less 21% of Black Households Without Vehicles**
Akron P.D.	2.05	2.76
Toledo P.D.	2.04	2.67
Dayton P.D.	1.67	2.32
Columbus/Franklin County***	1.77	2.34

*Source: U.S. Census Bureau.
**Source: Federal Highway Admin., U.S. Dep't of Transp., 1995 *National Personal Transportation Survey*, (visited Sept. 27, 1999) <http://www.bts.gov/ntda/npts>; Letters from Eric Hill, Research Associate, Center for Urban Transportation, to David A. Harris (Sept. 28 & Oct. 9, 1998).
***Includes all police agencies in Franklin County, not just Columbus.

Table 39.4 Combined Population Baselines and Likelihood Ratios

City	Black Driving Age Population*	Black Driving Age Population, Less 21% of Black Households Without Vehicles**
Akron	22.7%	17.9%
	2.05	2.76
Toledo	18%	14.2%
	2.04	2.67
Dayton	38%	30.0%
	1.67	2.32
Columbus/Franklin County***	16%	12.6%
	1.77	2.34

*Source: U.S. Census Bureau.
**Source: Federal Highway Admin., U.S. Dep't of Transp., 1995 *National Personal Transportation Survey*, (visited Sept. 27, 1999) <http://www.bts.gov/ntda/npts>; Letters from Eric Hill, Research Associate, Center for Urban Transportation, to David A. Harris (Sept 28 & Oct. 9, 1998).
***Data for all of Franklin County, not just the city of Columbus.

traffic violations.[37] In statistical terms, the biases in the assumptions are additive, not offsetting.

What do these figures mean? Even when conservative assumptions are built in, likelihood ratios for Akron, Dayton, Toledo, and Franklin County, Ohio, all either approach or exceed 2.0. In other words, blacks are about twice as likely to be ticketed as nonblacks. When the fact that 21% of black households do not own a vehicle is factored in, the ratios rise, with some approaching 3.0. Assuming that ticketing is a fair mirror of traffic stops in general, the data suggest that a "driving while black" problem does indeed exist in Ohio. There may be race-neutral explanations for the statistical pattern, but none seem obvious. At the very least, further study—something as accurate and exacting as Lamberth's studies in New Jersey and Maryland—is needed.

Why It Matters: The Connection of "Driving While Black" to Other Issues of Criminal Justice and Race

The interviews excerpted here show that racially biased pretextual traffic stops have a strong and immediate impact on the individual African-American drivers involved. These stops are not the minor inconveniences they might seem to those who are not subjected to them. Rather, they are experiences that can wound the soul and cause psychological scar tissue to form. And the statistics show that these experiences are not simply disconnected anecdotes or exaggerated versions of personal experiences, but rather established and persistent patterns of law enforcement conduct. It may be that these stops do not spring from racism on the part of individual officers, or even from the official policies of the police departments for which they work. Nevertheless, the statistics leave little doubt that, whatever the source of this conduct by police, it has a disparate and degrading impact on blacks.

But racial profiling is important not only because of the damage it does, but also because of the connections between stops of minority drivers and other, larger issues of criminal justice and race. Put another way, "driving while black" reflects, illustrates, and aggravates some of the most important problems we face today when we debate issues involving race, the police, the courts, punishment, crime control, criminal justice, and constitutional law.

The Impact on the Innocent

The Fourth Amendment to the United States Constitution prohibits unreasonable searches and seizures, and specifies some of the requirements to be met in order to procure a warrant for a search. Since 1961—and earlier in the federal court system—the Supreme Court has required the exclusion of any evidence obtained through an unconstitutional search or seizure.

I wish to point out a major difference between the usual Fourth Amendment cases and the most common "driving while black" cases. While police catch some criminals through the use of pretext stops, far more innocent people are likely to be affected by these practices than criminals. Indeed, the black community as a whole undoubtedly needs the protection of the police more than other segments of society because African-Americans are more likely than others to be victims of crime. Ironically, it is members of that same community who are likely to feel the consequences of pretextual stops and be treated like criminals. While whites who have done nothing wrong generally have little need to fear constitutional violations by the police, this is decidedly *untrue* for blacks. Blacks attract undesirable police attention whether they do anything to bring it on themselves or not. This makes "driving while black" a most unusual issue of constitutional criminal procedure: a search and seizure question that directly affects a large, identifiable group of almost entirely innocent people.

The Criminalization of Blackness

The fact that the cost of "driving while black" is imposed almost exclusively on the innocent raises another point. Recall that by allowing the police to stop, question, and sometimes even search drivers without regard to the real motives for the search, the Supreme Court has, in effect, turned a blind eye to the use of pretextual stops on a racial basis. That is, as long as the officer or the police department does not come straight out and say that race was the reason for a stop, the stop can always be accomplished based on some other reason—a pretext. Police are therefore free to use blackness as a surrogate indicator or proxy for criminal propensity. While it seems unfair to view *all* members of one racial or ethnic group as criminal suspects just because *some* members of that group engage in criminal activity, this is what the law permits.

Stopping disproportionate numbers of black drivers because some small percentage are criminals means that skin color is being used as evidence of wrongdoing. In effect, *blackness itself has been criminalized.* And if "driving while black" is a powerful example, it is not the only one. For instance, in 1992, the city of Chicago enacted an ordinance that made it a criminal offense for gang members to stand on public streets or sidewalks after police ordered them to disperse.[38] The ordinance was used to make over forty-five thousand arrests of mostly African-American and Latino youths [39] before Illinois courts found the ordinance unconstitutionally vague. In June of 1999, the U.S. Supreme Court declared the law unconstitutional, because it did not sufficiently limit the discretion of officers enforcing it.

The arrests under the Chicago ordinance share something with "driving while black": in each instance, the salient quality that attracts police attention will often be the suspect's race or ethnicity. An officer cannot know simply by looking whether a driver has a valid license or carries insurance, as the law requires, and cannot see whether there is a warrant for the arrest of the driver or another occupant of the car. But the officer *can* see whether the person is black or white. And, as the statistics presented here show, police use blackness as a way to sort those they are interested in investigating from those that they are not. As a consequence, every member of the group becomes a potential criminal in the eyes of law enforcement.

Rational Discrimination

When one hears the most common justification offered for the disproportionate numbers of traffic stops of African-Americans, it usually takes the form of rationality, not racism. Blacks commit a disproportionate share of certain crimes, the argument goes. Therefore, it only makes sense for police to focus their efforts on African-Americans. It only makes sense to focus law enforcement efforts and resources where they will make the most difference. In other words, targeting blacks is the rational, sound policy choice. It is the efficient approach, as well.

As appealing as this argument may sound, it is fraught with problems because its underlying premise is dubious at best. Government statistics on drug offenses, which are the basis for the great majority of pretext traffic stops, tell us virtually nothing about the racial breakdown of those involved in drug crime. Thinking for a moment about arrest data and victimization surveys makes the reasons for this clear. These statistics show that blacks are indeed overrepresented among those arrested for homicide, rape, robbery, aggravated

assault, larceny/theft, and simple assault crimes.[40] Note that because they directly affect their victims, these crimes are at least somewhat likely to be reported to the police and to result in arrests. By contrast, drug offenses are much less likely to be reported, since possessors, buyers, and sellers of narcotics are all willing participants in these crimes. Therefore, arrest data for drug crimes is highly suspect. These data may measure the law enforcement activities and policy choices of the institutions and actors involved in the criminal justice system, but the number of drug arrests does not measure the extent of drug crimes themselves. Similarly, the racial composition of prisons and jail populations or the racial breakdown of sentences for these crimes only measures the actions of those institutions and individuals in charge; it tells us nothing about drug activity itself.

Other statistics on both drug use and drug crime show something surprising in light of the usual beliefs many hold: blacks may *not*, in fact, be more likely than whites to be involved with drugs. Lamberth's study in Maryland showed that among vehicles stopped and searched, the "hit rates"—the percentage of vehicles searched in which drugs were found—were statistically indistinguishable for blacks and whites.[41] There is also a considerable amount of data on drug use that belies the standard beliefs. The percentages of drug users who are black or white are roughly the same as the presence of those groups in the population as a whole. For example, blacks constitute approximately twelve percent of the country's population. In 1997, the most recent year for which statistics are available, thirteen percent of all drug users were black.[42] In fact, among black youths, a demographic group often portrayed as most likely to be involved with drugs, use of all illicit substances has actually been *consistently lower* than among white youths for *twenty years running.*[43]

Nevertheless, many believe that African-Americans and members of other minority groups are responsible for most drug use and drug trafficking. Carl Williams, the head of the New Jersey State Police dismissed by the Governor in March of 1999, stated that "mostly minorities" trafficked in marijuana and cocaine, and pointed out that when senior American officials went overseas to discuss the drug problem, they went to Mexico, not Ireland. Even if he is wrong, if the many troopers who worked for Williams share his opinions, they will act accordingly. And they will do so by looking for drug criminals among black drivers. Blackness will become an indicator of suspicion of drug crime involvement. This, in turn, means that the belief that blacks are disproportionately involved in drug crimes will become a self-fulfilling prophecy. Because police will *look* for drug crime among black drivers, they will *find* it disproportionately among black drivers. More blacks will be arrested, prosecuted, convicted, and jailed, thereby reinforcing the idea that blacks constitute the majority of drug offenders. This will provide a continuing motive and justification for stopping more black drivers as a rational way of using resources to catch the most criminals. At the same time, because police will focus on black drivers, white drivers will receive less attention, and the drug dealers and possessors among them will be apprehended in proportionately smaller numbers than their presence in the population would predict.

The upshot of this thinking is visible in the stark and stunning numbers that show what our criminal justice system is doing when it uses law enforcement practices like racially-biased traffic stops to enforce drug laws. African-Americans are just 12% of the population and 13% of the drug users, but they are about 38% of all those arrested for drug offenses, 59% of all those convicted of drug offenses, and 63% of all those convicted for drug trafficking. While only 33% of whites who are convicted are sent to prison, 50% of convicted blacks are jailed, and blacks who are sent to prison receive higher sentences than whites for the same crimes. For state drug defendants, the average maximum sentence length is fifty-one months for whites and sixty months for blacks.[44]

The Expansion of Police Discretion

Police have nearly complete discretion to decide who to stop. According to all of the evidence available, police frequently exercise this discretion in a racially-biased way, stopping blacks in numbers far out of proportion to their presence on the highway. Law enforcement generally sees this as something positive because the more discretion officers have to fight crime, the better able they will be to do the job.

Police discretion cannot be eliminated; frankly, even if it could be, this would not necessarily be a desirable goal. Officers need discretion to meet individual situations with judgment and intelligence, and to choose their responses so that the ultimate result will make sense. Yet few would contend that police discretion should be *limitless*. But this is exactly what the pretextual stop doctrine allows. Since *everyone* violates the traffic code at some point, it is not a matter of *whether* police can stop a driver, but *which driver* they want to stop. Police are free to pick and choose the motorists they will pull over, so factors other than direct evidence of law breaking come into play. In the "driving while black" situation, of course, that factor is race. In other law enforcement areas in which the state has nearly limitless discretion to prosecute, the decision could be based on political affiliation, popularity, or any number of other things. What these arenas have in common is that enforcement depends upon external factors, instead of law breaking.

Distortion of the Social World

"Driving while black" distorts not only the perception and reality of the criminal justice system, but also the social world. For example, many African-Americans cope with the possibility of pretextual traffic stops by driving drab cars and dressing in ways that are not flamboyant so as not to attract attention. More than that, "driving while black" serves as a spatial restriction on African-Americans, circumscribing their movements. Put simply, blacks know that police and white residents feel that there are areas in which blacks "do not belong." Often, these are all-white suburban communities or upscale commercial areas. When blacks drive through these areas, they may be watched and stopped because they are "out of place." Consequently, blacks try to avoid these places if for no other reason than that they do not want the extra police scrutiny. It is simply more trouble than it is worth to travel to or through these areas. While it is blacks themselves who avoid these communities, and not police officers or anyone else literally keeping them out, in practice it makes little difference. African-Americans do not enter if they can avoid doing so, whether by dint of self-restriction or by government policy.

Undermining Community-Based Policing

Though the term sometimes seems to have as many meanings as people who use it, community policing does have some identifiable characteristics. The idea is for the police to serve the community and become part of it, not to dominate it or occupy it. To accomplish this, police become known to and involved with residents, make efforts to understand their problems, and attack crime in ways that help address those difficulties. The reasoning is that if the police become part of the community, members of the public will feel comfortable enough to help officers identify troubled spots and trouble makers.

As difficult as it will be to build, given the many years of disrespect blacks have suffered at the hands of the police, the community must feel that it can trust the police to treat them as law-abiding citizens if community policing is to succeed. Using traffic stops in racially disproportionate numbers will directly and fundamentally undermine this effort. Why should law-abiding residents of these communities trust the police if, every time they go out for a drive, they are treated like criminals? If the "driving while black" problem is not addressed, community policing will be made much more difficult and may even fail. Thus, aside from the damage "driving while black" stops inflict on African-Americans, there is another powerful reason to change this police behavior: it is in the interest of police departments themselves to correct it.

Ways to Address the Problem

With the Supreme Court abdicating any role for the judiciary in regulating these police practices under the Fourth Amendment, leadership must come from other directions and other institutions.

What other approaches might be fruitful sources of change?

The Traffic Stops Statistics Act

At the beginning of the 105th Congress, Representative John Conyers of Michigan introduced House Bill 118, the Traffic Stops Statistics Act of 1997.[45] This bill would provide for the collection of several categories of data on each traffic stop, including the race of the driver and whether and why a search was performed. The Attorney General would then summarize the data in the first nationwide, statistically rigorous study of these practices. The idea behind the bill was that if the study confirmed what people of color have experienced for years, it would put to rest once and for all the idea that African-Americans who have been stopped for "driving while black" are exaggerating isolated anecdotes into a social problem. Congress and other bodies might then begin to take concrete steps to channel police discretion more appropriately. The Act passed the House of Representatives in March of 1998 with bipartisan support, and then was referred to the Senate Judiciary Committee. When police opposition arose, the Senate took no action and the bill died at the end of the session. Congressman Conyers reintroduced the measure in April of 1999.[46]

The Traffic Stops Statistics Act is a very modest bill, a first step toward addressing a difficult problem. It mandated no concrete action on the problem; it did not regulate traffic stops, set standards for them, or require implementation of particular policies. It was merely an attempt to gather solid, comprehensive information, so that discussion of the problem could move ahead beyond the debate of whether or not the problem existed. Still, the bill attracted enough law enforcement opposition to kill it. But even if the Act did not pass the last Congress and subsequent bills also fail, it seems to have had at least one interesting effect: it has inspired action at the state and local level.

State Legislation

As important as national legislation on this issue would be, congressional action is no longer the only game in town. In fact, efforts are underway in a number of states to address the problem. [By mid-2001, thirteen states had laws that took some kind of action on racial profiling.]

While all of these measures differ in their particulars, they are all variations on Representative Conyers' bill—they mandate the collection of data and analyses of these data.

Local Action

Of course, legislative action is not required for a police department to collect data and to take other steps to address the "driving while black" problem. When a department realizes that it is in its own interest to take action, it can go ahead without being ordered to do so. This is precisely what happened in San Diego, California. In February 1999, Jerome Sanders, the city's Chief of Police, announced that the department would begin to collect data on traffic stops, without any federal or state requirement.[47] The Chief's statement showed a desire to find out whether in fact the officers in his department were engaged in enforcing traffic laws on a racially uneven basis. If so, the problem could then be addressed. If the numbers did not show this, the statistics might help to dispel perceptions to the contrary.

Thus far, San Diego, San Jose, Oakland, and Houston are the largest urban jurisdictions to do this, but they are not alone. Police in over thirty other cities in California, as well as departments in Michigan, Florida, Washington and Rhode Island, are also collecting data. Police departments, not courts, are in the best possible position to take action—by collecting data, by re-training officers, and by putting in place and enforcing policies against the racially disproportionate use of traffic stops. Taking the initiative in this fashion allows a police department to control the process to a much greater extent than it might if it is mandated from the outside. And developing regulations from inside the organization usually will result in greater compliance by those who have to follow these rules—police officers themselves.[48] This represents a promising new approach to the problem. The police must first, of course, realize that there is a problem, and that doing something about it is in their interest.

Litigation

Another way to address racial profiling is to bring lawsuits under the Equal Protection Clause and federal civil rights statutes. In *Whren*, the U.S. Supreme Court said that under the Fourth Amendment of the U.S. Constitution courts can no longer suppress evidence in pretextual stop cases. But the Court did leave open the possibility of attacking racially-biased law enforcement activity under the Equal Protection Clause with civil suits. There are a number of such suits around the country that are either pending or recently concluded, including cases in Maryland, Florida, Indiana, and Illinois.

It is important not to underestimate the difficulty of filing a lawsuit against a police department alleging racial bias. These cases require an "attractive" plaintiff who will not make a bad impression due to prior criminal record, current criminal involvement, or the like. They also require a significant amount of resources. For this reason, organizations interested in this issue, particularly the American Civil Liberties Union, have taken the lead in bringing these cases. Last but not least, it takes a plaintiff with guts to stand up and publicly sue a police department in a racially-charged case. Most people would probably rather walk away from these experiences, no matter how difficult and humiliating, than get into a legal battle with law enforcement.

Conclusion

Everyone wants criminals caught. Few feel this with more urgency than African-Americans, who are so often the victims of crime. But we must choose our methods carefully. As a country, we must strive to avoid police practices that impose high costs on law abiding citizens, and that skew those costs heavily on the basis of race.

Notes

1. *See* Traffic Stops Statistics Act of 1997, H.R. 118, 105th Cong. (1997). The bill was re-introduced in 1999 as the Traffic Stops Statistics Study Act, H.R. 1443, 106th Cong. (1999). The new bill limits data collection to a national sample of police departments.

2. Robert L. Jackson, "Push Against Bias in Traffic Stops Arrested." *Los Angeles Times,* June 1. 1998. A5.

3. Jackson 1998.

4. John Lamberth. 1996a. *Revised Statistical Analysis of the Incidence of Police Stops and Arrests of Black Drivers/ Travelers on the New Jersey Turnpike Between Exits or Interchanges 1 and 3 from the Years 1988 Through 1991.*

5. 734 A.2d 350.

6. *Soto* was a criminal case; the defendant and the others joining his motion had been stopped and contraband seized from them, resulting in their arrests. *See id.* at 352. There is no doubt that now this claim would not succeed if based on the Fourth Amendment to the Federal Constitution. Under *Whren v. U.S.,* the Fourth Amendment would play no part in the decision because the motivation of the officer is immaterial, as long as a traffic offense was, in fact, committed. 517 U.S. 806, 813 (1996). As the case was eventually decided, the trial court granted the motion to suppress based on New Jersey's own law and constitution. *See Soto,* 734 A.2d at 352.

7. Lamberth, 1996a.

8. Lamberth 1996a:2.

9. Lamberth 1996a:3–6.

10. Lamberth 1996a:6–7.

11. Lamberth 1996a: 14.

12. Lamberth 1996a:9.

13. Lamberth 1996a:26.

14. Lamberth's finding was supported by the testimony of several state police supervisors and officers. All said that blacks and whites drive indistinguishably. *See Soto,* 734 A.2d, 354.

15. *See Soto* 352.

16. Lamberth, 1996a:20.

17. Lamberth, 1996a:21.

18. This does not count those who are stopped *and arrested.*

19. Lamberth, 1996a:24.

20. Lamberth, 1996a:25.

21. Lamberth 1996a:25–26, 28.

22. John Lamberth. 1996b. Report, *Wilkins v. Maryland State Police,* Civil No. MJG–93–468.

23. David A. Harris, 1997. "Driving While Black and All Other Traffic Offenses: The Supreme Court and Pretextual Traffic Stops," *Journal of Criminal Law and Criminology,* 87:544–582.

24. Criminal Intelligence Report from Allegany County Narcotic Task Force to Maryland State Police (Apr. 27, 1992).

25. Lamberth 1996b, at 5 tbl. 1.

26. Lamberth 1996b, at 9. Statewide, State Police found drugs on virtually the same percentages of black and white drivers. This means that even though blacks were much more likely to get stopped and searched than whites were, they were no more likely to have drugs, putting the supposed justification for these stops in grave doubt.

27. Lamberth 1996b, at 9.

28. Lamberth 1996b, at 9–10.

29. Data from Akron Municipal Court, Dayton Municipal Court, Toledo Municipal Court, and Franklin County Municipal Court, which includes Columbus, were used.

30. For at least Toledo and Akron, these numbers represent the total number of traffic *cases,* not individual tickets; some cases include more than one ticket given to the driver on the same occasion. By sheer coincidence, the data for Toledo were produced twice—first, tabulating all *tickets,* and then all *cases.* The data tabulating cases came to me by accident. The data were different; in the data on tickets, blacks were 35% of those ticketed; in the data concerning cases, blacks were 31%. These data showed that blacks were more likely than nonblacks to receive more than one ticket in the same stop, an interesting fact in its own right. Because I am interested in measuring traffic *stops* and am using ticketing only as a way to estimate stops, I have used the data on cases; after all, even if more than one ticket is issued in any given encounter, the driver was only stopped once. It is of course possible that the fact that blacks receive more than one ticket per incident more often than whites is itself a reflection of race-based policing, but there may be other factors at work here as well, such as the fact that blacks tend to drive older cars than whites that may have more obvious safety violations, or the fact that blacks use seat belts less often than whites. Therefore, for purposes of this study, I have chosen to treat this difference as if it is not evidence of racial bias.

31. Data from Franklin County Municipal Court include only the years 1996 and 1997, but none from 1998.

32. Franklin County Municipal Court data include all communities in the county, not just Columbus, but were not listed in a way that allowed separate numbers to be broken out for individual police departments. *See* Memorandum from Michael A. Pirik, Deputy Chief Clerk, Franklin County Municipal Court, to David Harris (Aug. 28, 1998).

33. The data in this portion of the study were obtained from the Census Bureau's website: <http://www.census.gov>.

34. Federal Highway Admin., U.S. Dep't of Transp., *1995 Nationwide Personal Transportation Survey* <http://www.bts.gov/ntda/npts>.

35. Letter from Eric Hill, Research Associate, Center for Urban Transportation Research, to David A. Harris (Oct. 9, 1998).

36. E-mails from Joseph E. Jacoby, Bowling Green State University, to David A. Harris (Feb. 2 & 3, 1999).

37. Federal Highway Admin., 1995 (reporting that whites average 4.4 vehicle trips daily and blacks average 3.9).

38. Chicago Gang Congregation Ordinance, Chicago Mun. Code § 8–4–015 (1992).

39. Joan Biskupic, "High Court to Review Law Aimed at Gangs," *Washington Post,* Dec. 7, 1998, at A4 (reporting that while the law was enforced, 45,000 people, mostly African-Americans and Hispanics, were arrested); David G. Savage, "High Court May Move Back on 'Move On' Laws," *Los Angeles Times,* Oct. 5, 1998.

40. Bureau of Justice Statistics, 1997. *Source Book of Criminal Justice Statistics* 1997, U.S. Department of Justice, at 338.

41. Lamberth, 1996b, 7–8.

42. Substance Abuse and Mental Health Servs. Nat'l Admin., U.S. Dep't. of Health and Human Servs., *National Household Survey on Drug Abuse, Preliminary Results from 1997,* 13, 58.

43. National Inst. on Drug Abuse, *Drug Use Among Racial/Ethnic Minorities,* (1997) (showing past-year use of marijuana, inhalants, cocaine, and LSD by black twelfth graders lower than use by whites in every year from 1977 to 1997, and tobacco use by blacks lower since 1982); Bureau of Justice Statistics. U.S. Dep't of Justice, *Drugs, Crime, and the Justice System* (1992).

44. Bureau of Justice Statistics, 1997, at 338, 426, 428.

45. Traffic Stops Statistics Act of 1997. H.R. 118, 105th Cong. (1997).

46. Traffic Stops Statistics Study Act of 1999, H.R. 1443, 106th Cong. (1999).

47. Michael Stetz & Kelly Thornton, 1999. "Cops to Collect Traffic-Stop Racial Data," *San Diego Union-Trib.,* Feb. 5:A1.

48. Wayne R. LaFave, 1990. "Controlling Discretion by Administrative Regulations: The Use, Misuse, and Nonuse of Police Rules and Policies in Fourth Amendment Adjudication," *Michigan Law Review,* 89.

CHAPTER 40

The Decision to Prosecute

George F. Cole

What happens after an arrest has been made in a criminal case? An uninformed observer might assume that the arrestee is soon given his or her day in court, an opportunity to have innocence or guilt established before an impartial panel of peers, the jury. The more informed student of criminal justice realizes that the process is not quite that simple. The quality of justice depends on many factors, not the least of which are the decisions made by judicial officers, including prosecutors and judges. It also involves the police, defense attorneys, and community values and attitudes.

George F. Cole explores many of these variables in his examination of the decision to prosecute. It is the prerogative of the prosecutor's office to decide whether or not to prosecute a case. That decision is usually the product of a series of exchange relationships among justice-system personnel and even members of the community. Police try to influence prosecutors, defense attorneys negotiate for plea bargains or reductions in charge, and the lead prosecutor is sensitive to the feelings of judges and potential leaders. In addition, courts are congested, dockets are full, prosecutors are overburdened, and, in general, resources are scarce. What would happen to the courts if every person arrested were prosecuted before a jury?

The answer, of course, is paralysis and a denial of justice. Fortunately, prosecutors have a number of options they may employ throughout the proceedings that are designed to expedite the process of justice. Some cases are rejected for prosecution, others are plea bargained, and still others plead guilty. But the prosecutor's office must be careful about using these options because each decision has possible political ramifications. Justice-system constituencies cannot be alienated, and the public cannot believe that justice is not being served. Thus, the decision to prosecute is complex, involving more than perceived guilt or innocence.

This paper is based on an exploratory study of the Office of Prosecuting Attorney, King County (Seattle), Washington. The lack of social scientific knowledge about the prosecutor dictated the choice of this approach. An open-ended interview was administered to one-third of the former deputy prosecutors who had worked in the office during the ten year period 1955-1965. In addition, interviews were conducted with court employees, members of the bench, law enforcement officials, and others having reputations for participation in legal decision-making. Over fifty respondents were contacted during this phase. A final portion of the research placed the author in the role of observer in the prosecutor's office. This experience allowed for direct observation of all phases of the decision to prosecute so that the informal processes of the office could be noted. Discussions with the prosecutor's staff, judges, defendant's attorneys, and the police were held so that the interview data could be placed within an organizational context.

Reprinted from: George F. Cole, "The Decision to Prosecute." In the *Law & Society Review*, 4, pp. 331-343. Copyright © 1970 by the Law & Society Review. Reprinted by permission.

The primary goal of this investigation was to examine the role of the prosecuting attorney as an officer of the legal process within the context of the local political system. The analysis is therefore based on two assumptions. First, that the legal process is best understood as a subsystem of the larger political system. Because of this choice, emphasis is placed upon the interaction and goals of the individuals involved in decision-making. Second, and closely related to the first point, it is assumed that broadly conceived political considerations explained to a large extent "who gets or does not get—in what amount—and how, the good (justice) that is hopefully produced by the legal system" (Klonski and Mendelsohn, 1965:323). By focusing upon the political and social linkages between these systems, it is expected that decision-making in the prosecutor's office will be viewed as a principal ingredient in the authoritative allocation of values.

The Prosecutor's Office in an Exchange System

While observing the interrelated activities of the organizations in the legal process, one might ask, "Why do these agencies cooperate?" If the police refuse to transfer information to the prosecutor concerning the commission of a crime, what are the rewards or sanctions which might be brought against them? Is it possible that organizations maintain a form of "bureaucratic accounting" which, in a sense, keeps track of the resources allocated to an agency and the support returned? How are cues transmitted from one agency to another to influence decision-making? These are some of the questions which must be asked when decisions are viewed as an output of an exchange system.

The major findings of this study are placed within the context of an exchange system (Evan, 1965:218).[1] This serves the heuristic purpose of focusing attention upon the linkages found between actors in the decision-making process. In place of the traditional assumptions that the agency is supported solely by statutory authority, this view recognizes that an organization has many clients with which it interacts and upon whom it is dependent for certain resources. As interdependent subunits of a system, then, the organization and its clients are engaged in a set of exchanges across their boundaries. These will involve a transfer of resources between the organizations which will affect the mutual achievement of goals.

The legal system may be viewed as a set of interorganized exchange relationships analogous to what Long (1962:142) has called a community game. The participants in the legal system (game) share a common territorial field and collaborate for different and particular ends. They interact on a continuing basis as their responsibilities demand contact with other participants in the process. Thus, the need for the cooperation of other participants can have a bearing on the decision to prosecute. A decision not to prosecute a narcotics offender may be a move to pressure the United States' Attorney's Office to cooperate on another case. It is obvious that bargaining occurs not only between the major actors in a case—the prosecutor and the defense attorney—but also between the clientele groups that are influential in structuring the actions of the prosecuting attorney.

Exchanges do not simply "sail" from one system to another, but take place in an institutionalized setting which may be compared to a market. In the market, decisions are made between individuals who occupy boundary-spanning roles, and who set the conditions under which the exchange will occur. In the legal system, this may merely mean that a representative of the parole board agrees to forward a recommendation to the prosecutor, or it could mean that there is extended bargaining between a deputy prosecutor and a defense attorney. In the study of the King County Prosecutor's Office, it was found that most decisions resulted from some type of exchange relationship. The deputies interacted almost constantly with the police and criminal lawyers, while the prosecutor was more closely linked to exchange relations with the courts, community leaders, and the county commissioners.

The Prosecutor's Clientele

In an exchange system, power is largely dependent upon the ability of an organization to create clientele relationships which will support and enhance the needs of the agency. For, although interdependence is characteristic of the legal system, competition with other public agencies for support also exists.

Since organizations operate in an economy of scarcity, the organization must exist in a favorable power position in relation to its clientele. Reciprocal and unique claims are made by the organization and its clients. Thus, rather than being oriented toward only one public, an organization is beholden to several publics, some visible and others seen clearly only from the pinnacle of leadership. As Gore (1964:23) notes, when these claims are "firmly anchored inside the organization and the lines drawn taut, the tensions between conflicting claims form a net serving as the institutional base for the organization."

An indication of the stresses within the judicial system may be obtained by analyzing its outputs. It has been suggested that the administration of justice is a selective process in which only those cases which do not create strains in the organization will ultimately reach the courtroom (Chambliss, 1969:84). As noted in Figure 40.1, the system

operates so that only a small number of cases arrive for trial, the rest being disposed of through reduced charges, *nolle pros.*, and guilty pleas.[2] Not indicated are those cases removed by the police and prosecutor prior to the filing of charges. As the focal organization in an exchange system, the office of prosecuting attorney makes decisions which reflect the influence of its clientele. Because of the scarcity of resources, marketlike relationships, and the organizational needs of the system, prosecutorial decision-making emphasizes the accommodations which are made to the needs of participants in the process.

Police

Although the prosecuting attorney has discretionary power to determine the disposition of cases, this power is limited by the fact that usually he is dependent upon the police for inputs to the system of cases and evidence. The prosecutor does not have the investigative resources necessary to exercise the kind of affirmative control over the types

Figure 40.1 Desposition of Felony Cases—King County, 1964

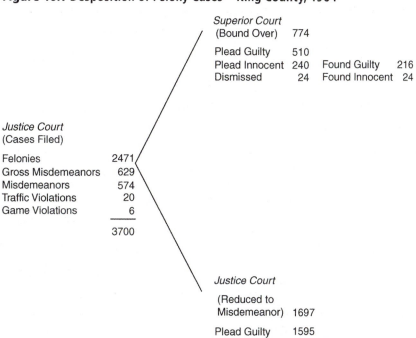

of cases that are brought to him. In this relationship, the prosecutor is not without countervailing power. His main check on the police is his ability to return cases to them for further investigation and to refuse to approve arrest warrants. By maintaining cordial relations with the press, a prosecutor is often able to focus attention on the police when the public becomes aroused by incidents of crime. As the King County prosecutor emphasized, "That [investigation] is the job for the sheriff and police. It's their job to bring me the charges." As noted by many respondents, the police, in turn, are dependent upon the prosecutor to accept the output of their system; rejection of too many cases can have serious repercussions affecting the morale, discipline, and workload of the force.

A request for prosecution may be rejected for a number of reasons relating to questions of evidence. Not only must the prosecutor believe that the evidence will secure a conviction, but he must also be aware of community norms relating to the type of acts that should be prosecuted. King County deputy prosecutors noted that charges were never filed when a case involved attempted suicide or fornication. In other actions, the heinous nature of the crime, together with the expected public reaction, may force both the police and prosecutor to press for conviction when evidence is less than satisfactory. As one deputy noted, "In that case [murder and molestation of a six-year-old girl] there was nothing that we could do. As you know the press was on our back and every parent was concerned. Politically, the prosecutor had to seek an information."

Factors other than those relating to evidence may require that the prosecutor refuse to accept a case from the police. First, the prosecuting attorney serves as a regulator of case loads not only for his own office, but for the rest of the legal system. Constitutional and statutory time limits prevent him and the courts from building a backlog of untried cases. In King County, when the system reached the "overload point," there was a tendency to be more selective in choosing the cases to be accepted. A second reason for rejecting prosecution requests may stem from the fact that the prosecutor is thinking of his public exposure in the courtroom. He does not want to take forward cases

which will place him in an embarrassing position. Finally, the prosecutor may return cases to check the quality of police work. As a former chief criminal deputy said, "You have to keep them on their toes, otherwise they get lazy. If they aren't doing their job, send the case back and then leak the situation to the newspapers." Rather than spend the resources necessary to find additional evidence, the police may dispose of a case by sending it back to the prosecutor on a lesser charge, implement the "copping out" machinery leading to a guilty plea, drop the case, or in some instances send it to the city prosecutor for action in municipal court.

In most instances, a deputy prosecutor and the police officer assigned to the case occupy the boundary-spanning roles in this exchange relationship. Prosecutors reported that after repeated contacts they got to know the policemen whom they could trust. As one female deputy commented, "There are some you can trust, others you have to watch because they are trying to get rid of cases on you." Deputies may be influenced by the police officer's attitude on a case. One officer noted to a prosecutor that he knew he had a weak case, but mumbled, "I didn't want to bring it up here, but that's what they [his superiors] wanted." As might be expected, the deputy turned down prosecution.

Sometimes the police perform the ritual of "shopping around," seeking to find a deputy prosecutor who, on the basis of past experience, is liable to be sympathetic to their view on a case. At one time, deputies were given complete authority to make the crucial decisions without coordinating their activities with other staff members. In this way the arresting officer would search the prosecutor's office to find a deputy he thought would be sympathetic to the police attitude. As a former deputy noted, "This meant that there were no departmental policies concerning the treatment to be accorded various types of cases. It pretty much depended upon the police and their luck in finding the deputy they wanted." Prosecutors are now instructed to ascertain from the police officer if he has seen another deputy on the case. Even under this more centralized system, it is still possible for the police to request a specific deputy or delay presentation of the case until the "correct" prosecutor is available. Often a prosecutor will gain a reputation for specializing in one type of case. This may mean that the police will assume he will get the case anyway, so they skirt the formal procedure and bring it to him directly.

An exchange relationship between a deputy prosecutor and a police officer may be influenced by the type of crime committed by the defendant. The prototype of a criminal is one who violates person and property. However, a large number of cases involve "crimes without victims" (Schur, 1965). This term refers to those crimes generally involving violations in moral codes, where the general public is theoretically the complainant. In violations of laws against bookmaking, prostitution, and narcotics, neither actor in the transaction is interested in having an arrest made. Hence, vice control men must drum up their own business. Without a civilian complainant, victimless crimes give the police and prosecutor greater leeway in determining the charges to be filed.

One area of exchange involving a victimless crime is that of narcotics control. As Skolnick (1966:120) notes, "The major organizational requirements of narcotics policing is the presence of an informational system." Without a network of informers, it is impossible to capture addicts and peddlers with evidence that can bring about convictions. One source of informers is among those arrested for narcotics violations. Through promises to reduce charges or even to *nolle pros.*, arrangements can be made so that the accused will return to the narcotics community and gather information for the police. Bargaining observed between the head of the narcotics squad of the Seattle Police and the deputy prosecutor who specialized in drug cases involves the question of charges, promises, and the release of an arrested narcotics pusher.

In the course of postarrest questioning by the police, a well-known drug peddler intimated that he could provide evidence against a pharmacist suspected by the police of illegally selling narcotics. Not only did the police representative want to transfer the case to the friendlier hands of this deputy, but he also wanted to arrange for a reduction of charges and bail. The police officer believed that it was important that the accused be let out in such a way that the narcotics community would not realize that he had become an informer. He also wanted to be sure that the reduced charges would be processed so that the informer could be kept on the string, thus allowing the narcotics squad to maintain control over him. The deputy prosecutor, on the other hand, said that he wanted to make sure that procedures were followed so that the action would not bring discredit on his office. He also suggested that the narcotics squad "work a little harder" on a pending case as a means of returning the favor.

Courts

The ways used by the court to dispose of cases is a vital influence in the system. The court's actions effect pressures upon the prison, the conviction rate of the prosecutor, and the work of probation agencies. The judge's decisions act as clues to other parts of the system, indicating the type of action likely to be taken in future cases. As noted by a King County judge, "When the number of prisoners gets to the 'riot point,' the warden puts pressure on us to slow down the flow. This often means that men are let out on parole and the number of people given probation and suspended sentences increases." Under such conditions, it would be expected that the prosecutor would respond to the judge's actions by reducing the inputs to the court either by not preferring charges or by increasing the pressure for guilty pleas through bargaining. The adjustments of other parts of the system could be expected to follow. For instance, the police might sense the lack of interest of the prosecutor in accepting charges, hence they will send only airtight cases to him for indictment.

The influence of the court on the decision to prosecute is very real. The sentencing history of each judge gives the prosecutor, as well as other law enforcement officials, an indication of the treatment a case may receive in the courtroom. The prosecutor's expectation as to whether the court will convict may limit his discretion over the decisions on whether to prosecute. "There is great concern as to whose court a case will be assigned. After Judge_____ threw out three cases in a row in which entrapment was involved, the police did not want us to take any cases to him." Since the prosecutor depends upon the plea-bargaining machinery to maintain the flow of cases from his office, the sentencing actions of judges must be predictable. If the defendant and his lawyer are to be influenced to accept a lesser charge or the promise of a lighter sentence in exchange for a plea of guilty, there must be some basis for belief that the judge will fulfill his part of the arrangement. Because judges are unable formally to announce their agreement with the details of the bargain, their past performance acts as a guide.

Within the limits imposed by law and the demands of the system, the prosecutor is able to regulate the flow of cases to the court. He may control the length of time between accusation and trial; hence he may hold cases until he has the evidence which will convict. Alternatively, he may seek repeated adjournment and continuances until the public's interest dies; problems such as witnesses becoming unavailable and similar difficulties make his request for dismissal of prosecution more justifiable. Further, he may determine the type of court to receive the case and the judge who will hear it. Many misdemeanors covered by state law are also violations of a city ordinance. It is a common practice for the prosecutor to send a misdemeanor case to the city prosecutor for processing in the municipal court when it is believed that a conviction may not be secured in justice court. As a deputy said, "If there is no case—send it over to the city court. Things are speedier, less formal, over there."

In the state of Washington, a person arrested on a felony charge must be given a preliminary hearing in a justice court within ten days. For the prosecutor, the preliminary hearing is an opportunity to evaluate the testimony of witnesses, assess the strength of the evidence, and try to predict the outcome of the case if it is sent to trial. On the basis of this evaluation, the prosecutor has several options: he may bind over the case for trial in Superior Court; he may reduce the charges to those of a misdemeanor for trial in Justice Court; or he may conclude that he has no case and drop the charges. The President Judge of the Justice Courts of King County estimated that about seventy percent of the felonies are reduced to misdemeanors after the preliminary hearing.

Besides having some leeway in determining the type of court in which to file a case, the prosecutor also has some flexibility in selecting the judge to receive the case. Until recently the prosecutor could file a case with a specific judge. "The trouble was that Judge _____ was erratic and independent, [so] no one would file with him. The other judges objected that they were handling the entire workload, so a central filing system was devised." Under this procedure cases are assigned to the judges in rotation. However, as the chief criminal deputy noted, "the prosecutor can hold a case until the 'correct' judge came up."

Defense Attorneys

With the increased specialization and institutionalization of the bar, it would seem that those individuals engaged in the practice of criminal law have been relegated, both by their profession and by the community, to a low status. The urban bar appears to be divided into three parts. First, there is an inner circle which handles the work of banks, utilities, and commercial concerns; second, another circle includes plaintiff's lawyers representing interests opposed to those of the inner circle; and finally, an outer group scrapes out an existence by "haunting the courts in hope of picking up crumbs from the judicial table" (Ladinsky, 1963:128). With the exception of a few highly proficient lawyers who have made a reputation by winning acquittal for their clients in difficult, highly publicized cases, most of the lawyers dealing with the King County Prosecutor's Office belong to this outer ring.

In this study, respondents were asked to identify those attorneys considered to be specialists in criminal law. Of the nearly 1,600 lawyers practicing in King County only eight can be placed in this category. Of this group, six were reported to enjoy the respect of the legal community, while the others were accused by many respondents of being involved in shady deals. A larger group of King County attorneys will accept criminal cases, but these lawyers do not consider themselves specialists. Several respondents noted that many lawyers, because of inexperience or age, were required to hang around the courthouse searching for clients. One Seattle attorney described the quality of legal talent available for criminal cases as "a few good criminal lawyers and a lot of young kids and old men. The good lawyers I can count on my fingers."

In a legal system where bargaining is a primary method of decision-making, it is not surprising that criminal lawyers find it essential to maintain close personal ties with the prosecutor and his staff. Respondents were quite open in revealing their dependence upon this close relationship to successfully pursue their careers. The nature of the criminal lawyer's work is such that his saleable product or service appears to be influence rather than technical proficiency in the law. Respondents hold the belief that clients are attracted partially on the basis of the attorney's reputation as a fixer, or as a shrewd bargainer.

There is a tendency for ex-deputy prosecutors in King County to enter the practice of criminal law. Because of his inside knowledge of the prosecutor's office and friendships made with court officials, the former deputy feels that he has an advantage over other criminal law practitioners. All of the former deputies interviewed said that they took criminal cases. Of the eight criminal specialists, seven previously served as deputy prosecutors in King County, while the other was once prosecuting attorney in a rural county.

Because of the financial problems of the criminal lawyer's practice, it is necessary that he handle cases on an assembly-line basis, hoping to make a living from a large number of small fees. Referring to a fellow lawyer, one attorney said, "You should see _____. He goes up there to Carroll's office with a whole fist full of cases. He trades on some, bargains on others and never goes to court. It's amazing but it's the way he makes his living." There are incentives, therefore, to bargain with the prosecutor and other decisionmakers. The primary aim of the attorney in such circumstances is to reach an accommodation so that the time-consuming formal proceedings need not be implemented. As a Seattle attorney noted, "I can't make any money if I spend my time in a courtroom. I make mine on the telephone or in the prosecutor's office." One of the disturbing results of this arrangement is that instances were reported in which a bargain was reached between the attorney and deputy

prosecutor on a "package deal." In this situation, an attorney's clients are treated as a group; the outcome of the bargaining is often an agreement whereby reduced charges will be achieved for some, in exchange for the unspoken assent by the lawyer that the prosecutor may proceed as he desires with the other cases. One member of the King County Bar has developed this practice to such a fine art that a deputy prosecutor said, "When you saw him coming into the office, you knew that he would be pleading guilty." At one time this situation was so widespread that the "prisoners up in the jail had a rating list which graded the attorneys as either 'good guys' or 'sell outs.'"

The exchange relationship between the defense attorney and the prosecutor is based on their need for cooperation in the discharge of their responsibilities. Most criminal lawyers are interested primarily in the speedy solution of cases because of their precarious financial situation. Since they must protect their professional reputations with their colleagues, judicial personnel, and potential clientele, however, they are not completely free to bargain solely with this objective. As one attorney noted, "You can't afford to let it get out that you are selling out your cases."

The prosecutor is also interested in the speedy processing of cases. This can only be achieved if the formal processes are not implemented. Not only does the pressure of this caseload influence bargaining, but also the legal process with its potential for delay and appeal, creates a degree of uncertainty which is not present in an exchange relationship with an attorney with whom you have dealt for a number of years. As the Presiding Judge of the Seattle District Court said, "Lawyers are helpful to the system. They are able to pull things together, work out a deal, keep the system moving."

Community Influentials

As part of the political system, the judicial process responds to the community environment. The King County study indicated that there are differential levels of influence within the community and that some people had a greater interest in the politics of prosecution than others. First, the general public is able to have its values translated into policies followed by law enforcement officers. The public's influence is particularly acute in those gray areas of the law where full enforcement is not expected. Statutes may be enacted by legislatures defining the outer limits of criminal conduct, but they do not necessarily mean that laws are to be fully enforced to these limits. There are some laws defining behavior which the community no longer considers criminal. It can be expected that a prosecutor's charging policies will reflect this attitude. He may not prosecute violations of laws regulating some forms of gambling, certain sexual practices, or violations of Sunday Blue Laws.

Because the general public is a potential threat to the prosecutor, staff members take measures to protect him from criticism. Respondents agreed that decision-making occurs with the public in mind—"will a course of action arouse antipathy towards the prosecutor rather than the accused?" Several deputies mentioned what they called the "aggravation level" of a crime. This is a recognition that the commission of certain crimes, within a specific context, will bring about a vocal public reaction. "If a little girl, walking home from the grocery store, is pulled into the bushes and indecent liberties taken, this is more disturbing to the public's conscience than a case where the father of the girl takes indecent liberties with her at home." The office of King County Prosecuting Attorney has a policy requiring that deputies file all cases involving sexual molestation in which the police believe the girl's story is credible. The office also prefers charges in all negligent homicide cases where there is the least possibility of guilt. In such types of cases the public may respond to the emotional context of the case and demand prosecution. To cover the prosecutor from criticism, it is believed that the safest measure is to prosecute.

The bail system is also used to protect the prosecutor from criticism. Thus it is the policy to set bail at a high level with the expectation that the court will reduce the amount. "This looks good for Prosecutor Carroll. Takes the heat off of him, especially in morals cases. If the accused doesn't appear in court the prosecutor can't be blamed. The public gets upset when they know these types are out free." This is an example of exchange where

one actor is shifting the responsibility and potential onus onto another. In turn, the court is under pressure from county jail officials to keep the prison population down.

A second community group having contact with the prosecutor is composed of those leaders who have a continuing or potential interest in the politics of prosecution. This group, analogous to the players in one of Long's community games, are linked to the prosecutor because his actions affect their success in playing another game. Hence community boosters want either a crackdown or a hands-off policy towards gambling, political leaders want the prosecutor to remember the interests of the party, and business leaders want policies which will not interfere with their own game.

Community leaders may receive special treatment by the prosecutor if they run afoul of the law. A policy of the King County Office requires that cases involving prominent members of the community be referred immediately to the chief criminal deputy and the prosecutor for their disposition. As one deputy noted, "These cases can be pretty touchy. It's important that the boss knows immediately about this type of case so that he is not caught 'flat footed' when asked about it by the press."

Pressure by an interest group was evidenced during a strike by drug store employees in 1964. The striking unions urged Prosecutor Carroll to invoke a state law which requires the presence of a licensed pharmacist if the drug store is open. Not only did union representatives meet with Carroll, but picket lines were set up outside the courthouse protesting his refusal to act. The prosecutor resisted the union's pressure tactics.

In recent years, the prosecutor's tolerance policy toward minor forms of gambling led to a number of conflicts with Seattle's mayor, the sheriff, and church organizations. After a decision was made to prohibit all forms of public gaming, the prosecutor was criticized by groups representing the tourist industry and such affected groups as the bartenders' union which thought the decision would have an adverse economic effect. As Prosecutor Carroll said, "I am always getting pressures from different interests—business, the Chamber of Commerce, and labor. I have to try and maintain a balance between them." In exchange for these considerations, the prosecutor may gain prestige, political support, and admission into the leadership groups of the community.

Summary

By viewing the King County Office of Prosecuting Attorney as the focal organization in an exchange system, data from this exploratory study suggests the market-like relationships which exist between actors in the system. Since prosecution operates in an environment of scarce resources and since the decisions have potential political ramifications, a variety of officials influence the allocation of justice. The decision to prosecute is not made at one point, but rather the prosecuting attorney has a number of options which he may employ during various stages of the proceedings. But the prosecutor is able to exercise his discretionary powers only within the network of exchange relationships. The police, court congestion, organizational strains, and community pressures are among the factors which influence prosecutorial behavior.

Discussion Questions

1. Why do the various criminal justice agencies cooperate with each other? Who are the prosecutor's clientele?

2. How is the prosecuting attorney dependent upon the police? What tools does the prosecutor have to motivate the police to be more effective on behalf of the prosecutor? How can police influence the prosecuting attorney's office? How are the police dependent upon the prosecutor?

3. What are the different types of defense attorneys? What is the relationship between the prosecutor and the defense attorney? What are the advantages of this relationship to each one? What are the disadvantages of this system, if any, to the concept of "justice for all"?

Notes

1. See also Levine and White (1961:583) and Blau (1955).
2. The lack of reliable criminal statistics is well known. These data were gathered from a number of sources, including King County (1964).

References

Blau, P. M. 1955. *The Dynamics of Bureaucracy.* Chicago: University of Chicago Press.

Chambliss, W. J. 1969. *Crime and the Legal Process.* New York: McGraw-Hill.

Evan, W. M. 1965. "Towards a Theory of Interorganizational Relations." *Management Sci.* 11 (August): 218-230.

Gore, W. J. 1964. *Administrative Decision Making.* New York: John Wiley.

King County (1964) Annual Report of the Prosecuting Attorney. Seattle: State of Washington.

Klonski, J. R. and R. I. Mendelsohn. 1965. "The Allocation of Justice: A Political Analysis." *Journal of Public Law* 14 (May): 323-342.

Ladinsky, J. 1963. "The Impact of Social Backgrounds of Lawyers on Law Practice and the Law." *Journal of Legal Education* 16, 2:128-144.

Levine, S. and P. E. White. 1961. "Exchange as a Conceptual Framework for the Study of Inter-Organizational Relationships." *Administrative Sci. Q.* 5 (March): 583-601.

Long, N. 1962. *The Polity.* Chicago: Rand McNally.

Schur, E. M. 1965. *Crimes Without Victims.* Englewood Cliffs, N.J.: Prentice-Hall.

Skolnick, J. E. 1966. *Justice Without Trial.* New York: John Wiley.

CHAPTER 41

Prostitution Control in America

Ronald Weitzer

A considerable amount of criminal justice resources is devoted to the enforcement of vice crimes, sometimes referred to as victimless crimes. The "War on Drugs" is widely known as the government's most public face in the fight against vice, but prostitution still accounts for nearly 100,000 arrests annually throughout the United States. It is estimated that America's police departments spend over $1 billion each year enforcing the nation's prostitution laws. Unfortunately, there is little return on this investment because law enforcement fails to effect any real decrease in prostitution activity and does little to alleviate its negative influence on communities.

In the following selection Ronald Weitzer examines the problems associated with America's prostitution policy. Weitzer argues that the current approaches employed by law enforcement fail to exert any real effect on prostitution outcomes, including the amount of prostitution, their ability to effectively protect prostitutes from victimization, and the community impact of prostitution zones. The author goes on to propose an alternative policy for the regulation of prostitution that includes redirecting control efforts from indoor to outdoor prostitution, gender-neutral law enforcement, and the provision of support for those who wish to leave the life of prostitution.

Reprinted from: *Crime, Law & Social Change* 32, no.1 (1999), pp.83–102. © 2000 Kluwer Academic Publishers. Reprinted by permission of Kluwer Academic Publishers.

Problems with Current Policy

Prostitution control in America involves the commitment of substantial criminal justice resources—with little impact on the sex trade or on collateral problems such as victimization of prostitutes and effects on host communites.

Criminal Justice System Costs

There are approximately 90,000 annual arrests in the United States for violations of prostitution laws (Bureau of Justice Statistics annual), in addition to an unknown number of arrests of prostitutes under disorderly conduct or loitering statutes. The fiscal costs are substantial. A study of the country's sixteen largest cities found that they spent a total of $120 million in 1985 enforcing prostitution laws (Pearl 1987). Data are unavailable on the costs of prostitution control nationwide, but extrapolating from the above figure on just a few cities, there is no question that the total expenditure is considerable.

What are the benefits of these expenditures? A San Francisco Crime Committee (1971: 20) concluded in 1971 that spending on prostitution control "buys essentially nothing of a positive nature," and Atlanta's Task Force on Prostitution (1986) concluded that this spending was a "waste" that burdened the courts and lowered police morale. Moreover, law enforcement has little effect on the amount of prostitution, offers little protection to prostitutes at risk, and gives little relief to communities besieged by street prostitution. At best, the problem is *contained* within a particular area where prostitutes are occasionally subjected to the revolving door of arrest, fines, brief jail time, and release, or *displaced* into another locale, begetting the same revolving-door dynamic. Containment is the norm throughout the United States; displacement requires sustained police intervention, which is rare. Instead, law enforcement typically consists of periodic arrests and occasional, sweeping crackdowns on prostitutes. Containment may be acceptable to residents of neighborhoods free of street prostitution, but is aggravating to many residents of prostitution zones.

Victimization

Street prostitutes are at considerable risk of violence from customers, exploitation from pimps, and drug and health problems. A survey of 200 street prostitutes in San Francisco found that two-thirds had been assaulted by customers and pimps and 70 percent had been raped by customers (Silbert and Pines 1982). Other studies report similar rates of victimization among street prostitutes (Barnard 1993; Davis 2000; Farley and Barkan 1998; James and Meyerling 1977). However, all of these studies relied on convenience samples (women who contacted service agencies or were interviewed in jail or on the streets), not random samples, which likely skews the results toward that part of the population experiencing the most victimization. This means that the high victimization rates reported are probably lower for street prostitutes as a whole. Having said that, all evidence indicates that street prostitutes are indeed vulnerable to abuse and that prevailing methods of prostitution control in most cities offer little protection against such victimization.

Workers involved in upscale prostitution, such as escorts and call girls, are relatively free of victimization (Perkins 1991:290). They are not immune to violence, but it is not the occupational hazard that it is for street workers.

Community Impact

It is street prostitution—not the more clandestine, indoor varieties of sex work—that generates the lion's share of citizen complaints about prostitution in America. A wide variety of sources (e.g., Clark 1993; Persons 1996) and my extensive search of newpaper articles in Lexis/Nexis (Weitzer 2000) identified a set of common claims made by residents of neighborhoods with street prostitution.

Unlike the antiprostitution reformers of the 19th and early 20th centuries, who made much of the immorality and sinfulness of prostitution as well as the exploitation of "fallen" women (Hobson 1987; Pivar 1973), neighborhood groups in contemporary America are driven less by moral indignation than by *overt street behavior* on the part of prostitutes, pimps, and customers. Stress is placed on the *tangible environmental effects* of sexual commerce on the street.

The degree to which prostitutes, pimps, and customers cause commotion in public places varies across time and place. Still, the public visibility of the enterprise increases the likelihood that it will have some adverse effect on the surrounding community. Similarities across cities in the manifestation of street prostitution produce similar complaints among residents. Standard complaints center on conduct such as streetwalkers' brazen flagging down of customers' cars, arguing and fighting with people on the street, visible drug use, performing sex acts in public, and littering with used condoms and syringes (both unsightly trash and a public health hazard). Children are frequently mentioned in the litany of grievances: they witness transactions and sex acts being consumated; they sometimes discover discarded condoms and syringes; and they are occasionally approached by prostitutes or customers.

Customers are scorned in these communities as much as the prostitutes (Persons 1996). Not only do they contribute to traffic congestion in their ritual cruising of prostitution strolls, they also harass and proposition women whom they mistake for prostitutes. Many communities have targeted the customers (by recording their license plate numbers, videotaping, etc.) more than the prostitutes, because the johns are seen as more vulnerable to public identification and shaming.

Residents define street prostitution not as a mere nuisance or "victimless crime" but instead as eroding the quality of life and contributing to neighborhood decay and street disorder (cf. Kelling and Coles 1996; Skogan 1990; Wilson and Kelling 1982). As a coalition of twenty-eight neighborhood and business groups in San Francisco declared, street prostitution "poses a very serious threat to the integrity of San Francisco's business and residential communities" (Coalition 1996).

No data exist on the magnitude of the problems due to street prostitution in American cities (aside from arrest rates and residents' claims that the problem is serious), but the literature on this topic indicates that street prostitution can present a real problem for host communities.

Alternative Policies

Soliciting for purposes of prostitution, pimping, and other prostitution-related activities are crimes throughout the United States, and this criminalization policy is seldom questioned. Rarely have policy makers shown a willingness to rethink the status quo and experiment with novel approaches.[1] No national commission of inquiry has examined prostitution, with the result that almost no public debate has taken place. Alternatives to the current policy of blanket criminalization are evaluated below.

Decriminalization

[Total] decriminalization would remove criminal penalties and result in a laissez-faire approach in which prostitution would be left unregulated. Prostitutes' rights groups, like COYOTE (Call Off Your Old Tired Ethics),[2] favor full decriminalization of adult prostitution because they define it as work, like any other work, and because decriminalization is the only policy that recognizes prostitutes' "right" to use their bodies as they wish. Regulations are opposed because they would allow government interference with this right and because they would only perpetuate the stigmatization of prostitutes (e.g., if restricted to brothels or red light districts).

There is virtually no public support for decriminalization. A 1983 survey found that only 7 percent of the public thought "there should be no laws against prostitution" (Merit 1983). Policy makers are almost universally opposed to decriminalization,

making this a nonstarter in any serious discussion of policy alternatives (Parnas 1981). Moreover, the logic behind decriminalization is shaky. Freed of regulation, prostitutes arguably would enjoy advantages unavailable to purveyors of other commercial services (Skolnick and Dombrink 1978:201; Decker 1979:463). A major Canadian commission held that prostitution should enjoy no special immunity from the law: "it is difficult to see how some degree of regulation could be avoided" in light of "the special risks inherent in the activity of prostitution" (Special Committee 1985:518). Taken to its extreme, decriminalization would permit prostitutes and their customers to engage in sexual exchanges without restriction, except for extant prohibitions on public nudity and sex.

Although decriminalization is roundly dismissed by the American public and policy makers, its advocates sometimes manage to get it onto the public agenda. A recent example illustrates the fate of a decriminalization proposal, in a city known for its tolerance. A Task Force on Prostitution was formed by San Francisco's Board of Supervisors in 1994 to explore alternatives to existing methods of prostitution control. Members included representatives of community and business groups, the National Lawyer's Guild, National Organization for Women, prostitutes' rights groups, the police department, and the district attorney's office. From the beginning, the prostitutes' advocates and their sympathizers set the agenda and dominated the proceedings, which led to chronic infighting. Supervisor Terence Hallinan was the driving force behind the panel but unsatisfied with the result: "I didn't ride herd on this task force. I would have liked a better balance...Instead of coming up with good, practical solutions, they spent months fighting about decriminalization and legalization."[3] After a majority of the members voted to recommend a policy of decriminalization in January 1995,[4] the six community and business representatives resigned. One of the latter later proclaimed that the departure of community members shredded the legitimacy of the panel and troubled the remaining members: "They were upset as hell because the task force lost credibility without the citizens' groups participating."[5] While the comment is not made from a disinterested position, the task force report itself expresses regret that consensus was not achieved on its main recommendation.

The panel's endorsement of decriminalization reflected the interests of prostitutes' advocates and their allies and doomed the report's prospect for serious consideration in official circles. The city's Board of Supervisors promptly shelved the report. It is possible, however, that a less radical recommendation would have been received more favorably by city officials; Supervisor Hallinan and even some community leaders had floated the possibility of legalization (zoning into red light areas) when the task force was first proposed.

Legalization

Legalization spells *regulation* of some kind: licensing or registration, confining prostitutes to red light districts, state-restricted brothels, mandatory medical exams, special business taxes, etc. Implicit in the idea of legalization is the principle of harm reduction: that is, that regulation is necessary to reduce some of the problems associated with prostitution. The American public is divided on the issue, with support for legalization ranging from a quarter to half the population in most polls (Gallup 1991, 1996; Harris 1978, 1990; Merit 1983; Weitzer 2000). This support has not, however, translated into popular pressure for legal change anywhere in the country, in part because most citizens see it as far removed from their personal interests and because policy makers are largely silent on the issue (Weitzer 1991).

Some advocates of legalization cite with approval Nevada's legal brothels. Confined to small-scale operations in rural areas of the state (and prohibited in Las Vegas and Reno due to opposition from the gambling industry), this model hardly solves the problem of street prostitution in urban areas. Streetwalkers flourish in Las Vegas and Reno, despite the existence of legal brothels in counties adjacent to these cities. What is needed is some kind of specifically urban solution to an essentially urban problem.

Since Nevada legalized brothels in 1971, no other state has seriously considered legalization. Legislators fear being branded as "condoning" prostitution, and see no political advantages in any kind of liberalization. The exceptions seem to prove the rule of futility. For example, bills to permit licensing of prostitutes and brothels were introduced in the California State Assembly in the 1970s, to no avail (Jennings 1976; Parnas 1981). In 1992 New York City Councilor Julia Harrison offered a resolution for licensing prostitutes, restricting legal brothels to certain parts of the city, and requiring HIV tests of the workers. The purpose was "to eliminate the pestilence of street activity in residential neighborhoods," as the resolution declared. Harrison told me that she got the "highest praise from the community" in her district, Flushing, but her proposal met with stiff opposition in the city council and never made it out of committee.[6]

A major determinant of the success of legalization is the willingness of prostitutes to comply with the regulations. Those who have pimps may not be allowed to work in most regulated systems, particularly if it means a dilution of the pimps' control over their employees. Where legalization includes stipulations as to who can and cannot engage in the sex trade, certain types of individuals will be excluded from the legal regime, forcing them to operate illicitly. Where underage or diseased or migrant prostitutes are ineligible, they would have no recourse but to work in the shadows of the regulated system. Moreover, every conceivable form of legalization would be rejected by some or many eligible prostitutes, who would see no benefits in abiding by the new restrictions and would resent the infringement on their freedom. It is precisely on these grounds that prostitutes' rights groups denounce licensing, mandatory health checks, and legal brothel systems. A possible exception would be zoning street prostitution into a suitable locale: away from residential areas but in places that are safe and unintimidating for prostitutes and customers alike. Many streetwalkers would be satisfied with this kind of arrangement, but others would not. Red light districts in industrial zones have been proposed, but most streetwalkers would reject confinement to these areas because they typically lack places of refuge and sustenance, such as restaurants, coffee shops, bars, parks, and cheap hotels—all of which are facilitative of street prostitution (Cohen 1980).

Even if an acceptable locale could be found, there is no guarantee that street prostitution would be confined to that area; market saturation in the designated zone would push some workers into less competitive locales. Moreover, while zoning presumably would remove street prostitution from residential areas, it would not necessarily remedy other problems associated with street work, such as violence and drug abuse.

Would a system of legal prostitution attract an influx of prostitutes into the host city? If limited to one or a few cities in the United States, the answer would be affirmative. Were it more widespread, each locale would hold less attraction to outside workers.

More fundamentally, would legalization, in any of its forms, institutionalize and officially condone prostitution and make it more difficult for workers to leave the business? Government officials, feminists, and prostitutes' rights advocates alike object to legalization on precisely these grounds. Whether legalization would indeed make it more difficult for workers to leave prostitution than is the case under criminalization would depend in part on whether the workers were officially labeled as prostitutes—via registration, licensing, special commercial taxes, a registry for mandatory health checks—or whether their identities would remain unknown to the authorities, as might be the case if legalization took the form of zoning.

A final consideration is the willingness and capacity of municipal authorities to actively regulate the sex trade and compel compliance with the rules. American officials are almost universally unprepared to assume this responsibility. Why would any American city assume the added burden of planning, launching, and managing a system of legal prostitution when the benefits are doubtful and when the logistical, resource, and moral costs would be envisioned as unacceptably high? Whatever the possible merits (health, safety, etc.) of any particular model of legalization, it is therefore imperative to consider its feasibility in the United States. Advocates face almost impossible odds trying to marshall support from legislators and the wider population. Proposals for legalization, while occasionally floated, will remain nonstarters in this country for the foreseeable future. A third policy alternative may have broader appeal.

A Two-Track Model

Policy makers often fail to draw the crucial distinction between street and off-street prostitution, partly because both types are criminalized by law throughout the United States. But since prostitution manifests itself in fundamentally different ways on the street and in indoor venues, it is only sensible to treat the two differently. One model would (1) *target resources exclusively toward the control of street prostitution* and (2) *relax controls on indoor prostitution* such as escort agencies, massage parlors, call girls, and brothels. A few blue-ribbon panels have recommended changes either consistent with or close to this two-track model. A San Francisco commission noted that whereas street prostitution has significant adverse consequences for public order and public health, the situation is quite the opposite for indoor prostitution—a situation warranting a dual approach (San Francisco Committee 1971). An Atlanta task force went a step further in recommending that law enforcement be directed against street prostitution rather than off-street prostitution and that city officials provide more assistance to neighborhoods affected by prostitution, in the form of greater liaison between neighborhood associations and the authorities and redevelopment of communities to discourage street prostitution and other crime (Atlanta Task Force 1986). And a landmark Canadian commission argued that abating street prostitution would require legislation allowing prostitutes to work somewhere else. It recommended (1) allowing unobtrusive street solicitation, (2) punishment of obnoxious behavior by streetwalkers (offensive language, disturbing the peace, disrupting traffic), and (3) permitting one or two prostitutes to work out of their residence (Special Committee 1985). (The third proposal was endorsed by a recent Canadian task force [Working Group 1998:71]). Indoor work by one or two prostitutes was seen as preferable to work on the streets or in brothels since it gives the workers maximum autonomy and shields them against exploitation by pimps and other managers. The commission also recommended giving provincial authorities the option of legalizing small, nonresidential brothels, subject to appropriate controls.

In all three cases, government officials rejected the recommendations—without explanation in San Francisco and Atlanta, and in Canada on the grounds that it would condone prostitution. Some Australian states, however, have recently implemented the two-track approach, i.e., decriminalizing brothels and increasing enforcement against street prostitution (Sullivan 1997).

Track One: Indoor Prostitution. Some cities already have an informal policy of de facto decriminalization of indoor prostitution—essentially ignoring call girls, escort agencies, and massage parlors unless a complaint is made, which is seldom. Police in other cities, however, devote substantial time and resources to this side of the sex trade, where it accounts for as much as half the prostitution arrests or consumes up to half the vice budgets. One study of sixteen cities found that indoor prostitution accounted for between a quarter and a third of all prostitution arrests in Baltimore, Memphis, and Milwaukee, and half the arrests in Cleveland.[7] Some cities (like Houston and Philadelphia) have shifted their emphasis from the street to indoor prostitution, ostensibly to go after the "big fish."[8] Some other police departments devote an entire branch to combatting outcall and escort services, e.g., the Pandering Unit in Detroit and the Ad Vice Unit in Los Angeles.

Efforts against indoor prostitution typically involve elaborate, time-consuming undercover operations to entrap the women. Such stings require considerable planning, and large-scale operations can last a year or two, becoming rather costly affairs. The Heidi Fleiss case in Los Angeles is only the most notorious recent example. There have been some federal actions as well. In 1990, for example, federal agents launched raids on more than forty upscale escort agencies in twenty-three cities. The sting was the culmination of a two-year undercover investigation, costing $2.5 million.[9]

An officer attached to the Ad Vice unit in Los Angeles justified his work with rather twisted logic: "We're trying to keep it from becoming rampant on our streets" (A&E 1997). In fact, crackdowns on indoor prostitution can have the opposite result—increasing the number of streetwalkers—thus unintentionally exacerbating the most obtrusive side of the prostitution trade. Closures of massage parlors and other indoor venues have had precisely this effect in some cities (Cohen 1980: 81; Larsen 1992; Lowman 1992; Pearl 1985), and a New Orleans vice officer noted that, "Whenever we focus on indoor investigations, the street scene gets insane."[10]

The success of a policy of nonenforcement regarding indoor prostitution would require that it be implemented without fanfare. A public announcement that a city had decided to take a "hands off" approach to this variety of sex work might serve as a magnet drawing legions of indoor workers and clients into the locale. But in cities where it is not already standard practice, an unwritten policy of nonenforcement might be a sensible innovation. It would free up resources for the more pressing problems on the street, and might have the effect of pushing some streetwalkers indoors, as one commission reasoned: "Keeping prostitutes off the streets may be aided by tolerating them off the streets" (San Francisco Committee 1971:44). Such an effect is far from certain, however. As a general rule, there is little mobility between the different ranks of prostitution (Benson and Matthews 1995; Heyl 1979), and each type has unique attractions to the workers. Advantages of street work include greater flexibility in working conditions than the more restrictive indoor work, rapid turnover of customers and lower time-commitment per trick, and the freedom and excitement of street hustling. Regarding the latter, "Many prostitutes say they prefer the constant action on the street...They enjoy the game aspect of the transaction and the intensity of life as a streetwalker, in contrast to work in a massage parlor or house" (James 1973:148). Some clients also prefer streetwalkers: advantages include easy access, anonymity, low cost, choice of women, and the thrill of cruising for sex on the streets—though other clients are attracted to indoor venues because they are safer and more discreet (Campbell 1998). Moreover, indoor work may not be an option for those streetwalkers who lack the social skills and physical attractiveness that may be required by such establishments or their clients. Indoor and outdoor prostitution serve different markets (Reynolds 1986). Having said that, greater police intervention on the street has at least some potential to induce some streetwalkers indoors, perhaps into massage parlors.

Compared to street prostitution, there is relatively little public opposition to indoor prostitution, provided it remains inconspicuous. Escort agencies and call girls are typically ignored by community groups, and even massage parlors and brothels arouse little concern relative to streetwalking—again, provided they remain discreet. In San Francisco, a leader of the neighborhood group Save Our Streets told me that most residents of his community would not be bothered by indoor prostitution: "My gut feeling is that, yes, that would be OK. No one has voiced concern over massage parlors" in the area.[11] And a Washington, DC, neighborhood activist remarked that "people wouldn't be too upset if prostitution went indoors."[12] Community groups rarely mobilize against indoor prostitution, and it appears that the general population is less concerned about this side of the trade. A 1988 survey of residents of Toledo, Ohio (a conservative, working-class city) found that 28 percent supported legal "government-controlled brothels" and 19 percent supported decriminalization of "private call-girl prostitution" (McCaghy and Cernkovich 1991). No national public opinion polls have asked about specific types of prostitution; instead, they ask vague questions about "legalization" or legal "regulation." Findings of a national Canadian survey may approximate American patterns: while only 11 percent of the population found street prostitution acceptable, a higher number accepted designated red light districts (28 percent), brothels (38 percent), escort and call girl services (43 percent), and prostitution on private premises (45 percent) (Peat Marwick 1984). Clearly, the *visibility* of prostitution shapes its public acceptability.

Is there a class bias in the two-track approach? Does it favor the higher class, indoor sector and unfairly target the lower-echelon streetwalkers? Inherent in any two-track approach are disparate effects on actors associated with each track, and with respect to prostitution there are legitimate grounds for differential treatment: (1) certain other types of commercial enterprise are prohibited on the streets, and there is no compelling reason why street prostitution should be permitted and (2) "this kind of policy may not be considered too inequitable if the costs inflicted on society by the street prostitutes are greater...than from those working in hotels" and other indoor venues (Reynolds 1986:194). The legal principle on which this proposal rests is that the criminal law should not interfere with the conduct of consenting adults, provided that this conduct does not *harm* the legally protected interests of others. Whereas street prostitution often involves violence against prostitutes, ancillary crime, disorderly behavior in public, and other adverse effects on host neighborhoods, indoor prostitution is in accord with the harm-reduction principle (Caughey 1974; Comment 1977). As the San Francisco Committee on Crime (1971:38) flatly concluded, "continued criminalization of private, non-visible prostitution cannot be warranted by fear of associated crime, drug abuse, venereal disease, or protection of minors." The Canadian commission (1985: 515) agreed: "The concern with the law is not what takes place in private, but the public manifestation of prostitution." Similarly, harms to prostitutes themselves are pronounced for street workers but much less so for workers in brothels and massage parlors and call girls and escorts (Bryan 1966; Exner et al. 1977; Farley and Davis 1978; Reynolds 1986). As a recent Canadian task force noted, "the two objectives of harm reduction and violence prevention could most likely occur if prostitution was conducted indoors" (Working Group 1998:35). The policy implication is clear: "reassign police priorities to those types of prostitution that inflict the greatest costs" (Reynolds 1986:192), namely, street prostitution.

Track Two: Restructuring Street Prostitution Control. One advantage of the two-track model is that resources previously devoted to the control of indoor prostitution can be transferred to where they are most needed: the street-level sex trade. Under this model, a policy of *more frequent arrests* of streetwalkers and johns would replace the current norm of sporadic, half-hearted enforcement. This is just the first step, however. What happens after arrest is equally important.

Most prostitution arrests in the United States require that offenders be caught in the act of solicitation, a labor-intensive form of control that limits enforcement efforts. In this legal context it would be naive to think that the "oldest profession" can be wholly eradicated from any major American city. The costs to the prostitute (fines, jail time) could be enhanced, but not dramatically for a misdemeanor offense. Moreover, stiffer penalties have the unfortunate side-effect of forcing prostitutes back onto the streets to recoup their losses, essentially becoming an added cost of doing business. Other, very different approaches are worth considering. A San Diego Task Force (1993), a British parliamentary committee (Benson and Matthews 1996), and the Association of Chief Police Officers in Britain (Bennetto 1996) have called for community service sanctions for prostitutes, and New York City has recently experimented with this penalty. If the policy of fining prostitutes simply encourages reoffending to recover losses, community service may open up avenues for a different line of work for at least some of the individuals who truly aspire to reintegration into conventional society. *Community service sanctions are superior to fines or incarceration for this population,* and any policy of intensified arrests should be coupled with a shift toward community service sanctions.

A third reform in the control of street-level prostitution is the need for a more *comprehensive program of meaningful job training and other needed services for those who want to leave prostitution* but eschew low-paying, dead-end jobs. It is not known what percentage of street prostitutes want to leave prostitution, but for those who do, resources are scarce (and even scarcer for sex workers who do not want to leave the industry, but need services). Services to women in the sex industry are woefully inadequate (Weiner 1996; Seattle Women's Commission 1995). For example, in Seattle,

> Existing services are not prepared to deal with the unique issues of sex industry women [e.g., stigma, sexual trauma, emotional problems]...Nor do women have the backup resources of family and education needed to reorganize their lives. (Boyer, Chapman, and Marshall 1993:20)

Getting prostitutes off the streets requires positive incentives and assistance in the form of housing, job training, counseling, and drug treatment, but the dominant approach is overwhelmingly coercive rather than rehabilitative. Past experience abundantly shows the failure of narrowly punitive intervention. Without meaningful alternatives to prostitution there is little opportunity for a career change.

What about the customers? Traditionally, the act of patronizing a prostitute was not a crime in the United States. This was largely due to the tremendous status disparity between male clients and "women of ill repute." Prostitutes were outcasts whereas patrons were seen as valuable members of society, even if they occasionally dabbled in deviant sexual liaisons. As Abraham Flexner wrote in 1920, the customer "discharges important social and business relations, is a father or brother responsible for the maintenance of others, has commercial or industrial duties to meet. He cannot be imprisoned without damaging society" (quoted in Little 1995: 38–39). This justification for gender discrimination persists in some quarters today. The renowned Model Penal Code reflects this double standard: The code stipulates that prostitution should be treated as a misdemeanor, while patronizing a prostitute should be punished as a mere violation—an infraction punishable by a fine rather than incarceration. The disparity was defended even as late as 1980, in the official commentary on the code:

> Authorization of severe penalties [jail time] for such misconduct [patronizing] is wholly unrealistic. Prosecutors, judges, and juries would be prone to nullify severe penalties in light of the common perception of extramarital intercourse as a widespread practice.... This level of condemnation [a violation and fine] would seem far more in keeping with popular understanding than would more severe sanctions. Furthermore, the lenient treatment of customers reflects the orientation of the offense toward the merchandizers of sexual activity. (American Law Institute 1980: 468)

The prevalence of extramarital sex, a "popular understanding" favoring the clients, and the notion that the law should target sellers, not buyers, of vice are all invoked to justify lenient treatment of clients. Most state penal codes now treat patronizing as a misdemeanor, not a mere violation as the Model Penal Code recommended.

Since the 1960s, the act of patronizing or soliciting a prostitute has been criminalized by all states, though many state laws continue to punish patronizing less severely than prostitution (Posner and Silbaugh 1996:156). And in most cities, enforcement against customers is either sporadic or lacking altogether. Although the double standard has eroded to some extent, it is still only in the exceptional jurisdiction where prostitutes and their patrons are treated equally. Elsewhere, gender bias persists in both arrest rates and penalties (Bernat 1985; Lowman 1990). Nationally, of the approximately 90,000 prostitution arrests every year, roughly one-third are males (Bureau of Justice Statistics annual), which breaks down to about 20 percent male prostitutes and 10 percent male customers. In light of the fact that customers greatly outnumber prostitutes, the gender disparity in arrests appears even more disproportional. Gender bias is also evident in sanctions. In Seattle from 1991 to 1993, for example, 2,508 prostitutes were arrested for solicitation while only 500 customers were arrested for patronizing (Seattle Women's Commission 1995). And in 1993, 69 percent of the prostitutes charged with solicitation were convicted whereas only 9 percent of the customers were convicted, largely because they were offered pre-trial diversion. Indeed, in most cities first-time arrested customers are routinely offered diversion rather than prosecution. And those customers who are prosecuted and convicted are less likely than prostitutes to receive fines or jail time (Lowman 1990). In Vancouver between 1991 and 1995, for example, only 0.5 percent of convicted customers were jailed and 9 percent fined; the remainder received absolute or conditional discharges. Convicted prostitutes were treated more harshly: 29 percent were jailed and 32 percent were given suspended sentences (Atchison et al. 1998).

An argument can be made for paying more attention to the *demand side* of prostitution. First, sheer numbers would seem to justify greater control of the customers, who are far more numerous than prostitutes. A major 1992 survey found that 16 percent of American men ages 18–59 said

they had ever paid for sex (Laumann et al. 1994). A question on something as stigmatized as one's personal involvement in prostitution is likely to yield some underreporting; still, it is clear that a significant proportion of the male population has had such encounters.

Second, demand-side prostitution controls can pay much higher dividends than supply-side controls. Prostitutes are dependent on this work for their livelihood and not easily deterred by sanctions. Customers, who have a greater stake in conventional society, are more fearful of arrest and punishment and more vulnerable than prostitutes to public shaming and stigmatization (Persons 1996). A British study found that arrested customers were unconcerned about fines but very worried about damage to their reputations if their activities were made public (Matthews 1993:14–15). A corollary is that customers are much less likely to recidivate after their first arrest. For example, in Washington, D.C., only 7 percent of the 563 males (mostly customers, some male prostitutes) arrested for prostitution offenses from 1990 to 1992 had previously been arrested for such an offense, whereas this was true of 47 percent of the 847 females arrested for prostitution offenses.[13] Similar findings were reported in Vancouver, Canada: 2 percent of the arrested customers and 49 percent of the arrested prostitutes were recidivists (Lowman 1990).

The large number of patrons and their greater susceptibility to deterrence are arguably good grounds for intensifying enforcement against them. Indeed, the customers may be uniquely qualified for deterrence:

> It is exactly in such situations, when the perpetrator is enmeshed in society and where the act is not central and integrated in his way of life, that punishment and deterrence have a positive effect...With a unilateral criminalization of the customers, we believe that a portion of the prostitution market will disappear. (Finstad and Hoigard 1993:222)

Others claim that cracking down on customers may even eradicate prostitution from a locale: "If communities really desire to eliminate prostitution, and not its side effects, customer control would be an obvious strategy to pursue" (Boles and Tatro 1978:76). And there appears to be substantial public support for targeting customers in some fashion, including public shaming. A 1995 national poll found that half of the public believed the media should disseminate the names and pictures of men convicted of soliciting prostitutes (*Newsweek* 1995). Residents of neighborhoods with street prostitution are especially likely to favor such controls (Weitzer 2000). As a member of one civic association noted, "These guys are the weak link in this chain. He's the one with the most to lose; that's why he's got to be kept out" (Gray 1991:25).

Though most cities continue to target their enforcement efforts against prostitutes rather than their customers, a few cities have begun to redirect control efforts toward the customers. One particularly innovative program is the "johns' school"—a program designed to educate and rehabilitate arrested customers. Since 1995, when San Francisco launched its First Offenders Prostitution Program for customers, several other cities have followed suit, including Buffalo, Las Vegas, Nashville, St. Paul, and some Canadian and British cities. San Francisco's school is a joint effort by the district attorney's office, the police department, the public health department, community leaders, and former prostitutes. The men avoid an arrest record and court appearance by paying a $500 fee, attending the school, and not reoffending for one year after the arrest. Every aspect of the all-day course is designed to *shame, educate, and deter* the men from future contact with prostitutes. The lectures are designed for maximum shock value: the men are frequently asked how they would feel if their mothers, wives, or daughters were "prostituted," and why they were "using" and "violating" prostitutes by patronizing them. The audience is also exposed to a graphic slide show on sexually transmitted diseases, horror stories about the wretched lives of prostitutes and their oppression by pimps, and information about the adverse impact of street prostitution on neighborhoods.

Unlike other shaming sanctions—such as printing customers' names or photos in local newspapers or on cable TV shows—where humiliation or "stigmatizing shaming" (Braithwaite 1989) of the offender is a goal, shaming in the johns' schools occurs in the context of a day of reeducation about the various harms of prostitution. This is closer to the "reintegrative shaming" model (Braithwaite 1989) linking punishment to rehabilitation, though this ends once the class concludes. A measure of rehabilitation is recidivism: of the nearly 2,200 graduates of San Francisco's school from March 1995 to February 1999, only eighteen were subsequently rearrested for solicitation. Toronto's program reports low recidivism as well.[14]

Low recidivism, or "specific deterrence" among the graduates of the johns' schools does not necessarily mean that the program is also having a larger "general deterrent" effect (on the never-arrested population of prospective johns), since in most cities with johns' schools, the number of johns on the streets is thus far unabated. Moreover, it is difficult to tell whether non-recidivism is due to the school experience per se or to the arrest. Official statistics show low recidivism among previously arrested customers generally (including those who had not attended a johns' school), suggesting that the arrest is the decisive deterrent.

Customers are also the focus of another innovative program. Inspired by drug forfeiture laws, a growing number of cities have passed ordinances empowering police to confiscate customers' cars when caught in the act of soliciting sexual favors on the street. Portland, Detroit, New York, Chicago, Washington, San Diego, Milwaukee, and Philadelphia are only a few of the cities where such laws have been enacted. After a car is seized a civil hearing is held to determine if there are grounds for forfeiture. Forfeited cars are sold at auction or retained as city property.

The laws vary substantially. Some are lenient with first-time offenders; others treat first-timers and repeat offenders the same. Most cities eventually return the car if the arrested driver is not the owner—if the car belongs to the driver's wife, employer, or a rental company. But some cities confiscate vehicles even if the owner was uninvolved in the crime. In St. Paul, Minnesota, for instance, an auto dealer's car taken on a test drive was used to solicit a prostitute and was seized by the police. (The Supreme Court ruled in *Bennis v. Michigan* in March 1996 that confiscation of property, even if the owner was not involved in the crime, is not unconstitutional.) Finally, in some cities (Oakland, California, Portland, Oregon, Washington, D.C.), a person may be acquitted of the criminal offense of soliciting a prostitute but lose his car in the civil case (where the standard of proof is lower), while in other cities the policy is to return the car if the criminal case fails.

Portland's 1989 forfeiture law has been the inspiration for other cities. Police seized 1,089 vehicles from 1990 through 1993, 52 of which (5 percent) were eventually forfeited; more recently, police have seized around 350 cars per year, only a few of which have been forfeited.[15] Most were first-time arrestees, who were allowed to sign a release agreement stipulating that they would refrain from any future street solicitation or automatically forfeit their car. The result is that the number of repeat offenders is almost nil. Between 1989 and May 1993, only 1 percent of the arrestees had been rearrested.[16]

The benefits of forfeiture laws may not be limited to their deterrent value but may also provide revenue for the police department. In Detroit, for instance, the proceeds have been used to buy police equipment and pay for officers' overtime. And even when cars are returned to their owners, some cities (e.g., Portland) recover the costs of police time, towing, and storage by charging a fee for the returned car. This is tantamount to a fine levied on all seized cars, whether or not the drivers are found guilty.

The forfeiture policy raises some obvious problems. Loss of a car penalizes not only the perpetrator but other family members who depend on it, and the punishment may not fit the crime. Permanent loss of a car worth perhaps thousands of dollars seems disproportionately harsh for a misdemeanor offense, and arguably violates the Eighth Amendment's prohibition on excessive fines. Moreover, there is a wide disparity in the value of the cars seized, from the worthless to the expensive. Such unequal punishment may violate the equal protection clause of the Fourteenth Amendment.

The car seizure policy and the johns' schools show that some cities (albeit a minority) have begun to take customers more seriously than in the past.

Moreover, the two programs are more imaginative than the arrest-and-fine approach and put more emphasis on deterring arrestees from recidivating. It remains to be seen whether sustained efforts to attack the demand for street prostitutes will pay dividends in reducing demand, as some analysts claim. But even if it does not have this effect, it can be justified by the principle that law enforcement should be gender neutral.

Conclusion

The two-track model outlined here has advantages over both the current policy of blanket criminalization and the alternatives of decriminalization and legalization. It is arguably superior to the other approaches in satisfying key tests: public preferences regarding the proper focus of law enforcement, efficient use of criminal justice resources, and the harm-reduction principle. Essential ingredients of the policy include (1) redirecting control efforts from indoor to street prostitution, (2) gender-neutral law enforcement, and (3) providing support services and assistance for persons who want to leave prostitution. Most effective implementation of the policy would require changes in all three areas simultaneously.

Discussion Questions

1. Drawing on the article by Albert DiChiara and John Galliher, why did some states pass legislation decriminalizing marijuana possession?

2. What do DiChiara and Galliher mean by "de facto decriminalization"?

3. In what ways did the Meese commission on pornography demonstrate its lack of impartiality, as documented by Carole Vance?

4. Based on the analysis of prostitution policy by Ronald Weitzer, identify the main problems with the policies of criminalization, legalization, and decriminalization of prostitution in the United States.

5. What are the potential advantages of the "two-track policy" outlined by Weitzer?

Notes

1. There has been more debate in official circles in Britain and Canada, where a number of cities have considered legalization.
2. Founded in 1973 by former prostitute Margo St. James, COYOTE is the premier prostitutes' rights group in the United States, and is affiliated with several lesser known organizations (Weitzer 1991). Although COYOTE claims to represent all prostitutes, it has been closely aligned with upper-echelon call girls, not streetwalkers.
3. *San Francisco Examiner.* December 6, 1995.
4. "The Task Force therefore recommends that the City stop enforcing and prosecuting prostitution crimes" (San Francisco Task Force 1996: 6).
5. Interview, April 29, 1997.
6. Interview, June 7, 1993.
7. Julie Pearl study, on file with *Hastings Law Journal.*
8. Interviews with vice officers in these cities by Julie Pearl; transcripts on file with *Hastings Law Journal.*
9. *San Francisco Chronicle.* April 6, 1990.
10. Vice sergeant interviewed by Julie Pearl, May 1985; transcript on file at *Hastings Law Journal.*
11. Interview, July 9. 1993.
12. Interview, July 27, 1993.
13. Figures provided by the U.S. Attorney's Office, Washington, DC.
14. Personal communication from Sergeant Doug Mottram, Metropolitan Toronto Police, August 7, 1997.
15. Interview with Sergeant Steve Larson, Portland Police Department, September 24, 1997.
16. *Newsday,* May 12, 1993.

References

A&E [Arts and Entertainment Network]. 1997. "Red Light Districts," Videotape.

American Law Institute. 1980. *Model Penal Code and Commentaries, Part II, Sections 240.0 to 251.4.* Philadelphia: American Law Institute.

Atchison. C., L. Fraser. and J. Lowman. 1988. "Men Who Buy Sex." In J. Elias, V. Bullough, V. Elias, and C. Brewer (eds.). *Prostitution.* Amherst: Prometheus.

Atlanta Task Force on Prostitution. 1986. *Findings and Recommendations.* Mayor's Office: Atlanta, Georgia.

Barnard, M. 1993. "Violence and Vulnerability: Conditions of Work for Street Working Prostitutes." *Sociology of Health and Illness* 15: 683-705.

Bennetto, J. 1996. "Community Work the Best Penalty for Vice, say Police." *The Independent* [London], October 21.

Benson, C. and R. Matthews. 1995. "Street Prostitution: Ten Facts in Search of a Policy." *International Journal of the Sociology of Law* 23: 395–415.

Benson, C., and R. Matthews. 1996. *Report of the Parliamentary Group on Prostitution.* London: Middlesex University.

Bernat, F. 1985. "New York State's Prostitution Statute: Case Study of the Discriminatory Application of Gender Neutral Law." In C. Schweber and C. Feinman (eds.), *Criminal Justice Politics and Women.* New York: Haworth.

Boles, J., and C., Tatro. 1978. "Legal and Extralegal Methods of Controlling Female Prostitution: A Cross-Cultural Comparison." *International Journal of Comparative and Applied Criminal Justice* 2: 71–85.

Boyer, D., L. Chapman, and B. Marshall. 1993. *Survivor Sex in King County: Helping Women Out.* Report submitted to the King County Women's Advisory Board, March.

Braithwaite, J. 1989. *Crime, Shame, and Reintegration.* Cambridge: Cambridge University Press.

Bryan, J. 1996. "Occupational Ideologies and Individual Attitudes of Call Girls." *Social Problems* 13: 441–450.

Bureau of Justice Statistics. Annual. *Sourcebook of Criminal Justice Statistics.* Washington, D.C.: Government Printing Office.

Campbell, R. 1988. "Invisible Men: Making Visible Male Clients of Female Prostitutes in Merseyside." In Elias, V. Bullough, V. Elias, and G. Brewer (eds.), *Prostitution.* Amherst: Prometheus.

Caughey, M. 1974. "The Principle of Harm and Its Application to Laws Criminalizing Prostitution." *Denver Law Journal* 51: 235–262.

Clark, C. 1993. "Prostitution." *Congressional Quarterly Researcher* 3: 505–527.

Coalition of San Francisco Business and Neighborhood Communities Impacted by Prostitution. 1996. *Resolution.*

Comment. 1977. "Privacy and Prostitution." *Iowa Law Review* 63: 248–265.

Cohen, B. 1980. *Deviant Street Networks: Prostitution in New York City.* Lexington, MA: Lexington.

Davis, N. J. 2000. "From Victims to Survivors: Working with Recovering Street Prostitutes." In R. Weitzer (ed.). *Sex for Sale: Prostitution, Pornography, and the Sex Industry.* New York: Routledge.

Decker, J. 1979. *Prostitution: Regulation and Control.* Littleton, CO: Rothman.

Exner, J. E., J. Wylie, A. Leura, and T. Parrill, 1977. "Some Psychological Characteristics of Prostitutes." *Journal of Personality Assessment* 41: 474–485.

Farley, F., and S. Davis. 1978. "Masseuses, Men, and Massage Parlors." *Journal of Sex and Marital Therapy* 4: 219-225.

Farley, M., and H. Barkan, 1998. "Prostitution, Violence, and Posttraumatic Stress Disorder." *Women and Health* 27: 37–49.

Finstad, L., and C. Hoigard. 1993. "Norway." In N. Davis (ed.), *Prostitution: An International Handbook on Trends, Problems, and Policies.* Westport, CT: Greenwood.

Gallup Organization. 1991. *Gallup Poll Monthly.* No. 313. October.

——. 1996. Public Opinion Online, Lexis/Nexis. Gallup poll. May 28–29.

Gray, K. 1991. "Prostitution Opponents Aim to Seize Johns' Cars." *Newsday,* December 5, p. 25.

Harris Poll, 1978. Public Opinion Online, Lexis/Nexis. N = 1,513, November 30–December 10.

——. 1990. Public Opinion Online, Lexis/Nexis. N = 2,254. January 11–February 11.

Heyl, B. 1979. "Prostitution: An Extreme Case of Sex Stratification." In F. Adler and R. Simon (eds.), *The Criminology of Deviant Women.* Boston: Houghton Mifflin.

Hobson, B. M. 1987. *Uneasy Virtue.* New York: Basic Books.

James, J. 1973. "Prostitute-Pimp Relationships." *Medical Aspects of Human Sexuality* 7: 147–160.

Jennings, M. A. 1976. "The Victim as Criminal: A Consideration of California's Prostitution Law." *California Law Review* 64: 1235–1284.

Kelling, G.. and C. Coles. 1996. *Fixing Broken Windows.* New York: Free Press.

Larsen, E. N. 1992. "The Politics of Prostitution Control: Interest Group Politics in Four Canadian Cities." *International Journal of Urban and Regional Research* 16: 169–189.

Laumann, E., J. Gagnon, R. Michael, and S. Michaels. 1994. *The Social Organization of Sexuality: Sexual Practices in the United States.* Chicago: University of Chicago Press.

Little, C. 1995. *Deviance and Control.* Itasca, IL: Peacock.

Lowman, J. 1990. "Notions of Formal Equality Before the Law: The Experience of Street Prostitutes and Their Customers." *Journal of Human Justice* 1: 55–76.

——. 1992. "Street Prostitution Control." *British Journal of Criminology* 32: 1–17.

McCaghy, C., and S. Cernkovich. 1991. "Changing Public Opinion toward Prostitution Laws." Paper presented at the World Congress of Sexology, Amsterdam.

Matthews, R. 1993. *Kerb-Crawling, Prostitution, and Multi-Agency Policing.* Paper no. 43. London: Home Office.

Merit Audits and Surveys. 1983. *Merit Report.* October 15–20.

Milman, B. 1980. "New Rules for the Oldest Profession: Should We Change Our Prostitution Laws?" *Harvard Women's Law Journal* 3: 1–82.

Newsweek poll. 1995. Public Opinion Online. Lexis/Nexis. N = 753, January 26–27.

Pearl, J. 1987. "The Highest Paying Customer: America's Cities and the Costs of Prostitution Control." *Hastings Law Journal* 38: 769–800.

Peat Marwick and Partners. 1984. *A National Population Study of Prostitution and Pornography.* Report no. 6. Ottawa: Department of Justice.

Perkins, R. 1991. *Working Girls.* Canberra: Australian Institute of Criminology.

Persons, C. 1996. "Sex in the Sunlight: The Effectiveness Efficiency, Constitutionality, and Advisability of Publishing Names and Pictures of Prostitutes' Patrons *Vanderbilt Law Review* 49: 1525–1575.

Pivar, D. 1973. *Purity Crusade.* Westport, CT: Greenwood

Posner, R., and K. Silbaugh. 1996. *A Guide to American Sex Laws.* Chicago: University of Chicago Press.

Reynolds, H. 1986. *The Economics of Prostitution.* Springfield: Charles Thomas.

San Diego Prostitution Task Force. 1993. *Report.* San Diego City Council, October.

San Francisco Committee on Crime. 1971. *A Report on Non-Victim Crime in San Francisco. Part 2: Sexual Conduct, Gambling. Pornography.* Mayor's Office.

San Francisco Task Force on Prostitution. 1996. *Final Report.* San Francisco Board of Supervisors, March.

Seattle Women's Commission. 1995. *Project to Address the Legal, Political, and Service Barriers Facing Women in the Sex Industry.* Report to the Mayor and City Council. Seattle: July.

Silbert, M., and A. Pines. 1982. "Victimization of Street Prostitutes." *Victimology* 7: 122–133.

Skogan, W. 1990. *Disorder and Decline.* New York: Free Press.

Skolnick, J., and J. Dombrink. 1978. "The Legalization of Deviance." *Criminology* 16: 193–208.

Special Committee on Pornography and Prostitution. 1985. *Pornography and Prostitution in Canada.* Ottawa: Dept. of Supply and Services.

Sullivan. B. 1997. *The Politics of Sex: Prostitution and Pornography in Australia since 1945.* New York: Cambridge University Press.

Weiner, A. 1996. "Understanding the Social Needs of Streetwalking Prostitutes." *Social Work* 41: 97–105.

Weitzer, R. 1991. "Prostitutes' Rights in the United States: The Failure of a Movement." *Sociological Quarterly* 32: 23–41.

——. 2000. 'The Politics of Prostitution in America." In R. Weitzer (ed.), *Sex for Sale: Prostitution, Pornography, and the Sex Industry.* New York: Routledge.

Wilson, J. Q., and G. Kelling. 1982. "Broken Windows." *Atlantic Monthly,* March, 29–38.

Working Group [Federal/Provincial Territorial Working Group on Prostitution]. 1998. *Report and Recommendations in Respect of Legislation, Policy, and Practices Concerning Prostitution-Related Activities.* Ottawa: Department of Justice.

CHAPTER 42

The Evidence in Favor of Prisons

Richard A. Wright

Once the accused has been arrested by the police, tried in a criminal court before a jury of peers or pleaded guilty, and sentenced by a judge, the state imposes some type of punishment as retribution for the misdeed. Although the state-imposed punishments may vary in type, ranging from death to a simple reprimand, crimes always call for a punishment. Criminal laws, as we saw earlier, are based on the principle of penalty. Through the years, this principle has been questioned as shortsighted and contrary to rehabilitative efforts. What should the state's objective be, then: to punish for past misdeeds or to resocialize for a future, noncriminal role in society? Does punishment play any positive role in making us more law abiding?

In this selection Richard A. Wright examines the objectives of punishment and, more specifically, the role of prisons in deterring crime. He concludes that prisons are not successful as either instruments of retribution or rehabilitation. Their use also fails to restore social solidarity to conformists who are demoralized by criminality. Prisons do, however, have beneficial functions. They "are effective agents of general deterrence, specific deterrence and incapacitation," he claims. In other words, the use of prisons has some effect on preventing crime among conformists and reducing future crimes among offenders. Although it can be argued that imprisonment prevents crime among those who are locked

up (except, of course, for some prison behavior that is illegal), it remains uncertain that the fear of being sent to prison prevents the average person from committing an offense.

Is imprisonment an effective means of punishment? That appears to be a question that may be answered in several ways, depending on one's objectives. It is certain, however, that a large number of citizens and policymakers believe it is, as the just deserts of those who violate the law and as a means of making us all more law abiding.

Of all the institutions in American society, prisons are perhaps the most vilified. The critics of prisons come in all shapes, sizes, political persuasions, and walks of life. Criticisms have been raised by political radicals (Wright, 1973), liberals (Currie, 1985) and neoconservatives (von Hirsch, 1976), and by attorneys (Stender, 1973), journalists (Wicker, 1975), novelists and playwrights (Shaw, 1946; Wilde, [1898] 1973), television scriptwriters (Bello, 1982), psychologists (Sommer, 1976), psychiatrists (Menninger, 1968), sociologists (Goffman, 1961), religious groups (American Friends Service Committee, 1971), ex-correctional officials (Fogel, 1975; Murton and Hyams, 1969; Nagel, 1973), ex-convicts (Johnson, 1970), current convicts (Abbott, 1982; Hassine, 1996) and criminologists far too numerous to list. Among academicians, only a handful of conservatives (see DiIulio and Logan, 1992; van den Haag, 1975; Wilson, 1985; Wright, 1994) staunchly support prisons.

The criticisms of prisons range from cautious reservations to virtual hysteria. Currie (1985:52)

Reprinted from: Richard A. Wright, "The Evidence in Favor of Prisons." In Martin D. Schwartz and Lawrence F. Travis III (eds.) *Corrections: An Issues Approach.* Copyright © 1997 by Anderson Publishing Company. Reprinted by permission.

moderately concludes that "although imprisonment is all too often an unavoidable necessity, it is not an effective way to prevent crime." (One must wonder, though, why Currie considers prisons necessary if they are so ineffective.) Among the less moderate, Menninger (1968:89) bluntly reviles prisons as "monuments to stupidity." He continues:

> [Prison] is a creaking, groaning monster through whose heartless jaws hundreds of American citizens grind daily, to be maimed and embittered so they emerge [as] implacable enemies of the social order and confirmed in their "criminality" (1968:89).

The title of Menninger's book—*The Crime of Punishment* (1968)—conveys the view that the injuries committed by criminals are relatively innocuous compared to the far more harmful social response of imprisonment.

I contend that the critics of prisons are wrong in their assessments (see Wright, 1994). Recent empirical research shows that punishments prevent crime and that prisons are at least modestly successful as a means of social control.

The Objectives of Punishment

Philosophers of punishment offer contradictory justifications—*retributive* and *utilitarian*—for inflicting pain on offenders (Wright, 1994). Retributivists (e.g., Fogel, 1975; Hospers, 1977; Lewis, [1948] 1971; von Hirsch, 1976, 1985) argue that the objective of punishment involves the repayment by the offender for his or her wrongs; the severity of punishment should be carefully calibrated to fit the seriousness of the offense. Retribution is considered a desirable end in itself: punishments are justly deserved by offenders as a consequence of the wrongfulness of their criminal acts. In addition, by seeking to right prior wrongs, retribution is directed toward punishing past offenses rather than toward preventing future crimes.

Utilitarians (e.g., Andenaes, 1974; Bentham, [1811] 1930; Hawkins, 1971; Wilson, 1985) are less concerned about offenders repaying their past "debts" to society; instead, they endorse punishment as a means (or instrument) to achieve certain desirable social ends (or benefits) in the future. In particular, utilitarians believe that punishment should prevent crime, through promoting such beneficial social outcomes as *rehabilitation, social solidarity, general deterrence, specific deterrence* and *incapacitation*. Correctional rehabilitation refers to the treatment of inmates through various counseling, educational, vocational, industrial and recreational programs. Those who claim that punishment promotes social solidarity argue that punishing the law-breaking minority reinforces and strengthens the commitment of the law-abiding majority to the dominant cultural norms, values and beliefs. General deterrence is the use of the threat of punishment to convince those who are not being punished not to commit future crimes. Specific deterrence is the use of punishment to convince those who actually are being punished not to commit future crimes. (In general deterrence, Peter is punished as an example to Paul that crime does not pay; in specific deterrence, Peter is punished as an example to convince Peter himself that crime does not pay.) Finally, incapacitation prevents crime in society-at-large through the use of punishment to remove criminals from uninhibited circulation in free society.

Here I briefly survey what modern research shows about the effectiveness of prisons in achieving the retributive and utilitarian objectives of punishment (for a much more extensive review of this evidence, see Wright, 1994). In general, research suggests that prisons are mostly ineffective as instruments of retribution, rehabilitation and social solidarity, but are moderately effective in promoting general deterrence, specific deterrence and incapacitation. I conclude with a policy recommendation based on this evidence.

The Failure of Prisons: Retribution, Rehabilitation and Social Solidarity

The critics of prisons usually depict them as total failures, or as Nagel (1973:177) contends, institutions that are "grossly ineffective [and] grossly dehumanizing." While Nagel's claims are grossly exaggerated, empirical evidence indicates that prisons do not effectively accomplish all their retributive and utilitarian objectives.

Retribution demands the equivalence of crimes and punishments, where the seriousness of crimes and the severity of punishments are closely matched (Fogel, 1975; von Hirsch, 1976). Certainly this is a laudable principle in the abstract, but probably impossible to accomplish in the real world of crime and imprisonment. For retributive-based sentencing to be successful, policymakers must be able to rank *both* the seriousness of crimes and the severity of punishments, and match them by degree. To date, though, empirical research shows that there is little public consensus on the seriousness of many crimes (especially vice, public order and white-collar offenses; see Miethe, 1982; Cullen et al. 1985; Warr, 1989); without basic social consensus in seriousness of crime rankings, it is impossible to fit punishments neatly to crimes.

There are other problems with using prisons as instruments of retribution. For example, retribution is modeled on the ancient rabbinical principal of *lex talionis* ("an eye for an eye and a tooth for a tooth"). But what about the offender who has a long history of eye-gouging and tooth bashing? Do we take into consideration his or her past record, or simply sentence on the basis of the current offense? Retributivists have never offered a satisfactory answer to this question (but for an attempt, see von Hirsch, 1985).

Retribution also ignores the social and personal contexts of crime and punishment. Variations in social class, demographic factors and personal backgrounds "mean that two different offenders guilty of similar crimes may experience the severity of supposedly identical punishments in very dissimilar ways" (Wright, 1994:45). A $50 fine is not the same thing to a millionaire as it is to a homeless person; likewise, a 65-year-old corporate executive would perceive a 10-year prison sentence much differently than a 20-year-old unemployed construction worker. For these and other reasons (see Wright, 1994), it is difficult to justify the use of imprisonment for the objective of retribution.

It is also sensible to be skeptical of the effectiveness of prisons as instruments of rehabilitation. The debate about the effectiveness of rehabilitation has been waged primarily through meta-evaluation (also called meta-analysis) studies, which judge the effectiveness of social programs by summarizing the findings of many individual studies (for longer reviews of meta-evaluation studies of correctional rehabilitation programs, see Wright, 1994, 1995). The most famous meta-evaluation study of rehabilitation is the "Martinson Report" (Lipton, Martinson and Wilks, 1975; Martinson, 1974), an analysis of 231 studies of the effectiveness of criminal justice treatment programs implemented between 1945 and 1967. This study found that rehabilitation programs have little to no effect on recidivism (defined as the percent of ex-convicts who commit subsequent offenses). Numerous other meta-evaluations of the impact of rehabilitation programs on offender recidivism have reached similar negative conclusions (for example, see Bailey, 1966; Greenberg, 1977; Lab and Whitehead, 1988; Sechrest, White and Brown, 1979; Whitehead and Lab, 1989; but see Andrews et al., 1990 for a more positive assessment of the effectiveness of rehabilitation programs). The balance of evidence seems to show that correctional rehabilitation programs are an ineffective means of preventing crime.

A number of prominent sociologists (see Durkheim, [1893] 1964; Erikson, 1966; Garfinkel, 1956) speculate that crime and punishment promote social solidarity by drawing law-abiding citizens together in a spirit of consensual outrage and indignation. For example, Erikson (1966:4) argues that crime and punishment create "a climate in which the private sentiments of many separate persons are fused together into a common sense of morality." He believes that the defense of moral boundaries that occurs through the punishment of criminals not only reinforces respect for the law among the already law-abiding, but also assists in the socialization of new generations.

Unfortunately, those who make this argument apparently underestimate the immense social injury that crime inflicts on communities. Current research shows that crimes and punishments tear us apart far more than they bring us together (Conklin, 1975; Lewis and Salem, 1986; Tittle, 1980). For example, Conklin's (1975:99) analysis of the impact of crime on 266 families in two Boston neighborhoods demonstrates that the fear of crime contributes to social disorder by promoting interpersonal suspicion, "insecurity, distrust, and a negative view of the community." Furthermore, there is no empirical evidence to suggest that even when offenders are apprehended by the police and eventually imprisoned, their punishments on balance restore *more* social solidarity than their crimes initially disrupted. In general, the empirical evidence suggests that prisons fail as instruments of retribution and as utilitarian agents promoting rehabilitation and social solidarity.

The Success of Prisons: General Deterrence, Specific Deterrence and Incapacitation

In his summary of research on deterrence and incapacitation, Currie (1985:52) argues that only "the more extreme proponents of an 'economic' view of crime" believe that crime can be prevented by incarceration. At the risk of being labeled an extremist, I think there is clear and compelling evidence to suggest that prisons are effective agents of general deterrence, specific deterrence and incapacitation.

Before discussing the research evidence relating to deterrence and incapacitation, it is necessary to define some key terms. Since the days of Cesare Beccaria ([1764] 1963) and Jeremy Bentham ([1843] 1962), scholars have argued that the effectiveness of punishments as deterrents depends on three properties: *celerity* (the promptness of punishment following a crime), *certainty* (the probability or likelihood that an offender will be arrested and punished) and *severity* (the painfulness of the punishment to an offender). More recently, deterrence theorists have distinguished between *actual deterrence* (or one's real probability of experiencing prompt, certain and severe punishments at the hands of criminal justice officals) and *perceptual deterrence* (or one's subjective estimation of the likelihood of experiencing prompt, certain and severe punishments; see Chiricos and Waldo, 1970; Jensen, 1969; Tittle, 1980; Wright, 1994). One other important distinction made by deterrence researchers concerns the relative effect of *formal*

social controls (exerted by criminal justice agencies) and *informal social controls* (exerted by one's family, friends, neighbors, teachers and employers) in deterring criminal behavior (see Tittle, 1980; Williams and Hawkins, 1986; Wright, 1994).

Punishment researchers distinguish between two forms of incapacitation, *collective* and *selective* (see Blumstein et al., 1986; Blumstein, Cohen and Nagin, 1978; Greenwood, 1982; Wright, 1994). Collective incapacitation refers to preventing crime by removing criminals from society-at-large through traditional forms of prison sentencing, which mostly emphasize the seriousness of the current offense, and to a lesser extent, one's prior criminal record. Selective incapacitation targets repeat offenders for removal from society-at-large.

General Deterrence

Many criminologists still dispute the idea that prisons can achieve the objective of general deterrence (see Biles, 1979; Brodt and Smith, 1988; Currie, 1985; Wright, 1996). These critics often cite research which shows that incarceration rates and crime rates frequently rise simultaneously; for example, Biles' (1979) historical study of the levels of imprisonment and crime rates in the United States, Canada and Australia shows a positive relationship between the variables.

Interestingly, these same critics conveniently ignore other bivariate evidence that suggests that punishment sometimes promotes general deterrence. For example, the United States faced a dramatic rise in bank robberies in the early 1930s (MacDonald, 1975). The FBI chose to attack this problem by pursuing a well-publicized "get tough" policy in which particularly notorious bank robbers (e.g., John Dillinger, Bonnie Parker and Clyde Barrow) were ambushed and shot to death. The result was a sharp drop in bank robberies, from a high of 609 in 1932 to 129 in 1937 (see MacDonald, 1975; Wright, 1994).

More important are two methodological shortcomings that render suspect any criticism of general deterrence that merely associates incarceration rates with crime rates. First, the causal order of the relationship must be specified: do higher incarceration rates cause higher crime rates, or vice versa? Only the former suggests the failure of general deterrence. Also, bivariate studies that simply relate incarceration and crime rates ignore many possible rival causal factors (e.g., the percent of the population unemployed and the percent of the population in crime-prone age groups) that might confound the relationship.

In my extensive survey of hundreds of deterrence studies published over the last 25 years (see Wright, 1994), I discerned a few clear trends about the effectiveness of punishments as general deterrents:

1. A moderate inverse relationship exists between crime rates and both the actual and perceived certainties of punishment.

2. The perceived certainty of punishment is more significant than actual certainty in deterring crime.

3. "Get tough" criminal justice policies that increase the perceived certainty of punishment to potential offenders have a moderate initial (immediate) deterrent effect on crime rates, but little residual (long-term) deterrent effect.

4. Little relationship exists between crime rates and either the actual and perceived severities of punishment.

5. Celerity plays little role in the effectiveness of punishments as general deterrents, because there is no logical reason why timeliness in the punishment of offenders should influence others.

6. Empirical evidence suggests that general deterrence effects vary for different types of offenders: for example, lower-class persons and older persons appear to be deterred more by the certainty of punishment than the affluent and the young (see Wright, 1994:90).

To mention a few specific studies showing the effectiveness of prisons as general deterrents, Gibbs (1968) and Tittle (1969) analyzed admissions to prisons to examine the effect of the probability of imprisonment (certainty) and the length of prison sentences (severity) on the rates of FBI index crimes in different states. Both of these early studies supported the argument that the certainty of punishment promotes general deterrence by showing that the probability of imprisonment, although not the length of time served, is inversely related to statewide crime rates for most index crimes.

More recently, in a methodologically sophisticated multivariate study that used advanced economic techniques, McGuire and Sheehan (1983) again found an inverse relationship between state imprisonment rates for one year and crime rates for subsequent years. In analyzing imprisonment and crime rate data for the years 1960 to 1979, these authors conclude that a one percent increase in incarceration rates results in a 0.48 to 1.1 percent reduction in crime rates.

Glassner et al.'s (1983) qualitative study of an unspecified number of older juvenile offenders from upstate New York suggests that imprisonment threats help to deter youth from committing adult crime. The authors try to explain why those interviewed usually curtailed their criminal activities at approximately age 16. Two-thirds of their subjects noted the fear of the harsher penalties (especially imprisonment) imposed by the criminal justice system on adults (compared to the lenient punishment of younger offenders by the juvenile justice system) as the reason for quitting crime. Glassner et al. (1983:221) conclude that most older youth make a "conscious decision" to abandon crime based on a rational calculation of risk, largely "because they fear being jailed if apprehended as adults."

Specific Deterrence

Critics who contend that prisons are ineffective agents of specific deterrence usually rely on recidivism to support their arguments. For example, Currie (1985) produces what he claims is "astonishing" evidence that between one-third and two-thirds of all released inmates eventually return to prison. He concludes: "High recidivism rates are a troubling, stubborn prima facie case that if imprisonment deters individual criminals at all, it clearly doesn't do so reliably or consistently" (Currie, 1985:70).

Simple recidivism rates, however, are invalid measures of the specific deterrent effect of prisons for three reasons. First, simple recidivism rates offer no comparisons of offenders who are arrested and incarcerated with those who avoid apprehension. While undoubtedly a large percent of those arrested and incarcerated continue to commit crimes, it is likely that a far larger percent of offenders who avoid arrest persist in crime (Packer, 1968).

In addition, for recidivism to be a valid indicator of specific deterrence, criminal justice personnel need to randomize the assignment of punishments to those apprehended (Sherman and Berk, 1984; Wilson, 1985). Otherwise, studies that compare various forms of intervention—e.g., arrest and detention versus nonarrest and informal mediation—may mistakenly conclude that the former fail only because higher risk offenders (who are more likely to recidivate) are arrested and detained.

Finally, simple recidivism rates ignore the "suppression effects" of various forms of punishment (Farrington, 1987; Murray and Cox, 1979). Using only one arrest after incarceration as an indicator of recidivism ignores the fact that the "recidivist" may be committing fewer or less serious crimes following imprisonment. To analyze suppression effects, researchers must have measures of the number and the seriousness of an offender's crimes both *before* and *after* incarceration. In a survey of the specific deterrence literature (see Wright, 1994), a number of conclusions emerge:

1. Formal social controls—including arrest, court processing, and brief periods of confinement—appear to have a moderate inverse relationship to subsequent individual offending.
2. No evidence exists to suggest that long prison sentences are more effective as specific deterrents than shorter prison terms.
3. Formal and informal social controls apparently work together as specific deterrents. Punishments are more effective in deterring future individual offending, the more one worries about reprisals from one's family and friends, or the loss of one's job and good reputation in the community.
4. Even when punishments fail to prevent simple recidivism, they may be effective in suppressing the number and the seriousness of future offenses (see Wright, 1994: 104-105).

Unquestionably, the most important evidence relating to specific deterrence is a cluster of studies on domestic assault sponsored by the National Institute of Justice (for a summary of this research, see Sherman, 1992). These studies offer considerable insight into the effect of punishments on individual offenders because all use research designs in which males apprehended for misdemeanor domestic assault are randomly assigned to alternative law enforcement strategies: advice or mediation, ordering offenders to leave the premises for a few hours, or arrest and short-term detention. The pioneering study in this area is Sherman and Berk's (1984) evaluation of the effectiveness of these three apprehension strategies in 314 domestic assault cases processed by the Minneapolis Police Department in the early 1980s. The cases were followed for six months to determine whether male offenders experienced a subsequent police contact for domestic assault and/or interviewed female victims reported subsequent assaults. In both the police and victim data, arrest/detained offenders were significantly less likely to recidivate than those who were informally processed.

Numerous studies attempted to replicate these findings in such widely dispersed places as Colorado Springs, Colorado (Berk et al., 1992), Miami (Pate and Hamilton, 1992), Milwaukee (Sherman et al., 1991; Sherman and Smith, 1992), Omaha, Nebraska (Dunford, Huizinga and Elliott, 1990) and San Diego (Berk and Newton, 1985). Although these studies have a less straightforward interpretation, they tend to show that an arrest/detention strategy only deters women batterers in conjunction with informal social controls, or the offenders' attachments and commitments to the community. Specifically, arrest/detention significantly decreases recidivism in domestic assault cases involving males who are employed and married, but has little effect on the recidivism of men who are unemployed and unmarried (see Sherman, 1992). It is crucial to note, though, that even when punishment fails as a specific deterrent, it still can have a beneficial effect as a general deterrent.

Incapacitation

Although there is fairly compelling evidence that arrest and short-term confinement can deter many potential and actual offenders, some types of criminals clearly are unafraid of punishment. The existence of "career" or "chronic" offenders—or a small number of criminals who commit a great number of crimes—shows that deterrence clearly is no panacea for the problem of crime in America. Researchers have for some time noted the problem of the career offender; for example, in their study of the arrest records of 9,945 Philadelphia boys born in 1945 and followed until their eighteenth birthdays, Wolfgang, Figlio and Sellin (1972) found that 6.3 percent of the cohort was responsible for 51.9 percent of the total arrests. A Rand Corporation study of 2,190 prison inmates in California, Michigan and Texas revealed that the most active 10 percent of burglars and robbers reported committing, respectively, 232 and 87 of these crimes in their last year on the streets (Chaiken and Chaiken, 1982; Greenwood, 1982). In a thorough survey of career offender studies, Blumstein et al. (1986) estimate that the most active 10 percent of offenders nationally commit about 100 crimes each per year. The career criminal problem suggests that the use of prisons for incapacitation is an important crime control strategy.

In an extensive review of the research evidence relating to collective incapacitation (see Wright, 1994), I estimate that current imprisonment strategies annually result in about a 20 percent reduction in the national crime rate. One way to estimate the overall effectiveness of collective incapacitation policies is to project this figure into the total number of offenses committed in the United States in any given year. For example, National Crime Victimization survey data show that 34,800,000 serious (FBI index) offenses were committed in the United States in 1990 (Bureau of Justice Statistics, 1991), so that an estimated 20 percent reduction in the crime rate would mean that collective incapacitation via imprisonment averted 6,960,000 offenses during the year. Certainly this suggests that prisons are at least moderately effective in reducing the amount of crime through collective incapacitation.

Policies of selective incapacitation—in which career criminals are specifically targeted for long-term imprisonment—may hold additional promise for reducing crime. The effectiveness of selective incapacitation on crime prevention depends on the accuracy of risk assessment instruments, or composites of factors that can predict an offender's future criminality. Greenwood (1982) and Forst (1984) have devised two important risk assessment instruments for selective incapacitation purposes. Based on the Rand Corporation study of 2,190 prisoners in three states, Greenwood (1982) discerned seven factors that could be used to predict high-rate offending: (1) conviction for offenses as a juvenile (before age 16); (2) time served in a facility for juvenile delinquents; (3) the use of illegal drugs as a juvenile; (4) the use of illegal drugs during the past two years; (5) unemployment for more than 50 percent of the last two years; (6) incarceration for more than 50 percent of the last two years; and (7) a previous conviction for the current offense. Using these factors, Greenwood (1982) originally estimated that California could reduce burglaries by 20 percent by pursuing a selective incapacitation sentencing strategy, but reanalyses of Greenwood's data have cut these burglary reduction estimates in half (Blumstein et al., 1986).

In his study of 1,708 parolees from the federal prison system, Forst (1984) reached conclusions similar to Greenwood's. Forst's (1984) risk assessment instrument includes two factors not considered by Greenwood: polydrug abuse (specifically alcohol and heroin) by an offender, and a recent conviction for a crime of violence. If federal sentencing were based on his instrument, Forst (1984) estimates that career offenders could be targeted for imprisonment with sufficient success to prevent five to 10 percent of all federal offenses (or as many as 45,000 serious crimes annually).

Despite evidence suggesting that prisons can be effective agents of selective incapacitation for career offenders, these proposals have been sharply criticized (see Currie, 1985; von Hirsch, 1985, 1988). The standard criticism is that risk assessment instruments used for selective incapacitation sentencing will produce an unacceptable number of false positives (or persons predicted to become career criminals who subsequently offend at low rates). False positives are certainly a problem in risk assessment instruments; various studies suggest that between 15 and 50 percent of those predicted to become career criminals by these instruments will not recidivate at high rates (see Wright, 1994). Still, Forst's (1984) analysis shows that traditional nonstatistical, "intuitive" prediction strategies for sentencing result in higher numbers of false postives than strategies using risk assessment instruments. Forst (1984:157–158—emphasis in the original) concludes that risk assessment instruments "not only do not 'cause' false positives where none existed before," but more importantly "generally *reduce* the rate of false positives." In the future, more sophisticated risk assessment instruments using additional prediction factors will undoubtedly further reduce the number of false positives (Wright, 1994).

Retributivists argue that selective incapacitation sentencing is unjust because the severity of the sentence will exceed the seriousness of the current offense (von Hirsch, 1985, 1988). Von Hirsch (1988) raises the disturbing specter of the trivial offender who receives a long prison term simply because of the diagnostic label of a risk assessment instrument. Ignoring such concerns, state legislatures recently have abandoned the logic of retribution by enacting "three-strikes-and-you're-out" laws (that mandate life sentences for a third felony conviction). Selective incapacitation sentences based on risk assessment instruments offer a more scientific and rational sentencing alternative to these draconian statutes.

Summary and a Policy Recommendation

On balance, the research evidence suggests that prison critics are wrong in their assessment that prisons have failed as a form of punishment. Although prisons are apparently ineffective in promoting the objectives of retribution, rehabilitation and social solidarity, they appear to be moderately effective in reducing the crime rate through general deterrence, specific deterrence and incapacitation. Elected officials who wish to implement a

rational correctional policy should deemphasize the former three objectives of imprisonment in favor of the latter three.

Furthermore, deterrence and incapacitation seem to be complementary objectives of imprisonment: sentencing strategies based on deterrence appear to be most effective in preventing crimes among nonoffenders and occasional offenders; incapacitation is ideally suited for career criminals. This suggests that a rational crime-reduction policy should involve a combination of *selective deterrence* sentencing (emphasizing the certainty of brief periods of detention) to threaten nonoffenders and occasional offenders and *selective incapacitation* sentencing (emphasizing severity through long-term incarceration) for career criminals (Wright, 1994). In practical terms, this means that the length of a convict's prison sentence should be determined primarily by the number of his or her prior offenses, and not by the seriousness of the current offense. This is my policy recommendation based on the evidence in favor of prisons.

Discussion Questions

1. What types of people are critical of prisons? Why? What are some of the criticisms?

2. According to Wright, do punishments prevent crime? Do prisons prevent crimes? Are they an effective means of social control?

3. Describe the various justifications for punishment. What are the problems associated with each? Which one is dominant in society today? Why? What is the difference between specific and general deterrence? Do they work?

References

Abbott, J. H. 1982. *In the Belly of the Beast: Letters from Prison.* New York: Vintage.

American Friends Service Committee. 1971. *Struggle for Justice.* New York: Hill and Wang.

Andenaes, J. 1974. *Punishment and Deterrence.* Ann Arbor: University of Michigan Press.

Andrews, D. A., I. Zinger, R. D. Hoge, J. Bonta, P. Gendreau and F. T. Cullen. 1990. "Does Correctional

Treatment Work? A Clinically Relevant and Psychologically Informed Meta-Analysis." *Criminology* 28(3):369-404.

Bailey, W. C. 1966. "Correctional Outcome: An Evaluation of 100 Reports." *Journal of Criminal Law, Criminology and Police Science* 57(2): 153-160.

Beccaria, C. ([1764]1963). *On Crimes and Punishments*. Indianapolis, IN: Bobbs-Merrill.

Bello, S. 1982. *Doing Life*. New York: St. Martin's Press.

Bentham, J. ([1843] 1962). *The Works of Jeremy Bentham, Volume 1*. New York: Russell and Russell.

——. ([1811]1930). *The Rationale of Punishment*. London: Robert Howard.

Berk, R. A., A. Campbell, R. Klapp and B. Western. 1992. "The Deterrent Effect of Arrest in Incidents of Domestic Violence: A Bayesian Analysis of Four Field Experiments." *American Sociological Review* 57(5):698-708.

Berk, R. A. and P. J. Newton. 1985. "Does Arrest Really Deter Wife Battery? An Effort to Replicate the Findings of the Minneapolis Spouse Abuse Experiment." *American Sociological Review* 50(2): 253-262.

Biles, D. F. 1979. "Crime and the Use of Prisons." *Federal Probation* 43(2):39-43.

Blumstein, A., J. Cohen and D. Nagin (eds.). 1978. *Deterrence and Incapacitation: Estimating the Effects of Criminal Sanctions on Crime Rates*. Washington, DC: National Academy of Sciences.

Blumstein, A., J. Cohen, J. A. Roth and C. A. Visher (eds.). 1986. *Criminal Careers and "Career Criminals," Volume 1*. Washington, DC: National Academy Press.

Brodt, S. J. and J. S. Smith. 1988. "Public Policy and the Serious Juvenile Offender." *Criminal Justice Policy Review* 2(1):70-85.

Bureau of Justice Statistics. 1991. *National Update*. Washington, DC: U.S. Department of Justice, Office of Justice Programs.

Chaiken, J. M. and M. R. Chaiken. 1982. *Varieties of Criminal Behavior*. Santa Monica, CA: Rand Corporation.

Chiricos, T. G. and G. P. Waldo. 1970. "Punishment and Crime: An Examination of Some Empirical Evidence." *Social Problems* 18(2):200-217.

Conklin, J. E. 1975. *The Impact of Crime*. New York: Macmillan.

Cullen, F. T., B. G. Link, L. F. Travis III and J. F. Wozniak. 1985. "Consensus in Crime Seriousness: Empirical Reality or Methodological Artifact?" *Criminology* 23(1):99-118.

Currie, E. 1985. *Confronting Crime: An American Challenge*. New York: Pantheon.

DiIulio, J. and C. Logan. 1992. "The Ten Deadly Myths about Crime and Punishment in the U.S." *Wisconsin Interest* 1(1):21-35.

Dunford, F. W., D. Huizinga and D. S. Elliott. 1990. "The Role of Arrest in Domestic Assault: The Omaha Police Experiment." *Criminology* 28(2): 183-206.

Durkheim, E. ([1893] 1964). *The Division of Labor in Society*. New York: The Free Press.

Erikson, K. T. 1966. *Wayward Puritans: A Study in the Sociology of Deviance*. New York: Wiley.

Farrington, D. P. 1987. "Predicting Individual Crime Rates." In D. M. Gottfredson and M. Tonry (eds.), *Crime and Justice: An Annual Review of Research, Volume 9*, pp. 53-101. Chicago: University of Chicago Press.

Fogel, D. 1975. "...We Are the Living Proof..." *The Justice Model for Corrections*. Cincinnati: Anderson Publishing Co.

Forst, B. 1984. "Selective Incapacitation: A Sheep in Wolf's Clothing?" *Judicature* 68(4 and 5):153-160.

Garfinkel, H. 1956. "Conditions of Successful Degradation Ceremonies." *American Journal of Sociology* 61(5):420-424.

Gibbs, J. P. 1968. "Crime, Punishment, and Deterrence." *Southwestern Social Science Quarterly* 48(4):515-530.

Glassner, B., M. Ksander, B. Berg and B.D. Johnson. 1983. "A Note on the Deterrent Effect of Juvenile Versus Adult Jurisdiction." *Social Problems* 31(2): 219-221.

Goffman, E. 1961. *Asylums: Essays on the Social Situation of Mental Patients and Other Inmates*. Garden City, NY: Anchor.

Greenberg, D. F. 1977. "The Correctional Effects of Corrections: A Survey of Evaluations." In D.F. Greenberg (ed.), *Corrections and Punishment*, pp. 111-148. Beverly Hills, CA: Sage Publications.

Greenwood, P. W. 1982. *Selective Incapacitation*. Santa Monica, CA: Rand Corporation.

Hassine, V. 1996. *Life Without Parole: Living in Prison Today*. Los Angeles: Roxbury.

Hawkins, G. 1971. "Punishment and Deterrence: The Educative, Moralizing, and Habituative Effects."

In S.E. Grupp (ed.), *Theories of Punishment*, pp. 163-180. Bloomington: Indiana University Press.

Hospers, J. 1977. "Retribution: The Ethics of Punishment." In R. E. Barnett and J. Hegel III (eds.), *Assessing the Criminal: Restitution, Retribution, and the Legal Process*, pp. 118-209. Cambridge, MA: Ballinger.

Jensen, G. F. 1969. " 'Crime Doesn't Pay:' Correlates of a Shared Misunderstanding." *Social Problems* 17(2):189-201.

Johnson, L. D. 1970. *The Devil's Front Porch*. Lawrence: University of Kansas Press.

Lab, S. P. and J. T. Whitehead. 1988. "An Analysis of Juvenile Treatment." *Crime and Delinquency* 34(1): 60-83.

Lewis, C. S. ([1948}1971). "The Humanitarian Theory of Punishment." In S. E. Grupp (ed.), *Theories of Punishment*, pp. 301-308. Bloomington: Indiana University Press.

Lewis, D. A. and G. Salem. 1986. *Fear of Crime: Incivility and the Production of a Social Problem*. New Brunswick, NJ: Transaction.

Lipton, D., R. Martinson and J. Wilks. 1975. *The Effectiveness of Correctional Treatment: A Survey of Treatment Evaluation Studies*. New York: Praeger.

MacDonald, J. M. 1975. *Armed Robbery: Offenders and Their Victims*. Springfield, IL: Charles C. Thomas.

Martinson, R. 1974. "What Works? Questions and Answers about Prison Reform." *The Public Interest* 35(Spring):22-54.

McGuire, W. J. and R. G. Sheehan. 1983. "Relationships Between Crime Rates and Incarceration Rates." *Journal of Research in Crime and Delinquency* 20(1):73-85.

Menninger, K. 1968. *The Crime of Punishment*. New York: Viking.

Miethe, T. D. 1982. "Public Consensus on Crime Seriousness: Normative Structure or Methodological Artificat?" *Criminology* 20(2-4): 515-526.

Murray, C. A. and L. A. Cox, Jr. 1979. *Beyond Probation: Juvenile Corrections and the Chronic Delinquent*. Beverly Hills, CA: Sage Publications.

Murton, T. and J. Hyams. 1969. *Accomplices to the Crime*. New York: Grove.

Nagel, W. G. 1973. *The New Red Barn: A Critical Look at the Modern American Prison*. New York: Walker.

Packer, H. L. 1968. *The Limits of the Criminal Sanction*. Stanford, CA: Stanford University Press.

Pate, A. M. and E. E. Hamilton. 1992. "Formal and Informal Deterrents to Domestic Violence: The Dade County Spouse Assault Experiment." *American Sociological Review* 57(5):691-697.

Sechrest, L., S. O. White and E. D. Brown (eds.). 1979. *The Rehabilitation of Criminal Offenders: Problems and Prospects*. Washington, DC: National Academy of Sciences.

Shaw, G. B. 1946. *The Crime of Imprisonment*. New York: Philosophical Library.

Sherman, L. W. 1992. *Policing Domestic Violence: Experiments and Dilemmas*. New York: The Free Press.

Sherman, L. W. and R. A. Berk. 1984. "The Specific Deterrent Effects of Arrest for Domestic Assault." *American Sociological Review* 49(2):261-272.

Sherman, L. W., J. D. Schmidt, D. P. Rogan, P. R. Gartin, E.G. Cohn, D. J. Collins and A. R. Bacich. 1991. "From Initial Deterrence to Long-Term Escalation: Short-Custody Arrest for Povery Ghetto Domestic Violence." *Criminology* 29(4):821-850.

Sherman, L. W. and D. A. Smith. 1992. "Crime, Punishment, and Stake in Conformity: Legal and Informal Control of Domestic Violence." *American Sociological Review* 57(5):680-690.

Sommer, R. 1976. *The End of Imprisonment*. New York: Oxford University Press.

Stender, F. 1973. "Violence and Lawlessness at Soledad Prison." In E. O. Wright (ed.), *The Politics of Punishment: A Critical Analysis of Prisons in America*, pp. 222-233. New York: Harper Torchbooks.

Tittle, C. R. 1980. *Sanctions and Social Deviance: The Question of Deterrence*. New York: Praeger.

——. 1969. "Crime Rates and Legal Sanctions." *Social Problems* 16(4):409-423.

van den Haag, E. 1975. *Punishing Criminals: Concerning a Very Old and Painful Question*. New York: Basic Books.

von Hirsch, A. 1988. "Selective Incapacitation Reexamined: The National Academy of Sciences' Report on *Criminal Careers and 'Career Criminals.'* " *Criminal Justice Ethics* 7(1):19-35.

——. 1985. *Past or Future Crimes: Deservedness and Dangerousness in the Sentencing of Criminals*. New Brunswick, NJ: Rutgers University Press.

——. 1976. *Doing Justice: The Choice of Punishments*. New York: Hill and Wang.

Warr, M. 1989. "What Is the Perceived Seriousness of Crimes?" *Criminology* 27(4):795-821.

Whitehead, J. T. and S. P. Lab. 1989. "A Meta-Analysis of Juvenile Correctional Treatment." *Journal of Research in Crime and Delinquency* 26(3):276-295.

Wicker, T. 1975. *A Time to Die.* New York: Ballantine.

Wilde, O. ([1898]1973). "The Ballad of Reading Gaol." In *De Profundis and Other Writings*, pp. 229-252. Middlesex, England: Penguin.

Williams, K. R. and R. Hawkins. 1986. "Perceptual Research on General Deterrence: A Critical Review." *Law and Society Review* 20(4):545-572.

Wilson, J. Q. 1985. *Thinking about Crime.* New York: Vintage.

Wolfgang, M. E., R. M. Figlio and T. Sellin. 1972. *Delinquency in a Birth Cohort.* Chicago: University of Chicago Press.

Wright, E. O. (ed.) 1973. *The Politics of Punishment: A Critical Analysis of Prisons in America.* New York: Harper Torchbooks.

Wright, R. A. 1994. *In Defense of Prisons.* Westport, CT: Greenwood Press.

——. 1995. "Rehabilitation Affirmed, Rejected, and Reaffirmed: Assessments of the Effectiveness of Offender Treatment Programs in Criminology Textbooks, 1956 to 1965 and 1983 to 1992." *Journal of Criminal Justice Education* 6(1):21-39.

——. 1996. "The Missing or Misperceived Effects of Punishment: The Coverage of Deterrence in Criminology Textbooks, 1956 to 1965 and 1984 to 1993." *Journal of Criminal Justice Education* 7(1):1-22.

CHAPTER 43

Decriminalization

Samuel Walker

One certain way of reducing crime is to reduce the number of behaviors that are defined as crime. This process, decriminalization, would not only lower the number and rate of crimes but would free police and judicial officers to concentrate on more serious offenses, while prisons and other correctional programs would be less crowded and capable of doing a better job rehabilitating convicted offenders. Advocates of decriminalization typically suggest it apply to victimless or public-order crimes, those that seem to hurt no one but consume a great deal of the time and resources of the criminal justice system. But if the process were so simple, it probably would have been tried by now. In fact, this is an enormously complex issue that raises passions on both sides.

In this selection Samuel Walker explores some of the arguments for and against the decriminalization of certain public-order offenses. He points out that this is essentially a moralistic debate, with opponents of decriminalization believing that certain behaviors are simply wrong and need to be deterred by threat of criminal penalty. Although the various rationales for decriminalization appear logical and reasoned, they cannot overcome the differences concerning moral standards that exist between proponents and opponents. Walker reaches no conclusion about the efficacy of decriminalization, concluding that predatory crimes, those that threaten us with

Reprinted from: Samuel Walker, "Decriminalization." In *Sense and Nonsense About Crime and Drugs*, pp. 237–242. Copyright © 1994 by Wadsworth Publishing Company. Reprinted by permission.

harm or loss, would not be affected by removing public-order offenses from the criminal statutes. Interesting though it may be, decriminalization is not the answer to America's crime problem.

... In their 1970 book, *The Honest Politician's Guide to Crime Control*, Norval Morris and Gordon Hawkins called decriminalization a "first principle." Specifically, they call for removing criminal penalties for (1) public drunkenness; (2) purchase, possession, and use of all drugs; (3) all forms of gambling; (4) disorderly conduct and vagrancy; (5) abortion; (6) private sexual activity between consenting adults; and (7) juvenile "status" offenses.[1]

It is important to clarify exactly what kinds of behavior are involved in this proposal. Public drunkenness is included but not drunk driving. The person drunk on the street may be a nuisance but poses no threat of harm to anyone else. The drunk driver does pose such a threat. Sexual activity between consenting adults is covered, but not sex between an adult and a child. In short, the standard decriminalization proposal covers a limited range of activity and not a general repeal of all criminal laws governing drinking or sex.

At this point in history there are two different approaches to decriminalization. We can call the items on Morris and Hawkins's agenda the "old" decriminalization. Something new arose in the 1980s: the notion of decriminalizing or legalizing drugs, including even those long considered the most dangerous drugs, heroin and cocaine.

We can call this the "new" decriminalization.... In this chapter let's examine the "old" decriminalization agenda to see what impact it might have on serious crime.

The Rationale for Decriminalization

Decriminalization was a response to what many liberals saw as the problem of the "overreach" of the criminal law. As Morris and Hawkins explained, too many different kinds of behavior are criminalized. The criminal law in America has traditionally been highly moralistic, covering gambling, many forms of sexual behavior, and alcohol-related problems.

According to the advocates of decriminalization, the broad reach of the criminal law has several undesirable consequences. First, it overburdens the justice system. The police spend too much time on relatively unimportant events, leaving them with less time for the really serious crimes of murder, rape, robbery, and burglary. These arrests fill the jails and clog the courts. In 1989 there were over 800,000 arrests for drunkenness. Since many of the 770,000 disorderly conduct arrests involved drunken people, the total number of alcohol-related arrests (not including drunk driving) is over a million a year.[2]

Second, there is not a strong public consensus about many of these crimes. In fact, the public is very ambivalent. We have many laws restricting gambling, but millions of people want to gamble and do so illegally. The laws prohibiting certain kinds of sexual activity hardly deter people from engaging in those forms of sex.

Ambivalent public attitudes send mixed signals to law enforcement officials, who are simultaneously told to enforce and not to enforce certain laws. The result is a pattern of selective and often arbitrary law enforcement. This violates the principle of equal protection of the law and leads to cynicism about law enforcement among the public and among police offenders.

Third, making various forms of recreation illegal brings into being criminal syndicates that provide the illegal goods and services that people want. Gambling was historically the principal source of revenue for organized crime, and America's demand for illegal drugs sustains vast international networks and neighborhood drug gangs. In this sense, the laws are criminogenic; they create forms of criminal behavior.

Fourth, the criminal syndicates corrupt both the justice system and the political system. The Knapp Commission investigation into police corruption in New York City found that police officers were receiving a weekly "pad" of between $300 and $1,500 a month for protecting illegal gambling.[3] In the 1980s the vast profits from the drug trade began to corrupt the banking system, as banks became involved in laundering drug profits.

Fifth, criminal penalties violate the right to engage in activities that many people believe are a matter of private choice among consenting adults. The overwhelming majority of Americans believe that sex between two adults of the opposite sex should not be a crime. About half of all Americans today now believe that sex between two adults of the same sex should not be a crime. About 80 percent of Americans believe that there is a right to terminate a pregnancy by abortion.[4]

Sixth, many criminal justice and public health experts believe that we have mistakenly attempted to deal with social, psychological, and medical problems through the criminal law. Arrest and prosecution do nothing to help the chronic alcoholic deal with his or her drinking problem, and in many cases they make matters worse. Medical and social services would be a far more effective response.[5]...

The Terms of the Debate

Debate over the old decriminalization has generally been framed in moralistic terms. Advocates of criminal penalties see certain kinds of behavior as wrong. The basic function of the criminal law, after all, is to define the boundaries of acceptable conduct. Robbery is a crime because taking something from another person by force violates our basic standards. Taking another person's life is also wrong. As Patrick Devlin put it, "the criminal law as we know it is based upon moral principle."[6]

Decriminalization is a bitterly controversial issue because of fundamental differences of opinion over moral standards. Opponents of abortion, for example, believe that human life begins at conception and therefore abortion is murder. Abortion rights supporters, on the other hand, believe that life begins at birth and therefore that abortion is a legitimate medical procedure. The same is true for sexual activities traditionally prohibited by the criminal law. Many people believe that adultery and homosexuality are wrong. Others believe that these are "victimless crimes," private matters that are none of the law's business.[7]

Decriminalization is also debated in terms of the personal and social consequences of certain kinds of behavior. We have always regulated drinking (restricting the place and hours of alcohol sale) on the grounds that the person who drinks to excess harms himself, his family, and his employer. Devlin argues that "Society is entitled by means of its laws to protect itself from dangers, whether from within or without."[8] The sum of all these harms damages society as a whole. Many people believe that public drunkenness harms society by lowering the quality of neighborhood life. Dealing with disorder problems of this kind is one of the central premises of community policing.

Advocates of decriminalization reply with a pragmatic argument of their own. The practical effect of criminalizing behavior is to make things worse. Arrest of the chronic alcoholic overburdens the justice system, doesn't help the problem drinker, and may actually aggravate the problem.[9]...

Public Drunkenness, Disorderly Conduct, and Vagrancy

Public drunkenness, disorderly conduct, and vagrancy are public nuisances rather than predatory crimes. They may offend the sensibilities of many people, but they do not inflict harm in the way that robbery and burglary do.

The crime control strategy underlying decriminalization in this area is indirect. The argument is that freeing the police from enforcing these laws will give them more time to concentrate on serious crime. These public order offenses do consume a great deal of police time and resources. In the nineteenth century they represented about 80 percent of all arrests, and they still make up the largest single group of arrests. In 1975 there were 1.2 million arrests for drunkenness, representing 13 percent of all arrests and three times the number of arrests for all violent crimes.[10]

The basic assumption about freeing up more police resources is flawed—that if the police quit making public drunkenness arrests and concentrated on serious crimes such as robbery and burglary, the availability of more time and resources would help to reduce crime.... We learned that simply adding more patrol officers will not prevent more crime. Adding more detectives will not produce higher clearance rates. The liberal crime control strategy behind decriminalization is ultimately identical to the traditional "more cops" proposal offered by conservatives. The proposal is just as unlikely to reduce serious crime.

In fact, we have already gone quite a ways in decriminalizing public nuisance offenses. Between 1975 and 1989 the total number of arrests for drunkenness, disorderly conduct, and vagrancy fell from 2 million to 1 million (the 2 million figure included drunkenness and a certain number of disorderly conduct and vagrancy arrests).[11] Several factors accounted for this drop. First, some court decisions held that arresting someone because of a medical condition—as opposed to some behavior—was unconstitutional. Second, some states decriminalized public intoxication. Third, the decline in public order arrests reflects informal decisions by police departments across the country to deemphasize minor crimes and concentrate on the more serious ones. In large part, this shift was in response to the high rate of serious crime....

Conclusions

There are many arguments for and against criminal penalties for the various forms of behavior we have discussed. Many people have serious moral objections to decriminalizing these behaviors. The anticipated advantages of decriminalization—reducing system overload, reducing corruption, and so on—may or may not be achieved. In either event, decriminalization will not necessarily have any effect on the predatory crimes of robbery and burglary that we are concerned about. If we are serious about reducing predatory crime, we have to keep our eyes focused on those crimes....

Discussion Questions

1. What is decriminalization? How does "old" decriminalization differ from "new" decriminalization? Why are some in favor of decriminalization? Why do some oppose it?

2. What problems are associated with criminalizing too many behaviors? How does criminalization of trivial matters affect equal protection of law? What effect does it have on the right to privacy?

3. How do laws such as the ones discussed by Walker create forms of criminal behavior? For actions such as drinking (alcoholic beverages), what might be a more effective policy than arrest?

Notes

1. Norval Morris and Gordon Hawkins, *The Honest Politician's Guide to Crime Control.* (Chicago: University of Chicago Press, 1970), p. 3.
2. Federal Bureau of Investigation, *Crime in the United States, 1989* (Washington, D.C.: Government Printing Office, 1990).
3. *The Knapp Commission Report on Police Corruption* (New York: George Braziller, 1973).
4. Bureau of Justice Statistics, *Sourcebook of Criminal Justice Statistics, 1990* (Washington, D.C.: Government Printing Office, 1991), pp. 195, 248.
5. Raymond T. Nimmer, *Two Million Unnecessary Arrests* (Chicago: American Bar Foundation, 1971).
6. Patrick Devlin, *The Enforcement of Morals* (London: Oxford University Press, 1965), p. 7.
7. Edwin M. Schur, *Crimes without Victims* (Englewood Cliffs, N.J.: Prentice-Hall, 1965).
8. Devlin, *The Enforcement of Morals*, p. 13.
9. Morris and Hawkins, *The Honest Politician's Guide to Crime Control.*
10. Federal Bureau of Investigation, *Crime in the United States, 1975* (Washington, D.C.: Government Printing Office, 1976), p. 179.
11. Nimmer, *Two Million Unnecessary Arrests.*

Index

A

M

N

CPSIA information can be obtained at www.ICGtesting.com
Printed in the USA
BVOW09s2344310815

415656BV00008B/17/P